उत्तररामचरितम्
UTTARARĀMACARITAM

भवभूतिविरचितः

उत्तररामचरितम्

BHAVABHŪTI'S

UTTARARĀMACARITAM

WITH

Sanskrit Commentary, English Translation, Critical and Explanatory Notes

BY

SARADARANJAN ROY
Vidyavinode, Siddhanta-Vacaspati,
Former principal, Vidyasagar College

BKP

BHARATIYA KALA PRAKASHAN
Delhi : : (India)

First Edition : 1926
Revised Edition : 2008

Published by **C.P. Gautam**
BHARATIYA KALA PRAKASHAN
3421-A, IInd Floor, Narang Colony Tri Nagar,
Delhi-110035. Phone : 32967505, Telefax : 27393083
E-mail : bkp3421@yahoo.co.in

ISBN : 978-81-8090-191-1

Printed by :
Salasar Imaging Systems
Delhi

Preface

In this volume the text is based mainly upon the late Pandit Vidyāsāgara's edition, though occasionally. I have adopted readings from (*i*) Vidyāsāgara's extracts from his four manuscripts, and (*ii*) the Bombay edition of Vīrarāghava.

While preparing the translation, I have derived much help from the late principal Tawney's precious little book. I am sorry Dr. Belvalkar's translation came in too late to be of much use in the earlier. Acts but it has saved me much trouble from the middle of Act V to the end.

The Commentary is my own. In its preparation I have often had occasion to consult Vīrarāghava, Vidyāsāgara, Goswami, etc. I have however, often ventured to differ from my predecessor. This has happened so often, that for sheer economy of space to keep down the price of the book, I do not say so (except in a few places) when I have a new explanation to offer. But I am sure the intelligent reader will be able to detect the omission at a glance.

For convenience of reference, the text has been divided into paragraphs. Where a paragraph end in the middle of a speech the initials of the speaker are given both at the end of the para and at the beginning of the next para.

My thanks are due to Pandit Kalikrishna Battacharya, Pandit Sudhakara Senior Professor of Sanskrit, Vidyāsāgara College, and to Professor Amujyacharan Vidyabhushana, Senior Professor of Pāli, Vidyāsāgara College, for hunting up certain references for me.

I shall be much obliged if my readers will kindly draw

my attention to errors and imperfection with a view to correction in the next edition.

This is a revised and meterially enlarged edition of our Uttararamacarit. Many notes and items are added here and there to make it more useful to its readers.

Saradaranjan Roy

Contents

Introduction

[*N.B.*—In the Summer of 1923, I read at the university institute an essay in Bengali on the "Fame of Bhavabhūti." The late lamented Sir Asutosh Mukhopadhyaya felt interested to such an extent that he wanted to forward, for an expression of opinion, a copy of the essay to Dr. Winternitz who then at Bolepur and he asked me to translate it into English. the translation was begun, but at its very commencement I was laid up for nearly two months with a serve attack of Pluerisy. The malady left me prostrate. As soon as I recovered a little I got Influenza and was down with it for nearly a month.

For these reasons I could not resume the work of translation during the life-time my honoured friend. Lately on taking up the work again I found reasons for extensive additions and alterations I have now. however, the melancholy satisfaction of having finished the task set me by the illustrious dead. The translation now appears as *Introduction* to this volume.]

1. The Uttararāmacarita

One of the most popular of sanskrit dramatists is Bhavabhūti. He is better knows and the author of the Uttararāmacarita.

The Uttararāmacarita is ususally considered by competent critics to be one of the best wrtten of Sanskrit dramas. It is in seven Acts and is based on the later history of Rāma commencing with his coronation after return from Laṅkā.

(i) The first Act tells us that soon after the coronation, people commence talking recklessly of Sītā with reference to her stay in the house of Rāvaṇa. The new reaches Rāma's ears and the king banishes his queen.

(ii) The second act opens with incidents that happen after a lapse of twelve years.

Rāma commences the Aśvamedha sacrifice. While preparation are going on for the sacrifice he is obliged to go out personally in quest of a certain Śūdra ascetic practising penance in the forest fo Daṇḍaka. At the sight of the place old association wake up the thorougly over whelm the king.

This Act and the Acts that follw describe events that take place within a day or two one another.

(iii) In the third Act we learn that Sītā is still alive through practically dead to the world. Delivered of twins (named Kuśa and Lava) on the day of her banishment she has been staying in the nether regions these twelve years with Prithvi and Gaṅgā. The boys were made over to Vālmīki by Gaṅgā herself for their training and education.

Gaṅgā knew that on his way back after meeting the Śūdra ascetic, Rāma would have to pass over the Panchavati the sight of which was bound to recall extremely painful memories.To relieve the shock she came over with Sītā to meet Godavari. From there she sent Sītā to gather flowers—a mere pretext—from the Panchavati making her invisible to morals.

As expected Rāma enters the Panchvati, meets Sītā there, feels her presence, but, being unable to see her, takes all this as a delusion, and with a heavy heart hastens towards his capital to get ready for the Aśvamedha.

(iv) Here commences the fourth Act. The sacrifical horse wanders into Vālmīki's hermitage and is seized by Lava.

(v) In the fifth Act, Chandraketu, Lakṣmaṇa's son, the guardain of the horse, meets Lava and forthwith the boys are attracted towards each other and become friends. Lava, however, makes certain remarks regarding Rāma and a regular fight follows.

(vi) The sixth act introduces Rāma again who notices the battle from the Puṣpaka, his aerial car, while proceeding towards his capital, comes down and prohibits the fight. Lava is then introduced to Rāma by Chandraketu. Next Kuśa arrives and is introduced by Lava. Hovering between hope and despair, Rāma notices the startling resemblance of the features of the boys with his own and those of Sītā.

(vii) Forthwith, in the seventh Act, Vālmīki comes to the rescue of the bewildered monarch. The sage invites the whole creation to witness the staging, by celestial nyhphs under the guidance of the sage Bharata, of a certain drama written by himself on the later hisory of Rāma. Lakṣmaṇa prepares a theatre and seats the audience. Rāma himself is present at the performance.

The performances discloses that Sītā was dilivered of twins on the very day of her exile and is still alive in Patala under the care of Prithvi and Bhāgīrathī. Her boys are with the sage Vālmīki. All see that they are no other than Kuśa and Lava.

The nymphs now retire, the acting ceases, and Vālmīki appears personally. He arranges for a declaration of Sītā's innocence and at his command Sītā herself emerges out of the waters of the Ganges led by Pṛthvī and Gaṅgā. Arundhati now delivers a well-merited snub to the people of Ayodhyā and the villages and asks Rāma to take back his spouse. The whole creation joins in the request, the people stand abashed and re-union follows.

II. The Auothor's name

In the prelude to the Uttararāmacarita the author introduces himself as "श्रीकण्ठपदलाण्छन...भवभूतिर्नाम"। Hence भवभूति was the name of the poet and he earned the title श्रीकण्ठ–one having the goddes of learning in his throat—possibly by his erudition.

So far as is at present known, Bhavabūti was not a prolific

writer. Two other books besides the Uttarachartia are ascribed to him—the Viracharita, a drama on the earlier history of Rāma ending with his return from Laṅkā, and the Mālati-Mādhava, a romance.

In all these, the personal matter in the prelude the three things in common, viz. (1) the author is Bhavabhūti who earned the title Srikantha, (2) the author comes of a Brāhmaṇa family of Padmapura in Vidarbha, (3) the dramas were all first staged on the occasion of the festival of the Kālapriyanātha.

Thus there can be no doubt that these three dramas were written by the same author.

The Viracharita adds that peot's father was Nilakantha and grand-father Bhattagopala.

Blinded perheps by the gloom of Nilakantha's "Kantha," some are misled into the belief that the poet's name was Srikantha and Bhavabhūti was a mere title, failing to see that Bhattagopala and his son Nilakantha have no "Kantha" in common in their names. Chapter and verse are cited by the supporters of this theory; thus—The poet while eulogising Gaurī sang "गिरिजायाः कुचौ वन्दे भवभूतिसिताननौ" also "साम्बा पुनातु भवभूतिषवित्रमूर्त्तिः" । This pleased Lord Bhava (शिव) to such an extent that he forthwith bestowed on the poet the title भवभूति ।

Against this may be noted that in old writings the poet is always referred to as भवभूति *not* as श्रीकण्ठ। Thus in the roth century, राजशेखर wrote in his बालचरित–

बभूव वल्मीकभवः पुरा कविस्ततः प्रपेदे भुवि भर्त्तमेण्ठताम्।
स्थितः पुनर्यो भवभूतिरेखया स वर्त्तते सम्प्रति राजशेखरः।

Next came कल्हन in the 12th century with the verse—

कविर्वाकपतिराजश्रीभवभूत्यादिसेवितः।
जितो ययौ यशोवर्मा तद्गुणस्तुतिवन्दिताम्।।

(Rājataraṅgiṇi, IV, 144)

In the 14th century Govardhanacharya in his आर्यासप्तशती wrote—

भवपूतेः सम्बन्धाद्भूधरभूरेव धारती भाति।
एतत्कृतकारुण्ये किमन्यथा रोदिति ग्रावा।।

But is quite unnecessary to hunt up these and similar references; "श्रीकण्ठपदलाण्छन....भवभूतिर्नाम" is decisive and seems to leave no room for discussion.

The Mālati Mādhava, as if to make assurance doubly sure, reads भवभूतिनामा for भवभूतिर्नाम। There is a deal of difference between भवभूतिर्नाम। The former is a compound of भवभूति and नामन् where नामन् means *name* and nothing else. The compound means "one whose *name* is Bhavabhūti". भवभूतिर्नाम is not a compound. भवभूतिः and नाम are separate words joined together by सन्धि। नाम is an अव्यय indicating प्राकाश्य publicity, celebrity etc. Hence भवभूतिर्नाम literally means knows as Bhavabhūti" This, however is a very common way of stating the *name* of a thing. Thus "हिमालयो नाम नगाधिराजः" "कालिन्दीतटवटः श्यामो नाम", "गिरि प्रस्त्रवणो नाम", चित्रकुञ्जवान् नाम दनुकबन्धाधिष्ठितो दण्डकारण्यभूभागः," "श्रमणा नाम सिद्धशवरी," etc.

III. His Home

The prelude to the वीरचरित supposes पद्मपुर in the दक्षिणापथ to be the poet's home (अस्ति दक्षिणापथे पद्मपरं नाम नगरम्। तव etc.) It is useal to render दक्षिणापथ as "the way to the South." This seems to require correction. The महाभारत in the वनपर्व says—

एते गच्छन्ति बहवः पन्थानो दक्षिणापथम्।
अवन्तिमृक्षवन्तञ्च समतिक्रम्य पर्वतम्।।
एष पन्था विदर्भाण्ममी गच्छन्ति कोशलान्।
अतः परञ्च देशोऽयं दक्षिणो दक्षिणापथः।।

"Here are several roads leading to दक्षिणापथ। They cross the hill ऋक्षवत् and go beyond अवन्ति। This road goes to विदर्भ,

those lead to कोशल। To the south beyond this place the land is known as दक्षिणापथ"। We shall not perhaps be much in the wrong if we say that दक्षिणापथ is the modern Deccan. *Deccan* is evidently a corruption of दक्षिण। "The town of पद्मपुर in the Deccan" is vague. The मालतीमाधव with more definiteness reads दक्षिणापथे विदर्भेष etc. The quotation from the महाभारत above places विदर्भ in the Deccan. विदर्भ is the modern Berars. We have it then that Bhavabhūti was born as Padmapura in the Berars. Padmapura has not yet been identified.

IV. His Age

Though born in the Berars, Bhavabhūti passed his best days at कान्यकुब्ज a one of the court-poets of king Yasovarman. The verse quoted above from the Rajatarangini may be freely rendered thus—"Yasovarman was a poet himself and commanded the services (सेवित) of a host of poets—Vakpatiraja, Bhavabhūti and others. When defeated by Lalitaditya, he made good use of his poesy by singing in praise of the victor'. From this and a few other minor considerations Bhavabhūti is supposed to have lived towards the latter part of the 7th century A.D.

V. His Creed

The Viracharita begins with a salutation to the absolute (ब्रह्मन्)।

"अथ स्वस्थाय देवाय नित्याय हतपाप्मने।
त्यक्तक्रमविभागाय चैतन्यज्योतिषे नमः।।"

This is colourless as regards the poet's creed. Every Hindu is a beliver in the Vedas; hence salutation to the सच्चिदानन्दस्वरूपं ब्रह्म is natural with him. This ब्रह्मन् is altogether unconditioned, and as such, cannot be the subject-matter of the devotee's meditation. The mind hankers after something conditioned—a personal god. Hence believers in ब्रह्मन् are also seen to be शैव, वैष्णव etc. in their creed. शिव, विष्णु etc. are the objects of their daily worship—they are भक्तs of शिव, विष्णु etc. which are to them but manifestations of ब्रह्मन् himself. What was Bhavabhūti—a शैव, or a वैष्णव, or What?

The उत्तररामचरित furnishes no clue; it opens with a salutation to the old masters—

इदं गुरुभ्यः पूर्वेभ्यो नमोवाकं प्रशास्महे।
विन्देम देवतां वीचममृतामात्मनः कलाम्।।"[1]

In the मालतीमाधव the poet makes salutation to शिव and गणेश। The case of गणेश may be left out of consideration; he is invoked by everybody to guard against hindrance in undertakings. Was then the poet a शैव?

There are considertations which cannot be ignored in giving an answer to this question. The prelude to the Viracharita has the following—

प्राचेतसो मुनिवृषा प्रथमः कवीनां यत् पावनं रघुपतेः प्रणिनाच वृत्तम्।
भक्तस्य तव समरंसत मेऽपि वाचस्तत् सुप्रसन्नमनसः कृतिनो भजन्ताम्।।

The first classical poet was Vālmīki. He has recorded the holy life of Rāma. I am a भक्त of Rāma. My speech also has revelled in recording that life. May the learned accept my record." In this, भक्त is a devotee, a worshipper; not a mere admirer.

To Bhavabhūti, Rāma was the Primeval Soul himself. Thus in the Viracharita he makes वशिष्ठ speak of Rāma as—

क्षमायाः स क्षेत्रं गुणमणिगणानामपि खनिः
प्रपन्नानां मूर्त्तेः सुकृतपरिपाको जनिमताम्।
कृपारामो रामो वहिरिह दृशोपास्यत इति
प्रमोदाद्वैतस्वाप्युपरि परिवर्त्तामह इमे।।

"In Rāma resides forbearence and all virtues. To those that report to him Rāma is prior-birth-merit embodied in this life. Rāma has to be seen within by meditation, but he revels in showing favour and is hence being seen without. From the consequent joy we are transported even above him."

Still more explicit is what in the वीरचरित comes from the presiding deity of Kuvera's Alaka; thus—

इदं हि तत्त्वं परमार्थभाजामयं हि साक्षात् पुरुषः पुराणः।
त्रिधा विभक्ता प्रकृतिः किलैषा त्रातु भुवि स्वेन सतोऽवतीर्णा ।।"

"This is the treasure of those that have acquired the Supreme Treasure. This is the Primeval Soul Himself. This is the First Cause (divided subsequently into Brahman, Viṣṇu and Maheśvara) which has come down on earth for the salvation of the good with a sight of its real self."

These and similar sentiments are those of genuine worship and are not compatible with mere admiration. Hence as he himself declares, Bhavabhūti was a भक्त of राम।

The question is likely to arise that if Bhavabhūti was a worship of Rāma, why does he salute Śiva in the Mālati Mādhava?

The answer is simple. The worshippers of विष्णु worship him either in the form of राम or as कृष्ण। These two classes of Vaiṣṇava are always of variance with each other. But Śiva's position is unique; nobody quarrels with Śiva. In public bathing *ghats* when a bather shout जय सीताराम, he is immediately challenged by dozens of voices with the counershout जय राधाश्याम, and *vice virsa*, while जय गौरीशङ्कर is at once taken up with alacrity by almost every one present. There is therefore no inconsisteny in a worshipper of Rāma saluting शिव। Or—it may be that as a dramatist Bhavabhūti saluted नटराज शिव the ideal lover at the beginning of his drama, for he was to depict the ardent love of Mālati and Mādhava. "आरोग्य भास्करादिक्च्छेत् धनमिच्छेद हुताशनात्" etc.,--As health is asked of Sun-god, wealth of Fire-god, so love is asked of Śiva. Thus this is no inconsistency with a रामभक्त।

VI. His works

As stated before, Bhavabhūti wrote three books, so far as is known at present, and they are all dramas. Two of these the Viracharita and the Uttararāmacarita, are based upon the Rāmāyaṇa of Vālmīki.

With reference to the genesis of these two books the poet himself explains, in the verse "प्राचेतसो मुनिबृषा प्रथमः कबीनाम्" etc., quoted before, that being a भक्त of राम he found it necessary to re-write the History of Rāma with certain alterations. The last line of the verse is "तत् सुप्रसन्नमनसः कृतिनोभजन्ताम्"। There तत् refers to the poet's own record. This record is in the form of a दृश्यकाव्य ; so the correct word with respect to it is पश्यन्त–let them *witness*. This the poet avoids and prefers भजन्ताम—let them *accept*. This is suspicious. It seems to suggest that his record apparently differs in places from that of Valmiki, and he exhorts the audience to accept his version of the story. Let us see what these differences, if any, are and what they have got to do with Bhavabhūti's भक्ति in राम।

(1) As a भक्त of राम the poet is shocked at the mean device adopted to slay the monkey-chief बाली। It casts a slur on his favourite diety which, as a भक्त, he is bound, he thinks, to try to wipe out. His version is that बाली was killed in fair fight wherein he himself was the aggressor.

(2) The poet cannot bear the idea that Sītā was banished without consultation with Vasiṣṭha and the elders. His divinity is incapable of taking such a hasty step. No, it was not that राम deliberately omitted to consult them, but, at the time, they were away from Ayodhyā and could not be consulted.

(3) Bhavabhūti's heart weeps to see Sītā go down to Pātāla leaving his Deity, his heart's idol, disconsolate. The very idea is repulsive to a भक्त । He thinks that the Rāmāyaṇa must be a comedy ; it must not be a tragedy. Accordingly he works towards that end.

(4) Incidentally he deems it necessary to absolve Kekayi of all responsibility in the matter of Rāma's exile.

The Vīracarita deals with रामवनवास and बालिवध and the Uttararāmacarita takes up सीताविवासन and पातालप्रवेश ।

The third line of the verse quoted before is "भक्तस्य तत्र समरंसत मेऽपि वाचः" । The past tense in समरंसत has to be noted. It implies that the poet's speech (वाचः) is no longer engaged in *recording* the story of राम ; the story is already *recorded*. This seems to suggest that, at the time the Viracharita was being staged, the Uttararāmacarita too was completed though the staging of it took place later on. Thus it appears that the verse "प्राचेतसी मुनिवृषा प्रथमः कवीनाम्" etc. warrants us to say that the poet's three dramas were staged in the order Viracharita, Uttararāmacarita, Mālati-Mādhava.

Sanskritists unanimously supposed that the Viracarita was staged first. But as regards the other two Dr. Sir Ramkrishna Gopala Bhandarkar in his preface to the Mālati-Mādhava says—"Mālati-Mādhava must have been his second work, and the Uttara-Rāmacarita the last. In the benedictory stanza at the end of this, the play is represented as the production of his mature intellect." Here in the foot-note is quoted the line "शब्दब्रह्मविदः कवैः परिणतप्रज्ञस्य वाणीमिमाम्" from the last verse in the Uttararāmacarita to justify the assertion "the production of his mature intellect" by "परिणतप्रज्ञस्य वाणीमिमां" । Later writers, including Prof. Lanman and Dr. Belvalkar, all follow Dr. Bhandarkar.

Here the reasoning is, because the poet was of *mature* intellect when he wrote the Uttararāmacarita, therefore the

Uttararāmacarita was the *last* work. It will perhaps strike many that when the intellect has matured it is just the time to *commence* writing, not to *stop* writing. There seems to be no bar to the supposition that after his intellect had matured, the poet first wrote the Vīracarita, then the Uttararāmacarita and last the Mālati-Mādhava. Maturiry of intellect does not necessarily imply old age and decrepitude that compel one to stop all work. वृद्धत्व is of two kinds, ज्ञानवृद्धत्व (maturity in knowledge or intellect or genius) and वयोवृद्धत्व (maturiy in age). Either is possible without the other "वृद्धत्वं जरसा बिना" is a current saying bequeathed unto us by Kālidāsa.

Moreover, before building upon the epithet परिणतप्रज्ञस्य it is necessary to see if परिणतप्रज्ञस्य, is by common consent the reading here and if so whether we all agree that it refers to भवभूति and no one else. Regarding the first point it may be noted that वीरराघव reads परिणतां प्राज्ञस्य for परिणतप्रज्ञस्य। This throws doubt on the authenticity of the reading. The reading itself being thus open to question it is not safe to base an inference upon it.

But for argument's sake, let us aceept the reading परिणतप्रज्ञस्य। Well, to whom does the epithet refer ? Not to भवभूति। Let me explain. Here there is another epithet शब्दब्रह्मविदः to qualify the poet. The poet, whoever he was, was both परिणतप्रज्ञ (of mature intellect) and शब्दब्रह्मविद् (enlightened in Brahman in the shape of speech). But भवभूति was not शब्दब्रह्मविद्, he himself says he was not. In the opening verse of the उत्तररामचरित he prays that he *might become* enlightened in Brahman in the shape of speech—"विन्देम देवतां वाचममृतामात्मनः कलाम्"। Hence, neither शब्दब्रह्मविदः nor परिणतप्रज्ञस्य in the line "शब्दब्रह्मविदः कवेः परिणतप्रज्ञस्यवाणीमिताम्" can refer to भवभूति।

The reference is to वाल्मीकि। The second half of the stanza as given by विद्यासागर is—

वाल्मीकेः परिभावयन्तुभिनयैर्विन्यस्तरूपां बुधाः
शब्दब्रह्मविदः कवेः परिणतप्रज्ञस्य वाणीमिमाम्।

In this the only possible construction is शब्दब्रह्मविदः परिणतप्रज्ञस्य कवेः वाल्मीकेः etc.

It is but fair to note that in the above some read तामेताम् for वाल्मीकेः। This reading also occurs in one of Vidyāsāgara's manuscripts. Sir Bhandarkar and others were probably misled by this reading.

A little reflection will show that तामेताम् cannot be the correct reading here. With तामेताम् the complete verse reads—

पाप्मभ्यश्च पुणातु वर्द्धयतु च श्रेयांसि सेयं कथा
मङ्गल्या च मनोहरा च जगतो मातेव गङ्गेव च।
तामेतां परिभावयन्त्वभिनयैर्विन्यस्तरूपां बुधाः
शब्दब्रह्मविदः कवेः परिणतप्रज्ञस्य वाणीमिमाम्।।"

The construction is "....सा इयं कथा। ताम् एताम् 'इमां वाणी परिभावयन्तु"। There are two separate sentences here. In the first sentence सा referes to something well-known (प्रसिद्धार्थ) and absent (परीक्ष). The word कवेः secure the presence (सन्निधि) of the absent thing before the vision of our mind. It so, the परोक्षता is gone, and the प्रसिद्धि too being already indicated the ताम् in the second sentences serves no purpose ; hence, it is objectionable.

Besides, as the second sentence is an अन्वादेश (subsequent assertion) एताम् there should be एनाम्। Moreover, the simulataneous presence of ताम्, एताम्, इमाम्, in similar senses, is extremely awkward and makes the sense obscure.

On the other hand with the reading वाल्मीकेः we have to construe—" .....सा इयंकथा। इमां वाल्मीकेः वाणी परिभावयन्तु" which leaves no doubt as to the sense intended. The absence of अन्वादेश in इमाम् is only a question of grammar and is not perhaps altogether indefensible as I have tried to show elsewhere (see Act. VII).

In these circumstances there is every likelihood that वाल्मीके: is the correct reading here and Sir Bhadarkar's conclusions do not follow. If then my interpretation of the verse "प्राचेतसी मुनिवृषा प्रथम: कवीनाम्" etc. be correct, it is safe to say that Mālati-Mādhava, not Uttararāmacarita, is the last work of the poet.

But one of our poets says "व्याख्या बुद्धिबलापेक्ष्या" (a keen wit can mould the interpretation any way it likes). Some clever critic might perhaps interpret my verse quite differently and thus vitiate my conclusion. Let us therefore see if independent evidence is available.

I. In the मालतीमाधव the style is purer and more attractive than what we find in the उत्तररामचरित। Now, the plot of a story depends largely upon inspiration. A happy idea may flash and illustrate the mind at any age. It cannot therefore be said that, of two stories by the same author, the more attractive is the product of a more advace age. But the style improves with age undoubtedly. Hence the style of मालतीमाधव is proof that it came after the उत्तररामचरित।

II. In the prelude to the Uttararāmacarita the Sūtradhāra, after stating the day's business says "एषोऽस्मि कार्यवशादायोध्यकस्तदानीन्तनश्च संवृत्त:"–"Owing to the requirements of my duties I have now become a citizen of Ayodhyā of Rāma's time."

Next Follows—"(समन्तादवलोक्य) "भो भो: etc"–(*Looking round*) Ho! Ho! etc." Now, who looks round here? Not the Sūtradhāra, but the citizen whom now the Sūtradhāra represents. This is defective. The Prelude should have ended with संवृत:। The stage-direction should have been something like thus—(परिक्रम्य निष्क्रान्त:)। इति प्रस्तावना। तत: प्रविशति कश्चिदायोध्यक:। आयोध्यक: (समान्तादवलोक्य)–भो भो: etc.

Referring to the Prelude to the Mālati-Mādhava we find—"सूत्रधारः-वाढ़म्। एषोऽसि कामान्दकी संवृत्तः। नटः-अहमप्यवलोकिता। (इति परिक्रम्य निष्क्रान्तौ)। प्रस्तावना। ततः परिवृत्य रक्तपट्टिकानेपथ्ये कामन्दक्यावलोकिते प्रविशतः" etc.—"*Sūtra*—All right. Here I have become Kāmandaki. *Actor*—I too have become Avalokita. (Exeunt after going round the stage.) *Then enter Kāmandaki and Avalokita dressed in scarlet*."

This is in perfect order. In order words the defect noticed in the Uttararāmacarita is corrected in the Mālati-Mādhava. This implies that the Mālati-Mādhava comes later than the Uttararāmacarita. Had the Uttararāmacarita been the later work, the defect avoided in the previous work would have occurred there at all.

III. Sanskrit poets often have in the prelude a kind word or two for the audience, In the Vīracarita, Bhavabhūti's first work, we read—

वश्यवाचः कवेः काव्यं सा च रामाश्रया कथा।
लब्धश्च वाक्यनिष्यन्दनिष्पेषनिकषो जनः।।

—"The poet is the master of speech, the theme is the supremely interesting stroy of Rāma, and the audience is one of connoisseurs of the merits of composition." Here the poet, a candidate for fame, is conscious of his own merit, is conscious of the merits of his work and has full confidence in the judgment of the audience. His expectations are therefore high.

In the Uttararāmacarita there is no mention of the audience; instead we have the cynical remark—"यथा स्त्रीणां तथा वाचां साधुत्वे दुर्जनो जनः-"People are wicked while judging of women and speech."

The language is that of dissappointment. The hopes with which the Vīracarita was launched have not been realised. The poet is therefore now indifferent towards his audience.

The prelude to the Mālati-Mādhava is in a differnt vein.

There the poet is furious and lets the audience have the full measure of his venom of abuse. Says he—

ये नाम केचिदिह नः प्रथयन्त्यवज्ञां जानन्ति ते किमपि तान् प्रति नैष यत्नः।

उत्पत्स्यतेऽस्ति मम कोऽपि समानधर्मा कालो ह्ययं निरवधिर्विपुला च पृथ्वी।"

"There are certain vile (नाम कुत्सायां क्रोधे च) no-bodies (केचित्) here who delight in airing their contempt of me. What do they know? I do not write for them. People there are surely elsewhere to appreciate me; even here, there will be a time when people will sing in my praise." To emphasise the wide difference in birth and training beween himself and his critics he belauds his own family, thus

ते श्रोत्रियास्तत्वविनिश्चयाय भूरि श्रुतं शाश्वतमाद्रियन्ते।

इष्टाय पूर्ताय च कर्मणेऽर्थान् दारानपत्याय तपोऽर्थमायुः।।

Now, mark the attitude of the poet towards the audience in the dramas. It is respectful in the Vīracarita, indifferent in the Uttararāmacarita, abusive in the Mālati-Mādhava. In what order did these chages in the attitude appear? That is our problem for solution.

Well, an author is always expected to be respectful towards his audience. Hence, it is natural to suppose that the Vīracarita was the poet's first work.

Assuming that the Vīracarita was a failure and remembering that the poet had a high opinion of himself and his work, we expect indifference towards the audience in the next work. This means that the Uttararāmacarita was the poet's second attempt.

If the Uttararāmacarita too was unfavourably recived then no wonder that the sensitive poet all patience and became abusive in his next venture. So Mālati-Mādhava naturally follows the Uttararāmacarita.

Another theory perhaps occur to some, viz., the Mālati-Mādhava was the poet's second work; it was a success and softened down his tone abuse into one of difference in the Uttararāmacarita. This does not seem to comment itself.

First, why should we suppose that the poet was *abnormally* sensitive like the writer of the "English poets and Sotch Reviewers" and that very first breath of criticism drove him mad?

Second, if he was really so impatient of criticism, then the poet's abuse was more likely to elicit from the audience counter-abuse than praise for the Mālati-Mādhava.

Third, if indeed the audience praised the Mālati-Mādhava, then, with his natural sensitiveness—sensitiveness which is touched equally by praise and abuse, the poet would be eager to make amends for his abuse and would come out with not indifference of cynicism, but a brimful of enthusiastic apprecation in the Uttararāmacarita.

It seems we have now enough materials before us to say with some amount of certainty that the sequence of the dramas is—Vīracarita, Uttararāmacarita, Mālati-Mādhava.

These dramas as we learn from the preludes were all staged at the festival of Kālapriyanātha (कालप्रियनाथस्य यात्रायाम्)। It is usual to make Kālapriyanātha as identical with the Mahākāla as Ujjayini. We are inclined to differ.

Mahākāla is a well-know name. Why should the poet alter it—persistently alter it—into the unheard of Kālapriyanātha? Besides, as shown above, Bhavabhūti was the court-poet of Yaśovarman at Kanauj. Why then should he go to Ujjayini to have dramas staged there? That would be an affront to his patron Yasovarman which that king would never forgive. The supposition seems absurd. It is more natural to take Kālapriyanātha as some deity enshrined some where in Yaśovarman's own territory.

The word Kālapriyanātha means "The guardian deity of Kālapriya." Again, Kālapriya would be a happy name for newly founded city. It means "The favourite of Time (Kāla)," *i.e,* "Imperishable" for it is "time" that destroys cities. It struck me a few days ago that the modern city of Kalpi might be the Kālapriya of Bhavabhūti. On referring to Dr. Belvalkar's

Translation I find that in this I had been anticipated by Mr. Lele of Bombay. Dr. Belvalkar rejects Mr. Lele's suggestion on the ground that it is based on mere surface resemblance beween the names Kalpi and Kālapriya I have not seen Mr. Lele's book and do not know if he cites reasons; but it seems what has been said above enables one to say that dramas were certainly not first staged at Ujjayini and Kālapriyanātha is not the Mahākāla of that city. Whether the resemblance between Kālapriya and Kalpilies on the surface only or goes any deeper cannot be decided until fresh materials are availble.

VII. His Fame

As appears from the preludes to his works, Bhavabhūti's carrer as a dramatist was one of disappointment. He recived no public favour during his life-time. But after his death came a time when people felt attracted towards his dramas. Gradually there arose a decent body of admirers. That was the time when the line. "कवयः कालिदासाद्या भवभूतिर्महाकविः"– "Kālidāsa etc. were poets but Bhavabhūti was the prince of poets"s used to be quoted and aswered by the opposite party with the cry "तरवः पारिजाताद्याः स्नुहिवृक्षी महातरुः"–"The Pārijāta etc. are trees but the Cactus is the prince of trees."

At the present time Bhavabhūti enjoys a world wide fame. Prof. Wilson says—"....brilliant thoughts occur—the justice and beauty of which are not surpassed in any literature." Pandit Vidyasagar remarks—"Noble and lofty sentiments abound in his works in a measure not to be useally seen in those of other poets." Sir Bhandarkar has—"He shows a just appreciation of the awful beauty and grandeur of Nature enthroned in the solitudes of dense forests, cataracts and lofty mountains. He has an equally strong perception of stern grandeur in human character, and is very succesful in bringing out deep pathos and tenderness. He is skillful in detecting beauty even in ordinary things or action and in distinguishing the nicer shades of feeling. He is a master of style and expression, and his cleverness in adapting his words to the sentiment is unsurpassed."

All this is very high praise and renders prophetic the poet's words "उत्पत्स्यतेऽपि मम कोऽपि समानधर्मा"। These appreciations reach us with reasons assigned for them, whereas we do not know what made his books unpopular during the poet's life-time. We ppropose to make an attempt to know. We shall try to see if there is anything, ven in the poet's best work with which the critic is likely to be dissatisfied.

The Uttararāmacarita is by common consent supposed to be the masterpiece of Bhavabhūti. There is the current saying "उत्तरे रामचरिते भवभूतिर्विशिष्यते"–"Bhavabhūti excels himself in the later history of Rāma." Are these any deffects, any serious defects in the drama? Let us search for the reply.

At the very outset it appears that the language is heavy; often it is unmusical; in places is is repulsive. It jars and grates to such an extent that Govardhanācārya in the verse from the Ārya-Saptaśati quoted before compares Bhavabhūti's composition to a rocky soil. In a jesting mood he remarks—

भवभूतेः सम्बन्धात् भूधरभूरेव भारती भाति।
एतत्कृतकारुण्ये किमन्यथा रोदिति ग्रावा।।

"—Coming in contact with Bhavabhūti goddess speech has turned into a rocky soil. Hence it is that when Bhavabhūti's speech weeps the poets says that the rock itself weeps"—

We are aware that sometimes this very verse is interpareted as a high tribute to the pathos of Bhavabhūti's writing. The text of the verse does not seem to justify this interpretation. Besides, the context shows that Govardhana here is not at all anxious to make any profound remark; he merely wants to say someting smart. Thus in the very next verse he says of Bāṇa—

जाता शिखण्डिनी प्राक् यथा शिखण्डी तथावगच्छामि।
प्रागल्भ्यमधिकमाप्तुं वाणी बाणही बभूवेति।।

"Bāṇa is Vāṇī herself with the female suffix ङीप् dorpped to acquire geater boldness of speech (for the sake of the joke he chooses to forget that Bāṇa begins with B and Vāṇī with V so that the mere absence of ङीप् does not chage the one into the other[1]). Change of sex is not unknown in history, for, did not sex-transmution covert शिखण्डिनी Into शिखण्डी in the good old days?"

It is impossible to take this, and along with this the previous verse also, as spoken in earnest. Govardhana does not like Bhavabhūti's style and cuts a joke.

But unattractiveness of style is a minor-offence in a dramatist. Like every story-teller, he has other more important ends to meet the foremost of which is to make the incidents appear natural and consistent with one another. In other words the dramatist has first of all to secure a perfect techinique. If the technique is defective all interest in the story is gone; lofty ideals and masterly delineation of character fail to make a permanent impression.

Bhavabhūti's technique in the Uttararāmacarita leaves much to be desired. I shall cite a few instances, only a few out of a lot.

(i) In the Prelude the Sūtradhāra says—

एषोऽहं कार्श्यवशादायुोयकस्तदानौन्तनश्च संवृत:। (समन्तादवलोका) भी भो..... किमिति विश्रान्तचारणानि चत्वरस्थानानि?"

This has already been cited as a defect because the acting begins which the entry of the citizen of Ayodhyā. The prelude threrfore should have ended immediately before and the Sūtradhāra should have left the stage. The Daśarūpaka

---

1. Some lexicographers do indeed read बाण and वाणी with both व and ब !

says—"प्रस्तावनान्ते निर्गच्छेत् ततो वस्तु प्रपञ्चयेत्"–"The Sūtradhāra must leave the stage after the prelude and *thereafter* the staging should commence." Strictly speaking this only offends against the rules of dramaturgy and is not an instance of defective technique. But all the same no orthodox critic would tolerate it.

(ii) After the above follows—"(प्रविश्य) नटः भाव, प्रषिता हि इतः स्वगृहान् महाराजेन लङ्कासमरसुहृदः etc. "(*Entering*) Naṭa—Honoured Sir, the allies in the war at Laṅkā have been sent aways to their homes by the Mahārāja etc." This too is defective; no Naṭa can come in after the Prelude has ended.

Again this Naṭa addresses the Sūtradhāra as Bhava and the Sūtradhāra returns the compliment with Mariṣa. But Bhava, Mariṣa etc., are terms allowed in the prelude only. Thus here the poet offers us the choice beween Scylla and Charybdis. If the Prelude has ended, Sūtradhāra, Naṭa, Bhava, Mariṣa etc. are out of place. If the Prelude continues, then "किमिति विश्रान्तचारणनि चत्वरस्थानानि," वेदेशिकोऽस्मीति पृच्छामि" etc. are inconsistent.

The dilemma certainly cannot escape the vigilance of the critic.

(iii) In answer to the Sūtradhāra's query "किमिति विश्रान्तचारणानि etc."—"Why are the yards idle etc." the Naṭa says—"प्रषिता हि इतः etc." the guests have left etc. He also adds—

वशिष्ठाधिष्ठिता देव्यो गता राघवमातरः।
अरुन्धतीं पुरस्कृत्य यज्ञे जामातुराश्रमम्।।

—"Vasiṣṭha has gone to Ṛṣyaśṛṅga's place taking the queen-mothers with him." This is irrelevant. We can understand music in honour of guests, but Vasiṣṭha and the queen mothers can have nothing to do with it. Their presence or absence cannot start or stop music.

The poet wants to keep them away at the moment of

Sītā's exile as explained before and informs the audience accordingly, forgetting, however, that the information is irrelevant at this stage. The technique is faulty here.

(iv) Next we are told that Vasistha etc. have reached Ṛṣyaśṛṅga's place and sent word thought Aṣṭāvakra to explain why Rāma and Sītā were not invited. Aṣṭāvakra says—"वत्से, कठोरगर्भेति नानीतासि। वत्सोऽपि राममद्रस्त्वद्विनोदनार्थमेव स्थापित:"–"—Child, your term is full, so you have not been brought over; Rāma too has been left there to entertains you."

The fulness of Sītā's term requires explanation. The queen-mother left in the morning; Aṣṭāvakra reached Ayodhyā that very day at about noon; Sītā was exiled soon after noon and in the afternoon was delivered of twins. If delivery is to take place in the afternoon the elders will guess it from looks etc. in the morning Sītā was the darling of the elders, was given up for lost and was recovered unexpectedly after a lapse of 14 years. That was her first conception. In the circumstances the elders cannot think of leaving her on the day of delivery even for a few hours, whereas this absence was to be for 12 years. Any Hindu mother-in-law would unhesitatingly decide to stay on till delivery and then go. This is another defect in the technique.

(v) Further, Aṣṭāvakra reports that the queen-mother etc. have asked to Rāma to satisfy without delay any *dohada* (puerperal longings) Sītā might have. It is queer to think of *Badhumata's dohada* after the expiry of the whole term on the day of delivery. The request was unnatural at this stage.

(vi) Rāma's reply to the above is—"क्रियते यद्येषा कथयति"—"It will be done if she discloses it." Rāma doubts if she would tell him at all, such was her bashfulness. But Sītā falisifies his doubts by immediately declaring her wish and even uses the owrd *dohada* itself without a blush.

The *dohada* was—to roam in the forests once again and to bathe in the Bhāgīrathī; and this on the day of delivery!

Rāma does something stranger still. He orders Lakṣmaṇa to take her over to Vālmīki's hermitage, forgetting that her term being full it was not deemed advisable to take her over to Ṛṣyaśṛṅga's place. Sītā now asks Rāma to accompany her. Rāma retorts that it was cruel of her think that a request for it was necessary. Yet when getting on into the car she finds Lakṣmaṇa alone there, she does not even ask where Rāma was and why he did not come.

All this is extremely unnatural. The unnaturalness arises from assuming that Sītā's terms was full. It is worth while to see if this is at all a possible assumption.

In the Viracarita we find that after having killed Rāvaṇa, Rāma starts that very day for Ayodhyā which he reaches in the evening. Coronation follows the next day. Festivities continue for a little over two weeks. Ashtavakra comes on the day the festivities cease. Including that day we see that since her deliverance Sītā has been living wiht her husband for about a fortnight. yet the poet says Sītā's terms was full when Aṣṭāvakra came! This is a glaring incongruity which no critic can tolerate.

Bhavabhūti has left us no materials of judge if Sītā has conceived before her abduction by Rāvaṇa, which supposition alone can remove the incongruity here. The Rāmāyaṇa of Vālmīki does not allow the suposition as will be abvious on references to the Sundarakāṇḍa.

(vii) A very crurious feature of Aṣṭāvakra'a visit is that the messages sent throught him did not occur to the elders at the time. they left Ayodhyā. Foregetfulness is pardonable in the queen-mother. Foregetfulness is pardonable in the queen-mothers; but why should Vasiṣṭha forget? He too has sen through Aṣṭāvakra this very urgent and important piece of adivce of Rāma—

जामातृयज्ञेन वयं निरुद्धास्त्वं बाल एवासि नवञ्च राज्यम्।
युक्त्रं प्रजानामनुरञ्जने स्यास्तस्माद् यशो यत् परम धनं वः।।

"I am detained here for 12 years. You are a mere boy and only recently crowned. So try to please your subjects by all means. This will make you popular and popularity is what your ancestors have all prized." The nervousness of Vasiṣṭha about Rāma's abilities as displayed in this verse makes it imperative for him to add here—"In matters of moment do nothing without consulting me." But this he omits.

On the other hand, Vasiṣṭha had no reason to think so lightly of Rāma. He knew who Rāma was as is obvious from the verse "क्षमायाः स क्षेत्रं गुणमणिगणानामपि खनिः" etc. quoted before, Hence, the advice sounds inconsistent in his mouth.

This much is enough to show the nature of the technique of the Uttararāmacarita. I will, however, before leaving this subject add two more instances.

(viii) In Act II we learn that the elders have been dismissed by Ṛṣyaśṛṅga but Arundhati has declined to go back to Ayodhyā which is now bereft of her beloved Sītā.

The queen-mothers approve. Vasiṣṭha advises them to go and live in Vālmīki's hermitage. Why? Vasiṣṭha had a hermitage of his own. There they could all go and thus avoid going back to Ayodhyā. Of course Vasiṣṭha knew what was going to happen at Vālmīki's hermitage as described in Act VII and was perhaps actuated by that knowledge to make the suggestion. But the suggestion should have come with all the appearence of naturalness in it, and this it fails to do.

(ix) In Act VII, on hearing a hubbub, Vālmīki explains उत्खातलवणो मधुरेश्वरः प्राप्तः–"Śatrughna is returnining from Madhura after having killed Lavaṇa." The expedition against Lavaṇa had started 12 years before as we know from Act I. We have then to suppose that a regular war has been in progress against Lavaṇa these 12 years, the Rākṣasa defying Rāma's forces all the while. In that case the Aśvamedha becomes an impossibility because the conqueror of the whole world alone has the right to it.

As I have already said these are only illustrative of the defects of technique and do not make an exhaustive list.

Modern critics have however learnt to shut their eyes to defects of technique. We do not know how they learnt it, but the art is there and in a highly improved form, for, not only do they now wink at defects but actually see beauty in them. Thus Dr. Belvalkar and Prof. Lunman speak of the "almost perfect development in form and technique" of the Uttararāmacarita and of "the advance which Bhavabhūti had made in his tecnique" in "the first act of the Uttararāmacarita."

Here let me not be misunderstood. My objects in noticing these defects, as stated at the outset, is only to see if the poet's detractors—those who came out purposely to condemn—got any real hold against him, and thus to explain why the poet was unpopular during his life time. In time, the play of passions and prejudices ceased and admireres arose. If I am asked to speak on the ground for admiration, I think little would remain unsaid if I said "The man who can read through the Uttararāmacarita without being moved to tears more than once स योगी ह्यथवा पशु:–is either a sage or a brute."

VIII. The Sources of the Uttararāmacarita.

The general outlines of the story of the Uttararāmacarita are obviously derived from the Rāmāyaṇa of Vālmīki. For the details Bhavabhūti is largely indebted of Kālidāsa and to certain extent to Bhāsa also. The Ālekhyadarśana of Act I only an amplification of Kālidāsa's—

तयोर्यथाप्रार्थितमिन्द्रियार्थानासेदुषः सद्मसू चित्रवत्सु।
प्राप्तानि दुःखान्यपि दण्डकेषु सञ्चिन्त्यमानानि सुखान्यभूवन्।।

—"They are now enjoing life. On the walls of the mansions are painted scenes of their sojourn in the Daṇḍaka. Many of these recall painful memories; but now, while contemplating on them in the picture, they give more pleasure then pain."

Both Sītā and Śakuntalā are abandoned *when with child*. At the time of abandonment Kālidāsa's Rāma laments—

राजर्षिवंशस्य रविप्रसूतेरुपस्थितः पश्यत कीदृशोऽयम्।
मत्तः सदाचारशुचे कलङ्कः पयोदवातादिव दर्पणस्य।।"

—"This illustrious race is soiled throught contact with me"

Bhavabhūti's Rāma think exactly along smilar lines—

यत् सावित्रैर्दीपितं भूमिपालैर्लोकश्रेष्टैः साधु शुद्धं चरित्रम्।
मत्सम्बन्धात् कश्मला किंवदन्तौ स्याच्चेदस्मिन् हन्त धिङ्मामधन्यम्।।

—"My ancestores have rendered therace pure, my luckless self has solied it"

Both the queens, Sītā and Śakuntalā, depart *leaving no trace behind* the thier husbands meet their sons *unexpectedly after the lapse of years in a hermitage.* Both the poets dweel on the resemblance of the features of the boys of those of their sires and on the *thrill of joy* caused to their sires *from the touch of the boys.* Thus—"अस्य बालकस्य रूपसंवादिनी ते आकृतिः" in Śukuntala, VII; and—"अये केवलमस्मत्संवादिनी आकृतिः" in the Uttararāmacarita, VI; also—

अनेन कस्यापि कुलाङ्करेण स्पृष्टस्य गात्रेषु सुखं ममैत्रम्।
कां निर्वृतिं चेतसि तस्य कुर्याद यस्यायमङ्गात् कृतिनः प्ररूढः।।

in Śakuntala, VII; and....

"अङ्गादङ्गात् स्नुत इव निजः स्नेहजो देहसारः
प्रादुर्भूय स्थित इव बहिश्चेतनाधातुरेव।
सान्द्रानन्दक्षुभितहृदयप्रस्नवेनेव सृष्टो
गात्रं श्लेषे यदमृतरसस्रोतसा सिञ्चतीव।।"

in the Uttararāmacarita slightly disguised by Bhavabhūti's fondness for the prolix.

Both the pairs pine away after separation and suffer in their person. When husband and wife accidentally meet for the first time after the separation, Kālidāsa's Śukantala exclaims ....'न खलु आर्यपुत्र इव" and Bhavabhūti's Sītā remarks... "हा कथं प्रभातचन्द्रमण्डलापाण्डुराकृतिः etc."

As for the queens, Duṣyanta remarks of Śukantala...

वसने परिधूसरे वसाना नियमक्षाममुखी धृतैकवेणिः।
अतिनिष्करुणस्य शुद्धशीला मम दीर्घं विरहव्रतं बिभर्त्ति।।

and Tamasā says almost the same thing of Sītā in the Uttararāmacarita....

परिपाण्डुदुर्बलकपोलसुन्दरं दधती विलोलकवरौकमाननम्।
करुणस्य मूर्त्तिरिव वा शरीरिणी विरहव्यथेव वनमेति जानकी।।

Both the kings are re-united with their queens *in a hermitage* in presence of a sage of exceptional spiritual eminence.

In Act V. Bhāsa's Svabhavasavadatta, king Udayana. (whose beloved queen Vasavadatta was supposed to have perished in a fire though she was really alive unknown to all in the world except Yaugandharayana) sees Vasavadatta in a dream and commences talking in sleep. By chance Vasavadatta herself arrrives there, speaks to the sleeping king and touches his hand. The touch rouses the king and Vasavadatta hastily withdraws. This seems to be the germ out of which Bhavabhūti unflods his Act III of the Uttararāmacarita.

The talk Udayana has with the Vidūṣaka on awaking strongly reminds one of Rāma's talk with Vāsantī in the Uttararāmacarita Act. III. Thus Bhāsa writes—"*King* I have good news for you, Vasavadatta is alive. *Vid.*—Alas, Vasavadatta! Where is Vasavadatta? She is long dead. King—No, friends no I was half awake, she aroused me and left. Rumanvat has deceived me saying she was dead." Bhavabhūti has—"*Rāma*—Friends Vāsantī, you are lucky. *Vas.*—How so, Sire? *Rāma*—Sītā has come back to me. *Vas.*—

Well, Sire, Where is she? *Rāma*—Why, she is standing before you."

IX. Bhavabhūti, The Man

We often judge a man by his writings, by the trend of his thoughts. This is not safe and often likely to mislead. We shall however apply the test to me case of Bhavabhūti to see what results it yields. In the Uttararāmacarita the verses—

इयं गेहे लक्ष्मीरियममृतवर्त्तिनेयनयो-
रसावस्याः स्पर्शो वपुषि बहलश्चन्दनरसः।
अयं कण्ठे बाहुः शिशिरमसृणो मौक्तिकसरः।
किमस्या न प्रेयो यदि परमसह्यस्तु विरहः।।

and अद्वैतं सुखदुःखयोरनुगुरणं सर्वास्वस्थासु यद्
विश्रामो हृदयस्य यत्र जरसा यस्मिन्न हार्य्यो रसः।
कालेनावरणात्ययात् परिणते यत् स्नेहसारे स्थितं
भद्रं प्रेम सुमानुषस्य कथामप्येकं हि तत् प्राप्यते।।

paint perfect pictures of conjugal love.

The verse "अङ्गादङ्गात् स्रुत इवनिः स्नेहजो देहसारः" etc. quoted before is again a happy delineation of parental affectoin. Very likely then Bhavabhūti was a loving husband and an affectionate father.

In his description of nature it is the somber and the terrible that usually attract his where others see aesthetic beauty alone. In keeping with this, in the region of mind also, Nature in agony, not in ecstasy, he likes to depict. He prefers the shades keeping away from the sun-shine. The inference ought to be that the poet was a pessimist of a morose temperament. This is supported by the absence of the jester in his drama.

From the absence of the jester some argue that the poet had no sense of humour. In the Uttararāmacarita only once he cracks a joke. That is when Lakṣmaṇa points out the pictures of the wives of the four brothers skipping over that of his own wife Sītā laughingly asks—"वत्स, इयमपि अपरा का"–"Dear child, Who is this other girl?"

I think this a bit unfair to the poet. Sense of humour cannot be absent where there is the sense of the ludicrous; and the latter the poet did possess undoubtedly. Thus, in the Mālati-Mādhava, the poet, describing Śiva's delirious dance (ताण्डव), says—

सानन्दं नन्दिहस्ताहतमुरजरवाहूतकौमारवर्हि-
त्रासान्नासाग्ररन्ध्रं विशति फणिपतौ भोगसङ्कोचभाजि।
गण्डोड्डीनालिमालामुखरितककुभस्ताण्डवे शूलपाणे-
र्वैनायक्यश्चिरं वो वदनविधुतयः पान्तु चीत्कारवल्यः।।"

—"Nandi is playing the tabor. The bee notes he is eliciting resemble the rumble of a water-laden cloud. This attracts Kārtikeya's peacock at whose sight the frightened serpent-king on the head of the Lord beats a hasty retreat, and for shelter closes its hood and runs up one of the nostrils of Gaṇeśa! Poor Gaṇeśa is shrieking and sneezing and giving violent jerks to his head to shake off the intruder who had stuck fast in the hole. May these jerks of Gaṇeśa be to your salvation for ever."

It seems to me that the absence of the jester only shows that the poet was always serious in his undertakings and eschewed frivolities.

X. The Characters in the Play

Of the several characters in the play, Rāma and Sītā stand prominent. The others i.e. Lakṣmaṇa, Janaka, Chandreketu, Lava, Kuśa, Vālmīki, Kauśalya, Arundhati, Gaṅgā, Pṛthvī etc. are of minor importance So, we Shall here note a few traits in Rāma and Sītā's characters.

[*N.B*: As this edition had to be published in a very short time owing to the great demand of the book, so we have dealt with a few salient points only of the important characters and hastily pass over others.]

Rāma: Bhavabhūti paints Rāma as an ideal householder.—both physically and morally. As regards his strength etc. Sambhuka extols him as the destroyer of terrible demons. As a strong warrior he goes forward to save the elephant reared by Sītā herself. Even his majestic appearance commands respect. Thus Kuśa says "आशंसनीयपुण्यदर्शनः स महात्मा"। Rāma was ब्रह्मकोषस्य गोप्ता। And his aim was to protect the world more so the subject on moral principles (c.p. "इदं विश्वं पाल्यं विधिवदभियुक्तेन मनसा" etc.). In fact duty was the great aim of Rāma. He followed duty for duty's sake. As a prince of the solar race प्रजारञ्जन was his highest duty (युक्तः प्रजानामनुरञ्जने स्यास्तस्माद्यशो यत् परमं धनं वः); for this duty he even abadoned Sītā and bore everything manfully ("स्नेहं दयाञ्च सौख्यञ्च यदि वा जानकीमपि। आराधनाय लोकानां मुञ्चतो नास्ति मे व्यथा।।"). Thus his aim was greatest good of the greatest number. He could not brook vice in his kingdon. Thus he saves the dead Brāhmaṇa boy by killing Sambuka the Śūdra ascetic. In fact he duly behaves to all and knew the power of religion (लौकिकानां हि साधूनामर्थं बागनुवर्त्तते।ऋषीणां पुनराद्यानां वाचमर्थोऽनुधावति।।"). In public capacities he brilliantly discharged his duties to the entire satisfaction of all. Great as a moral ruler, he was also great as a loving husband. He abandoned Sītā, but all the while brooded over her affection. Sītā's thought ruled supreme in his mind. Throughtout his life he evinced his unbounded and pure affection for his wife and ever tried to minister to her happiness. His heart-rending cries and frantic utterings on account of sepration from his wife disclose the depth of his love. But in this respect his sentimentalism carries hism away and brings him down to the level of ordianry lovers. He had great regard for Sītā's merits and chastity (इयं गेहे लक्ष्मीः etc.). As a father also he is very affectionate. Thus thought Lava molested his soliders still he is filially disposed towards him; Rāma is soft to his relations. Indeed his filial affection inclined him to Lava and Kuśa though the relation was not known. Rāma's fondness for Chandraketu should not also pass unnoticed.

Thought Rāma is the foremost hero of is age, he was devoied of all pride. Thus while seeing the pictures he avoids self-praise (लक्ष्मणः–पश्य अयमसौ आर्य्येणा–इत्यर्द्धोक्ते) रामः–वत्स, बहुतरं

द्रष्टव्यमस्ति etc.). Rāma was also an ardent admirer of the sublime aspects of nature. see Rāma's description of Panchavati in Act II.

Thus though yong in age Rāma was just in his judgements and never swerved from the path of duty.

Sītā—As Rāma was a perfect type of manhood so Bhavabhūti depicts Sītā as an ideal woman. Here we see her as a wife. Her character as mother or daughter is not so painted as to deserve serious consideration. She did all for Rāma's good and she followed him in joy and in sorrow like a shadow; though banished still she thought of Rāma alone. Thus she was really a पतिव्रता। Even in her banishment, she curses her luck and not Rāma; thus though wronged she uttered not a single reproach against her husband. Such an ideal picture of self-abnegation and undeviating submission to the will of the husband is rare indeed. Even though विमानिता the addresses आर्यपुत्र to Rāma. She restores back Rāma to consciousness by the words—"जं भोदु तं होदु"।

There is more meaning here than what meets the ear. In fact the Third Act gives us a clear picture of Sītā's deep love and great concern for her husband. After the birth of Lava, of Kuśa, her consideration of husband was greather than that of sons. Of a spotless charcter she feels for others grief. As a being of purity she sanctifies all by her chaste character ("उत्पत्तिपरिपूतायाः किमन्यैः पावनान्तरैः। "हा चारित्रदेवते"।"अर्पितेयं तवाभ्यासे सीता पुण्यब्रतावधूः!") We conclude by saying that her love for husband was amply rewarded when Rāma was about to perform अश्वमेध by a हिरण्मयी सीताप्रतिकृति। Thus Arundhati addresses Rāma (as he was taking back Sītā)......

"जगत्पते...रामचन्द्र! नियोजय यथाधर्मं प्रियां त्वं धर्मचरिणीम्।
हिरण्मयाः प्रतिकृतेः पुण्यप्रकृतिमध्वरे।।"

In fact, Sītā is ver a sobre devoted wife; only once has cuts joke with Lakṣamaṇa (e.g, "इयमपि अपराका")।

Lakṣmaṇa is depicted as an unselfish brother following Rāma obediently. *Chandraketu* is his worthy son and a befitting fighter of the solar race.

Lava and *Kuśa* are worthy sons of a worthy Kṣattriya father and act as true disciples of a great sage like Vālmīki.

Janaka is here painted as a great saint overcome with grief for his daughter's misfortune.

Kauśalyā as a noble queen of Dasaratha is all tenderness.

Arundhati, Gaṅgā, Pṛthvī as God-like women and plays part in briging re-union of Sītā and Rāma.

Vālmīki is all kindness (cp. मा निषाद etc. Act. II.) and acts here like providence and manages everything to unite Rāma and Sītā.

Chapter - 1

(*i*) इदं गुरुभ्यः पूर्वेभ्यो नमोवाकं प्रशास्महे।
विन्देम देवतां वाचममृतामात्मनः कलाम्।।1।।

With the utterance of *Names* unto the old masters, we pray that we might attain Speech Divine, the immutable digit of *Brahman*. Or—Here, we utter word *Namas* unto the old masters that we might....*Brahman*.

मितभाषिणी। अन्वयः–पूर्वेभ्यो गुरुभ्यो नमोवाकम् "आत्मनः अमृतां कलां देवतां वाचं विन्देम" इद्रं प्रशास्मेह। यथा–इदं पूर्वेभ्यो गुरुभ्यो नमोवाकं प्रशास्मेह। आत्मनः अमृतां कला देवतां वाचं विन्देम।।

व्याख्या–'पूर्वेभ्यः' प्राचीनेभ्यः 'गुरुभ्यः' रामायणादिप्रवन्धमुखेन उपदेष्टृभ्यः वाल्मीकिभासकालिदासादिभ्यः 'नमः' नमः शब्दस्य 'वाकः' उच्चारणं यास्मिन् कर्मणि अन्ति तत् यथा तथा (मत्वर्थीयः अच्। न हि बहुव्रीहिः, षष्ट्या वैयधिकरणस्य तत्र अनाकरत्वात्) 'आत्मनः' ब्रह्मणः 'अमृताम्' अनपायिनीं 'कला' षोडशभागत्मिकां 'देवतां' देवस्वरूपां 'वाचं' वाणीं शब्दब्रह्मणः "सूक्ष्मा"–संज्ञितां तुरीयां भिदाम् (उक्तञ्च–"वैखरी शब्दनिष्पत्तिर्मध्यमा श्रुतिगोचरा। द्योतितार्था च पश्यन्ती सूक्ष्मा वागनपायिनी।।" इति) 'विन्देम' लभेमहि 'इदम्' एतत् 'प्रशास्महे' आशास्महे प्रार्थयामहे। इति कवेरात्माकाधनिवेदनम् ('अस्मादो द्वयोश्च" इति बहुवचनम्)। एष गुरुभ्यः प्रणामः तत्प्रसादात् शब्दब्रह्मणः सूक्ष्मा कला मे स्फुरतु ततो जीवन्मुक्तो विषयेषु स्वतन्त्रः स्याम् इति फलितम् (तदुक्तम्–"तस्यां विज्ञातमात्रायामधिकारो निर्वत्तते। पुरुषे षोडशकले तामाहुरमृतां कलाम्।।" इति)। पक्षे व्याख्यानम्–'इदम् एतत् 'पूर्वेभ्यो गुरुभ्यो नमः' एव 'वाकः' शब्दः (कर्म्मणि घञ्) तं 'प्रशास्महे' उच्चारयामहे। एषोऽहं गुरून् नौमि इत्यर्थः। किमर्थे प्रणाम इत्याह–'आत्मनः अमृतां कलां देवतां वाचं विन्देम' इत्यादि प्राग्वत्। उभयव–अमृताकलाविज्ञानफलं सर्वविषवेषु विभुतां कामये। तच्च विज्ञानम् ऋते गुरुप्रसादात् न सम्भवति तत् प्रथमं गुरुनेव नौमि इति तात्पर्यम्। कविवचनमिदं नटमुखेन।

Notes. I. उत्तरामचरितम्–चरितम् is रामस्य चरितम्। the deeds of Rāma. उत्तरं चरितम्, the *later* deeds of Rāma, कर्मधा– । उत्तररामचरितम् अधिकृत्य कृतं नाटकम् इति उत्तररामचरित+अण् उत्तररामचरित्, the अण् disappearing by the Vattika "लुबाख्यायिकाभ्यो बहुलम्"। Or, by transference of epithets (लक्षणा) 'the later deeds of Rāma' are taken to mean *to book* on the later deeds of Rāma. Or again चरित is चरितर्णन by लक्षणा। उत्तरं चरितमस्मिन् उत्तररामचरितम्, बहु– । Here, *later*, means those happening after Rāma's return from Laṅkā. The *prior* deeds are described by the poet in another work named वीरचरितम् or महावीरचरितम्। The name of the drama is sometimes given as उत्तररामचरितम्। But as the other drama is never *spoken* of as वीररामचरितम् we prefer here the simple उत्तररामचरितम्।। 2. अङ्कः–Act. The अङ्क Continues untill *all* the actors leave the stage. "अन्तनिष्क्रान्तनिखिलपात्रोङ्कः परिकीर्त्तितः"।। 3. इदम्–In the alternative Tika this refers to the *act* of salutation, the वाक्यार्थ of गुरुभ्यः .... प्रशास्महे। Hence *neuter* as in "किमिदं द्यतिमात्मीयां न विभ्रति यथा पुरा "– Kumara. Also "इदमशरणैरद्याप्येवं प्रसीदत रुद्यते"–Act III, sl. 32. 4. गुरुभ्यः–चतुर्थौ सम्प्रदाने by the rule "कर्माणा यमभिप्रैति स सम्प्रदानम्"। नसस् is the कर्म in the Ist व्याख्या and it is intended for गुरु। In the second, the कर्म is नमोवाक which again is meant for गुरु। The चतुर्थी has nothing to do with the नमस् शब्द here, because we still get चतुर्थी if नमस् is replaced by some other word. Thus गुरुभ्यः नमः वक्ति, गुरुभ्यः अभिवादनं वक्ति, गुरुभ्यः वन्दनं वक्ति, etc. It is the क्रिया that regulates the विभक्ति here. 5. नमोवाकम्–वचनम् इति वच+घञ् भावे वाकः। नमः इत्यस्य वाकः, द्वतत्– । नमोवाकः अस्ति अस्मिन् इति नमोवाक+अच् मत्वथ नमोवाकम्, containing the utterance of नमस्। तत् यथा तथा। Qual. प्रशास्मेह। this suits the Ist व्याख्या। For the 2nd, उच्यते इति वच+घञ् कर्मणि वाकः word नमः इति वाकः नमोवाकः, the word नमस्, कर्मधा– । तम्। कर्म of प्रशास्मेह। See next note. In the Ist व्याख्या, the मत्वर्थौय अच् is a necessity, beacause the व्यधिकरण बहु–, *viz*, नमः इत्यस्य वाकः अस्मिन्, goes against panini and should be avoided if possible. 'सामनाधिकरणनां बहुव्रीहिर्वक्ताव्यः व्यधिकरणनां मा भूत्"–*Bhāṣya*. 6. प्रशास्महे–शास् is परस्मैपदौ। The गणसूत्र "आत्रः शासु इच्छायाम्" gives आत्मनेपद to आ+शास only, *not* to प्र+शाम also. So प्रशास्महे। Should be प्रशास्मः। But there are some who do not consider "आङः शासु– " to be always binding. This will justify प्रशास्महे। Madhava attributes this view to आत्रेय। Thus—"प्रायेणयमाङ्

पूर्व इति 'नमोवाकं प्रशास्मेह इति भवभूतिप्रयोगोपपत्तिरित्यात्रेयः''–*Dhātu-Vṛtti*. This implies that शासु to mean इच्छा is usually (प्रायेण) preceded by आङ् (sometimes by other prefixes also) and then it has the आत्मनेपद। Nāgeśa takes the प्रायिकता in a wider sense. He belives that not only may the उपसर्ग change but the meaning also. Hence he says प्रशास्महे means कुर्महे। Thus—''नमोवाकमिति वचेर्धञि वाकः। नम इति वचनमित्यर्थः, नमस्कारमिति यावत्। प्रशास्महे कुर्महे इत्यर्थः। धातूनामनेकार्थत्वात्''–*Śabdendusekhara*. Viraraghava says ''प्रशासनन्तु निर्देशः''।। 7. विन्देम–विद here is लाभार्थक (तदादि, उभयपदौ)। ''सत्तायां विद्यते ज्ञाने वेति विन्ते विचारणे। विन्दते-विन्दतौ लाभे श्यन् लुक-श्रम शेष्विदं क्रमात्।।'' शकि लिङ्। The सूक्ष्मा कला is gained by कर्मयोग and ज्ञानयोग (See note 10). 8. देवतां वाचम–देव एत इति देव+तल् स्वार्थे देवता। देव is masculine and देवता is feminine because sometimes स्वार्थिक affixes do give different gender and number to the resultant word. क्वचित् स्वार्थिकाः प्रकृतितो लिङ्गवच नान्यतिवर्तन्ते''। देवता वाक् here is a particular कला of ब्रह्मन् or आत्मन्। It is वाक् or शब्द in its subtlest form (सूक्ष्मा वाक्) and is different from what is popularly called वाग्देवौ (See under यं ब्रह्माणम् etc.—below) 9. असृताम्–सृतं मरणम् अपायः। अविद्यमानं सृतमस्याः बहु–ताम्। The सूक्ष्मा कला is supposed to be immutable (असृता, *i.e* अविकारा)। ''सूक्ष्मावागनपयिनी''। 10. आत्मनः कलाम्–कला is the 16th part. This कला is supposed to reside at मूलाधार। ''सा हि सर्वस्यप्राणापानान्तरालवर्त्तिनी विगतप्रादर्भावतिरोभावा सम्यक्- प्रयोगपरिशीलनात्मना कर्मयोगेन, मननादिना ज्ञानयोगेन च, सम्यगधिगम्यते''–*Ratneśvara*.

(*ii*) (नान्द्यन्ते) सूत्रधारः–अलमतिविस्तरेण। अद्य खलु भगवतः कालप्रियनाथस्य यात्रायाम् आर्य्यमिश्रान् विज्ञापयामि। एवमत्रभवन्तो विदाङ्कर्वन्तु–अस्ति तत्रभवान् काश्यपः श्रीकण्ठपदलाञ्छनः पदवाक्यप्रमाणतत्त्वज्ञो भवभूतिर्नाम जातुकर्णीपुत्रः (सू–)

(*After the Nandi*) Manager—Away with much prolixity. I address honourable gentlemen to-day at the festival of the mighty Kālapriyanātha. Let these respectable people know it thus—There is an illustrious descendant of Kaśyapa, marked with the epithet Śrīkantha, versed in the essence of the regulations on words and sentence (Grammar), born of the mother of the Jātukarṇya *Gotra*, Bhavabhūti by name, (MA)—

मित–।'नान्द्याः पूर्वरङ्गाख्याया मङ्गलक्रियायाः' अन्ते' अवसाने सूत्र कथासूत्रं धारयतीति 'सूवधारः' नटानां नेता स्थापकनामा नटः कथयति।। अलमितिकिं कथयति इत्याह– 'अतिविस्तरेण' बाहुलोन 'अलम्' संक्षेपतः कर्तव्य निवेदयामि। 'अद्य खलु भगवतः कालप्रियनाथस्य अत्रैव स्थापितस्य शिवलिङ्कविशेषस्य 'यात्रायाम' उत्सवे समवतेतान् 'आर्यमिश्रान्' पूज्यान् महानुभावान् 'विज्ञापयामि' बोधयामि। 'अत्रभवन्तः' पूज्या इमे 'एवं' विदाङ्कुर्वन्तु इत्थं जानन्तु। वेद्याञ्चाह–तत्रभवान् काश्यपः' कश्यपसगोचः पूज्याः 'श्रीकण्ठः' इति 'पदं लाच्छनं' चिह्न यस्य ताहशः श्रीकण्ठोपाधिक इत्यर्थः 'पदानां सूप्तिङन्तानां' वाक्यानां सूम्भूयार्थामिधायिना पदकदम्बानाञ्च यानि 'प्रमाणानि' अनुशासनानि तेषां 'तत्त्वज्ञः' मर्मवि् 'भवभूतिर्नाम' भवभूतिः इति प्रसिद्धः 'जातूकर्ण्याः' जातूकर्ण्यगोवोद्भवायाः। कस्याचित् ब्राह्मण्याः 'पुत्रः अस्ति'।

Notes. 1. नान्दान्ते–नन्दनं नन्दः rejoicing, भावे घञ्। नन्दे, नन्दात्, नन्देन वा क्रियते पठ्यते वा इति नन्द+अण् शैषिकः स्त्रियां नान्दी। It is often only a benedictory verse. "देवद्द्विजनृपादीनामाशीर्वादपरायणा। नन्दन्ति देवात यस्मात्तस्मान्नान्दी प्रकीर्त्तिता।।" Here by नान्दी the poet refers to *all* those observances which precede the acting. The benedictory verse is only one of them. Collectively these are known as पूर्वरङ्ग। "यन्नाठ्यवस्तुनः पूर्वरङ्गविघ्नोपशान्तये। कुशीलवाः प्रकुर्वन्ति पूर्वरङ्ग स उच्यते।। प्रत्याहारादिकान्यङ्गान्यस्य भूयांसि यद्यपि। तथाप्यवश्यं कर्त्तव्या नान्दौ विघ्नोपशान्तेय।।" The drift is—The ceremonies are numerous. But the benedictory verse (नान्दी) is indispensable though the rest may be omitted. The verse "इदं गुरुभ्यः–" does not satisfy the definition of a नान्दी as given above. It merely expresses the wish of the poet himself and is not the नान्दी। We have to suppose that the ceremonies have been observed and the नान्दी verse, whatever it was, recited *outside* the stage. But the ways of Bhavabhūti are sometimes so unothodox that is quite possible that this very verse was meant to pass as नान्दी। The procedure then would be that the सूत्रधार should enter the stage, recite the verse "इदं गुरुभ्यः–" and thereafter commence the प्रस्तावना। 2. सूत्रधारः–सूत्र+धृ+णिच् स्वार्थे+अण् कर्त्तरि। "पूर्वरङ्ग विधायादौ सूत्रधारे विनिर्गते। प्रविश्य तद्वदपरः काव्यमासूत्रयेन्नटः।।" Hence the पूर्वरङ्ग is performed *outside*, the सूत्रधार enters *thereafter* (नान्दान्ते)। 3. विस्तरेण+वि+स्त्+अप् भावे विस्तरः। With घञ् we get विस्तारः। Both refer to expanse, but the Ist to that of words only. Thus वाक्यस्य विस्तारः but पटस्य विस्तारः। The rule is प्रथमे वावशब्द"। 4. आर्यमिश्रान्–मिश्र is प्रशंसावचन। "मतल्लिकोद्घमिश्राः स्युः प्रकाण्डस्थलभित्तयः" इति गणव्याख्याने। प्रशस्या आर्याः

आर्यमिश्राः, the परनिपात of मिश्र being due to the rule ''प्रशंसावचनैश्च''। 5. अत्रभवन्तः–एतद्+जस् (1 मा)+चल स्वार्थे अत्र, meaning एते। अत्र भवन्तः (कर्माधा–) need not necessarily be a compound. अत्रभवत् तत्रभवत् etc. imply पूजा। 6. विदाङ्कुर्वन्तु–विद+लोट अन्तु निपातनात्। Optionally विदन्तु by the rule ''विदाङ्कुर्वन्त्वित्यन्यतरस्याम्''। 7. श्रीकण्ठ etc.—श्रीः सरस्वती कण्ठे अस्य श्रीकण्ठः a learned degree implying vast eruditicn. 8. भवभूतिः–This is the name of the poet. Viraragava, however, suggests that श्रीकण्ठः is the proper name given him by his father and भवभूति the name under which he is known to the word. He states the origin of the name thus—''एतत्कृत–साम्बा पुणातु भवभूतिपवित्रमुर्त्तिः–इति श्रीकश्रवणसन्तुष्टो राजा भवभूतिरित्येनं ख्यापयामास....किञ्चास्मै कवये ईश्वर एव भिक्षुरूपेण आगत्य भूति दत्तवान्... एवञ्च भवात् भगवतो भूतिर्यस्य इति भवभूतिरित्यन्वर्थ इत्याहुः।'' We suppose भवभूति was the name and श्रीकण्ठ the title. 9. जातूकर्णी etc.—जतूकर्णस्य ऋषेगोर्वेत्रापत्यं स्त्री इति जतूकर्ण+यञ्+ङीप्=जातूकर्ण्य+ङीप्=जातूकर्णी the य disappering by the rule ''हलस्तद्धितस्य''। पिता काश्यपः माता जातूकर्णी इति उभयोः कुलयोर्महानयं कविरिति फलितम्।

(*iii*) **(सू–) यं ब्रह्माणमियं देवी वाग् वश्येवानुवर्त्तते।**

उत्तरं रामचरितं तत्प्रणीतं प्रयुज्यते।। 2।। (सू–)

(Ma—) Which Brahman this goddess speech obeys like one ensalved. The later deeds of Rāma recorded by him (in the form of a drama) are being staged. 2. (Ma—).

मित–अन्वयः–यं ब्रह्माणम् इयं देवी वाक् वश्या इव अनुवर्तते। तत् प्रणीतम् उतरम् रामचरितं प्रयुज्यते।

व्याख्या–'यं ब्रह्मणं' विरिञ्चिमिव द्वितीयं यं भवभूतिम् 'इयं दैवी वाक्' सरस्वती 'वश्या इव' अनुरक्ता इव रमणी 'अनुवर्त्तते' सेवते इति पूर्वेण सम्बन्धः (यच्छब्दस्य उत्तरवाक्यगतत्वेन अन्वयात् न तच्छब्दव्यपेक्षा)। भूपृष्टे ब्रह्मा एवायं भवभूतिः। नाकपृष्ठस्य ब्रह्मण इव अस्यापि भार्या सरस्वती। परन्तु एष भेदः–नाकस्य ब्रह्माणमियं पातिव्रत्यानुरोधात् सेवते, इमं पुनर्भूतलगतं ब्रह्माणं प्रेमविह्वला सती इत्याशयः। इयञ्च रूढाहङ्कारकत्थना। श्लोकार्द्धमिदं पूर्वेण अन्वितम्–भवभूतिरस्ति यं ब्रह्माणम् इत्याद्यवन्यः। उत्तरार्द्धं तु–'तेन' भवभूतिना 'प्रणीत' नाटकाकारेण निबद्धम् 'उत्तरम्' अर्वाचीनम् अयोध्याप्रत्यावर्त्तनात् परं भूतं 'रामचरितं' रामचरितकथा 'प्रयुज्यते' अमिनीयते। इति विज्ञापयामि भवन्तोऽपि जानन्तु इति पूर्वेण सम्बन्धः।

Notes. 1.ब्रह्माणम्–ब्रह्मन् means both प्रजापति and विप्र। "ब्रह्मा विप्रः प्रजापतिः" इत्यमरः। विप्र is not intended here, for then the poet would have written the more familiar word ब्राह्मणं। 'यं ब्राह्मणमियं देवी' suits the metre well. Besides, after what has gone before any one can infer that भवभूति was a विप्र without being explicity told of it. In fact ब्रह्मणम् is deliberately used here to mean प्रजापति। The poet brags that he too is ब्रह्म having सरस्वती for his wife ! 2. दैवी वाक–This is सरस्वती the wife of प्रजापति। देवतां वाचम् of sl. 1 is different, because सरस्वती (देवी वाक्) the poet already commands (वेश्येवानुवर्त्तते), While he is only hopping to acquire देवतां वाचम् (विन्देम प्रशास्महे)। It is not any one and every one than can entertain such hope. Even Vālmīki was inspired in अमृता कला after years of toil. The inspiration came to him quite unawares when he saw a fowler shoot down a heron. He did not know that he was inspired and had actually to be told of it by Brahman himself. Comp. "पद्मयोनिरवोचत् ऋषे प्रबुद्धोऽसि वागात्मनि ब्रह्मणि" (Act II,para viii). 3. यं ब्रह्माणम् etc.—This half has to go with the prose preceding; for, otherwise, the meaning becomes that the drama is the work of प्रजापति himself. At any rate the author is not identified. The work is of some ब्रह्मन् whom देवी वाक्अनुवर्त्तते, nothing showing that *that* ब्रह्मन् is भवभूति। On other grounds too it is necessary that यम् etc. be predicated of भवभूति। For, then he audience at once feels interested in the poet. Of such prowess is the poet! His drama is indeed worth staging on an occasion like this in preference to dramas by older poets. Also यमित्यादिकस्य विधेयत्वेन उपस्थापनात् सामाजिकानामुन्मुखीकरणाम्। 4. तत्प्रणीतम्–As explained above the तद् here connot go with the यम् preceding. यम् going with the prose preceding, the second half of the verse must be taken as an independent sentence. तद् in the second half will not require the cerrelative यद् because it then becomes प्रक्रान्तार्थ (contextual)– भवभूतिरस्ति, तत्प्रणीतम् प्रयुज्जते is the context. 5. *Remark*—The audacious brag of the poet embodied in this verse taken along with the fact that the poet does not flatter the audience with any such compliment like "अभिरूपभूयिष्ठाः परिषत्," "परिषदप्येषा गुणग्रहिणी" or his own "लब्धश्च वाक्यनिस्यन्दनिष्पेषनिकषो जनः" (in the Viracharita) is significant. The poet has lost respect for audience. See *Remark* under Para xi.

(iv) **(सू–) एषोऽसि कार्यवशादायोध्यकस्तदानीन्तनश्च संवृत्तः। (समन्तादवलोक्य) भो भोः! यदा तावत् तत्रभवतः पौलस्त्यकुलधूम-केतोर्महाराजरामस्य अयमभिषेकसमयः रात्रिन्दिवमसंहतानन्दनान्दीकः, तत् किमिति विश्रान्तचारणानि चत्वरस्थानानि ?**

(Ea) Here, for the sake of my work I have become one of Ayodhyā and of that time. (*Looking, all round*) Ho! Ho! As this occasion for the coronation of the illustrious and mighty king Rāma, a veritable Dhūmaketu to the race of Paulastya, is indeed to have uninterrupted music of joy day and night, why then are the sites of court-yards deserted by bards?

मित–एषः' 'कार्य्यवशात्' प्रयोगनुरोधात् अभिनयहेतोः इत्यर्थः 'आयोध्यकः' अयोध्यायां दृष्टः कश्चित् पुरुषः ("धन्वयोपधात्–" इति बुञ्) 'तदानीन्तनश्च' रामसमकालोऽपि 'संवृत्तः' जातः। इतः प्रभृति मां सूत्रधारं मा मन्यध्वं किन्तु कञ्चिदायोध्यकम् तदानीन्तनञ्च। रामाभिषेकसमये कश्चिदयोध्यां प्रविश्य वक्ष्यमाणं ब्रवीमि इति जानीत इति भावः। तदेवाह–भो भोः' पुरुषाः 'यदा तावत्' यतश्च 'पौलस्त्यकुलस्य' रावणवंशस्य 'धूमकेतोः' उत्पातग्रहरूपस्य 'तत्रभवतः' मान्यस्य 'महाराजस्य' राजचक्रवर्त्तिनो 'रामस्य अयम् अभिषेकसमयः रात्रिन्दिवम्' अहर्निशम् 'असंहता' अविच्छिन्ना'' आनन्दनान्दी' उत्सवतूर्य्यघोषः यस्मिन् तथाविधो वर्त्तते 'तत्' तख्यात् 'किमिति' कथं 'चत्वरस्थानानि' अङ्गनभूमयः "विश्रान्तचारणानि' नटविरहितानि लक्ष्यन्ते? उत्सवस्य अविच्छेदो युक्तः तथापि अङ्गनेषु नटा न दृश्यान्ते, कथमेमत् इति प्रश्नः।

Notes. 1. एषोऽस्मि etc.—Henceforth सूत्रधार behaves as a man at Ayodhyā. This is irregular. The सूत्रधार should have left the stage after sl. 2. and entered again dressed as a man at Ayodhyā. The stage direction should have been something like this:–(निष्क्रान्त। ततः प्रविशति कश्चिदायोध्यकः:)। आयोध्यकः (समन्तादवलोक्य)–भो भोः etc. Instead, the man stays on and, dressed still as सूत्रधार, declares that he is no longer the सूत्रधार but a man of Ayodhyā! A most primitive method of stage-management undoubtedly. Practically पात्रप्रवेश has taken place here and the प्रस्तावना has ended. 2. अयोध्यक–अयोध्यायां जातः दृष्टो वा इति अयोध्या+वुञ् शैषिकः। This is Viraraghava's reading. Others have आयोध्यिकः with ठञ् of the अध्यात्मादि class. The sense is तत्र भवः ('lives there' not *born* there') on which the Vṛttikāra remarks—"सता भवत्यर्थो

गृह्यते न जन्म, तत्र जात इति गतार्थत्वात्"। Hence आयोध्यिक means 'lives in Ayodhyā'. But later (Para vii) सूत्रधार says he is a वैदेशिक–resident of a foreign country—which contradicts आयोध्यिक here. We therefore perfer आयोध्यकः। 3. तदानीन्तनः–तस्मिन् काले इति तद+ङि(७मी)+दानीम् स्वार्थे तदानीम्। तदानीं भव इति तदानी+ट्युल्। The तद् here refers to राम in रामचरितम् of sl. 2. The maxim "सर्वनाम्नानुसन्धिर्वृत्तिछन्नस्य" allows such reference even though the word referred to is compounded. Comp. "पटीलपत्रं पितघ्नं मूलं तस्य कफापहम्" where तस्य refers to पटोल not पटोलपच। 4.यदा–अव्यय indicating हेतु। Comp. "यदा वुधैः सर्वगतस्त्वमुच्यसे न वेत्सि भावस्यमिमं कथं जनम्"–*Kumara*. with the reading यदि, translate—If, as you say, the time is etc. This expresses some doubt as to the character of the time, which is not desirable. 5. पौलस्त्य etc.—पुलस्ति or पुलस्त्य is one of the Saptarṣis, a son of Brahman. तस्य गोत्रापत्यं पुमान् इति पुलस्ति +यञ् (or पुलस्त्य+अण्) पौलस्त्यः। धूमकेतु is a comet. Comets are supposed to augur misery to the world. By transference of epithets धूमकेतु means *like* धूमकेतु, *i.e.*, पीड़ाकार। Some take धूमकेतु as अग्नि। "अग्रात्पातौ धूमकेतू" इत्यमरः। 6. रात्रिन्दिवम्–दिवा is an अव्यय meaning दिवसे। रात्री च दिवा च इति रात्रिदिवा+अच् समासान्त रात्रिन्दिवम्। The द्वन्द्व, the समासान्त and the मकरान्तता of रात्रि are by निपातन in the rule "अचतुरविचतुर–" (P.5.4.77). 7. असंहृत etc.—नान्दी here is तौर्यत्रिक music or दुन्दुभि drum. Com. "नान्दीनादप्रभृति हि कृतं मङ्गलं तैस्तदानीम्", "दिष्ट्या देवदुन्दुभिध्वनिः"etc.—Viracharita. आनन्द festival rite. आनन्दस्य नान्दी music accompanying a festiverite. असंहृता आनन्दनान्दी यस्मिन्। बहु–"नद्यृतश्च" इति कप् समासान्तः। This is predicated of अभिषेकसमयः अयम्। The actor does not mean by समय the exact moment of coronation, but the whole period from a little before to a little after that moment. This is abvious from इयतो दिवसान् उत्सव आसीत् (para v.) 8. विश्रान्त etc.—विश्रान्त absent. Comp. "विश्रान्तविग्रहकथो रतिमान् जनानाम्", "विरोधी विश्रान्तः प्रसरति रसो निर्वृतिघनः" (Act VI, Sl. II). चारण bard. विश्रान्ताः चारणाः येषु बहु–। As अभिषेकसमयः is to be असंहतानन्दनान्दीकः why are चत्वरस्थानानि विश्रान्तचारणानि? Evidently this cannot be a part of the prelude (प्रस्तावना)।

(*v*) (प्रविश्य) नटः–भाव, प्रेषिता हि स्वगृहान् महाराजेन लङ्कासमर-मुह्रदो महात्मानः प्लवङ्गराक्षसाः, सभाजनोपस्थायिनश्च नानादिगन्तपावना ब्रह्मर्षयो यदाराजर्षयञ्चधनाय इयतो दिवसान उत्सव आसीत्। (न–)

(Entering) Actor—Sir, by the great king have been sent back to their homes the high-souled Monkeys and Rākṣasas who where allies in the war in Laṅkā the Brahmarṣis and Rājarṣis too—sanctifiers of the various quarters—that came for congratulation, in whose honour festivities lasted all these days. (Ac—)

मित– । "प्रविश्य नेपथ्यात् रङ्गमारुह्य 'नट' आह हे 'भाव' विद्वान् सूत्रधार ('भावो विद्वान्" इत्यमरः) 'लङ्कायां वृत्तो यः 'समरः' रणः तत्र ये 'सुहृदः' मित्राणि उपकारिण इत्यर्थः ते 'महात्मानः' उदाराशया भूरिविक्रमाश्च 'प्लवङ्गराक्षसाः' सुग्रीवविभीषणादयः सहैव रामेण ये लङ्कायाः समागताः, तथा 'सभाजनाय' अभिषेककर्मणि अभिनन्दनाय 'उपस्थायिनः' समागताः 'नानादिगन्तपावनाः' पूरिपूतदशदिशः 'ब्रह्मर्षयो रातजर्षयश्च महाराजेन, रामेण सम्राजा 'स्वगृहान् हि' निजभवनान्येव 'प्रेषिताः' प्रेरिताः (ण्यन्तात् प्रजोज्ये कर्मणि क्तः), 'यदाराधनाय' येषां ब्रह्मर्षिराजर्षिप्लवङ्गराक्षसानाम्'आराधनाय' सत्कृतये''इयतो दिवसान्' व्याप्य 'उत्सव आसीत्'। गतेषु तेषु उत्सवो विरतः विश्रान्तचारणानि च चत्वरस्थानानि इति भावः।

Notes—1. नटः–This is irregular. No नट should enter the stage after one of the *Dramatis Personae* has made his appearance. Here an आयोध्यक has already entered in the person of the सूत्रधार, and the नट is now entering to represent a second. These two are वैतालिक (bards) by profession as is abvious from "राजद्वारमेव स्वजातिसमयेन उपतिष्ठाव:" below (Para ix). 2. भाव–This is how a सूत्रधार has to be addresed by his companions. सूत्रधारं वदेद्भाव इति वै पारिपार्श्विकः"। Hence the नट takes the first comer as सूत्रधार and not as an आयोध्यक। By implication he himself too enters not as an आयोध्यक but as a नट of the stage set up at the यात्रा of कालप्रियनाथ। This is a glaring contradiction of "एषोऽस्मि कार्यवशात्–" above. Besides, as a नट of the local stage, he is utterly incompetent to explain the absence of चारण is in the quadrangles at the time of Rāma's coronation. "प्रेषिता हि–" etc. are therefore misplaced in his mouth. He can of course alter them if he enters as—acts the part of—another आयोध्यक। 3. प्रेषिताः–प्र+इष गतौ+णिच्+क्त कर्मणि। "गतिबुद्धि–" इत्यादिना द्विकर्मकत्वम्। 4. स्वगृहान्–"गृहं गृहाः पुभूम्निः" इति बहुत्वं पुंसि। The sense is—If taken in themasculine गृह *must* be in the plural. But if the plural is used it is not *necessarily* in the masculine. Comp. "नीवारसुष्टिपचना गृहिणो गृहाणि"–Act I, sl. 25. 5. लङ्का etc.—शोभनं हृदयमस्य gives सुहृदय also मुहृद्। The latter is by निपातन in the rule "सुहृद्दुर्हृदौ मित्रामित्रयोः" which restricts सुहृद् to a मित्र and दुर्हृद् to an अमित्र (enemy). सुहृदय means 'one with a good heart' whoever he may be—friend or foe, 6. प्लवङ्ग etc.—प्लव leap. प्लवेन गच्छन्ति इति प्ल+गम+खच् कर्त्तरि प्लवङ्गा or प्लवङ्गमाः। The खच् optionally elides the अम् of गम् by the Vārttika "खश्च डिद्वा वक्तव्यः"। रक्षांसि एव राक्षसाः। अण् स्वार्थे (See देवताम्, sl. I.) प्लवङ्गाश्च राक्षसाश्च। उक्त अणिकर्त्तकर्म of the क्रिया in प्रेषिताः। 7. सभाजन etc.—सभाज to greet चुरादि+णिच् स्वार्थे+लुाट् भा‌े सभाजनम् greeting सभाजनाय उपतिष्ठन्ते इति सभाजन+उप+स्था+णिनि साधुकारिणि क र्तरि। Qual. both ब्रह्मर्षयः and राजर्षयः। 8. नाना etc.—नाना is an अव्यय meaning विभिन्न। दिशाम् अन्तः। नाना दिगन्ताः। तान् पावयन्ति इति नानदिगन्त+पू+णिच्+ल्युट् कर्त्तरि बाहुलकात्। Or, पाव्यन्ते एभिरिति ल्युट् करणे। This too refers to both ब्रह्मर्षयः and राजर्षयः। 9. ब्रह्मर्षयः–ब्रह्मकल्पा ऋषयः, शाकपार्थिवादि। 10. राजर्षयः–राजान इमे ऋषय इव, उपमितकर्मधा–II. च–This *twice* occurs here. The first (सभाजनोपस्थायिनश्च) implies समुच्चय of ब्रह्मर्षि and राजर्षि with प्लवङ्ग and राक्षस in प्रेषणक्रिया। The second indicates समुच्चय of राजर्षि with ब्रह्मर्षि in पावनक्रिया। 12. यदारा etc.—आ+राध+णिच्+ल्युट् भावे आराधनम्। येषां आराधनम्। तस्मै। तादथ्ये चतुर्थी। 13. इयतः–इदं परिमाणमेषाम् इति इदम्+वतुप्=ई+वतुप् ई+घतुप्=इयत् (प्रातिपदिक) which in the second case plural becomes इयतः। Qual, दिवसान्। 14. दिवसान्–अत्यन्तसंयोगे 2या। These long continued festvities were a necessity as much in celebration of the unique coronation as in honour of the renowned guests. The सूत्रधार recognises only the importance of the coronation iteself (पौलस्त्यकुलधूमकेतोः अभिषेकसमयः), the नट draws attention to the high character of the guests—one set were the mighty allies of war and the other the sanctifiters of the whole universe. These are gone and the coronation has long been over hence the festivities cease.

(*vi*) **(न–) सम्प्रति हि**

(Ac) Now again,—

वशिष्ठाधिष्ठिता देव्यो गता राघवमातरः।
अरुन्धतीं पुरस्कृत्य यज्ञे जामातुराश्रमम्।। 3।

The dowager queens, the mothers of the Rāghavas, led by Vasiṣṭha, have gone to the house of their son-in-law, at a sacrifice, with Arundhati at their head.

मित– । एकं मिमित्तमुक्तमनुत्सवस्य अपरमपि शृणु–वशिष्ठेति ।

अन्वयः–देव्यो राघवमातरः वशिष्ठधिष्ठिताः (सत्यः) अरून्धतीं पुरस्कृत्य यज्ञे जामातुराश्रमं गताः ।

व्याख्या–'देव्यः' दशरथमहिष्यः 'राघवाणां' रामादीनां 'मातरः' कौसल्याकेकयी- सुमित्राः 'वशिष्ठेन' कुलगुरुणा 'अधिष्ठिताः' गोपिता नीयमाना वा सत्य 'अरुन्धती पुरस्कृत्य' गुरुपत्नीत्वेन तामेव अग्रतो निधाय 'यज्ञे जामातुः' ऋष्यशृङ्गस्य 'आश्रमं गताः' । यज्ञेऽपि जामातुरेव इत्यार्थादायाति । निमन्त्रितैर्वियुक्ता, दैवीमिश्च विरहिता राजधानी, तत् कथमुत्सव इति भावः ।

Notes. 1. वशिष्ठ etc.—अतिशयेन वशी इति वशिन्+इष्ठन् वशिष्ठः । अतिशयेन वसुमान् gives वसिष्ठ with a dental. अधि+स्था+क्त कर्मणि अधिष्ठिताः ruled over. Vasiṣṭa was the guide of the royal house in *all* matters. Comp."हा कष्टम्! अरुन्धतीवशिष्ठधिष्ठितेषु रघुकदम्बकेषु.....कथमिदं जातम्"–Act II, para xiii, 2. राघव etc.—रामस्य मातरः is also seen. But it looks disrespectful for an ordinary bard (चारण) to refer to the king by name without some much qualifying epithet as देवस्य, महाराजस्य etc. Hence too we avoid the exposition राघवस्य मातरः, मातरः, because राघवस्य in the singular refers specifically to राम। 3. पुरस्कृत्य–पुरस् is an अव्यय meaning अग्रे। पुरस+कृ+ल्यप्, गतितत्–The स of पुरस् becomes विसर्ग and is then restored (to स) by the rule "नमसुपुरसोर्गत्योः"। 4. यज्ञे–यज्ञ here by लक्षण is यज्ञकाल। तस्मिन्। अधि 7मी। 5. Remark—This verse gives an additional reason why festivities have ceased—why विश्रान्तचारणानि चत्वरस्थानानि। But is may well be asked if the festivities had anything to do with the dowager queens, or with वशिष्ठ and अरुन्धती either. On the other hand, if we suppose that the verse has no reference to the festivities, a reason has to be found why the नट unasked, speaks of the absence of the queens etc. here. The fact is, as explained in the Introduction, Bhavabhūti is anxious to remove the queen-mothers, Vasiṣṭha and Arundhati from the capital and seizes the earliest opportunity to inform the audience of their absence witout caring much to see if the information suits the occasion.

(*vii*) सूत्र–वैदेशिकोऽस्मीति पृच्छामि कः पुनर्जामाता।

Ma.—Who again is the son-in law? I ask because I live in a foreign land.

नटः–कन्यां दशरथो राजा शान्तां नाम व्यजीजनत्।
अपत्यकृतिकां राज्ञे लोमपादाय यां ददौ।।4।। (न–)

Ac.—King Daśaratha begot a dauther, Śānta by name, whom he gave unto king Lomapāda as an adoptive child.

मित–। कन्यामिति। 'राजा दशरथः शान्तां कन्यां व्यजीजनत्' जनमयामास 'यां' शान्तं 'लोमपादाय राज्ञे' अपत्यकृत्तिकां' दत्रिमां कन्यां 'ददौ'। अनपत्येन राज्ञा लोमपादेन याचितः स दशरथः स्वतनयां शात्मामस्मै कृत्रिमकन्यारूपेण ददौ इत्यर्थः।

Notes. I. बैदेशिकः–विदेशे भव इति विदेश+ठज्, अध्यात्मादि। भवः means वर्त्तमानः। "सत्ता भवत्यर्थो गृह्यते न जन्म" (see under आयोध्यकः, para 4). I am a man of Ayodhyā; but as I live in a forgeign land I am ignorant of the events of my own country and do not know who the son-in-law is. 2. व्यजीजतन्–वि+जन+णिच्+चङ्+लुङ् तिप्। 3. अपत्य etc.—कृता एव इति कृत+कन् स्वार्थे+टाप स्त्रियाम् कृतिका aritifical, adopted. अपत्यञ्च तत् कृतिका च अपत्यकृतिका, कर्मधा–। ताम्। कृतक, कृत्तिका etc. may appear either as विशेष or विशेषण in a कर्मधा–। The पूर्वनिपात is thus unrestricted. Comp. "सोऽनं न पुत्रकृतकः पदवी। मृगस्ते'–Śakuntala, Act IV; "कृतककलहं कृत्वा"–*Mudrārākṣasa;* "यस्योपान्तं कृतकतनयः कान्तया वर्द्धितो मे"–*Meghadūta* Or अपत्यं कृतिका, सुप्सुपा। Or again अपत्यं कृतकम् अपत्यकृतकम्, सुप्सुपा। स्त्रियाम् अपत्यकृतक+टाप्।

(*viii*) **(न–)। विभाण्डकसुतस्तामृष्यशृङ्ग उपयेमे।**

तेन च साम्प्रतं द्वादशवार्षिकं सत्रमारब्धम्। तदनुरोधात् कटोरगर्भामपि वधूं जानकीं विमुच्य गुरुजनस्तत्र गतः।

(Ac—) Bibhandaka'a son, Ṛṣyaśṛṅga, married her. And by him is now begun a sacrifice that will last for twelve years. For its sake, the mother-in-law have gone, leaving behind the daughter-in-law Jānakī though her period of gestation is full (Or—though with a fully developed foetus).

मित–। 'तां' शान्तां मुनेः 'विभाण्डकस्य सुतः ऋष्यशृङ्ग उपयेमे' उदवहत् ("उपादयमः स्वकणे" इत्यात्मनेपदम्)। 'तन च' ऋष्यशृङ्गेण 'साम्प्रतम्' अधुना 'द्वाशवर्षिक' द्वादशवर्षाणि भावि 'सत्रमारब्ध' यागः प्रक्रान्तः।'तस्य' यज्ञस्य जामातुर्वा 'अनुरोधात्' गौरवाद्धेतोः कठोरगर्भामपि' पूर्णगर्मामपि 'वध' जानकी विसुच्य एकाकिर्नी परित्यज्य 'गुरुजनः' श्वश्रूवर्गः 'तत्र गतः'।

Notes. I. द्वादश etc.—द्वौ च दश च द्वादश, द्वन्द्वः। Now द्वादशन् and वर्ष cannot be compounded into द्वादशवर्ष by "दिक्संख्ये संज्ञायम्" because द्वादशवर्ष is not a संज्ञा। We compound by "तद्धितार्थोत्तरपदसमाहारे च"। Thus द्वादशवर्षाणि भविष्यति इति द्वादशवर्ष+ठञ् (तद्धितार्थे द्विगुः)=द्वादशवर्षिकम्। उभयपदवृद्धि by "अनुशतिकादीनाञ्च"। The prohibition "वर्षस्याभष्यति" does not apply, because that is for those cases only in which उत्तरपदवृद्धि *alone* is enunciated. 2.तदनु etc.—अनुरोध is प्रतिबन्ध restraint. तस्य अनुरोधः the restraint put by it. तस्मात्। The sense is—The secrifice put a check to their free movements and forced them to be in attendance. The तद् here is better taken as referring to सत्र than to ऋष्यशृङ्ग। वशिष्ठ says "जामातृयज्ञेन वयं निरुद्धा" (sl. II). So the निरोध (अनुरोध), restraint, comes from जामातृयज्ञ *not* from जामातृ। 3. कठोर fully developed, advanced Comp. "कठोरताराधिपलाच्छनच्छविः" "कठोरीभूतस्तु दिवसः", "परिणतकठोरपुष्कर" "कठोरपारावलकण्ठ" etc.—गर्भ foetus, or, by लक्षण, the whole period of gestation. कठोरः गर्भः अस्याः, बहु- । ताम्। This is absurd (See Intro—). 4. जानकी विमुच्य–The words are ominous. Fore-cast of जानकीविमोचन? 5. गुरूजनः etc.—This refers to Sītā's mother-in-law. This is not possible. No Indian mother-in-law would think of it (See Intro—).

(*ix*) सूत्र– । तत् किमनेन। एहि राजद्वारमेव स्वजातिसमयेन उपतिष्ठावः।

Ma.—So away with this. Come let us attend at the royal gate as is the practice with our own caste.

नट–तेन हि निरूपयतु राज्ञः सुपरिशुद्धामुपस्थानस्तोत्रपद्धतिं भावः।

Ac.—Then let your honour think out some absolutely faultless lines of panegyrics of attendace.

मित– । सूत्रेति–अनेन उत्सवविरामहेतुचिन्तनेन। 'स्वा जातिः' चारणजातिः तस्याः 'समयः' आचारः तेन हेतुना 'राजद्वारमेव उपतिष्ठावः' उपसृत्य तिष्ठावः। वैतालिका वयम्, राजद्वारे स्थित्वा राज्ञः स्तुतिपठनमस्माकमाचारः, 'तत् एहि' आचारं पालायामः, अलमुत्सवालोचनरूपया अनधिकारचर्चया च।। नटेति–'तेन हि' निमित्तेन स्तुतिः पठनीया इति हेतोः 'भावः' मान्यो भवान् 'राज्ञः' सुपरिशुद्धाम् उपस्थानस्य' सेवायाः या 'स्तोत्रपद्धतिः' स्ततिपदावलिः तां निरुपयतु चिन्तयतु।

Notes. सूत्रधारः-This is irregular. He is no longer सूत्रधार now. Say आयोध्यकः। 2. खजाति etc.—Here सूत्रधार describes himself and the नट as two bards (वैतालिक) of अयोध्या। This is all right. 3. उपस्थान etc.—उपस्थान attendacne. पादाभ्यां हन्यते इति पाद+हन+क्तिन् कर्मणि पद्धतिः track; hence, line, string of panegyrics for attendance. सुपरिशुद्धाम् is important as giving occasion for सूत्रधार's remark and the नट's hint at the slander of the queen. 4. *Remark*—We expect the bards to recite some verses, but they do not do it. (see Sl.7).

(x) **सूत्रधारः—मारिष,**

सर्वथा व्यवहर्त्तव्यं कुतो ह्यवचनीयता।
यथा स्त्रीणां तथा वाचां साधुत्वे दुर्जनो जनः।। 5।।

Ma—Good man, we have to work, by all means. Whence, pray, is escape from criticism? People are wicked in the matter of the purity of speeches as of women.

मित—। 'मारिष' आर्य 'सर्वथा' सर्वप्रकारेण येन केनापि प्रकारेण इत्यर्थः 'व्यवहर्त्तव्यं' व्यवहारः कर्त्तव्य आचारो रक्षितव्यः। यथाशक्ति कर्त्तव्योऽनुष्ठेयः। 'कुतो हि' कुत एव 'अवचनीयता' निन्दाभावो भवेत, न कुतोऽपि इत्यर्थः। निन्दा स्यादेव, अतः सुपरिशुद्धया वा अपरिशुद्धया वा यया कथापि पद्धत्या स्तोतव्यम्। स्तुतिः कृता इत्येवालम्, शुद्धा वा अशुद्धा वा पदावलिरित्यकिञ्चित्करमिति भावः। कारणमाह,—'जनः यथा स्त्रीणां तथा वाचां साधुत्वे दुर्जनः खलः। सुपरिशुद्धामपि वाचम अशुद्धा इति वर्णयेत्।

Notes. 1. मारिष—The सूत्रधार has to address this attendants as मार्ष or मारिष। Here the सूत्रधार himself forgets that he is an आयोध्यक। 2. सर्वथा—By all means, after all, any how etc. Comp. "सर्वथा पीतं दुःशासनस्य रक्तम्"। 3. व्यवहर्त्तव्यम्—वि+अव+हृ+तव्य भावे। व्यवहार routine, conduct etc. व्यवहर्त्तव्यम् the routine has to be followed. सर्वथा व्यवहर्त्तव्यम्—The routine has after all (by all means etc) to be followed. We must any how do our work. Duty must not be omitted; whether done properly or imporperly is immaterial. 3. अवचनीयता—वच+अनीयण्कर्मणि वचनीयम् that which is to be condemned. न वचनीयम् not to be condemned, irreproachable. तस्य भावः। The sense is—Any way you cannot escape criticism; why then this solicitude for a सुपरिशृद्धा स्त्रोत्रपद्धतिः? 4. *Remark*—Here 'वाचां साधुत्वे दुर्जनो जनः" seems to be a fling at the audience. The audience is fault-finding; my previous work वीरचरित

has been unjustly criticised. See *Remark* under Para 'iv'. This has an important bearing on the sequence of Bhavabhūti's dramas (See *Intro*).

(*xi*) **नटः। अतिदुर्जन इति वक्तव्यम्–**

Ac.—you should say "extremely wicked";

देव्यामपि हि वैदेह्यां सापवादो यतो जनः।
रक्षोगृहस्थितिर्मूलमग्निशुद्धौ त्वनिश्चयः।। 6।।

For, people have evil words even in the matter of Queen Vaidehi. This stay in the house of the Rākṣasa is the root of it. Incredulity indeed prevails in the declaration of purity by Fire.

मित–। अतिदुर्जनत्वे हेतुमाह–'यतः' यस्मात् 'जनः देव्यां वैदेह्यामपि' या हि स्वयं देहवतीव साधुता तस्यमापि 'सापवादो हि' असाधुतासमारोपपर एव। किं तादृशस्य समारोपस्य वीजम् इत्याह–'रक्षसः' रावणस्य 'गृहे' या 'स्थितिः' निवासः सा एव 'मूलं' वचनीयवीजनम्। ननु अग्नौ शुद्धा सा, कुतो वचनीयता इत्याह–अग्नौ या 'शुद्धि' तत्र 'तु अनिश्चयः' अप्रत्यय एव। इति शङ्कास्थानस्य सूचना।

(*xii*) **सूत्रधारः–यदि पुनरियं किंवदन्ती महाराज स्पृशेत् ततः कष्टं स्यात्।**

Ma—It would be painful if this gossip reached the Mahārāja.

नटः–सर्वथा ऋषयो देवताश्च श्रेयो विधास्यन्ति। (परिक्रम्य) भो भोः क्वेदानीं महाराजः? (आकरर्ण्य) एवं जनाः कथयन्ति–

Ac—The saints and the gods will, by all means, promote welfare. (*Going round the stage*) Ho! Ho! Where is the Mahārāja now? (*Listening*) Thus do people say,—

स्नेहात् सभाजयितुमेत्य दिनान्यमूनि
नीत्वोत्सवेन जनकोऽद्यः गतो विदेहान्।
देव्यास्ततो विमनसः परिसान्त्वनाय
धर्मासनाद्विशति वासगृहं नरेन्द्रः।। 7।।
(इति निष्क्रान्तौ)। प्रस्तावना।

Through affection having come to greet and having passed these days in festivities, Janaka has gone back to-day to Videha; to console the queen, who is sad thereat, the lord of men enters the bed-room from the seat of justice (*Exeunt*).

मित–। सूत्रेति–नाहं जनानां सापवादतां गणयामि। 'पुन:' पक्षान्तरे 'यदि इयं किवंदन्तौ' एष लोकापवाद: 'महाराजं' स्पृशेत् तस्य कर्णगोचरा भवेत् 'तत् कष्टं स्यात्' विपद्भावेत्। इति भाविन्या विपत्ते: सूचना।। नटेति–सत्यं कष्टं स्यात् परम् 'ऋषय:' वाल्मीकिप्रभृतय: 'देवताश्च' पृथ्वीभागीरथ्यादय: 'सर्वथा' सर्वप्रयत्नेन 'श्रेयो विधास्यन्ति' कष्टमपनुद्य मङ्गलं करिष्यन्ति। इति सप्तमाङ्कप्रतिविम्बनम्। तत: उपस्थानस्तोत्रपाठार्थं 'परिक्रम्य' रङ्गमञ्चं परितो गत्वा असन्निहिते राजनि वृथा स्तव इति तत्रत्यान् जनान् पृच्छति 'भो: भो:' इत्यादि। आकाशभाषितमेतत्, उत्तरं श्रुत्वा आह–'जना:' इत्यादि। स्नेहादिति–अन्वय:। स्नेहात् सभाजयितुम् एत्य अमूनि दिनानि उत्सवेन नीत्वा अद्य जनक: विदेहान्! गत:। नरेन्द्र: तत: विमनसो देव्या: परिसान्त्वनाय धर्मासनात् वासगृहं विशति।

व्याख्या–'स्नेहात्' प्रीत्या 'सभाजयितुम्' परमकठोर-सत्यपालनत्रैलोक्यकरण्टकोद्धारप्रभृतिषु कर्मसु अभिनन्दितुम् 'एत्य' अयोध्या प्राप्य 'अमूनि' दिनानि उत्सवेन प्रमादेन 'नीत्वा अद्य जनक:' विदेहाधिपति: देव्या: पिता इति शेष: 'विदेहान्' निजजनपंद प्रति 'गत:'। नरेन्द्र: राम: 'तत:' तस्मात् जनकगमनात् 'विमनस:' 'क्षुब्धाया:' 'देव्या:' महिष्या: सीताया: 'परिसान्त्वााय' विनोदनाय् 'धर्मासनात्' सभामण्डपस्थितात् राजपीठात् धर्मासनं परित्यज इत्यर्थ: (ल्यब्लोपे पञ्चमी) 'वासगृहं' शयनमन्दिरं 'विशति'। 'एवं जना: कथयन्ति' इति पूर्वेण सम्बन्ध:। नास्त्यत्र महाराज: स्त्रोत्रपाठेन एहि याम: इति 'निष्क्रान्तौ' नटसूत्रधारौ।

Notes.—1. किंवदन्ती–किं वदति इति किम्+वद+झच् कर्त्तरि स्त्रियाम्=किंवदन्त+ङीष् गौरादि। Rumour. वर्द्धमान seems to suggest—वद+शतृ स्त्रियां वदन्तौ that which says, '*i.e* a rumour. कुत्सिता वदन्ती or किञ्चित् वदन्ती। 2. कष्टं स्यात्–This hints at the impending separation of the royal pair related towards the end of the first Act. 3. सर्वथा–By every means. 4. ऋषयो देवताश्च–The reference is to the vage Vālmīki (ऋषि:) and the goddesses Earth and Gaṅgā (देवता) as we find in the Seventh Act. 4. श्रेय:–अतिशयेन प्रशस्य इति प्रशस्य+इयसुन्। कष्टं स्यात् is assumed, but it will end happily through the intervention of Vālmīki, Earth and Gaṅgā. 5. परिक्रम्य–This is go to the gate of the audience chamber (राजद्वार, para *ix*). 6. भो भो: etc.—The नट undertakes to gather all the information, because he is the man on the spot while the other is a foreigner (वैदेशिक, para *vii*). This is addressed to people outside the stage. 7. आकर्ण्य–आ सम्यक् कर्णेन गृहीत्वा इति आ+कर्प+णिच्+ल्यप्। The reply is not heard by the audience. The enquirer feigns that he has heard the reply and translates it to the audience.This is just the characterstic of an आकाशभाषित। "किं ब्रवीर्ष्यवमित्यादि बिना पात्रं ब्रवीति यत्। श्रुत्वानुक्तमष्येकस्तत् स्यादाकाशभाषितम्।।" The stage direction shold have been—(परिक्रम्य–आकाशे) । Comp. Śakuntala, Act III, विष्कम्भक। As a rule there is no आकाशभाषित before actual staging has commenced. 8. उत्सवेन–The उत्सव was in honour of अभिषेक and also in honour of the august visitor (para *v*). 9. विदेहान्–निमि the old ancestor of जनक, the founder of his race, lost his body through a curse and was thence-forward know as विदेह। By transference of epithes विदेहस्य अनुचरा विदेहाः। Next विदेहानां निवासो जनपदः becomes विदेहः+अण् विदेहाः the अण् disappearing by the rule "जनपदे लुन्"। Lastly the resultant word is masculine plural by the rule "लुपि युक्तवद्व्यक्तिवचने"। 10. विमनसः–विक्षुब्धं मनो यस्याः सा विमनाः बहु–। तस्याः She was sorry for the parting with her father whom she had met after such a log and evenful inteval. 11. परिसान्त्वनाय–देवीं परिसान्त्वयितुम् gives देव्याः परिसान्त्वाय with लुयट। The चतुर्थी being by "तुमार्थाच्च भाववचनात्"। 12. धर्मासनात्–धर्म justice. धर्मस्य आसनम् the seat of justice—judgment-seat. 13. प्रस्तावना–प्र+स्तु+णिच्+युच् भावे स्त्रियाम् That which introduces, Prelude आमुख। "नटो विदूषको वापि पारिपार्श्विक एव वा। सूत्रधारेण सहिताः संलापं यत्र कुर्वते।। चित्रैर्वाक्यैः स्वकार्योत्थैः प्रस्तुताक्षेपिभिर्मिथः। आमुखं तत्तु विज्ञेयं नाम्ना प्रस्तावनापि सा।।"–*Sāhitya-darpaṇa.* The word प्रस्तुता–क्षेपिभिः has to be noted carefully. What is the प्रस्तुत–matter in hand—here? It is the acting of the उत्तररामचरित (para *iii*). That acting—the प्रस्तुत–has not become अक्षिप्त here in Sl. 7. It became अक्षिप्त wiht the word एषोऽहम् etc in para *iv*. The प्रस्तावना shold have ended there. There can be little or no doubt that the poet had really intended to close his प्रस्तावना there; and all that follows was ment by him to be a विष्कम्भक conducted by two men of Ayodhyā. Subsequently purists perhaps thought in unorthodox for the सूत्रधार alone to introduce the acting—सूत्रधारेण सहिताः suppose the presence of others along with the सूत्रधार। Accordingly with more zeal than thought they, it seems, altered the whole of the text from (समान्तदवलोक्य) भो भोः etc. down to इति निष्क्रान्तौ here. The result has been a mass of inconsistencies as noted during our progress above. Unorthodoxy surely is not desirable; but it is no doubt a much lesser evil than inconsistency.

Again, in the matter of the introduction of the acting by सूत्रधार *alone*, भवभूति can be supported by the case of भास as precedent. Bhāsa's dramas are all intorduced by सूत्रधार *alone*, The canons of dramatugy were formulated, not perhaps even excluding the नाट्यशास्त्र of Bharata, long after भास। But even after these cannos had taken entire possesion of the Indian s ages, भास was not despised for his unorthodoxy. Thus Bāṇa says—"सूत्रधारकृतारम्भैर्नाटकैर्बहुभूमिकैः। सतपाकं यशो लेभे भासो देवकुलैरिव।।" Here सूत्रधारकृतारम्भैः is not intended to imply a blemish. Before Bāṇa, Kālidāsa has said "प्रशितयशसां भाससौमिल्ल- कविपुत्रादीनां स्थितेष्वपि प्रबन्धेषु" etc. It is thus difficult to see what moved the purists to alter Bhavabhūti's text and imcorporate his विष्कम्भक into the प्रस्तावना। It has made the प्रस्तावना by no mens a short one as is expected from his अलमतिविस्तरेण in para *ii*. If on the other hand it be contended that all this work is the poet's own and purists had nothing to do with it, whn we must say that Bhavabhūti was a poet who cared little for his reputation.

(*xiii*) **(ततः प्रविशत्युप्रविष्टो रामः सीता च)**

(*Then enter Rāma and Sītā seated*)

रामः–देवि वैदेहि, समाश्वसिहि। ते हि गुरवो न शक्न वन्ति विमोक्तुमस्मान्।

Rāma.—Queen Vaidehi, cheer up. Such elders cannot indeed leave us.

किन्त्वनुष्ठाननित्यत्वं स्वातन्त्र्यमपकर्षति।
सङ्कटा ह्याहिताग्नीनां प्रत्यवायैर्गृहस्थता।। ८।।

But obligatory observances (lit. obligatoriness of observance) curtail freedon. The position of a householder who cherishes fire is risky on account of sin (through lapses).

मित–। 'ते' तथाविधाः स्नेहमयाः गुरवः पित्रादयः 'अस्मान् विमोक्तुं न हि शक्नुवन्ति'।। कथं तर्हि विमुक्ता एव वयमित्यत्राह किन्त्रिति।

अन्वयः–किन्तु अनुष्ठाननित्यत्वं स्वातन्त्र्यम् अपकर्षति। आहिताग्नीनां गृहस्थता प्रत्यवायैः सङ्कटा हि।

व्याख्या–'किन्तु' पक्षान्तरे 'अनुष्ठानानां' कर्त्तव्यविधीनां 'नित्यत्वम्' अनुल्लङ्घ-नीयता 'स्वातन्त्र्य' यथेच्छप्रवृत्तिम् 'अपकर्षति' नियमयति सङ्कोचयति। स्नेहात् इहैवावस्थाने जनकस्य प्रवृत्तिरमसित किन्तु नित्यानुष्ठेयानां विधीनामनुरोधात् सः अस्मान् परित्यज्य गतः। परतन्त्रेण सता तेनायं परित्यागः अत्र तस्य स्नेहाभावं मा शङ्किष्ठाः। धीरा भव, पुनरेष्यति तत्रभवान् पिता ते। इत्यचिरभाविनि रामकर्त्तकसीता-परित्यागे रामसुखेणैव दैवप्रेरिता काव्यपूर्वा सामाश्वासनवाणी वैदेह्याः। कुतः पुनर्जनकस्य अनुष्ठाननित्यता इत्यत्राह–'आहिताग्नीनां' साग्निकानां 'गृहस्थता' गार्हस्थं 'प्रत्यवायैः' पापैः नित्यानुष्ठानविधातजनितैः 'सङ्कटा हि' आपत्करी एर। तस्य हि राजर्षेर्वैवाहिको-ऽग्निराहित आस्ते तत्र नित्यहोमस्तेन अनुष्ठेयः अननुष्ठानेतु प्रत्यवाय इति भावः।

Notes. 1. ते गुरवः–This refers either to Janaka alone or to all elders of his type. If to Janaka alone, say गौरवे बहुवचनम्। 2. स्वातन्त्रम्–स्वम् आत्मा तन्त्र प्रधानं यस्म स स्वतन्त्रः one to whom his self is the final authority, '*i.e.*' Independent, बहु–। तस्य भाव इति स्वतन्त्र+ष्यञ्। Independance. 3. आहिताग्नीनाम्–आ+धा+क्त कर्मणि आहितः set up. आहितः अग्निः अनेन आहिताग्निः or अग्राहितः। The पूर्वनिपात of आहित is optional by the rule "वाहिताग्नादिषु"। 4. प्रत्यवायैः–प्रत्यवायते निम्नं प्रति गच्छति एभिः इति+प्रति+अव+अय+घञ करणे=प्रत्यवायाः those that cause one's downfall, '*i. e*'. sin.

(*xiv*) **सीता–जाणामि अज्जउत्त किन्दु सन्दावआरिणो बन्धुअण-विप्पओओ होन्ति। (जानामिआर्यपुत्र, किन्तु सन्तापकारिणो बन्धुजनविप्रयोगा भवन्ति)।**

Sītā—I know it, my husband, but separation from kinsmen causes grief.

रामः–एवामेतत्। एते हि हृदयमर्मभिदः संसारभावाः येभ्योः बीभत्समानाः सन्त्यज्य सर्वान् कामान् अरण्ये विश्राम्यन्ति मनीषिणः।

Rāma—So it does. These are just those heart rending traits of the world revolting from which the wise rest in the woods having renounced all cravings.

(प्रविश्य) कञ्चुकी–रामभद्र–(इत्यर्द्धोक्ते साशङ्कम्) महाराज–

(*Entering*) Chamberlain—Rāmabhadra—(*At this part utterance—With timidity*) Great king—

रामः (सस्मितम्)–आर्यः ननु रामभद्र इत्येव मां प्रति उपचारः शोभते तातपरिजनस्य। तत् यथाभ्यस्तमभिधीयताम्।

Rāma (*With smile*)—But, Noble Sir, this Rāmabhadra is indeed the form of address towards me that becomes the attendants of my father. So speak as is your wont.

कञ्चुकी–ऋष्यशृङ्गाश्रमादष्टावक्र सम्प्राप्तः।

Chamberlain—Aṣṭāvakra has come from the hermitage of Ṛsyaśṛṅga.

सीता–अज्ज तदो किं विलम्बीअदि (आर्य ततः किं विलम्ब्यते)?

Sītā—Noble Sir, why then delay?

रामः–त्वरितं प्रवेशय। (कञ्चुकी निष्क्रान्तः)।

Rāma—Usher him in quick (*Exit Kanchuki*)

मित–। जानामीति–कर्त्तव्यानुरोधात् शिष्यजनपरित्यागो न हि स्नेहस्तज्यते गुरुभिरिति 'जानामि किन्तु' सत्यपि ज्ञाने 'बन्धुजनै' पित्रादिभिः ये 'विप्रयोगाः' विरहाः ते 'सन्तापकारिणो भवन्ति'। परित्यक्ता वैदेही गुरुदुःखा अपि स्नेहोऽपि भवता त्यक्त इति नैव मन्यते इति रामं प्रति तस्यैव दैवस्य जानकीमुखेन आश्वासवचनम्।। एवमिति–'एतत्' बन्धुजनविप्रयोगरूपं वस्तु 'एवम्' ईदृशं सत्पापकारि इति भावः। 'एते हि' इमे एव ते 'हृदयस्य मर्म भिन्दति' ये तादृशाः 'संसारस्य' जीवलोकस्य 'भावाः' धर्माः 'येभ्यो बीभत्समानाः' जुगुप्समानाः, यद्वा–'येभ्यः' यैः हेतुभिः 'बीभत्समानाः' बैरूप्यं भजमानाः 'मनीषिणः सर्वान् कामान् सन्त्यज्य अरण्ये ब्राह्मणः। अर्द्धम् उक्तम्, तस्मिन्।। आर्येति–'ननु' इत्याक्षेपे। 'उपचारः' आमन्त्रणपादम्। 'तातस्य दशरथस्य 'परिजनः' रामस्य पैतृको भृत्य इत्यर्थः।।

Notes. 1. हृदय etc.—हृदयस्य मर्म हृदयमर्म। तत् भिन्दति इति हृदयमर्म+भिद्+किप् कर्त्तरि। 2. येभ्यः बीभत्समानाः–बैरूप्यं भजमाना इति बध (भ्वादि वैरूप्ये)+सन्+लटः स्थाने शानच् कर्त्तरि बीभत्समानाः lit. undergoing a change of attitude. Hence remotely जुगुप्सा is implied. Thus येम्भः has अपादाने पञ्चमौ by the Varttika

"जुगुप्साविरामप्रमादार्थनासुपसंख्यानम्"। Or हेतौ 5मी। 3. उपचारः– उपचरत्यनेन इति उप+चर+घञ्करणे उपचारः mode of address. 4. तापपरिजनस्य–शेषे षष्ठी। तातपरिजनस्य सम्बन्धे शोभते। The Chamberlain has to be an old Brāhmaṇa. He is employed in the harem and is the senior officer there. "अन्तः पुरचरो विप्रो बृद्धो गुणगणन्वितः। सर्वकार्येषु कुशलः कञ्चुकीत्यमिधीयते"।। 5. यथाभ्यस्तम्–अभ्यस्तम् practised. तत् अनतिक्रम्य यथाभ्यस्तम्, अव्ययी–। 6. किं विलम्ब्यते–Here in her eagerness Sītā commits a breach of etiquette. "Why delay" is an—order to lead him in at *once*—A peremptory order involving censure for the delay already made. But the king alone, as he is personally present there, is competent to pass such an order. 7. त्वरितम् etc.—Sītā's words have created an awkward situation for the Chamberlain. Should he wait to hear Rāma or should he fortwith go back as desired by Sītā? Rāma relivers the situation by formally ordering him to do with Sītā wants.

(*xv*) **(प्रविश्य) अष्टावक्रः–स्वस्ति वाम्।**

(*Entering*) Aṣṭāvakra—Blessing unto you both.

रामः–भगवन्रेभिवादये, इत आस्यताम्।

Rāma—I bow unot you, Worshipful Sir; be seated here.

सीता–भअवं णमो दे। अवि कुशलं मे सअलगुरुअणस्म अज्जाए अ सन्ताए (भगवन्नमस्ते। अपि कुशलं मे सकलगुरूजनस्य आर्यायाश्च शान्तायाः)?

Sītā—Salutation to thee, Mighty Sir. Is it all well with my elders and with noble Śānta?

रामः–निर्विघ्नः सोमपीती आवुत्तो मे भगवान् ऋष्यश्रृङ्गः आर्या च शान्ता?

Rāma—Is my brother-in-law, Worshipful Ṛṣyaśṛṅga, as well as noble Śānta, drinking Soma without let?

सीता–अम्हे वा सुमरइ (अस्मान् वा स्मरति)?

Sītā—I wonder if she remembers me.

मित–। 'सकलगुरुजनस्य' निखिलश्वश्रूजनस्य।। 'आवुत्तो मे' भगिनौपतिर्मम 'सोमपीती' सम्प्रति सोमरसपाननिरतः 'भगवान् ऋष्यश्रृङ्गः निर्विघ्नः कुशली किम्

इति प्रश्नकाकुः। 'आर्या च शान्ता' सोमपीतिनी निर्विघ्न किम्।। "सस्त्रीको धर्ममाचरेत्" इति शान्तायाः सोमपाने योगः।। अस्मान् इति–'वा' इति वितर्के। आर्या शान्ता 'अस्मान्' मां 'स्मरति वा'। चिरादर्शनात् स्मरणां प्रति वितर्केः।।

Notes. 1. वाम्–"नमः स्वस्ति–" इति स्वस्तिशब्दयोगे चतुर्थी। 2. सकल etc. गुरुश्वासौ जनश्च गुरुजनः। सकलो गुरुजनः। तस्य। This includes शान्ता। शान्ता however is specially mentioned to show Sītā's regards for her. 3. सोमपीतो–पीतं पानम्। भावे क्त। सोमस्य पीतं सोमपीतम् the drinking of the Soma juice. तत् अस्ति अस्य इति सोमपीत+इनि मत्वर्थे। He has to drink the juice on account of the याग। सोमपीती निर्विघ्नः implies सोमपानकर्म निर्विघ्नम्, hence यागो निर्विघ्नः। In other words Rāma wants to know if the sacrifice is proceeding smoothly without let or hindrance from Rākṣasas or toerh molester. As king it ishis duty to make such enquiry. 4. अस्मान् etc. The question is natural after seperation of 14 Years.

(*xvi*) **अष्टावक्रः (उपविश्य)–अथ किम्। देविभगवान् वशिष्ठस्त्वामाह–**

Aṣṭa. (*Having sat down*)—O yes (lit. What else) Queen, Mighty Vasiṣṭha say this unto you—

विश्वम्भरा भगवती भवतीमसूत
राजा प्रजापतिसमो जनकः पिता ते।
तेषां वधूस्त्वमसि नन्दिनि पार्थिवानां
येषां गृहेषु सविता च गुरुर्वयञ्च।। ९।।

The mighty sustainer of all (Earth) gave birth to you; King Janaka, a peer of Brahman, is your father. My child you have become a daughter-in-law to those kings in whose house Savita is the Guru as well as myself.

तत् किमन्यदाशास्मेह केवलं वीरप्रसवा भूयाः।

So what else shall I wish of you? Only be you the mother of heroes.

मित–। विश्रेति। अन्वयः–नन्दिनि, भगवतौ, विश्वम्भरा भवतीमसूत। प्रजापतिसमो भाजा जनकस्ते पिता। येषां पार्थिकानां गृहेषु सविता च गुरुः वयञ्च तेषां त्वं बधूः असि।)

व्याख्या–हे 'नन्दिनि' आनन्ददायिनि वत्से सीते 'भगवती विश्वम्भरा' देवी धरित्री 'भवतीम् असूत त्वां सुषुवे। पूतं महच्च ते मातृकुलम्। 'प्रजापतिना' ब्रह्मण 'समः' तुल्यः भुवि ब्रह्मवादप्रवर्त्तकत्वात् ब्रह्मकल्पः 'राजा जनकः ते पिता।' यथा माता तथा पिता च श्लाघ्यः। एबंविधायाः सम्बन्धे अनुरूपं श्वशुरकुलं भवतु इत्येव प्राथ्यर्ते। तदपि ते सिद्धं यतः 'येषां' पार्थिवानां गृहेषु सविता च गुरुः' वंशप्रवर्त्तकः 'वयञ्च' गुरुवः अहमपि नेता 'तेषां' त्वं वधूः' स्नुषा 'असि'। एवं पितृकुलेन मातृकुलेन श्वशुरकुलेन च महीयस्याः ते सन्ततिसौभाग्यमेव आशास्यं शिष्यते। 'तत् केवलं वीरप्रसूवा भूयाः' प्रवीरं जनय इत्येव 'आशास्महे' प्रार्थयामहे किम्' आशास्यमन्यत् नास्त्येव ते।

Notes. 1. विश्व विभर्त्तीति–विश्व+भृ+खच् कर्त्तरि संज्ञायां स्त्रियाम् विश्वम्भरा the earth. Here विश्व means सर्व and is a सर्वनाम्। Refers to the earth. For force see मित–। 2. प्रजापतिसमः–प्रजापतिना समः। For force see मित–। 3. नन्दिनि–नन्दयति इति नन्द+णिच्+ल्यु कर्त्तरि स्त्रियाम् नन्दिनी the daughter. 4. पार्थिवानाम्–पृथिव्या ईश्वराः इति पृथिवी+घञ् पार्थिवाः lords of the earth. तेषाम्। 5. सविता च etc.—Supply गुरुवः thus–सविता च गुरुः वयञ्च गुरूवः। The first गुरु here means 'progenitor.' The solar race of kings started with मनु who was a so of सविता। The second गुरु means 'spiritual guide' or 'adviser'. Plural because of वयम् of वयन् which used for the singular अहम् by the rule "अस्मदो द्वयोश्च"। गुरवः is a विधेय and not an ordinary विशेषण; hence the prohibition "सविशेषणानां प्रतिषेधः" does not apply. 6. वीरप्रसवा–प्रसूयते इति प्र+सू+अप् कर्मणि प्रसवः offspring. वीरः प्रसवो यस्याः। This is important, see sl. 10.

(*xvii*) **रामः–अनुगृहीताः स्मः।**

Rāma—We are favoured.

लौकिकानां हि साधूनामर्थं वागनुवर्त्तते।
ऋषीणां पुनराद्यानां वाचमर्थोऽनुधावति।।10।।

Of those that are deemed wise in the world, the speech follows facts; but of the primal seers facts, hasten after the speech.

मित–। अनेन आशीर्वचनेन वयम् अहञ्च जानकी च 'अनुगृहीताः' महान् हि एषोऽस्माकं प्रसादः। एतदेव स्फुटीकरोति लौकिकेति–'लौकिकानां' लोके विदितानां 'साधूनां सतां प्राकृतानां मुनीनामित्यर्थः' 'वाक् हि' वाणी तु 'अर्थं' वस्तु, यत् वृतं

यद्वा वर्त्तिष्यमाणं तदित्यर्थः 'अनुवर्त्तते' वृतवर्त्तिष्यमानानुयायी तेषां वाक्प्रयोगः। 'पुनः' पक्षान्तरे, आद्यानाम् ऋषीणां' वशिष्ठप्रमुखाणां पुराणनां महामुनीनां 'वाचं' वाणीम् 'अर्थः' वस्तु 'अनुधावति' अनुसरति वागनुरूपं परिणमति। एकत्र अर्थसापेक्षा वाक्, अन्यच वाकसापेक्षः अर्थः इति भेदः। तन्नूनं महामुनेः प्रसादात् गर्भस्थमिदमपत्यं मे पुत्र एव न कन्या, पुत्रोऽपि पुनः प्रवीरः न हि प्राकृतः कश्चित् क्षत्रियः, इति महान् अनुग्रही मम च सीतायाश्च। अस्मादेव विनिश्चयात् अनुपदमुच्यमानं जन्मकास्त्रप्रदानं सङ्गच्छते। कन्यापक्षे प्राकृतक्षत्रियपक्षे च स्पष्टैवासङ्गतिः।

Notes. 1. लौकिकानाम्–लोके विदिताः इति लोक+ठञ् लौकिकाः। तेषाम्; 2. अर्थम्–अर्थ is वस्तु fact 3. आद्यानाम्–आदौ भवा इति आदि+यत् आद्याः primeval. वशिष्ट, a son of Brahman himself, was indeed an आद्य ऋषिः।

(xviii) **इदं भगवत्या अरुन्धत्या देवीभिः शान्तया च भूयोभूयः सन्दिष्टम्–यः कश्चिद्गर्भदोह्वदः अस्याः सः अचिरात् सम्पादयितव्यः।**

Aṣṭa.—It has been repeatedly enjoined by Illustrious Arundhati, the queen-mother and Śānta that whatever puerperal longings this one may have, has to be forthwith provided.

रामः–क्रियते यद्येषा कथयति।

Rāma—It will be done forthwith if she speaks out.

अष्टावक्रः–ननान्दुः पत्या च देव्याः सन्दिष्टमृष्यश्रृङ्गेण–

वत्से कठोरागर्भेति नानीतासि, वत्सोऽपि रामभद्रस्तवद्विनोदार्थमेव स्थापितः। तत् पुत्रपूर्णोत्सङ्गामायुष्मतीं द्रक्ष्यामः।

Aṣṭa.—And unto the queen has. been said by Ṛsyaśṛnga, her sister-in-law's husband,—My child, you have not been brought here because your terms is full, and darling Rāma too has been left there solely for your entertainment. So I shall see your long-lived self with your lap occupied by your boy.

मित–। यः कश्चिदिति–यदा 'यः कश्चित्' य एव 'गर्भहेतुकः दोहदः' इच्छा 'अस्या' देव्याः सञ्जायते 'सः अचिरात' तत्क्षणं 'सम्पादयितव्यः'। ननान्दुरिति–'ननान्दुः' भर्त्तृभगिन्याः शान्तायाः। 'स्थापितः' अयोध्यायामिति शेषः।

Notes. 1. गर्भदोहदः–दोहम् आकर्ष ददाति इति दोहदः that which creates a hankering, इच्छा desire. गर्भस्य दोहदः, *i. e.,* गर्भजनितो दोहदः गर्भदोहदः puerperal longing. दोहद is इच्छामात्र। Thus "अथ दोहदम्। इच्छा काङ्क्षा स्पृहेहा तृड् etc."—*Amara.* Bhānuji remarks "अयमिच्छामात्रवाची अपि विशेषण गर्भिणीच्छायां प्रयुज्यते"। Bhavabhūti here differs. Again Amara makes the word neuter. Bhānuji quotes हेमचन्द्र for the masucline—"दोहदो गर्भलक्षणे। अभिलाषे तथा गर्भे"। Unfortunately the word is not one of the अर्द्धर्चादि class taking both the genders, and as Amara is a much higher authority than हैम we have to take this masucline use of Bhavabhūti as a license. For the neuter compare—"सनूपुररवेण स्त्रीचरणेनाभिताड़नम्। दाहदं यदशोकस्य ततः पुष्पोद्गमो भवेत्"।। 2. यद्येषा–The 'if' (यदि) implies that Sītā will not speak out. Some read यद् यदेषा। That implies—Every now and then I am supplying what she demands. It is preposterous to suppose that अरुन्धती etc. remained ignorant of this fact so long. Their request thus becomes superfluous. I therefore prefer यद्येषा which, implying doubt on Rāma's part about her disclosing the desire to him is quite in keeping with Sītā's bashfulness. 2. कठोर etc.—See para ix. 3. त्वद्विनोदार्थम–तव विनोदः त्वद्विनोदः। तस्मै, or स अर्थः प्रयोजनं यस्मिन् कर्मणि तत् यथा तथा। If Rāma too had gone Sītā would have felt very lonely. For objections See Intro.

(*xix*) **रामः (सहर्षस्मितम्)–तथास्तु। भगवता वशिष्ठेन न किञ्चिदादिष्टोऽस्मि?**

Rāma—(*With a smile of joy*)—So may it be! Havn't I been commissioned any way be Illustrious Vasiṣṭha?

अष्टावक्रः–श्रूयताम्–

Aṣṭa.—Listen—

जामातृयज्ञेन वयं निरुद्धा–
स्त्वं बाल एवासि नवञ्च राज्यम्।
युक्तः प्रजानामनुरञ्जने स्या–
स्तस्माद् यशो यत् परमं धनं वः।।11।।

I am detained by the sacrifice ofthe son-in-law; you are but a boy and your sovereignty of recent date. Be intent upon pleasing your people. Thence comes fame which is the highest treasure of your race.

मित–। राम इति। 'हर्षस्य' यत् 'स्मित' तेन 'सह'। वशिष्ठेन सीतायै प्रदत्तात् आशीर्वादात् पुत्रोत्पत्ति प्रति यो रामस्य निश्चयो जातः तस्येदमृष्यशृङ्गवचनं समर्थनम् इति 'हर्षः'। 'तथा' यथा भगवता ऋष्यशृङ्गेण अभिहित पुत्रर्णोतृसङ्गत्वं सीताया इति यावत् 'अस्तु' भूयात्। आशिषि लोट्।। जामात्रिति। वयं जामातृयज्ञेन निरुद्धाः। त्वं बाल एवासि राज्यञ्च नवम्। प्रजानामनुरञ्जने युक्तः स्याः तस्मात् यशः यत् वः परमं धनम्।

व्याख्या–'वयम्' अहं ते उपदेष्टा 'जामातुः' ऋष्यशृङ्गस्य 'यज्ञेन निरुद्धाः' नियन्त्रिताः। परिहीणोऽसि मदीयैरुपदेशैः कर्त्तव्योपदेष्टा च भवतो नास्ति कश्चिदपर इति मे शङ्कास्थानमिति भावः। स्वयमेवाहं समर्थ इति मा संस्थाः–'त्वं बाल एवासि' कुतो भवतः सामर्थ्यम्। भवतु, कर्त्तव्यञ्च गुरुतरं किमपि नास्ति तत् का शङ्का इत्यत्राह–'राज्यञ्च' ते 'नवम्' अचिरप्राप्तम् तत् प्रशमनानि बहूनि कार्याणि सन्ति, बालस्तुं कथं तानि कुर्याः इति युक्ता शङ्का। तर्हि किमत्र कार्यम् इत्याह–'प्रज्ञानामनुरञ्जने प्रीणने 'युक्तः स्याः' निरतो भवे 'तस्मात्' प्रजारञ्जनात् 'यशः' कीर्त्तिर्भवति 'यत्' यशः 'वः' इक्षाकूणां 'परमं धनम्'। प्रीताः प्रजास्तां स्तोष्यन्ति शङ्का च मे अपयास्यति कुलप्राप्ता कीर्तिश्च ते न हास्यति इत्यर्थः।

Notes. 1. जामातृ etc. त्वं लालः etc. नवश्च etc.—For force see मित–। 2. युक्तः–युक्ते समाधौ दिवादि+क्त कर्त्तरि। Or युजिर योगे रुधादि+क्त कर्मणि। In the latter case the nominative is कर्त्तव्यव्रुद्धि; thus कर्त्तव्यबुद्धिस्त्वां प्रजारञ्जने युनाक्ति=कर्त्तव्यबुद्धा त्वं प्रजारञ्जने युक्तः। 3. तस्मात् यशः etc.—We may also consture तस्मात् यत् यशः (तत्) वः परमं धनम्। In the construction adopted, यत्, being in a subsequent clause (उत्तरवाक्यगत), does not require the direct mention of तद्। 4. *Remark*—Here the first half of the verse states Vasiṣṭha's apprehension of mismanagement in his absence. Naturally, we expect the second half to suggest some way to avoid mismanagement. Instead, the second half exhorts the king to seek popularity. This seems incongruous. A defence may be given assuming that a popular king may sagely bungle state-affairs. Again, while speaking thus, Vasiṣṭha himself discards consistency (See. *Intro*). The fact is, for the development of his plot, the poet needs this exhortation to gain popular favour (See *Intro*).

(*xx*) **रामः–यथाह भगवान्मैत्रावरुणिः।**

Rāma—As the Illustrious Maitravaruṇi says.

स्नेहं दयाञ्च सौख्यञ्च यदि वा जानकीमपि।
आराधनाय लोकानां मुञ्चतो नास्ति मे व्यथा।। 12।।

There is no pain unto me sacrficing love, pity and bliss, nay even Jānakī, for the service of the poeple.

मित– । मित्रः सूर्यश्च वरुणाश्च मित्रावरुणौ । तयोरपत्यं मेत्रावरुणिः वशिष्ठः ('देवतान्द्वन्द्वे च" इत्यानङ् । "अत इञ्" इति इञ्) । 'यथा मेत्रावरुणिः' आह तथैव करिष्यामि, प्रजानामनुरञ्चने युक्तः स्यामित्यर्थः । स्नेहमिति–'लोकानाम् आराधनाय' प्रजानामनुरञ्चनाय' 'स्नेह दयाञ्च' खीखश्च सुखादि च, किं बहुना, यदि वा जानकीमपि' सर्वस्वभूतां मम 'मुञ्चतो मे व्यथा नास्ति' । इति सीताविविासनच्छ्रया ।

Notes. 1. मैत्रावरुणिः–मित्र in the masucline means the sun, वरुण is the water-god. मितश्च वरुणाश्च मित्रावरुणौ । मित्र becomes मित्रा by the rule "देवताद्वन्द्वे च" । तयोरपत्यं पुमान् इति मित्रावरुण+इञ् । But is not वशिष्ठ the son of ब्रह्मन्? He is; the tradition however is that वशिष्ठ lost this body through a curse. His spirit entered the Sun and Varuna through whom he was re-endowed with a body, got a re-birth. 2. स्नेहं दयाम्–स्नेह implies *pleasure,* the pleasure one feels at the sight of the beloved; दया imvolves *pain,*the pain casued by another's distress. 3. सौख्यम्–सुखमेव इति सुख+ष्यञ् स्वार्थे । 4. जानकीम्–In renouncing जानकी Rāma did indeed renounce स्नेह, दया and सौख्य ।

(*xxi*) **सीता–अदो एब्ब राहबधुरन्धरो अज्जउक्तो (अतएव राघवधुरन्धर आर्यपुत्रः) ।**

Sītā—Hence is that my husband leads among the Rāghavas.

रामः–कः कोऽत्र भोः? विश्राम्यतां भगवानष्टावक्रः ।

Rāma—Who is here, Ho! Well, Who? Let Illustrious Aṣṭāvakra be rested.

अष्टावक्रः–(उत्थाय परिक्रम्य च) अये कुमारलक्ष्मणः प्राप्तः (इति निष्क्रान्तः) ।

Aṣṭā.—(Rising and going round the stage)—Ha! Prince Lakṣmaṇa has come. (Exit).

(प्रविश्य) लक्ष्मणः–जयति जयत्यार्यः । आर्य तेन चित्रकरेण अस्मदुपदिष्टमस्यां वीथिकायामार्यस्य चरितमभिलिखितम् । तत् पश्यत्वार्यः ।

(Entering) Lakṣmaṇa—Prosper, let noble brother prosper. Noble brother, the experiences of your noble self, as instructed by me, have been painted along this walk by that painter. Let your noble self have a look at it.

मित– । अत इति–धुरं यानमुस्वं धारयतीति धुरन्धरः धानाग्रयायी वाहः, लक्षणया इह अग्रेसरः। राघवाणां धुरन्धरः रघुश्रेष्ठः। अविचारयतैव पराथेय आत्मत्यागस्तेन श्रेष्ठता। जयतीति–वीथिः पन्थाः इह तु प्रकोष्ठवत् आवृतः पन्थाः। सा एव वीथिका। तस्याम वीथिकाया भित्तौ इत्यर्थः। चरितं चित्रितम्, अपि च प्रासङ्गिकं यद्यत् वृत्तं सर्वम्। अभिलिखित चित्रितम्। तत् चित्रम् आर्यः पश्यतु।।

Notes. 1. राघव etc.—धुरं धारयति इति धुर्+णिच् संज्ञायाम् कर्त्तरि धुरन्धरः a संज्ञा of beasts of buden. By transference of epithets this is here used to mean the *formost.* राघवाणां धुरन्धरः। 2. कः etc.—It is curious that no one responds to Rāma's shout. 3. विश्राम्यताम्–वि+णिच्+लोट् ताम कर्मणि। विश्रम्यताम् is expected because श्रम is मित्; hence with णिच the rule "मितां ह्रस्वः" gives श्रामि not श्रमि। Hence while commenting on "धुर्यान् विश्रामयेति सः" In Raghu I, Malli takes up the Vṛttikāra's hint "केचिदत्र वा इत्यनुवर्त्तयन्ति। सा च व्यवस्थितविभाषा" *i. e.,* वा follows from the previous rule "वा चित्तविरागे" attaching aptionality to "मितां ह्रस्वः", but the option has to be व्यवस्थित, restricted. In other words we have to consider that some roots allow ह्रस्व, some do not. श्रश् is one of those roots that do not allow ह्रस्व। Thus विश्राम्यताम् not विश्रम्यताम्। But the केचित् of the Vṛtti's shows that the Vṛttikāra does not like this defence. So too Mādhava. They should have विश्रम्यताम् only. We may say श्रम श्रामः with the तद्धित affix अण् (प्रज्ञादि)। विगतः श्रामः अस्य विश्रामः refreshd. विश्रामः क्रियताम् इति विश्राम+णिच् (नाम धातु)+लोट् ताम् कर्मणि। 4. निष्क्रान्तः–Here again no one leads अष्टावक्र out. 5. चित्रकरेण–चित्र painting . चित्रं करोति इति चित्र+कृ+ट कर्त्तरि ताच्छील्ये चित्रकरः a painter. 6. अस्मदुपदिष्टम्–अस्माभिः, *i .e.,* मया उपदिष्टम्। Lakṣmaṇa as eyswitness gave him the deails, 7. तत्–This refers not to चरितम् but to अभिलेखनम्।

(xxii) **रामः–जानासि वत्स दुर्मनायमानां देवीं विनोदयितुम्। तत्कियन्तमवधि यावत्?**

Rāma—Darling, you know how to divert the sorrowing queen. To What extent is that?

लक्ष्मणः—यावदार्याया हुताशेन विशुद्धिः।

Lak.—Up to noble sister's purification in fire.

रामः—शान्तम्।

Rāma—peace!

उत्पत्तिपरिपूतायाः किमस्याः पावनान्तरैः।
तीर्थोदकञ्च वह्निश्च नान्यतः शुद्धिमर्हतः।।13।।

Of this one, sanctified by birth, what can be done by other sanctifiers? Holy water and fire do not require purification from other sources.

देवि देवयजनसम्भवे प्रसीद एष ते जीवितावधिः प्रवादः।(रा–)

Queen, speare me; sprung as thou art from the ground for offering oblations to the gods, this is a life-long slur on thee.

मित–। जानामीति–दुःस्थितं मनो यस्याः सा दुर्मना। दुर्मना इव आचरति इति दुर्मनायमाना पितृविरहात् विमर्षा। ताम्।। तत् चित्रं कियन्तम् अवधि पर्यन्तं यावत् केन वृत्तान्तेन परिसमाप्तः तत् अवधिरिह अन्तवचनः। कियदिति परिमाणवचनम्, तत्तु, अवधौ न सङ्गच्छते। ''कमवधि यावत्'' इति युक्तम्। यावदित्यधिकारवचनमव्यम्। कमवधिमधिकृत्य इतर्थे अवधि यावदिति। सकर्मिकाया अधिकरणक्रियाया अन्तर्भावात् अवधिम् इति कर्मणि द्वितीया।। यावदिति–अत्र तु सीमवचनो यावच्छब्दः। आर्याया हुताशने विशुद्धिश्चित्रस्य सीमा इत्यर्थो गम्यते। अधिकरणक्रियाया अभावात् भवति इत्याह्यायाः क्रियायाः कर्त्तरि विशुद्धिरिति प्रथमा।। शान्तमिति–अव्ययमेतन्पकारान्तं निषेधे वर्त्तते। हुताशने विशुद्धिः'' मा ब्रूहि ''हुताशने विशुद्धिप्रकटनम्' इति युक्तम् इत्यर्थः।। निषेधे कारणमाह उत्पत्तिरिति–अन्वयः। उत्पत्तिपरिपूताया अस्याः पावनान्तरैः किम्? तीर्थोदकञ्च वह्निश्च अन्यतः शुद्धिं न अर्हतः।

व्याख्या–'उत्पत्या' जन्मना या 'पूरिपूता' सम्यक विशुद्धा तथा विधाया 'अस्या' सीतायाः पावान्तरैः' अन्यैः शोधनैः हुताशनादिभिः 'किं' क्रियते न किमपि। तत् शान्तम् हुताशने विशुद्धिरिति। पश्य 'तीर्थोदकञ्' गङ्गादीनां पुण्यसलिलञ्च 'वह्निश्च' पुण्यश्च हुताशनः 'अन्यतः' अन्यस्मात् पावानान्तरात् 'शुद्धिं' शोधनं 'न अर्हतः' न क्षमेते। एवं सीता अपि अग्निशुद्धिं न अर्हति इत्यबेहि।। उत्पत्तिपरिपूतत्वे हेतुमुपस्थापयति देवीति–इज्यते अस्मिन् इति यजनम् यज्ञभूमिः। ल्युट् अधिकरणे। देवानां यजनम् तत्

सम्भवः उत्पत्तिस्थानं यस्याः तत्संबुद्धौ देवयजनसम्भवे। योनिजाया अयोनिजा शुद्धतरा। अयोनिजासु पुनर्दे वयजनसम्भवा शुद्धतमा, अतएव 'उत्पत्तिपरिपूता' सीता, सार्थकश्च "परिपूता" इत्यत्र परिशब्दयोगः। जीवितम् अवधिः सामा अस्य जोवितावधिः जीवनान्त इतत्यर्थः। प्रहीणो वादः प्रवादो निन्दा। इयमसौ यस्या हुताशने विशुद्धिरासीत् इति यावज्जीवं ते निन्दा स्थास्यति इत्यर्थः। तत्र मद्वचनमेव हेतुः इति तदर्थं मह्यं मा कुप्य 'प्रसीद'।

Notes. 1. दुर्मनायमानाम्–दुर्मनस्+क्यङ्+लटः शानच् कर्त्तरि। The स disappears by the rule "कर्तुः ख्यङ् सलोपश्च"। जानासि etc.—is a compliment to लक्ष्मण। Sītā was feeling disconsolate when लक्ष्मण introduced this diversion, hence the compliment. 2. तत्–Refers to अभिलेखनम्, *i. e,* चित्रम्। तत् कियन्तम् etc. seem to be rather un-called-for. This is introduced to give Rāma an opportunity to explain his attitude towards Sītā, after her release. He qs apparently inexplicably rude; but the reason is "जनः कुलधनैरनुरञ्जनीयः। If Sītā bears this in mind it will also explain to her impending renunciation. 3. पावनान्तरैः–अन्यानि पावनानि पावनान्तरणि। मयूरव्यंसकादि तत्–। तैः। But अन्य (Other) is a relative term. "Other than what? Other than सीता herself. But सीता is not described as पावन, She is called here as पूत only which is quite different. 4. प्रसीद–Be pacified, *i.e.,* excuse. The reason for the importunity is that Rāma had offered the occasion for this slur.

(*xxiii*) **(रा–) कष्टं जनः कुलधनैरनुरञ्जनीय-**
स्तन्मे दुरुक्तमशिवं न हि तत क्षमं ते।
नैसर्गिकी सुरभिणः कुसुमस्य सिद्धा
मूर्ध्नि स्थितिन चरणैरवताड़ितानि।। 14।।

(R.—) It is a pity people have to be humoured by those who value the fame of their family. Hence, the evil and ungracious speech of mine. Surely that was not fit for you. What is naturally accorded to fragrant flower is a seat on the head, not trampligs under feet. (Or—The seat on head accorded to the fragrant flower—and not tramplings under feet—is what comes natural to it).

सीता–होदु अज्जउत्त होदु। एहि पेकखम्ह दाव दे चरिदं (भावतु आर्यपुत्र भवतु। एहि प्रेक्षामहे तावत् ते चरितम्)।

Sītā—Let that go, my husband, let that go. Come let us see (the painting of) your experiences. (*They get up and go round the stage*).

मित–। कष्टमिति।

अन्वयः–कष्टम्! कुलधनैः जनः अनुरञ्जनीयः। तत् मे अशिवं दुरुक्तम्। तत् ते क्षमं न हि। सुरभिणः कुसुमस्य नेसर्गिकी सिद्धा मूर्द्धि स्थिति, (यद्वा–सुरभिणः कुसुमस्य सिद्धा सूर्द्धि स्थितिः नैसर्गिकी) न चरणैरवताड़ितानि)।

व्याख्या–'कष्टम्' अहो दुःखम्! 'कुलं धनं' येषां तादृशैः पुरुषै प्रजारञ्जनलब्धायाः कुलकीर्तेः रक्षणपरैः राघवैः जनः अनुरञ्जनीयः, प्रीणयितव्यः। शोच्चमेतत् व्रतं तेषाम्। 'तत्' तस्मात् एतद्व्रतानुरोधात् 'मे अशिवम्' अभव्यं 'दूरक्तं' दुर्वचनम्, आत्मानं वचनीयात् मोचय इति यत् लङ्कायामुक्तम्। व्रतेनैतेन परतन्त्रोऽमेवमवोचं न हि स्वेच्छया, तत् 'देवि प्रसीद' इति पूर्वेण सम्बन्धः। तत्' दुरुक्तं 'ते क्षम न हि' नैव योग्यम्। अयोग्यत्वे दृष्टान्तमाह–'सुरभिणः कुसुमस्य नैसर्गिकी, स्वाभाविकी 'सिद्धा' निसर्ग जातात् सौरभादेव लोके लब्धा 'मूर्द्धि स्थितिः' शिरसि स्थानम्। सैव तस्य क्षमा। 'न' न तु 'चरणैः अवताड़ितानि' आघाताः तस्य कुसुमस्य क्षमाणि। एवं नैसर्गिकेण पातिव्रत्यसौरभेण समन्वितायास्तवापि अभिनन्दनमेव तदानीं क्षममासौत् न दुरुक्तमशिवम्। तत् देवि प्रसीद (पक्षे–'सुरभिणः कुसुमस्य सिद्धा' लोके प्रसिद्धा 'मूर्द्धि स्थितिः' तस्य सम्बन्धे 'नैसर्गिकी' स्वाभाविकी इत्यादि प्राग्वत्)।। भवत्विति–'भवतु' यातु यत्, अलं तच्चिन्तया नाहं स्मरामि तत्। अहं ते हृदयं जानामि त्वमपि मम। तत् 'एहि तावत् पेक्षामहे ते चरितं' चरिताश्रयमालेख्यम्। परिक्रामतः वीथिकागमनमभिनयतः।

Notes. 1. कष्टम्–कष+क्त भावे कष्टम् क्लेशः। This is an exclamation here. 2. कुलधनैः–कुल here is by transference of epithets कुलकीर्त्ति। Also without such transference we have in a different sense "इक्ष्वाकूणं कुलधनमिदं यत् समाराधनीयः-Act VII, Sl.6 3. तन्मे–तत् is an अव्ययः implying हेतु। 4. दुरुक्तम्–व्च+क्त कर्मणि or भावे उक्तम् speech (कर्नणि) act of saying (भावे)। दुष्टमुक्तम्, प्रादितत्–।5. तत् क्षमम्–तत् refers to दुरूक्तम्। 6. नैसर्गिकी–नितरां सृज्यते इति नि+सृज+घञ् कर्मणि निसर्गः nature. निसर्गात् आगता इति निसर्ग+ठक्+ङीप् स्त्रियाम्। This is better taken here as a विधेय। If taken as an ordianry attributive (नैसर्गिकी सिद्धा) tautology seems unavoidable, because what is नैसर्गिकी is of course सिद्धा also.

(*xxiv*) **लक्ष्मणः–इदं तदालेख्यम्।**

Lak.—This is the painting.

सीता (निर्वर्ण्य)—के एदे उपरि णिरन्दरठ्ठिदा उवत्थु वन्दि विअ अज्जउत्तं (के एते उपरि निरन्तरस्थिता उपस्तुवन्ति इव आर्यपुत्रम्)?

Sītā *(observing)*—who are these, crowded together in the air, belauding as it were my husband?

लक्ष्मणः–एतानि तानि सरहस्यजृम्भकास्त्राणि यानि भगवतः कृशाश्वात् कौशिकमृषि विश्वस्य मित्रं विश्वामित्रमुपसंक्रान्तानि तेन च ताड़कावधे प्रसोदीकृतान्वार्थ्यस्य।

Sak.—These are the famed Jṛmbhaka weapons, having secret spells, which from the mighty Kṛśāśva devloved upon sage Viśvāmitra, the benefactor of the world, the son of Kauśika, and by him were made into a gift a pleasure to my noble brother at the slaying of Tāḍakā.

मित– ।इदमिति–आलेख्यं चित्रम्।। निर्वर्ण्येति–निर्वर्णनं सूक्ष्ममीक्षणम्। निर्वर्ण्य निरीक्ष्य। उपरि आकाशे। अन्तरम् अवकाशः। निर्गतमन्तरं यस्मिन् कर्मणि तत् यथा तथा स्थिताः निरन्तरस्थिताः परम्परसंपर्षेण वर्त्तमानाः।। एतानीति–रहसि भंवरहस्य गूह्यं मन्त्र इत्यर्थः। स च मन्त्रो द्वेधा, प्रयोगमन्त्रः संहारमन्तश्च। जृम्भन्ते प्रयोक्तुरिच्छया इति जृन्भकाणि। तथाविधानि अस्त्राणि जृम्भकास्त्राणि। रहस्येन सह वर्त्तमानानि सरहस्यानि। सरहस्यानि जृम्भकास्त्राणि। उपसंक्रान्तानि गतानि। प्रसादीकृतानि प्रीतिदत्तानि, हतायां ताड़कायां प्रसन्नेन मुनिना दत्तानि।।

Notes. 1. उपस्तुवति–The weapons appeared in person and looked like ordinary human beings engaged in singing the praise of Rāma. 2. विश्वस्य मित्रम्–Benefactor of the whole world. Weapons to such a person had nouse except to further the welfare of the world. Hence, they are made over to Rāma as the fittest person for this sort of work. विश्वामित्र is the संज्ञा of the sage. In the विश्व becomes विश्वा by the rule ''मित्रे चर्षौ''।

(*xxv*) **रामः–वन्दस्व देवि दिव्यास्त्राणि।**

Rāma—Queen bow unto these divine weapons.

ब्रह्मादयो ब्रह्महिताय तप्त्वा परमहस्त्राः शरदस्तपांसि।
एतान्यपश्यन् गुरवः पुराणाः स्वान्येव तेजांमि तपोमयानि।15।।

The old master, headed by Brahman, having practised penance for over a thousand years, for the good of the Vedas, saw these the very fire of their austerities.

मित–। वन्दस्वेति–दिवि भवानि दिव्यानि। दिव्यरूपतां दर्शयति ब्रह्मेति। अन्वयः–ब्रह्मादयः पुराण गुरुवः ब्रह्महिताय परःसहस्राः शरदः तपांसि तप्त्वा तपोमयानि स्वानि तेजांसि एव एतानि अपश्यम्।

व्याख्या–'ब्रह्मादयः' विरिञ्चिप्रभृतयः 'पुराण गुरुवः' आद्या आचार्याः 'ब्रह्मणो' वेदस्य 'हिताय' मङ्गलाय वेदद्रोहिषणां राक्षसादीनां प्रशमाय 'परः सहस्रा' सहस्रात् पराः अधिकाः 'शरदः' संवत्सरान् व्याप्य 'तपांसि तप्त्वा स्वानि तेजांसि एव' तपस्तेजांसि एव जाज्जवल्यमानानि अस्त्ररूपेण च परिणतानि 'एतानि अपश्यन् ऐक्षन्त। एवं दिव्यानि एतानि वन्दस्व।।

Notes. 1. ब्रह्महिताय–तादर्थ्ये चतुर्थी। 2. परःसहस्राः–पर is अधिक। सहस्रात् पराः is to be compounded by योगविभाग of पञ्चमी in the rule "पञ्चमी भयेन"। We the expect सहस्रपराः। But Vardhamāna places it under the राजदन्तादि list, so परा leads. The form then should have been परासहस्राः। Next by the dictum "सर्वनाम्नो वृत्तिमात्रे पुंवद्भावः" we get परसहस्राः। Lastly assuming that the word is of the पारस्करादि class, as is done by भानुजि, we have परम सहस्राः which yields परःसहस्राः। Vardhamāna however makes it of the पृषोदरादि class and introduces सकरागम at the last stage. 3. शरदः–व्याप्त्यर्थ्ये 2 या। 4. पुराणाः–पुरा भवा इति पुरा+ट्युल् पुरातनाः; or by निपातन in the rule "पूर्वकालैकसर्वजरत् पुराण–" also पुराणः।

(*xxvi*) **सीता–णमो एदाणं (नम ऐतभ्यः)।**

Sītā—Salution to these.

रामः–सर्वथेदानीं त्वत्प्रसूतिमुपस्थास्यन्ति।

Rāma—They will certainly serve your child now.

सीता–अणुगहीद म्हि (अनुगृहीतास्मि)।

Sītā—I am favoured.

लक्ष्मणः–एष मिथिलावृत्तान्तः।

Lak.—This is the scene at Mithilā.

सीता–अम्महे दलन्तणवणीलुप्पलसामलसिणिद्धमसिणसोहमाण-मंसलेण देहसोहग्गेण विम्हअत्थिमिदतादद‍ीसमाणसोम्मसुन्दरसिरी

अनादरक्ख ड़िदसङ्करसराणो सिहण्डअमुद्धमु हमण्डलो अज्जउत्तो आलिहिदो (अम्महे! दलन्नवनीलोत्पलश्यामलस्निग्धमसृणशोभमान-मांसलेन देहसौभाग्येन विस्मयस्तिमिततातदृश्यमानसोम्यसुन्दरश्रीः अनारदरखण्डितशङ्करशरासनः शिखण्डकमुग्धमुखमण्डलः आर्यपुत्र आलिखितः)।

Sītā—Ha! Here is my husband painted is his charming. fame—muscular, appearing midly glossy, blue as a fresh blue-lotus blooming—with the orb of his face lovely through the youthful locks, with the bow of Śankara snapped without effort and with his graceful and attractive beauty being scanned by father motionless in wonder.

मित–।सर्वथेति–'सर्वथा' सर्वप्रकारेण, अव्यमिचारेण इत्यर्थः 'इदानीम्' अधुना, प्रसूताया त्वसिय इत्यर्थः।। प्रसूयते इति प्रसूतिः अपत्यम्। कर्मणि क्तिन्। उपस्थास्यन्ति उप समीपे स्थित्वा तथा निदेशं कृत्वा सेविष्यन्ते। 'एतानि' इति कर्त्तृपदमुह्यम्।। अमेह इति–'अमेह' इत्यव्ययम् आश्चर्ये। स्तीषुनियतमेतत्। केषाञ्चिन्मते प्राकृते एव अस्य प्रयोगः। तेषां तु 'अहो' इति संस्कृते अनुवादः।। 'दलत्' प्रस्फुटत् यत् 'नवनीलोत्पलं नीलपद्मकोरकम् तदिव 'श्यामलं' किञ्च 'स्निग्धमसृणं' कोमलोज्जवलं यथा तथा 'शोभमानम्' अपि तु 'मांसलं' परिपुष्टं प्रचुरमित्यर्थः यत् 'देहसौभाग्यं' वपुःप्रकर्षः तेन सह तद्विशिष्ट इत्यर्थः तथा 'शिखण्डकैः' बालोचितैः का पक्षकैः 'मुग्ध' मनोहरं 'मुखमण्डलं' आननविम्ब यस्य तथाविधः बाल एव इत्यर्थः तथापि 'अनादरेण' अवलीलया 'खण्डितं' भग्रं 'शङ्करशरासनं' हरधनुः येन तथाविधः अतएव 'विस्मयेन स्तिमितः' निश्चलो यः 'तातः' पिता जनकः तेन 'दृश्यमाना सौम्या' सुभगा 'सुन्दरी च श्रीः' कान्तिर्यस्य तथाविधः 'आर्यपुत्र आलिखितः'।। अत्रैदं द्रष्टव्यम्–श्यामलतादयो दहधर्माः, सौभाग्यस्य पुनः कीदृशी श्यामलातादयः उच्यते–"भावानयने द्रव्यनयानम्" इति भाष्यवचनात् "देहसौभाग्यम्" इत्यती "सुभगदेहः" इत्यस्य बोधः। तेन–मांसलेन देहसौभाग्येन" इति न काचिदयुक्ता।

Notes. 1. सर्वथा etc.—Here the weapons are given away. This will play in important part in the recognition of Sītā's children hereafter. But there is an imcongruity here. The वीरचरित makes the weapons a gift of *both* राम and लक्ष्मण। Thus राम says of विश्वामित्र–"दिव्यास्त्रसम्प्रदायोऽयं लक्ष्मणेन सहास्तु मे" and विश्वामित्र agrees. In that case राम *alone* has no right to make the gift now. This goes against the development of the plot. 2. अस्मेह–Some think that this word is not at all used in Sanskrit. In that case translate अहो। 3. दलत् etc.—This is a compound of the three words दलन्नवनीलोत्पलश्यामलम्, स्निग्धमसृणाशोभमानम् and मांसलम् all qualifying देहसौभाग्यम्। But the compounding has to be done in *two* stages. Thus, get a कर्मधा–of the 1st two and then add the 3rd for onother कर्मधा–; or first compound the 2nd and 3rd and then add the 1st. This is because a कर्मधा–has to be two words only, never more than two. The three constituents have to be treated thus नोलीत्पलम्, क्रमधा–। नवनीलोत्पलम, कर्मधा–। दलन्नवनीलोत्पलम् कर्मधा–दलन्नवनीलोत्पश्यामलम्, उपमानसमास।। स्निग्धमसृणम्, कर्मधा–। Next सुसुपा।। मांसंलाति इति मांस+ला+क+कर्त्तरि or मासम् अस्त्यस्मिन् इतिमांस+लच् मत्वर्थे मांसलम् muscular. By transference of epithets this means here 'plentiful' प्रचुर। Also see मित–।। 4. देह etc.—सुभगस्य भावः इति सुभग्+ष्यञ् सौभाग्यम् good luck. We have वृद्धि in both components by the rule "हृद्भगसिन्ध्वते पूर्वपदस्य च"। देहस्यसौभाग्यम्, तेन। सहार्थे तृतीया। Also see मित–।।5. विस्मय etc. —बिस्मयेन स्तिमितः, सुप्सुपा। तादृशस्तातः, कर्मधा–। तेन दृश्यमाना, 3 तत्–। तादृशी सौम्या सुन्दरी श्रीर्चस्य, a बहु–of four constituents. Note that श्रयति पुरुषम् इति श्रि+क्विप् कर्त्तरि श्रीः by the Vārttika "किप् वचिप्रच्छि–". Thus the ई not being ङीप् the rule "नदृयतश्च" does not apply and we do not get श्रीकः in the बहु–। Also see under—वटुपरिषदं पुण्यश्रीकः श्रियेव सभाजयन्–Act IV, Sl. 19. 6. अनादर etc.—This, taken with शिखण्डक etc., causes wonder in Janaka. So young yet so powerful !

(*xxvii*) **लक्ष्मणः–आर्ये पश्य–**

Lak.—Look, Noble lady, look—

सम्वन्धिनो वशीष्ठादीनेष तातस्तबार्चति।

गौतमश्च शतानन्दो जनकानां पुरोहितः।।16।।

Here is thy father honouring his bridal connections and Gotama's so Śatānanda, the priest of the house of Janaka, honouring Vasiṣṭha and others.

मित–।सम्बन्धित इति।अन्वयः (एष तव तातः सम्बन्धिनः, जनकानां पुरोहित गौतमः शतानन्दश्च वशिष्ठादीन्, अर्चति।)

व्याख्या–'एष तव तातः' पिता जनकः 'सम्बन्धिनः' वैवाहिकान् दशरथादीन्, तथा जनकानां जनककुलजानां 'पुरोतिः गौतमः' गौतमपुत्रः 'शतानन्दश्च वशिष्ठदीन् अर्चति पूजयति।। अत्र "तात शतानन्दश्च वशिष्ठदीन् सम्बन्धिनः अर्चति" इति बहूनां व्याख्यानम्।।

Notes. 1. सम्बन्धिनः–सम्बन्धः विवाहसम्बन्धः अस्ति एषाम् इति सम्बन्ध+इनि मत्वर्थे सम्बन्धिनः those that are connected by the marriage-tie, 2. जनकानाम्–जनक here, by transference of epithets, stands for all members of the family of Janaka. 3. *Remark.*—The usual construction (see *Mita*—) makes वशिष्ट etc. also सम्बन्धी of जनक which is not desirable. Beside the अर्चनक्रिया is done simultaneously by both सम्बन्धिन्s. Ths should give the dual अर्चतः not the singular. In the construction adopted by us जनक honours दशरथ etc. and शतानन्द separetely does the same to वशिष्ट etc. Hence, the singular अर्चति is correct. Also it is met that the पुरोति should honour the पुरोहित। In the Śakuntala when Kanva's disciples arrive the king deputes his पुरोहित to honour them.

(*xxviii*) **रामः–द्रष्टव्यमेतत्।**

Rāma—This is worth seeing.

जनकानां रघूणाञ्च सम्बन्धः कस्य न प्रियः।
यत्र दाता ग्रहीता च स्वयं कुशिकन्दनः।।17।।

To whom is not gratifying the union of Janakas and the Raghus wherin the son of Kuśika is himself the offers and the acceptor as well?

मित–'द्रष्टव्यं' दर्शनीय दर्शनात् प्रीतिरित्वर्थः।। जनकानामिति। सुगमम्।।

Notes. 1. जनकानाम् etc.—Here also we have transference of epithets as in Sl. 16. 2. कुशिकनन्दनः–This is विश्वामित्र।

(*xxix*) **सीता–एदे क्ख़ तक्कालकिदगोदाणमङ्गला चत्तारो भादरो विआहदिक्खिदा तुम्है। अम्मा जानामि तस्मिं एव्व पदेसे तस्मिं एव्व काले वत्तामि (एते खलु तत्कालकृतगोदानमङ्गलाः चत्वारो भ्रातरो विवाहदीक्षिता यूयम्। अहो जानामि तस्मिन्नेव व प्रदेशे तस्मिन्नेव काले वर्त्ते)।**

Sītā— Here are you four brothers under the vow of marrige with the auspicious ceremony of tonsure performed just before. Ah! Methinks I am at the very same place now and at the very hour.

रामः–एवम्।

Rāma—Yea,

समयः स वर्त्तत इवैष यत्र मां
समनन्दयत् सुमुखि गौतमार्पितः।
अयमुद्गृहीतकमनीयकङ्कण-
स्तव मूर्त्तिमानिव महोत्सवः।। 18।।

Here O fine-faced girl, time has it seems returned—the time when your hand] carrying the attractive nuptial thread, onbeing placed on mine by Gautama, delighted me like sepreme bliss embodied.

मित–।एते।गावः केशाःस्वनामख्याताः पशवो वा।गत्रां दानं छेदनं वितरणं वा गोदानम्।तदेव मङ्गलं शुभकर्म गोदानमङ्गलम्।स कालः तस्कालः।तस्मिन् कृतं तत्कालकृतम्। 'तत्कालकृतं गोदानमङ्गलं' यैः ते।। दीक्ष नियमग्रहणे भूादिषु आत्मनेपदी। कर्त्तरि क्तः दीक्षिताः। 'विवाहे दीक्षिताः'।। समय इति।

अन्वयः- सुमुखि, एष स समयः वर्त्तते इव यत्र अयं तव करः उद्गृहीतकमनीयकङ्कणः (सन्) गीमार्पितः (भूत्वा) मूर्त्तिमान् महोत्सव इव मां समनन्दयत्।

व्याख्या–हे 'सुमुखि' सूवदने सीते सुष्ठु उक्तं त्वया तस्मिन्नेव काले वर्त्ते इति। ममापि 'एष स समयः वर्त्तते इव यत्र' यस्मिन् समये 'अयं तव करः' दक्षिणो हस्तः 'उद्गृहीतं' धृत 'कमनीयं कङ्कणं' वैवाहिक्र करसूत्रं येन तादृशः सन् 'गीतमेन' गौतमपुत्रेण जनकपुरोहितेन 'अर्पितः' मम करे निवेशितो भूत्वा 'मूर्त्तिमान्' धृतदेहः 'महोत्सव इव' परमानन्दसन्दोह इव 'मां' समनन्दयत्' सम्यक् प्रीणयामास। तत् अहमापि "जानामि तस्मिन्नेव काले वर्त्ते" इति।।

Notes. 1. तत्काल etc.—गोदान is differently explained as "Shaving and "Gift of cows." केशान्त is a synonym of गोदान। Hence some offer the derivation गावः केशाः दीयन्ते छिद्यन्ते अस्मिन् इति अधिकरणे ल्युट्। This seems a bit far-fatched. We notice that the ceremony of केशान्त has the peculiarity that its दक्षिण is a pair of cows. "गोमिथनं दक्षिणा"

–*Aśvalāyana* quoted by वाचस्पति। It is quite possible that owing to this distinctive charactei, केशान्त itself has come to be known as गोदान। Hence, it seems better not to strain गोदान as above but take it in its plain sense "Gift of cows" as this gift accompanies tonsure, let गोदान secondarily refer to केशान्त, tonsure. 2.समय: etc—Here Rāma echoes Sista's sentiment "जानामि etc."

(*xxx*) **लक्ष्मणः–इयमार्या इयमप्यार्या माण्डवी इयमपि वधूः श्रुतकीर्तिः।**

Lak.—This is my noble sister-in-law, this again is noble Māṇḍavī and this is daughter in-law Śrutakīrti.

सीता–वच्छ इअ वि अवरा का (वत्स, इयमपि अपरा का)?

Sītā—Child, who is this other one again?

लक्ष्मणः–(सलज्जस्मितमपावार्य)–अये ऊर्मिलां पृच्छंत्यार्या। भवतु अन्यतः सञ्चारयामि। (प्रकाशम्) आर्य दृश्यतां द्रष्टव्यमेतत्, अयञ्च भगवान् भार्गवः।

Lak. (Aside with a bashful smile)—Ho! Her noble self is asking of Urmilā. well, I will direct her elsewhere. (Aloud) Noble sister-in-law, look here this is worth seeing. This again is Worshipful Bhārgava.

सीता–(ससम्भ्र मम्)–कम्पिदन्हि (कम्पितस्मि)।

Sītā (*In alarm*)—I am startled.

रामः–ऋषे नमस्ते।

Rāma—Salutation to thee, O sage.

मित–। इयमिति। 'आर्य्य' इति सीता लक्ष्यते। 'माण्डवी' इति भरतपन्नी जनकानुजस्य कुशध्वजस्य कन्या। तदनुजा शत्रुघ्नपन्नी श्रुतकीर्तिः।'आर्या माण्डवी'' इति भरतस्य ज्येष्ठत्वं प्रतीयते। प्राचीनानां तु मतं लक्ष्मणो ज्यायान् इति।। वत्सेति। चतसृष्वपि कन्यकासु लिखितासु ऊर्मिला न कथिता इति लक्ष्मणं इति सीतायाः परिहासः।। सलज्जेति। लज्जया सह सलज्जम्। 'सलज्जं स्मितम्,। तत् यथा तथा। 'अपावार्य अन्यैरश्रु तं यथा तथा आत्मानां प्रत्युक्त्वा। अन्यतः' अन्यस्मिन् विषायान्तरे इत्यर्थः।'सञ्चारायामि' करोमि इत्यर्थः।'भार्गवः' परशुरामः।। ससम्भ्रमेति। सम्भ्रमो

भयम्। तेन सहं यथा तथा। 'कम्पिता' भयेन इति शेषः। अतीतस्मरणात् भयं ततः कम्पः।।

Notes. 1. सलज्ज etc.—स्मित् becuase he has been found out by Sītā; लज्जा because the matter relates to his wife. 2. आपवार्य–अप+वृ+णिच्+ल्यप् literally having screened. Technically it is a stage direction when an actor turns his back on the other actors and speak out something which is not intended for them. Thus—"तद्भवेदपवारितम्। रहस्यन्तु यदन्यस्य परावृत्य प्रकाश्यते।।"

(*xxxi*) **लक्ष्मणः–आये पश्य पश्य, अयमसावार्येण (इत्यर्द्धोक्ते)–**

Lak—, Look noble lady, look; here, by my noble brother, that *(When half-uttered)*—

रामः (साक्षेपम्)–अयि, बहुतरं द्रष्टव्यमस्ति, अन्यतो दर्शय।

Rāma. *(Deprecatingly)*—Well tere is a good deal remaining to see, guide us elsewhere.

सीता (सस्नेहबहुमानं निर्वर्ण्य)–सुठ्ठ, मोहसि अज्जउत्त एदिना विणअमाहप्येण (सुष्ठ, शोभसे आर्यपुत्र एतेन विनयमाहात्मेयन)।

Sītā *(Eyeing with regard and affection)*—My husband you show will in this immensity of modesty.

लक्ष्मणः–एते वयमयोध्यां प्राप्ताः।

Lak.—Here are we arrived at Ayodhyā.

रामः–(सास्त्रम्)–स्मरामि हन्त स्मरामि।

जीवत्सु तातपादेषु नवे दारपरिग्रहे।
मातृभिश्चिन्त्यमानानां ते हि नो दिवा गताः।।18।।

Rāma (*With tears*)—I remember, alas! I remember, gone are those days of ours when, our revered father living, with our acceptance of wives fresh, we were anxioushly cared for by our mothers. (R.—)

मिति–। आर्ये इति। अर्द्धः अंशमात्रम्। अर्द्धश्चासौ उक्तय 'अर्द्धोक्तः' तस्मिन्। असमाप्ते लक्ष्मणावाक्ये इत्यर्थः। अयमसावार्येण जित इति वाक्यसमाप्तिः। अनुच्चारिते एव जितशब्दे।। साक्षेपेति। आक्षेपो निन्दा। तेन सह 'साक्षेपम्'। समक्षमेव "भार्गवो जितः" इति प्रशंसावाक्योच्चारणम् अनुचितम्। अतो निन्दन् रामो ब्रवीति।। सस्नेहेति।

महान् विपुलः आत्मा स्वरूपं यस्य स महात्मा।' तस्य भावः 'माहात्म्यं परिपूर्णता। 'विनस्य माहात्म्यं'' तेन। प्रकर्षगतेन विनशेय इत्यर्थः। हेतो तृतीया। ''शोभसे" इति बहुमानः', ''आर्यपुत्र इति 'स्नेहः'। तदाह 'सस्ने हमहुमानम्' इति।। स्मरामीति। 'हन्त' इति विषादे अव्ययम् जीवत्स्विति। अन्वयः तातपादेषु जीवत्सु (सतसु) दारपरिग्रहे नवे (सति) मातृभिः चिन्त्यमानानां नः ते दिवसा गता हि।

व्याख्या–'तातपादेषु जीवत्सु' पूज्ये ताते जीवति 'दारपरिग्रहे' पाणिपीड़नकर्मणि 'नवे' अचिरसम्पन्ने सति 'मातृभि, चिन्त्यमानानाम्' अनुध्यायमानानां 'नः ते' पूर्वानुभूता आनन्दमयाः 'दिवसा मता हि' गता एव।।

Notes. 1. अयम् etc.—This points at the picture before them. असौ refers to भार्गव। 2. अयि–This here expresses निन्दा। Comp. ''अयि कठोरयशः किल ते प्रियम्''–Act III, Sl. 27. 3. अन्यतः–अन्यस्मिन्, i.e. elsewhere in the gallery. अन्य+ङि (7मी)+तसि स्वार्थे। 4. सस्नेह etc.—बहुमननं बहुमानः regard. This is because of his self-effacement. स्नेह because the possessor of this sublime virtue is her own husband. 4. विनयमहात्म्येन–This is equivalent to महता विनयेन। ''भावानयने द्रव्यानयनम्''। 5. एते–Again points at the scene in the picture. 6. हन्त–An अव्यय implying विषाद। 7. तातपादेषु–A कर्मधा–of तात and पाद। पाद, when an उत्तरपद in such compounds, indicates प्रशंसा (प्रशंसावचन)। The समास is regulated by the rule ''प्रशंसावचनैश्च'' Which also directs the परनिपात of पाद। The plural is due to गौरव। गौरवे बहुवचनम्। Note that पाद is प्रशंसावचन *only* when it is the उत्तरपद in these compounds. When the word is uncompounded, it does not imply प्रशंसा। Thus पादाः ताताः will not mean तातपादाः–revered father. Hence पाद has to be avoided in the वाक्य of the compound. In other words the compound is of the नित्य–समाप्त class with अस्वपदविग्रह (See मित–above). The couplet ''मतल्लिकोद्वमिश्राः ख्युः प्रकाण्डस्थलभित्तयः। हस्तपाशतटाः पादपालीमचर्चिकादयः।'' gives the प्रशंसावचन words in general use.

(xxxii) **(रा–) इयमपि तदा जानकी,**

प्रतनुविरलैः प्रान्तोन्मीलन्मनोहरकुन्तलै–
दर्शनमुकुलैर्मुग्धालोकं शिशुर्दधती मुखम्।
ललितललितैज्योत्स्नाप्रायैराकृत्रिमविभ्रमै–
रकृत मधुरैरम्बानां मे कुतूहलमङ्गकैः।। 20।।

Rāma—Thus Jānakī too, then.

A child, wearing a face lovely to look at by reason of her bud-like teeth and showing off (by contrast) at the sides with beautiful locks that were fine and not over-dense, afforded joy to my mothers with her small limbs that were very delicate and charming with unassumed grace that resembled the moon beam.

मित– । इयमिति । परवर्त्तिना पद्येन अन्वितमिदम् ।। **अन्वयः**–तदा प्रतनुविरलैः मनोहरकुन्तलैः प्रान्तोन्मीलत्, दशनमुकुलैः मुग्धालोकं सुखं दधती शिशुः इयं जानकी अपि ललितललितैः ज्योत्स्नाप्रायैः अकृत्रिमविभ्रमैः मधुरैः अङ्गकैः मे अम्बानां कुतूहलम् अकृत ।

व्याख्या–'तदा' तस्मिन् काले मातृचिन्तासमकाले इत्यर्थः 'प्रतनुभिः' सूक्ष्मैः विरलैः' अनतिनिविड़ैश्च अतएव 'मनोहरैः कुन्तलै' केशैः 'प्रान्तयोः' गण्डयोः 'उन्मीलत् शोभमानम्, तथा 'दशनमुकुलैः' दन्तकुट्मलैः 'मुग्धालोकं' कान्तदर्शनं 'मुखं दधती' धारयन्तौ 'शिशुः इयं जानकी अपि ललितललितैः' अति सुकुमारै 'ज्योत्स्नाप्रायाः' चन्द्रिकाकल्पा ये अकृत्रिमविभ्रमाः' सहजविलासाः तैः हेतुभिः 'मधुरैः' रुचिरेः 'अङ्गकेः' ह्रस्वैरङ्गैः 'मे अम्बानां' जननीनां 'कुतूहलम्' आनन्दम् 'अकृत' अकरोत् । मातृभिश्चिन्त्यमाना वयम्, आनन्दश्चानुभूतस्ताभिः सीतारूपविलोकनात् इति भावः। वीरचरितविरुद्धमेतत् । तत्र तु प्राप्तयौवना सीता परिणीता रामेण ।।

Notes. 1. इयमपि etc.—अपि implies समुच्चय of कुतूहलकरण and चिन्तन, the construction being जानकी अपि अम्बानां कुतूहलमकृत । मातृभिश्चिन्तनक्रियायाः जानक्या च कतूहलकरणक्रियायाः एकस्मिन् काले (तदा) समुच्चयः। 2. प्रतनुविरलैः– Qual. मनोहरकुन्तलैः। 3. प्रान्तोन्मीलत्–प्रान्त is पार्श्व the sides of the face. उद्+मील+शतृ उन्मीलत् lit. opening up, here showing off शोभमानस् as Vidyasagara has it. Compare "उन्मीलितं तलिकयेव चित्रम्"–*Kumāra*. Now see *Tika*. Qual. मुखम् । 4. मनोहर etc.—हेती ३या। This is the reason why the face was प्रान्तोन्मीलत् । 5. दशनमुकुलैः–दशना मुकुला इव teeth looking like white flower buds, उपमितकर्मधा– । तैः। हेती ३या। This is the reason why the face was मुग्धालोक। 6. मुग्धालोकम्–मुग्धः मनोहरः आलोको दर्शनं यस्य तत् beautiful to look at, बहु– । Qual. मुखम् । 7. दधती–No नुम् because the root is अभ्यस्त। 8. ललितललितैः–ललितेभ्यो ललितानि, ललितललितानि सुप्स पा। तैः। Qual अङ्गकैः।9. ज्योत्स्नाप्रायेः–प्राय here means 'like' तुल्य। ज्योतिरस्त्यस्याम्

इति ज्योतिस्+न मत्वर्थे स्त्रियाम् ज्योत्स्ना moon-beam. The इ of ज्योतिस् disappears by निपातन in the rule "ज्योत्स्नातमिश्रा–'। ज्योत्स्नया प्रायाणि ज्योत्स्नाप्रायाणि, सुप्सुपा। तैः। Qual. अकृत्रिमविभ्रमैः। See next note. 10. अकृत्रिम etc.—क्रियया निर्वृत्ता इति कृ+क्त्रि=कृत्रिमाः with मप् attached. न कृत्रिमाः अकृत्रिमाः not artificial, "i. e." natural. विभ्रम is शोभा, विलास etc. अकृत्रिमाः विभ्रमाः natural grace. तैः। हेतौ 3या। The gives the हेतु why the limbs (अङ्गकः) were मधुर। The natural grace of the limbs resembled the natural brilliancy of the moon; *i. e.*,the विभ्रम resembled ज्योत्स्ना and rendered the limbs मधुर। 1. *Remark.*—The description of सीता as a शिशु at the time of marrige contradicts the वीरचरित where on the day after the marrige राम speaks thus to सीता–"उन्नद्धस्तनकुम्भकुटनलगुरूच्छ्वावभुगनस्य ते मध्यस्य त्रिवली तरङ्गकजुषो भङ्गः प्रिये मा च भूत्।" This is does not suit a शिग्र।

(*xxxiii*) **लक्ष्मणः–एषा मन्थरा।**

Lak.—Here is Mantharā.

रामः (अनुत्तरमन्यतो गत्वा)–देवि वैदेहि

Rāma—(*passing on to another point without comment*)—Queen Vaidehi.

इङ्गुदीपादपः सोऽसं शृङ्गबेरपुरे पुरा।
निषादपतिना यत्र स्निग्धेनासीत् समागमः।। 21।।

This is that Ingudi tree in the city of Sringavera where formely chanced my meeting wity my friend the king of the Nishadas.

लक्ष्मणः (विहस्य स्वगतम्)–अये मध्यमाम्बाबृत्तान्तोऽन्तरित आर्येण।

Lak.—(*Laughing and to himself*)—Ha! The incident of our second mother is screened over by my noble another.

मित–। अनुत्तरमिति। अविद्यमानम् उत्तरं प्रतिवचनं यस्मिन् गमने तत् यथा तथा इङ्गुदीति। अन्वयः–सः अयं शृङ्गवेरपुरे इङ्गुदीपादपः यत्र पुरा स्निग्धेन निषादपतिना समागम आसीत्।

व्याख्या–'सः' पूर्वानुभूतः अयम्' एष चित्रे हश्यनानः 'शृङ्गवेर पुरे इङ्गुदीपादपः'।

'यत्र' यस्मिन् इङ्गुदीपादपे इङ्गुदीपादपतले। यद्वा 'यत्र' यस्मिन् शृङ्गवेरपुरे 'पुरा' पूर्वं वपयाणसमये इत्यर्थः। 'स्निग्धेन वयस्येन' निषादपतिना' निषादराजेन गुहेन 'समागम आसीत्' मेलनमभूत।। द्वितीयार्द्धे 'यत्र' इति उत्तरवाक्य- गतत्वात् तच्छब्दोपादानं नापेक्षते। तथा अनुभूतार्थत्वात् 'सः' इति यच्छब्दनिरपेक्षम्।। विहस्येति। स्वस्मिन् आत्मनि गते 'स्वगतम्' अन्यैरश्रुतं स्वरसंयोगं विनैव भाषितम्। तत् यथा तथा। आह इत्यूह्यक्रियाविशेषणम्। 'मध्यमा अम्बा' जननी केकयी। तस्या 'वृत्तान्त' व्यापारः रामवनवासादिकः। 'अन्तरितः' गोपितः, तत् तस्या निन्दितमाचरणम् उपस्थापितं मा भूत इति परिहृतः।। इदमपि वीरचरित विरुद्धम्। तत्र हि मृषा कैकेया अपवादः, सर्व एव रामवनवासवृतान्तो माया शूर्पणखायाः सेव मन्थरावेषेण दशरथमुपमृत्य रामस्य निर्वासनं भरतस्य चाभिषेचनं याचितवती इत्युक्तम्।।

Notes. 1. अन्यतः–To another part of the walk. 2. शृङ्गवेरपुरे–Consture शृङ्गवेरपुरे इङ्गुदीपादपः not शृङ्गवेरपुरे यत्र etc. Comp. वर्त्मनि वनस्पतिः–Para xxxvi, विन्ध्याटवीमुखे विराधसंरोधः–Para xxxvii, etc. 3. स्निग्धेन–स्निह्यतीति स्निह+क्त कर्त्तरि वर्तमाने स्निग्धः friend. "स्निग्धो वयस्यः सवयाः इत्यमरः। 4. मध्यमा etc.— मध्यमाम्बायाः केकय्याः वृत्तान्तः वार्त्ता रामवनवासादिकं दुष्कर्म। 5. अन्तरितः–अन्तर is अन्तर्द्धि screening, or screen. अन्तरेण गोपितः इति अन्तर+णिच् (नामधातु)+क्त कर्मणि।

(*xxxiv*) **सीता–अम्हो एसो जडासञ्जमणबुत्तन्तो (अहो! एष जटासंयमनवृत्तान्तः)।**

Sītā—Ha! Here is the incident of matting the locks.

लक्ष्मणः–

पुत्रसंक्रान्तलक्ष्मीकैर्यद्वृद्धेक्ष्वाकुभिर्धृतम्।
धृतं बाल्ये तदार्येण पुण्यमारन्यकं व्रतम्।।22।।

Lak.—The holy vow of the forester which had been observed by the Ikṣavākus with their sovereignty transferred to their sons when old, was, by my noble brother, taken up in childhook.

मित–। अहो इति। 'जटानां संयमन' बन्धनं तदेव 'वृतान्तः' व्यापारः। पुत्रेति। अन्वयः–(वृद्धेक्ष्वाकुभिः पुत्रसंक्रान्तलक्ष्मीकैः (सद्भिः) यत् धृतं तत् पुण्यमारण्यकं व्रतम् आर्य्येण बाल्ये धृतम्)।

व्याख्या–'वृद्धैः इक्ष्वाकुभिः' इक्ष्वाकुकुलजैः नृपैः 'पुत्रे संक्रान्तां संक्रमिता

'लक्ष्मीः' राजश्रीः यैः (अन्तर्भावितण्यर्थः क्रामतिः)। यद्वा 'संक्रान्तां' सङ्गता 'लक्ष्मीः' येषां तादृशैः सद्भिः 'यत्' धृतम्' अवलम्बितं 'तत् पुण्यं' पवित्रम् 'आरण्यकं व्रतं' वनवासरूपा तापसवृतिः 'आर्येण' पूज्येन रामेण 'बाल्ये' शैशवे एव 'धृतम्'। अहो त्यागः।

Notes. 1. पुत्र etc.—लक्षयति पश्यति नीतिविद पुमांसम् इति लक्ष+णिच्+ई (औणदिक) कर्त्तरि स्त्रियाम् लक्ष्मीः Fortune. Royalty etc.; now see मित–। त्रिपदबहु–। Or पुत्रे संक्रन्ता पुत्रसंक्रान्ता, सुप्सुपा। तादृशी लक्ष्मीः येषाम्ः। कप् is added by the rule "उरःप्रभृतिभ्यः कप्"। "नद्यृतश्च" has no scope because लक्ष्मी is not नदीसंज्ञक। Witness लक्ष्मीः with a विसर्ग which would have disappeared if the word were नदीसंज्ञक। 2. वृद्धेक्ष्वाकुभिः–इक्ष्वाकु is an ancestor of the race. By transference of epithets the decendants of इक्ष्वाकु are also called इक्ष्वाकु। वृद्धा इक्ष्वाकवः etc. The word वृद्ध here is significant. They did it when *old* after having fully enjoyed the sweets of royal power etc. Noble brother did the same when quite young, when enjoyment was just coming within his reach. Hence the magnitude of the sacrifice. 3. *Remark*—It would have been better to leave वृद्ध uncompounded. Compounded, the word loes the prominence which is necessary for the force as exlplained in note.

(*xxxv*) **सीता–एसा पसणपुणमसलिला भअवदी भाईरही (एषा प्रसन्नपुण्यसलिला भगवती भागीरथी)।**

Sītā—This is mighty Bhāgīrathī with her clear and holy waters.

रामः–देवि रघुकुलदेवते नमस्ते

Rāma—Salutation to thee, Illustrious Detiy, of the race of Raghu.

तुरगविचयव्यग्रानुर्वीभिदः सगराध्वरे
कपिलमहसामर्षात् प्लुष्टान् पितुः प्रपितामहान्।
अगणिततनूपातं तप्तवा तपांसि भगीरथी
भगवति एव स्पृष्टानद्भिश्चिरादुददीधरत्।। 23।।

O mighty one, Bhāgīratha, having practised penance, heedless of the loss of body saved after a lone time, with the touch of my waters, the great-grand-fathers of his father who, intent upon the search for the horse at the sacrifice of Sagara, had rent the earth and got consumed by Kapila's fire from wrath.

सा त्वमम्ब स्नु षायामरुन्धतीव सीतायां शिवानुध्यानपरा भव।

With such traditions, Mother do thou be, like Arundhati, watchful over the welfare of thy daughter-in-law Sītā.

मित–। एषेति। 'प्रसन्नं' विमलं 'पुण्यं' 'सलिलं' यस्याः। देवीति। कुलस्य देवता, विशेषेण पूजिता देवी, कुलदेवता। रघूणां रघुवंशीयानां कुलदेवता रघुकुलदेवता। यद्वा–रघुकुलस्य देवता। कुलदेवतात्वं समर्थायते तुरगेति।' अन्वयः–भगवति, भगीरथः अगणिततनूपातं तपांसि तप्त्वा तव अद्भिः स्पृष्टान् सगराध्वरे तुरगविचयव्यग्रान् उर्वीभिदः अमर्षात् कपिलमहसा प्लुष्टान् पितुः प्रतिमहान् चिरात् उददीधरत्।

व्याख्या–हे 'भगवति' महिममयि गङ्गे पूर्वपुरूषोऽस्माकं दिलीपतनयो 'भगीरथः अगणितः' उपेक्षितः 'तनूपातः' देहनाशो यस्मिन् कर्मणि तत् यथा तथा 'तपांसि तप्त्वा' तपश्चरित्वा तेनैव तपोबलेन त्वां प्रसाद्य स्वर्गात् भूतलमानीय 'तव अद्भिः' सलिलैः 'स्पृष्टान्' संसृष्टान् 'सगरस्य' तेषामेव पितुः 'अध्वरे' यागे अश्वमेधे 'तुरगस्य' यज्ञियाश्वस्य इन्देण चोरितस्य रसातलञ्च कपिलसमीपे नीतस्य 'विचये' अन्वेषणे 'व्यग्रान्' व्यापृतान् भुवि चाश्वमनासाद्य पतति विचयार्थम् 'उर्वीभिदः' महीं विदार्य कपिलसमीपं गतान् कपिलञ्च अश्वचौर इति धर्षणपरान् 'अमर्षात्' रोषाञ्च ज्वलितं यत् 'कपिलस्य महः' तेजः तेन 'प्लुष्टान्' भस्मीभूतान् 'पितुः' दिलीपस्य 'प्रपितामहान्' पितामहान् (''पितुश्च पितामहान्'' इति कर्तव्य ''पितुः प्रपितामहान्'' इति लिपिकरप्रमाद इव प्रतिभाति) 'चिरात्' बहोः कालात् परम् 'उददीधरत्' उद्धारयामास।। 'सा' तपसा कुलदेवतारूपेण अर्जिता कुलमङ्गलकारिणी च 'त्वम् अरुन्धतीव' तदाख्यकुलगुरुपत्नी इव 'स्नुषायां' बन्धां 'सीतायां शिवानुध्यानपरा' मङ्गलचिन्तननिरता 'भव'। अस्य वचनस्य उपयोगं सप्तमाङ्कके स्फुटीभविष्यति।।

Notes. 1. तुरग etc.—तुरेण वेगेन गच्छतीति तुर+गम+ड कर्त्तरि तुरगः horse. विशिष्ट्म अग्रमेषाम् इति व्यग्राः keen. तुरगस्य विचयः। तस्मिन् व्यग्राः, सुप्तुपा। 2. उर्वी–etc.—उर्वी is मही earth. तां भिन्दन्ति इति उर्वी+भिद+छिप् कर्त्तरि उर्वीभिदः, ताम्। They dug up the earth at the command of their father—''यावत्तुगसन्दर्शस्तावत् खनत मेदिनीम्''। 3. सगर etc.—सगर was an old ancestor of the Raghus. अध्वर is याग (अध्वानं स्वर्गमागे राति ददाति इति क प्रत्ययः)। This was an अश्वमेध। The sacrifical horse was stolen by Indra and left tied near the sage Kapila who was practising penance in Pātāla. 60000 of Sagara's sons went out in search of the horse. They dug up the earth, saw the horse hear near Kapila whom they insulted and were all consumed in the fire of Kapila's wrath. The hole dug by Sagara's sons is the सागर, sea (सगरस्य अयम् इति अण्)। 4. अमर्षात्–मृष+घञ्+भावे मर्षः चमा। न मर्षः अमर्षः। तस्मात्। हेतरै 5मी। हेतु of कपिलमहः। Kapila's ire was due to the intolerance (अमर्ष) caused by the arrogance of the princes. 5. प्रपितामहान्–This should be पितामहान् as is seen from the रामायण quoted by विद्यासागर–"सगरस्यासमञ्जस्तु असमञ्जादथांशुमान्। दिलीपोऽंशुमतः पुत्रो दिलीपस्य भगीरथः।।" The princes were प्रपितामह of भगीरथ not of his father. Hence विद्यासागर suggests the reading पुरा प्रपितामहान्। This attaches oversight to the poet himself because it is difficult to believe that the scribes misread पितुः for पुरा। I am inclined to think that the poet had written पितुश्च पितामहान् which agress with the रामायण। The scribes, however misread श्च and wrote प्र, a very likely error. With च, construe उर्वीभिदः प्लुष्टांश्च–rent the earth and got burnt up. 6. चिरात्–An अव्यय meaning चिरेण कालेन। अपवर्गे तृतीया which has disappeared. They lay long undelivered. Their great-grandson भगीरथ brought down गङ्गा was thenceforth called भागीरथी (भगीरथस्य इयं तेन आनीता इति, or—तस्य कुलदेवता इति)।

(xxxvi) **लक्ष्मणः–अयमसौ मरद्वाजवेदितश्चित्रकूटयायिनि वर्त्मनि वनस्पतिः कालिन्दीतटवटः श्यामो नाम।**

Lak. —This is the fig three, Śyāma by name, on the bank of the Kālindī] on the road to the Citrakūṭa, mentoined by Bharadvāja.

सीता–सुमरेदि एदं पदेसं अज्जउत्तो (स्मरति एतं प्रदेशमार्यपुत्रः)?

Sītā—Does my husband remember this spot?

रामः–अयि कथं विस्मर्यते?

Rāma—How could it be forgotten, dear?

अलसलुलितमुग्धान्यध्वजसञ्जातखेदा–
दशिथिलपरिरम्भैर्दत्तसंवाहनानि।
परिमृदितमृणालौदुर्बलान्यङ्गकानि
त्वमुरसि मम कृत्वा यत्र निद्रामवाप्ता।।24।।

(This is) where you fell asleep laying on my bosom your slim limbs powerless like crushed stalks of lotus, Languid bruised and thus charming Or—and 'Palsied') through the fatigue caused by the journey—limbs to which shampooings were done by close embraces.

मित–। अयमिति। मुनिना 'भरद्वाजेन आवेदित:' चित्रकूटं याति इति 'चित्रकूटयायि' तस्मिन् 'वर्त्मनि' स्थित: 'अयमसौ वनस्पति:' वृक्ष:। वृक्षस्य विस्तरमाह–वर्त्मन: कस्मिन् प्रदेशे इत्याह–'कालिन्द्य:' यमुनाया: तटे' जात:। किंजातीयो वनस्पतिरित्याह–'वट:' वटजातीयो वनस्पति:, किमाख्य इत्याह–'श्यामोनाम' श्याम इति प्रसिद्ध:।। अयीति। प्रदेश: कर्म। कथं विस्मर्यते एष प्रदेश:। स्मरणे कारणमाह अलसेति।

अन्वय:–यत्र त्वम् अध्वसञ्जातखेदात् अलसलुलितमुग्धानि परिमृदितमृणालीदुर्वलानि (ततश्च) अशिथिलपरिरम्भै: दत्तसंवाहनानि अङ्गकानि मम उरसि कृत्वा निद्रामवाप्ता।)

व्याख्या–कथं विस्पर्यते एष प्रदेश: 'यत्र' यस्मिन् प्रदेशे त्वम् अध्वन: अध्वातिक्रमणात् 'सञ्जाता' य: खेद: क्लान्ति तेन 'अलसानि' स्तिमितानि 'लुलितानि' मृदितानि 'मुग्धानि' मनोहराणि तेन च 'परिमृदिता' निष्पिटा या 'मृणाली' विसकिसलयं सा इव 'दुर्बलानि ततश्च श्रममपनुद्य बलमाधातु मया 'अथिशिलै:' गाढ़ै 'परिरम्भै: आलिङ्गनै: 'दत्त संवाहनम्' अङ्गचर्या मर्दनरूपा येषु तथाविधानि 'अङ्गकानि' ह्रस्वाङ्गानि 'मम उरसि वक्षसि 'कृत्वा' निधाय निद्राम् आवाप्ता' निद्रिता। भरद्वाजाश्रमात् चित्रकूटं प्रति चलिता पथि परिश्रान्ता अस्यैव वटस्य तले मम वक्षसि त्वं प्रसुप्ता, सुखातिशयश्च तेन ममाभूत, तत् कथं विस्मर्यति एष प्रदेश:?

Notes. 1. वनस्पति:–वनस्य पति: वनस्प्रति:। The word is of the पारस्करादि class and takes सुट् changning पति into स्पति। This means here a tree in general. ''वनस्प्रतिर्वक्षमात्रे''। 2. कालिन्दी etc.—कालिन्द्यास्तटम्। तस्मिन् वट:, सुप्सुपा। 3. अलस etc.—अलसानि च लुलितानि च अलसलुलितानि, कर्मधा–। तानि च मुग्धानि च, कर्मधा–See next. 4. अध्व etc.—अध्वन: or अध्वनि सञ्जात: अध्वसञ्जात:, सुप्सुपा। तादृश: खेद: कर्मधा–। तस्मात्। हैतौ 3या। हेतु of अलस etc. सञ्जात seems superfluous,अध्वखेदात् is enough. 5. अशिथिल etc.—परि+रभ+घञ् भावे परिरम्भ embrace. करणे 3या। 6. दत्त etc.—सम्+वह+णिच्+ल्युट् करणे संवाहन that with which to remove (fetigue), shampoo. 7. परिमृदित etc.—परिमृदिता मृणाली, कर्मधा– सा इव दुर्बलानि, उपमान कर्मधा–। Evidently Sītā's limbs were not naturaliy so powerless. They were then rendered powerless because they had become अलसलुलितमुग्धानि through अध्वसञ्चातखेद। But मुग्धानि (charming) has nothing to do with दुर्बलानि। Hence explain मोहमुपगतानि इति मुह+क्त कर्त्तरि मुग्धानि palsied. Or, if we agree to put up with a little

दूरान्वय we may consture—यत्र त्वम् अध्वसञ्जातखेदात् परिमृदितमृणालीदुर्बलानि अलसलुलितमुग्धानि अशिथिलपरिरम्भैः दत्तसंवाहनानि अङ्गकानि etc, which again is not altogether free from objection. अङ्गकानि–ह्रस्वानि अङ्गानि इति अङ्ग+कन् ह्रस्वे अङ्गकानि। We suppose the ह्रस्वता here to be opposed to stoutness, *i, e,* it is slimness.

(*xxxvii*) **लक्ष्मणः–एष विन्ध्याटवीमुखे विराधसंरोधः।**

Lak.—Here is our capture by Viradha at the entrance to the Vindhya forest.

सीता–अलं दाव एदिणा। तेक्खामि दाव अज्जउत्तहत्थ-धरिदतलवेरण्ठादवत्तं अत्तणो दक्खिणारणप्पबेसारम्भं (अलं तावदेने। प्रेक्षे तावत् आर्यपुत्रहस्तधृततालवृन्तातपत्रम् आत्मानो दक्षिणारण्य-प्रवेशारम्भम्)।

Sītā—Away with this. I am looking at (scene of) my attept to enter the southern forests with a palm-leaf umbrella held (over me) in the hand of my husband.

रामः–। एतानि तानि गिरिनिर्झरिणीतटेषु
वैखानसाश्रिततरूणि तपोवनानि।
येष्वातिथेयपरमाः शामिनो भजन्ते
नीवारमुष्टिपचना गृहिणो गृहाणि।। 25।।

Rāma—These are those penance groves on the banks of mountain-streams with trees restorted to by hermits where house-holders retired from the world (Or—self-restrained) occupy huts, cooking handfuls of wild rice, and consider hospitality the highest duty.

मित–। एष इति। 'विन्धस्य' तदाख्यस्य गिरेः या 'अष्टवी' वन तस्याः 'मुखे' प्रवेशमार्गे 'विराधेन तदाख्येन रक्षसा आर्यस्य मम च 'संरोधः' निरुध्य ग्रहणम्।। अलमिति। 'आर्यपुत्रस्य हस्तेनधृत' यत् तालवृन्त' तदेव 'आतपत्र' यस्मिन् तम्। विन्ध्यारणयादारभ्य 'दक्षिणास्यां दिशि प्रमृत यत् 'प्रवेशस्य' आरम्भम्' उद्योगम्। । एतानीति।

अन्वयः–गिरिनिर्झरिणीतटेषु वैखानसाश्रिततरूणि एतानि तानि तपोवनानि येषु नीवारमुष्टिपक्षनाः आतिथ्येपरमाः शमिनो गृहिणाः गृहणि भजन्तो।

व्याख्या–निर्झरा विद्यन्ते आसां निर्झरिणयः नद्यः। 'गिरिनिर्झरिणीनां' गिरिनदीनां 'तटेषु तीरेषु 'वैखानसैः' वानप्रस्थैः यतिभिः 'आश्रिताः' अधिकृताः 'तरवो' वृक्षाः वृक्षमूलानि इत्यर्थः येषु तानि 'एतानि' चित्रितानि' तानि तपोवनोनि येषु नीवारमुष्टोः' नियताहारत्वात् मुष्टिमात्रस्य नीवारसंग्रहस्य 'पचनं पाको येषां तथाविधाः, एवं स्वल्पेऽप्योदने' आतिष्येयम् अतिथिसत्कारः 'परम' प्रधानं कर्म येषां तादृशाः 'शमिनः' शमप्रधानाः 'ग्रहिणाः ग्रहस्था मुनयः गृहाणि भजन्ते कुटौः समाश्रयन्ते कृतकुटीरा निवसन्ति।।

Notes. 1. विराध etc.—विराध is the कर्त्ता of संरोध ; the कर्म्म is easily guessed, *viz.,* राम and लक्ष्मण। Also the घञ् in संरोध (सम्+रूध+घञ्)is भावे। Hence there is उभयप्राप्ति here and विराध takes अनुक्ते कर्त्तरि 3या। Thus आवयोः विराधेन संरोधः। Compounding आवयोः विराधसंरोधः 3तत्–। Or avoid the rule 'उभयप्राप्तौ कर्मणि' and apply the Vārttika "शेषे विभाषा"। This gives आवयोः विराधेन विराधस्य वा संरोधः yielding as before विराधसंरोधः as a 3तत्–or 6तत्–। 2 अलं तावत् etc.—She wants to avoid the painful sight. 3. आर्यपुत्र etc.—see मित–। Qual. दक्षिणारण्य etc. 4. दक्षिणारण्य etc.—See मित–। आरम्भ is here आरम्भाश्रयं चित्रम् by transference of epithets. 5. वेखानस etc.—वैखानस is वानप्रस्थ an anchorite. The derivation is uncertain. The Bhagavata in the रामपञ्चाध्याय uses विखनस् or विखनस as a name for ब्रह्मन्। If this is accepted, we may say विखनसः विखनसस्य वा इमे वैखानसाः those who have renounced the world for ब्रह्मन्। They get seated at the foot of trees and practise penance in these penance-groves (तपोवनानि)। 6. आतिथेय etc.—अतिथिषु साधु इति अतिथि+ढञ् (एय) आतिथेयम् hospitality. Now see मित–। Also see next two. 7. शामिनः–शम+घञ् भावे शमः restraint. सः अस्ति एषाम् इति शम+इमि शमिनः। Owing to their restraint they could they could eat very sparingly or renounce a few meals altogether when necessity arose. 8. नीवार etc.—नितरां व्रियन्ते मुनिभिः इति नि+वृ+घञ् कर्मणि नीवारः wild paddy. नि becomes नी by "उपसर्गस्य घञि–"। मुष्टि shows the scantiness of the supply. Even thus were अतिथेयपरमाः। How was that possible with such a meagre supply? They themselves were शमिनः so could afford to hand over their all to the guests. 9. गृहणि–"गृहं गृहाः पुंभूम्नि" does not bar the plural use in the neuter.

(xxxviii) **लक्ष्मणः–अयमविरलानोकहनिवहनिरन्तरस्निग्धनीलपरि–**

सरारण्यपरिणद्धगोदावरीमुखरकन्दरः सन्ततमभिष्यन्दमानमेघमेदुरित-नीलिमा जनस्थानमध्यगो गिरिः प्रस्रवणो नाम।

Lak.—Here is the hill Prasravana by name extending to the heart of Janasthāna whose darkness is deepened by perpetually pouring clouds and whose caves ring with the (flow of the) Godāvarī which is embraced by the forests at the skirts that are of a umiformly mild blue colur because of dense rows of tress.

रामः— स्मरसि सुतनु तस्मिन् पर्वते लक्ष्मणेन
प्रतिविहितसपर्यास्वस्थयोस्तान्यहानि।
स्मरसि सरसतीरां तत्र गोदावरीं वा
स्मरसि च तदुपान्तेष्वावयोर्वर्त्तनानि।। 26 ।।(रा–)

Rāma.—Fair-limbed girl, do you remember those days on that mountain where we rested at ease with comforts provided by Lakṣmaṇa? Do you also remember the Godāvrī there with its attractive (i.e. shady and cool) banks? Do you remember our strolls as well in its neighbourhood? (R—)

मित–। अयमिति। 'अयं प्रस्त्रवणो नाम गिरिः'। किम्भूतः प्रस्तवणः? 'जनस्थानस्य तदाख्यस्य अरणस्य 'मध्यं' मध्यभागपर्यन्तं' गच्छति' प्रसरति यस्तादृशः। पुनः किम्भूतः? 'सन्ततं' सततम् 'अभिष्यन्दनानैः' वर्षद्भिः 'मेघैः मेदुरितः' स्निग्धतामापादितो 'नीलिमा' श्यामता यस्य तथाविधः। पुनः किम्भूतो गिरिः? गोदावर्या' तदाख्यया नद्या हेतुभूतया, तज्ज्लप्रवाहेण इत्यर्थः 'सुखराः' नदन्तः 'कन्दराः' गृहाः यस्य तथाविधः। किम्भू ता गोदावरी? निरन्तराः अविच्छिन्नाः 'भ्निग्धनीलाः' मसृण श्यामाः 'परिसराः' पर्यन्तभागाः येषां तादृशैः 'अरण्यैः परिणद्धा' आलिङ्गिता गोदावरी। तच्च कथम्? 'अविरलैः' निविड़ैः 'अनोहकहनिवहैः' वृक्ससासमूहैः हेतुभिः। गोदावरीसुलिलपर्यन्तप्रमृता वृक्षराजिरित्यर्थः।। स्मरसीति।

अन्वयः–सुतनु, तस्मिन् पर्व्वते लक्ष्मणेन प्रतिविहितसपर्यास्वस्थयोः (आवयोः) तानि अहानि स्मरसि? तत्र सरसतीरां गोदावरीं वा स्मरसि? तदुपान्तेषु आवयोर्वर्त्तनानि स्मरसि च?

व्याख्या–हे 'सुतनु' कान्तवपुः सीते 'तस्मिन् पर्व्वते' गिरौ प्रस्रवणे 'लक्ष्मणेन प्रतिविहिता' उत्पेक्ष्य उत्प्रेक्ष्य प्रार्थनां विनैव कृता या 'सपर्या' या परिचर्य्या तया 'स्वस्थयोः' सुखमवस्थितयोः आवयोः 'तानि अहानि' दिनानि 'स्मरसि' किम्? 'तत्र' तस्मिन् गिरी गिरिप्रान्ते इत्यर्थः 'उपान्तेषु' पर्यन्तभागेषु 'आवयोः' वर्त्तनानि' भ्रमणानि 'स्मरसि च'।।

Notes. 1. अविरल etc.—Qual. गिरिः। 'अनसां' शकटानाम् 'अकः' गतिः अनोकः। तं घ्नन्ति इति अनोकः+हन+ड कर्त्तरि अनोकहाः tress. Long lines of carts are often seen held up by tress blown down by gales and lying across roads. परिसरत्यस्मिन् इति परि+मृ+घ संज्ञायांपरिसरः skirts. *Cf.*"सद्यः पुरोपरिसरेषु शिरीषमृद्वी"। परि+नह बन्धनेः+क्त कर्मणि परिणद्ध embraced. In this sense comp. "ताम्बूलवल्लीपरिणद्धपूगस्वेलालतालिङ्गितचन्दनासु"–*Raghu.* न विरलाः अविरलाः not sparse, *i.e.*, dense. निर्गतम् अन्तरम् अवकाशः एभ्यः निरन्तराः continuous. अनोहकानां निवहः अनोकहनिवहः। स्निग्धाश्च नीलाश्च स्निग्धनीलाः, कर्मधा–। निरन्तराश्च स्निग्धलीलाश्च निरन्तरस्निग्धनीलाः, कर्मधा–। तादृशाः परिसरा एषां निरन्तरस्निग्धनील- परिसराणि बहु–। अविरलाः अनोहनिवहाः, कर्मधा–। अविरलानोकहनिवहैः निरन्तरस्निग्ध- नीलपपिसराणि, सुप्सुपा–। तथाविधानि अरण्यानिए कर्म–। परिणडा या गोदावरी तया मुखराः सुप्सुपा–। तथाविधाः कन्दरा यस्य। 2. सन्ततम्–सम्+तन+क्त कर्म कर्त्तरि सन्तत or सतत। The म of सम् disappears optionally by the कारिका "समो वा ततहितयोः"। Qual. the क्रिया in अभिष्यन्दमान। 3.अभिष्यन्दमान etc.—अभि+स्यन्द+शानच् कर्त्तरि अभिस्यन्दमान or अभिष्यन्दमान, the ष being optional by 'अनुविपर्य्यभिनिभ्यः स्यन्दतेरप्राणिषु"। मिद (स्नेहेन भूादि)+घुरच् कर्मकर्त्तरि मेदुरः mild स्निग्ध। मेदुरः कृतः इति मेदुर+णिच् (नामाधातु)+क्त कर्मणि मेदुरितः subdued. नीलस्य भाव इति नील+इमनिच् नीलिमा blueness. अभिष्यन्दमाना मेघाः, कर्मधा–। तै मेदुरितः, 3 तत्–। तादृशो नीलिमा यस्य, बहु–। Qual. गिरिः। Mark that मेदुरितनीलिमा गिरिः is the same as स्निग्धनीलो गिरिः। +. जनस्थान etc.—जनस्थान was the old name of the central part of the Deccan. तस्य मध्यम्। तत् गच्छतीति जनस्थानमध्य+गम+ड कर्त्तरि। 5. प्रतिविहित etc.—सपर (अदन्त) is a root of the करण्डवादि class meaning to 'honour' (पूजायाम्)। सपर+यक् स्वार्थ सपर्य which also is a root. The यक् is by the rule—कण्डादिभ्यो थक् सपर्य+अ भावे स्वियाम् सपर्या पूजा, i.e., all those attentions to minister to their comforts. स्वस्मिन् तिष्ठतः इति स्व+स्था+क कर्त्तरि स्वस्थौ at ease. प्रतिविहिता सपर्यया, कर्मधा–। तया स्वस्यौ। तयोः। Qual. आवयोः। 6. तानि–No यच्छद is necessary because the reference is to अनुभूतार्थ। 7.अहानि–No शेष विवक्षा, hence "अधोगथ–" does not apply, and we get कर्मणि 2या not षष्ठी। 8. सरस etc.—रस is स्वाद। रसेन सह सरसम् tasteful, *i.e.*, attractive, बहु–। सरस तीर यस्याः ताम्। बहु–Qual. गोदावरीम्। 9. उपान्तेषु–अन्त is समीप। उपगता अन्तम् उपान्ताः close tothe margin, प्रादितत्–। तेषु। 10. आवयोः–अहञ्च त्वञ्च आवाम्, एकशेष by the Vārttika "त्यदादीनां मिथः सहोक्तौ यत् पर तच्छिष्यते", *i.e.,*when words of the त्यदादि class are spoken of together (as in a द्वन्द्व) that which is subsequent in the list is retained and the other dropped, युष्मद् and अस्मद् are त्यदादि and युष्मद् precedes

अस्मद् in the list. Hence अस्मद् is the शेष here giving आवाम्। तयोः। शेषे षष्ठी। 11. वर्त्तनानि–वृत+लुट् भावे। वर्त्तते is usually revolution as in "मेरोरूपान्तेष्विव वर्त्तमानम्"। Here it means motion in general, *i.e.*, walk, stroll etc.

(xxxix) **(रा–) अपि च**

(R.—) And (do you remember) also that.

किमपि किमपि मन्द मन्दमासत्तियोगा–
दविरलितकपोल जल्पतोरक्रमेण।
अशिथिलपरिरम्भव्यापृतैकैकदोष्णो–
रविदितगतयामा रात्रिरेव व्यंगसीत्।। 27।।

Night itself passed unto us with its watches unnoticed, an arm of each of us engaged in clasping the other close, we through proximity talking low and aimlessly with our cheeks in contact?

मित–। अपीति। स्मरसीति योज्यम्। स्मरसि चापि यत् राचिरेव व्यरंसीत् इति परवर्त्तिना श्लोकेन सम्बन्धः।। किमपीति।

अन्वयः–अशिथिलपरिरम्भव्यापृतैकैक- दोष्णोः आसत्तियोगात् अविरालितकपोलं मन्दं मन्दं किमपि किमपि अक्रमेण जल्पतोः (आवयोः) रात्रिदेव अविदितगतयामा (सती) व्यरं सीत्।

व्याख्या–अशिथिलः' गाढ़ः यः 'परिरम्भः' आलिङ्गनं तत्र 'व्यापृतः' नियुक्तः मम 'एकः' तव च 'एक दोः' बाहुः ययोः तादृशयोः अतएव 'आसत्तेः' परस्परसान्नियस्य 'योगात्' सङ्गावात् 'अविरलितौ' मिलितौ 'कपोलौ' गण्डौ यस्मिन् कर्म्मणि तत् यथा तथा 'मन्द मन्द'' सान्निध्यादेव नीचैर्नीचैः 'किमपि किमपि' अचिन्तितोपस्थितं वस्तु अचिन्तितत्वादेव 'अक्रमेण क्रमस्य परिपाव्या अभावेन विशृङ्खलं यथा तथा इत्यर्थः 'जल्पतोः' गदतोः आवयोः 'रात्रिरेव' समग्रा एव रात्रिः न तु तस्या एकदेशमावम् 'अविदितम्' अज्ञातं यथा तथा 'गताः' याताः 'यामाः' प्रहराः यस्याः तादृशौ सती 'व्यरंसीत्' व्यतीता। विनिद्रयोर्जल्पनपरयोरेव अक्ष्णोः प्रभाता रजनी इत्यर्थः। इत्येतत् स्मरसि किम् इति पूर्वेण सम्बन्धः।।

Notes. 1. किमपि–One किमपि refers to राम the other to सीता। Each was talking at random. 2. मन्दं मन्दम्–मन्द is अनुज्ञ। It is गुणवचन qualifying जल्पनक्रिया। The duplication by the rule "प्रकारे गुणवचनस्य" the sense being मन्दप्रकारं जल्पतोः–talking *rather* low. The double form has to be treated like a कर्मधा–compound by the rule "कर्म धारयवदुत्तरेषु"। This requires the elision of the विभक्ति with the form मन्दमन्दम्। This irregularity is common with poets. Comp. "मन्दं मन्दं नुदति पवनः"–*Kālidāsa*. A defence may be attempted—मन्दं जल्पतोः talking low, मन्द being कर्म or क्रियाविं–। मन्दं यथा तथा मन्दं जल्पतोः–Softly talking low, *i.e.,* talking very low. 3. आसत्ति etc—आ+सद्+क्तिन् भावे आसत्तिः आसन्नता closeness. तस्या योगः तस्मात् (हेतौ 5मी. हेतु of अविरलित &.) 4. अविरलित and—विरल spares, here separated न विरलौ अविरलौ not separated, i.e., in contact. अविरलौ क्लती इति अविरल+णिच् (नाम धातु)+क्त कर्म्मणि अविरलितौ। Next बहु–। 5. अक्रमेण–क्रम order. न क्रमः अक्रमः random, नञ् तत्–। तेन। प्रकृत्यादि or सहार्थे 3या। 6. अशिथिल &.—न शिथिलः अशिथिलः। तादृशः परिरम्भः, कर्मधाः–। तस्मिन् वापृतम, सुप्सुपा। एकम् एकम् एकैकम् one of each. कर्मव्यतिहारे द्विरुक्तिः। The whole is treated as a बहुव्रीहि compound, hence the first एकम् drops its विभक्ति। एकैकं दोः एकैकदोः, कर्मधा–। दोस् is both masculine and neuter. अशिथिलपरिरम्भव्यापृतम् एकैकदोः ययोः तथाविधयोः। Qual. आवयोः of verse 26. This compound explains the reason for आसत्तियोग। दोस् becomes दोषन् optionally (by the rule "पद्दन्नोमास्–") in *Bibhaktis* beginning with शस्। Hence—"व्यापृतैकैकदोषोः" is also correct. 7. अविदित &.—अविदिताश्च गताश्च यामाः यस्याः, त्रिपदबहु–। 8. रात्रिदेव–एव implies अवधारण। In other words it adds emphasis to रात्रि, *'i.e.,'* रात्रिदेव means the whole night. जल्पतोः रात्रिरेव व्यरंसीत् implies, by virtue of the शतृ in जल्पतोः, that day dawned before the जल्पन had finished. Compare वादिनः धेनुरावव‍ृते in "इति वादिन एवास्य होतुराहुतिसाधनम्। अनिन्द्या नन्दिनी नाम धेनुराववृते वनात्॥"–Raghu.

(xl) **लक्ष्मणः–एषा पञ्चवटयां शूर्पणखा।**

Lak.—Herer is Śūrpaṇakhā in the Pañcavaṭī.

सीता–हा अज्जउत्त, एतिअं दे दंसणं (हा आर्यपुत्र, एतावत् ते दर्शनम्)।

Sītā.—Alas, my husband this much is my sight of you.

रामः–अयि विप्रयोगत्रस्ते, चित्रमेतत्।

Rāma—Ah! You frightened-by (thoughts of) separtion, this is but a picture.

सीता–जहा तहा होदु, दुज्जणो असुहं उप्पादेइ (यथा तथा भवतु, दुर्जनः असुखम् (अशुभम्?) उत्पादयति)।

Sītā.—Be it as it may, the wicked cause evil.

रामः–हन्त वर्तमान इवमे जनस्थानवृतान्तः प्रतिभाति।

Rāma.—Ha! The events at Janasthāna appear as if present before me.

मित–। एषेति। 'पञ्चवट्याम्' आलिखिता इति योज्यनम्।। हा इति। "एतावत् ते दर्शनम्" इति भाविन्या विपत्तेश्छाया। 'ते' इति कर्म्मणि षष्ठी।। अयीति। 'विप्रयोगो' विरहः। तस्मात् 'त्रस्ता' भीता 'विप्रयोगत्रस्ता'। पूर्वानुभूतो विप्रयोगः शूर्पणखाकृत आसीत् इति भयम्। नह्यत्र तत्वतः शूर्पणखाया आगमः 'चित्रमेतत्' तस्याः तत् कुतो भयम्।। चित्रगता वा पारमार्थिकी वा 'यथा तथा भवतु' तस्याः प्रसङ्गोऽपि 'अशुभम् उत्पादयति' परम् अश्रेयसे भवति। तथा चोक्तं "कथापि खलु पापानामलमश्रेयसे यतः"; मन्वे अमङ्गलं किञ्चिन्मे भविता।। हन्तेति। हन्त' इत्यव्ययमिह विषादे। विषादकाराणमाह–'जनस्थानस्य वृत्तान्तः' सीताहरणरूपः अतीतोऽपि प्रतिकृतोऽपिअद्य 'मे वर्तमान इव प्रतिभाति' प्रत्यक्षमिव दृश्यते। अयमपि आसन्नस्य सीताविरहस्य छायापातः।।

Notes. 1. शूर्पणखा–शूर्पा इव नखा अस्याः, बहु–। ङीष् is prohibted by "नखमुखात् संज्ञायाम्" because this is the संज्ञा of Rāvaṇa's sister. न becomes ण by "पूर्वपदात् संज्ञायामगः"। 2. एतावत् &.—The mention of शूर्पणखा alarms her. 3. असुहं–This is usually translated as असुखम्। But अशुभम् seems better, अशुभ अमङ्गलं। This is a foecast of the great अमङ्गल (banishment) which was impending. Again we have already had a warning against दुर्ज्जन in Sl. 7. It seems the same word दुर्ज्जन is repeated here to show that the mishap is going to happy through दुर्ज्जन। 4. वर्त्तमान इव–I too am reminded of those heart-rending incidents at Janasthana and feel as if those sufferings I am again going through now.

(xli) **लक्ष्मणः–**

अथेदं रक्षोभिः कनकहरिणच्छद्मविधिना
तथा वृतं पापैर्व्यथयति यथा क्षलितमपि।
जनस्थाने शून्ये विकलकरणैरार्यचरितै–
रपि ग्रावा रोदित्यपि दलति वज्रस्य हृदयम्।। 28।।

Lak.—Now. here is what happened through the vile Rākṣasa's (Or—what was dealt by the vile Rākṣasas with the) adoption of the strategem of the golden deer in such a manner as to pain even though wiped out. Even rocks weep, even the heart of adamant breaks, at my noble brother's doings with the sense dazed in lonely Janasthāna.

सीता (सास्त्रमात्मगतम्)–अह देव दहुउलानन्द, एव्वं मम कारणदो किलिट्ठो सि (अयि देव रघुकुलानन्द, एवं मम कारणात् क्लिष्ट आसीः)।

Sītā.—(*With tears—within herself*)—O king, the joy of Raghu's race, so much were you afflicted for my sake!

मित– । अथेति।

अन्वयः–अथ पापैः रक्षोभिः कनकहरिणच्छद्मविधिना इदं तथा वृतं यथा क्षालितमपि व्यथयति। शून्ये जनस्थाने विकलकरणैः आर्यचरितैः ग्रावा अपि रोदिति वज्रस्य अपि हृदयं दलति।

व्याख्या–'अथ' इति आरम्भे। दारुणतरस्य प्रदर्शनमारभ्यते मया इत्यर्थः। पापैः दुराचारैः 'रक्षोभिः राक्षसैः कर्त्तृभिः 'कनकहरिणः' सुवर्णमृग एव 'छद्म' छलं मायामृग इत्यर्थः तस्य 'विधिना' अनुष्ठाने हेतुना ('उभयप्राप्तौ कर्मणि'' इति रक्षोभिरित्यत्र तृतीयैव। परं ''कर्मणि च'' इति कर्मषष्ठाः समासनिषेधात् कनकहरिणछद्मविधिना इति चिन्त्यः प्रयोगः) 'इदम्' एतत् चित्रे दृश्यमानं वस्तु 'तथा वृत'' तेन प्रकारेण पर्यवसितम् 'सीताहरणावसानमित्यभिप्रायः) 'यथा क्षालितमपि विशेधितमपि प्रतिकृतमपि इत्यर्थः 'व्यथयति' तापयति, तदा इदं वृतमिति स्मृतिपथमायातमपि पीड़यति इत्यर्थः (''आर्य्या अपह्रियते रावणेन'' इति रूक्षं परिह्रत्य ''तथा वृतं यथा क्षालितमपि व्यथयति'' इति मसृणमुक्तम्)। 'शून्ये' मानुषसञ्चारविरहिते 'जनस्थाने विकलानि' अवशनि 'करणानि' इन्द्रियाणि येषु तादृशैः आर्यस्य चरितैः अनुष्ठानैः हेतुभिः 'ग्रावा' गिरिः 'अपि रोदिति' समवेदनो भूत्वा अश्रणि मुञ्चति, 'वजस्य अपि हृदयं दलति' विदीर्यते। अयीति। 'रघुकुलम् आनन्दयति' यः सः। 'क्लिष्टः' क्लेशं प्राप्तः।।

Notes. 1. अयः–Implies आरम्भ। A different subject is begun. Comp. ''अर्थतस्मन्वन्तरपुराण etc.''—Para xliv. 2. इदम्–There is a gesture here, the index finger pointing at the scene 3. रक्षोभिः–तृतीया in the अनुक्तकर्त्ता of विधानक्रिया, thus—इदं रक्षांसि कनकहरिणच्छद्म विदधति (इति) इदं रक्षोभिः कनकहरिणच्छद्मनः विधिः (इति)=इदं रक्षोभि कनकहरिणच्छद्म विधिः (इति)। But the grammer is bad, because the 6तत्–in the last stage is prohibited by the rule ''कर्मणि च''। We therefore propose the following—इदं रक्षांसि वृत्तवन्तः=इद्र रक्षोभिः वृतम्। (भावे)। How वृत्तम्?–कनकहरिणच्छद्मविधिना

(करणे 3या) with अविवक्षा of the कर्तृता (?) of the Rākṣasas in the विधानक्रिया। The prose may be given thus—अथ इदं कनकहरिणच्छद्मविधिना पापैः रक्षोभिः तथा वृत्तम् etc. Translate—Now, here the vile Rākṣasas, with the adoption of the stratagem of the golden deer, have so manourved that it pains even though etc. 4. तथा वृत्तम् etc.—This is an indirect way of saying—"Now here sister-in-law is being carried away by Rāvaṇa." The direct statement is too harsh to be repeated just now when feelings are strung to such high pitch. 5. शून्ये-शून्ये is 'void'. Here 'destitute of human beings.' Hence none to weep for Rāma. 6. अपि ग्रावा etc.—But Rāma received full sympathy from the lower creations—birds, beasts and trees. "नृतं मयूराः कुसुमानि वृक्षा दुर्भानुपाताान् विजहुर्हरिणयः"-says Kālidāsa. Elsewhere he has "उद्गलितर्भकवला मृगाः परित्यक्तनर्त ना मयूराः। अपसारिपाण्डुपत्रा सुञ्चन्त्यश्रूणि इव लताः।।"-Śakuntala. 7. रोदिति दलति-The वर्त्तमानकाल shows that भवभूति goes a step further and says—Even to-day at narrations of brother's mad doings even (अपि) rocks weep and the adamant bursts, what to say of birds, beasts and trees? 8. मम कारणात्-'मम' मत्सम्बन्धि यत् 'कारणां' तस्मात्। शेषे षठी and हेतो 5मी।

(*xiii*) **लक्ष्मणः-(रामं निर्वर्ण्य साकूतम्)-आर्य, किमेतत्?**

Lak.—(Meaningly, after watching Rāma)—How is this, noble brother?

अयं ते वाष्पौघस्त्र टित इव मुक्तामणिसरो
विसर्पन् धाराभिलुठति धरणीं जर्जरकणः।
निरुद्धोऽप्यावेगः स्फुरदधरनासापुटतया
परेषामुन्नेयो भवति च भराध्मातहृदयः।। 29।।

This mass of thy tears flowing in streams rolls in the ground being divided into drops like a broken string of pearls. The emotion which by its volume has filled your heart, though checked, can be guessed by others also from the quivering lower lip and nostrils.

मित-। राममिति। 'रामं निर्वण्य' सूक्ष्म वीक्ष्य तस्य आवेगं दृष्ट्वा 'साकूतं' साभिप्राय यथा तथा आह। स्वयमावेगकारणं जानन्नपि राममुखात् तच्छ्रवणमभिप्रायः अतएव साभिप्रायम्।। अयमिति।

अन्वयः—धाराभिः विसर्पन् अयं ते वाष्पौधः जर्जरकणः (सन्) त्रुटितः मुक्तामणिसर इव धरणीं लुठति। भराध्मातहृदयः आवेगः निरुद्धोऽपि स्फुरदधरनासापुटतया च परेषासुन्नेयो भवति।

व्याख्या—'धाराभिः प्रवाहैः विसर्पन्' 'अयं ते वाष्पौधः' अश्रुराशिः भुवमागत्य 'जर्जरकणः' सन् विन्दुजालरूपेण परिणमन् इत्यर्थः 'त्रुटितः' छिन्नः 'मुक्तामणिसरः इव गलितमणिः मुक्ताहार इव 'धरणीं लुठति' धरणयामावृर्तते (अकर्म्मकस्य लुठतेर्देशस्य कर्मसंज्ञा। "देशकालाध्व- गन्तव्याः कर्मसंज्ञा ह्यकर्मणाम्") एतदेव हृदयावेगोन्नयनाय अलम् परमन्यदप्यस्ति इत्याह—'भरेण' आतिशयेन 'आत्मातम्' आपूरितं 'हृदयं' येन तादृशः 'आवेगः' विचलितता 'निरुद्धः अपि' नियन्त्रितोऽपि विलापरूपेण अप्रकटितोऽपि इत्यर्थः 'स्फुरन्' कम्पमानः 'अधरः नासापुटञ्च' यस्य तद्र पत्वात् 'च' न केवलमश्रुभिः 'परेषाम्' अन्येषां द्रष्टणमित्यर्थः 'उन्नेयो भवति' अनुमेयो भवति।।

Notes. I. मुक्ता etc.—सर is 'a string. मुक्त एव मणयः, कर्म्मधा–तेषां सरः। The smilie is defective in the usual construction मुक्तामणिसर इव धाराभिः विसर्पन् etc. Hence we have given a different prose order (see above.) The tears can be compared to beads of pearls if they stand distinct in the shape of drops. But ओध (steam प्रवाह), as well as धाराभिः (in streams) goes against it. 2. धाराभिः–प्रकृत्यादि तृतीया। 3. धरणीम्–कर्म्म of लुटति। लुट though अकर्मक can have its site (देश) as कर्म्म by the कारिका "देशकालाध्वगन्तव्याः कर्मसंज्ञा ह्यकर्मणाम्"। 4. जर्जर etc–जर्जराः पृथक्तया उपलब्धाः कण यस्य सः, बहु–। Before reaching the ground—the whole was one continuous stream and by its transparence etc. looked like a string of pearls. Or reaching the ground it broke up into particles and then looked like a *broken* string of pearls each separate drop of tears now resembling a bead of the broken string. 5. निरुद्ध–Rāma was not making loud lamentations, hence his आवेग was indeed निरुद्ध। 6. स्फुरत् etc.—नासायाः पुटं नासापुटम्। अधरञ्च नासापुटञ्च अधरनासापुटम्। प्राणयङ्गत्वात् समाहारः, तत एकवचनम्। स्फुरत् अधरनासापुटं यस्य तस्य भावः। तया। हेतौ 3या। 7. च–Construe स्फुरदधरनासापुटतया च the च implying समुच्चय of वाष्पवर्षण with स्फुरदधरनासापुटता। People can guess the आवेग from स्फुरदधरनासापुटता and also (च) from the fact that वाष्पीधो धरणीं लुटति। Usually च is construed as उन्नेयी भवति च with च implying अवधारण–become inferrable indeed. This should be avoided, because the tears spoken of in the first half of the verse have already declared the emotion to observers, why then go to the quivering lips etc. in the second half ?

(xliii) **रामः–वत्स,**

Rāma—Darling.

तत्कालं प्रियजनविप्रयोगजन्मा
तीव्रोऽपि प्रतिकृतिवाञ्छया विसोढ़ः।
दुःखाग्निर्मनसि पुनर्विपच्यमानो
हृन्मर्मव्रण इव वेदनां करोति।। 30।।

The fire of anguish caused by loss of my beloved and at the time, endured, though intense, through a desire for retaliation being rekindled in my mind, is causing pain like a wound in the vitals of the heart.

सीता–हद्धी हद्धी अहं वि अदिभूमिं गदेण रणरणएण अज्जउत्तसूणं विअ अत्ताणं पेक्खामि (हा धिक्, हा धिक्, अहिमपि अतिभूमिं गतेन रणरणकेण आर्यपुत्रशून्यमिव आत्मानं प्रेक्षे)।

Sītā—O fie! O fie! Through distress reaching its climax I too deem myself as if devoid of my husband.

मित–। तत्कालमिति। (प्रियजनविप्रयोगजन्माः तीव्रः अपि प्रतिकृतिवाञ्छया तत्कालं विसोढ़ दुखाग्निः पुनः मनसि विपच्यमानो हृन्मर्मव्रण दूवं वेदनां करोति)।

व्याख्या–'प्रियजनेन' प्रेमपात्रेगण सीताया इति यावत् यः 'विप्रयोगः' विरहः तस्मात् 'जन्म' यस्य अतएव 'तीव्रः अपि' दारुणोऽपि 'प्रतिकृतेः' प्रतिकारस्य वैरनिर्यातनस्य इति यावत् या 'वाञ्छा' आकाङ्क्षा तया प्रतिकारचिन्तनपरतया इत्यर्थः तं कालं व्याप्य 'तत्कालं' तस्मिन् काले इति यावत् 'विसोढ़' कृतविसहनः 'दुखाग्निः' शोकपावकः 'पुनः' भूयोऽपि अघ 'मनसि विपच्यमानः' विपाकं गच्छन् सन् 'हृन्मर्मणि' हृदयस्य जीवस्थाने जातोयो 'ब्रणः' सघःप्राणहरः स्फोटक स 'इव वेदनां करोति' पीड़यति। अतएव हे वत्स अश्रुप्रवाहः अधरनासस्फुरणञ्च।। हा इति। 'अतिगता' सर्वोपरि गता 'भूमिः' स्थानम् 'अतिभूमिः' प्रकर्षः। तां 'गताः' प्राप्तः अत्युत्कट इत्यर्थः यः 'रणरणकः' उद्वेगः तेन। 'आर्यपुत्रशून्यमिव आत्मानं प्रेक्षे इति अचिरप्राविन्धा विपदञ्छाया।।

Notes. 1. तत्कालम्–स कालः तत्कालः, कर्मधा–। तम्। व्याप्तार्थे 2या। 2. प्रिय

etc.—प्रियः जनः कर्मधा–। तेन विप्रयोगः, सुपसुपा। तस्मात् जन्म यस्य सः, बहु–। This sort of व्यधिकरणबहु–though irregular, is unavoidable. "अवर्ज्यो बहुव्रीहिर्व्यधिकरणो जन्माद्य तरपदः"–*Vamana*. 3. विसोढ़–वि+सह+क्त कर्मणि। The स does not become ष though the rule 'परिनिविभ्यः सेत्रसित–" directs the change. This is because "सोढ़" makes an exception in the case of सह when its स become सो। दुःखाग्निः–दुःखम् अग्निरिव, उपमितकर्मवा–। 4. विपच्यमानः–वि+पच+शानच् कर्मकर्त्तरि। Being developed. Formerly it was विप्रयोगजन्मा, now it is विप्रयोगस्मृतिजन्मा। This and प्रियजनविप्रयोगजन्मा go against a रूपकर्मधा–in दुःखाग्नि 5. हृन्मर्म्म etc.—हृद् heart, नर्मन् vital point. हेदो मर्म। तस्मिन् व्रणः, सुपसुपा। If like fire, the pain should be grater than that of हृन्मर्मव्रण? Not necessarily. The likeness is not in तीव्रता, for then we cannot have the compound दुःखाग्नि, the rule "उपमितं व्याघ्रादिभिः सामान्याप्रयोगे" prohibiting it when the common attributive (सामान्य) is directly mentioned. Hence we say दुःख and अग्नि are compared through their दाहकता; they both consume their subject. The तीव्रता in तीव्रोऽपि is *predicated* afterwards. If was not though of (अविवक्षा) when compounding. 6. अतिभूमिम्–भूमि is तल storey-अत्युन्नता भूमिः इत्यर्थे अतिभूमिः is a प्रादितत्–(नित्यसमास)। अतिभूमि गतः then means reched the 'top-floor' i. e., excessive. 7. *Remark*—Both Rāma and Sītā are here represented as already feeling the pangs of separation. This is not without a purpose. *It perpares then for the coming blow.*

(xliv) **लक्ष्मणः (स्वगतम्)–भवतु अन्यतः क्षिपामि। (चित्रं विलोक्य प्रकाशम्) अथैतन्मन्वन्तरपुराणस्य गृध्नराजस्य तत्रभवतस्तातजटायुषः चरित्रविक्रमोदाहरणम्।**

Lak. (*To himself*)—well, I wil trun them to something else. (*Looking at the painting*—Aloud). Here is the exhibition of the nature and valour of that Manvantara-old vulture-king the revered father Jatayus.

सीता–हा ताद निव्वूढो दे अबच्चसिणेहो (हा तात, निर्व्यूढस्ते अपत्यस्नेहः)।

Sītā—Alas ! Father, your filial love has been fully demonstrated !

रामः–हा तात काश्यप शकुन्तराज, क्व पुनस्त्वादृशस्य महतस्तीर्थस्य साधोः सम्भवः ?

Rāma—Alas ! Father Kaśyapa, king of birds, where again will appear such a highly worthy saint as thyself ?

मित–। भवत्विति। 'अन्यतः' अन्यविषये। 'क्षिपामि' नयामि। अन्यदुप-स्थापयामि इत्यर्थः।। 'अन्तरम्' अवकाशः व्याप्तिकालः। मनोः अन्तरं 'भन्वन्तरम्' स्वायन्भुवादीनां चतुर्दशानामेकैकस्य राज्यकालः। 'मन्वन्तरेण' मन्वन्तरमितकालेन यः 'पुराणः' प्राचीनः अतिवृद्ध इत्यर्थः। तस्य 'चरितस्थ आचरणस्य सद्धृतस्य इत्यर्थः, येन चरित्रेण प्रेरितः अतिवृद्धोपि सीतार्थे दुर्दान्तं रावणमपि रुरोध इति हृदयम्। तथा 'विक्रमस्य' शौर्यस्य येन शौर्येण रावणास्यापि प्राणसंशयो जात इत्याशयः। तयोः 'चरित्रविक्रमयोः उदाहरण' प्रदर्शनं चित्रे लेखनर्मि ति यावत्।। सीतेति। 'ते तव 'अपत्यस्नेहः सन्ततिवात्सत्यं निर्व्यूढ़ महता हि वैशिष्ठेन 'उढ़' अङ्गीकृतः। प्राणव्ययेनैव त्वया मद्‌गतस्य स्नेहस्य आणृन्यमङ्गीकृतमिति भावः।। राम इति। 'काश्यप' कश्यपसगोत्र। देवर्षेरिव कश्यपस्य ते हृदयम् इत्याशयः। 'शकुन्तानां पक्षिणं 'राजा' त्वम्। राज्ञ इव आश्रितरक्षाविधिस्ते इति भावः। 'तीर्थस्य' पुण्यनिलयस्य इत्यर्थः। 'क सम्भवः' न क्वापि। न कोऽप्यन्यः प्राणशङ्काभवमत्य ईदृशे देष्करे यतेत इत्यर्थ।।

Notes. 1. मन्वन्तर etc.—The Manus are 14 in number each of whom is in the ascendant (राजा) for a certain number of years which is known as a मन्वन्तर। मन्वन्तरेणः पुराणः (Deriv ante) सुप् सुपा। Jatayus had lived a whole मन्वन्तर। 2. जटायुषः–जटायुस् was the second son of गरुड़। The name is also spelt जटायु ending in उ। 3. निर्व्यूढ़–निर्+वि+वह+क्त कर्मणि। नि is intensive, वि distinctive. The love you felt was not like that of ordinary people (वि distinctive) and it was felt in a vast measure (निर intensive), वह to carry here means 'to feel and show it.' 4. त्वादृशस्य–त्वमिव दृश्यमानः त्वामिव आत्मानं दर्शयति इति युष्मद्+हश+कञ् कर्म कर्त्तरि त्वादृशः। This is after the भाष्य। Usually the affix is taken as कर्त्तरि–त्वमिव पश्यतीति। The Vṛtti says—'ताहगादयो हि रूढिशब्दप्रकारा नैत्रात्रदर्शनक्रिया विद्यते''।

(xlv) **लक्ष्मणः–अयमसौ जनस्थानपश्चिमतः चित्रकुञ्जवान् नाम दनुकबन्धाधिष्ठतो दण्डकाररण्यभागाः। तदिदमृष्यमूकपर्वते मतङ्गस्याश्रमपदम्। इयञ्च श्रमणा नाम सिद्धशवरी। तदेदत् पम्पाभिधानं सरः।**

Lak.—Here is the tract of the forest Daṇḍaka known as Citrakuñjavat, to the west cf Janasthāna, haunted by the headless gaint Danu; this is the site of the hermitage of Mataṅga on the hill Ṛsyamuka; this again is the emancipated Caṇḍāla woman named Śramaṇa; this is the celebrated lake called Pampā.

सीता–एत्थ किल अज्जउत्तेण विसज्जिदाामरिसधीरत्तणं पमुक्ककण्ठं रुदिअं आसी (अत्र किल आर्यपुत्रेण विसृष्टामर्ष-धीरत्वं प्रमुक्तकण्ठं रुदितमासीत्)।

Sītā—Here, you say, wrath and fortitude were given up by my husband and lamentation made at the top of his voice.

मित–। अयमिति। 'जनस्थानस्य' तदाख्यस्य महावनस्य 'पश्चिमतः' पश्चिमे दिग्बिभागे। 'दनुः' नाम यः 'कबन्धः' निष्कन्धरो राक्षसः तेन 'अधिष्ठितः' अध्युषितः। 'दण्डकारणयस्य भागः' अशविशेषः। 'सिद्धा' तपसः पारं गता 'शवरी' चण्डाली।। अत्रेति। 'किल' इत्यव्ययमिह ऐतिह्ये। श्रुतमात्रे श्रुतमात्रे विषये। श्रुतं मया यत् इह इत्यादि। 'विसृष्टः' परित्यक्तः 'अमर्षः' मदपहारिणि रिपौ रावणे यः कोपः (येन च मद्वियोगजः शोको विस्मृतः) 'धीरत्वं धैर्यञ्च (येन पुनः स्मृतोऽपि शोको नियन्त्रित आसीत्) यस्मिन् कर्मणि तत् यथा तथा। कण्ठप्रमोचनक्रियाविशेषणमेतत्। 'प्रमुक्तः' उदौरितः 'कण्ठः' स्वरः यस्मिन् कर्मणि तत् यथा तथा। रोदनक्रियाविशेषणमेतत्।।

Notes. 1. जनस्थान etc.—पश्चिमे इति पश्चिम+ङि (सप्तमौ)+तसि स्वार्थे पश्चिमतः to the west, आघादि। 2. चित्रकुञ्जवान् is the proper name of the tract.3. ऋष्यमूक etc.—ऋष्यमूक is the hill where Rāma met सुग्रीव। 4. मतङ्गव etc.—The mention of the sage reminds us of his curse on Bali. वाली after killing the monster दुन्दुभि flung away his carcase to a considerble distance causing blood from it to defile the sage Matanga's hermitage and person. Thereupon the sage pronounced instant death on बाली if he came to ऋष्यमूक। Thenceforth बाली always shunned the hill and सुग्रीव who had offended बाली took up his residence there secure from Bali's wrath. 5. तद्देतत्–तत् is प्रसिद्धार्थक। Or तत् एतत् यस्य मयाा बहुशः कथिता ते कथा। See under किल above. अत्र किल–अत्र refers to पम्पा। किल इत्यैतिह्ये–Such is the rumour. She means that she has heard of it since very likely from Lakṣmaṇa himself.

(xlvi) **रामः—देवि, रमणीयमेतत् सरः।**

Rāma—Charming is this lake, my Queen.

एतस्मिन् मदकलमल्लिकाक्षपक्ष–
व्याधूतस्फुरदुरुदण्डपुणरीकाः।
वाष्पाम्भः परिपतनोद्गमान्तराले
सन्दृष्टाः कुवलयिनो भुवो विभागाः।। 31।।

Here, at intervals between the shedding and the show of tears, I noticed tracts studded with blue lotuses and with long stalked white lotuses becomig manifest when shaken by the wings of the Mallikākṣa cackling sweetly from joy.

मित–। एतस्मिन्निति।

अन्वयः–एतस्मिन् मदकलमल्लिकाक्षपक्षव्याधूतस्फुर- दुरुदण्डपुणडरीकाः कुवलयिनो विभागः वाष्पाम्भः परिपतनोद्गमान्तराले सन्दृष्याः।

व्याख्या–'एतस्मिन्' सरसि 'मदेन' हर्षेण प्रिथसन्निधानजनितेन आनन्देन 'कलाः' मधुरं रुवन्तः ये 'मल्लिकाक्षाः' धवलदेहाः मलिनचञ्चुचरणा राजहंसाः तेषां 'पक्षैः व्याधूतानि' कम्पितानि एतएव 'स्फुरन्ति आर्विर्भवन्ति' प्राक् वर्णसाम्यात् मल्लिकाक्षेभ्यः पृथक्तया अगृहितानि कम्पितेषु च पुण्डकरूपेण प्रकटीभवन्ति 'उरुदण्डानि' दीर्घनालानि अतः पुनरुद्गदीवराजहंसवत् प्रतीयमानानि 'पुण्डरीकाणि' श्वेतपद्मानि येषु तादृशः 'कुवलयिनः' प्रचुरनीलोत्पलाः 'भुवो विभागाः' भूखण्डाः पम्पाजलप्रदेशाः इति यावत् 'वाष्पाम्भसाम्' अश्रुजलानां यत् 'परिपतनं' निःशेषेण भूप्राप्ति भूयश्च यस्त षाम् 'उद्गमः' नेत्रयोराविर्मावः इत्येतयोः 'अन्तराले' अवकाशे 'सन्दृष्टाः' सम्भगवलोकिताः। इन्दीवरैनीलं क्वचित् क्वचित् पुण्डरीकैः सितमिति वर्णवैचित्र्यात् रमणीमेतत् सरः। मम तु दुःखायैवाभूत् सा रमणीयता। तत्र विहरतां द्वन्द्वचराणां सानन्दानां मधुरञ्च गायतां मल्लिकाक्षाणां दर्शनात् आत्मनो दयितया वियोगः प्रत्यग्र इव प्रतिभातो मे, दुःखेन च प्रसृता तनयनयोर्वारिधारा। एवं सावरणे लोचने विलुप्तं क्षणं पम्पादर्शनम्। अश्रूणि विमुच्य तु मया भूयोऽपि दृष्टा पम्पा च पुनरेव अश्रुधारा। एवमेव नीतं मया समग्रमहः इति भावः। उक्तञ्च ग्रन्थान्तरे–''अनुदिनमपूरि पम्पा मदक्षिसम्पातिभिः सलिलैः'' इति।।

Notes. 1. मदकल etc.—मदेन कलाः सुप् सुपा। मदकला मल्लिकाक्षाः कर्मधा–तेषां पक्षः तेन व्याधूतानि, 3तत्–। उरुः दण्डः उरुदणडानि, बहु–मदकलमल्लिकाक्षपक्षव्याधूतानि स्फुरन्ति उरुदण्डानि पुण्डरीकाणि येषु, बहु–। For propriety etc. see Tika. 2.

वाष्पाम्भः वाष्प is the vapour (उष्मा) that is supposed to proceed from the eyes before the flow of tears. वाष्पपाम् अम्भः। परिपतनञ्च उद्धमश्च, द्वन्द्वः। तयोः अन्तरालम्। वाष्पाम्भसां परिपतनोद्‌गमान्तरालम्। तस्मिन्। 3. सन्दृष्टा–सम् implies साकल्य। It seems misplaced here. Under the circumstances Rāma could have a proper view of the lake.

(xlvii) **लक्ष्मणः–अयमार्यो हनूमान्।**

Lak.—This is noble Hanumat.

सीता–एसो सो चिरणिव्विणजीअलोअसमुद्धरणगुरुओबआरी महाभाओ मारुदी (एष स चिरनिर्विणजीवलोकसमुद्धरणगुरुकोपकारी महाभागो मारुतिः)।

Sītā—Of the long-suffering world of beings, this is the great benefactor by rescue—the highly talented son of the wind-god.

रामः– दिष्टया सोऽयं महाबाहुरञ्जनानन्दवर्द्धनः।
यस्य वीर्येण कृतिनो वयञ्च भुवनानि च।।32।।

Rāma—O joy ! This is the mighty-armed contributor to Anjana's joy through whose valour myself and the world gained our ends.

मित–। एष इति। 'चिरं' यथा तथा 'निर्विणः' दुःखितः 'चिरनिर्विणः' रावणेन दीर्घकालं क्लेशमापादितः। 'गुरु' महत् एव 'गुरुकम्'। 'गुरुकं' यथा तथा 'उपकारी गुरुकोपकारी'। 'समुद्धरणेन रावणवधं विधाय दुःखमोचनेन 'गुरुकोपकारी समुद्धरणगुरुकोपकारी। 'चिरनिर्विणस्य' जीवलोकस्य त्रिभुवनस्य 'समुद्धरण-गुरुकोपकारी'।। महान् भागः' विधिदत्तः सद्‌गुणरर्शिर्यस्य' सः। 'मारुतस्य' पवनस्य अपत्यं 'मारुति' हनूमान्।। दिष्ट्या इति। (अन्वयः दिष्ट्या ! अयं सःमहाबाहु, अञ्जनानन्दवर्द्धनः यस्य वीर्येण वयञ्च भुवनानि च कृतिनः।)

व्याख्या–दिष्ट्या इत्यव्ययमिह हर्षे। अहो हर्षः 'अयम्' एष चित्रे लिखितः 'स महामाहुः' आजानुलस्वितभुजः उदग्रभुजः शूर इत्यर्थः 'अञ्जनायाः' केशरिपप्नाः 'आनन्दवर्द्धनः' हर्षजननः सुतः हनूमान् 'यस्य वीर्येण', सीतासमुद्धरणात् 'वयञ्च', रावणावधात् 'भुवनाानि च कृतिनः' कृतकृत्या जाताः।।

Notes. 1. हनुमान्–हनुरस्याति कुत्सितः इति हनु+मतुप् निन्दायाम्। It is a संज्ञा of the monkey-chief, hence "शरादीनाञ्च" lengthens the उ of हनु। Comp.

"शङ्के हनुमल्कथितप्रवृतिः", एष श्रीलहनूमता विचचिते श्रीमन्महानाटके" etc. sometimes हनुमत् with a short उ is also seen. Thus "वसन्तकालो हनुमानिवागतः", "गाढ़ वक्षसि ताड़िते हनुमता द्रोणाद्रिरत्राहत" etc. 2. चिरनिर्विण etc.— निर्+विद+क्त कर्त्तरि निर्विणः distressed. The ण is by "निर्विणस्योपसांख्यानम्"। गुरु एव इति गुरु+कन् स्वार्थे गुरुकम्। गुरुकं यथा तथा उपकारौ गुरुकोपकारी, सुप्तुपा। चिरं निविणः, 2तत्–। तादृशो जीवलोकः कर्मधा–। तस्य समुद्धरणम। तेन गुरुकोपकारी, सुप्सुपा। 3. मारुतिः–मारुतस्य अपत्यं पुमान् इति मारुत+इञ्। Refers to हनुमान् who was the Wind-god's son by अञ्जना the wife of the monkey-chief केशरी। 4. दिष्ट्या–An अव्यय Indicatting हर्ष। 5. कृतिनः–कृतमेभिः इति कृत+इनि। Rāma did his work (सीतासमुद्धरण) and the worlds did their work (रावणवध) through the powess of हनुमान्। For भुवनानि change कृतिनः to कृतीनि।

(xlviii) **सीता–वच्छ, एसो कुसुमिदकअम्बतरुतण्ठविदबरहिणो किस्णामामहेओ गिरी जत्थ अणुभावसोहग्गमेत्तपरिसेसधूसरसिरी मूहत्तं मुच्छन्तो तुए परुदिएण अवलम्बिदो तरुअले अज्जउत्तो आलिहिदो (वत्स, एष कुसुमितकदम्बतरुताण्डवितबर्हिणः किन्नामधेयो गिरिः यत्र अनुभावसुभाग्यमात्रपरिशेषधूसरश्रीः मुहूर्त्तं मूर्च्छन त्वया प्ररुदितेन अवलम्बितः तरुतले आर्यपुत्रः आलिखितः)।**

Sītā.—Brother, of what name is this hill where peacocks, are in a giddy dance on Kadamba tress in flower and on which is painted, under a tree, with looks pale, the exuberance of majesty alone remaining, my husband fainting and supported by yourself weeping for the moment ?

मित–। वत्सेति। 'वत्स किन्नाधेयः एष गिरिः' किं नामधेयम् अस्य गिरेः 'यत्र तरुतले आर्यपुत्रः आलिखितः' ? किम्भूतः आर्यपुत्र ? 'मूच्छर्न आर्यपुत्र मुहूर्ते प्ररुतिदेन त्वया अवलम्बितः'। पुनः किम्भूत आर्यपुत्रः ?–'अनुभावस्य' प्रभावस्य यत् सौभाग्यम्' आतिशय्य 'तस्मात्र' तदेव 'परिशेषः' अवशिष्ट यस्याः तादृशी 'धूसरा' भूमौ लुण्ठनात् रेणदिग्धा 'श्रीः' शोभा यस्य तादृशः, अनुभावमात्र शिष्यते सर्वमन्यद्रामणीयकमपगतं यस्य तादृशः आर्य्यपुत्र इत्यर्थः। किम्भूतो गिरिः?–'कुसुसितः' प्रफुल्लः यः 'कदम्बतरु' तत्र 'ताण्डवितः' कृतोद्धतनृत्यः 'बर्हिणः' कश्चिन्मयर यस्मिन् स गिरिः।।

Notes. 1. कुसुमित etc.–कुसुमानि सञ्जातानि अस्य इति कुसुम+इतच कुसुमित in flower. ताण्डवं प्रकृतः इति ताण्डव+णिच् (नामधातु)+क्त कर्त्तरि आदि कर्मणि (वर्त्तमाने)

ताण्डवितः dancing। वर्हम् अस्य इति बर्ह+इनच् वर्हिणः having fine tail, *i.e.*, peacock. कुसुमितः कदम्वतरुः कर्मधा–तस्मिन् ताण्डवितः, सुप्सुपा। तादृशो बर्हिणो यस्मिन्, बहु–। 2. किन्नामधेयः–नाम एव इति नामन्+धेय स्वार्थे नामधेयम् name. किं नामधेयं यस्य, बहु–। 3. अनुभाव etc.—अनुगतो भावः अनुभावः, प्रादितत्–। सुभगस्य भावः इति सुभग+ष्यञ् सौभाग्यम् affluence. "हृद्भगसिन्ध् वन्ते पूर्वपदस्य च" इत्यूभयपदवृद्धिः। अनुभावस्य सौभाग्यम्। तदेव इति अनुभावसौभाग्यमात्रम्। नित्यसमास of the मयूरव्यंसकादि class मात्र implies अवधारण। "मात्रं कार्त्स्न्येऽवधावेणे"। Of the मयूरव्यं सकादि compounds the भाष्य says "समासान्तरं न भवति"। This is interpreted to mean that these compounding may *lead* in a समास but cannot follow. Hence compounding again अनुभावमात्रं परिशेषं परिशेषो वा यस्याः सा अनुभावमात्रपरिशेषा, बहु–। तादृशी धूसरा श्रीः यस्य, त्रिपदबहु–। 3. प्ररुदितेन–प्र+रुद क्त कर्त्तरि प्ररुदितः weeping aloud, तेन।

(xlix) **लक्ष्मणः–सोऽयं शैलः ककुभसुरभिर्माल्यवान् नाम यस्मिन्**
नीलः स्निग्धः श्रयति शिखरं नूतनस्तोयवाहः।

आर्येणस्मिन्–

Lak.—This is that hill fragrant with Arjuna flowers, Mālyavat by name, where the first cloud (of the season), dark and moist, settles on the top. Here by my noble brother—

रामः– विरम विरमातः परं न क्षमोऽस्मि
प्रत्यावृत्तः पुनरिव स मे जानकीविप्रयोगः।।33।।

Rāma.—Stop ! Stop ! I can endure no more. That loss of Jānakī seems to have come back to me.

मित–। स इति।

अन्वयः–अयं स ककुभसुरभिः माल्यवान्नाम शैलः यस्मिन् नीलः स्निग्धः नूतनस्तोयवाहः शिखरं श्रयति। अस्मिन् आर्य्येण–।

व्याख्या–'अयं सः ककुभैः अर्जुनपुष्पैः सुरभिः माल्यवान्नाम शैलः यस्मिन्' सजलत्वात् 'नीलः स्निग्धः' नेत्रानन्दः नूतनः' ऋतौ प्रथमोदितः 'तोयवाहः' जलदः 'शिखरं श्रयति' अध्यास्ते।'अस्मिन्' गिरौ 'आर्येण'–इत्यन्यत् किञ्चित् प्रकान्तमाचिप्तं रामेण।। विरमेति। (अन्वयः–विरम विरम। अतः परं न क्षमोऽस्मि। स जानकीविप्रयोगः पुनः प्रत्यावृत इव मे।)

व्याख्या–हे लक्ष्मण, 'विरम विरम' निवृतो भव, गिरौ माल्यावति किं किं मया कृतं तत्प्रसङ्गे नालम्। 'अतः' अस्मात् 'परम्' "आर्येणस्मिन्" इति कथनात् परं यत् कथनीयं तत् श्रोतु 'न क्षमः अस्मि' सर्वथा असमर्थोऽहम्। कारणमाह–"आर्येणस्मिन्" इत्येतात्येव प्रोक्ते यत् यत् विरहकातरेणमया कृतं तस्मिन् तत् सर्वं स्मृतं मया। तेन मन्ये 'सः' पूर्वानुभूतो जानकीविप्रयोगः' सीताविरहः 'पुनः प्रत्यावृत इव मे' मम समागत इव। इति आसन्नस्य सीताविरहस्य छाया।।

Notes. 1. सोऽयम् etc.—This is in reply to Sītā's question किनामधेयो गिरिः। 2. ककुभसुरभिः–Scents are supposed to be unendurable to the विरहिन्। Comp. "गन्धश्च धाराहतपल्वलानां कादम्बमर्द्धोद्गतकेशरञ्च। स्निग्धाश्च केकाः शिखिनां बभूवुर्यस्मिन्नसहानि विना त्वया मे।।"–*Raghu.* 3. नूतनस्तोयवाहः–This is as trying as the गन्ध। Thus "नव पयो यच्च धनैर्मया च त्वद्विप्रयोगाश्रुसमं विसृष्टम्।"–*Raghu.* 4. आर्येनास्मिन्–Some read वत्सैतस्मात् as coming from राम। This is an interruption to लक्ष्मण। But as लक्ष्मण has finished his scentence with नूतनस्तोयवाहः the interruption seems misplaced. आर्येणस्मिन् on the other hand evidently wants to introduce a painful subject and the interruption comes in very well there. Also see next. 5. विरम विरम–"व्याङ्परिभ्यो रमः" इति परस्मैपदम्। सम्भूमि द्विरुक्तिः। The repetition shows Rama's impatiensce. Hence the repetition is expected to be *abrupt*. The endearing epithet वत्स in वतसै-तत्मात् takes from the abruptness and does not seem to suit the repetition विरम विरम। The interruption beginnig with the plain विरम विरम emphasises the abruptness. We therefore perfer the reading आर्येणस्मिन् attirbuted to लक्ष्मण by वीरराघव।

(*l*) **लक्ष्मणः–अतः परम् आर्यस्य तत्रभवतां कपिराक्षसानाञ्च असंख्यातानि उत्तरोतराणि कर्माश्चर्याणि। परिश्रान्ता चेयमार्या। तद्विज्ञापयामि विश्राम्यतामिति।**

Lak.—Hereafter (follow) countless wonderful deeds of my noble brother and the honoured monkeys and Rākṣasas one exceliing another. But my noble sister here is tired. So I say let up stop here.

सीता–अज्जउत्त एदिणा चित्तदंसणेण पच्चुपणदोहदाए अत्थि मे विणप्पं (आर्यपुत्र, एतेन चित्रदर्शनेन प्रत्युत्पन्नदोहदाया अस्ति मे विज्ञाप्यम्)।

Sītā—My husband, with a longing arising from this inspection of the picture, I have a prayer, to make.

रामः—नन्वाज्ञापय।

Rāma—Well, command me.

सीता—जाणे पुणो वि पसणगम्भीरासु वणराइसु विहरिस्सं पवित्तसोम्मसिसिरावगाहां च भअवदीं भाईरहीं अवगाहिस्सं (जाने पुनरपि प्रसन्नगम्भीरासु वनराजिषु विहरिष्यामि, पवित्रसौम्यशिशिरावगाहाञ्च भगवतीं भागीरथीमवगहिष्ये)।

Sītā.—I hope I shall once again room in those safe though sombre lines of forests, and shall bathe in the mighty. Bhāgīrathī a plunge in which is sanctifying, delightful and cool.

मित—। अत इति। 'संख्यातं' संख्या। भावे क्तः। 'असंख्यातानि' असंख्यानि, अद्य निःशेषेण द्रष्टमशक्यानि इत्यर्थः। 'उत्तरं' प्रकृष्टम्। 'उत्तरेभ्य उत्तराणि'। बालिवधः इति प्रकष्टं कर्म, लङ्कादाहस्तु, प्रकृष्टतरं, प्रकृष्टततमं पुनः सागरबन्धनम्। एवं परं परं प्रकर्षमापद्यमानानि कर्माणि'। 'कर्माणि' च तानि 'आश्चर्याणि'। क्रियाकृतं निसर्गकृतञ्च इति द्विविधमाश्चर्यम्। आद्यमिह कर्माश्चर्यमिति निर्दिष्टम्। एतेन आश्चर्यमिति विशेष्यं कर्मेति विशेषणं भवति, "विशेषणं विशेषेण बहुलम्"। इति च समाप्तः। 'विश्राम्यताम्' अस्माभिरिति कर्त्तृपदमूह्यम्।। आर्यपुत्रेति। 'प्रत्युतपन्नः' सञ्जातः 'दोहदः' मनोरथी यस्यास्तयाः। 'विज्ञाप्यं' विज्ञापनीयम् आवेदनीयं त्वयि। कश्चिदभिलाषो मे जातः तं विज्ञापयितुमिच्छामि इत्यर्थः।। नन्विति। 'आज्ञापय' आदिश। विज्ञापिते एव अविलम्बितं करिष्यते इति भावः।। जाने इति। 'प्रसन्ना' प्रशान्तश्वापदा अतएव विस्रम्भकर्यः तथा 'गम्भीराः' अप्रधृष्याः या 'वनराजयः' तासु। एतेन तपोवनं, किञ्चिल्लक्ष्यते कथमन्यथा प्रशान्ताः श्वापदाः ? 'पवित्र' पावनः 'सौभ्यः सुभगः आनन्दन इत्यर्थः 'शिशिरः' शीतलश्च 'अवगाहः' मज्जनं स्नानमित्यर्थः यस्यां ताम्। एतेन भागीरथीतीरस्थं तपोवनमायाति। तादृशञ्च तपोवनं वाल्मीकेः। अतएव वाल्मीकितपोवने परित्यागो वैदेह्याः।।

Notes. 1. असंख्यातानि—अविद्यमानं संख्यातम् एषाम बहु—। 2. विश्राम्यताम्—see ante, "विश्राम्यतामष्टावक्रः। 3. विज्ञाप्यम्—वि+ज्ञा+णिच्+यत् कर्मणि। 4. ननु etc.—ननु implies आक्षेप, disapproval. What you say in the matter of दोहद is not a विज्ञापना but an आज्ञा to me. Hence you should have said आज्ञाप्यम् not विज्ञाप्यम्। Now आज्ञापय, command me. 5. जाने—ज्ञा+लट्ए। Here ज्ञा means to wish. The result of the wish is her own विहार and स्नान।

Hence the क्रियाफल goes to the कर्त्ता। The आत्मनेपद seems compulsory by "अनुपसर्गात् ज्ञः" though ज्ञा is परस्मैपदी। But here विहरिष्यामि and अवगाहिष्ये being in the उत्तमपुरुष directly states that the क्रियाफल attaches to the कर्त्ता of ज्ञानक्रिया। Hence the आत्मनेपद is optional by the rule "विभाषोपदेन प्रतीयमाने"। Thus also जानासि पुनरपि etc. just like स्वम अश्वं जानीते, स्वम् अश्वं जानाति etc. 6. *Remark*—On the propriety of this para see *Intro.*

(*li*) **रामः–वत्स लक्ष्मण।**

Rāma—Dear Lakṣmaṇa.

लक्ष्मणः–एषोऽस्मि।

Lak.—Here I am.

रामः–अचिरं सम्पादनीयोऽस्या दोहद इति सम्प्रत्येव गुरुभि सन्दिष्टम्। तत् अस्खलितसमुखसम्पातं रथमुपस्थापय।

Rāma—Her longings have to be gratified without delay; this has just now been urged by the elders. So brings here a car with an easy uninterrupted roll.

सीता–अज्जउत्त तुम्हेहिं बि तहिं गन्तवं (आर्यपुत्र, त्वयापि तत्र गन्तव्यम्)।

Sītā—My husband, you also will have to go there.

रामः–अयि कठिनहृदये, एतदमि वक्तव्यमेव ?

Rāma—O hard-hearted girl, needs this be said really ?

सीता–तेण हि पिअं मे (तेन हि प्रियं मे)।

Sītā—Then indeed is joy to me.

लक्ष्मणः–यथाज्ञापयत्यार्यः। (इति निष्क्रान्तः)।

Lak.—As my noble brother commands (*Exit*).

मित–। अचिरमिति। 'न स्वलितः व्याहतः अतएव 'सुखः' सुखकरः 'सम्पातः' गमनं यस्य तादृशं गर्भिणीवहनयोग्यमित्यर्थः 'रथम् उपस्थापय' आनय।। अयीति। 'वक्तव्यमेव इति अनुक्तमपि सिद्धमेव तत् वृथा उक्तिः। अपरञ्च, आसन्नप्रसवायास्ते सहयायी न वा स्यामिति ते शङ्का जाता तत् नूनं 'कठिनहृदया' असि।। तेनेति। 'तेने त्वद्गमनेन। अन्यथा तपोवनगमनं मे प्रियं न स्यात्।।

Notes. 1. सम्प्रत्येव–see ante "यः कश्चिद्गर्भदोहदोऽस्याः etc." 2. अस्खलित etc.–स्खल+क्त कर्त्तरि स्खलितः। न स्खलितः। This qualifles सम्पातः। स्खलित literally 'slipped; hence 'changed' अस्खलित is therefore uninterrupted, सुखयतीति सुख+णिच् (नाम धातु)+एच् कर्त्तरि सुखः pleasant. सम्+पत+घञ् भावे सम्पातः motion, progress. अस्खलितः सुखः सम्पातः अस्य, चिपदबहु–Rāma does not want a jolting car which is dangerous to a woman whose term is full. 2. उपस्थापय–उप समीपवचन। उप+स्था+णिच्+लोट् हि। Bring such a car up to her. 3. *Remark*—After, this, transfer लक्ष्मणः,–यथाज्ञापयत्यार्यः etc. from below which is clearly misplaced there. 4. आर्यपुत्र etc.—This has introduced an inconsistency (see *Intro.)* 5. लक्ष्मणः etc.We have retained this here because all available text have it here. There is clearly no need for लक्ष्मण to wait so long after Rāma's order रथमुपस्थापय। As it stands, it is irrelvent and looks like a rude interruption to राम and Sītā's talk.

(*lii*) **रामः–प्रिये इतो वातायनोपकण्ठे मुहूर्तं संविष्टा भव।**

Rāma—Darling, you lie down for a while (*lit.*—a moment) here near the window.

सीता–एवं होदु। ओहिंरिज्जामि क्खु, परिस्समजणिदाए णिद्दाए (एवं भवतु। अपह्रिये खलु परिश्रमजनितया निद्रया)।

Sītā—So be it. I am indeed being drifted by sleep caused by fatigue.

मित–। प्रिये इति। 'वातायनस्य' गावाक्षस्य 'उपकण्ठे' समीपे। 'संविटा' शयाना 'भव' शयित्वा चित्रदर्शनजनितं श्रमं नीदय इति शेषः। श्रान्ता एव सीता आसीत्, तथा च लक्ष्मणोनोक्तं "परिश्रान्ता चेयमार्या" इति।। एवमिति। 'एव भवतु तथास्तु' संविष्टा एव भवामि इत्यर्थः। 'अपह्रिये' आकृष्टा भवामि। श्रमात् निद्रा एव मे प्राप्ता।।

Notes. 1. वातायन etc.—अयते अनेन इति अय गतौ+ल्युट् करणे अयनम् passage. वातस्य अयनं वातायनम् passage for air, *i.e.*, window उपगतः कणठम् उपकण्ठः that which has come up to the neck, i.e., that which is near, neighbourhood. समीपस्थः प्रदेशः प्रादितत्–। Or कण्ठस्य समीपे उपकण्ठम् or उपकण्ठे, अव्ययी–। The प्रादितत्–is better because the अव्ययी–is unnecessarily cumbrous. For, we want समीपे, but for this we deliberately avoid the simple word समीपे and complicate matters by adding कण्ठस्य at start, dropping कण्ठस्य at the last stage!! वातायनस्य उपकण्ठः वातायनीपकण्ठः। तस्मिन् Sītā was tired would be refreshed by the breeze near the window. 2. *Remark*—Vidyasagara reads वातायनावर्त्त के मुहर्ते संविष्टौ भवावः। We have adopted Virarāghava's reading, which is in part the same as that of Vidyasagara's manuscript No. 2. Our reasons are—(i) Sītā was really tited. लक्ष्मण has already noticed this. Comp. "परिश्रान्ता क्षेयमार्या," para 2. She was so tired that she felt drowsy. Comp. "अपह्निते खलु परिश्रमजनितया निद्रया" below. Hence is was necessary that she should lie down. No reason has been adduced to suppose that Rāma too was fatigued and felt the need for stretchig himself. Hence Virarāghava's संविष्टा भव seems to be more reasonable that संविष्टौ भवावः। See next Para. (ii) आवर्त्तक is a cover. Vidyasagara explains "यत्र स्थिता नीन्यैर्लक्ष्यन्ते तादृशे स्थानम्"। The neccessity is pinted out saying "निभृते स्थाने......शयानौ भवावः"। But they were in the inner apartments where outsiders were not usually allowed. Besides, as will appear, while lying with Sītā Rāma freely admits his officers of the inner appartments. Hence there is no neccesity for seeking निभृतस्थान–a cover. We therefore prefer उपकण्ठे to आवर्त्तके।

(*liii*) रामः–तेन हि निरन्तरमवलम्बस्व मामत्र शयनाय। जीवयन्निव साध्वसश्रमस्वेदविन्दुरधिकण्ठमर्प्यताम्। बाहुरैन्दवमयूखचुम्बितस्यन्दिचन्द्रमणिहार विभ्रमः।।34।।

(तथा कारयन् सानन्दम्) प्रिये किमेतत्? (रा–)

Rāma—Then do hold me close to lie down here.

Let your arm, shwing drops of perspiration through shock and fatigue, hence having the beauty of a neck-lace of moongems kissed by lunar rays and dripping, be placed on my neck as if enlivening me.

(*Making her do so—In joy*) Darling, what is this? (R.—)

मित–। तेनेति। 'तेन हि' यदि निद्रा प्राप्ता तदा। 'निरन्तरं' गाढ़म् 'अवलम्बस्व' आलिङ्ग। ततः शेष्व तेन सुलभा निद्रा भविष्यति इत्यर्थः।। जीवयन्निति।

अन्वयः– ससाध्वसश्रमस्वेदविन्दुः (अतएव) ऐन्दवयमयूखचम्बितस्यन्दिचन्द्र मणिहारविभ्रमः बाहुः जीवयन्निव अधिकण्ठम् अर्प्यताम्।)

व्याख्या–'साध्वसेन' वासेन भार्गवशूर्पणखदीनां चिन्नदर्शनजनितेन इति यावत् तथा 'श्रमेण' चित्रात् चिनान्तरगमनार्थे वीथिकापरिभ्रमणजनितेन कल्मेन जाता ये 'स्वेदविन्दवः' धर्मजालकं, तैः 'सह' वर्त्तमानः अतएव 'ऐन्दवेन' चान्द्रेण 'मयूखेन' किरणेन 'चुम्बितः' स्पृष्टः ततश्च 'स्यन्दौ' जलवन्दिुवर्षी यः, 'चन्द्रमणीनां' चन्द्रकान्तामणीनां 'हारः' माला तस्य यो 'विश्रमः' स इव शोभा यस्य तादृशो 'बाहु' तवार्य भुजः 'जीवयन्निव' विरहीत्पेक्षणात् अवसन्न मां सामश्वसयन्निव 'अधिकण्ठं' मदीये कण्ठे 'अर्प्यतां' न्यस्ताम्। "प्रत्यावृतः पुनरिव स मे जानकीविप्रयोगः" इत्यर्थ दूये। तत् बाहुना सामवलम्बस्य तेन समाश्वसिमि इति भावः। (कण्ठे करार्पणस्य फलं जीवनम्, तेन 'जीवयन' इति हेती शतृ)।। तथेति।। 'तथा' तादृशी सीतां कण्ठर्पितबाहु 'कारयन्'।।

Notes. 1. तेन हि etc.—In saying संविष्य भव राम meant सीता merely to stretch herself. But she says she would sleep. Hence (तेन हि) राम has to lie down himself. 2. ससाध्वस etc.—साध्वस fright. साध्वसश्च श्रमश्च साध्वसश्रमौ, द्वन्द्व। The पूर्वनिपात of श्रम was expected, but sometimes the rule of पूरनिपात are violated, अनित्यः पूर्ननिपातविधिः। साध्वसश्रमाभ्यां स्वेदविन्दु सुप्सुपा। तेन सह। 3. अधिकण्ठम्–कण्ठे इति अधिकण्ठम् विभक्तार्थे अव्ययी–। 4. अर्प्यताम्–ऋ+णिच्+लोट् ताम् कर्मणि। विधौ लोट्। 5. ऐन्दव etc.—ऐन्दवमयूखेन चुम्बितः, 3तत्। तादृशश्चासौ स्यन्दी च, कर्मधा–। तादृशश्चन्द्रमणिहारः, कर्मधा–। तस्य विभ्रमः। स इव विभ्रमो यस्य, 'सप्तस्य पमान–" इति बहुन्रोहिः। 6. किमेतत्–। This is a question to सीता। The touch of Sītā's arm on his neck has produced indescribale sensations which राम can identify as pleasure or pain etc. and he refers to सीता for an answer.

(*liv*) **(रा–)**

विनिश्चेतुं शक्ये न सुखमिति वा दुःखमिति वा दुःखमिति वा
प्रबोधो निद्रा वा किमु विषविसर्पः किमु मदः।
तव स्पर्शे स्पर्शे मम हि परिमूढेन्द्रियगणो
विकारश्चैतन्यं भ्रमयति समुन्मीलयति च।।35।।

(R—) I cannot take it as bliss or as woe either, as waking or as sleeping, coursing of poison or of liquour. Verily, at every touch of thine, an emotion, having benumbed all my senses, stupefies consciousness also revives it.

सीता (विहस्य)–त्थिरप्पसादा तुम्हे इदो दाणिं किं अबरं (स्थिरप्रसादा यूयम् इत इदानीं किमपरम्)।

Sītā (Laughing)—You are of unwavering kindness; what else could it be?

मित–।

अन्वय–(एतत्) सुखमिति वा दुःखमिति वा, प्रबोधो निद्रा वा, किमु विषविसर्पः किमु मदः, विनिश्चेतु न शक्ये। तव स्पर्शे स्पर्शे हि परिमूढ़ेन्द्रियगणे विकारः मम चैतन्य भ्रमयति समुन्मीलयति च।

व्याख्या–यदेतदनुभूयते मया तत् सुखमिति वा' सुखरूपेण वा 'दुःखमिति वा' दुःखरूपेण वा 'विनिश्चेतुम्' अवधारयितुं न शक्ये न क्षमोऽहम्, प्रबोधः जागरणं 'निद्रा वा' सुषुप्तिर्वा विनिश्चेतु न शक्ये 'किमु विषविसर्पः' सन्मोहनं किषं मे शरीरे सञ्चरति 'किसु मदः' आनन्दनो मदः सुरा वा, विनिश्चेतु नं शक्ये। कथमेवमेकस्मिन्नपि विरुद्धबोध इत्याह–'तव स्पर्शे स्पर्शे हि' प्रतिस्पर्शमेव, त्वया स्पृष्टमात्रं परिमूढ़ः' विह्वलः 'इन्द्रियगणो' यस्मात् तादृशः कश्चित् 'विकारः' चित्तविक्षेपः मम चैतन्य भमयति' चेतनां हरति 'समुन्मीलयति च' करोत्यति। यदैव चेतनस्य मे भवति कश्चिद्बोधः, तदैव लुप्यते चेतना बोधस्य च विपर्य्ययो जायते, एवमेकस्मिन्नपि विरुद्धबोधः। तत् निश्चयाय त्वामेव पृच्छामि "किमेतदति", चलितचेतनोऽहं स्वयं कथं विनिश्चिनुयाम्? स्थिरेति। प्रन्नस्य पृच्छामि "किमेतादिति", चलिततनोऽहं स्वयं कथं विनिश्चिनुयाम्? स्थिरेति। प्रन्नस्य उत्तरमाह–'स्थिरः' अचलः 'प्रसाद' अनुग्रहो येषां तादृशा 'यूयं' मयि। इतः अस्मात् 'अपरम् अन्यत् किम् इदानीं भवेत् । नेतत् सुखं न वा दुःखं न हि प्रबोधो न वा निद्रा, नापि विषविसर्पो न च मदः किन्तु एतत् खलु प्रसन्नता ते मयि।।

Notes. 1. शक्ये–शक of the दिवादि classic उभयपदी। Hence शक्यामि, शक्ये। 2.सुखम् etc.—सुख and दुःख are contraries. If it is not taken as the one it is almost sure to be taken as the other. But no, I cannot call it either. 3. प्रबोधः etc.—Again contraries. If not प्रबोधः it is likely to be taken as निद्रा। But I cannot decide which. 4. विष etc.—विष and मद also are contraries—one stupefies the other stimulates. Here the wordig seems defective. The contraries are विष and मद। If विसर्प is to be added, it should go with *both* (विषविसर्प and मदविसर्प) and not with one only. वि+सृप+धञ् भावे विसर्प not विसर्प। "सात्पदाद्योः" इति षत्वनिषेधः। 5. तत्र स्पर्श etc.—This explain why he cannot decide. Difficulty in a decision usually arises when the two sides present similar characteristics. But here though the characters are widely different

I am unable to decide *because* तव स्पर्शे स्पर्शे etc. (see *Mitabh*—). I have lost control of my senses, how can I decide? You tell me what it is. This is a compliment to सीता। 6. विहस्य etc.—Sita laughs and pays back the compliment. I know what it is; it is simply your unfalling kindness to me and nothing else. There is nothing in my touch (स्पर्शे स्पर्शे): your enduring love (स्थिरप्रसाद) for me makes you fell and talk thus. इदानीम् is वाक्यालङ्कारे as in "क इदानीम् उष्णोदकेन नवमालिकां सिञ्चति"–*Śakuntalā*. The verse and Sītā's remark have been differently explained by commentators.

(*lv*) **रामः–** **म्लानस्य जीवकुसुमस्य विकाशनानि**
सन्तर्पणानि सकलेन्द्रियमोहनानि।
एतानि ते सुवचनानि सरोरुहाक्षि
कर्णामृतानि मनसश्च रसायनानि।।36।।

Rāma—O lotus-eyed girl, these sweet words of thine, that are nectar to the ears a tonic that gratifies all the senses ; (they) impart strength to the mind also and thus cause the blooming of the withered flower of life.

सीता–पिअंवद सइस्सं (प्रिर्यवद शयिष्ये)। (इति शयनाय समन्ततो निरूपयति)।

Sītā—Sweet -speaker, I will lie down (*Looks round for a pillow)*.

मित–। म्लानस्येति।

अन्वयः–सरोरुहाक्षि, एतानिते कर्णासृतानि सुवचनानि सकलेन्द्रियमोहनानि सन्तर्पणानि मनसः रसायनानि च (अतएव) म्लानस्य जीवकुसुमस्य विकाशनानि।

व्याख्या–हे 'सरोरूहाक्षि' कमललोचने जानकि 'एतानि' एवंविधानि "स्थिरप्रसादाः" इत्यादि प्रकारकाणि ते कर्णमृतानि' श्रोत्रमुखानि 'सुवचनानि' मञ्जुभाषितानि चाटुकारणामिव न केवलं श्रोचसुखानि अपि तु 'सकलेन्द्रियाणां' श्रोतृनैत्रादीनां निखिलकरणानां 'मोहनानि' मधुरतया आत्मविस्मृतिविधायकानि 'सन्तर्पणनि' बलवर्द्धनानि औषधानि। सर्वेन्द्रियतर्पणात् देहोत्कर्षविधायकानि ते वक्षनान्येतानि इति भावः। न हि एतावति पर्यवसित एतेषा गुणः, परमेतानि 'मनसः' रसायनानि च' आप्यायनान्यपि। एवं देहमनसोरुभयोरप्याप्यानात् 'म्लानस्य' संसारदुःखतापैर्विशुष्कस्य 'जीवकुसुमस्य' जीवनरूपस्य पुष्पस्य 'विकाशनानि' फुल्लताविधायकानि (सर्वत्र बाहुलकात् कर्त्तरि ल्युट्) ते सुवचनानि। एष नवीभूतोऽहं

तवानेन वक्षसा इति भावः।। प्रियवदेति। यथा मद्वचनं प्रति भवान् भणति तथैव मद्विषये भवतो वचनं जीवकुसुमविकाशनं तत् हे 'प्रियंवद' मधुरालापिन् निद्रा मां बाधते कालात्ययमकृत्वा एव 'शयिष्ये'। शेते अस्मिन् इति 'शयनम् उपधानम्। तस्मै 'निरुपयति नेत्र' पातयति।।

Notes. 1. *Remark*—Note the allocation of the qualifying epithets. म्लानस्य जीवकुसुमस्य विकाशनानि is the final chracter given to the सुवचनानि; it is the last predicate (विधेय)। They are such becuase they are सकलेन्द्रियमोहनानि सन्तर्पणानि also becuase they are मनसश्च रसायनानि। कर्णमृतानि is an ordinary विशेषण of सुवचनानि। Commentators see here only a jumble of qualifying epithets thoughtlessly brought togehter. 2. प्रियवद–प्रियं वदतीति प्रिय+वद+खच् कर्त्तरि। Here again we have an exchange of compliments. You prize my words (सुवचनानि), but your words gratify me (प्रियंवद)–they are to me म्लानस्य जीवकुसुमस्य विकाशनानि।

(*lvi*) **रामः–अयि किमन्वेष्टव्यम ?**

Rāma—What have you go to seek, darling.

आविवाहसमयाद्गृहे वने शैशवे तदनु यौवने पुनः।
स्वापहेतुरनुपाश्रितोऽन्यया रामबाहुरुपधानमेष ते।। 37।।

The pillow is this arm of Rāma, unresorted to by any other woman, the producer of thy sleep since the time of marrige, at home in childhood and thereafter in the woods agian in youth.

सीता (निद्रा नाटयन्ती)–अत्थि एदं अज्जउत्त अत्थि एदं (अस्त्येतत् आर्यपुत्र अस्त्येतत्)। (इति स्वपिति)।

Sītā *(Acting drowsiness)*—So it is, my husband, so it is (Falls asleep).

मित–। अयीति। 'किमन्वेष्टव्य्' अन्वेष्टव्यं नान्ति ते। यदन्विष्यते तदिहैवास्ति इति भावः। या इति।

अन्वयः–आ विवाहसमयात् शैशवे गृहे तदनु पुनर्यौवने वने ते स्वापहेतुः अन्यया अनुपाश्रितः पर एषा रामबाहुः उपधानम्।

व्याख्या–'आ विवाहसमयात्' विवाहकालात् परं तत्कालविधि इत्यर्थः। 'शैशवे गृहे' अयोध्यायां 'तदनु' ततः पर शैशवान्ते 'पुनः यौवने वने' दण्डकादिषु 'ते स्वापहेतुः निद्राविधायकः 'अन्यया' रमण्या 'अनुपाश्रितः' असेवितः अतो बहुभिः सेवितात्, कृत्रिपादुपधानात् विशिष्टः 'एष रामबाहुः' मदीयो भुजः 'उपधानं' वर्त्तते एव। एवं

विशिष्टे स्थिते निकृष्टे कः प्रयत्नः। एहि इहैव उपधेहि इति भावः। निद्रामिति। 'निद्रां नाटयन्ती नाट्येन निद्राबाधां दर्शयन्ती। 'एतत्' भवदुक्तम् 'अस्ति' सत्यमेव।।

Notes. 1. विवाह etc.—'आ' इति कर्मप्रवचनीययोगे पञ्चमी by the rule "पञ्चम्यपाङ्परिभिः"। An अव्ययी-compound is optionally available giving आविवाहसमयम्। 2. तदनु–Not a compound. तत् has 2या owing to अनु which is a कर्मप्रवचनीय by the rule "हीने"। The हीनता is in respect of time. 3. यौवने–यूनो भाव इति युवन्+अण् यौवनम्। तस्मिन्। We take शैशवे यौवने and गृहे वने in order, i.e.,' शैशवे गृहे, यौवने वने। This supposes that सीता was married when a child and went to the woods with राम when an adult. Those who are opposed to this view should suppose a च understood after वने and construe—आ विवाहसमयात् स्वापहेतु; गृहे वने च (this specifies the *place*); शैशवे तदनु यौवने पुनः (this gives the *time*) 4.स्वापहेतुः–हेतु is कर्त्ता। स्वापस्य हेतुः। 5. रामबाहुः–Sītā was looking for a pillow. राम offers his arm for one. This is better than an ordinary pillow, because a pillow, if found there, must have been used by several other ladies. But this one is अनुनाश्रितोऽन्यया। You are used to it शैशवे तदनु यौवने and it is better than any other, hence किमन्वेष्टव्यम्–What are you looking for ? 5. अस्त्रेतत् etc.—Here both lie down and forthwith सीता falls asleep.

(*lvii*) **रामः–कथं प्रियवचना वक्षसि प्रसुप्तैव। (निर्वर्ण्य सस्नेहम्)–**

Rāma—Ha ! The sweet-speaker has really fallen asleep on my bosom. *(Marking—with tenderness)*—

इयं गेहे लक्ष्मीरियममृतवर्त्तिर्नयनयो–
रसावस्याः स्पर्शो वपुषि बहलश्चन्दनरसः।
अयं कण्ठे बाहुः शिशिरमसृणो मौक्तिकसरः
किमस्या न प्रेयो यदि परमसह्यस्तु विरहः।।38।।

She is grace is my house—She is a brush of ambrosia to my eyes—This touch of here is a liberal supply of essence of sandal to my body—This arm is a cool smooth string of pearls on my neck. What of hers is not sweet, if her absence alone is indeed unendurable ? (Or—If her absence is indeed unendurable, what else of here is not sweet).

मित–। इयमिति।

अन्वयः–इयं गेहे लक्ष्मीः इयं नयनयोः अमृतवर्त्तिः। अस्याः असौ स्पर्श वपुषि बहलश्चन्दनरसः, अयं बाहुः कण्ठे शिशिरमसृणो मौक्तिकसरः। अस्याः परमस्याः किं न प्रेयः)।

व्याख्या–'इयं जानकी मदीये 'गेहे' गृहे 'लक्ष्मीः' कान्त्यधिष्ठात्री देवता, गृहस्य शोभा मे जानकी इत्यर्थः। 'इयं' मे नयनयोः अमृतवर्त्तिः सुधामयी शलाका तद्वत् सुखकरी इत्यर्थः। न केवलम् ''इयम्'' एव स्वरूपतः सुभगा मे, किन्तु ''अस्या'' सम्बन्धि सर्वमेव सुभगम् इत्याह–'अस्याः' जानक्याः 'असौ'' अयं बाहुः' अवलम्बनार्थं न्यस्तो भुजः 'कण्ठे शिशिरमसृणः' शीतलः अपरुषश्च यः 'मौक्तिकसरः' मुक्ताहारः तथाविधः प्रेयान्। स्पर्शबाहुप्रभृतयः कति पुनः पृथगुच्यन्ताम्, संक्षेपतो ब्रवीमि 'अस्याः, किं' किमिव वस्तु 'न प्रेयः' न मे प्रीतिप्रदम्, सर्वमेव प्रेय इत्यर्थः 'यदि तु' पक्षान्तरे नूनं 'परं' केवलं विरहः असह्यः' सोढ़ मशक्यः (यद्वा–'यदितु विरहः असह्यः' असह्य एव 'परं विरहव्यतिरिक्तम् 'अस्याः किं न प्रेयः')।।

Notes. 1. कथम्–An अव्यय implying surprise. राम did not expect that she would fall asleep so soon. 2. गेहे, नयनयौः, वपुषि, कण्ठे–Thus she was everywhere a source of joy to राम। The two were lying together. Hence राम was actually feeling her स्पर्शो वपुषि and the moment before (see sl. 35) he had placed her arm on his neck (कण्ठे बाहुः)। 3. शिशिर etc.—शिशिरश्चसौ मसृणश्च, कर्मधा–। 4. मौक्तिक etc.—मुक्ता एव इति मुक्ता+ठक् (विरयादि) मोक्तिकम्। Neuter by the dictum ''क्वचित् स्वार्थिकाः प्रकृतितो लिङ्गवचनान्यतिवर्त्तन्ते''। 5. प्रेयः–अतिशतेन प्रियम् इति प्रिय+ईयसुन्। No comparison is implied. 6. यदि–अव्यय implying पक्षान्तर। 7. परम्–अव्यय meaning केवल। Qual. विरहः। परं विरहः-Separation alone. Or पर–else अन्य।'परं किम् अन्यत् किम् (न प्रेयः)'। 8. तु–अव्यय implying अवधारण, निश्चय। Take it alone with असह्यः। असह्यस्तु असह्य एव really unendurable.

(*lviii*) **(प्रविश्य) प्रतीहारी–देव उबट्ठिदो (देव उपस्थितः)।**

(*Entering*) Warder—Sire, waiting close by.

रामः–अयि कः ?

Rāma—Well, who ?

प्रतीहारी–आसणापरिचारओ दुम्मुहो देवस्म (आसन्नपरिचारको दुर्मुखो देवस्य)।

Warder—Sire's personal attendant Darmukha.

रामः (स्वगतम्)–शुद्धान्तचारी दुर्मुखः। स मया पौरजानपदान् अपसर्पितुं प्रयुक्तः। (प्रकाशम्) आगच्छतु। (प्रतीहारी निष्क्रान्ता)।

Rāma (To *himself*)—Durmukha is employed in the harem. He was detailed by me to spy out citizens and villagers. (*Aloud*) Let him come in. (*Exit Warder*).

मित–। देव इति। 'उपस्थितः' समीपे वर्त्तमानः।। अयीति। क उपस्थित इति नोक्तम्। तत् आत्मना अनन्तरोक्तं यत् "असह्यस्तु विरहः" इति वदनुपदमेव प्रतीहार्या प्रोक्तम् "उपस्थितः" इति एतयोः परम्परान्वये "असह्यस्तु विरहः उपस्थितः इति वासकरोऽर्थ आयाति। तेन सन्त्रन्तो रामः पृच्छति 'अयि कः उपस्थितः इति। इयमपि भाविन्या विपत्तेश्छाया।। आसन्नेति। 'आसन्नः' सदैव समीपे वर्त्तमानः।। शुद्धेति। 'शुद्धान्ते' अन्तःपुरे 'चरति' व्यवहरति। 'दुर्मुखः' अन्तः पुरे नियुक्त इत्यर्थः। 'पौरान्' पुरवासिनः पुरुषान् 'जानपदान्' जनपदवासिनश्च ग्रामनगरवासिनः सर्वान् इत्यर्थः। 'अपसर्पितु' प्रच्छन्नं परीक्षितुम्।।

Notes. 1. उपस्थितः–Has come. प्रतीहारी does not say *who* has come. To Rāma this sounds ominous, because his last word uttered aloud is विरहः (sl. 30) and the warder's उपस्थितः utteed immediately after it presents to his already disturbed mind the context विरहः उपस्थितः। He is startled by the coincidence. 2. अयि etc.— अयि here implies सम्भ्रम caused by the coincidence विरहः उपस्थितः। This sort of coincidence is in dramatic parlance known as पताकास्थानक। "यत्रार्थे चिन्तितेऽन्यस्मिन् तल्लिङ्गोऽन्यः प्रयुज्यते। आगन्तुकेन भावेन पताका स्थानकं तु तत्।।" पताकास्थानक is sometimes मङ्गलार्थ sometimes अमङ्गलार्थ। Here it is अमङ्गलार्थ; it bodes evil—the विरह that is imminent. 3. अपसर्पितुम्–अप+सृप+तुमुन्। This is a poetical licence the correct form bein अपसुर्प्तुम् or अपस्रप्तुम्। सृप occurs in the अनिट्कारिका–"तृप्यतिदृप्यती सृपिम्"। अप+सृप means 'to spy'. "अपसर्पश्चरः स्पशः" इत्यमरः। The reading 'पीरजानपदचरितमुपगन्तुम्" seems better. —

(*lix*) **(प्रविश्य) दुर्मुखः (स्वगतम्)–हा कथं सीदादेईए ईरिसं अचिन्तणिज्जं जणाबवादं देअस्म कथइस्मं। अहवा णिओओ क्खु मे ईरिसो मन्दभाअस्म [हा कथं सीतादेव्या ईदृशम् अचिन्तनीयं जनापवादं देवस्य कथयिष्यामि। अथवा नियोगः खलु मे ईदृशो मन्दभागस्य]।**

(*Entering*) Durmukha (*To himself*)—Alas ! How shall I

report to Sire this inconceivable slander of Queen Sītā by the people? Or such indeed is the duty of me the ill-starred.

सीता (उत्स्वप्नायते)–हा अज्जउत्त सोम्म कहिं सि [हा आर्यपुत्र सौम्य कुत्र असि]।

Sītā (*Talks in her sleep*)—Ah ! my husband, where art thou, O gentle one?

मित– हा इति। 'अचिन्तनीयं' चिन्तयितुमशक्यम्। 'जनापवादम्' लोकनिन्दाम्। 'नियोग' अधिकारः, कर्तव्यं कर्म।। सीतेति। स्वप्नः स्वापः निद्रा। 'उद्बुद्धः स्वप्लात्' उत्स्वप्नः विगतनिद्रो जनः। 'उत्स्वप्न' इव आचरति 'उत्स्वप्नायते' सुप्ता अपि प्रवुद्धा इव आचरति वाचं प्रयुङ्क्ते इत्यर्थः। 'कुत्र असि' इति स्वप्न तथा रामविरहो दृष्ट इत्यर्थः। दुर्मुखागमनात् आसन्नं वियोगम् अन्तरात्मा तस्या जानाति इति विपदः सूचना।।

Notes. 1. जनापवादम्–अप+वद+घञ् भावे अपवादः slander जनानाम् अपवादः। 2. देवस्य–देवाय is expected. षष्ठी शेषे। 3. ईदृश –Of this nature, *i.e.*, to spy and report. 4. उत्स्वप्नायते–उतस्वप्न is a प्रादितत्–(see Tika). स इव आचरति इति उत्स्वप्न+काङ (नामधातु)+लट् ते b the rule "कर्त्तुः काङ् सलोपश्च"।

(*lx*) **रामः–अये सैवेयं रणरणकदायिनो चित्रदर्शनात् विरहभावना देव्याः स्वप्नोद्वेगं करोति। (सस्नेह परामृशन्)–**

Rāma—Ha ! It is that distressing thought of separation suggested by the inspection of the painting that is disturbing the queen's sleep. (*Affectionately caressing her*)—

अद्वैतं सुखदुःखयोरनुगुणं सर्वास्ववस्थासु यद्-
विश्रामो हृदयस्य यत्र जरसा यस्मिन्न हार्यो रसः।
कालेनावरणात्ययात् परिणते यत् स्नेहसारे स्थितं
भद्रं प्रेमसुमानुषस्य कथमप्येकं हि तत् प्राप्यते।।39।।

With great difficulty indeed is gained that unique and benificent love of a good creature that is unchanged in weal and woe, obliging under all circumstances, where there is the heart's repose, the ardour of which is not to be mitigated with age, which develops into the mature core of affection through the wearing off of the coating (of reserve) by time.

मित–। अये इति। 'सैव' पूर्वप्रदर्शिता 'विरहभावना' विप्रयोगशङ्का या शूर्पणखाया: 'चित्रदर्शनात्' ज्ञाता 'रणकदायिनी' उद्वेगकारिणी सा 'इयं' देव्या: स्वप्नोद्वेगं करोति। अद्वैतमिति।

अन्वय:–यत् सुखदु:खयो: अद्वैतम् (अतएव) सर्वासु अवस्थासु अनुगुणम्, यत्र हृदयस्य विश्राम:, यस्मिन् जरसा रस: न हार्य:, यत् कालेन आवरणत्ययात् परिणते स्नेहसारे स्थितम्, तत् एकं सुमानुषस्व भद्रं प्रेम कथमपि हि प्राप्यते।

व्याख्या–'यत् सुखदु:खयो अद्वैतं' द्विरूपतावर्ज्जितम् यथा सुखे तथा दु:खे यस्य एकरूपता अतएव 'सर्वासु अवस्थासु' सम्पदि च विपदि च 'अनुगुणम्' अनुलोमम्, 'यत्र' यस्मिन् प्रेम्नि 'हृदयस्य विश्राम:' संसारयातनाक्लिष्टस्वंमनस: क्लानिविगम:, 'यस्मिन्' प्रेम्नि 'जरसा' वाद्धकेन 'रस:' स्वाद: 'न हार्य्य:' अनपनेय:, 'यत्' प्रेम 'कालीन आवरणस्य' सङ्कोचादीनामाच्छादनस्य 'अत्ययात्' विगमात् 'प्ररिणते' परिपाकमुपेयषि 'स्नेहसरि' स्नेहस्य स्थिरांशे 'स्थितं' तदूपेण वर्तमानम्, 'तत् एकम्' इतरविलक्षणं 'भद्रं' कल्याणकरणं 'सुमानुषस्य' सज्जनस्व 'प्रेम कथमपि हि' अतिकृच्छ्रेणैव हि 'प्राप्यते' लभ्यते। दुर्लभं खलु तत् जगति मम तु सिद्धम अहो मे भाग्यम् इति भाव:।।

Notes. 1.रणरणकदायिनी–रणरणक is उद्वेग। No satisfactory derivation is available, वंददातीति रणरणक+दा+णिनि कर्त्तरि तच्छैलि साधुकारिणि वा स्त्रिाम्। 2. विरह etc. –भू+णिच्+युच् भावे स्त्रियां भावना thought. विरहस्य भावना apprehension of separation. स्वप्नस्व उद्वेग:। 4. अद्वैतम्–द्वयोर्भाव इति द्वि+तल् हिता। सा एव इति द्विता+अण् स्वार्थे द्वैतम् double character ; प्रज्ञादि, which is आकृतिगण। The derivation from (द्वि+इत)+णि) अण् as is suggested by Mallinātha in Bhāravī is round about and undesirable, a simpler derivation as above being available. अविद्यमानं द्वैतनस्मिन् अद्वैतम्, बहु–। 5. अनुगुणम्–गुण here is भर्तृगण। अनुगतं गुणम् अनुगुणम् adapting itself to the husband's state. प्रादितत्–। Here it is not the wife's love that is अनुगुण, but the wife herself. 6. विश्राम:–See ante on विश्राम्यताम् अष्टावक्र:। 7. हार्य:–हृ+ण्यत् कर्मणि capable of mitigation. 8. आवरणत्ययात्–आ+वृ:ल्युट् करणे आवरण veil, cover, अति+इ+अच् भावे अत्यय removal. आवरणस्य अत्यय:। तन्मात्। हेतौ 5मी। आवरण here is लज्जा etc. which conceal the प्रेम and which wear off in time as familiarity grow. 9. प्रेम–प्रियस्य भाव इति प्रिय+इमनिच् प्रेमन् (प्रातिपदिक)। इमनिच् usually gives a masculine derivative, such as लघिमा, गरिमा, महिमा etc. we thus expect प्रेमा। But poet often make it neuter, as here. Also compare "तथाविधं प्रेम पतिश्च तादृश:।" Bhavabhūti has it in the masculine also, thus "अनिबन्धनं प्रेमाणमामनन्ति"–Act. V. para xvii.

(*lxi*) दुर्मुखः (उपसृत्य)–जअदि जअदि देओ [जयति जयति देवः]।

Durmukha (*Advancing*)—Prosper, let Sire prosper.

रामः–ब्रूहि यदुपलब्धम्।

Rāma—Tell me what has been gathered.

दुर्मुखः–उबत्थुवन्ति देअं पौरजाणवदा विशुमरिदा अम्हे महाराअदसरहस्म रामभद्देणत्ति [उपस्तुवन्ति देवं पौरजानपदा विस्मारिता वयं महाराजदशरथस्य रामभद्रेण इति]।

Dur.—"We have been by Rāmabhadra made to forget the great king Daśaratha"—thus do citizens and villagers belaud Sire.

रामः–अर्थवाद एषः। दोषन्तु कञ्चित् कथय येन स प्रतिविधीयते।

Rāma—This is praise. But tell me of any defect that it may be remedied.

दुर्मुखः (सास्रम्)–सुणादु देओ [शृणोतु देवः]। (कर्णे–एवम् एवम्)।

Dur. (*With tears*)—Let Sire listen (*Whispers into his ears* — Thus and thus)

रामः–अहह तीब्रसंवेगो वाग्वज्रः। (इति मूर्च्छति)।

Rāma—Oh ! A thunder-bolt-of-words of intense energy (*Faints away*).

दुर्मुखः–आस्मसदु देओ [आश्वसितु देवः।]

Dur.—Let Sire take courage.

मित–। उपस्तुवन्तीति। 'उपस्तुवन्ति' प्रशंसन्ति। 'इति' अनेन प्रकारेण 'पौरजानपदाः देवम उपस्तुवन्ति'।। 'अर्थवादः प्रशंसा। 'प्रतिविधीयते' निराक्रियते। 'कर्णे' रामस्य कर्णे कथयति। 'एवम् एवम्' इति गुप्तभाषितस्य उपलक्षणम्। रहस्वं किञ्चित् कथयन्ति जनाः इत्यर्थः। तच्च कर्णे कथितं श्रोष्यति देवी यदि बुध्यते इति। अहहेति। 'तीव्रः' दुःसहः 'संवेगः' प्रपातः अस्य। 'वागीव वज्रः'।

Notes . 1. विस्मारिता:–वि+स्मृ+णिच्+क्त कर्मणि made to forget स्मृ means to remember. But वि being *privative,* वि+स्मृ means to forget. In this sense the root is not मित् and we do not get ह्रस्व with णिच्। मित्त्व is compulsory when meaning उत्कण्ठाः पूर्वकस्मरण। Thus स्मरयति forces to yearn after, but स्मारयति forces to remember. 2. महाराजदशरथस्य–Originally this was कर्म of स्मृ। But the कर्मत्व is here ignored (अविवक्षा) and we have शेषे षष्ठी। Now if there is अविवक्षा of कर्म the root becomes अकर्मक and by the rule 'गतिबुद्धिप्रत्यवसानार्थ–'' the अणिकर्त्ता becomes कर्म when णिच् is attached. Thus वयं विस्मृतवन्तः=रामभद्रः अस्मान् विस्मारितवान्=रामभद्रेण वयं विस्मारिताः। But this is against the comentators of पाणिनि। They exclude अविवक्षित कर्म roots from the operation of the rule "गतिवुद्धि–"। Thus–"येषां देशकालदिभिन्नं कर्म न सम्भवति ते अत्र अकर्मकाः न तु अविवक्षितकर्माणोऽपि तेन 'मासमासयति देवदत्तम्' इत्यादौ कर्मत्वं भवति 'देवदत्तेन आचयति' इत्यादौ तु न"–*Bhaṭṭoji* Hence we should get –वयं विस्मृतवन्तः= रामभद्रः अस्माभिः विस्मारितवान्=रामभद्रेण अस्माभिः विस्मारितम् (भावे)। 3. अर्थवादः–वदनम् इति वद+घञ् भावे वादः। अर्यस्य प्रयोजनस्य वादः a statement made through necessity, *i.e.,* with the object of gaining some end. Hence it, is flattery or प्रशंसा। 4. येन–येन कथनेन। Unless you say I cannot remedy. प्रतिविधान is owing to your report हेतौ 3या। 5. कर्णे etc.–What is said, is there suppressed and the suppression indicated by एवम्–एवम्–Thus (say people), thus. This is whispered into Rāma's ear because he apprehends that सीता might hear him.

(lxii) रामः (आश्वस्य)–

Rāma (*Recovering*)—

हा हा धिक् परगृहवासदूषणं यदु-
वैदेह्याः प्रशमितमद्भुतैरुपायैः।
एतत् तत् पुनरपि दैवदुर्विपाका-
दालर्कं विषमिव सर्वतः प्रसृप्तम्।। 40।।

Alas ! Alas ! Cursed be this slander of Vaidehi through residence in another's house which has been suppressed by miraculous means. Through an evil turn of fate the same has once again spread all round like the venom of a rabit dog.

तत् किमत्र मन्दभाग्यः करोमि। (रा-)

[*Or.* —Alas ! Alas ! How accursed ! The very same slander of Vaidehi... means, has again.... dog]. (R—)

Now what can I ill-starred as I am, do in lthis matter ?

मित-। हा हेति।

अन्वयः–हा हा धिक ! वैदेह्याः यत् परगृहवासदूषणम् अद्भुतैः उपायैः प्रशमितम्, दैवदुर्विपाकात् तत् एतत् पुनरपि आलर्कं विर्षामिव सर्वतः प्रसृप्तम्।

व्याख्या–'हा हा धिक्' अहो दुर्गतिः। 'वैदेह्याः यत् परगृहे' भर्तृभिन्नजनमन्दिरे 'वासात् दूषणं' जनैः कलङ्कारोपः 'अद्भूतैः उपायैः विचिवैः साधनैः अग्निशुद्धादिभिः 'प्रशमितम्' अपनीतम् 'दैवस्य' हतविधेः 'दुर्विपाकात्' दुष्परिणमात् 'तत् एतत् पुनरपि आलर्कं मत्तकुक्कुरसस्वन्धि 'विषमिव सर्वतः' समन्तात् 'प्रसृप्तं' मञ्चरितम्।।

Notes. 1.परगृह etc. –दुष+णिच्+ल्युट् करणे दूषणम् cavil, slander प्ररगृहवासात् दूषणम्, सुप्सुपा। Here दूषण is not any blemish in वैदेही। She is without blemish–उत्पत्तिपरिपूता। It is the idle and reckless talk of the people. Hence, the णिच् ; otherwise the poet would have said दोषण or दोष। 2. प्रशमितम्–प्र+शम्+णिच्+क्त कर्मणि प्रशान्तम् or प्रशमितम्। 3. दैव etc.–दुष्टो विपाकः दुर्विपाकः, प्रादितम्–। दैवस्य दुर्विपाकः। तन्मात्। हेतौ 5मी। 4. आलर्कम्–अलर्क a mad dog. तस्य इदम् इति अलर्क+अण। 5. *Remark.*–This is an adaptation of Kālidāsa's "पौरेषु सोऽहं वहुलोभवन्तमपां तरङ्गेष्विव तैलविन्दुम्। सोढ़ं न तत्पूर्वमवर्ण मीरो आलानिकं स्थाणमिव छिपेन्द्रः।" Like Kālidāsa's, Bhavabhūti's verse implies that something must be done and that immediately.

(lxiii) (रा-) (विमृश्य सकरुणम्) अथवा किमन्यत्?

(R—) (*Reflecting—Piteously*)—Or, what else?

सतां केनापि कार्येण लोकस्याराधनं व्रतम्।
यत् पूरितं हि तातेन माञ्च प्राणांश्च मुञ्चता।।41।।

The service of the people by any means is the vow of all good (kings),—vow which was indeed redeemed (kept) by father by renouncing me and life as well.

सम्प्रत्येव भगवता वशिष्ठेन सन्दिष्टम्। (रा-)

Even now this has been urged by Worshipful Vasiṣṭha.

मित– ।'विस्मृश्य' ध्यात्वा ।'अथवा' लोकानां तुष्टिमेव विधास्ये 'अन्यत् किं' करणीयमस्ति ।। निश्रयेऽस्मि् हेतुमाह सतामिति ।

अन्वयः–के अपि कार्येण लोकस्य आराधनं सतां व्रतम यत् तातेन माञ्च प्राणाञ्च मुञ्चता पूरितं हि ।

व्याख्या–'के अपि' सुदष्करेण च 'कार्येण' कर्मणा लोकस्य' प्रजानाम 'आराधनम्' अनुरञ्चनं 'सतां व्रतं' साधनामनुष्ठेयो विधिः' 'यत्' व्रतं 'तातेन' पित्रां दशरथेन 'माञ्च प्राणांश्च मुञ्चता' सुदुष्करं कुर्वता इति भावः 'पूरितंहि' उद्यापितमेव । तत् मयापि प्रजारञ्जनानुरोधात् सुदुष्करं सीतापरित्यागमेव कुवंता तत् व्रतं पूरयियते इति भावः। अत्र सीतापरित्यागसमर्थनार्थ दशरथचरितस्योपस्थापनं रामायणविरुद्धं वीरचरित- विरुद्धञ्च। तत्र केकायीप्रीतये रामविवासन्मुक्तं न प्रजारञ्जनार्थनम् ।। सम्प्रतीति। 'सन्दिष्टं' 'युक्तः प्रजानामनुरञ्जने स्थः।'' इत्यादिष्टम्। तत् सर्वथा अपरिहार्य्यः सीता- परित्यागः।

Notes. 1. विमृश्य–वि+मृश means to reflect. The preceding verse establishes the necessity for instant action. Two courses present themselves–a course of conciliation of the people which means renunciation of सीता, and a course of repression. Rāma *reflects* (विमृश्य) –weighs the pros and cons of the two and decides on the adoption of the former. The decision breaks his heart and what follows now is said सकरुणम्–piteously. 2. केनापि–The अपि implies indescribability, inconceivability etc. 3. पूरितम्–Vidyasagara's reading is पूजितम् honoured. But something more definite than that is required. One may honour (पूजित) a custom yet not observe it ; actual observance is necessary. Hence पूरित seems better. 4. *Remark.*–सताम् etc. cites precedent to justify this apparently atrocious decision. Similar sacrifies are not rare in our family-father made such sacrifice, why then should I not be equal to it? सम्प्रत्येव etc. referes to Guru's command which is above all other considerations.

(*lxiv*) **(रा–) अपि च–**

(R—) Moreover.

यत् सावित्रैर्दीपितं भूमिपालै
लोकश्रेष्ठैः साधु शुद्धं चरित्रतम्।
मन्सम्बन्धात् कश्मला किंवदन्ती
स्याच्चेदस्मिन् हन्त धिङ् मामधन्यम्।।42।। (रा–)

If to this—the pure record, well rendered illustrious by the solar race of kings, the best among men—a foul slander attaches through my connection, then, alas ! woe be to te luckless self on mine.

मित– । एवं सीतायाः परित्यागे गुणमुक्त्वा अपरित्यागे दोषमाह–यदिति।

अन्वयः–लोकश्रेष्ठैः सावित्रैः भूमिपालैः यत् शुद्धं चरित्रं साधु दीपितम् अस्मिन् मत्सम्बन्धात् कश्मला किंवदन्ती चेत् स्यात् हन्त अधन्यं मां धिक्।

?व्याख्या–'लोकश्रेष्ठैः' पुरुषसिंहैः 'सावित्रैः' सूर्य्यवंशीयैः 'भूमिपालैः' महीपतिभिः 'यत् शुद्धं चरित्रं विमलं वृत्तं 'साधु दीपितं' सम्यगुद्भासितम् 'अस्मिन्' [लिपिकरप्रमादोऽयम् 'तस्मिन्' इति कबेरभिप्रायः स्यात्] 'मत्सम्बन्धात्' मम सम्पर्कात् एतस्मिन्न् अन्तरे सीतापरित्यागमकुर्वता मया योगात् 'कश्मला' मलिना 'किंवदन्ती' जनवादः 'चेत् स्यात्' यदि प्रसजोत तदा 'हन्त' अहो दुःखम 'अधन्यं हतभाग्यं 'मां धिक्'। तत् कुलचरितं दीपितमेव तिष्उतु इति करणीय एव सीतापरित्यागः इति भावः।।

Notes. 1. सावित्रैः–सूते इति सू+तृन् कर्त्तरि सविता Sun. सवितुरपत्यानि पुमांसः इमि सवितृ+अण, सावित्राः।2. भूमिपालैः–भूमिं पालयन्ति इति भूमि+पा+णिच+अण् कर्त्तरि भूमिपालाः। तेः। 3. लाकश्रेष्ठैः–अतिशयेन प्रशस्या इति प्रशस्य+इष्टन् श्रेष्ठाः, लोकेषु श्रेष्ठा। सुप्सुपा। तैः। 5. साधु–Qual. दीपनक्रिया। Comp. "तत् साधु कृतसन्धानं प्रतिसंहर शायकम्"–*Śakuntala.* 5. कश्मला–कश्मल is पाप। तत् अस्ति अस्मिन् इति कश्मल+अच् मत्वर्थे स्त्रियाम् कश्मला sinful ; secondarily 'dark' मलिना। 6. किंवदन्ती–किं कुत्सितं वदति इति किम्+वद+झच् स्त्रियाम्। 7. अस्मिन्–Seems to be a copyist's slip for तस्मिन्। 8. *Remark*–This verse gives the evil consequences of the non-observance of the व्रत referred to in sl. 41. If सीता is not abandoned a slur attaches to the race–the race originated by the resplendent Sun himself–the race of which the deeds are as resplendent sun. Hence by the maxim 'त्यजेदेकं कुलस्यार्थे' the abandonment of सीता is unvavoidable. This is an adaptation of "राजर्षिवंशस्य रविप्रसूतेरुपस्थितः पश्यत कीदृशोऽयम्। सत्तः सदाचारणशुचेः कलङ्कः पयोदवातादिव दर्पणस्य।।" –*Raghu.*

(*lxv*) **रा– हा देवि देवयजनसम्भवे, हा स्वजन्मानुग्रहपवित्रितवसुन्धरे, हा निमिजनकवंशनन्दिनि, हा पावकवशिष्ठारुन्धतीप्रशस्तशीलशालिनि,**

हा रामभयजीविते, हा महारण्यवासप्रियसखि, हा प्रियस्तोकवादिनि, कथमेवंविधायास्तव ईदृशः परिणामः।

(R—) Ah, my queen sprung from the ground for sacrifice to the gods ! Ah, thou by whom the earth was sancitified through the favour of thy birth ! Ah, thou the delighter of the race of Nimi and Janaka ! Alas, thou with a character belauded by fire, Vasiṣṭha and Arundhati ! Alas, thou that lived in Rāma ! Alas, my dear companion at stay in the great forest ! Ah, thou of sweet and spare speech ! Such as thou art, how is it that such is thy end?

त्वया जगन्ति पुण्यानि त्वयपुण्या जनोक्तयः।
नाथवन्तस्त्वया लोकास्त्वमनाथा विपत्स्यसे।। 43।

Through thee the worlds are holy, on thee are people's unholy tattle ! Through thee the worlds are provided with a guardian, thou art to perish without a guardian !

दुर्मुख ब्रूहि लक्ष्मणम्–एष ते नूतनो राजा रामः समाज्ञापयति (कर्णे–एवमेवम्)।

Durmukha, tell Lakṣmaṇa—Here, your new king Rāma commands (*Whispers into his ears*—Thus and thus).

मित–। हा इति। 'देवानां यजनं' यागस्थली 'सम्भवः' उत्पत्तिस्थानं यस्याः तादृशी सीता जन्मा पूता इत्यर्थः। अतएव 'स्वजन्म' एव यः 'अनुग्रहः' तेन 'पवित्रिता' विशोधिता 'वसुन्धरा' पृथिवी यया तादृशी सीता। अतएव सा 'निमेः' जनकवंशकर्त्तुः 'जनकस्य' च वंशस्य नन्दिनी' आनन्ददायिनी सीता [मन्थे–'रघुजनक' इति कवेः पाठ आसीत्, 'निमिजनक' इति लिपिकरप्रमादः। रघोः जनकस्य' च यौ 'वंशौ' तोः 'नन्दिनी' इति व्याख्यानम्]। 'पावकेन वशिष्ठेन अरुन्धत्या' च 'प्रशस्तं' स्तुतं सत् 'शीलं' तेन 'शालते' शोभते सीता। जन्मना शीलेन च अवला सीता इति भावः तस्यापि पुनर्लोकवादः इति खेदः। 'राममयं' रामैकपरं 'जीवितं' जीवनं यस्याः तादृशी। यस्या जीवने सर्वकर्मसु रामभावना तादृशी सीता, तस्या अपि परपुरुषसंसर्गशङ्का इति खेदः। महारण्ये दण्डकासु 'वासे प्रिया सखी' सहचरी तादृश्यामपि सन्देहः इति खेदः। 'प्रियं स्तोकम्' अल्पञ्च 'वदति' या सा 'ईदृशः' अचिन्ताः 'परिणामः' अन्तिमा दशा।। परिणाममेव दर्शयति त्वयेति।

अन्वयः–सुगमः।

व्याख्या—सुगमा। 'त्वया जगन्ति पुण्यानि' न केवलं त्वं पवित्रितवसुन्धरा किन्तु पवित्रितभुवनत्रयासि। 'अपुण्याः' जुगुप्सिता। 'त्वया' हेतुभूतया 'लोकाः नाथवन्तः' पुरा रावणपीड़िता असहाया आसन् अधुना रावणविनाशात् ससहायाः। अनाथा अशरणा' विपद्यसे' मरिष्यसि। उभयव असामञ्जस्यं प्रदर्शते। या पावनी सा अपवित्रीक्रियते, या शरणं सैव अशरणा इति।। नूतन इति+नूतनः' इति साभिप्रायम्। राजा नूतनः कर्मापि तस्य नूतनम्। न हि सूर्यवंशीयेन केनापि भूपालेन परित्यक्त्वा आसन्नप्रसवा धर्मपत्नी। तदपि नृतं नूतनेन राज्ञा क्रियते इत्यभिप्रायः।।

Notes. 1. स्वजन्म etc.—पवित्रा कृता इति पवित्र+णिच् (नाम धातु)+क्त कर्मणि पवित्रिता। 2. निमिजम etc.—रघुजनक seems to be the correct reading. 3. पावक etc.—प्र+शंस+क्त्व कर्मणि प्रशस्तम् belauded. पावक belauded her शील at the time of the ordeal in Laṅkā. वशिष्ठ and अरुन्धती were constant admirers. 3. राममय etc.—रामः प्रचुरः अस्मिन् इति राम+मयट् राममयम्। 4. ईदृशः परिणामः—Here राम anticipates events—what will happen to her if abandoned. 5. नाथवन्तः—नाथ is रक्षक protector, guardian etc. 6. रामः—mentions himself by name to show that राम alone is capable of such a villainous deed. 7. *Remarks*—for propriety of the various epithets here see *Mitabh*—above.

(*lxvi*) दुर्मुखः—कहं दाणीं अग्गिपरिशुद्धाए गब्भट्ठिदपवित्तरहुउल-सन्दानाए देईए दुज्जणवअणादो एवं अज्झवसिदं देएण [कथमिदानीम् अग्निपरिशुद्धाया गर्भस्थितपवित्ररघुकुलसन्तानाया देव्या दुर्जनवचनादेव-मध्यवसितं देवेन?

Dur.—How is it that through the slander of the wicked thus is now being contemplated by Sire regarding the queen who was cleared by fire (tested in fire?) and in whose womb rests the hallowed progency of the race of Raghu?

रामः—शान्तम्। कथं दुर्जनाः पौरजानपदाः ?

Rāma—Peace ! How are the citizens and villagers wicked ?

इक्ष्वाकुवंशोऽभिमतः प्रजानां जातञ्च दैवाद्वचनीयवीजम्।
यच्चाद्भुतं कर्म विशुद्धिकाले प्रत्येतु कस्तद्ध्यातिदूरवृत्तम्।। 44।।

Ikṣvāku's race is liked by the people, but through fate

has occured cause for slander. On the other hand, the miraculous deed (development) at the time of vindicatioin happened far off indeed. Who would believe in it ?

तद्गच्छ।

Do Go.

दुर्मुखः–हा देई [हा देवि]। (इति निष्क्रान्तः)।

Dur.—Alas, our queen ! (*Exit*).

मित। कथमिति। 'अग्नौ परिशुद्धौ' तस्याः 'देव्याः' सम्बन्धे। शेषे षष्ठीत इत्येकम् अनध्यवसायकारणम्। 'गर्भे स्थितः पवित्रः रघुकलसन्तानः' यस्याः यद्वा 'पवित्रस्य रघुकुलस्य सन्तानः' यस्याः तस्याः देव्याः। इत्यनयवसायकारणं द्वितीयम्। तथापि 'कथं देवेन अध्वसितं' व्यापृतमेतस्मिन् परिहार्ये कर्मणि। एवमनेके स्थिते अनध्यवसायकारणे मा भूदध्यवसायो देवस्य।। इक्ष्वाक्विति।

अन्वयः–इक्ष्वाकुवंशः प्रजानामभिमतः। दैवाच्च वचनीयबीजं जातम्। यच्च विशुद्धिकाले अद्भुतं कर्म, अतिदूरवृत्तं तत् कोहि प्रत्येतु।

व्याख्या–इक्ष्वाकोः वंशः प्रजानाम् अभिमतः तत्र अनुरक्ताः प्रजाः कथं मयि दुर्जनाः स्युः। नोचेत् दुर्जनाः, कथं जनवादः ?'दैवाच्च समैव हतभाग्यतया 'वचनीयस्य' निन्दायाः 'बीजं' कारणं 'जातम्' उपस्थितम्। अग्नौ दग्धं हि तत् बीजमिति चेत् 'यच्च' यत पुनः 'विशुद्धिकाले अद्भुतं कर्म' प्रदीप्तवह्निप्रविष्यापि कुशलिनी देवी अग्निप्रभृतीनाञ्च साक्षात्कारः अभूत् 'अतिदूरे' लङ्कायां वृत्तं' जातं 'तत् को हि प्रत्येतु' न कोऽपि। तत् अस्त्येव कारणं जनवादस्य, न हि दुर्जना प्रजाः।।

Notes. 1. अग्नि etc.–परिग्रहा means परिशुद्धा इति ज्ञाता found out to be pure *not* cleansed of impurities. No impurity could ever attach to her, she was उतपत्तिपरिपूजा। As such the slander may be ignored. 2. गर्भस्थित etc. –सन्तन्यते सातत्यं गम्यते वंशः अनेन इति सम्+तन+घञ् करणे सन्तानः progency. The whole is a चतुष्पद बहुव्रीहि (see *Mitabh*–). Or पवित्र रघुकुलम्, कर्मधा–। तस्य सन्तानः। गर्भेस्थितः पवित्ररघुकुलसन्तानो यस्याः, त्रिपदबह–। तस्याः। 3. देव्याः–देव्याः सम्बन्धे। शेषे षष्ठी। 4. अध्यवसितम–सी is सकर्मक meaning 'to destroy' etc. But अधि+अव+सो is अकर्मक meaning 'to make an effort' to make to one's mind' etc. and सकर्म्मक when meaning 'to attempt' etc. Here it is अकर्मक। अधि+अव+सो+क्त भावे वर्तमाने अध्यवसितम्। The reading अनार्यमध्यवसितम् is objectionable. अनार्य is too strong a word to come to the king from a menial. 5. अभिमतः–अभि+मन+क्त कर्मणि वर्तमाने। Hence प्रजानाम has अनुक्ते कर्त्तरि षष्ठी by "क्तस्य च वर्तमाने"। 6. अद्भुते कर्म–सीता

came out of fire unscathed. All the leading gods appeared in person to testify to the sancitfy of सीता। 7. विशुद्धिकाले–Here again विशुद्धि is विशुद्धिप्रख्यापन। 8. प्रत्येतु–प्रति+इ+लोट् तु। विधर्थे लोट्। 9. तत्–कर्म्म of प्रत्येतु। Very often प्रति+इ is used as अकर्मक and the object of प्रत्यय as its अधिकरण। Thus ''आत्मन्यप्रतययं चेतु:''–*Śakuntala*. 9. *Remark*–Note that here again we have the word दुर्जन। We have met with it already in ''साधुत्वे दुर्जनो जनः'', ''दुर्जनः अशुभमृतुपादयति" etc.

(*lxvii*) **रामः–हा कष्टम्। अतिबीभत्कर्मा नृशंसोऽस्मि संवृत्तः।**

Rāma—O woe ! I have bcome a murdered of extremely loathesome ways.

शैशवात् प्रभृति पोषितां प्रियां
सौहृदादपृथगाशयामिमाम्।
छद्मना परिददामि मृत्यवे
सौनिको गृहशकुन्तिकामिव।।45।। (रा–)

This dear one—brought up from childhood—never, through affection, having a different mind—I am consigning to death under a pretext as does the butcher a domestic bird. (R—)

मित–। हा इति। 'नृशंसः' घातुकः 'अस्मि' नास्ति सन्देहः, परं तत्रापि 'अतिबीभत्सं' घृणिततमं 'कर्म्म' यस्य तादृशोऽहम्।। कारणमाह शैशवादिति।

अन्वयः–शैशवात् प्रभृति पोषितां सौहृदात् अपृथगाशयां प्रियाम् इमां सौनिकः गृहशकुन्तिकाम् इव छद्मना मृत्यवे परिददामि।

व्याख्या–'शैशवात् प्रभृति' बाल्यादारभ्य 'पोषितां' लालिताम् अतः स्नेहपात्रम् 'सौहृदात्' प्रेमवशात् न तु भयादिना 'अपृथक्' अभिन्नः 'आशयः' अभिप्रायो यस्याः तादृशी प्रेम्ना मदनुवर्त्तिनीमित्यर्थः अतश्च वात्सल्यभाजनं 'प्रियां' मम प्रीतिकरीम् इत्थं बहुभिरेव निमित्तैः सदा यत्नतः प्रतिपाल्याम् 'इमां' प्ररूढ़विश्वासां मत्पार्श्वगतां सीता 'सौनिकः' मांसविक्रयौ 'गृहशकुन्तिकां' प्रयत्नपोषितां पक्षिणीम् 'इव छद्मा' छलेन तपोवनप्रदर्शनरूपेण 'मृत्यवे' यमाय 'परिददामि' प्रयच्छामि। किमतः परं बीभत्सं स्यात्।।

Notes. 1. अतिबीभत्स etc. –बीभत्सते अनेन इति वध वैरूप्ये स्वादि+सन्+घञ् करणे=बीभत्स+घञ्=बीभत्सम् that which causes disgust, i.e., revolting, loathsome etc. वैरूप्य is the sense given by the वृत्ति। Bhaṭṭoji interprets

वैरूप्य as चित्तविकार। Hence बीभत्सते means चित्तविकारं लभते। In this sense सन् after वध is compulsory and स्वार्थे and इच्छार्थे। The rule is "मान्वधदान्शान्भ्यो दीर्घश्चाभ्यासस्य"। दीर्घश्चाभ्यासस्य change बीभत्व into बीभत्स। 2. नृशंसः–नृन् शंसति हन्ति इति नृ+शंस+अच् कर्त्तरि नृशंसः a murderer. By abandoning सीता in this condition I am certainly going to become a murderer (नृशंस)। The murder again is being committed in a peculiarly : disgusting manner (बीभत्स)। The verse following explains the बीभत्सता। 3. शैशवात् etc.–Hence she ought to be an object of affection, and I am going to kill her. Is not this loathsome ? 4. प्रियाम्–She is an object of delight to me, yet I am going to kill her. This is revolting. 5. सौहृदात्–सुहृदयस्य भावः इति सुहृदय+अण=सुहृद्+अण् by the rule "हृदयस्य हृद् लेखयदणलासेषु"=सौहृदम्। The rule "हृद्भगसिधुवन्ते पूर्वपदस्य च" does not apply and we do not get सौहार्दम् (See addendum in our edition of *Śakuntala*). The rule–"सुहृद्दुर्हृदौ मित्रामित्रयोः" has no scope because सीता is not being looked upon here as a mere मित्र। 6. अपृथगाशयाम्–The thought is the same as in 'अनुगुणं सर्वास्ववस्थासु यत्" (sl. 40). Such a one is being killed by me ! How disgusting !! 7. इमाम्–Here he points at सीता sleeping in confidence on his bosom. Even such a one I am killing. I am really अतिबीभत्सकमा। 8. छद्मना–Again I am killing her under a pretext. She is not being plainly told of her fate. She goes out delighted at my kindness to her ! O woe !! 9. परिददामि–परि implies सर्वतोभावः। There is not the least doubt that she will die. 10. सौनिकः–सना is वधस्थान or मांसविक्रयस्थान meat-stall. By लक्षणा (transference of epithets) it is here विक्रेयं मांसम्। सूना पण्यमस्य इति सूना+ठक् सौनिकः। The derivation सूनायां नियुक्तः does not suit us, because the butcher is not posted or employed (नियुक्त) by one at his post.

(*lxiii*) (रा–) तत् किम् अस्पर्शनोयः पातकी देवीं दूषयामि। (सीतायाः शिरः खैरमुन्नमय बाहुमाकर्षकन्)–

(R)—Why then do I, an untouchable sinner, defile the queen? *Withdrawing his arm after having gently lifted Sītā's head)*—

अपूर्वकर्मचाण्डालमयि मुग्धे विमुञ्च माम्।
श्रितासि चन्दनभ्रान्त्या दुर्विपाक विषद्रुमम्।।46।।

Loose hold of me, O simple girl—of me a Cāṇḍāla by

this unheard of deed. You have taken hold of a poison-tree of dire tendencies under the delusion that it is sandal-tree.

(उत्थाय) हन्त विपर्यस्तः सम्प्रति जोवलोकः पर्यवसितं जीवितप्रयोजनं रामस्य। शून्यमधुना जीर्णारण्यं जगत्। असारः संसारः। कष्टप्रायं शरीरम्। अशरणोऽस्मि किं करोमि का गतिः। (रा–)

(*Getting up*) Alas ! To Rāma now is upset the land of the living, the end of the life has vanished ; the earth is now a withered wilderness —a void ; he world is bereft of its best ; this body is now almost an infliction. I am helpless, what shall I do ? What recourse ? (R.—)

मित–। तदिति। 'तत् तस्मात् बीभत्सकर्मनृश् सत्वात् 'अस्पर्शनीयः पातकी स्पृष्टु मप्ययोग्यः पापी अहं 'किं' कथं स्वगाचसंसर्गेण चारित्रपूतां 'देवीं दूषयामि'। अस्या दूरे इव स्थास्यामि।। सीताया इति। 'सीतायाः शिरः स्वैरं' जागरणभयात्, शनैः शनैः 'उन्नमय्य' उत्तोल्य 'वाहुम्' उपधानीकृतं स्वभुजम् 'आकर्षन्' अपनयन आह।। अपूर्वेति।

अन्वयः–अयि मुग्धे अपूर्वकर्मचाण्डालं मां विमुञ्च। चन्दनभ्रान्त्या दूर्षिपाकं विषद्रुमं श्रितासि।

व्याख्या–'अयि मुग्धे' सरलेसीते 'अपूर्वम्' अन्येन अकृतम् अतिबीभत्सं 'कर्म' यस्य तथाविधं 'चाण्डालं' मां विमुञ्च' मद्गत्रसंस्पर्श त्यज। कारणमाह–'चन्दनभ्रान्तया' मुखस्पर्शयन्दनोऽयसिति भ्रमेण 'दुर्विपाकम्' असुखप्रवणं 'विषद्रुमं श्रितासि' दुःखमेवास्य स्पर्शः तत् विमुश्च माम्।। [अतः परं मन्धे स्खलितो ग्रन्थः। स्वबाहुमाकृष्य ''विमुञ्च माम्'' इत्युक्तम्। विमोचनञ्च न भवति यावत् रामस्य कण्ठे प्रदत्तः सीताया बाहुर्नावतार्यते। अनुपदमुक्तम् ''उत्थाय'' इति च न सङ्गच्छते। तदित्थं भवतु–सीताया बाहुं स्वैरं स्वकण्ठादवतार्य्य उत्थाय–इति]।। हन्तेति। 'हन्त' अहो खेदः 'रामस्य' सम्बन्धे 'सम्प्रति' अधुना सीतायाः परित्यागात् 'जीवलोकः' प्राणिजगत् 'विपर्य्यस्तः' विपर्य्यासं जातः आकुलः संवृत्त 'जीवितस्य' प्राणधारणस्य 'प्रयोजनम्' अर्थः फलं 'पर्यवसितं' विगतम्। सीताविरहितस्य जगदन्यथा जातं मे' तत् मरणमेव श्रेयः इति भावः। 'अधुना' सीताविरहे 'जगत्' इयं धरा मे 'जीर्णारण्यम्' उक्तिन्नं काननम् अतएव 'शून्यं' जीवसम्पर्कविहीनं जातम् ; 'संसारः असारः' सारहीनः सहस्तुविरहितः प्रतिभाति 'शरीरं कष्टप्रायं पीड़ाविशेषमिव मन्धे। 'अशरणोऽस्मि' घोरस्यास्य विपत्पातस्य प्रतीकारी मे नास्ति।।

Notes. 1. अस्पर्शनीयः etc.–स्पृश्+अनीयर् कर्मणि स्पर्शनीयः। न स्पर्शनीयः

अस्पर्शनीयः। पातयति इति पत+णिच्+खलु कर्त्तरि पातकम् that wihch causes downfal, sin. तदस्य अस्तीति पातक+इनि पातकौ sinner. I am an untouchable sinner, I should not defile the queen with my touch. 2. स्वैरम्–ईरणम् इति ईर+घञ् भावे ईरः। स्वः ईर स्वैरः, कर्म्मधा–। The वृद्धि is due to the Vārttika "स्वात् ईरिरिणीः तत् यथा तथा। Qualifies उन्नमनक्रिया। 3. अपूर्व etc.–अविद्यमानं पूर्वं पूर्व वर्त्ति यस्य तत् अपूर्वम् unprecedented, बहु–। तादृशं कर्म यस्य। चण्डाल एव इति चण्डाल+अण् स्वार्थे चाण्डालः (प्रज्ञादि)। अपूर्वकर्मा चाण्डालः कर्मधा–। तम्। 4. चन्दनभ्रान्त्या–चन्दनस्य भ्रान्तिः। तया। 5. दुर्विपाकम्–वि+पच+घञ् भावे विपाकः development, दृष्टो विपाकः अस्य दुर्विपाकः that which developes into something very undesirable, बहु–। 6. विषद्रु मम्–विषस्य द्रुमः। 7. विपर्यस्तः–वि+परि+अस+क्त कर्मणि। Become topsy-turve. 8. जीवलोकः–जीवानां लोकः। What was one thing in the land of the living has become to me (रामस्य) something different now. 9. पर्यवसितम्–परि–अव+सी+क्त कर्त्तरि। 10. जीर्णारण्यम्–जीर्णम् अरण्यम्, कर्मधा–। The world is now to me a wildernes in which all vegetation has withered away. 11. असारः+सृ+घञ् कर्त्तरि सारः that which lasts, the best. अविद्यमानः सारः अस्मिन्। 12. संसारः–संसरत्यस्मिन् इति सम्+सृ+घञ् अधिकरणे संसारः the world of re-birth. The best in the world was सीता। She is doomed, so the world is bereft of its best. 13. कष्टप्रायम्–कष्ट pain ; प्राय is बाहुल्य। प्रायेण कष्टं कष्टप्रायम् mostly an infliction or a great inflection, सुप्सुपा। The reason why प्राय does not lead in the compound is that when entering a वाक्य the विभक्ति in always remains तृतीया (एकविभक्ति) while that in कष्ट changes. Thus प्रायेण कष्टं शरीरं मे प्रायेण कष्टं शरीरं वहामि, प्रायेण कष्टेन शरीरेण किम्, etc. Hence प्राय does not get पूर्वनिपात (though an उपसर्जन) owing to the prohibition. "एकविभक्ति च अपूर्वनिपाते"। Comp. एवम्प्रायाः in "प्रबलतमसामेवम्प्रायाः शुभेषु हि वृत्तयः"– *Śakuntala*. Or say प्राय means तुल्य। कष्टेन तुल्यम् कष्टप्रायम्, सुप्सुया। "प्रायो मरणानशने मृत्यौ बाहुल्यतुल्ययोः" इति मेदिनौ। 14. *Remark*–As pointed out in the मितभाषिणी the text here is defective. राम makes up his mind to avoid touch with Sītā's body. (किमस्पर्शनीयः पातकौ etc.). Hence, he withdraws his arm (बाहुमाकर्षन्). But this does not cut off touch because Sītā's arm is still on his neck (अयं कण्ठे बाहुः शिरमसृणो मौक्तिकसरः–sl. 38). This has to be removed. Sl. 46 is preliminary to its removal. विमुञ्च माम् etc.– let me go–cannot refer to the withdrawal of Rāma' arm, for by withdrawing *his* arm it is

Rāma that lets go Sītā. She can be said to have let राम go when her own hold of राम is released. Besides, so long as Sītā's arm is on his neck, उत्थाय following becomes incongruous. Hence it seems a part of the text is missing here (see मितभाषिणी)।

(*lxix*) (रा–) अथवा–

(R.—) Or,

दुःखसंवेदनायैव रामे चैतन्यमाहितम्।
मर्मोपघातिभिः प्राणैर्वज्रकोलायितं स्थिरैः ।। 47 ।।

In Rāma, for the full preception of pain indeed, was concious:ıess instilled, and by life—steady life striking at the vitals—has been played the part of a peg of adamant.

हा अम्ब अरुन्धति, हा भगवन्तौ वशिष्ठविश्वामित्रो, हा भगवन् पावक, हा देवि भूतधात्रि, हा तात जनक, हा तात, हा मातरः, हा परमोपकारिन् लङ्काधिपते विभीषण, हा प्रियसख सुग्रीव, हा सौम्य हनूमन्, हा सखि विजटे, मुषिताः स्थपरिभूताः स्थ रामहतकेन। (रा–)

Alas, mother Arundhati ! Alas, worshipful Vasiṣṭha and Viśvāmitra ! Alas, mighty sanctifier (fire) ! Alas, Goddess the sustainer of beings (Earth) ! Alas, father Janaka ! Alas, father ! Alas, mother ! Alas, my great benefactor Vibhīṣaṇa, the king of Laṅkā ! Alas, dear friend Sugrīva ! Alas, gentle Hanumat ! Alas, fried Trijaṭā ! You are all robbed and insulted by wretched Rāma. (R.—)

मित– । दुःखेति।

अन्वयः–दुःखसंवेदनाय एव रामे चैतन्यम् आहितं मर्मोपघातिभिः प्राणैः स्थिरैः (सद्भिः) वज्रकीलायितम्।

व्याख्या–'दुःखस्य संवेदनाय' सम्यक् ज्ञानाय 'एव रामे चैतन्यम् आहितम्' अर्पितम्। न हि अचेतनस्य ज्ञानं सम्भवति इति धावा प्रथमं रामे चैतन्याधानं कृतम्, प्राणप्रतिष्ठा विहिता। चेतनोऽपि यदि मुहूर्त्तमात्रं जीवति, तस्य ज्ञानं स्याद्वा, परं सम्यक् ज्ञानं न स्यात्। इति धातुरेव इच्छया 'मर्मणि' जीवस्थाने ये 'उपघ्नन्ति' प्रहरन्ति तादृशैः 'प्राणैः' असुभिः 'स्थिरैः' अचलैः सद्भिः 'वज्रकीलः' वज्रप्रस्तरनिर्म्मितः सुदृढ़ः य शङ्कुः तेन इव आचरितम्। चेतनोऽहं प्राणाश्च मां न मुञ्चन्ति तत् अनन्तं

दुःखमनुभवामि। एष एव धातुरभिप्रायः तत् 'किं करोमि का गतिः'।। हा इति। 'अरुन्धती' स्नेहवती सीतायाम्। 'वशिष्ठविश्वामित्रौ' गुरू। 'पावकः' शीलसाक्षी सीतायाः। 'भूतधात्री सीताया माता शीलसाक्षिणी च। 'परमोपकारी' सीतासमुद्धरणे सहाय इति। विस्मृतः स उपकारः कृतघ्नेन मया। 'विजटा' स्नेहवती सीतायामशोकवनिकासु। 'मुषिताः' भवतां सीतारूपरत्नोत्तमनाशनात्। 'परिभूताः' युष्मभ्यम् अनिवेद्य एक सीताविनाशनात्। 'हतकेन' दुष्कम कुर्वता 'रामेण'।।

Notes. –1. दुःख etc. –सम्+विद+ल्युट् भावे संवेदनम् full perception. The सम् is intensive. दुःखस्य संवेदनम्। तस्मै। तादर्थ्ये अर्थी। 2. रामे–Goes with both आहितम् and वज्रकीलाश्रितम्। 3. आहितन्–ओ+धा+क्त कर्मणि। The nom. is धात्रा understood. The object was to make me feel the misery. चैतन्यमाहितम्=प्राणः प्रतिष्ठापिताः। The प्राण तिष्ठा gives sensation ; I feel the pain. The complete the feeling the प्राण is rendered enduring. 4. मर्मीप etc.–मर्मणि उपघ्नति इति मर्म्+उप+हन+णिनि कर्त्तरि ताच्छील्ये। तैः। Hence, they bring me pain. 5. etc.–वज्र adamant, a kind of very hard stone. कील plug. वज्रस्य कीलः। तेन इव आचरितम् इति वज्रकील+क्यङ्+क्त भावे=वज्रकीलाय (नामधातु)+ क्त=वज्रकीलायितम् acted like a plug of adamant. 6. मुषिताः–Sītā was dear to all of these. Here loss would be a personal loss to each of them. 7. परिभूताः–परि+भू means 'to insult'. The loss is being caused without reference to them, hence the insult. 8. रामहतकेन–हत+कन् इवार्थे हतकः a wretch. रामश्चासौ हतकश्च, कर्म्मधा –। तेन। One who robs (मुषिताः) and insults (परिभृताः) is indeed a wretch. The समास is by "कुत्सितानि कुत्मनैः" though strictly speaking the rule does not apply. The rule wants that हतकत्व should attach a slur on रामत्व which it does not. [*N.B.*–The slur may be established with a little twisting. Thus–राम is one who pleases (रमते or रम्यते अनेन). For such a one it is slur to behave like a wretch. But witness विष्णुगुप्तहतक, चानक्यवटु, etc. where it is not easy to detect slur. It seems the rule is rather loosely applied by poets.

(*lxx*) **(रा–) अथवा कश्च तेषामहमिदानीमाह्वाने ?**

(R.—) Or who indeed am I now in the matter of their invoction.

ते हि मन्ये महात्मानः कृतघ्नेन दुरात्मना।
मया गृहीतनामानः स्पृश्यन्त इव पाप्मना।। 48।।

योऽहम्–

> विश्रम्भादुरसि निपत्य लब्धनिद्रा-
> मुन्मुच्य प्रियगृहिणीं गृहस्य शोभाम्।
> आतङ्कस्फुरितकठोरगर्भगुर्वी
> क्रव्याद्भ्यो वलिमिव निर्घृणः क्षिपामि।।49।।

Methinks those noble souls are being touched by Sin itself with their names uttered by me - me, ingrate and vilehearted, who, heartless, lifts up and throws as an offering into the carnivora his beloved wife, the jewel of his house, that in confidence, had gone to sleep by casting herself down on his bosom—wife heavy with the full foetus that is quivering through fright. (R.—).

मित–। अथवेति।'अथवा' पक्षान्तरे।'इदानीम्' अधुना अतिवीभत्सकर्मा नृशंसः 'अहं तेषाम्' अरुन्धतीप्रभृतीनाम्'आह्वाने' संबोधनकर्मणि 'कश्च' कः खलु, न कोऽपि, अनधिकारी खल्वह तेषामाह्वाने।। कारणमाहते इति।

अन्वयः–महात्मानः ते कृतघ्नेन दुरात्मना मया गृहीतामानः (सन्तः) पाप्मना स्पृश्यन्ते इव (इति) मन्थे।

व्याख्या–'महात्मानः' उदाराशयाः 'ते' अरुन्धतीप्रभृतयः 'कृतघ्नेन' उपकारकापकारिणा 'दुरात्मना' नीचाशयेन 'मया' अपूर्वकर्म्मचाण्डालेन रामेण 'गृहीतं नाम' येषां तथाविधाः सन्तः 'पाष्मना' मूर्ति यतापापेन 'स्पृश्यन्ते इव' 'हि' एतदेव अहं मन्थे' मम मतम्। अतस्तेषां नामग्रहणपरिहारो मया कर्त्तव्यः। कृतघ्नता दुरात्मता च दर्शिता अपि भूयः प्रदर्श्यतेविश्रम्भादिति।

अन्वयः–(यः अहम्) गृहस्य शोभां विश्रम्भात् उरसि निपत्य लब्धनिद्रां प्रियगृहिणीम् उन्मच्छ निर्घुणः (सन्) आतङ्कस्फुरितकटोरगर्भगुर्वी' (ताम्) वलिमिव क्रव्याद्भ्यः क्षिपामि। किम्भूतेन मया गृहीतनामानः ? (यः अहम्) 'गृहस्य शोभां' भूषणस्वरूपां गृह भूषयित्वा हितकारिणीं मे अपि च 'विश्रम्भात्' मयि प्रत्ययात् निशःशङ्कम् 'उरसि निपत्य' वक्षसि निर्भरं संविश्य 'लब्धनिद्रां' सुप्तां 'प्रियगृहिणीं' प्रिया पत्नीम्, 'उन्मुच्य' परित्यक्तुमनाः वक्षसः उत्तोल्य अकृतज्ञतायाः परां काष्ठां प्रदर्श्य इति भावः। अथ पुनः 'निर्घृणः' सन् करुणापरिहौणो भूत्वा। 'आतङ्केन वासेन चित्रदर्शनजनितेन 'स्फुरितः' कम्पमानः 'कठोरः' परिपूर्णे यो 'गभंः' तेन 'गुर्वी' मन्थरगमनाम् अतएव पलायितुम क्षमां तां 'वलिमिव' भक्षणार्थम् आमिषपिण्डमिव 'क्रव्याद्भ्यः' सिहव्याघ्नादिहि सेभ्यः 'क्षिपामि' दूरादेव व्यस्य ददामि। किमतः परं दुरात्मा स्यात्। एवं कृतघ्नेन दुरात्मना च मया गृहीतनामानस्ते स्पृश्यन्त इव पाष्मना।।

Notes. 1. मन्ये–This is his candid opinion, not a surmise. 2. महात्मान:–Contrast with दुरात्मना। Such being the contrast, I am an untouchable with regard to them. 3. कृतघ्नेन–कृ+क्त कमणि कृतम् the service done उपकार:। कृतम् हन्तीति कृत+हन+टक् कर्त्तरि कृतघ्न:। This is owing to च in "अमनुष्यकर्त्तके च"। "चकारात् क्वचिन्मनुष्यकर्तृकेऽपि"। In the case of राम however his मनुष्यत्व may be ignored. Or say after माधव (i) the affix टक् is बाहुकात् in a wider sense than usual ; (ii) take the word as of the मूलविभुजादि class and attach क। The difference between the two is seen in the faminine–कृतघ्नी with टक् and कृतघ्ना with क। 4. मया etc.–My tongue utters their names. This seems to me like sin personified touching their person (and defiling them). 5. विश्रम्भात्–वि+श्रम्भ+घञ् भावे विश्रम्भ: confidence. तस्मात्। हेतौ 5मी। Hence my विश्वासघातकता। 6. उन्मुच्य–Having lifted up just as a lump of meat is picked up and thrown at lions, tigers, etc. in a zoo. 7. प्रिय etc.–Comp. पोषितां प्रियाम्, sl. 46. 8.गृहस्य शोभाम्–Comp. इयं गेहे लक्ष्मी:, sl. 39. क्रव्याद्भ्या:–क्रव्य raw meat. क्रव्यम अदन्ति इति क्रव्य+अद+विट् कर्त्तरि क्रव्याद (प्रातिपदिक)। तेभ्य:। अर्थी सम्प्रदाने।

(lxxi) **(रा–) (सीताया: पादौ शिरसि कृत्वा) देवि, देवि, अयं पश्चिमस्ते रामस्य शिरसा पादपङ्कजस्पर्श:। (इति रोदिति)**

(R—) (*Placing Sītā's feet on his head*) Queen, my Queen, this is the last touch of thy lotus-feet with Rāma's head. (*Weeps*).

(नेपथ्ये)–अव्रह्मण्यम् अव्रह्मण्यम्।

(In the tiring room)—Murder ! Murder !

राम:–ज्ञायतां भो: किमेतत्।

Rāma—Ho ! Let it be known what this is

(पुनर्नेपथ्ये)–

(Again in the tiring room)—

ऋषीणामुग्रतपसां यमुनातीरवासिनाम्।
लवणत्रासित: स्तोम: शरण्यं त्वमुपस्थित:।।50।।

The body of ascetics of grim austerities dwelling on the

banks of the Yamunā, terrorised by Lavaṇa, has come to you the protector.

मित–। देवीति। 'पश्चिम:' पश्चाद्भव: अन्तिम इत्यर्थ:। 'शिरसा पादपङ्कजम्पर्श:' प्रसादनार्थम्। एतत्ते चरम' प्रसादनम्। दुर्लभमत: परमावयो: परस्पर दर्शनमिति भाव:।। ब्रह्मणमिति। ब्रह्मणि वेदे साधु ब्रह्मण्यम्। न ब्रह्मण्यम्। वेदविरुद्धम्, हिंसा इत्यर्थ:। आवेगे द्विरुक्ति:। घातो ब्रह्महत्या वा वर्त्तते त्रायतां भो: इत्याशय:।। ऋषीणमिति।

अन्वय:–यमुनातीरवासिनाम् उग्रतपमाम ऋाीणां स्तोम: लवणत्रासित: (सन्) शरण्यं त्वाम् उपस्थित:।

व्याख्या–'यमुनातीरवासिनां कालिन्दीतटसद्मनाम् 'उग्रतपसां' कटोरव्रतानाम् 'ऋषीणां स्तोम: समूह: 'लवणेन' रावणभागिन्धा: कुम्भीनस्या: पुत्रेण 'त्रासित:' सन् 'शरण्य' रक्षणसमर्थ 'त्वाम् उपस्थित:' वाणार्थ त्वत्सकाशमागत:।।

Notes. 1. पश्चिम:–पश्चात् भव इति पश्चात्+डिमच्। Final. 2. शिरसा etc.–This is to propitiate for the injury done. 3. नेपथ्ये–नेपथ्य is the dressing room of the actors. 4. अब्रह्मण्यम्–ब्रह्मन् is वेद। ब्रह्मणि वेदे साधु इति ब्रह्मन्+यत् ब्रह्मण्यम् that which is sanctioned by the Vedas. न ब्रह्मण्यम् अब्रह्मण्यम्, that which is not sanctioned by the Vedas 'i.e.', प्राणिहिंसा। The Vedas teach "मा हिंस्यात् सर्वभूतानि"। सन्भ्रमे द्विरुक्ति:। The exclamation implies that some one is craving protection against हिंसा by some one else. प्राणिहत्या भवति त्रायतां भो: is the sense. 5. उग्रतपसाम्–Hence deserving protection. 6. लवण etc.–त्रस+णिच्+क्त कर्म्मणि। 7. शरण्यम्–शरणे रक्षणे साधु: इति शरण+यत् शरण्य: a good protector. "शरणं गृहरक्षित्रोर्वधरक्षणयोरपि" इति मेदिनी। 8. उपस्थित:–उप+स्था+क्त कर्त्तरि has approached. उप+स्था is सकर्म्मक when meaning सङ्गतिकरण and is then आत्मनेपदी। Comp. 'अथैनं ससुपस्थिता' 'महामात्रान् उपतिष्ठते' etc.

(*lxxii*) **राम:–आ: कथम्! अद्यापि राक्षसत्रास:। तद् यावद् अस्य दुरात्मन: कुम्भीनसीपुत्रस्य उन्मूलनाय शत्रुघ्नं प्रेषयामि। (कातिचित् पदानि गत्वा पुनर्निवृत्य) हा देवि, कथमेवङ्गता भविष्यसि। भगवति वसुन्धरे, श्लाघ्यां दुहितरमवेक्षस्व जानकीम्–**

Rāma.—Ha ! How so ! fear of Rākṣasas even now ? Well then I will send Śatrughna for the up-rooting of this vile-hearted son of Kumbhīnasī. (*Having gone a few steps and come back*) Alas ! my Queen ! Thus circumstanced how will you live ? O mighty repository of riches (Earth), look after your worthy daughter Jānakī—

जनकानां रघूणाञ्च यत् कृतस्नं गोत्रमङ्गलम्।
यां देवयजने पुण्ये पुण्यशीलामजीजनः ।।51।।

(इति निष्क्रान्तः)

Who is the sum total of the blessings of the race of Janaka and Raghu and whom, of holy habits, you brought forth in the holy sacrificial ground of the gods. (51).

(*Exit*).

मित–। आः इति। 'अद्य' अधुना। हते रावणे प्रशमिता राक्षसा इत्येव जानामि तत् कथं तेभ्यस्त्रासः। विपन्नानां ब्राह्मणानां परित्राणे यतिष्यमाणमीहतः विपदं गतायाः आत्मपत्न्याः स्मर् करुणभिभूत आह 'एवम्' ईदृशीमवस्थां 'गता' प्राप्ता आतङ्कस्फुरतिकठोरगभगुर्वी क्रव्याद्भ्यः क्षिप्ता अशरणा 'कथं भविष्यसि' केनोपायेन आत्मानं रक्षित्वा जीविष्यसि। असमर्थोऽहं भवत्या रक्षणे तत् त्वदर्थे मातरं वसुन्धरामाक्रन्दामि इत्याह भगवतीति। 'अवेक्षस्व' स्या शिवानुध्यानपरा भव। सर्वथा प्रयत्नर्हा सः इत्याह जनकानमिति।

अन्वयः–त् जनकानां रघूणाञ्च कृत्स्नगोत्रमङ्गलम्। पुण्यशीलां या पुण्ये देवयजने अजीजनः।

व्याख्या–'यत्' सीतारूपं वस्तु 'जनकाना' जनकवंशीयानां 'रघूणाञ्च' रघूवंशीयानामपि 'कृतस्मं' समयं 'गोवमङ्गलं' कुलकल्याणम वंशयोर्यत् यत् कल्याणकरं तत्समुदायरूपेण या सीता स्थिता अतएव यवेन रक्षणीया ते। कारणन्तरञ्च त्वत्सम्न्धे प्रकृष्टतरमस्ति इत्याह–'पुण्यशीला' पूतचरितां 'यां पुण्ये देवयजने' देवानां यज्ञभूमौ 'अजीवन' जनितवत्यसि। कन्या किल मातुः रक्षणीया एव। सा च कन्या शीलेन श्लाघ्या इत्यात्मनापि रक्षामर्हति "श्लाध्यांदुहितरमवेक्षस्व जानकीम्" इति भावः।

Notes. 1. कुम्भीनसी etc.–कुम्भी a small pitcher. कुम्भी इवनासिका अस्याः इति कुम्भीनस्+अच्+ङीष्=कुम्भीनसी a woman with nose like a small pitcher. नासिका becomes नस् and अच् comes in by "अच, नासिकाया नसञ्चास्थ लात्"। ङीष् is optional by "नासिकोदर–"। Hence कुम्भीनसा is also correct. 2. कतिचित् etc. –The poet removes राम because his emotion at the so called Sītā's departure for तपोवन would betray him. 3. भगवति etc. –This appeal to वसुन्धरा is important as will be seen in Act VII. 4.

जनकानां रघूणम्–जनक and रघु here stand for the *progeny* of जनक and रघु by transference of epithets. 5. गोवमङ्गलम्–Whatever is beneficial to the races is embodied in Sītā. It she perishes both the races perish with her. Hence for those weighty reasons guard her careflly in my absence. 6. पुण्यशीलम्–People's slander makes no impression on his high opinion of her character. She is abandoned solely to please the people as commanded by the गुरु। 7. अजीवनः–You gave birth to her, she is your own child ; hence, besides the consideration for the two leading races of kings, you have a personal interest in her welfare.

(*lxxiii*) सीता–हा सोम्म अज्जउत्त कहिंसि [हा सौम्य आर्यपुत्र कुत्रासि]। (सहसोत्थाय) हद्धी हद्धी दुस्मिविणएण विप्पलद्धा अहं अज्जउत्तं आक्कन्दामि [हा धिक्, हा धिक्, दुःस्वप्नेन विप्रलब्धाहमार्यपुत्रमाक्रन्दामि]। (विलोक्य) हद्धी हद्धी एआइणीं मं पसुत्तं उज्झिअ गदो अज्जउत्तो। किं दाणीं एढं। भोदु से कुबिस्सं ऊइ तं पेक्खन्ती अत्तणो पहविस्मं। को एत्थं परिअणो [हा धिक्, हा धिक् एकाकिनो मां प्रसुप्ताम् उज्झित्वा गत आर्य्यपुत्रः किमिदानीमेतत्। भवतु तस्मै कोपिष्यामि यदि तं प्रेक्षमाणा आत्मनः प्रभविष्यामि। कोऽत्र परिजनः] ?

Sītā—Alas ! Gentle husband whither art thou ? (*Suddenly getting up*) O fie, O fie, deceived by a bad dream I am shouting for my husband. (*Looking round*) O fie ! O fie ! my husband has left leaving me alone and asleep. What is this? Well, I will be angry with him if seeing him I can control myself. Who attends (Lit.—is the waiter) here?

मित–'दुःस्वप्नेन' अप्रियेण आर्यपुत्रविरहं प्रदर्शयता स्वप्नेन 'विप्रलब्धा' प्रतारिता। 'आक्रन्दामि' आह्वयामि। प्राप्त एव विरहः स्वप्नेदृष्टः न ह्ययं विप्रलम्भः। 'एकाकिनीम् उजझित्वा गतः' इत्येकं कोपकारणम्, 'प्रसुप्तामुजझित्वा गतः' इति द्वितीयम्। 'आत्मः प्रभविष्यामि' यदि आत्मा मे वशः स्यात्। प्रणयस्य गाढ़तया असम्भवः कोपः, तत् सत्यपि कोपकारणे, कृते च सङ्कल्पे, 'तं प्रेक्षमाण' कोपं विस्मारिष्यामि इत्याशयः।

Notes. 1. हा धिक् etc. –धिक् implies निन्दा। She censures herself for the mistake. In the sentence following we have again हा धिक् etc. ; there she censures राम for his apparent want of consideration for her. 2. तस्मै–सम्प्रदाने चतुर्थी। सम्प्रदान in connection with कीपिष्यिामि by the rule 'क्रुधद्रुह–a'. But this is against the spirit of the Bhāṣya. There a distinction is made between क्रोध and कोप। कोप is the first stage ; its *further development* is क्रोध। "न हि अकुपितः क्रुध्यति"–*Bhāṣya.* That being so, कुप् does not make a सम्प्रदान। Hence it is that the rule itself says "यं प्रति कोपः" not "यस्मै कोपः" which would have saved a syllable. We therefore propose to read तस्य for तस्मै। The प्राकृत word से may be rendered तस्य also. The षष्ठी would be शेषे–तस्य सम्बन्धे कोपिष्यामि।

(*lxxiv*) **(प्रविश्य) दुर्मुखः–देई कुमारलक्खणो विस्मबेजि सज्जो रहो आरुहदु देई त्ति [देवि, कुमारलक्ष्मणो विज्ञापयति सज्जो रथः आरीहतु देवी इति]।**

(*Entering*) Durmukha—Queen, Prince Lakṣmaṇa begs to say that the car is ready, let Queen get in.

सीता–इयं आरुहामि [इयमारोहामि]। (उत्थाय) परिपफुरइ विअ मे गम्भभारो ता सिहिल गच्छ्मह [परिस्फुरतीव मे गर्भसारः तत शिथिलं गच्छामः]।

Sītā—Here, I am getting in. (*Rising*) The burden of my womb seems to throb, so I will go slowlyl.

दुर्मुखः–इदो इदो देई [इत इतो देवी]।

Dur.—This way Queen , this way.

सीता–णमो तबोधणाणं, णमो रहुउलदेवदाणं, णमो अज्जउत्त-चरणकमलाणं, णमो सअलगुरुअणाणं, [नमस्तपोधनेभ्यः, नमोरघुकुल-देवताभ्यः, नम आर्यपुत्रचरणकमलेभ्यः, नमः सकलगुरुजनेभ्यः]। (इति निष्क्रान्ता)

Sītā—Salutation to those that are rich in penance, salutation to the deities of the race of Raghu, salutation to the lotus-feet of my husband, salutation to all my seniors. (*Exit*).

इति चित्रदर्शनो नाम प्रथमोऽङ्कः।

Here ends the First Act named "Inspection of the Painting?".

मित–। "शिथिलं मन्दं 'गच्छामः'।। तपोवनं गच्छतीति प्रथममेवं तपोधनान्

प्रणमति। ततः कुलदेवताः प्रणमति। ततो भर्त्तारम्। इह स्थानान्तरं गन्तमुद्यता मर्त्तारमंपश्यन्ती अपि तद्दर्शनार्थं न यतते इत्यसमञ्जसम।।

Notes. 1. परिस्फुरित etc.–This is some new experience. Had it been the usual quickening felt from the fourth month onwards it would not have been the subject of her remark. She marks it because it is unusual. It was the day of delivery. 2. आर्यपुत्र etc.–When she says this she does not notice that राम should have accompanied her but keeps himself absent. See *Intro.*

Chapter - 2

(*i*) (नेपथ्ये)—स्वागतं तपोधनायाः।

(In the tiring Room)—Welcome to thee rich in asceticism.

(प्रविश्य अध्यगवेषा) तापसी—अये वनदेवतेयं पलकुसुमपलवार्ध्येण मामुपतिष्ठते।

(*Entering in the garb of a traveller*) Female Ascetic—Ha! Here is a sylvan deity meeting me with an offering of fruits, flowers and fresh leaves.

(प्रविश्य) वनदेवता (अर्घ्यं विकीर्य)—

(*Entering*) Sylvan Deity (Exhibiting the offerings)—

यथेच्छं भोग्यं बो वनमिदमयं मे सुदिवसः
सतां सद्भिः सङ्गः कथमपि हि पुण्येन भवति।
तरुच्छया तोयं यदपि तपसो योग्यमशनं
फलं वा मूलं वा तदपि न पराधीनमिह वः।।1।।

This forest is for you to enjoy any way you wish ; a happy day is this for me. Through merit and with great difficulty indeed does a meeting of the good come off with the good. The shade of a tree, water and what food suits your vow, be it fruit or root, all this is not for you at another's disposal here.

मित—।'तपोधनायाः स्वागं' शुभागमनं भवतु।। अध्वानं गच्छतीति 'अध्वगः' पथिकः। तस्य 'वेष' इव वेषो यस्याः।। –'फलैः कुसुमैः पल्लवैश्च' कल्पितः यः 'अर्घ्यः' पूजोपहारः तेन सह 'माम् उपतिष्ठते' मया सङ्गता भवति।।'विकीर्य' तापस्याः पुरो निधाय।। यथेच्छमिति।

अन्वयः—इदं वनं यथेच्छं भोग्यं वः। अयं मे सुदिवसः। पुण्येन हि कथमपि सतां सद्भिः सङ्गः भवति। इह वः तरुच्छाया, तोयं, यदपि तपसी योग्यमशनं फलं वा मूलं वा तदपि, न पराधीनम्।

व्याख्या—सुगमा।'पुण्येन हि' पुण्येनैव 'भवति'। तच्च 'कथमपि' अतिकृच्छ्रेण कदाचिदेव भवति इत्यर्थः।।

Notes. 1.स्वागतम्–आ+गम+क्त भावे आगतम् arrival. सुष्ठु आगतं स्वागतम् auspicious arrival. This is the usual word of welcome to a guest. 2. तपोधनायाः–शेषे षष्ठी। चतुर्थी is also seen thus–"कल्पितार्घ्याय तस्मैः....स्वागतं व्याजहार", "तस्मै ते परमेशाय स्वागतं स्वागतञ्च मे" etc. 3. अध्वगेषा–अध्वन्+गम+ड कर्त्तरि अध्वग traveller. तस्य वेषः। स इव वेषो यस्याः। "सप्तम्युपमान–"इति बहुव्रीहिः। 4. फल etc.–अर्घ honour, honouring. अर्घाय इदम् इति अर्घ+यत् अर्घ्यम् offerings of honour फलकुसुमपलवानि, द्वन्द्व। तत्कल्पितम् अर्घ्यम्, कर्मधा–of the शाकपार्थिवादि class. तेन। सहार्थे 3या। 5. उपतिष्ठते–meets. "उपद्देवपूजा–" इति सङ्गतिकरणे आत्मनेपदम्। We do not say उपतिष्ठते देवता बुद्ध्या पूजयति because the वनदेवता has not yet entered. The अर्घ्य is offered after her entrance (see below). 'She meets me' may be said as soon as a start is made to meet. But 'she honours me' seems a bit premature before honour is actually offered. 6. यथेच्छम etc.–The whole forest is at your disposal. 7. सुदिवसः–An auspicious day ; the reason follows. 8. सताम् etc.–सताम् of meritorious people like myself, सद्भिः with people of your stamp. It is not good taste to describe one's self as one of the सत्। पुण्येन–हेतौ 3या। Merit is the cause that produces the meeting as its effect. Again, that merit must be of an extraordinar type, hence such meetings do rarely happen (कथमपि भवति)।9. तरुच्छाया–तरोः छाया। तरुणाम् would give तरुच्छायम् by "छाया बाहुल्ये"। 10. पराधीनम्–परस्मिन् अधि इति पर+अधि+ख। सप्तमी तत्–with ख attached compulsorily by "आषड्क्ष–आशितङ्गु–अलकर्म–अलंपुरुष–अध्युत्तरपदात् खः।" The 7मी तत्–is by "सप्तमी शौण्डैः" अधि being of the शौण्डादि class.

(*ii*) **तापसी–किमत्रोच्यते।**

Ascetic—What do I say to this ?

प्रियप्राया वृत्तिर्विनयमधुरो वाचि नियमः
प्रकृत्या कल्याणी मतिरनवगीतः परिचयः।
पुरो वा पश्चाद्वा तदिदमविपर्यासितरसं
रहस्यं साधूनामनुपधि विशुद्धं विजयते।।2।।

(इत्युपविशतः)

Deeds highly agreeable, restraint in speech pleasing from modesty, heart naturally benevolent, acquaintance never denounced—this well-known guileless and stainless secret cf the good of which the flovor is unchanged at the beginning and at the end [Or—before and behind], rules triumphant.

(*They sit down*)

मित–।'अत्र' अस्मिन् विषये इमां भवत्या उदारतां प्रति इत्यर्थः मया 'किमुच्यते' किम् अन्धत् उच्यताम्? एकमेवात्र वक्तव्यं "साधूनां रहस्यं विजयते" इति। तदेवाह प्रियप्रायेति।

अन्वयः–वृत्तिः प्रियप्राया। वाचि विनयमधुरो नियमः। मतिः प्रकृत्या कल्याणी (अतएव) परिचयः अनवगीतः। इदं तत् पुरो वा पश्चाद्वा अविपर्य्यासितरसं साधूनाम् अनुपधि विशुद्धं रहस्यं विजयते।)

व्याख्या–'वृत्तिः' व्यापारः कर्म इत्यर्थः 'प्रियप्राया' प्रायेण बाहुल्येन प्रिया अतिप्रिया इत्यर्थः। साधूनां कर्मभिः जना न केवलं नोद्विजन्ते परन्तु सुप्रीता भवन्ति इति भावः। आस्तां कम रमणीयम्, वाक् पुनरुद्वेगकरीस्यात् इत्याह 'वाचि' साधूनां 'विनयेन' नम्रतया हेतुना 'मधुरः' प्रीतिप्रदः 'कोऽपि यिमः' संयमो वर्त्तते। साधवो हि पारुष्यं परिहृत्य रमणीयाञ्च कोमतामाधाय वाचं प्रयुञ्चते, तत् वाचापि तेषां सुप्रीता एव भवन्ति जनाः। भवतु सुशिक्षिततया तेषां कर्मणि वाचि च नियमः स्यात् परं मनः क्रूरं वा भवेत् इत्याह 'मतिः' साधूनां मनः 'प्रकृत्या' स्वभावेनैव न हि शिक्षावशात् 'कल्याणी' शिवा परेषां मङ्गलचिन्तनपरा इत्यर्थः अतएव 'परिचयः' सद्यः परिचितोऽपि जनः 'अनवगीतः' अनिन्दितः येन साधवः परिचिता भवन्ति तस्य निन्दां ते कदापि न कुर्वन्ति इत्यर्थः। मनोवाक्कसर्मसु मधुराः साधव इति भावः। 'इदम्' उक्तप्रकारकं 'तत्' प्रसिद्ध 'पुरो वा पश्चाद्वा' प्रथमपरिचये परिचयपरिणतौ चं यद्वा समक्षे च परोक्षे च 'अविपर्यासित' व्यत्ययमभजमानम् अतएव 'अनुपधि' अकपटं 'विशुद्धं' विमलं 'साधूनां रहस्यं' चरितं 'विजयते' सर्वान् विजित्य वर्त्तते। साधूनां चरित।वजितं हि त्रिभुवनम् इति भावः।

Notes. 1. किम् etc.–There is an intonation here (काकु). Do you want to know what I have got to say in this matter ? Her reply follows in the verse. 2. प्रियप्राया–Very pleasing. For grammar etc. See कष्टप्रायम्। I. Ixvii. 3. वाचि etc.–नि+यम+अप् करणे नियमः restraint. This is usually taken to mean that the *Sadhus* are men of few words. The restraint seems better taken with respect to the *quality* of the words used than *quantity*. The speechof the *Sadhus* is weeded of all undesirable words. 3. अनवगीतः–अव means अनुच्च low. अवगीत that which is spoken low. But निन्दा is spoken low (whispered). Hence अवगीत is निन्दित। न अवगीतः not condemned. 4. परिचयः–परि+चि+अच् कर्मणि परिचयः an acquaintance. The *Sādhus* never condem an acquaintance. The reason is their मति is प्रकृत्या कल्याणी, they cannot think ill of others. 5. पुरः etc. –पूर्वस्मित् काले इति पूर्वं+ङि (7म)+असि स्वार्थे पुरः at the beginning. वा implies, समुच्चय *i.e.,* means च। Comp. "सा वा शम्भोस्तदीया वा मूर्तिर्जलमयी मम"–*Kumāra.* अपरस्मिन् काले इति अपर+ङि (7मी) +अस्ताति स्वार्थे पश्चात् at the end. Both पुरस् and पश्चात् are अव्यय। Here the two together mean 'at the beginning and at the end', 'before and behind,' 'in presence and in absence' etc. 6. अविपर्यासितरसम्–वि+परि+अस+घञ् भावे विपर्यास reversal. विपर्यासं गमित इति विपर्यस+णिच् (नाम धातु)+क्त कर्मणि विपर्यासितः changed. न विपर्यासितः। तादृशो रसो यस्याः। The *Sādhus* speak well of one in one's presence as well as in absence (अनवगीतः परिचयः) ; hence their ways are *always* sweet (अविपर्यासितरसम्)। 7. रहस्यम्–रहसि भवम् इति रहम्+यत्। A secret. It is a *secret* because those who are not *sādhus* cannot acquire it. 8. अनुपधि–उप+धा+कि कर्मणि उपधि deceit. अविद्यमानम् उपधि अस्मिन्, बहु–। अविपर्यासितरस hence अनुपधि। They feel, speak and work sincerely. 9. विजयते–जि to conquer is सकर्मक and we have to take भुवन as the कर्म understood. It also means 'to prosper' उत्कर्षप्राप्ति। In this sense it is अकर्मक। The आत्मनेपद is by "विपरायां जेः"। विजयते conquers (people), prospers rules triumphant etc.

(iii) **वनदेवता–कां पुनरत्रभवतीमवगच्छामि।**

Deity—Well whom do I see in your honoured self ?

तापसी–आत्रेयस्मि।

Ascetic—I am Ātreyī.

वनदेवता–आर्ये आत्रेयि, कुतः पुनरिहागम्यते किम्प्रयोजनो वा दण्डकारण्यप्रचारः।

Deity—Noble Ātreyī, whence do you come here ? what again is the object of your wandering in the forest of Daṇḍaka?

आत्रेयी–

Ātreyī—

अस्मिन्नगस्त्यप्रमुखाः प्रदेशे भूयांस उद्गीथविदो वसन्ति।
तेभ्योऽधिगन्तुं निगमान्तविद्यां वाल्मीकिपाश्र्वादिह पर्यटामि।।2।।

In this quarter live many Vedic scholars with Agastya at their head. To learn from them the doctrine of the Vedānta I come here from the side of Vālmīki.

मित–।कामिति–किं नाम भवत्या इत्यर्थः।। आर्ये इति–कुतः कस्मात् स्थानात्। किं प्रयोजनम् अस्मिन् किम्प्रयोजनः। दण्डकारण्ये प्रचारः। दण्डकारण्यप्रवेशे को हेतुरिति भावः।। अस्मिन्निति। सुगमम्। वाल्मीकेः शिष्या किलाहम्, सम्प्रति अगस्त्यादृषेः उपनिषदः पठितुमिहागता इति भावः।

Notes. 1.अत्रभवतीम्–एषा भवती इति अत्र भवती compounded or uncompounded. Also see जयमत्रभवान्नूनं''etc.–Kirat XI 2. दण्डका etc.–The word is differently written दण्डक also दण्डका। Comp. ''दण्डकायां वने वः'', sl. 13. below ; also ''प्राप्तानि दुःखान्मपि दण्डकेषु''–*Raghu.* 3. अगस्त्य etc. प्रकृष्ट सुखं प्रमुखम् the head, top etc. अगस्ताः प्रमुखे एषाम्। Agastya was the most prominent amont them, hence she means to say that she wants to go to Agastya himself. Comp. ''विश्रान्तास्मि भद्रे, सम्प्रत्यगस्ताश्रमस्य पन्थानं ब्रूहि'', para ix. below. 4. भूयांसः–अतिशयेन बहव इति बहु+ईयसुन=भू+यस्=भूयस्। This is by ''वहोः लोपो भू च वहोः''। 5. उद्गीथ etc. –उच्चैर्गीयते इति उद्+गी+थक् कर्मणि भावे वा उद्गीथः a section of the सामवेद। तं विदन्ति इति उद्गीथ+विद+क्विप् कर्त्तरि those that are versed in उद्गीथ। Hence, a Vedic scholar in general. 6. तेभ्यः–''आख्याता उपयोगे'' इत्यपादाने 5मी। 7. निगम etc.नितरां गम्यते बुध्यते परतत्त्वम् अनेन इति न+गम+अप् करणे निगमः the Vedas. तस्य अन्तः निगमान्तः sequel to the Vedas. 'i.e.', the Upaniṣads. विद्यते ज्ञायते इति विद+क्यप् भावे विद्या knowledge ज्ञानम्। निगमान्तस्य विद्या a knowledge of the Upaniṣads. 8. वाल्मीकि etc.–वाल्मीकिः पार्श्व समीपं वाल्मीकिपार्श्वम्। तस्मात्। ल्यब्लोपि कर्मणि 5मी। वाल्मीकिपार्श्व परित्यज्य इत्यर्थः। Or गम्यमानापययोगे अपादाने 5मी as in 'कृतो भवान्? पाटलिपुत्रात्।'

(*iv*) **वनदेवता–यदा तावदन्येऽपि सुनयस्तमेव हि पुराणब्रह्मवादिनं प्राचेतसमृषिं ब्रह्मपारायणाय उपासते, तत् कोऽयमार्याया दीर्घप्रवास-प्रयासः ?**

Deity—When indeed others, even *Munis,* approach that

wery sage, Prācetasa, that old discourser on Brahman for going through the end of the Vedas, why is this attempt of yourself for a long stay away from home?

आत्रेयी–तत्र महानध्ययनप्रत्यूह इत्येषदीर्घप्रवासोङ्गीकृतः।

Ātreyī—There is great hindrance to study there, hence this long stay out has been decided upon.

वनदेवता–कीदृशः?

Deity—What sort of hindrance?

आत्रेयी–तस्य भगवतः केनापि देवताविशेषेण सर्वप्रकाराद्भुतं स्तन्यत्यागमात्रके वयसि वर्तमानं दारकद्वयमुपनीतम्। तत् खलु न केवलमृपीणाम् अपि तु सचराचराणां भूतानाम्। आन्तराणि तत्त्वान्युपस्नेहयति।

Ātreyī—Unto that mighty sage were brought by a certain goddess, two infants marvellous in every way, of an age when just weaned from breast-milk. They truly soften the internal entities, not of Ṛṣis only, but of all creatures movable and immovable.

मित–। यदा इति–'यदा तावत् अन्ये' जनाः 'मुनयः अपि' न केवलं प्राकृता जनाः 'ब्रह्मणः' वेदस्य 'पारायणय' अन्तगमनाय 'पुराणब्रह्मवादिनम्' आद्यं वेदगुरु 'तम् ऋषि' प्राचेतसमेव उपासते तत् आर्यायाः अयं दीर्घप्रवासप्रयासः कः' कीदृशः असमीचीन इति आशयः।। तत्रेति–अध्ययनस्य प्रत्यहः विघ्नः।। तस्येति–'देवताविशेषेण भगवतः उपनीतम्' इत्यन्वयः। सर्वप्रकारेण अद्भुतम्। स्तने भवं स्तन्यं दुग्धम्। तस्य त्यागः स्तन्यत्यागः लक्षणया स्तन्धत्यागकालः। स मात्रा परिमाणं यस्य तत् 'स्तन्धत्यागमात्रकम्'। कप् समासान्तः। तादृशे वयसि वर्तमानं 'दारकद्वयं' कुमारयगलम्। 'उपनीतं' समोपमानीय दत्तम्। 'तत्' दारकद्वयम्। 'चरैः' जङ्गमैः 'अचरैः' स्थावरेः 'सह' निखिलानां 'भूतानाम् आन्तराणि' मनोबुद्ध्यादीनि 'तत्त्वानि' पदार्थान् 'उपस्नेहयति' आवर्जयति।।

Notes. 1. यदा–A meaning यतः because . Comp. ''यदा बुधैः सर्वगतस्तुमुच्से''–*Kumara.* 2. अन्येऽपि मुनयः–Construe अन्ये, मुनयोऽपि। 3. पुराण etc. –पुराणश्चासौ ब्रह्मवादी च कर्मधा–। 4. प्राचेतसम्–प्रचेतस is वरुण। तस्य अपत्यं पुमान् प्राचेतसः। This is वाल्मीकिः। 5. ब्रह्मपारायणाय–ब्रह्मणः वेदानां पारम्, तस्मिन्

अयनं गमनम्। तस्मै। तादर्थ्यो 4अर्थी। 6. दीर्घ etc.–प्रवास is staying away from home. 7. कीदृशं–This is meant to refer to अध्ययनप्रत्यूहः। But as दीर्घ प्रवासः immediately precedes it and अध्ययनप्रत्यूहः is more remote it naturally goes with दीर्घ प्रवासः। Hence it seems better to write कीदृशः अध्ययन प्रत्यूहः। 8. देवता etc.–विशेष्यते इति वि+शिष+णिच्+घञ् कर्मणि विशेषः variety. देवतानां विशेषः।

(*v*) **वनदेवता–अपि तयोर्नामसंविज्ञानमस्ति ?**

Deity—Is there any information about their names?

आत्रेयी–तयैव किल देवतया तयोः कुशलवाविति नामनी प्रभावश्च आख्यातः।

Ātreyī—It is said that their names, *viz.*, Kuśa and Lava, and their might were revealed by the goddess herself.

वनदेवता–कीदृशः प्रभावः ?

Deity—What kind of might ?

आत्रेयी–तयोः किल सरहस्यजृम्भकास्त्राणि आजन्मसिद्धानि इति।

Ātreyī—What are told, that the Jṛmbhaka weapons with their secret have been achieved unto them since birth.

वनदेवता–इति हि भोश्चित्रम्।

Deity—Ho ! This is really strange.

मित–। अपीति–अपि प्रश्ने। 'तयोः' इत्यनन्तरं 'दारकयोः' इति ग्रन्थः स्खलितः प्रतिभाति। अन्यथा 'दाकद्वयम्' इति प्रस्तुतम्, तदिह 'तस्य' इति स्यात्। एवमुत्तरत्रापि। नाम इति–सम्यक् विज्ञानं संविज्ञानं विशेषबोधः। नाम्नोः संविज्ञानम्। नाम तयोर्जानासि किम् इति प्रश्नार्थः। किल इत्यैतिह्ये। जना एवं कथयन्ति इत्यर्थः।

Notes. 1. अस्ति–She means अस्ति ते, do you know ? If you do, tell me. 2. आख्यातः–आ+चक्ष or ख्या+क्त कर्मणि। Construe नामनी आख्याते प्रभावश्च आख्यातः। 3. *Remark*–It seems दारकयोः has been inadvertently omitted by copyists here after the first तयोः। Otherwise the reference being to दारकद्वयम् we expect तस्य।

(*vi*) **आत्रेयी–तौ च भगवता वाल्मीकिना धात्रीकर्म वस्तुतः परिगृह्य पोषितौ परिरक्षितौ च। वृत्तचूडौ च त्रयीवर्जम् इतरा विद्याः सावधानेन**

परिपाठिती। समनन्तरञ्च गर्भैकादशे वर्षे क्षात्रेण कल्पेन उपनीय तौ त्रयीविद्यामध्यापितौ। न ह्येताभ्यामतिप्रदीप्तप्रज्ञामेधाभ्याम् अस्मदादेः सहाध्ययनयोगोऽस्ति। यतः।

Ātreyī—And the two were reared and guarded by worshipful Valmiki literally undertaking the work of a nurse; again, with the ceremony of tonsure performed, they were carefully [lit. — by him with care] taught the other sciences except the Vedas ; and then, in the eleventh year from conception, they were initiated after the manner of the Kṣatriyas and taught the Vedas. Of such as myself there can indeed be no joining at study with these two of excessively bright grasp and memory ; for —

वितरति गुरुः प्राज्ञे विद्यां यथैव तथा जड़े
न च खलु तयोर्ज्ञाने शक्तिं करोत्यपहन्ति वा।
भवति च पुनर्भूयान् भेदः फलं प्रति तदु यथा
प्रभवति शुचिर्बिम्बोन्द्रहे मणिर्न मृदां चयः।।4।।

The teacher gives lessons to the sharp as well as to the dull ; surely he does not also increase or decrease their aptitude for grasping. Yet towards the result, there indeed arises a great difference. It is like this—A flawless gem, not a lump of earth, succeeds in receiving an image.

मित–।धात्रीत्यादि–'वस्तुतः' स्वरूपतः 'धात्रीकर्म' उपमातुः कार्य्यं 'परिगृह्य' स्वीकृत्य। स्वयमेव धात्री भूत्वा' इत्यर्थः। 'परिरक्षितौ' विपद्भ्य इति शेगः।। वृत्तेत्यादि–'वृत्ता' निष्पन्ना 'चूड़ा' तृतीये वर्षे काय्यः' संस्कारविशेषः ययोः तौ। 'सावधानेन' कृतमनः संयोगेन वाल्मीकिना 'त्रय्या' ऋग्यजुःसामरूपस्य वेदत्रयस्य 'वर्जः' वर्जनं यस्मिन् कर्म्मणि तत् यथा तथा 'परपाठितौ' ["गतिबुद्धि–" इत्यणिकर्त्तुः कर्मसंज्ञा]।। समनन्तरमित्यादि–'गर्भात्' गर्भाधानात्' 'एकदशे वर्षेक्षात्रेण' क्षत्रियजात्युक्तेन 'कल्पेन' विधिना 'उपनीय' उपनयनसंस्कारेण योजयित्वा।। न हीत्यादि–'अतिप्रदीप्ता' प्रखरा 'प्रज्ञा' बुद्धिः 'मेधा' स्मृतिः ययोः ताभ्यां 'सहाध्ययने' एकत्रं पाठे 'योगः न हि अस्ति' न सम्भवति।। कुत इत्याह वितरतीति।

अन्वयः–गुरुः यथा प्राज्ञे तथा एव जड़ेविद्यां वितरति, न खु तयोर्ज्ञाने

शक्तिञ्चकरोति अपहति वा। फलं प्रति पुनः भूयान् भेदो भवति च। तथा शुचिर्मणिः बिम्वोद्ग्राहे प्रभवति मृदां चयः न (तथा) तत्।

व्याख्या–अव सहाध्ययोगाभावे आचार्यदोषः शिष्यदोषो वा इत्यवाह 'गुरुःयथा प्राज्ञे' तीक्ष्णबुद्धौ शिष्ये तथा एव जड़े' मन्दबुद्धौ 'विद्यां वितरति' शास्त्रार्थ विवृणोति। विशेषेण अनुपक्षितौ युगपदुपस्थितौ हावपयसौ अविशेषेणैव पाठयति, तत् कुत आचार्यदोषः। भवतु यद्येवं स्यात् यत् स एकस्य बुद्धिं पुष्णाति इतरस्य च नाशयति? न इत्याह–'न खलु' अतिविशेषेण विद्यावितरणव्यतिरिक्तं स 'तयोः ज्ञाने' विब्रुतार्थबोधे 'शक्तिञ्च' सामर्थ्य मपि एकस्य 'करोति' इतरस्य 'अपहन्ति वा' नाशयति वा। यद्येवं फले अविशेषः स्यातु, फलं प्रति पुनः पक्षान्तरे फलसम्बन्धे तयोः 'भूयान् भेदः' महत् वैलक्षण्यं 'भवति च' भवत्येव। तन्मन्धे गुरुगतमपि किञ्चिदिहास्ति। मैवम्–'यथा शूचिर्मणिः' विमलं रत्नं 'विम्बोद्ग्राहे' छायाग्रहणे 'प्रभवति' शक्तो भवति 'मृदां चयः' लोष्ट'न' प्रभवति तथा 'तत्' स भेदाविर्भावः। स्वभाव एवाव कारणम्। यथा अन्यो मणिस्वभावः अन्यश्च मृतस्वभावस्तेन च एकत्र प्रतिबिम्ब दृश्यते नान्यत्र तथा एकः प्राज्ञस्वभावः अन्यश्च जड़स्वभावः तेन प्राज्ञे विद्या स्फुरति न जड़े। न हि कश्चिदत्र गुरोर्दोषः इति भावः।

Notes. 1. वस्तुतः–वस्तु is स्वरूप the reality. वस्तुना इति वस्तु+टा (श्या)+तसि स्वार्थे। In reality, actually, Vidyasagara reads धात्रीकवस्तुतः as a compound and explains धात्रीकरूपात् व्यापारात् with तस् पञ्चम्यर्थे। 2. परिरक्षितौ–Guarded against accidents. वीरराघव belives that ants are a menace to infant life and परिरक्षण is from the attack of ants. 3. वयीवर्जम् etc.–This may also be derived as वयौ वर्जयित्वा इति त्रयी+वर्जि (चुरादि)+ णमुल् भावे by he rule "द्वियायाञ्च"। The rule means that when the कर्ता of वर्जनक्रिया and final क्रिया is in a hurry णमुल् may be attached with a द्वितीयान्त word as उपपद। We have to suppose there tha Vālmīki quickly did the वर्जनक्रिया and पाठनक्रिया। as difference of opinion is possible in this supposition we give an alternative in the Tika. वयीवर्जम् इतराः seems a bit tautologous. त्रयीवर्ज विद्याः or त्रयौतरा विद्याः seems to serve the purpose eqally well. The *Vidyas* are 14 in all –"अङ्गानि वेदायत्वारो मीमांसा न्यायविस्तरः। पुराणे धर्मशास्त्रञ्च विद्याह्येताश्चतुर्दश।।" The boys were taught all these excepting त्रयौ, i.e., the Vedas, ऋच, यजुस, सामन् 4. सावधानेन–अवधान careful attention. तेन सह, बहु–। तेन। Qual. वाल्मीकिना। 5. परिपाठितौ–Here we had originally वृत्तकूडौ (कर्त्ता) विद्याः परिपठितवन्तौ= सावधानः (प्रयोजक) वृत्तचूडौ (प्रयोज्यकर्ता as कर्म) विद्याः परिपाठितवान् (with

णिच्). Changing the voice –मावधानेन वृत्तचूड़ौ विद्याः परिपाठितौ। The rule 'गतिबुद्धिप्रत्यवसामार्थशब्दकर्माकर्मकाणमणिकर्त्ता स णौ' applies because परिपठन is शब्दकर्म। Also note that by the diction "बुद्धिभक्षार्थयोः शब्दकर्मणाञ्च निजेच्छया" we may optionally make वृत्तचूड़ौ or विद्याः the reverse. 6. गर्भैकादशे–एकश्च दश च एकादश, एक becoming एका by निपात। एकादशानां पूरणम् इति एकादशम्+डट् एकादशम्। गर्भात् एकादशम्, सुप्सुपा। 7. उपनयी–त्रयी should not be taught *before* उपनयन। 8. त्रयीविद्याम् etc.–The changes are in Note. 5. above. 9. एताभ्याम्–सहार्थे श। 10. अतिप्रदीप्त etc. –To understand a lesson is one thing, to retain it is another ; the first is the work of प्रज्ञा and the second that of मेधा। 11. अस्मदादेः–वयम् (*i.e.*, अहम्) आदिः (आदयः?) अस्य जड़समूहस्य सः अस्मदादिः, बहु–। तस्य। 12. सह etc.–सह अध्ययनं सहाध्ययनम्, सुपसुपा etc. 13. वितरति etc.–प्रजानातीति प्र+ज्ञा+क कर्तरि प्रज्ञः। स एव इति प्रज्ञ+अण् स्वार्थे प्राज्ञः। Delivery of the lecture alone is the Guru's work ; he does nothing beyond it. प्राज्ञे जड़े do note take चतुर्थी because there is no सम्प्रदानविवक्षा। विषयाधिकरणे 7मी। 14. न च etc. –च is समुच्चये। He does not at the same time quicken the intellect of one and deaden that of the other. 15. भवति च–च is अवधारणे। 16. तत्–Refers to the manifestation of difference. 17. प्रभवति–Becomes capable. It does not mean 'lords it over', hence cannot govern the 4th case-ending by "नमः स्वस्तिः– "। 18. बिम्बोद्ग्राहे–बिम्ब is image. उद्+ग्रह+घञ् भावे उद्ग्राहः reception. विषयाधिकरणे 7मी। चतुर्थी has no scope (see note 17). 19. *Remark*–The verse is introduced with a यतः ; hence it professes to be a *reason* why न सहाध्ययनयोगोऽस्ति। She means to say the teacher goes on lecturing ; only the bright ones follow him, we lag behind. Hence न सहाध्ययनयोगोऽस्ति।

(*vii*) **वनदेवता–अयमसावध्ययनप्रत्यूहः?**

Deity—Is this the hindrance to study.

आत्रेयी–अपरश्च।

Ātreyī—Yet another.

वनदेवता–अथापरः कः?

Deity—Well, what is the other ?

आत्रेयी–अथ स ब्रह्मर्षिरेकदा माध्यन्दिनसवनाय नदी तमसा-मनुप्रपन्नः। तत्र च युग्मचारिणोः क्रौञ्चयोरेकं व्याधेन विध्यमानमपश्यत्।

आकस्मिकप्रत्यवभासाञ्च देवीं वाचमव्यतिकीर्णवर्णम् आनुष्टुभेन छन्दसा परिणतामभ्युदैरयत्–

Ātreyī—Now, that Brahman-like sage on a certain occasion went to the river Tamasa for his mid-day bath. There, out of two herons roaming together, he saw one being shot down by a fowler and forthwith delivered himself of Goddess Speech that suddenly flashed within him measured in Anushtup metre without any syllable in excess or defect (thus)—

मा निषाद प्रतिष्ठां त्वमगमः शाश्वतीः समाः।
यत् क्रौञ्चमिथुनादेकमवधीः काममोहितम्।। 5।।

Thou shalt have no home, O Niṣāda, for years eternal ; for, of a pair of herons, thou slayest one that is mad with love.

मित–। माध्यन्दिनेति–मध्ये भवम् माध्यन्दिनम्। इह "मध्यन्दिनसमये" इति केषाञ्चित् पाठः, तत्र वृद्ध्यभावश्चिन्त्यः। "माध्यन्दिन" इति दिनमध्यभवे रूढ़म्। 'माध्यदिनसवनाय मध्याह्नस्नानाय।"मध्यो मध्यो दिनण्चास्मात्" इति दिनण् प्रत्ययः। अनुप्रपन्नः गतः स्नानार्थमिति शेषः।। युग्मेन चरतोः "युग्मचारिणेः" सहविहरतोः।। 'अकस्मात्' अतर्कितं भवः 'आकस्मिकः' अचिन्तितोपनतः 'प्रत्यवभासः स्फुरणं यस्याः ताम्।। 'देवीं वाचम्' असृताम् आत्मनः कलाम्।। 'अव्यतिकीर्णाः' न्यूनत्वाधिकत्वरहिताः 'वर्णाः' यस्याम्। चतुर्ष्वपि अनुष्टुभो वा। मा निषादेति।

अन्वयः–निषाद, यत त्वं क्रौञ्चमिथुनात् काममोहितम् एकमवधीः (तत्) शाश्वतौः समाः प्रतिष्ठां मा अगमः।

व्याख्या–हे 'निषाद' व्याध 'यत्' यस्मात् 'त्वं क्रौञ्च- मिथुनात्' वकद्वन्द्वात् 'काममोहितम् एकम्' पुमांसमित्यर्थः 'अवधीः' तस्मात् 'शाश्वतीः समाः' अनन्तान् वत्सरान् व्याप्य 'प्रतिष्ठाम्' आस्पदं वासस्थानं 'मा अगमः' मा प्राप्नुहि। क्रूरेण त्वया एकमनयोर्निहत्य विहता अनयो गृहचर्य्या तत् तवापि गृहं न भविषयति, अयितनिलया एव निषादजातिर्विचरिष्यति इति शापः।।

Notes. 1. माध्य etc.–मध्य+दिनण् माध्यदिनम्। मध्य becomes मध्यम by the Varttika "मध्यो मध्यम्–"। स+ल्युट् भावे सवनम् bath. माध्यन्दिन is what occurs in the middle of any thing whatever, but it is restricted (रूढ़)

to mean what happens at the middle of the day. Our reading is from Virarāghava ; the usual reading is मध्यदिनसमये। मध्यन्दिन without वृद्धि has to be defended saying the वृद्धि is अनित्य। It seems better to avoid this reading. 2. युग्म etc.–युग्मेन चरतः इति युग्म+चर+णिनि कर्त्तरि ताच्छील्ये युग्मचारिणौ roaming : in pairs. 3. एकम्–The masculine implies that the male bird was shot down. 4. आकस्मिक etc.–अकस्मात् is an अव्यय meaning अतर्कितम् unexpectedly. अकस्मात् भव इति अकस्मात्+ठञ्, आकस्मिकः happening unexpectedly. प्रति+अव+भास घञ् भावे प्रत्यवभास। Next कर्मधा–। 5. अव्यति etc.–वि+अति+कृ+क्त कर्मणि व्यतिकीर्ण irregularly scattered scattered. न व्यतिकीर्णः, नञ् तत। Regular. Next बहु–। Having the same number of syllables in each line. 6. आनुष्टुवेव इति अनुष्टुभ्+अण् स्वार्थे प्रज्ञादि। 7. परिणताम्–The सूच्छा कला of शब्दब्रह्मन् suddenly flashed within him and came out in the shape of a verse in the अनुष्टुभ् metre. 8. निषाद–निषीदति पापमस्मिन् इति नि+स्था अङ् अधिकरणे प्रतिष्ठा habitation आलय। The Niṣadas are a criminal tribe leading a nomad life because, says the poet, doomed to it by this curse of the sage. 9. अगमः–भविष्यदर्थे लुङ् by the rule "माङि लुङ्"। But "न माङ्योगे" prohibits अट् and the from ought to be गमः। Some propose to meet the difficulty by taking the मा here as different from माङ् and thus avoiding the rule "न माङ्योगे"। The defence though good in cases like मा कुरु धनजयौवनगर्वम् etc. is not available here because if the मा here is not माङ् the लुङ् itself becomes inadmissible in a भविष्यत् sense the rle for it being "माङि् लुङ्"। The best defence is to say this is आर्ध। to. शाश्वतीः–शश्वत् is an अव्यय meaning सदा। शश्वत् भवाः इति शश्वत्+अण् स्त्रियां शाश्वत्यः or शश्वत् ठञ् स्त्रियां शाश्वतिकाः। ताः। अण् is available from निपातन in the Vārttika "शाश्वते प्रतिषेधः" and ठञ by "कालात् ठञ्"। 11. क्रौञ्च etc.–क्रौञ्चमिथुनम् आसाद्य इति ल्यबुलोपे कर्मणि 5मी। Or say when one is singled out there is mental separation from the group (बौद्ध अपाय) ; hence अपादाने 5मी। 12. *Remark*–The curse is for his wickedness in destroying the domestic felicity of the pair of herons. You have rendered the female heron homeless so homeless you go for ever. Even to this day the hunting tribes (वेदिया) have no fixed habitation.

(viii) **वनदेवता–चित्रम् ! आम्नायादन्यो नूतनश्छन्दसामवतारः!**

Deity—O marvel ! A fresh incarnation (manifestation) of the metres other than those in the Vedas !

आत्रेयी–तेन खलु पुनः समयेन ते भगवन्तमाविर्भूतशब्द-ब्रह्मप्रकाशमृषिमुपगम्य भगवान् भूतभावनः पद्मयोनिरवोचत्–"ऋषे, प्रबुद्धोऽसि वागात्मनि ब्रह्मणि। तत् ब्रूहि रामचरितम्। अव्याहतज्योतिरार्षं ते प्रातिभं चक्षुः। आद्यः कविरसि"। इत्युक्त्वा तत्रैवान्तर्हितः। अथ भगवान् प्रचेतसः प्रथमं मनुष्येषु शब्दब्रह्मणस्तादृशं विवर्त्तमितिहासं रामायणं प्रणिनाय।

Ātreyī—Again mightly Padmajoni, the creator of beings, having approached that worshipful sage unto whom the ligh of Brahma as Sound had appeared by that time, said—"O sage, you have become enlightened in Brahman in the shape of Speech, so narrate the deeds of Rāma. Your saintly eye of inspiration has its light unobstructed. You are the first poet." Having said this, even there and then he vanished. Thereupon the mighty sage Prācetasa composed the historical poem Rāmāyaṇa, the first evolution of Sound Brahma in that shape among men. [Or better—Thereupon......Prācetasa first composed....the evolution of .....men].

मित–।'अस्नायात् अन्यः' वेदात् भिन्न 'नूतनः' अदृष्टपूर्वः 'छन्दसाम् अवतारः' छन्दोदेवताया आविर्भावः। वह्वीभिर्मूर्त्तिभिः किल वेदेषु अवतीर्णा छन्दोदेवता, इयं पुनरस्या नूतनोऽवतारः।। 'तेन समयेन आविर्भूतशब्दब्रह्मप्रकाशम्' इत्याद्यवयः। 'आविर्भूतः' प्रकटः शब्दब्रह्मणः प्रकाशः' ज्योतिः यस्य यस्मिन् वा तम्। आविर्भवनं प्रति अपवर्गे तृतीया। जन्मनः प्रभृति तन्मुहूर्त्ते यावत् यः 'तेन समयेन' तावता कालेन इत्यर्थः।। भूतानि भावयति उत्पादयति इति 'भूतभावन' त्रिभुवनविधाता।। 'वागात्मनि' शब्दस्वरूपे 'ब्रह्मणि' विषये 'प्रबुद्धः असि' प्रकर्षेण बोधस्ते जातः, शब्दब्रह्मणः स्वरूपं सम्यगुपब्धवानसि। 'आर्ष ते प्रातिभं' प्रतिभारूपं चक्षः 'अव्याहतज्योतिः' सर्वदर्शि जातम्। 'आद्यः कविरसि' लोके।। 'अथ भगवान् प्राचेतसः मनुष्येषु' लोके 'शब्दब्रह्मणः तादृशं प्रथमं विवर्तं परिणामम् 'इतिहासं रामयणं प्रणिनायं'। [यद्वा–अथ ....प्राचेतसः प्रथमं मनुष्येषु शब्दब्रह्मणः तादृशं विवर्त्तम् इत्यादि]।

Notes. 1. आम्नायात्–आ+म्ना+घञ् कर्मणि आम्नाय: the Vedas अनाशब्दयोगे 5मी। 2. नूतन:–New. The poet intends to say that this is the first time a meter not found in the Vedas is introduced. As worded the line implies that metres outside the Vedas have been invented. This one, however, is a fresh invention. The ambiguity is removed if we read चित्रम् आम्नायादन्य: प्रथमश्छन्दसामवतार:। 3. छन्दसाम्–छन्दम् here includes all *possible* metres ; it is a group which is personified. 4. अवतार:–अवतरत्येन इति अव+तृ+घञ् करणे। An incarnation. 5. समयेन–Refers to the whole time from birth to the manifestation of the metre. अपवर्गे श्या। The आविर्भाव of शब्दब्रह्मन् was attained (फलप्राप्ति) by that length of time. 6. भूत etc.–भावयति जनयति इति भू+णिच+ल्युट् कर्त्तरि बाहुलकात् भावन:। Next इतत्–Also see note. 7.7 पद्मयोनि:–पद्म: विष्णोर्नाभिपद्मं योनि: कारणं यस्य स:। A name of ब्रह्मन्। As this implies that ब्रह्मन् is *born*, we may also derive भूतभावन: thus–भूतानि भाव्यन्ते अेन इनि भूति+भावि+ल्युट् करणे the कर्त्ता being विष्णु। 7. अव्याहत etc. –अव्याहतं अविघ्नितं ज्योति: यस्य तत्। The light of your will penetrate everthing unobstructed. You will see all ; the entire life of Rāma will stand revealed to you. This is predicated of चक्षु:। Compare Rāmāyaṇa–"रामस्य सह सौमित्रे राक्षसानाञ्च सर्वश:। वैदेह्यायैव यदृतं प्रकाशं यदि वा रह:। तच्चाप्यवितथं सर्वं ते भविष्यति।।" 9. प्रातिभम्–प्रतिभाति अनया इति प्रति+भा+अङ् करणे प्रतिभा inspiration. प्रतिभा एव इति प्रतिभा+अण् स्वार्थे प्रातिभम्। We have neuter by the maxim "क्वचित् स्वार्थिका:प्रकृतितो लिङ्गवचनान्यतिवर्त्तन्ते"। The आर्थ प्रतिभा of the sage is taken as his चक्षुस्। 10. अथ–अनन्तरम्। This was after the twins had finished their course of the Vedas. Hence this was the time when they should have been taken through the Vedānta. 11. प्रथमम्–construe प्रथमं विवर्त्तम् the first evolution, or प्रथमं प्रणिनाय first composed. The latter has to be preferred (see next para). 12. मनुष्येषु–Construe मनुष्येषु विवर्त्तम्। This is according to the theory that nothing new is created, every thing is in existence from eternity; what we call creation in but a manifestation of something pre-existent in Brahman. This इतिहास named रामायण had its germ in शब्दब्रह्मन् but that was देवेषु not मनुष्येषु। The sage had mastered शब्दब्रह्मन् (प्रबुद्धोऽसि etc.) hence he saw all and made it known मनुष्येषु in that form (तादृशम्)। 13. विवर्त्तम्–विवर्त्तते विभिन्नरूपेण वर्त्तते अनेन इति वि+वृत+घञ् करणे विवर्त्त: manifestation, evolution. 14.

इतिहासम्–इतिह is an अव्यय meaning पारम्पर्योपदेशः–a statement of succession of events स आस्ते अस्मिन् इति इतिह+आस+घञ् अधिकरणे इतिहासः a book containing narration of past events, *i.e.,* पुरावृत्तम्। This is the explanation of Amara's commentators. Vardhamāna says. "इतिहं इति लोकप्रवादागमयोः"। लोकप्रवाद is what people say *i.e.,* tradition story current in word. The rest as before. This makes इतिहास a systematic collection of stories and traditional knowledge regarding any matter in hand.

(*ix*) **वनदेवता–हन्त पण्डितः संसारः।**

Deity—Bravo ! The world will become wise.

आत्रेयी–तस्मादवोचम् "महानध्ययनप्रत्यूहः" इति।

Ātreyī—Hence I said there was great hindrance to study.

वनदेवता–युज्यते।

Deity—Rightly said.

आत्रेयी–विश्रान्तास्मि भद्रे, सम्प्रत्यगस्त्याश्रमस्य पन्थानं ब्रूहि।

Ātreyī—I am rested, gentle friends. Now, tell me the way to the hermitage of Agastya.

वनदेवता–इतः पञ्चवटीमनुप्रविश्य गम्यतामनेन गोदावरौतीरेण।

Deity—Having entered the Pañcavaṭī here, proceed along this bank of the Godāvarī.

आत्रेयी (सवाष्पम्)–अप्येतत्तपोवनम्? अप्येषा पञ्चवटी? अपि सरिदियं गोदावरी ? अप्ययं गिरिः प्रस्त्रवणः ? अपि जनस्थानदेवता वासन्ती त्वम्।

Ātreyī—(*With tears*) is this tapovana ? Is this Pañcavaṭī ? Is this hill the Prasvaṇa ? Are you Vāsantī the deity of Janasthāna ?

वासन्ती–अस्त्येतत् सर्वम्।

Vāsantī—All this is so.

मित–। पण्डित इति–रामायणपाठात् सर्वे प्राज्ञा भविष्यन्ति इति भावः। मण्डित इति पाठान्तर दृश्यते। तत्र 'मण्डितः' भूषितः। गुणरिस्ना रमयणो ग्रन्थः जगत्या

अलङ्कार इति भावः।। तस्मादित्यादि–तस्मात् कस्मात्? पूर्वत्र "प्रथमं विवर्त्तम्" इत्यन्वये अध्ययनप्रत्यूहो नैव दृश्यते। "प्रथमम् इतिहासं प्रणिनाय" इति पक्षे तु "प्रथमम् इतिहासं परस्ताच्च अन्यत् किञ्चित् आरब्धम्" ते सम्प्रति कार्यान्तरे व्यासक्तो मुनिः निगमान्तविद्या तु नाध्याप्यते इत्यध्यनप्रत्यूहः।। अप्येतदिति–तपोवनमिति तत्रत्यस्य कस्यचित् प्रदेशस्य नाम स्यात्।।

Notes. 1.अध्ययन etc.–In the para preceding consture प्रथमम् इतिहासं प्रणिनाय। Now, "*First* composed the history" implies that something other than history is engaging his attention now. Hence अध्ययनप्रत्यूहः, because the teacher is busy. The construction शब्दब्रह्मणः प्रथमं विवर्त्तं प्रणिनाय does not explain the प्रत्यूह, because the sage has then finished his work and is free to lecture to his pupils. Hence prefer प्रथमम् इतिहासं प्रणिनाय। That the sage was really busy with something else will be evident from प्रणीतो न प्रकाशितः etc. in Act. IV. paras xxxvii-xxxviii. 2. तपोवनम्–A separate अपि with तपोवनं indicates that तपोवन was a proper name like पञ्चवटी, गोदावरी, प्रस्रवण, वासन्ती। It evidently referred to a tract of land including the spot where the two speakers were seated.

(*x*) **आत्रेयी–वत्से जानकि,**

Ātreyī—Child Jānaki.

स एष ते वल्लभबन्धुवर्गः प्रासङ्गिकीनां विषयः कथानाम्।

त्वां नामशेषामपि दृश्यमानः प्रत्यक्षदृश्यामिव नः करोति।। 6।।

This group of your friends and favourite objects, the object of incidental remarks, on being seen, makes you as if before my eyes and visible though your name alone is left to us.

मित–। स इति।

अन्वयः–प्रासङ्गिकीनां कथानां विषयः स ते एष वल्लभबन्धवर्गः दृश्यमानः (सन्) नामशेषामपि त्वां नः प्रत्यक्षदृश्यामिव करोति।

व्याख्या– 'प्रासङ्गिकीनां' कथांन्तरप्रसङ्गे भवानां 'कथानां विषयः' वस्तु 'स ते एष वल्लभानां तपोवनपञ्चवटीगोदावरीणां 'बन्धोः' वासन्त्याश्च 'वर्गः' समूहः 'दृश्यमानः' सन् 'नाम' सीतेति नाममात्रं 'शेषः' इह लोके स्थितं यस्याः तादृशीम् 'अपि' लोकान्तरगतामपि 'त्वां नः प्रत्यक्षदृश्यामिव' लोचनगोचरीभूतामिव 'करोति'। चतुर्षु एषु दृष्टेषु मधे त्वामेव सशरीरां पश्यामि इत्याशयः।।

Notes. 1. वल्लभ etc.–वल्लभ is favourite बल्लभाश्च बन्धूश्च वल्लभबन्धवः द्वन्द्व। बन्धु should have come first in the compound because it is अल्पाचतर। But the rule is often violated. Com. "समुद्राभ्रात्""लक्षणहेत्वो", etc. of पाणिनि himself. वल्लभबन्धूना वर्गः। Or say बन्धूनां वर्गः बन्धुवर्गः group of friends. वल्लभो बन्धुवर्गः the favourite group of friends. This counts तपोवन, पञ्चवटी and गोदावरी among friends. Whether this is reasonable or nor it is not easy to say. Trees and animals are often seen regarded as friends. Thus–"यत्र द्रुमा अपि मृगा अपि बन्धवो मे"–Act III. sl. 9. But that very verse excludes the tract of land from among friends and treats it as mere आधार of the friends (यत्र)। Besides, there is no reason to suppose that the four now spoken of, *viz.*, तपोवन, पञ्चवटी, गोदावरी, वासन्ती, were favourites among friends. For these reasons the first exposition has to be preferred. Against this, however, note पूर्वसुहृदो भूमिभागान् of para xxxii which justifies the inclusion of तपोवन etc.–among friends. 2. प्रासङ्गिकीनाम्–प्र+सञ्ज+घञ् भावे प्रसङ्ग context, course of conversation. प्रसङ्गे भवा इति प्रसङ्ग+ठञ् प्रासङ्गिक्यः। तासाम्। 3. प्रत्यक्ष etc.–अक्ष्णः प्रति इति प्रति+अक्षि+टच् समासान्त प्रत्यक्षम् before the eye. अव्ययी–by the गणसूत्र "प्रतिपरसमनुभ्योऽक्ष्णः"। प्रत्यक्षं दृश्या, सुप्सूपा।

(*xi*) वासन्ती (सभयं स्वगतम्)–कथं नामशेषामित्याह? (प्रकाशम्) आर्ये किमत्याहितं सीतादेव्याः?

Vāsantī. (*With alarm to herself*)—Why does she say "name alone is left"? (*Aloud*) Noble lady, has my calamity befallen queen Sītā?

आत्रेयी–न केवलमत्याहितं सापवादमपि।

Ātreyī—Not a mere calamity, but with a scandal too.

वासन्ती–कथमिव?

Vāsantī—How so ?

आत्रेयी–(कर्णे–एवमेवम्)।

Ātreyī—(*Whispers in the ear*—Thus and thus.

वासन्ती–अहह ! दारुणो दैवनिर्घातः। (इति मूर्च्छति)।

Vāsantī—Oh ! A terrible bolt from the blue ! (*Faints away*).

आत्रेयी–भद्रे, समाश्वसिहि समाश्वसिहि !

Ātreyī—Courage, gentle friend, courage.

वासन्ती–हा प्रियसखि, हा महाभागे, ईदृशस्ते निर्माणभागः ! रामभद्र, रामभद्र ! अथवा अलं त्वया। आर्ये आत्रेयि, अथ तस्मादरण्यात् परित्यज्य निवृत्ते लक्ष्मणे सीतादेव्याः किं वृत्तमिति काचिदस्ति प्रवृत्तिः?

Vāsantī—O ! Dear friend, O! supremely endowed lady was such the lot at your creation ? Rāmabhadra, Rāmabhadra, or no use of thee. Noble Ātreyī, is there any information as to what happened to queen Sītā after Lakṣmaṇa had returned from that forest abandoning her.

आत्रेयी–न हि न हि।

Ātreyī—No, indeed no.

मित– । अत्याहितमिति–"अत्याहितं महाभीतिः कर्म जीवानपेक्षि यत्" इत्यमरः। यत्र प्राणशङ्काः तत् अत्याहितम्।। अहहेति–अहह इति गुरुदुःखसूचकमव्ययम्। 'निर्घातः' नितरां घातः वज्रपात इत्यर्थः। तथाच–"निर्घातोग्रैः कुञ्जलीनान् जिघांसुर्ज्यानिर्घोषैः क्षोभयामास सिंहान्" इति रघौ। दैवप्रेरितो निर्घातः 'देवनिर्घातः'।। हा इति–महान् भागः अंशः नेसर्गिको गुणराशिः इत्यर्थः यस्याः तत्संबुद्धौ 'महाभागे'। 'निर्माणे' सृष्टिकाले विहितो 'भागः' भाग्यम्। प्रवृत्तिः' वार्त्ता।

Notes.–1. अत्याहितम्–अतिशयेन आहितम् इति अति+आ+धा+क्त कर्मणि something that is laid heavy on one's mind a calamity that threatens life. अत्याहितं जातं किम् is the construction. 2. दैव etc.–दैव is Destiny. निर+हन्+घञ् भावे निर्घातः a violent stroke, hence thunder. दैवस्य निर्घातः thunder-bolt sent down by fate. Here वासन्ती mourns Sītā's luck. Alas ! Sītā was struck by a veritable bolt from the blue. Thus thinking of the plight of her friends she herself faints away. 3. प्रियसखि–प्रियसखी gives प्रियसखी+टच् by "राजाहः सखिभ्यः टच्"। This is because by the maxim "प्रातिपदिकग्रहणे लिङ्गविशिष्टस्यापि गृहणम्" what is enjoined of सखि affects सखी also. Next by पुंवद्भाव we get प्रियसखि+टच्। The final इ disappearing (टिलोप) we have प्रियसख which in the feminine becomes प्रियसखी। तत्संबुद्धौ। Apparently there seems to exist a short cut to the form प्रियसखी if we assume that समासान्तविधि being अनित्य the poet has not affixed टच् at all. So that प्रिया सखी प्रियसमुखी, तत्संबुद्धौ is quite plain sailing. But this assumption is not justified if there is a way to the correct form without अनित्यता। अनित्यता has to be assumed only when there is no other solution. 4. महाभागे–भाग here is अंश share ; 'i.e., the share of virtues allotted to her. "एकदेशांशयोर्भागः" इति विकाण्डशेषः। 5. निर्माणभागः–निर्माण is सृष्टि। भाग now is भाग्य, भागधेय lot निर्माणे भागः the lot assigned by विधाता at creation ; सुप्सुपा। "भागो रूपार्द्धके प्रोक्तोभागधेयैकदेशयोः" इति विश्वः।

(*xii*) **वासन्ती–हा कष्टम् ! अरुन्धतीवशिष्ठाधिष्ठितेषु रघुकदम्बकेषु जीवन्तौषु च प्रवृद्धासु राज्ञीषु कथमिदं जातम्?**

Vāsantī—O woe ! How could this happen, Arundhati and Vasiṣṭha guiding the princes of Raghu's race and the old queens living?

आत्रेयी–ऋष्यश्रृङ्गसत्रे गुरुजनस्तदासीत्। सम्प्रति तु परिसमाप्तं तत् द्वादशवार्षिक सत्रम् ऋष्यश्रृङ्गेण विसर्जिताच सम्पूज्य गुरवः। ततो भगवत्यरुन्धती नाहं वधूविरहितामयोध्यां गमिष्यामि इत्याह। तदेव राममातृभिरनुमोदितम्। तदनुरोधात् भगवतो वशिष्ठस्य परिशुद्धा वाचः–वाल्मीकितपोवनं गत्वा तत्र वत्स्यामः–इति।

Ātreyī—The elders were then at the sacrifice of Ṛṣyaśṛṅga. But now that twelve year-old sacrifice has ended and the elders have been dismissed by Ṛṣyaśṛṅga with due honours. Thereafter Worshipful Arundhati has said—I shall not enter Ayodhyā which is bereft of my daughter-in-law. The same has been fully approved by Rāma's mothers. Out of regard for all this, mighty Vasiṣṭha's unimpeachable words are these—We shall go to the hermitage of Vālmīki and live there.

मित–। हा इत्यादि–'अरुन्धत्या वशिष्ठेन' च 'अधिष्ठितानि' अधिकृतानि कर्त्तव्योपदेशैः परिचालितानि तेषु।'कदम्बकं' वृदं समूहः। रघूणां कदस्वकानिः तेषु। रघुवंशीयेषु। भावे सप्तमी। रघुकदम्बकेषु अरुन्धतीवशिष्ठाधिष्ठितेषु सप्त, राज्ञीषु जीवन्तीषु सतीषु इत्यन्वयः।। ऋष्येत्यादि–सत्रं यज्ञः। 'परिसमाप्तम्' इत्यनेन वंदेह्यास्त्यागत् द्वादश वत्सरो गताः त्रयोदशो वर्त्तते इत्यायाति।'तयो' अरुन्धती वचनस्य

राममातृवचनस्य च 'अनुरोधः बाधा' तस्मात्। 'वाल्मीकितपोवनम्' इति तु कथमुच्यते नविगच्छामः। वशिष्ठस्यापि तपोवनमास्ते तव वासेऽपि अयोध्यागमनं परिह्रियते एव।।

Notes. 1. अरून्धती etc.–कदम्ब is समूह। "वृन्दें कदम्ब नीपि ना" इति त्रिकाण्डशेषः। कदस्वानि एव इति कदम्ब+क् स्वार्थे कदम्बकानि। रघु by transference of epithets, stands for the members of Raghu's race. The idea is – Arundhati and Vasiṣṭha guiding the affairs, the renunciation becomes well nigh impossible ; these two cannot possibly approve of it ; supposing, however that they do approve the old queens will interfere. Hence कथमिदं जातम्। 5. द्वादश etc. – 12. years have passed from the commencement of the सत्र। Sītā was exiled the very day it commanced. Hence this is the 12th year of Sītā's exile. 3. वाल्मीकि etc.–It is not clear why Vālmīki's hermitage was selected. The reason assigned is तदनुरोधात् i.e., because अरुन्धती and the queens do not like to go to Ayodhyā. This is not sufficient reason because वशिष्ठ has own hermitage, he could have easily taken them over there to avoid going to Ayodhyā.

(xiii) **वासन्ती–अथ स राजा किमारम्भः सम्प्रति?**

Vāsantī—Well, how is that king engaged now?

आत्रेयी–तेन राज्ञा क्रतुरवमेधः प्रकान्तः।

Ātreyī—The sacrifice Asvamedha has been commenced by that king.

वासन्ती–हा धिक् ! परिणीतमपि।

Vāsantī—O shame ! Wedded again !'

अत्रेयी–शान्तं शान्तम्।

Ātreyī—Peace ! Peace !

वासन्ती–का तर्हि यज्ञो सहधर्मचारिणी ?

Vāsantī—Who then is the colleague at the sacrifice ?

आत्रेयी–हिरणमयी सीताप्रतिकृतिः।

Ātreyī—A golden image of Sītā.

वासन्ती–हन्त भोः–

Vāsantī—O joy !

वज्रादपि कठोराणि मृदूनि कुसुमादपि।
लोकोत्तराणां चेतांसि को न विज्ञातुमर्हति।। 7।।

Of the superhuman, who indeed is worthy enough to know the hearts that are harder than even adamant, softer than flower even ?

मित–। अथेति–'अथ' इति प्रश्ने। 'राजा' इति रामस्य प्रजारञ्जनपरताया गर्हा। "राजा प्रकृतिरञ्जनात्" इति तु प्रसिद्धम्। प्रकृतिरञ्जनानुरोधात् प्रियामपि तदवस्थामपि, पत्नीं परित्यजति अहो "राजा"। इति गर्हा। 'कः आरम्भः' व्यापारः कर्म इत्यर्थः अस्य। एतदप्याक्षेपपरम्। कृतमेकमनेन जुगुप्सितं कर्म सधे अपरमपि तादृशमेव किञ्चित् प्रस्तुतम् इत्यभिप्रायः।। हा इति–'परिणीतम्' तेन इति कर्त्तृपदमूह्यम्। "सस्त्रीको धर्ममाचरेत्" इति वचनात् अश्वमेधे अपरिहार्य पत्नीसाहचर्यम् तन्मन्धे पत्न्यन्तरं गृहीत्वा कृतं सीहापरित्यागानुरूपं कर्म तेन इति भावः।। का इति–'सह' एकत्र 'धर्म' चरति' या सा 'सहधर्मचारिणी'।। हिरण्यमर्यीति–हिरण्यस्य विकारः हिरण्मयीति निपातनात् यलोपः।। हन्त इति हर्षे। वज्रादिति।

अन्वयः–लोकोत्तराणां चेतांसि को नु विज्ञातुमर्हति? (तानि) वज्रादपि कठोराणि कुसुमादपि मृदूनि। यद्वा–लोकोराणां चेतांसि वज्रादपि कठोराणि कसुमादपि मृदूनि। की नु (तानि) विज्ञातुमर्हति?

व्याख्या–ये 'लोकात्' जगतः भूतलगतजनसमुदायादित्यर्थः 'उत्तराः' ऊर्द्धतराः जगहिलक्षणा इति यावत् तेषां 'चेतांसि' हृदयानि 'को नु' कस्तावत् 'विज्ञातु' विशेषेण ज्ञातुम् 'अर्हति' योग्यो भवति, न कोऽपि इत्यर्थः। अविज्ञेयत्वे, कारणमाह–तानि च सति प्रयोजने कदाचित् 'वज्रादपि कठोराणि' लक्ष्यन्ते, तेन कठोरत्वेन विज्ञायन्ते। अन्धदा पुनः प्रयोजनभेदात् 'कुसुमादपि मृदूनि' दृश्यन्ते ततश्च मृदुतया विज्ञायन्ते। इत्थं मृदुत्वकठोरत्वादि विरुद्धधर्मोपितानि तानि न मृदुतया न च कठोरतया विज्ञातुं शक्यन्ते। रामोऽपि लोकोत्तर एव हि प्राकृती मानवः। अथ स सीतापरित्यागे यदि कठोरः, तस्याः प्रतिकृतिग्रहणे नूनं मृदुः। तत् कथं ब्रूयां कठोरो रामो मृदुर्वा प्रकृत्या। इति वासन्त्या रामं प्रति कलुषतां परिहृत्य उदासीनतया स्थितिः।।

Notes. 1. राजा किमारम्भः–For force see मित–above, 2. अश्वमेधः–मेध्यते हन्यते अस्मिन् इति मेध+घञ् अधिकरणे मेधः sacrifice. अश्वस्य मेधः horse-sacrifice. 3. परिणीतम्–परि+नी+क्त भावे। Nom. तेन understood, for reasons for the inference see मित–।4. शान्तम्–अव्यय ending in म implying prohibition. "Do not say so" is the sense. The duplication (द्विरुक्ति) implies आवेग, impatience. Vāsantī's inference is hasty and Ātreyī impatiently checks her. 5. सह etc.–धर्म्म चरतीति धर्म+चर णिनि कर्त्तरि स्त्रियाम् धर्मचारिणी। सह धर्मचारिणी, सुप्सुपा। 6. हिरण्मयी–हिरण्मयी। The य of हिरण्य disappears by निपातन in the rule "दाण्डिनायन–"। This information surprises Vāsantī. She sees the injustice of her remark, and in joy exclaims हन्त भोः etc. 7. लोकोत्तराणाम्–उदू means ऊर्द्ध। अतिशयेन उत् इति उद्+तरप् उत्तरः higher. लोक is लोकसमुदाय। लोकात् उत्तराः लोकोत्तराः occupying a level higher than that of men. तेषाम। The उत्तर is different from उत्तर meaning 'north'. Hence this is not a सर्वनाम and we have उत्तराः like दक्षिणः in दक्षिणा गाथकाः। Also compare उत्तरे प्रत्युत्तरे च शक्तः। 8. को नु–नु implies आक्षेप। Who can i.e., I challenge if anybody can. Here Vāsantī's harshnes towards Rāma is gone ; she admits she cannot judge him.

(*xiv*) **आत्रेयी–विसृष्टश्च वामदेवाभिमन्त्रितो मध्योऽश्व उपकल्पिताश्च यथाशास्त्रं तस्य रक्षितारः, तेषामधिष्ठाता च लक्ष्मणात्मजश्चन्द्रकेतुः अवाप्तदिव्यास्त्रसम्प्रदायश्चतुरङ्गबलान्वितः प्रहितः।**

Ātreyī—And the sacrificial hose has been let loose consecrated by Vāmadeva; its guards too have been appointed in accordance with the Śāstras; moreover Candraketu the son of Lakṣmaṇa, who had received initiation in heavenly weapons, has been told off as their leader followed by a force in four divisions.

वासन्ती (सस्नेहकौतुकास्त्रम्)–कुमारलक्ष्मणस्यापि पुत्रः। हन्त मातर्जीवामि।

Vāsantī (*With tears of joy and affection*)—A son unto prince Lakṣmaṇa too ! Hurrah ! Mother I am living.

मित–। विसृष्टेत्यादि–'विसृष्टः' मोचितः। वामदेवेन मन्त्रैरभिपूजितः 'वामदेवाभिमन्वितः'। मेधंयागमर्हतीति 'मेध्यः' यज्ञियः। 'उपकल्पिताः नियुक्ताः। 'यथाशास्त्रं' शास्त्रानुसारतः। 'रक्षितारः' प्रत्येकं शतसंख्या दण्डिनः कवचिनो निषङ्गिण इति। 'अधिष्ठाता' नायकः नेता इत्यर्थः। सम्प्रदीयते इति 'सम्प्रदायः' गुरुपरम्परागतः सदुपदेशः। कर्मणि घञ्। 'अवाप्तः' गुरोर्लब्धः 'दिव्यास्त्राणां' सुरायुधानां 'सम्प्रदायः' उपदेशः येन सः। चतुरङ्गेण हस्त्वश्वरथपादातसमन्वितेन 'बलेन' सैन्धेन 'अन्वितः' अनुगतः। 'प्रहितः' प्रेरितः। एतत्तु बलम् अश्वरक्षितृभ्यो भिन्नम। अयमासीत् प्रयाणक्रमः–प्रथमम् अश्वः, ततस्तस्य रक्षितारः, पश्चाच्च चतुरङ्कः बलान्वितश्चन्द्रकेतुः।। सस्नेहेत्यादि–अस्त्रं नेत्रजलम् आनन्दजनितं जलमिति यावत्। 'स्नेहस्य

कौतुकस्य' हर्षस्य च यत् 'अस्रम' तेन सह। 'कुमारलक्षणस्यापि पुत्रः' इति आनन्दहेतुः। 'हन्त' इति हर्षे। 'जीवामि' इति हर्षः। अयि 'मातः' यत् त्वया मां प्रति बाल्ये बहुशोऽप्युक्तम् "पुत्रि जीव" इति, अद्य जीवित्वा तस्य फलं मया प्राप्तं, कुमारलक्षणस्य पुत्रप्राप्तिं श्रुत्वा आनन्दानुभव इति। तत् जीवामीति महान् हि मे हर्षः। मृता चेत् स्याम् अद्यायमानन्दो न स्यात्॥

Notes. 1. वामदेव etc. –Vāmadeva did the duty in the absence of Vasiṣtha. 2. रक्षितारः etc.–शास्त्रमनतिक्रम्य यथाशास्त्रम्, अव्ययी– । See Act IV, Para xliii, "प्रत्येकं शतसंख्याः etc." . They duty of these was to guard the horse only. 3. अधिष्ठाता–The leader. Comp. "वशिष्ठाधिष्ठिता देव्यो", Act. I. sl. 3. 4. अवापत etc.–सम्प्रदाय may also be derived with घञ् भावे without any material alteration of meaning. 5. प्रहितः–प्र+हि+क्त कर्मणि। 6. सस्नेह etc. कौतुक is तथा। 7. हन्त etc.–You wished me long life, mother, and I am glad mother that I am living still. For joy has come to me to day at the news of Lakṣmaṇa's son. Comp. "एति जीवन्तमानन्दा नरं वर्षशतादपि"–Live, and you are bound to be happy some day.

(*xv*) आत्रेयी–अत्रान्तरे ब्राह्मणेन मृतं पुत्रमारोप्य राजद्वारि सोरस्ताड़मब्रह्मण्यमुद्घोषितम्। ततो "न राजापचारमन्तरेण प्रजास्वकालमृत्युश्चरति" इत्यात्मदोषं निरूपयति करुणामये रामभद्रे सहसैवाशरीरिणी वागुदचरत्–

Ātreyī—At this juncture a Brāhmaṇa, laing down his son's dead boy at the royal gate, shouted 'Murder' beating his breast. Thereupon, as compassionate Rāmabhadra was looking for some misconduct of himself, because untimely death does not prevail among people without lapse in the ruler, suddenly there arose a voice without a body—

शम्बूको नाम वृषलः पृथिव्यां तप्यते तपः।

शीर्षच्छेद्यः स ते राम तं हत्वा जीवय द्विजम्॥ 8॥

A Śūdra namdes Śambūka is practising penance on earth. He has to be unhesitatingly beheaded by you personally, O Rāma, Revive the Brāhmaṇa by killing him.

इत्युपश्रुत्य कृपाणपाणिः पुष्पकं विमानमारुह्य सर्वा दिशो विदिशश्च शूद्रतापसान्वेषणाय जगत्पतिश्चरितुमारब्धवान्।

Having heard this, the lord of the earth, sword in hand,

mounting the aerial car Puṣpaka, has commenced to scour in all the principal and secondary directions for a search for the Śūdra ascetic.

वासन्ती–शूद्रः शम्बूको नाम धूमपः अस्मिन्नेव जनस्थाने तपश्चरति। तत् अपि नाम रामभद्रः पुनरपीदं वनमलङ्कुर्यात्।

Vāsantī—A Śūdra named Śambūka, practises penance in this very Janasthāna inhaling smoke. Could it then be that Rāmabhadra would once again grace this forest?

मित–। अत्रेत्यादि–'अत्र' अस्मिन् 'अन्तरे' अवकाशे मेध्याश्वविसर्जनात् परमित्यर्थः। 'मृतम्' अकाले मृतम्। 'राजद्वारि आरोप्य' राजद्वारस्य पार्श्वस्थितायां वेदिकायां निधाय। 'उरसः' आत्मवक्षसः 'ताडः' ताड़ने तेन 'सह' वक्षसि कराघातं कृत्वा इत्यर्थः। 'अब्रह्मण्यम्' अवध्यता 'उद्घोषितम्' उदीरितम् 'पुत्रशोकात् म्रिये त्रायस्व माम्'' इति उच्चैरुच्चारितम्। 'ततः तदनन्तरं तच्छ्रुत्वा इति शेषः। 'राज्ञः अपचारः' दुर्व्यवहारः तम् 'अन्तरेण' विना। 'चरति' प्रसरति। राजदोषेणैव अकाले प्रजा म्रियन्ते इत्यर्थः। 'इति अतो हेतोः। 'आत्मदोषं' कमपि आत्मनः सूखलनं 'निरूपयति' पर्यालोचयति। 'करुणमये' ब्राह्मणेन समवेदने। 'रामभद्र' इति भावे सप्तमी। 'शरीरम्' नास्ति अस्या उत्पत्तिस्थानत्वेन इति 'अशरीरणि वाक्' आकाशवाणी इत्यर्थः 'उदचरत्' आविर्भूता। का सा इत्याह शम्बूकेति।

अन्वयः–सुगमः।

व्याख्या–हे 'राम शम्बू कोनाम वृषलः' कश्चित् शूद्रः तपसि अनधिकारी इति शेषः 'पृथिव्यां' त्वदीये राज्ये 'तपः तप्यते' चरति। अपचारोऽयं, परं प्रजासु ते न हि त्वयि। 'सः' अपचारवृत्तः शूद्रः 'ते शीर्षच्छेद्यः' शिरश्छेदेन नित्यं त्वया स्वहस्तेन दण्डनीयः। तं हत्वा द्विजं ब्राह्मणबालकं 'जीवय'। तस्य हननेनैव ब्राह्मणबालको जीविष्यति इति भावः। दण्ड्यः स इयन्तं कालं न दण्डितस्त्वया इत्ये तन्मावस्ते अपचारः नाधिकः।। 'इति' इमां वाचम् 'उपश्रुत्य' आकर्ण्य 'कृपाणपाणिः' खड्गहस्तः। 'दिशः' पूर्वादयः। 'विदिशः' उत्तरपूर्वादयः कोणाः।। शूद्र इत्यादि। 'धूमं' धूममात्रं 'पिवति' इति 'धमपः' निराहार इत्यर्थः। तद्धि कठोरतरं तप इत्थमनुष्ठीयते–कस्यचित् तरोः शाखाया अवाक्शिरा लम्बते तापसः। अधश्च तस्य भूमौ अग्निर्ज्वलति तदुत्थं धूमं स पिवति तेनैवनशनो तीवति। 'रामभद्रः' इति कोमलेन आख्यामपदेन रामंप्रति वासन्त्याः प्रसन्नतामापन्नं चेत इति गम्यते। तच्च हिरण्यमय्याः प्रतिकृतेः श्रवणादिति मन्तव्यम्। 'अलङ्कुर्यात्' भूषयेत् आत्मन उपस्थित्या इति शेषः।।

Notes. 1.अब्रह्मण्यम्–See Act I, Para lxxi, Here अब्रह्मण्यम् उद्दोषितम् is equivalant to अब्रह्मण्यम् इति शब्द उद्घोषितः। 2. राजापचारम्–अप+चरं+घञ् भावे अपचारः misconduct, राज्ञः अपचारः misconduct on the king's part. तम। अन्तरेण्युक्ते द्वितीया। 3. निरूपयति–नि+रूप+णिच् स्वार्थे (चुरादि) + शतृ निरूपयन्। तस्मिन्। He was searching within himself for some lapse of his. 4. करुणामये–This epithet is used to imply that his pity was excited at the plight of the Brāhmaṇa. 5. अशरीरिणी–शरीरम् अस्ति अस्या इति शरीर+इनि सत्वर्थे। न शरीरिणी Speech cannot actually possess a body, it has the body for its source. 6. वृषलः–A Śūdra. As such he was not eligible for practising penance. 7. पृथिव्याम्–This is to say, in Rāma's own kingdom. Hence, the misdeed of the शूद्र indirectly affects his king राम also. 8. तप्यते etc.–Originally we had शम्बूकः तपः तपति with तपः as कर्म्म। If we want to imply ease in his practise of penance (सौकर्यद्योतन), we may treat तपः as कर्त्ता, but this कर्ता will have to be regarded as *like* कर्म by the rule "तपस्तपः कर्मकस्यैव"। The लट् now is neither कर्त्तरि nor कर्मणि but कर्मकर्त्तरि, the form being तप्यते with यक्। The case is peculiar as तपः still has कर्माविभक्ति and not कर्तृविभक्ति as is usual (witness भिनत्ति कुशलम्=भिद्यते कुशलः) in such cases. 9. शीर्षच्छेद्यः–शीर्ष means शिरः head. "उत्तमाङ्गं शिरः शीर्षम्" इत्यमरः। शीर्षस्य वेदः शीर्षच्छेदः। तं नित्यमर्हति इति शीर्षच्छेद+यत् शीर्षच्छेद्यः one always deserving to be beheaded. Followers of Pāṇini, however, suppose that शिरस् has here become शीर्ष in connection with यत्। Thus "शिरश्छेदं नित्यमर्हति शीर्षच्छेद्य. . . .प्रत्ययसन्नियोगेन शिरसः शीर्षभावो निपात्यते"–*Vṛttikāra* under the rule "शीर्षच्छेदात् यच्च"। Bhaṭṭoji also has the same. 10. ते–This is emphasised. तत्रैव, you have to do it personally. It is the duty of the king to punish sinners, hence you have to punish him and that without fail (नित्यम्), 11. विदिशः–विभिन्ना दिग्भ्यः विदिशः (विदिश् is the प्रातिपदिक) other than the four cardinal points, 'i.e.' the intervals between consecutive cardinal points. "दिशोर्मध्ये विदिक् स्त्रियाम्"। ताः। चर is सकर्मक। Comp. "तपश्चरति", 'उभौ लोकौ सञ्चरसि इमञ्चामुञ्च देवल" etc.

(*xvi*) आत्रेयी–भद्रे गम्यतेऽधुना।

वासन्ती–आर्ये आत्रेयि एवमस्तु। कठोरीभूतस्तु दिवसः।

तथाहि–

कण्डूलद्विपगण्डपिण्डकषणोत्कम्पेन सम्पातिभि-
घर्मस्त्रं सितबन्धनैः स्वकुसुमैरर्चन्ति गोदावरीम्।
छायापरिकरमाणविष्करमुखव्याकृष्टकीटत्वचः
कूजत्क्लान्तपोतकुक्कुटकुलाः कूले कुलायद्रुमाः।। 9।।

(इति निष्क्रान्ते)।

विष्कम्भकः

Ātreyī—Gentle friends, I go now.

Vāsantī—Be it so, noble Ātreyī, but the day has advanced. Thus (As you see)—

Nesting trees on the bank, on which rest flock of weary pigeons and of wood-cocks cooning and from the bark of which worms are pulled out with their beaks by birds scratching the trunk in the shade, are worshipping Dodāvarī with their own flowers which having their stalks loosened by the heat drop through the shake given by the rub of the itching lumps on the cheeks of elephants. (*Exeunt*).

Here ends the Viṣkambhaka.

मित–।'कठोरीभूतः' प्रौढ़तामन्नः। मध्याह्नो वर्त्तते इत्यर्थः। कण्डूलेति।

अन्वयः–छायापस्किरमाणविष्किरमुखव्याकृष्टकीटत्वचः कूजत्कान्तकपोत–कुक्कुटकुलाः कूले कलायद्रुमाः घर्मस्त्रंसितबन्धनैः कण्डूलद्विपगण्डपिण्डकषणोत्कस्पेन सम्पातिभिः स्वकुसुमैः गोदावरीम् अर्चन्ति।

व्याख्या–पश्य प्रखर रविकर परिहृत्य 'छायासु' अपस्किरमाणाः' भोज्यसंग्रहार्थं नखैरितस्तत आलेखनतत्पराः ये 'विष्किराः' पक्षिणः तेषां 'मुखैः' चञ्चुभिरिति यावत् 'व्याकृष्टाः' बहिर्निष्काशिताः 'कीटाः' याभ्यः तादृश्यः 'त्वचः' वल्कलानि येषां तथाविधाः, किञ्च 'कूजन्तः' रुवन्तः 'क्लान्ताः' आतपखिन्नाः ये 'कपीताः कुक्कुटाः' च तेषां 'कुलानि' समूहाः येषु तादृशाः ये 'कूले' तट स्थिताः 'कुलायद्रुमाः' पक्षिणाम् आवासवृक्षाः ते 'घर्मेण' आतपेन 'स्त्रंसितं' शिथिलितं 'बन्धनं' हन्तं येषां तैः अतएव

'कण्डू लानां कण्डूतियुक्तानां' 'द्विपगण्डपिण्डानां' वनगजगण्डस्थलीनां यत् 'काणं घर्षणं ततो जातो यः 'उत्कम्पः' दोलनं तेन 'सम्पातिभिः' बन्धशैथियात् पतद्भिः 'स्वकुसुमः' निजपुष्पराशिभिः 'गोदावरीम् अर्थन्ति' पूजयन्ति मध्याह्नकृत्यं गोदावर्य्याः कुर्वन्ति। एवमातपखिन्नाः पक्षिणो गजाः वृक्षाय। भवत्याः पुनरध्ववाहने अध्यवसायः। तत् शनैः शनै खेदं परिहृत्य गम्यताम् इति भावः।। 'विष्कम्भकः' इति कथांशानां योजकः।'वृत्तवर्त्तिष्यमाणानां कथांशानां निदर्शकः। संक्षिप्तार्थस्तु त्रिष्कम्भ आदावङ्कस्य दर्शितः।।"

Notes. 1. कण्डूल etc.–कण्डू is itch. कण्डूः लातः इति कण्डू+ला+क कर्त्तरि कण्डूलौ promoting itch. गण्डयोः पिण्डा वण्डपिण्डो the two lumps on the cheeks. द्वाभ्यां पिबन्ति इति द्वि+पा+क कर्त्तरि द्विपाः elephants. द्विपानां गण्डपिण्डौ द्विपगण्डपिण्डौ। कण्डूलौ द्विपगण्डपिण्डी itchy lumps of cheeks of elephants. उत्कम्प is due to the काषण।–कषणात् उत्कम्पः or–कषणस्य उत्कम्पः, सुप्सुपा or द्वतत्–। तेन। हेतौ श्या। It is the हेतु or सम्पतन। 2. सम्पादिभिः–साधु सम्पतन्ति इति सम्+पत्+णिनि साधुकारिणि कर्त्तरि सम्पातीनि invetiably falling. The reason is they are already loosened from their stalks by the heat, and then the shake given by the elephants drop them. 3. धर्म etc.–स्रंस+णिच्+क्त कर्मणि स्रंसितानि loosened. धर्म is heat. 4. छाया etc.–अप+कृ+शानच् कर्त्तरि अपस्किरमाणः scratching the cover off in quest of food. Here we have the आत्मनेपद by the Varttika "किरतेर्हर्षजीविकाकुलायकरणेषु इतिवक्तव्यम्"। जीविकाकरण s भक्ष्यसंग्रह। Next सुट् comes in before क by the rule "अपात् चतुष्पाच्छकुनिषु आलेखने"। व्याकृष्टकीट indicates भक्ष्यसंग्रह ; the worms are their food. 5. कूजत् etc.–The reading कान्त for क्लान्त has little to recommend it. कान्तता of the birds seems irrelevant in describing the effects of the solar heat. क्लान्त is preferable. 6. कुलाय etc.–The कुलाय here refers to the birds only. They were out in quest of food and have now come back oppressed by the heat. 7. *Remark.*–The verse describes the effect of heat. कण्डूल etc. is to show that elephants have come back to the shade after the fore-noon grazing. धर्म etc. describe the effect on trees in general. छाया etc. and कूजत् etc. explain how the birds are affected. All this is to warn Ātreyī of the risk she was running by venturing out in a sun that so much affects birds, beasts and trees in the forest. She has to proceed carefully. The time evidently was summer. 8. विष्कम्भकः–Sometimes the connection between what is about to follow and what has gone before is shown by something like an introduction to the Act following. This introduction is called विष्कम्भक (see मित–)

(xix) **(ततः प्रविशति सदयोद्यतशङ्गो रामभद्रः)।**

(*Then enters Rāmabhadra with sword but overcome by pity*).

रामः– रे हस्त दक्षिण मृतस्य शिशोर्द्विजस्य
जीवातवे विसृज शूद्रमुनौ कृपाणम्।
रामस्य गात्रमसि दुर्वहगर्भखिन्न-
सीताविवासनपटोः करुणा कुतस्ते ।।10।।

Rāma——Heigh ! Right-hand, drop the sword on the Śūdra ascetic for the resuscitation of the dead boy of the Brāhmaṇa. You are a limb of Rāma who easily banished Sītā drooping under her hardly bearable womb, whence can there be pity in you?

(कथञ्चित् प्रहृत्य) कृतं रामसदृशं कर्म। अपि जीबेत् स ब्रह्मण-शिशुः?

(*Striking with great unwillingness*) A deed is done becoming Rāma. Would the Brāhmaṇa boy revive ?

मित–। सदयेति–'दयया' सह 'उद्यतः' उच्छ्रितः उन्नमितः 'खङ्गी' येन यस्य वा। रे इति।

अन्वयः–रे दक्षिण हस्त द्विजस्य मृतस्य शिशोः जीवातये शूद्र सुनौ कृपाणं विसृज। दुर्वहगर्भखिन्नसीताविवासनपटोः रामस्य गात्रमसि, कुतसे करुणा।

व्याख्या–'रे दक्षिण द्विजस्य' ब्राह्मणस्य 'मृतस्य शिशोः जीवातवे' जीविताय जीवनाय [''जीवातरस्त्रियां भक्ते जीविते जीवनौषधे'' इति मेदिनी। तादर्थ्यै चतुर्थी] 'शूद्रमुनौ कृपाणं विसृज खङ्गं पातय। 'दुर्वहेणं' अतिगुरुणा 'गर्भेण खिन्ना' 'तदुदूवहनक्लिष्टा या 'सीता' तस्यः यत् 'विवासनं' बने परित्यागः तत्र 'पटोः' निपुणस्य अक्लेशेन तदवस्थामपि सीतां त्यक्तवतो 'रामस्य गात्रम् असि' तत् 'कुतः ते करुणा' नास्त्ययेव व करुणा, अतो ''विसृज शूद्रमुनौ कृपाणम्''। एतत्तु प्रहारकाले आत्मनि करुणासञ्चारमनुभूय हस्तं प्रत्याह।। कथञ्चिदिति–'कथञ्चित्' अतिक्लेशेन करुणमभिभूय इत्यर्थः।'सदृशम्' अनुरूपम्। प्राक् निरपराधा पत्नी परित्यक्ता सम्प्रति निरपराधी सुनिर्हितः। अन्योऽन्धानुरूपमेवैतत् द्वयम् इति भावः।

Notes. 1. सदय etc.–सदयम् उद्यतः सदयोद्यतः raised with pity. तादृशः

खड्गो यस्य, बहु- । 2. जीवातवे-जीव to live + आतु भावे जीवातुः (masc.) living. *i.e.,* coming back to life. तस्मै । The word is both masc. and neuter. 3. प्रहृत्य-The blow kills the ascetic. This is against stage-etiquette which prohibits the staging of death etc. 4. जीवेत्-सम्भावनायां लिङ् । अपि adds शङ्का to the सम्भावना । Would he revive, *i.e.,* I am not sure if he would.

(xx) **(प्रविश्य) दिव्यपुरुषः-जयति जयति देवः ।**

(*Entering*) A divine being—Prosper, Sire prosper.

दत्ताभये त्वयि यमादपि दण्डधारे
सञ्जीवितः शिशुरसौ मम चेयमृद्धिः ।
शम्बूक एष शिरसा चरणौ नतस्ते
सत्सङ्गजानि निधनान्यपि तारयन्ति ।। 11 ।।

With protection even from Yama promised, thou inflicting punishment, that child has revived and mine too is this glory. This is Śambūka bowed down to thy feet with his head. Resulting from contact with the good, even execution saves !

मित- । दत्तेति ।

अन्वयः-एष शम्बूकः शिरसा ते चरणौ नतः । यमादपि दत्तभये त्वयि दण्डधारे (सति) असौ शिशुः सञ्जीवितः मम च इयमृद्धिः । सतसङ्गजानि निधनान्यपि तारयन्ति ।

व्याख्या-'एषः' अयमहं शम्बूकः शिरसा ते चरणौ नतः' मूर्द्धा ते पादौ नमामि । कथं शम्बूकः ! कुतः पुनस्ते दिव्यं वपुः इत्याह-'यमादपि अभयं' भयाभावो 'दत्तं' येन तादृशे अचिन्तनीयप्रभावे 'त्वयि दण्डधारे' स्वहस्तेन शसितरि सति 'असौ शिशुः' ब्राह्मणबालकः 'सञ्जीवितः' यमात् मोचितः प्राप्तजीवनो जातः, प्रसङ्गात् पुनः 'मम च' ममापि इयम् ऋद्धिः' एषा दिव्यदेहधारणरूपा सम्पद् । देहनाशात् देहनाशात् देहलाभ इति नेतदाश्चर्य्यमित्याह 'सतां' माधूनां 'सङ्गात्' समागमात् 'जातानि निधनानि अपि' देहपाता अपि 'तारयन्ति' जीवयन्तेय्व न नाशयन्ति। ततु साधोर्भवत्तो देहनाशो मे प्रकृष्टतरदेहलाभायैव जात इति भावः ।।

Notes. 1. दिव्य etc.-दिवि भव इति दिब्+यत् दिव्यः । Hence Rāma did not at sight know who he was. 2. यस्मात्-पञ्चमी in connection with अभय by "भीत्रार्थानां भयहेतुः" । 3. दण्डधरि-दण्ड धारयति इति दण्ड+धारि+अण् कर्त्तरि दण्डधारः personally inflicting punishment. तस्मिन् । 4. सञ्चीवितः-This removes Rāma's doubt about the revival of the boy. शम्बूक knows of this revival becuse he is a दिव्यपुरुष now. 5. ऋद्धिः–Prosperity. The punishment secures me a promotion. This refers to his resplendent frame (दिव्यदेह)। 6. निधनानि–नि+धा+क्यु भवि निधनं death. Even death is life. 7. *Remark*–It seems the thought is improved if we transpose the halves of the verse. The salutatioin should be the first act on meeting the king. Hence जयति जयति देवः। शम्बूक एष शिरसा चरणौ नतस्ते seems quite natural. Besides unless परिचय proceds, मम चेयमृद्धिः is unintelligible.

(xxi) **रामः–द्वयमपि प्रियं नः तदनुभूयतामुग्रस्य तपसः फलम्।**

Rāma—Both are joy to me. So enjoy the fruit of your grim austerities.

यत्रानन्दाश्च मोदाश्च यत्र पुण्याभिसम्भवाः !
वैराजा नाम ते लोकास्तैजसाः सन्तु ते ध्रुवाः ।।11।।

May those luminous regions secured by merit known as Vairājā, where there is bliss and where there is joy, be yours for ever.

मित–। द्वयमिति–शिशोः सञ्जीवनं तव च ऋद्धिः इति द्वयम्। तदेव फलं दर्शयति यत्रेति।

अन्वयः–यत्र आनन्दाय यत्र मोदायं भोदाश्च ते पुण्याभिसम्भवाः वैराजा नाम तैजसाः लोकाः ते ध्रुवाः सन्तु।

व्याख्या–'यत्र' येषु लोकेषु 'आनन्दाश्च' मुखानि च 'मोदाश्च' हर्षा अपि अनुभूयन्ते 'ते' प्रसिद्धाः 'पुण्याभिसम्भवाः' सुकृतनिर्जिता उगस्य तपसः फलरूपाः 'वैराजा नाम' वैराजशब्देन आख्याताः 'तैजसाः' ज्योतिर्मयाः 'लोकाः ते' तव सम्बन्धे 'ध्रुवाः' सन्तु स्थिरा भवन्तु मा ते तेभ्यः कदापि प्रच्युतिभूत्। लोकास्ते सिद्धास्तपोभिः, आशसि ध्रुवास्ते भवन्तु इति भावः।।

Notes. 1. आनन्दाः–आनन्द here is 'bliss सुखप्रवाह। 2. मोदाः–is हर्ष joy. पुण्याभिसम्भवाः–पुण्य is तपस्। अभि+सम+भू+अप् अपादाने अभिसम्भव that from which something devolves i.e., source. पुण्यम् अभिसम्भवः एषाम्। The region (वैराज) are secured by merit (पुण्य)। 4. वैराजाः–विशेषेण राजते इति वि+राज+क्विप् कर्त्तरि विराज् the eternal soul. तस्य इमे इति विराज्+अण् वैराजाः। 5. तैजसाः–तैजस इमे तेजस्+अण् तैजसाः luminous. 6. सन्तु etc. –This embodies Rāma's wish (आशंसा) on behalf of शम्बूक। आशंसायां लोट्। This seems out of place because the regions are described as तपसः फलम्, hence they are independent of Rāma's आशंसा। Their permanency too is assured by तपस्। शम्बूक himself in the next para saying एष महिमा takes everything as already achieved and leaves nothing to आशंसा। In fact सन्तु here appears to be a copyists slip for सन्ति। With सन्ति construe –वैराजा नाम ध्रुवाः तैजसा लोकाः ते सन्ति। Explain –'वैराजा नाम ध्रुवाः' नित्याः 'तैसा लोकाः ते सन्ति' तपःसिद्धा वर्त्तन्ते। Those regions await you, to and अनुभूयताम् उणस्य तपसः फलम्। Translate thus –Those luminous eternal regions, secured by merit, where there...joy, are assured unto you. 7. *Remark* –The reading यवानन्दाय मोदाश्च यत्र पुण्याश्च सम्पदः is rejected because it goes against the प्रक्रम here. The verse begins with a यत्र and a च in the first predication. This style should be preserved if possible. It is seen preserved in the last statement यत्र पुण्याश्च सम्पदः। Hence मोदाश्च instead of यत्र मोदाय is objectionable.

(xxii) **शम्बूकः–युष्मत्पादप्रसादोपाय एष महिमा न तु तपसः फलम्। अथवा महदुपकृतं तपसा।**

Śambūka —This greatness has the favour of thy revered self for its source, and is not surely the result of penance. Or a great service has been rendered by penance.

अन्वेष्टव्यो यदसि भुवने भूतनाथः शरण्यो
मामन्विष्यन्निह वृषलकं योजनानां शतानि।
क्रान्त्वा प्राप्तः स इह तपसां सम्प्रसादोऽन्यथा चेत्
क्वायोध्यायाः पुनरुपगमो दण्डकायां वने वः ॥13॥

That thou, the lord of beings, the refuge, the one to be sought after in the world, hast come here having done hundreds of *yojanas* seeking me, this is the favour of penance in this matter. If otherwise, where is thy presence again in the forest of Daṇḍaka from Ayodhyā. 13.

मित–। युष्मदित्यादि। मान्या यूयं 'युष्मात्पादाः' ["प्रशंसावचनैश्च इति समासः]। युष्मत् पदानां पूज्यानां भवतां नः 'प्रसादः' अनुग्रहः स एव 'उपायः' पन्थाः आगममार्गः यस्य तादृशः 'एष महिमां अयं मे महान् उत्कर्षः। अथ भवान् मयि न प्राहरिष्यत् लोकानहं न प्राप्याम्। तत् भवदनुग्रहान्मे लोकप्राप्तिः न कि तपसा इत्यर्थः॥ अन्वेष्टव्य इति।

अन्वयः–इह भूतनाथः शरण्यः भुवने अन्वेष्टव्या असि वृषलकं माम् अन्विष्यन् योजनानां शतानि क्रान्त्वा इह प्राप्तः (इति) यत् स तपसां सम्प्रसादः। अन्यथा चेत् अयोध्याया दण्डकायां वने वः पुनरुपगमः कृ?

व्याख्या–'इह' अस्मिन् विषये मम लोकप्राप्तौ इति यावत् 'भूतनाथः' जगदीश्वरः 'शरण्यः' जगत्त्राता अतएव 'भुवने' जगति 'अन्वेष्टव्यः' परसंश्रयत्वेन योगिभिरपि विचेतव्यः। मानवदेहेन गूढस्वरूपः सन् न अन्विष्यसे अन्वेष्यथा वा किन्तु सम्प्रति दिव्यरूपोह जानामि अन्वेष्टव्य इति। एवंविधः 'असि' त्वम् [अव्ययमेतत् त्वमर्थे, यद्वा–'प्राप्तः असि' इति योज्यम्।] 'वृषलकं' असत्यपि अधिकारे तपश्चरन्तं कुत्सितं वृषलं यद्रं 'माम् अन्विष्यन्' विचिन्वन् 'योजनानां शतानि क्रान्त्वा' अतिक्रम्य 'इह' अस्यां दण्डकायां 'प्राप्तः' आगतः इति 'यत् स तपसां सम्प्रसादः' अनुग्रहः। 'अन्यथा चेत्' यदि विपरीतं स्यात् तपश्चेत् नाचरितम् 'अयोध्यायाः 'दण्डकायां वने' सुदूरे दण्डकारण्ये 'वः पुनः उपगमः क्व' पुनरागमनं कुत्र स्थितम्। असम्भवः उपगम इत्यर्थः। ममास्मिन्नभ्युदये भवता दण्डपातनं हेतुः। दण्डपाताने पुनः तपो हेतुः। अत उच्यते मया "महदुपकृतं तपसा" इति।।

Notes. 1. युष्मत् etc. –पाद is प्रशंसावचन। "हस्तपाशतटाः पादपालीम-चर्चिकादयः" so says गणकार। But is प्रशंसावचन only when final in a compound. Hence uncompounded it does not imply प्रशंसा। Thus no वाक्य with पाद can be given ; consequently we have a नित्यसमास with अस्वपदविग्रह। प्रशस्ता यूयं युष्मत्पादा। उपेयते फलं प्रति गच्छति अनेन इति उ+इ (or अय) + घञ् करणे उपायः means. Now see मित–। 2. महिमा–महती भाव इति महत्+इमनिच् महिमा greatness, *i.e.*, accession *to* divine status, 4. उपकृतम्–उप+कृ+क्त भावे। 5. अन्वेष्टव्यः etc. –अनु+इष+तव्य कर्मणि to be sought after. The तव्य is significant. The whole word has to search for you –"has to" search, not that it "has searched" or 'is searching'. This is because no one knows you yet as भूतनाथ and शरण्य screened as you are in human frame. I know because I am divine now. भूतनाथ and शरण्य explain why अन्वेष्टव्य। 6. असि–अव्यय meaning त्वम्। Or construe प्राप्तः असि। 7. वृषलकम्–कुत्सितो वृषल इति वृषल+कन् कुतसिते। 8. सद्रह etc. सः is masculine because it goes with समासादः which is the विधेयः and prominent (विधेय प्राधान्यात्)। इह refers to the matter in hand, *i.e.*, the lift of शम्बूक। 9. दण्डकायाम्–Both दण्डक and दण्डका are seen.

(*xxiii*) रामः–कि नाम दण्डकेयम् (सर्वतोऽवलोक्य) आम।

Rāma—Really, is this the Daṇḍaka ? (*Looking round*) Yea—

स्निग्धश्यामाः क्वचिदपरतो भीषणाभोगारूक्षाः
स्थाने स्थाने मुखरककुभो झाङ्कृतैर्निर्झराणाम्।
एते तीर्थाश्रमगिरिसरिद्गर्त्तकान्तारमिश्राः
सन्दृश्यन्ते परिचितभुवो दण्डकारण्यभागाः।।14।

These I see before me are tracts of the Daṇḍaka forest—a jumble of watering-places, hermitages, hills, streams, lakes, woods of which the grounds are familiar—somewhere attracitvely blue, elsehwhere repulsive in their awful expanse, in places again resounding the quarters with the wash of rushing springs.

मित–। किं नमिति–'किं प्रश्ने।'नाम' सम्भाव्ये। वितर्के पर्यवसानम। दण्डका न वा इति वितर्कः।'आम्' इति प्रतिवचनावधारण्योरव्ययम्, इह अवधारणे। दण्डवैव इत्यवधाणम्।। अवधारण्स्य समर्थनमाह स्निग्धेति।

अन्वयः–एते परिचितभुवः तीर्थाश्रगिरिसरिद्त्तकान्तारमिश्राः (अतएव) क्वचित् स्निग्धयामाः अपरतः भीषणभोगरूक्षाः स्थाने स्थाने निर्भराणां झाङ् कृतेः मुखरककुभः दण्डकारणभागाः सन्दृश्यन्ते।

व्याख्या–'एते' पुरोवर्त्तिनः 'परिचिता' दृष्ट्पूर्वा 'भूः' येषां तादृशाः विदितसन्निवेषाः 'तीर्थैः जलावतारैः शैलैः 'सरिद्भिः' नदीभिः 'गर्त्तः विलैसरोभिरित्यर्थः 'कान्तारैः वनैश्च 'मिश्राः' सङ्कुलाः अक्रमसन्निविष्टैस्तीर्थादिभिः परिव्याप्ताः अतएव 'क्वचित् स्निग्धश्यामाः' निविडतरुराजिभिः प्रसन्नहरिताः 'अपरतः' स्थानान्तरे 'भीषणेन' भीमेन महता इत्यर्थः 'आभागेन' विस्तारेण 'रुक्षाः' अप्रियदर्शनाः 'स्थाने स्थाने निर्झराणां वारिप्रवाहाणां 'झाङ् कृतैः' अधः पतनशब्दैः 'मुखराः' निनादिताः 'ककुभः' दिशः येषु तादृशाः 'दण्डकारण्यस्य भागा' प्रदेशाः 'सन्दृश्यन्ते' लक्ष्यन्ते।।

Notes. 1. स्निग्धश्यामाः–स्निह+क्त कर्त्तरि स्निग्ध lit. *wet* here *attractive.* श्याम blue, here *green.* स्निग्धाश्च तेश्यामाश्च *attratively green* through an exuberance of foliage. 2. भीषण etc. –आभोग is पूर्णता full extension "पूर्णन्वयतवाभागौ" इत्यनेकार्थः। भीषणभोगः, कर्म्मधा–। तेन रूक्षाः, सुप्सुपा। A vast expanse of a monotonous nature is not at all pleasant. स्थाने स्थाने–At proper places, *i.e.,* places where the springs form something like water-falls. Hence, there is अवधारण and "स्वार्थे अवधार्यमाणे–" इति द्विर्वचनम्। वीस्मा is not intended because that would make *all* places resound with the noise of water falls. 4. झाङ् कृतैः–झाङ् is an imitation of the splash–an onomatopoeia –अनुकरणशब्द। It is a गतिसंज्ञक word by the rule "अनकरणञ्चनितिपरम्"। झाङ्+कृ+क्त भावे झाङ् कृतानि utterance of the sound झाङ्, गतितत्पुरुष। 5. तीर्थ etc.— गर्त literally is a hole बिल। It stands for natural lakes. In some parts of Bengal these lakes still go by name of बिल। मिश्रयन्ते इति मिश्र+णिच् स्वार्थे (चुरादि)+घञ् कर्मणि मिश्राः jumbled up. तीर्थ, आश्रम गिरि etc. are all in a confused mass here. Hence here स्निग्धश्यामाः, there भीषणभोगरूक्षाः, elsewhere सुखरककुभः। 6. *Remark* — The verse is ordinarilly construed thus–क्वचित् स्निग्धयामाः अपरतः भीषणभोगरूक्षाः स्थाने स्थाने निर्झरारणां झाङ्कृतै मुखरककुभः तीर्थाश्रमगिरि सरिद्गर्त्तकान्तारमिश्राः परिचितभुवः एते दण्डकारण्यभागाः सन्दृश्यन्ते। This ignores the force of the different attributives in the verse. We have therefore altered the Prose Order.

(*xxiv*) **शम्बूकः–दण्डकैवेयम्। अत्र किल पूर्वं निवसता देवेन–**

Śambūka—This is indeed the Daṇḍaka. Formerly by Sire, living here, we are told (Or—to be sure)—

चतुर्दश सहस्त्राणि रक्षसां भीमकर्मणाम्।
त्रयश्च दूषणखरत्रिमूर्धानो रणे हताः।। 15।।

Were killed at fight fourteen thousand of Rākṣasas of dire deeds, also the three—Khara, Dūṣaṇa and Trimūrdhan. (Trisiras).

तेन सिद्धक्षेत्रे जनस्थाने मादृशामपि भीरुजनानाम् अकुतोभयः सञ्चारो जातः।

Whence in Janasthāna, the land of those that are successful at penance, fearless passage has been secured even unto timid people like himself.

मित–। 'किल' इति वार्त्तायाम् अधारणे वा 'पूर्व हताः पूर्वं निवसतां इति वा अन्वयः।। 'सिद्धानां' तपःसिद्धानां 'क्षेत्रं' स्थानं तपश्चरणभूमिः, यन तपस्तप्तासिद्धा भवन्ति तत्।। 'मादृशां भीरुजनानामपि' इत्यन्वयः। 'अविद्यमानं कुतोऽपिभयं' यस्मिन् 'सञ्चारे' विचरणे स 'जातः' सम्पन्नः।।

Notes. 1. मादृशम्–अहमिव दृश्यमानाः मामिव आत्मानं पश्यन्ति इति अस्मद्+दृश+कञ् कर्मकर्त्तरि मादृशाः। तेषाम्। 2. अकुतीभयः–This is a तत् पुरुष (by निपातन in the मयूरव्य संकादि class) although the वाक्य (see *Mitabh—*) tempts one to call it a बहुव्रीहि। Qual. सञ्चारः।

(*xxv*) रामः—न केवलं दण्डका जनस्थानमपि।

Rāma—Janasthāna too, not Daṇḍaka alone.

शम्बूकः—वाढ़म्। एतानि खलु सर्वभूतलोमहर्षणानि उन्मत्तचण्डश्वापदकुलसङ्कुलगिरिगह्वराणि जनस्थानपर्य्यन्तदीर्घारण्यानि दक्षिणां दिशमभिवर्त्तन्ते। तथाहि—

Śamb.—Certainly. These are indeed the long lines of forest at the outskirts of Janasthāna, stretching away to the south, that put up the hair of all beings on end, where the mountain-dens are full of mad and ferocious beasts of prey. Thus (Here are)—

निष्कूजस्तिमिताः क्वचित् क्वचिदपि प्रोच्चण्डसत्त्वस्वनाः
स्वेच्छासुप्तगभीरघोष भुजगश्वासप्रदीप्ताग्नयः।
सीमानः प्रदरोदरेषु विलसत्स्वल्पाम्भसो यास्वयं
तृष्यद्भिः प्रतिसूर्य्यकैरजगरस्वेदद्रवः पीयते।।16।।

The borders, where a little water shines at the bottom of mountain clefts and yet this running sweat of the python is drunk by thirsty chameleons, are somewhere still and noiseless, elsewhere again, though full of terrible roars of wild beasts have fire kindled by the breath of deep-throated snakes sleeping at ease.

मित–।'वाढ़म्' दृढ़म् जनस्थानमपि।'बाढ़' इति अनन्तरोक्तं द्रढ़यति। [''बाढं दृढ़े प्रतिज्ञायाम्'' इति विश्वः,'एतानि' दृश्यमानानि 'खलु जनस्थानस्य' यः 'पर्यन्तः' प्रान्तभागः तव स्थितानि 'दीर्घारण्यानि सुदूरप्रसृतानि काननानि 'दक्षिणांदिशम् अभिवर्त्तन्ते' तां प्रति गच्छन्ति। किम्भूतानि? –अरण्यानि ?–'सर्वभूतानां लोहमहर्षणानि' भयङ्कराणि। पुनः किम्भूतानि 'उन्मत्तैः' मदोदग्रैः 'चण्डैः' प्रकृति कीपनैः 'श्वापदकुलैः सङ्कुलानि' व्याप्तानि 'गिरिगह्वराणि' येषु तादृशानि दीर्घारण्यानि। लोमहर्षणत्वं दर्शयति निष्क्जेति।

अन्वयः—प्रदरोदरेषु विलसत्स्वल्पाम्भसः सीमान्–यासु तृष्यद्भिः प्रतिसूर्य्यकैः अयम् अजगरस्वेदद्रवः पीयते–क्वचित् किुजस्तिमिताः क्वचित् प्रोचण्डसत्वस्वनाः अपि स्वेच्छासुप्तगभीरघोषभुजश्वासप्रदीप्ताग्नयः।

व्याख्या– 'प्रदरीदरेषु' विलगर्भेषु 'विलसन्ति' प्रकाशमानानि 'स्वल्पानि अम्भांसि' जलानि यासु तादृश्यः 'सीमानः' प्रान्तभूमयः–'यासु 'सीमसु 'तृष्यद्भिः'

पिपासितैः 'प्रतिसूर्यकैः' क्लकलासैः 'अयम्' एष 'अजगराणां' महाकायानां सर्पाणां 'स्वेदद्रवः' प्रवाहेण सवत् प्रभूतं धर्मजलं 'पीयते' प्रदरस्थस्थ जलस्य स्वल्पतया तत् परित्यज्य प्रभूतमिदं धर्म्मजलं पीयते तादृयः सीमानः-'छचित्' छापि 'निष्क् जस्तिमिताः' निश्चलाश्च माणिपरिस्पन्दबिरहात् निःशब्दाः 'क्वचित्' कुत्रचित् पुनः 'प्रोच्चण्डाः' अतिभीमाः 'सत्त्वस्वना' सिंह व्याघ्रगजादिगर्जनानि यासु तादृश्यः 'अपि स्वेच्छयां' यथेच्छं 'सुप्तानां गभीरघोषाणां' गुरुगर्जनानां 'भुजगानाम्' अजगराणां 'श्वासेन' सविषेण निःश्वासवायुना 'प्रदीप्तः अग्नि' यासु [यद्वा-'भुजगश्वासः' एव 'प्रदीप्तः अग्निः' यासु] तादृश्यः दृश्यन्ते। क्वचित् "निष्कम्पवृक्षा निभृतद्विरेफा मूकाण्डजाः शान्तमृगप्रचाराः" चित्रार्पिता इव सीमानः, अन्यत्र श्वापदानां भैरवरवः तथापि सुखसुप्ता अजगराः, गुरु च तेषां निःश्वासर्गर्जनं नासाविवराच्च वायुना सह निःसृतः प्रदीप्तो वह्निः सुप्तानां प्रवहत् धर्मजलञ्च पीयते कृकलासैः इति परा काष्ठा भयानकस्य।।

Notes. 1. वाढ़म्-वाह+क्त कर्मणि वाढ़ admitted. This is an emphatic confirmation. Certainly this is Janasthāna. Some take this as an अव्यय ending in म। But the चादि and स्वरादि lists do not include it. However, as those lists are only illustrative not exhaustive (आकृतिगण), we may treat it as an अन्वय implying उक्तिदार्ढ्य। 2. सर्वभूत etc.-लोमानि हर्ष्यन्ते एभिः इति लोमन्+हृष+ण्चि्+ल्युट् करणे लोमर्हाणणि those that raise the hairs on end, *i.e.,* terrible. 3. etc.-उन्मत्त referes to a temporary display of temper, चण्ड speaks of their nature. Hence उन्मत्त etc. means-ferocious beasts in a state of excitement. शुनः पदमिव पदमेषां श्वापदाः। श्वपद is expected, but "शुनो दन्तदंष्ट्राकर्णकुन्दवराहपुच्छपादेषु दीर्घो वाच्यः" lengthens the vowel yielding श्वपदाः। Now see *Mitabh*-4. जनस्थान etc.-परिगतः अन्तः पर्य्यन्तः the border-land. Now see *Mitabh*— 5. निष्क्ज etc.-The very stillness is awful. 6. कचिदपि-Here again we have differed from commentators and taken अपि with what follows thus completely altering the sense of the verse. We believe this is an improvement. 7. प्रोच्चण्ड etc.-For समास see *Mitabh*—The uproar not disturb the huge snakes. See next. 8. स्वेच्छ्र etc.-स्वेच्छासुप्त shows that they were sleeping undisturbed by the howling of the beasts of prey. गभीरघोष shows that the snakes were adding to the noise. The breathing of snakes is noisy, श्वासप्रदीप्ताग्नि may be taken in two ways as suggested in the *Mitabh*—

It may mean that fire was lighted by their breathing ; or that the breath itself was blazing fire. The latter is preferable, because with the first explanation we get a forest fire which will at once rouse the अजगर and cause a general stampede among beasts and birds. 9. विलसत् etc.—The water स्वल्प, because the time was summer (see verse 9. कण्डूल etc.). Either through scantiness or from its quality it was beneath notice of the thirsty chamleons. 10. अजगर etc.—The अजगरs were the very snakes that were स्वेच्छासुप्त। Once sweats profusely when one sleeps in the summer at mid-day. The sweat of the sleeping snakes ran in streams (स्वेदद्रव) and was too tempting a delicacy for the thirsty chameleons to refuse ! ! They shunned the waters in the caves and slaked their thirst here.

(xxvi) **रामः—**

पश्यामि च जनस्थानं भूतपूर्वखरालयम्।
प्रत्यक्षानिव वृत्तान्तान् पूर्वाननुभवामि च।। 17।।

Rāma—I see Janasthana, Khara's abode of old, and simultaneously all the old incidents I feel as if before my eyes.

(सर्वतोऽवलोक्य) प्रियारामा हि सर्वथा वैदेह्यासीत्, एतानि तानि नाम कान्ताराणि। किमतः परं भयानकं स्यात्। (सास्रम्)। – (राम–)

(*Looking round*) Verily Vaidehī was ever fond of the woods, and these are those very forests ! What coule be more dreadful (to me) than this ? (*With emotion*) (Rāma).

मित–।

अन्वयः–भूतपूर्वस्वरालयं अनस्थानं पश्यामि च पूर्वान् वृत्तान्तान् प्रत्यक्षानिव अनुभवामि च।

व्याख्या–'भूतपूर्व' पूर्व भूतं 'खरस्य' रावणभ्रातुः 'आलयं निवासं 'जनस्थानं पश्यामि च' तत्क्षणं 'पूर्वान् वृत्तान्तान्' शूर्पणखासमागमं खरादिनिधनं सीताहरणम् इत्येतत् प्रासङ्गिकञ्च सर्वम् 'प्रत्यक्षान् इव' लोचनपथे वर्तमानान् इव 'अनुभवामि च'। खरालयदर्शनेन युगपत् पूर्ववृत्तान्तानुभव इति हौ चकारौ द्योतयतः। 'सर्वथा' सर्वप्रकारेण वासकृच्छ्रेऽपि सति इति भावः 'वैदेही प्रियारामाहि' वनप्रिया एव 'आसीत्'। 'एतानि' दृश्यमानानि 'तानि नाम' तान्येव प्रियारामाया वैदेह्याः प्रियाणि 'कान्ताराणि'

वनानि, कुत्र पुनः सा प्रिया मे। अहो दुखम्, अतः परै एतद्दर्शनादधिकं मृतसम्बन्धे 'किं' भयानकं स्यात्' न किमपि। असह्यमेतद्दर्शनं मे इत्यर्थः।।

Notes. 1. भूतपूर्व etc.–पूर्व भूतः भूतपूर्वः, सुप्सुपा। भूत leads in the compound (पूर्वनिपात) by निपातन in the rule "भूतपूर्वे चरट्"। भूतपूर्वः खरालयः or भूतपूर्वः खरालयो यस्मिन्। तम्। He speaks of खरालय because he is reminded of it by शम्बूक in sl. 15. above. 2. प्रत्यक्षान्–For प्रत्यक्ष see ante. 3. पूर्वान्–By पूर्व he referes generally to all the incidents of his stay in Janasthana. 4. प्रियारामा–आरमति अस्मिन् इति आ+रम+घञ् अधिकरणे आराम: garden, here, forest, because refers to it by कान्ताराणि। प्रियः आरामः अस्या प्रियारामा or आरामप्रिया। The पूर्वनिपात of प्रिय is optional by "वा प्रियस्य"। 5. तानि–Those that were dear to वैदेही। 6. नाम–निण्श्चये। Tee very same that were dear etc. 7. कान्तराणि–कान्तार is कानन। "कान्तारं काननं प्रोक्तम्" इत्यनेकार्थः। This refers to the आराम in प्रियारात्मा। Hence आराम there has to mean not उपवन but वन। 8. भयानकम्–Because the sight awakens painful memories. 9. सास्रम्–अस्र is अश्रु। "असमश्रुणि शोणिते"। But the अश्रु here is to be taken as emotion only—emotion that chokes the voice, not actual tears. Rāma is careful that his emotion be not noticed by शम्बूक ; hence in para xxix we find सवाष्पस्तम्भम्। 9. *Remark*—This could not have been within Śambūka's hearing. The thought is such as a sufferer usually reserves to himself or communicates to a close friend only. Perhaps the text was रामः (स्वगतम्) which has been altered by copyists.

(xxvii) **(राम–)**

त्वया सह निवत्स्यामि वनेषु मधुगन्धिषु।
इति चारमतेहासौ स्नेहस्तस्याः स तादृशः।।18।।

(Rāma—) 'With thee I will live in sweet-scented forest" on this view alone she enjoyed it here. Such was that love of hers.

अकिञ्चिदपि कुर्वाणः सौख्यैर्दुःखान्यपोहति।
तत्तस्य किमपि द्रव्यं यो हि यस्य प्रियो जनः।।19।।

He is indeed one's indescribable treasure who is one's beloved. (He) chases away one's sorrows with joy though doing nothing whatsoever.

मित–। इह किं वस्तु तस्याः प्रियमासीदित्याह त्वयेति।

अन्वयः–त्वया सह मधुगन्धिषु वनेषु निवत्स्यामि इति च इह असौ अरमत। तादृशः तस्याः स स्नेहः।

व्याख्या–'त्वया' प्रियेण 'सह' त्वत्साहचर्य्यादेव मत्सम्बन्धे 'मधुगन्धिषु' मकरदवासितेषु 'वनेषु निवत्स्यामि इति च' इत्येव 'इह' अस्मिन् दुरासदे कान्तारे 'असौ' सीता 'अरमत' ननन्द। वासस्त्वया सह इत्येव मे पर्य्याप्तम्, एतन्मात्रेणापि काननं सर्वम् उद्गन्धि अपि मधुगन्धि मम सस्पत्स्यते इति तस्या आनन्दः। 'तादृशः तथाविधः अनिर्वचनीय इत्यर्थः 'तस्याः सः' मयि 'स्नेहः आसीत्।। किं कृतं त्वया यत् त्वत्साहचर्ये एवं तस्या बहुमानः इत्याह अकिञ्चिदिति।

अन्वयः–यः यस्य प्रियः जनः तत् तस्य किमपि हि द्रव्यम्। (सः) अकिञ्चित् अपि कुर्वाणः सौख्यैः दुःखानि अपोहति।

व्याख्या–'यो यस्य प्रियो जनः' प्रीतिपात्रं 'तत्' प्रीतिपात्रं 'तस्य सम्बन्धे 'किमपि हि' इतरविलक्षणम् अनिर्वचनीयमेव द्रव्यं' वस्तु। इतरविलक्षणतां दर्शयति–'अकिञ्चित्' न किञ्चित् 'अपि कुर्वाणः' आचरन् 'सौख्यैः' सुखसन्तानैः 'दुःखानि अपोहति' दूरीकरोति। सामान्यतो हि लोके कश्चित् प्रीतिकर किञ्चित् कुर्वन् सुखयति अयन्तु अकिञ्चिदपि कुर्वाणः इति इतरविलक्षणता। प्रियोऽहमासं सीतायाः अतः किञ्चितकरणनपेक्षया अपि "मया सहं" इत्येव सा अप्रीयत इति श्लोकयोराशयः।।

Notes. 1. मधुगन्धिषु–मधुनः गन्ध इव गन्धः एवाम् एषु वा मधुगन्ध+इत् समासान्त by "उपामनाच्च"। Forest-life is bitter ; with you (त्वया सह) it will be honey-scented to me. The compound is usually taken as a स्वरूपकथन, thus–मधुनो गन्धः मधुगन्धः। स अस्ति एषु इति मधुगन्ध+इनि मत्वर्थे। This is because sweet-scented flowers are always blooming in forests. This interpretation lacks the poetryof the first. 2. इति च etc.–इति gives the reason. The त्त implies अवधारण। This much only, nothing more. इह in the forest. The reason why she enjoyed it here was that she had my company. This is the reading in the Bombay edition with Virarāghava's Commentary. With this, the future in निवस्त्यामि is rather awkward, निवसामि in the present suits better. Vidyasāgara has इव for इह (इति चारमतेवासौ) which suits निवत्स्यामि if we suppose that the verse speaks of the time of leaving Ayodhya. But the इव–as if she enjoyed it—takes from the स्नेह which is not desir-able. One of Vidyasāgara's manuscripts reads इति हा रमते सीता। There the present in रमते is troublesome the reference still being to the moment of leaving Ayodhyā. The choice seems to lie between इति चारमतेहासौ

and इति हा रमते सीता। 3. अकिञ्चित् etc.—The whole पाद is not a compound because अपि intervenes. अकिञ्चित्कुर्वाणः may be allowed as a rare instance of an असमर्थसमास। 4. सौख्यैः–सुखमेव इति सुख+ष्यञ् स्वार्थे सौख्यम्। The plural implies a succession of सुख। 5. तत्– The विधेय is द्रव्य which isneuter and prominent here. The प्रियो जनः is taken not as a प्रियो जनः but as किमपि द्रव्यम्। Hence विधेयप्राधान्यात् क्लीवत्वम्। 6. किमपि–The पि adds अनिर्व्वचनीयता। Comp. "स्फुरत हृदये कोऽपि पुरुषः", "किमपि हृदये कृत्वा मन्त्रयेथे" etc.

(*xxviii*) **शम्बूकः–तदलमेभिर्दुरासदैः। अथैतानि मदकलमयूरकण्ठ-कोमलच्छविभिवकीर्णानि पर्वतैः, अविरलनिविष्टनोलबहलच्छायतरुण-तरुषमण्डितानि, असम्भ्रान्तविविधमृगयूथानि पश्यतु महानुभावः प्रशान्तगम्भीराणि मध्यमारण्यकानि।**

Śamb.—Then away with these inacessible regions [*Or*—this repulsive scenery]. Now, let Your Eminence behold these still and sombre forests in the interior with herds of deer of different kinds (roaming) undistrubed, adorned with groups of densely grown dark and very shady young trees, strewed with hillocks having the soft look of the throat of a peacock cooing with joy.

इह समदशकुन्ताक्रान्तवाणीरवीरुत्-
प्रसवसुरभिशीतस्वच्छतोया वहन्ति।
फलभरपरिणामश्यामजम्बूनिकुञ्ज-
स्खलनमुखरभूरिस्त्रोतसो निर्झरिण्यः।। 20।। (शम्बू–)

Here flow hill stream having clear and cool waters scented by the flowers of cane-twigs that are lighted upon by hilarious birds and whose strong currents murmur as they glide through groups of Jambu trees that are blue through the ripening of their load of berries. (Samb.—)

मित–। तदिति। 'तत्' तस्मात् यतो भवतामनाग्रह एतेषु लक्ष्यते तस्मात् 'दुरासदैः' दुर्गमैः अप्रीतिकरैः 'एभिः पर्यन्तकाननैः अलम्'। रामं निरुक्तरं पश्यन् एवमाह शम्बूकः।।'अथ महानुभावः' भवान्'एतानि' इतो दृश्यमानानि 'प्रशान्तानि' निष्कम्पाणि 'गम्भीराणि' अप्रधृष्याणि उदाराणि 'मध्यमानि' जनस्थानमध्यवर्त्तीनि 'अरण्यकानि' वनानि। किम्भुतानि तानि? –'मदेन' हर्षेण 'कलः' मधुरं रुवन् यः 'मयुरः' तस्य 'कण्ठस्य' इव 'कोमला' स्निग्धनीला 'छविः' येषां तादृशैः 'पर्वतैः अवकीर्णानि'

व्याप्तानि। पुनः किम्भूतानि? –'अविरलनिविष्टाः' निविडसंरूढाः 'नीलाः' हरितवर्णाढ्याः 'बहलच्छायाः' छायाप्रधानाः ये 'तरुणतरवः' नवपादपाः तेषां 'षण्डैः' समूहैः 'मण्डितानि' भूषितानि। पुनः किम्भूतानि? –असम्भ्रान्तानि' अत्रस्तानि 'विविधमृगाणां नानाहरिणानां 'यूथानि' येषु तानि।। इहेति।

अन्वयः–इह समदशकुन्ताक्रान्तवाणीवीरुत्पसवसुरभिशीतस्वच्छतोयाः फलभरपरिणामश्यामजम्बू- निकुञ्जस्वलनमुखरमूरिस्रोतसः निर्झरिण्यः वहन्ति।

व्याख्या–'इह' एषु मध्यमारण्य केषु 'समदैः' मदमत्तैः 'शकुन्तैः' पक्षिभिः 'आक्रान्ताः उत्पत्य श्रिताः याः 'वाणीरवीरुधः' वेतसलताः:तासां 'प्रसवैः पुष्पैः शकुन्ताश्रयणत् कम्पितानां लतानां वृन्त्यच्युतैः पुष्पैरित्यर्थः 'सुरभीणि' वासितानि 'शतानि अस्मिन् ग्रीष्मेऽपि अनुष्णानि 'स्वच्छानि' विमलानि सुरभित्वशीतत्वस्वच्छत्वैः निदाधे सुखपेयानि इति शेषः तोयानि' जलानि यासां तादृश्यः किञ्च 'पलभरस्य' फलराशेः 'परिणमेन' वक्वतया 'श्यामेषु' फलानां कृष्णत्वात् कृष्णेषु 'जम्बूनिकुञ्जेषु' जम्बू पादपगुल्मेषु यत् 'स्खलनं' प्रसरणं तेन 'मुखराः' पादप्रतिघातैः शब्दायमानाः 'भूरिस्रोतसः' प्रवलप्रवाहाः यासां तादृश्य 'निर्झरिण्यः' गिरिनद्यः 'वहन्ति' प्रसरन्ति। अनातपे जम्बू निकुञ्जे विश्रान्ताः क्लान्ता अध्वगाः पक्वानि फलानि उपभुज्य सुरभीणि शीतानि स्वच्छानि च तोयानि निपीय झटिति स्वस्था भवन्ति, तत् रमणीयानि इमानि मध्यमारण्यकानि पश्यतु देवः इति।।

Notes. 1. तदम् etc.—Rāma was musing not replying to Śambūka's remark "एतानि खलु etc." Hence Śambūka thought that his terrible picture of the outskirts (निष्कूजस्तिमिताः etc.) was not inviting to Rāma. So, he drops he subject (तदलम् etc.) to take up something more agreeable. 2. दुरासदैः–दुःखेन आसद्यन्ते इति दुर्+आ+सद+खल् कर्मणि दुरासदाः etc. cp. "दुरासदवनज्यायान् गम्यस्तुङ्गोपि भूधरः" —*Kirāt* XI. 3. मदकल etc.—This shows the attractiveness of the scenery. 4. पर्वतैः–Here the reading पर्यन्तैः seems unsuitable. It sounds queer to say पर्यन्तैः अवकीर्णानि (strewn with outskirts). Besides the पर्यन्त has been dropped with the words तदलम् etc. 5. अविरल etc.—अविलरनिविष्ट closely grown. The epithet shows that it was pleasant here in मध्यमारण्य to roam about because the walks were abundantly shady. 6. असम्भ्रन्त etc.–असम्भ्रान्त not scared. They were accustomed to human presence. One can enjoy it here by watching the different kinds of deer (*Or better*—of animals in a general) grazing at ease. 7. इह etc.—The verse adds another attraction to those mentioned in the prose preceding. When you are tired with the inspection of mountain scenes and of the animals at ease, rest in the shade of one of the numerous Jambugroves. You will find plenty of excellent-eating ripe fruits there if you are hungry (फलभर etc.) and water as well—nice, cool, limpid, scented water—so allay your thirst. 8. समद etc. Comp. ''उपान्तवानीरवनोपगूढ़ान्यालक्ष्यपारिप्लवसारसानि''–*Kālidāsa.* The water possessed all the requirements of an agreeable drink in summer. The time was about mid-summer as already pointed out. 9. फलभर etc.–भूरि is बहुल plentiful ; here 'strong'. It is the strenth of the current that causes the murmur by striking against the trees with force.

(*xxix*) **(शम्बू–) अपि च**

(Samb.—) Moreover,

दधति कुहरभाजामत्र भल्लू कयूना-
मनुरसितगुरूणि स्त्यानमम्बूकृतानि।
शिशिरकटुकषायः स्त्यायते शल्लकीना-
मिभदलितविकीर्णग्रन्थिनिष्यन्दगन्धः।।21।।

Here the spluttering whines of bear-cubs lying in dens, magnified by echoes, acquire volume ; the cool, pungent and agreeable odour of the gum oozing from the knots of the Sallaki crushed and scatterd by elephants, is intensified [*Or*—prevades all round]

मित–। दधतीति।

अन्वयः–अव कुहरभाजां भल्लूकय्नाम अनुरसितगुरुणि अम्बूकृतानि स्तयानं दधति। शल्लकीनां शिशिरकटुकषायः इभदतिविकीर्ण- ग्रन्थिनिष्यन्दगन्धः स्तायते।

व्याख्या–'अत्र' एषु मध्यमारण्यकेषु 'कुहरभाजां' गुहागतानां 'भल्लूकयूनां' तरुणभल्ल्कानाम् 'अनुरसितैः' प्रतिध्वनिभिः 'गुरूणि' महान्ति 'अम्बूकृतानि' थुत्कारसमेताध्वनयः 'स्त्यानं दधति' वृद्धिं भजन्ते। किञ्च 'शलकानां करिप्रियाणं तरुविशेषाणां 'शिशिरः' शीतलः 'कटः' तीव्रः 'कषायः' सुरभिश्च 'इभैः' गजैः 'दलिताः' मर्दिताः 'विकीर्णाः' इतस्ततो विक्षिप्तायये 'ग्रथयः शाखासन्धयः तेषां 'निष्यन्दस्य' क्षीरद्रवस्य 'गन्धः स्त्यायते' वर्द्धते। भल्लूकैर्नादितानि गजैर्वासितानि च नातिभीमानि वनानि इति भावः।।

Notes.—1. कुहर etc.–कुहर is गह्वर cave. कुहरं भजन्ते इति कुहर+भज+णिव कर्त्तरि कुहरभाः, तेषाम्। 2. भल्लूक् etc.–भल्लूकायश्चामी युवानश्च। तेषाम्। 3. अनुरसित

etc. —अनु+रस+क्त भावे अनुरसितम् echo. 4. स्त्यनम्–स्तै+ल्युट् भावे। Intensity सङ्क्षात। 5. अम्बृकृतानि–अनम्बु अम्बु कृतानि इति अम्बु+चि+कृ+क्त कर्मणि growls resembling the sound of spitting. 6. स्त्यायते–स्तैय+लट्ते कर्त्तरि। The root is परस्मैपदौ, the आत्मनेपद seems to be irregular. Or say स्तैय here means 'to intensify' (अनेकार्थत्वद्धातूनाम्). Hence we have लट् ते कर्मणि। स्त्यायते becomes intensified.

(*xxx*) **रामः (सवाष्पस्तम्भम्)–भद्र शिवास्ते पन्थानः। देवयानं प्रतिपद्यस्व पुण्येभ्यो लोकेभ्यः।**

Rāma (*Checking his tears*)—Gentle friend, may your journey be safe. Take to the divine car for the holy regions.

शम्बूकः–यावत् पुराणब्रह्मवादिनम् अगस्त्यमृषिमभिवाद्य शाश्वतं पदमनुप्रविशामि। (इति निष्क्रान्तः)।

Śamb.—I will enter the eternal region after having saluted Agastya, that old discouser on Brahman. (*Exit*).

रामः– एतत्तदेव हि पुनर्वनमद्य दृष्टं
यस्मिन्नभूम चिरमेव पुरा वसन्तः।
आरण्यकाश्च गृहिण्श्च रताः स्वधर्मे
सांसारिकेषु च सुखेषु वयं रमज्ञाः।।12।। (रा–)

Rāma—Today, here, is seen again that very forest where formerly, we, residing for a long time indeed, continued as foresters devoted to our duty and as householders as well enjoying the taste of wordly pleasures. (R—).

मित–। सवाष्पेत्यादि–वाष्प इति कण्ठगतो वाष्पः न तु अक्षिगतः। 'वाष्पस्थ स्तम्भः' निरोधः' ते सह।। एकाकौ सीतागतं चिन्तयितुकामः शम्बकस्व साहचर्यं परिहर्त्तुमिच्छन् तं विसृजति भद्रेति। 'देवयानं' देवैः प्रेरितं विमानं 'प्रतिपद्यस्व' स्वीकुरु। 'पुण्येभ्यो लोकेभ्यः' पुण्यान् लोकान् प्राप्तुमित्यर्थः।। 'यावत्' अवधारणे। 'श्वावतं' नित्यम् अनपायि 'तं' स्थानम्।। एतदिति।

अन्वयः–तदैव हि एतत् वनम् अद्य पुनर्दुष्टं यस्मिन् पुरा चिरमेव वसन्तः आरण्यकाश्च गृहिण्य वयं स्वधर्मे रताः सांसारिकेषु सुखेषु रसज्ञाश्च अभूम।

व्याख्या–'तदैव हि' पूर्वपरिचितम् 'एतत् वनम् अद्य पुनर्दृष्टं यस्मिन् पुरा' दण्डकाप्रवासकाले 'चिरमेव' कालं 'वसन्तः आरण्यकाश्च' मुनिवृत्तयश्च 'गृहिण्य'

गृहस्थाश्च 'वयं स्वधर्मे' मुनिव्रते 'रताः सांसारिकेषु सुखेषु विषये 'रसज्ञाश्च' ज्ञातास्वादा अपि 'अभूम'।।

Notes. 1. सराष्प etc.—Śambūkua's enthusiasm made no impression on Rāma. He liked to be left alone to brood over his lot and wanted to utter the words of dismissal to Śambūka. But he knew that in speaking he would run the risk of betraying his emotion by the tremor in his voice. Hence, he checks the emotion (सवाष्पस्तम्भम्) and utters the customary formula of farewell (शिवास्ते पन्थानः). The वाष्व is in the throat not in the eyes. Comp. "कण्ठः स्तम्भिवापवृत्तिकलुषश्चिन्ताजड़ं दर्शनम्"–*Śakuntala.* 2. शाश्वतम्–शश्वत्+अण् निपातनात्। शाश्वतिक is also allowed (see *ante*). 3. *Remark*—Here it is strange that Rāma does not think of himself going over to Agastya to pay his respects to that august sage. Contrast "अनतिक्रमणीयानि श्रेयांसि" of Duṣyanta when in the neighbourhood of हेमकूट on his way back to earth from heaven. The fact is the poet wants Rāma to linger and open his heart to the audience and thus prepare them for the touching scene in Act III. But however desirable this may be the means employed for this end would have been more acceptable had they not made Rāma discourteous and wanting in manners towards his superiors. 4. आरण्यकाः etc. –रताः स्वधर्मे as आरण्यकाः and सांसारिकेषु सुखेषु रसज्ञाः as गृहिणः। अरण्ये वसन्ति इति अरण्य+कुञ् शेषे आरण्यकाः यतिनः। संसारे भवानि इति संसार+उञ् सांसारिकाणि, अध्यात्मादि। 5. *Remark*—we may also construe रताः रसज्ञाश्च वयं चिरमेव वसन्तः अभूम।

(*xxxi*) (रा–)–अपि च–

(R—) Besides,

एते त एव गिरयो विरुवन्मयूरा-
स्तान्येव मत्तहरिणानि वनस्थलानि।
आमञ्जुवञ्जुललतानि च तान्यमूनि
नीरन्ध्रनीलनिचुलानि सरित्तटानि।। 23 ।। (रा–)

These are really the same hills with peacoks crowing the same woodlands indeed with the deer wild (with joy). Yonder are the very same river-banks with beautiful Vañjula creepers and (overgrown) with dark Nichula clumps without an opening. (R—).

मित–। एते इति

अन्वयः–एते ते एवं विरुवन्मयूरा गिरयः। (इमानि) तानि एव मत्तहरिणानि वनस्थलानि। अमूनि च तानि एव आमञ्जुवञ्जुलललतानि नीरन्ध्रनीलनिचुलानि सरित्तटानि।

व्याख्या–'एते' पुरोवर्त्तिनः 'ते एव' पूर्वपरिचिताः 'विरुवन्तः' नदन्तः 'मयूराः' येषु तथाविधाः 'गिरयः' पर्वताः। इमानि 'तानि एव' पूर्वदृष्टानि 'मत्तहरिणानि' प्रहृष्टकुरङ्गाणि 'वनस्थलानि' काननप्रदेशाः। अमूनि च' दूरे दृश्यमानानि 'तानि एव' पूर्वानुभूतानि 'आमञ्चवः' परमरमणीयाः 'वञ्जुललताः' वेतसलताः येषु तादृशाणि किञ्च 'नीरन्ध्राः' निविडप्ररूढ़ा 'नीलाः' श्यामाः हरितापत्रबहुला इत्यर्थः 'निचुलाः' हिज्जलवृक्षाः येषु तादृशानि 'सरित्तटानि' नदीतीराणि।।

Remark—The eithets show that the place was very suitable for strolls at ease.

(*xxxii*) **(रा–)–**

मेघमालेव यश्चायमारादपि विभाव्यते।
गिरिः प्रस्त्रवणः सोऽयं यत्र गोदावरी नदी।। 24।।

(R—)—And this hill, which even from near looks like a row of clouds, is the same Prasravaṇa near which is the river Godāvarī.

अस्यैवासीन्महति शिखरे गृध्रराजस्य वास-
स्तस्याधस्ताद्वयमपि रतास्तेषु पर्णोटजेषु।
गोदावर्याः पयसि विततश्यामलानोकहश्री-
रन्तः कूजन्मखरशकुनो यत्र रम्यो वनान्तः।। 25।।(रा–)

On the giant peak of this very hill was the home of the vulture-king. Below the same we too lived happily in those leaf huts near which the forest-skirts was charming with singing-birds cooing under the foliage and the beauty of its green trees displayed in the waters of Godāvarī. (R—).

मित–। मेघेति।

अन्वयः–अयञ्च यः आरादपि मेघमालेव विभाव्यते सोऽयं गिरिः प्रस्त्रवणः यत्र गोदावरी नदी।

व्याख्या–'अव्यञ्च' दृश्यमानः 'यः आरादपि' समीपस्थादपि देशात् 'मेघमाला इव विभाव्यते' अत्युच्चत्वात् शिखराणां वारिदावलिभ्रान्तिं जनयति 'स अयं गिरिः प्रसवणः यत्र' यस्य समीपे 'गोदावरी नदी' प्रवहति।। अस्येति।

अन्वयः–अस्यैव महति शिखरे गृध्रराजस्य वासः आसीत्। तस्य अधस्तात् वयमपि तेषु पर्णोटजेषु रताः यत्र गोदावर्याः पयसि वितश्यामलानोकहश्रीः अन्तःकूजम्मुखरशकुनः वनान्तः रम्यः।

व्याख्या–'अस्यैव' प्रस्रवणस्य 'महति शिखरे' तुङ्गे शृङ्गे 'गृध्रराजस्य' जटायुषः 'वासः' निलयः 'आसीत्'। 'तस्य' गृध्रराजनिवासस्य 'अधस्तात्' निम्ने 'वयमपि तेष पर्णोटजेषु' पत्रकुटीरेषु 'रताः' रममाणः अभूम 'यत्र' येषु येषां समीपे इत्यर्थः 'गोदावर्याः पर्यास वितता' बिम्बेन विस्तारिता 'श्यामलानाम् अनोकहानां वृक्षानां 'श्रीः' यस्य तादृशः किञ्च 'अन्तः' पत्रमध्ये 'कूजन्तः' शब्दायमानाः 'मुखराः' गायन्तः 'शकुनाः' पक्षिणः यस्मिन् तादृशः सन् 'व ान्तः रम्यः' रमणीय आसीत्। इह पित्रा जटायुषा परिरक्षिताः रम्ये वनान्ते रममाणा एव वयमास्म इति भावः।

Notes. 1. आरादपि–आरात् is an अव्यय meaning दूर also समीप। It is usual here to take आरात् as दूर। But then अपि loses its force and the statement falls flat on the ears because every hill looks like a cloud from a distance. Hence we take आरात् meaning समीप। The line then means that while other hills give the impression of a cloud only from a distance, प्रस्रवण does it even (अपि) from near, its शिखर is so high (see महति शिखरे below). 2. सोऽयम्–अयम् occurs twice in the verse; one of these looks like superfluous. 3. यत्र–अधिकरणे ७मी। The आधार here implies सामीप्य as in गङ्गायां घोषः। 4. वासः–उष्यते अस्मि् इति वस+घञ् अधिकरणे वासः house. 5. तस्य–May be construced either as तस्य रामस्य or तस्य शिखरस्य। 6. अधस्तात्–अधर is निम्न। अक्षरस्मिन् इति अधर+ङि (7मी)+अस्ताति स्वार्थे। अधर becomes अध् by "पूर्वाधरावराणम् असि पुर् अध् अवश्च एषाम्" and "अस्ताति च" (also when अस्ताति follows). The word is an अव्यय। 7. रताः–रम+क्त कर्त्तरि वर्तमाने रत enjoying रममाण। 8. तेषु–In those etc. तेष केषु? "यत्र रमे वनान्तः"। 9. वितत etc.–वि+तन+क्त कर्मणि वितत spread out, exhibited etc. Where exhibited ? गोदावर्याः पथसि in the water of the Godāvarī. That is possible only by reflection. For अनोकह tree (see *ante*). श्रि+क्विप् कर्त्तरि वी beauty शोभा। ङीष् is not added, hence the word is not नदीसंज्ञक। Consequently the rule "नद्यतय" does not apply and कप् is not attached as a समासान्त in the final बहु–। ङीप् is optional by "कृदिकारादक्तिनः"। If attached, the form becomes विततश्वामलानोकहश्रीकः with कप्। The forest-beauty is transferred to the waters by reflection Comp. "विम्वागतैस्तीरवनैः समृद्धिं निजां विलोक्यपहृतां पयोभिः etc."–*Bhaṭṭi.* "यत्र–येषु इति यद्+सुप् (7मी)+वल् स्वार्थे। Refers to पर्णोटजेषु। अधिं 7मी the आधार impling सामीप्य as in "यत्र गोदावरी नदी" above II. रम्यः–रमते अस्मिन् इति रम+यत् अधिकरणे बाहुलकात् ; or रमयतीति रम+णिच्+यत् कर्त्तरि बाहुलकात्। The वनान्त was रम्य because it appealed to the sense of sight through the charming reflections (विवत–) and to the sense of hearing by reason of अन्तःकूजत्–। Over and above these there was that sense of security that we were being looked after by father जटायुस्। Hence we really enjoyed life there (रताः)।

(xxxiii) **(रा–) अत्रैव सा पञ्चवटी यत्र चिरनिवासेन विविध-विश्रम्भातिप्रसङ्गसाक्षिणः प्रदेशाः प्रियायाः प्रियसखी वासन्ती च प्रतिवसति। तत् किमिदमापतितमद्य रामहतकस्य ! सम्प्रति हि–**

(R—) Here indeed is that Pañcavaṭī the sites in which through long residence, are witneses to the excess of our familiarity in many ways and where lives Vāsantī the dear friend of my darling. What then is this that has befallen wretched Rāma to-day?

At this moment—

चिराद्वेगारम्भी प्रसृत इव तीव्रो विषरसः
कुतश्चित् संवेगाच्चलित इव शल्यस्य शकलः।
व्रणो रूढग्रन्थिः स्फुटित इव हृन्मर्मणि पुन-
र्घनीभूतः शोको विकलयति मां नूतन इव।। 26 ।। (रा–)

After a long time indeed, grief intensified, as if fresh, overpowers me like some quick-acting violent poison coursing in the system; like a splinter of a shaft, for some reason or other, moving with great force ; like an ulcer in the vitals of the heart re-opened after the cicatrix had been formed (healed) (R—).

मित–। अत्रेत्यादि। 'विविधानां' नानाप्रकाराणां' विश्रम्भाणां विश्वस्तकर्मणां यः 'अतिप्रसङ्गः' दूरप्रसरः आतिशव्यमित्यर्थः तस्य 'साक्षिणः' साक्षाद्दृष्टारः 'प्रदेशः' सन्ति। तत्तत्प्रदेशानां दर्शनेन वासन्त्याश्च स्मरणेन विकलीकृतोऽहम्। 'किमिदम्' अतिदुःसहं किमपि इत्यर्थः। चिरादिति।

अन्वयः–चिरात् घनीभूतः नूतन इव शोकः प्रसृतः तीव्रो वेगारम्भी विषरस इव, कुतयित् संवेगात् चलितः शल्यस्यशकल इव, हृन्मणि रूढ़ग्रन्थिः पुनः स्फुटितः व्रणः इव, मां विकलयति।

व्याख्या–'चिरात्' वहोः कालात् परम अद्य तत्तत्प्रदेशदर्शनात् 'घनीभूतः' गाढतामापन्नः 'शोकः' सीताविरहसन्तापः 'प्रसृतः' प्रसर्त्तुमारब्धः [आदिकर्मणि क्तः] शिराभिः सञ्चरमाणः 'तीव्रः' दारुणः 'वेगारम्भी' क्षिप्रकर्मा 'विषरस इव' देहे विद्धः शङ्कुखण्ड इव अथवा 'हृन्मर्मणि' हृदयस्य मर्मस्थाने 'रूढग्रन्थि' सञ्जाबन्धनः विरोपित इत्यर्थः किन्तु 'पुनः स्फुटितः' भूयोऽपि मुक्तवन्ध न। व्यात्तमुखः 'ब्रण इव मां विकलयति' विवशं करोति।

Notes. 1. विविध etc.–विश्रम्भ is विश्वास familiarity ; hence *deeds* of familiarity. अतिप्रसङ्ग long continuance, hence *excess.* साक्षात् is an अव्यय meaning प्रत्यक्ष। 'साक्षात् अस्ति एषाम् इति सत्वात्+इनि साक्षिस्त्रः eye-witnesses. Hence, their sight recalls the incidents. 2. वेगारम्भी–वेगेन आरब्धुं शीलमस्य इति वेग+आ+रभ+णिनि कर्त्तरि। 3. कुतश्चित् etc.—The idea is that the splinter is embedded within the body, invisible and therefore cannot be removed. For some inexplicable reason the spliner has commenced to burrow on and is causing pain. 4. रूढ़ग्रन्थिः–रूढ़ formed ग्रन्थि knot. रूढ़ः ग्रन्थिः अस्य of which the knot has formed, *i.e.,* which is no longer a gaping wound. The edges of the wound have united and the wound has healed. 5. विकलयति–कला is कलना comprehension. विगता कला अस्य विकलः destitute or perception, senseless. विकलं करोति इति विकल+णिच् (नाम धातु)+ल्युट् तिप्। 6. नूतन इव–Some read मूर्च्छयति च। मूर्च्छा and वैकल्य are almost the same. If मूर्च्छा is a grade higher, then विकलयति becomes sperfluous. नूतन् इव seems to be the better reading.

(*xxxiii*) **(रा–) तथापि तान् पूर्वसुहृदो भूमिभागान् पश्यामि। (निरूप्य) अहो अनवस्थिता भूमिसन्निवेशः।**

(R—) Even so, I will see my old friends, those tracts of land. (*Looking attentively*) Ha ! the disposition of the ground has changed. Thus—

तथाहि–पुरा यत्र स्त्रोतः पुलिनमधुना तत्र सरितां
विपर्यासं यातो घनविरलभावः क्षितिरुहाम्।
बहोर्दृष्टं कालादपरमिव मन्थे वनमिदं
निवेशः शैलानां तदिदमिति बुद्धिं द्रढ़यति।। 27।।

Where formerly was the current, there now are the sands of the streams ; the denseness and sparseness of trees have undergone reversal. This forest, seen after a long time, I deem as if another ; the position of the hills strengthens the surmise that it is the same.

मित– । 'तथापि' सत्यामपि विकलतायाम् । 'अवस्थित:' अविचलित: । न तथा 'अनवस्थित:' परिवर्त्तित: । 'भूमे: सन्निवेश:' विन्यास: ।। पुरेति ।

अन्वय:–सरितां पुरा यत्र श्रोत: अधुना तत्र पुलिनम् । क्षितिरुहां घनविरलभाव: विपर्यासं यात: । वहो: कालात् दृष्टम् इदं वनम् अपरमिव मन्थे । शैलानां निवेश: इदं तत् इति बुद्धिं द्रढ़यति ।

व्याख्या–'सरितां' नदीनां 'पुरा' प्राक् दण्डकावासकाले 'यत्र' यस्मिन् देशे 'स्रोत:' आसीत् 'अधुना' अद्य 'तव पुलिनम्' सैकतम् । 'क्षितिरुहां' वृक्षाणां 'घनविरलभाव:' घनत्वं विरलत्वञ्च 'विपर्यसं यात:' वैरीत्यं प्राप्त: । वृक्ष यव पुरा घना: तव अधुना विरला: यत्र च विरला: तत्र पुनर्घना इत्यर्थ: । एवं सरितृसु वृक्षेषु च अपरविघत्वे जाते 'वही: कालात्' परं 'दृष्टम् इदं वनम्' एष 'अपरमिव मन्धे' । तत् कथमुक्तं "एतत्तेव हि पुनर्वनमद्य दृष्टम्" इति तत्राह–'शैलानां निवेश:' पर्वतानाम् यथा पुरा अवस्थानाम् 'इदं तत्' तदेव वनम् 'इति बुद्धि द्रढयति' ईदृशं ज्ञानं व्यवस्थापयति समर्थयते ।।

Notes. 1. अनवस्थित:–अवस्थित: unchanged न अवस्थित: । 2. भूमि etc.–सम्+नि+विश्+घञ् भावे सन्निवेश: location, भूमै: सन्निवेश: । 3. विपर्यासम्–वि+परि+अस+घञ् भावे विपर्यस interchange. 4. घन–etc. घन dense is विरल sparse घनश्च विरलश्च घनविरलौ, इन्दृ । तयोर्भाव: । What was dense is now sparse, and the sparse has become dense. 5. चितिरुहाम्–क्षितौ रोहन्ति इति चिति+रुह+किप् कर्त्तरि क्षितिरुह: । The प्रातिपादिक is क्षितिरुह् । तेषाम् । 6. द्रढ़यति–दृढ़ strong. दृढं करोति इति दृढ़+णिच् (नाम धातु)+लटय् तिप् । दृढ़ becomes द्रढ़ as in इष्ठन् by the Vārttika --णविष्ठवत् प्रातिपदिकस्य" ।

(*xxxiv*) **(रा–) हन्त परिहरन्तमपि मामित: पञ्चवटीस्नेहो बलादीकार्षतीव । (सकरुणम्)**

(R—) Alas ! Though I am avoiding it, the love for Pañcavaṭī draws me hence as if by force. (*Pathetically*).

यस्यां ते दिवसास्तया सह मया नीता: पुन: स्वे गृहे
यत्सम्बन्धिकथाभिरेव सततं दीर्घाभिरस्थीयत ।

एकः सम्प्रति नाशितप्रियतमस्तामद्य रामः कथं
पापः पञ्चवटीं विलोकयतु वा गच्छत्वसम्भाव्य वा ।।28।।

How can my vile self—Rāma—after having caused the loss of his darling, now see alone, or leave without honouring, that Pañcavaṭī where those days were by me passed and with long talks of which indeed I ever kept myself enaged with her in my own home ?

मित– । हन्तेति । 'हन्त' इत्यव्ययमिह विषादे । 'परिहरन्तम्' अतिक्रम्य गच्छतम् ।। यस्यामिति ।

अन्वयः–तया सह मया यस्यां ते दिवसा नीताः पुनः स्वे गृहे दीर्घाभिर्यत् सम्वन्धिकथाभिरेव सततमस्थीयत तां पञ्चवटी सम्प्रति नाशितप्रियतमः पापः रामः कथमद्य एक विलोकयतु वा असम्भाव्य गच्छतु वा ।

व्याख्या–'तया' सीतया 'सह मया यस्यां' पञ्चवट्यां 'ते' पूर्वानुभूता आनन्दमया 'दिवसा नीताः' अतिवाहिताः 'पुनः' भूयः' 'स्वे गृहे' प्रत्यावृत्य अयोध्यायां 'दीर्घाभिः यत् सम्बन्धनीभिः' यदाश्रयाभिः 'कथाभिरेव सततम्' अविच्छेदन 'अस्थीयत' यापितम् 'तां' तथाविधां सर्वकालप्रियां 'पञ्चवटीं सम्प्रति' अधुना 'नाशिता' विनाशं गमिता 'प्रियतमा' येन तथाविधः अतएव 'पापः रामः कथम् अद्य एकः' प्रियाविरहितः 'विलोकयतु वा असम्भाव्य' तस्या विलोकनरूपां सम्माननामकृत्वा 'वा गच्छतु' ।

Notes. 1. तया सह मया–These go with both नीताः and अस्थीयत। तया सह मया नीताः–तया सह मया अस्थीयत। 2. यत्सम्बन्धि etc.–यस्या सम्बन्धः यत् सम्बन्धः। स अस्ति आसु इति यत् सम्बन्ध+इनि मत्वर्थे यतुसम्बन्धिन्यः। तादृश्यः कथाः, कर्मधा– । ताभिः। 3या करणे। 3. अस्यीयत–स्था+लङ् त भावे। 4. एकः–Formerly it was तया सह, now एकः। Hence, the painfulness of the situation. 5. सम्प्रति–This refers to the whole time from the banishment of Sītā's to the present. 6. नाशित etc.—Note the णिच्। It is नाशित, not नष्ट। I have myself killed her. प्रियतमा नष्टा। –मयसा प्रियतमा नाशिता। एकः is painful enough ; add to that the fact that I am myself the cause for it ; the situation becomes unbearable. 7. *Remark.* The language is rather unhappy here. यस्यां मया नीताः तां रामः विलोकयतु makes the speaker different from राम। The identity of the two cannot be restored even if we supply an अहम्। यस्यां मया नीताः ताम् अहं रामः विलोकयतु is bad grammar ; the लोट् should be in the 1st person–यस्यां मया नीताः ताम् अहं रामः विलोकयानि।

(*xxxv*) (प्रविश्य) शम्बूकः–जयति जयति देवः। देव, भगवानगस्त्यो मत्तः श्रुतभवत्सन्निधानस्त्वामाह–परिकल्पितमिनावतरणमङ्गला प्रतीक्षते वत्सला लोपामुद्रा सर्वे चु महर्षयः, तदेहि सम्भावयाम्मान्। अथ प्रजविना पुष्पकेण स्वदेशमुपगम्य अश्वमेधाय सज्जो भविष्यसि–इति।

(*Entering*) Śamb.—Prosper, let Sire prosper. Sire, mighty Agastya having heard from me of your presence (here) says to you this :—With auspicious arrangements made for your dismounting from the divine car, awaits affectionate Lopāmudrā, likewise all the sages. So come and honour us. Thereafter having reached our own country, in the swift Puṣpaka you will get ready for the Aśvamedha.

रामः–यथाज्ञापयति भगवान्।

Rāma—As his mighty self commands.

शम्बूकः–इतस्तर्हि देवः प्रवर्त्तयतु पुष्पकम्।

Śamb.—Then let Sire direct the Puṣpaka this way.

रामः–भगवति पञ्चवटि गुरुजनोपरोधात् क्षणं क्षम्यतामतिक्रमो रामस्य।

Rāma—Worshipful Pañcavaṭī, for a moment, excuse Rāma's lapse through pressure from superiors.

मित–।जयतीत्यादि।'श्रुतं भवतः सन्निधानं सन्निध्यं येन। आश्रमसमीपे भवानास्ते इति श्रुत्वा इत्यर्थः। 'परिकल्पितानि' आहृत्य सम्भृतानि 'विमानात् अवतरणाय मङ्गलानि' मङ्गलद्रव्याणि यया तादृशी सती 'प्रतीक्षते' भवदागमनप्रतीक्षां कुरुते। 'सर्वे च महर्षयः' आश्रमवासिन सुनयः प्रतीक्षन्ते।'अथ' अनन्तरम् अस्मान् सम्भाव्य इत्यर्थः।'प्रजविना' द्रुतगामिना। इहागमनेऽपि यागकालो नातिवर्त्तिष्यते द्रुतगामित्वात् पुष्पकस्य इति भावः।। भगवतीति। 'गुरुजनस्य' अगस्त्यस्य यः 'उपरोधः' आग्रहः तन्मात् 'क्षणम्' इति प्रत्यावर्त्तन सूचयति।'अतिक्रमः उपेक्ष्य गमनम्। गुरुजनोपरोधात् अतिक्रमः इत्यन्वयः न तु गुरुजोपरोधात् क्षम्यताम् इति।

Notes. 1. मत्तः–अपादान of the क्रिया in श्रुत। अपादाने पञ्चमी। Next अस्मद+असि (5मी)+ङसि स्वार्थे। An अव्यय।2. परिकल्पित etc.–विमानात् अवतरणम् विमानावतरणम्, सुपसुपा। तस्य मङ्गलानि the auspicious arrangements necessary for alighting. परिकल्पितानि विमानावतरणमङ्गलानि यया। 3. महर्षस्यः-Supply प्रतीक्षन्ते। 4. एहि etc.—This is something like a command. After this Rāma could not refuse the request. 5. अथ etc.-Here Agastya takes a very charitable view of Rāma's omission to visit him. He supposes that Rāma thinks he would be late for the sacrifice if he tarried here. The sage allays Rāma's apprehension by pointing out the speed of the car—There would be ample time left to get ready for the sacrifice. 6. गुरुजन etc.-उप+रुध+घञ् भावे उपरोध importunity. गुरुः जनः, कर्मधा-। तस्य उपरोधः। तस्मात्। हेतौ 5मी। हेतु of अतिक्रम।

(*xxxvi*) **शम्बूकः-देव पश्य पश्य-**

Śamb.—Behold, Sire, behold.

गुञ्जकुञ्जकुटीरकौशिकघटाघुत्कारवत्कीचक-
स्तम्वाडम्बरमूकमौकुलिकुलः क्रौञ्चावतोऽयं गिरिः।
एतस्मिन् प्रचलाकिनां प्रचलतामुद्वेजिताः कूजितै-
रुद्वेल्लन्ति पुराणरोहिणतरुस्कन्धेषु कुम्भीनसाः।। 29।। (श-)

This is hill Krauñcavaṭa where crowds of crows are silenced by the uproar of the clumps of whistling bamboos which is mingled with the hootings of noisy arrays of owls in their bower-like thickets. On this, huge sepents, on the trunks of old sandal trees, swing about being troubled by the notes of peacocks on the move. (Samb.—)

मित-। गुञ्जदिति।

अन्वयः-अयं गुञ्जत्कुञ्जकुटीरकौशिकघटाघुत्कारवत्- कौचकस्तस्वाड़म्बर मूकमौकुलिकुलः क्रौञ्चावतो गिरिः। एतस्मिन् प्रचलतां प्रचलाकिनां कुजितैः उद्वेजिताः कुम्भीनसाः पराणरोहिणतरुस्कन्धेषु उद्वेल्लन्ति।

व्याख्या-'अयम्' एष दृश्यमानः 'गुञ्चत्यः' नदन्त्यः याः 'कुञ्जकीराश्रयिण्यः' लतागृहवर्त्तिनाः 'कौशिकघटाः' पेचकसमूहाः तासां यः 'घुत्कारः' घुत्-इत्यव्ययक्तध्वनिः तेन मिथः यः 'कौचकस्तम्बानां वेणगुच्छानाम् 'आडम्बरः' तुसुध्वनिः तेन 'सूकम्' भयनिःशङ्क' 'मौकुलिकुलं' काकवर्गः यस्मिन् तथाविधः 'क्रौञ्चावतो गिरिः'। 'एतस्मिन्' गिरौ 'प्रचलताम्' परिपततां 'प्रचलाकिनां' मयूराणम् 'कूजितैः' केकाभिः 'उद्वेजिताः' त्रासिताः 'कुम्भीनसाः' अजगरः 'पुराणनां रोहिणतरुणं' चन्दनवृक्षाणां 'स्कन्धेषु' प्रकाण्डेषु 'उद्वेल्लन्ति' दोदुल्यन्ते।।

Notes. 1. गुञ्जत–etc.–कुञ्ज is an enclosure of creepers (लतादि-पिहितोदर)। कुटीर is a leaf-hut. कुञ्जकेव कुटीरं कुञ्जकुीरम् leaf-hut of a bower. कौशिक is owl. घटा a crowd. कौशिकानां घटाः। कुञ्जकुटीरस्थाः कौशिकघटाः, कर्मधा–of the शाकपार्थिवादि class. गुञ्जन्ताः कुञ्जकुटीरकौशिकघटाः, कर्म्मधा– । धुत् is an imitation of the owl's note. *Ghoot* (घुत्) is the same as the English *Hoot.* घुत्++क्लः घञ् भावे घत्कारः the sound घुत्। गुञ्जत्कुञ्जकुटीरकौशिकघटानां घुत्कारः। सः अस्ति अस्मिन् इति मतुप्=गुञ्जत्कुञ्जकुटीरकौशिकघटाधुत्कारवान्। कीचक whistling bamboo. स्तम्ब clump. आढम्बर is पटहध्वनि ; here, the hubbub created by innumerable bamboos whistling together but not in unison. कीचकानां स्तम्बाः। तेषाम् आड़म्बरः। गुञ्जत्कुञ्जकुटीरकौशिकघटाघुत्कारवान् कीचकस्तम्बाडम्बरः कर्म्मधा– । मौकुलि is काक। The crows are a proverbially-clamorous lot, and bamboo clumps are their favourite resort. Here they were on the bamboos, but did not open their mouth at all, not becauseof the whistling noise of the bamboos, but because owls held revelry and were hooting in very dark thickets close by. The two sounds got mingled and over-awed them. 2. *Remarks.*—Note Bhavabhūti's preference of the uncommon to the common. He would have कौशिक not पेचक, मौकुलि not वायस, प्रवलाकिन् not मयूर, रोहिण not चन्दन कुम्भीनम् not अजगर।

(*xxxvii*) **(शम्बू–) अपि च**

(Śamb.) —Moreover,

एते ते कुहरेषु गद्गदनदद्गोदावरीवारयो
मेघालङ्कृतमीलिनीलशिखराः क्षीणीभृतो दक्षिणाः।
अन्योऽन्यप्रतिघातसङ्कुलचलत्कल्लोलकोलाहलै-
रुत्तालास्त इमे गभीरपयसः पुण्याः सरित्सङ्गमाः।।30।।

(इति निष्क्रान्तौ)

इति पञ्चवटीप्रवेशो नाम द्वितीयोऽङ्कः।

These are those southern mountains that have the waters of the Godāvarī gurgling in their caves and have their peaks blue because the top is adorned with clouds. Here are those holy deep watered river-confluences resounding with the roar of billows that rush along mixed up through mutual impact.

(*Exeunt*).

This is the Second Act styled—
Entrance into the Pañcavaṭī.

मित–। एते इति।

अन्वयः–एते ते कुहरेषु गद्गदनदग्दोदावरीवारयः मेघालङ्कृतमौलिनीशिखराः दक्षिणाः क्षीणीभृतः। इमे ते गभीरपयसः अन्योन्यप्रतिघात सङ्कुलचलत् कल्लोलकोलाहलैः उत्तालाः पुण्याः सरित्सङ्गमाः।

व्याख्या–'एते' इमे दृश्यमानाः 'ते' पूर्वदृष्टाः 'कुहरेषु गह्वरेषु 'गद्गदम्' अव्यक्त 'नदन्ति' शब्दायमानानि 'गोदावर्या वारीणि' जलानि येषु तादृशाः किञ्च 'मेघैः' अलङ्कृताः' ये 'मौलयः' शिरीभागाः तैः 'नीलानि शिखराणि' शृङ्गाणि येषां तथाविधाः 'दक्षिणः' दक्षिणदिग्वर्त्तिनः 'क्षीणभृतः' पर्वताः। इतश्च पुनः 'इमे' दृश्यमाना 'ते' पूर्वदृष्टाः 'गभीरपयसः' अगाधजलाः 'अन्योऽन्यप्रतिघातेन' परम्परसंघर्षेण 'सङ्कुलं' मिश्रं यथा तथाः चलतां' प्रसर्पतां 'कल्लोलानां' तरङ्गाणां 'कोलाहलैः' आरावैः 'उत्तालाः' उत्कटाः अहृद्या इत्यर्थः 'पुण्याः' पावनाः 'सरित्सङ्गमाः' नदीसन्निपाताः।।

Notes. 1. गद्गद् etc.—For समास see टीका। This shows that the hills had partially entered the waters of the गोदावरी। 2. मेघ etc.–मौलि head. शिखर peak. In the case of a hill the head is peak and the peak is head. But to avoid the consequent tautology we have to think of मौलि in a general sense and then refers to शिखर। 3. दक्षिणः–दक्षिण here means दक्षिणस्थ by transference of epithets. We cannot have आंच in the sense दक्षिणस्यादिशि because आच् gives an अव्यय and the विसर्ग elides. 4. अन्योन्य etc.–प्रति+हन+घञ् भावे प्रतिघात impact. अन्यस्य अन्यस्य प्रतिघातः इति अन्योऽन्यस्य प्रतिघात=अन्योऽन्यप्रतिघातः the सु in the first अन्य being retained बाहुलकात्। The Vārttika's bearing on this point are "कर्पव्यतिहारे सर्व नाम्नो द्वे वाच्ये समासवच्च बहुलम्" which doubles अन्यस्य "अन्यपरयोर्न समावत्" prevents the elision of the षष्ठी in अन्यस्य। Next "असमासवद्भावे पूर्व पदस्थस्य सुपः सुर्वाच्यः" gives अन्यः अन्यस्य=अन्धीन्यस्य। 5. उत्तालाः–उद्गतस्तालात् उत्तालः। "उत्तालो विकटे श्रेष्ठे" इति मेदिनी। We get श्रेष्ठ if ताल is a palm-tree, and विकट when ताल means time-measure. The English equivalent in that case is *discordant*, disagreeable. The कोलाहल makes the place disagreeable.

Chapter - 3

(*i*) **(ततः प्रविशति नदीद्वयं तमसा मुरला च)**

(*Then enter two streams Tamasā and Murala*)

तमसा–सखि मुरले किमसि सम्भ्रान्तेव?

Tam.—Friend Murala, why do you seem to be in hurry (agitated)?

मुरला–भगवति तमसे, प्रेषितास्मि भगवतः अगस्त्यस्य पत्न्या लोपामुद्रया सरिद्वरां गोदावरीमभिधातुम्–(मु–)

Mur.—Mightly Tamasā, I am sent by Lopamudrā, the wife of Worshipful Agastaya, to Godāvarī to say (this) (Mur—).

मित–1. सम्भ्रमस्त्वरा आवेग्री वा। 'सम्भ्रान्ता' त्वरावती आवेगवतौ वा।

Note. 1. नदीद्वयम्–By नदी is here meant नदीदेवता, presiding deity of a river. 2. भगवति तमसे–The address भगवति shows मुरला was much lower in status than तमसा। She was quite an ordinary individual, so there is nothing strange in her running errands for लोपामुद्रा।

(*ii*) **(मु–) जानास्येव यथा वधूत्यागात् प्रभृति**

(Mur.—)"You surely know that, since the renunciation of his wife (*Or*—of our daughter-in-law).

अनिर्भिन्नो गभीरत्वादन्तर्गूढ़घनव्यथः।
पुटपाकप्रतीकाशो रामस्य करुणो रसः।। 1।।

(मु–)

Rāma's tender feelings, unrevealed through calmness but with the intense anuish hidden within, have been like the bakings in a closed vessel.—" (Mur).

मित–। 'बध्वाः' पत्न्या तु षायाः सीताया वा 'त्यागात् प्रभृति' त्यागकाल-मारभ्य।। अनिर्भिन्नेति।

अन्वयः–गभीरत्वात् अनिर्भिन्नः अन्तर्गूढ़घनव्यथः रामस्य करुणो रसः पुटपाकप्रतीकाशः।

व्याख्या–'गभीरत्वात्' आत्मनः अलौकिकात् गाम्भीर्यात् 'अनिर्भिन्नः' हृदयं निर्भिद्य बहिरनागतः किन्तु 'अन्तः' मध्ये हृदये इत्यर्थः 'गूढ़ा' निलीना 'घना' गुर्वी 'व्यथा' हृदयवेदना यस्य तथाविधः 'रामस्य करुणो रसः' शोकजो मनीविकारः 'पुटे' रुद्धमुखे पात्रे यत् 'पच्यते' तत्तुल्यः 'पुटपाकप्रतीकाशः' पुटपाक्द्रव्यवत् प्रतीयते। अत्र राभो रुद्धमुखं मुखं पात्रम्, करुणो रसः अन्तःस्थित पच्यमान वस्तु। परं पच्यमानस्यैववेदना न्याय्यसा, इष्यते तु पुटतुल्यस्य रामस्य इत्युपाक्लेशः।

Notes. 1. वधूत्यागात्–वधू wife जाया also स्नुषा daughter-in-law "वधूजोयास्नषा स्त्री च" इत्यमरः। प्रभृतियोमे 5मी। 2. अनिर्भिन्नः–निर्+भिद+क्त कर्त्तरि निर्भिन्नः, issued out. भिद usually means 'to pierce'; here the meaning has changed. The गति which is implied in piercing has become more prominent. Hence गत्यर्थवात् कर्त्तरिक्तः। Or say निर्+मिद्+क्त भावे निर्भिन्नम्। तत् अस्ति अख्य इति निर्भिन्न+अच् मत्यर्थे निर्भिन्नः। This applies both to करुणो रसः and the thing baked (पाक)। 3. गम्भीरत्वात्–गभीरत्त्र is गाम्भीर्य imperturbability. This belongs to रामः। This applies to पुट also, गभीरत्व then meaning depth. The vessel must be deep enough to hold the thing baked and have room to spare. Otherwise the heat will burst it open ; there will be निर्भेद, an overflow, and the baking will no longer be अनिर्भिन्न। 4. etc.—For समास see मित–। The heating affects the thing baked; hence the व्यथा belongs to the thing baked which changes colour and does a lot of other things indicative of the heat. Now as the thing baked is compared to करुणो रसः the व्यथा should also go with it. But what sort of व्यथा does the करुणो रसः feel in this case? अन्तः refers to both राम and पुट। 5. पुट etc.—प्रति+कश्+घञ् कर्मणि करणो वा प्रतिकाशः प्रतीकाशः। पच्यते इति पचः घञा कर्मणि पाकः। पुटे पाकः backings in a closed vessel, सुप्सुपा। Or पुटे पाकः (घञ् भावे) अस्य पुटपाकः, बहु–। Amara's "स्युरुत्तरपदे त्वमी। निभसङ्काशनीकाशप्रतकाशोपमादय।।" implies that प्रतीकाश means *like* (तुल्य) *only* when it is final in a compound. Hence though पुटपाकप्रतीकाशः means पुटपाकतुल्यः, yet when uncompounded, पुटपाकेन प्रतीकाशः does not mean पुटपाकेन तुल्यः। Consequently the वाक्य should not contain प्रतीकाश। Thus पुटपाकेन तुल्य इत्यर्थे पुटपाकप्रतीकाशः a

नित्यसमास of the सुप्सुपा class. 6. *Remark*— राम and पुट are compared, also पाक and करुणरस। The defects in the simile are already noted (see Mitabh—and note 4 above).

(*iii*) (मु–) ''तेन च तथाविधेष्टजनकष्टविनिपातजन्मना प्रकर्षगतेन दीर्घशोकसन्तापेन सम्प्रति नितरां परिक्षीणो रामभद्रः। तमवलोक्य कम्पितमिव मे हृदयम्। अधुना च प्रतिनिवर्त्तमानेन रामभद्रेण नियतमेव पञ्चवटीवने बधूसहवासविश्रम्भसाक्षिणः प्रदेशा द्रष्टव्याः। तेषु च निसर्गधीरस्यापि एवंविधायामवस्थायाम् अतिगम्भीराभोगशोकक्षोभसंवेगात पदे पदे महान्ति प्रमादस्थानानि शङ्कनीयानि रामभद्रस्य। तत् भगवति गोदावरि, त्वया सावधानया भवितव्यम्–।। (मु–)

(Mur.—) "Hence indeed Rāmabhadra is now extremely emaciated all over through the torture of lasting grief arising from the lamentable loss of such a dear one and which has reached its climax. My heart trembles as it were on seeing him. Now again, while returning, sites have surely to be seen by Rāmabhadra in the forest of Pañcavaṭī that are witneses of familiarities while living there, with wife. And in them, under such conditions, great occasions of danger from the intensity of the shock of grief of very deep reach have to be appre-hended at every step of Rāmabhadra though naturally firm.

So mighty Godāvarī, you have to be watchful.—" (Mur.)

मित–। 'तेन च' करुणस्य पुटपाककल्पत्वहेतुना 'प्रकर्षगतेन' सातिशयेन 'दीर्घशोकस्य' चिरदुःखस्य 'सन्तापेन' ज्वालया 'सम्प्रति नितराम्' अतीव 'परिक्षीणः' कृशतामपन्नः रामभद्रः'। किम्भूतेन सन्तापेन ?–'तथाविधः' तादृशः यः 'इष्टः जनः' प्रियजनः सीतारूपः तस्य यः 'कष्टः' कष्टकरः दारुणः तस्यामवस्थायाम् अभावनीयत्वात् सुदुःसहः इत्यर्थः 'विनिपातः' विनाशः तस्मात् 'जन्म' यस्य तादृशेन सन्तापेन। असहायायाः पूर्णगर्भाया विश्वस्तायाः प्रियेण स्नेहवता च भर्त्रा कृतो विनाशः इति भर्त्तुः सम्बन्धे कष्टत्वं विनिपातस्य। दुःखञ्च रामस्य, न हि दुःखमापन्ना सीता इति, किन्तु मृतैव सा इति। तत् ''कष्टविनिपातः'' इत्यनेन मरणं लक्ष्यते न तु क्लेशमाचम्। प्रतिनिवर्त्तमानेन जनस्थानात् राजधानीं प्रतिगच्छता। 'नियतं' निश्चितम्। बध्वा स वासे' ये विश्रम्भाः' स्वच्छन्छविहाराः तेषां 'साक्षिणः'। 'तेषु च' प्रदेशेषु

'निसर्गेण' प्रकृत्या 'धीरस्यापि' अविचलनशीलस्थापि 'रामभद्रस्य एवंविधायाम-वस्थायां कार्य्यान्तरचिन्ताशून्ये काले पूर्ववृत्तान्तस्मारकपदार्थपरिव्याप्ते देशे च 'अतिगम्भीरः' अन्तस्तलस्पर्शो आभोगः' विस्तारो यस्य तादृशो यः 'शोकः' तस्मात् यः 'क्षोभः' चेतोविकारः तस्य 'स वेगात् वेगातिशयात् 'पदे पदे' प्रतिपदं 'महान्ति प्रमादस्थानानि' भयविषयाः। 'शङ्कनीयानि' उहितव्यानि। शोकवेगात् यत्र कुत्रासौ व्यापद्येत इति मे भयम् इति भावः। 'सावधानया' अवधानपरया सतर्कया।।

Notes 1. तेन च–हेतौ 3या। Because पुटपाकप्रतीकाशः, therefore. 2. तथाविध etc.—तथा विधा प्रकारः अस्य तथाविधः of that type, बहु–। इष्यते इति इष+क्त वर्त्तमाने इष्टः favoutire, इष्टजन is सीता। तथाविधेष्टजनः, कर्म्मधा–। कष्टविनिपात is rendered अनिष्टसङ्घटन by Vidyāsāgara. But Rāma grieved because Sītā was dead and under such tragic circumstances. Hence, though seers like वशिष्ट, अरुन्धती, अगस्त्य, लोपामुद्रा etc. knew that Sītā was not dead, yet it seems better here to suppose that लोपामुद्रा was speaking with referencee to Rāma's estimation of the matter. Bedsides from the conversation that follows, it is obvious that Muralā herself thought Sītā was dead and Lopāmudrā's कष्टविनिपात did not make her think otherwise. We therfore treat कष्टविनिपातः as a कर्मधा–। तथाविधेष्टजनकष्टविनिपातः, 6तत्–। तस्मात् जन्म यस्य तेन, बहु–। The final व्यधिकरणवहु–is unavoidable (अवर्ज्य) though against पाणिनि। "अवर्ज्यो बहुब्रीहिर्व्यधिकरणो जन्माद्यचरपदः" so says Vāmana. 3. नितराम्–नि implies प्रकर्ष excess. Further प्रकर्ष is added by तरप् and आम् comes in by "किमेत्तिङव्ययघात् आसु अद्रव्यप्रकर्षे"। The प्रकर्ष lies in क्षीणत्वगुण, hence there is गुणप्रकर्ष not दव्यप्रकर्ष and the rule applies. 4. परिक्षीणः–परि+क्षि+क्त कर्त्तरि=परि+क्षी+क्त=परिक्षीण। The परि here does not imply excess because the excess is already expressed fully by नितराम्। It declares सर्वतोभाव of the क्षीणता, *i,e.,* Rāma was *lean all over*, 5. वधू etc.—Refers to both time and place. The time was against him because in the first place he was so weak in body and therfore unable to stand a shock; secondly because having nothing to keep him engaged (the hunt after Sambuka having ended) he was likely to brood. The place, full of reminiscents, was obviously against him. 5. अतिगम्भीर etc.—अतिगम्भीरः, प्रादितत्–। अतिगन्धीराभोगः, बहु– । etc. see *Mitabh*— 6. महान्ति प्रसाद etc.—प्र+मद+घञ् भावे प्रमाद carelessness; hence *danger* which usually results from care lessness. Here the meaning is *danger* as in

"नेपथ्ये-प्रमाद: प्रमाद:" (Para xii below). प्रमादस्थानानि। A प्रमादस्थान is deemed महत् if it is *most likely* to cause प्रमाद।

(*iv*) (मु–)

वीचीवातैः शीकरक्षोदशीतैराकर्षद्धिः पद्मकिञ्जल्कगन्धान्।
मोहे मोहे रामभद्रस्य जीवं स्वैरं स्वैरं प्रेषितैस्पर्तये"–ति"।।2।।

(Mur.—) "You refresh the life on Rāmabhadra at every swoon with breezes sent gently from your waves —breezes that are cool through the pounding of particles of spray and wafting fragrance from lotus filaments."

मित–। वीचीति।

अन्वय:–"मोहे मोहे शीकरक्षोदशीतैः पद्मकिञ्चल्कगन्धान् आकर्षद्धि स्वैरं स्वैरं प्रषितैः वीक्षीवातैः रामभद्रस्य जीवं तर्पय" इति (अभिधातु' प्रषितास्मिन्।

व्याख्या–'मोहे मोहे' प्रतिमोहं यदैव मूर्च्छितो रामभद्रस्तदैव त्वं 'शीकराष्णां' जलकाणनां 'क्षोदेन' पेषणेन 'शीतैः' शीतलैः अतो जीवतर्प णसमर्थेः 'पद्मकिञ्चल्कानां कमलककेशरानां 'गन्धान् आकर्षद्धिः' वहद्भिः सुरभिभिरित्यर्थः अतश्च नीवतर्पणैः स्वैरं स्वैरं' मन्दं मन्दं 'प्रषितैः प्रेरितैः अतोऽसि जीवतर्पणैः 'वीक्षीवातैः तरङ्गवायुभिः 'रामभद्रस्य जीवं" चेतनाधातुं तर्पय प्रीणय 'इति' एतत् अभिधातुम् इति पूर्वेण सम्बन्धः।।

Notes. 1. वीची etc.—वीचि is both masc. and neuter. The ङीप् is optional; hence वीचि or वीची in the feminine. वीचीसङ्गता वाताः वीचीवाताः। तैः। 2. शीकर etc.—क्षुद to pound+घञ् भावे क्षोद pounding. शीकर is जलविन्दु। These come from the वीची। शीत is better left to be inferred instead of being broadly stated. For समाप्त see मित–। The breeze is acceptable if it is mild, cool, and fragrant. This epithet attaches coolness to the breeze. 3. पद्म etc.—This makes the breeze fragrant. 4. स्वैरं स्वैरम्–स्वः ईरः प्रेरणा अस्मिन् स्वैरम् self-determined, hence mild. The duplication is by "प्रकारे गुणचनसा"। स्वैरं स्वैरम् मन्दप्रकारम्। But then the double form has to be treated as a कर्म्मधारय by the rule "कर्मधारयवदुत्तरेषु"। This gives स्वैरस्वैरम्। स्वैरं स्वैरम् seems to be a poetical license.

(*v*) **तमसा–उचितमेव दाक्षिण्यं स्नेहस्य, सञ्जीवनोपायस्तु मौलिक एव रामभद्रस्याद्य सन्निहितः।**

Tam.—This kidness is indeed worthy of her affection.

The very foundamental means of reviving Rāmabhadra, how ever, is at hand to-day.

मुरला–कथमिव ?

Mur.—How so ?

तमसा–श्रूयताम्। पुरा किल वाल्मीकितपोवनोपकण्ठात् परित्यज्य गते लक्ष्मणे सीतादेवी प्राप्तप्रसववेदनमात्मानम् अतिदुःखसंवेगात् गङ्गाप्रवाहे निक्षिप्लवती। तदैव तत्र दारकद्वयं प्रसूता भगवतीभ्यां पृथ्वीभागीरथीभ्यामभ्युपपन्ना रसातलञ्च नीता। स्तन्यत्यागात् परेण च तत् दारकद्वयं तस्याः प्राचेतसस्य महर्षेर्गङ्गादेवी स्वयमर्पितवती।

Tam.—Listen. In the past, queen Sītā (Lakṣmaṇa having returned from the neighbourhood of the penance grove of Vālmīki, leaving her there) under the impulse of violent grief, threw herself into the currents of Gaṅgā with the labour-pains on ; that every moment there she gave birth to two boys, and favoured by mighty Earth and Bhāgīrathī, was taken to the nether regions. After they had been weaned from mother's milk, again, those two boys of hers were delivered unto the great sage Prācetasa by the goddesss Gaṅgā herself.

मित–। उचितमिति–'दाक्षिण्यम्' उदारता। एतत् 'दाक्षिण्यम्' इयमुदारता रामं प्रति तस्याः 'स्नेहस्य उचितमेव' योग्यमेव। 'तु' पक्षान्तरे 'अद्य रामभद्रसा मौलिकः' मूले सीतारूपे प्रधानायतने भवः 'सञ्जजीवनोपायः' जीवनतर्पणविधिः 'सन्निहितः' करप्राप्तः।। श्रूयतामित्यादि–उपगतः कण्ठम् 'उपकण्ठः' समीपवर्ती देशः। 'वाल्मीकितपोवनस्य उपकण्ठः' तस्मात्। 'अतिदुःखस्य' प्रबलवेदनायाः यः 'संवेगः' दारूणता तस्मात्। 'अभ्युपपन्ना' अनुगृहीता। 'तस्याः तत् दारकद्वयं स्तन्यत्यागात् पेरणं कालेन स्तन्यत्यागमात्रमेव इत्यर्थः 'स्वयं गङ्गादेवी प्राचेतसस्य महर्षेः वाल्मीकेः [सम्बन्धसामान्ये षष्ठी] 'अर्पितवती'।।

Notes. I. मौलिकः–मूले भव इति मूल+ठञ् मौलिकः original, fundamental. मूल is here सीता। 2. प्रमूता–प्र+सू+क्त कर्त्तरि आदि कर्मणि स्त्रियाम्। Or सू means प्राणिप्रसव which implies motion of the foetus. Hence, the root is in a manner गत्यर्थ and as such takes क्त in the कर्त्तृवाच्य by the rule "गत्यर्थाकमंक–"–। 3. परेण–पर here is परवर्त्तिकाल। तेन। अपवर्गे 3या। No definite period of time is meant. No sooner परिवर्त्तिकाल came they were brought to Vālmīki. 4. प्राचेतसस्य–प्राचेतम् is वरूण। तस्य अपत्यं पुमान् इति प्रचेतम्+अण् प्राचेतसः। तस्य सम्बन्धसामान्ये षष्टी as in राजकस्य वस्त्रं ददाति।

(*vi*) **मुरला (सविस्मयम्)—**

Mur.—(*In wonder*)—

ईदृशानां विपाकोऽपि जायते परमाद्भुतः।
यत्रोपकारणीभावमायात्येवंविधो जनः ।। 3 ।।

Of such persons, adversity too becomes highly interesting—adversity in which people of this stamp play the part of servers.

मित– । ईदृशानामिति।

अन्वयः–ईदृशानां विपाकोऽपि परमाद्भुतः तः जायते, यत्र एवंविधो जनः उपकरणीभावम् आयाति।

व्याख्या–'ईदृशानाम्' एवंविधानाम् अप्राकृतानां जनानां सीताप्रमुखाणामित्यर्थः 'विकोऽपि विषमोऽपि परिणमः 'परभाद्ध तः' अत्याश्चर्य्यो 'जायते' भवतिः 'यत्र' विपाके एवंविधः ईदृशः गङ्गाप्रमुखः 'जनः उपकरणीभावम्' उपकारकताम् आयाति' भजते, उपकारको भवति। स्वयं गङ्गा उपकारिणी पृथिवी च इत्यद्भुताया सीताया विपदः इति भावः।।

Notes. I. विपाकः–पच+घञ् भावे कर्मणि वा पाकः development परिणतिः। विषमः पाकः विपाकः an untoward turn, a calamity. प्रादिवत्– । उपकरणीभावम्– उपक्रियते अनेन इति उप+कृ+ल्युट् करणे उपकरणम् help hence benefactor उपकारकः। Or उप+कृ ल्यट् कर्त्तरि बाहुलक त् उपकरणम् benefactor उपकारकः। अनुपकरणम् उपकरणं भवति *i.e.*, उपकरणस्य भावम् आयाति इति उपकरण+चिव+भू+लट् ति उपकरणीभवति (*i.e.*, उपकरणीभावम् आयाति)। This is directly expressed with घञ् thus अनुपकरणस्य उपकरणस्य भाव इति उपकरण+चिव+भू+घञ् भावे उपकरणाभवः। तम्।

(*vii*) **तमसा–इदानीन्तु शम्बूकवृत्तान्तेनानेन सम्भावितजनस्थानागमनं रामभद्रं सरयूमुखादुपश्रुत्य भगवती भागीरथी यदेव भगवत्या लोपामुद्रया स्नेहादशङ्कितं तदेवाशङ्क्य सीतासमेता केनचिदिव गृहाचारव्यपदेशेन गोदावरीं विलोकयितुमागता।**

Tam.—But just now, having heard from the mouth of Sarajū that, through his Śambūka affair, Rāmabhadra's visit to Janasthāna is assured, mighty Bhagīrathī, apprehending just what is feared by Worshipful Lopāmudrā through affection, has, under the pretext of some family observence, come to see Godāvarī, accompanied by Sītā.

मित– । 'इदानीं तु' सम्प्रति पुनः 'सरव्याः' नद्याः 'मुखात् अनेन शम्बुकस्य वृत्तान्तेन "तदाख्यो वृषलस्तपस्तप्यते तं हत्वा जीवय द्विजम्" इति वृत्तान्ते न 'सम्भवितं' सम्यक् भावितं निश्चितमित्यर्थः 'जनस्थानागमनं' यस्य तादृशं 'रामभद्रम् उपश्रुत्यं' नूनं शम्बेकं हन्तुं जनस्थानं गमिष्यति रामभद्र इत्येव सरव्या विज्ञापिता 'भगवती भागीरथी केनचिदिव येन केनचित् 'गृहाचारस्य कुलक्रियायाः 'व्यपदेशेन' छ्लेन इदं मे कुलकर्म गोदावरीसमीपे कर्त्तव्यम् इति यथा ागति किञ्चित् छ्लमवलम्ब्य इत्यर्थः 'गोदावरी विलोकयितुमागता' तत्रैव रामेण सीता समेर्ष्यति इति ।।

Notes. 1. शम्बूक etc.—This does not refer to the beheading of शम्बूक, but to the prediction made by the voice in the air. See next. 2. सम्भावित etc.—सम+भू+णिच्+क्त कर्मणि सम्भावित। Usually this means *likely*, here *sure, fully guessed* etc. (सम्यगूहित)। In this sense compare सम्भावनीय in—सम्भावनीयनुभावा अस्या आकृतिः–*Śakuntala*. The voice in the air having declared the condition of the boy's revival, Rāma was bound to go to जनस्थान where शम्बूक was and his presence there could be clearly seen (सम्भावित)। But whether we mean *likely* or *sure*, शम्बूकवृत्तान्त cannot refer to the beheading of शम्बूक। For in that case राम has to be taken as already come to जनस्थान, because शम्बूक was practising penance in जनस्थान। Comp. Vāsantī's "अस्मिन्नेन जनस्थाने तपश्चरति" in Act II, p. 32. Hence, he being already there, it is absurd to say he is *likely* or sure to come.) 3. गृहाचार etc.––This आचार is not the ग्रन्थिबन्धन referred to by तमसा below. But something that came up to her at the time—it was altogether imaginary, a hoax, as is obvious from इव in केनचिदिव। भागीरथी gave सीता a plausible reason for the visit and asked her to accompany which सीता did.

(viii) **मुरला–सुविचिन्तितं भगवत्या–"राजधानीस्थितस्य खलु तैस्तैर्जगतामाभ्युदयिकैः कार्यैर्व्यापृतस्य रामभद्रस्य नियताश्चित्तविक्षेपाः। अव्यग्रस्य पुनरस्य शोकमात्रद्वितीयस्य पञ्चवटी-प्रवेशो महाननर्थः" इति। तत् कथमिदानीं सीतादेव्या रामभद्र आश्वासनीयः स्थात् ?**

Mur.—it is well guessed by her mighty self that the commotions of Rāmabhadra's mind are indeed checked while staying in his capital occupied with all those measures of benificence to the world; but entrance into the Pañcavaṭī is highly undesirable (a great mishap) for him unoccupied, with grief alone for his second. Well then how is Rāmabhadra to be consoled now by queen Sītā?

मित–। 'राजधान्यां स्थितस्य जगताम् आभ्युदयिकैः' मङ्गलविधायकैः कार्यैः व्यापृतस्य' आसक्तचित्तस्य 'रामभद्रस्य चित्तविक्षेपाः' जानकीविरहभावनाजनिताः मनसः क्षोभः 'नियताः' नियन्त्रिताः। 'अव्यग्रस्य पुनः' किन्तु विषयान्तरेः अनासक्तस्या 'शोकमात्रं द्वितीयं' सहाय इत्यर्थः यस्य तादृशस्य 'अस्य पञ्चवटीप्रवेशो महान् अनर्थः अनिष्ट् 'इति' एतत! 'भगवत्या' भागीरथी 'सुविचिन्तितं' निपुणमवधारितम्। 'तत् तस्मात् अनर्थः' पञ्चवटीप्रवेश इति हेतोः पृच्छामि सति च अनर्थे 'सीतादेव्या कथं रामभद्रः आश्वासनीयः स्याात्'। गोदावरीह्रदे स्थितया सीतया रामभद्रस्य समागम एव न स्यत्, आस्ताम् आश्वासनम् इति भावः।।

Notes. 1. सुविचिन्तितम्–Well thought of. The कर्म is इति following; and इति refers to the whole from राजधानी to अनर्थः। 2. आभ्युदयिकैः–अभि+उद्+इ+अप् भावे अभ्युदय prosperity. अभ्युदयः प्रयोजनम् एषाम् इति अभ्युदय+ठञ् आभ्युदयिकानि। 3. नियताः–नि+यम+क्त कर्मणि Checked. 4. अव्यग्रस्य–न व्यग्रः अव्यग्रः unoccupied. 5. शौक etc.—शोक एव शोकमात्रम्, मय रव्यं सकादि तत्–। तत् द्वितीयं without any other companion but शोक। He will then brood over शोक। 6. अनर्थः–अर्थ is प्रयोजन the end, the wished for. न अर्थः अनर्थः What is not wished for, hence a mishap. 7. कथम् etc.—I do not see how Sītā could console Rāma. She is under water with गोदावरी while राम is here in पञ्चवटी।

(*ix*) तमप्सा–उक्मत्र भगवत्या भागीरथीदेव्या–"वत्से देवयजनसम्भवे सीते, अद्य खलु आयुष्मतोः कुशलवयोर्द्वादशसंवत्सरस्य संख्यामङ्गल ग्रन्थिरभिबध्यते। तत् आत्मनः पुराण श्वशुरम् एतावतो मानवस्य राजर्षिवंशस्य प्रसवितारं सवितारम् अपहतपाप्मानं देवं स्वहस्तावचितैः पुष्पैरूपतिष्ठस्व। न च त्वामवनिपृष्ठचारिणीम् अस्मत्प्रभावात् वनदेवता अपि द्रक्ष्यन्ति किं पुनर्मर्त्याः" इति। अहञ्च

आज्ञापिता–"तमसे, त्वयि प्रकृष्टप्रेमेव बधूर्वत्सा जानकी। अतस्त्वा-मेवास्याः प्रत्यन्तरीभव" इति। साहमधुना यथादिष्टमनुतिष्ठामि।

Tam.—In this matter has been said this by the mighty goddess Bhagīrathī:—

"Child Sītā, sprung from the ground for divine sacrifice, this very day is being tied the auspicious knot for the enumeration of the twelth year of Kuśa and Lava of long life. So do you worship, with flowers plucked with your own hand, your primeval father-in-law the god sun, the destroyer of sin, the progenitor of this race of royal sages descended from Manu. Through my power, even forest-deities shall not see you moving on the surface of the earth, how again mortals? And I have been comanded thus:—Tamasā, our daughter-in-law, child Jānakī, is indeed greatly attached to you; so be you her close companoin." (Thus commissioned) I now do as bid.

मित–।'अत्र' अस्मिन् विषये सीताकर्तृकरामसमाश्वासनप्रस्तावे।'द्वादशस्य संवत्सरस्य' या 'संख्या' गणना तस्या 'मङ्गलकरो ग्रन्थिः' बन्धः अभिबध्यते ग्रथ्यते यो हि ग्रन्थिः प्रतिवर्षमायुष्मतोर्जन्तिथौ सूत्रे तस्मिन् बध्यते, एकादश च येषां ग्रन्थीनां बद्धा तेषां द्वादशो ग्रन्थिर्वध्यते इत्यर्थः।'पुराणम्' प्राचीनम् आद्य मित्यर्थः 'श्वशुरम्'। 'मानवस्य' मनुसम्बन्धिनः वैवस्वतमनोर्जातस्य।'अपहतः' विनाशितः 'पाप्सा' पापं येन तम् 'स्वहस्तेन अवचितैः पुष्पैः उपतिष्ठस्व' पूजय। ननु जले कुतः पुष्पाणि, तत् पुष्पार्थं मया समीपवर्त्तिनि जनस्थाने भ्रमितव्यम्। जनाश्च मां मृतां जानन्ति, तत् यदि केनचित् दृष्टा स्याम् अनिष्ठं प्रसज्येत इत्यत्राह–अवन्याः पृष्टे विचरन्तीं त्वाम् अस्माकं प्रभावात्' मभैव महिम्ना 'वनदेवताः अपि न द्रक्ष्यन्ति किं पुनमर्त्त्याः' कुतो वा मानुषाः पश्येयुः तन्निशङ्कं गच्छ।'प्रकष्ठप्रेमा' परमानुरागा।'प्रत्यन्तरीभव' अनुचरीभव।।

Notes. 1. कुशलवयोः–मुरला does not knot now who कुश and लव are. a. द्वादश etc.—द्वौ च दश च 'द्वादश' twelve. द्वि becomes द्वा by "द्व्यष्टनः संख्यायाम्–" द्वाशानां पूरण इति द्वादशन्+उट्–द्वादशः twelfth. A knot is tied on a silk string at the completion of each year of the child's age. The twelfth year is complete to-day (अद्य खलु)। The boys were born on the day सीता was abandoned. That very day Rishyasringa's sacrifice commenced. It was to last 12 years. We are already infromed that the sacrifice is over (see Act II, बिष्कम्भक) । Hence, we have to suppose that तमप्सा and मुरला met on the day of the completion of the sacrifice. 3. उपतिष्ठस्व–देवपूजायाम् आत्मनेपदम् owing to the Vārttika "उपाद्देवपूजा–"। 4. प्रकृष्टप्रेमा–प्रकृष्टः प्रेमा or प्रकृष्टं प्रेम यस्याः सा । Here the प्रातिपादिक is प्रकृष्टप्रेमन् in the original masucline. In the fem. ङीप् is barred by "मनः' । Hence, the fem. form is also प्रकृष्टप्रेमन् । 5. प्रत्यन्तरीभव–No समाप्त, we have two distinct words प्रत्यन्तरी and भव by the rule "उपपदमतिङ्" । अन्तर is अवकाश interval, opportunity etc. प्रतिगता अन्तरं प्रत्यन्तरा on that is ready at the right moment, *i.e.*, a companion; प्रादितत्– । अप्रत्यन्तरा प्रत्यन्तरा भव इति प्रत्यन्तरा+च्वि+भू+लोट्हि।

(*x*) मुरला–अहमप्यमुं वृत्तान्तं भगवत्यै लोपामद्रायै निवेदयामि। रामभद्रोऽपि आगत एव इति तर्कयामि।

Mur.—I too will communicate this news to mighty Lopāmudrā Rāmabhadra also I guess has indeed arrived.

तमप्ता–तदियं गोदावरीह्लदान्निसाष्क्रम्य–

Tam.—Well, then here, emerging from Godāvarī's pool—

परिपाण्डुदुर्बलकपोलसुन्दरं दधती विलोलकवरीकमाननम्।
करुणस्य मूर्त्तिरिव वा शरीरिणी विरहव्यथेव वनमेति जानकी।। 4।।

Jānakī enters the wood with her beautiful face wan and lean the cheeks, with her braid of locks dangling about—like the very person of the sentiment Karuṇa, or like the pang of separation embodied.

मित– । अहमित्यादि–रामभद्रोऽपि आगत एव इति तर्कयामि' प्राप्त एव समाश्वसनकालः कुत्र नु सीता इति भावः। यत् त्वं राममागत्मेव मन्यसे 'तत्' ब्रवौमि तदिति–सीतापि आगता एव मा शङ्क्ष्ठिाः। परीति।

अन्वयः–परिपाणुदुर्बल- कपोलसुन्दरं विलोलकवरीकम् आननं दधती जानकी करुणस्य मूत्तिरिव शरीरिणी विरहव्यथा इव वा वनमेति।

व्याख्या–'परिपाण्डू' पाण्डुरवर्णौ 'दुबंलौं' क्षामौं 'कपोलौ गन्डौ यस्मिन् तथाविधं 'सुन्दरं' मनोहरञ्च अतएव द्रष्ठृणां करुणोद्दीपकम् तथा 'बिलोला' बन्धनाभावात् दोदुल्यमाना 'कबरी' यस्मिन् तथाविधम् अतएव विरहिणीत्वं प्रख्यापयत् 'आनन'

मुखं दधती धारयन्ती 'जानकी करुणस्य मूत्तिरिव' मूत्तिमानिव करुणो रसः 'शरीरिणी' धृतदेहा 'विरहव्यथा इव वा' अथवा सशरीरा वियोगवेदना इव वनम् एति' जनस्थानकाननं प्रविशति।।

*Notes.*I. रामभद्रोऽपि etc.—She fancies she sees signs of Rāma's arrival. Hence her apprehension that disaster is imminent while ther are no signs of Sītā's presence to avert it. Tamasā reassures her with तदियम् etc. 2. तदिव्यम् etc.—Be not alarmed, here is Sītā coming. 3. परिपाण्डु, etc.—पाण्डु pale. परिपाण्डु very pale. दुर्बली weak, here *emaciated*. परिपाण्डु च तौ दुर्बलौ च परिपाण्डु दुर्बली pale and emaciated. कर्मधा-। तादृशौ कपोलौ यस्मिन्। तच्च तत् सुन्दरञ्च, कर्मधा-। Usually this is taken to mean that though the cheeks were pale and hollow yet the face looked beautiful (Vidyāsāgara); or, beautiful because it was pale and emaciated (Vīrarāghava). Both these make the सौन्दर्य्य prominent, *i.e.,* the observer is impressed by the सौन्दर्य at its sight. In other words he seen no करुणास्य मूर्त्तिः। We therfore take the सौन्दर्य as a natural attribute and परिपाण्डुता and दुर्बलता striking the observer as merely incidental and holding up to him an image of the havoc done by paleness etc. to a beautiful face. This is करुण्य मूर्त्तिः। 4. विलोल etc.—विलोल dangling. कबरौ a braid of hair. The कप् is समासान्त। The कवरी was विलोल, *i.e.,* it was not tied up as in dressing the hair at toilet. This is the usual singn of the विरहिणी। It gives the observer the image of शरीरिणी विरहव्यथा। The comparison is thus two-fold-करुणस्य मूर्त्तिरिव through परिपाण्डु etc. and शरीरिणी बिरहव्यथेव from बिलोल etc. It is not that the epithet परिपाण्डु etc. plays no part in the second comparison. There is the word व्यथा joined to विरह and परिपाण्डु etc. imdicates व्यथा। It is the व्यथा, the torment of बिरह, that has taken the colour off the cheeks and hollowed them out. The second comparison is an improvement over the first.

(*xi*) मुरला—इय हि सा।

Mur.—Thus is indeed she!

किसलयमिव मुग्धं बन्धनाद्विप्रलूनं
हृदयकुसुमशोषी दारुणो दीर्घशोकः।

ग्लपयति परिपाण्डु क्षाममस्याः शरीरं
शरदिज इव घर्मः केतकीगर्भपत्रम्।। 5।।

(इति परिक्रम्य निष्क्रान्ते)

विष्कम्भकः

Just as the heat development in autumn does with respect to the leaf at the cure of the Ketakī, so the terrible and lasting grief, that has blasted her flower-like heart, is drying up her extermely wan and lean bodys which resembles a beautiful new leaf picked from its stalk.

(Exeunt going round the stage).

Here ends the Viṣkambhaka.

मित– । 'इयं हि सा' इति प्रत्यभिज्ञा ।। किसलयेति ।

अन्वयः–हृदयकुसुमशोषी दारुणः दीर्घशोकः (हृदयकुसुमशोषी) शरदिजः धर्मः केतकीगर्भपत्रमिव अस्याः वन्धनात् विप्रलून मुग्धं किसलयमिव परिपाण्डु क्षाम शरीरं ग्लपयति।)

व्याख्या–द्विविधमस्निमन् श्लोके साम्यम्, शरीरग्लपनं केतकीगर्भ पत्रग्लपनमिव इत्येकम्, शरीर किसलयमिव परिपाण्डु क्षामम् इति द्वितीयम्। 'कुसुमतुल्य' हृदय शोषयति' यस्तादृशः 'दारुणः' कठोरः 'दीर्घशोकः' चिरविरहवेदना 'हृदयस्थितं' पत्रकोषगं 'कुसुमं' केतकीकुसुमं 'शोषयति' यस्तादृशः ' शरदिजः धर्म्मः' शरतकालसम्भव आतपः 'केतक्या गर्भपत्रमिव' पुष्मारवक पत्रमिव 'अस्याः बन्धनात् विप्रलूनं' वृन्तात् छिन्न 'मुग्धं' सुन्दरं किसलयमिव 'नवपल्लमिव 'परिपाण्डु' छिन्नत्वात् स्लानं 'म्लामं' शौर्णञ्च 'शरीर ग्लपयति' पीड़यति ।।

Notes. 1. किसलयम्–The sibilant is dental not palatal. Compare the यमक in "किसलयैः सलयैरिव पाणिभिः"–*Raghu*. 2. बन्धनात् etc.— Hence it is परिपाण्डु क्षाम। 3. हृदय etc.—This goes with both दीर्घ शोक and धर्म्मं See *Mitabh*—हृदय *heart* (दीर्घशोक); also *interior* (धर्म्म), by transference of epithets. हृदयं कुसुममिव (दीर्घशोक) ; also हृदये कुसुमम् (सुप्सुपा), or हृदयस्थितं कुसुमम् (शाकपार्थिवादि कर्मधा–) in the case of धर्मं तत् शोपयतीति हृदयकुसुम+शष+णिच्+णिनि कर्त्तरि तीच्छील्ये। 4. ग्लपयति–ग्लै+णिच्+लट् तिप्=ग्लापि+ति=ग्लापयति or ग्लपयति the आ becoming अ optionally by "ग्लास्नावनुक्मां च"। 5. परिपाण्डु etc.—Lean and pale as she is like a fresh twig plucked and exposed to the sun, the terrible grief is still gnawing at the core of her heart. 6. शरदिजः–शरदि जात इति शरद+जन ड

कर्त्तरि शरदिजः the सप्तमी being retainted by "ततपुरूषे कुति बहुलम्"। 7. धर्म–This is आतप sun-light, i.e., heat. 8. केतकी etc.—केतकी is the flower together with its casing of leaves. The core is the flower, the casing next to the flower is the गर्भपत्र and outside there are the other leaves. These with the flower encased within are the केतकी of the market. The flower is here supposed to have withered through heat (हृदयकुसुमशोषी)। 9. *Remark*—It is strnage that मुरला can see सीता। भागीरथी has declared that not even a वनदेवता can see her. The following are compared—(a) Sītā's heart is tender like a flower. (b) Her pale and lean body is like a fresh twig that has been plucked and has become discoloured and shrivelled through heat. (c) Her torment of grief is like the onslaught of autumnal heat on the innermost leaves of the Ketakī flower.

(*xii*) **(नेपथ्ये)–प्रमादः प्रमादः।**

(In the tiring room)—(A) mishap! (A) mishap!

(ततः प्रविशति पुष्पावचयव्यग्रा सकरूणीत्सुक्यमाकर्णयन्ती सीता)।

(Then enters Sītā occupied with gathering flowers and listening with sorrow and anxiety).

सीता–अम्महे जाणामि पिअसही मे वासन्दी वाहरदि [अहो जानामि प्रियसखी मे वासन्ती व्याहरति]।

Sītā—Ha! My dear friend Vāsantī is shouting I belive (Again in the tiring room)—

(पुनर्नेपथ्ये)–

सीतादेव्या स्वकरलितैः शल्लकीपल्लवाग्रै-
रग्रे लोलः करिकरभको यः पुरा पोषितोऽभूत्।

The young elephant, full of fun in her presence, that was reared formerly queen Sītā with tops of Śallakī twings collected with her own hand—

सीता–कि तस्म [कि तस्य]?

Sītā—What of him?

(पुनर्नेपथ्ये)–

(Again in the Tiring Room)—

बध्वा सार्द्धं पयसि विहरन् सोऽयमन्येन दर्पा-
दुद्दामेन द्विरदपतिना सन्निपत्याभियुक्तः ।। 6 ।।

He, the same sporting in water with his mate, is attacked by an irresistible leader of tuskers defiantly rushing in through sheer insolence.

मित– । 'प्रमादः' विपदित्यर्थः । एतत वासन्त्या भाषितम् ।। 'पुष्पाणमवचयः' हस्तेन सङ्कलनं तत्र 'व्यग्रा' व्यापृता । वासन्तीसन्निधानात् 'करुणा' । प्रमादवर्णनात् विशेषविज्ञानार्थम् 'औत्सक्यम्' ।। 'पुनर्नैपथ्ये' इत्यत्र पुनरिति व्यर्थम् ।। सीतेति ।

अन्वयः–पुरा सीतादेव्या यः अग्रे लोलः करिकरभकः स्वरकलितैः शल्लकीपल्लवाग्रेः पोषितः अभूत् सः अयं बध्वा सार्द्ध पयसि विहरन् अन्येन उद्दामेन द्विरदपतिना दर्पात् सन्निपत्य अभियुक्तः ।

व्याख्या–'पुरा' दण्डकावासकाले 'सीतादेव्या यः अग्रे' सीतासमक्षं 'लोलः, चपलः शैशवोचितचाञ्चल्यविशिष्टः 'करिकरभकः' गजपोतः 'स्वकरकलितैः स्वहस्तावचितैः 'शल्लकीपल्लवानां' कोमलैः 'अग्रैः पोषितः' वर्द्धितः 'अभूत् सः अयं बध्वा' करेणकया 'सार्द्धं पयसि विहरन्' जले क्रीडम् 'च्यन्येन' अपरेन् न तु येन केनचित् अपरेण किन्तु 'उद्दामेन द्विरदपतिना' अमितबलेन केनचित् गजेन्द्रेण 'दपात्' गर्वात् 'सन्निपत्य' अभिधाब्य 'अभियुक्तः' आक्रान्तः । इति प्रमादो- ऽयमापतिनः ।।

Notes. 1. पुष्प etc.—अव+चि+अच् भावे अवचयः plucking. This is irregular. घञ् is enjoined in this sense by "हस्तादाने चेरस्तेये" । Compare कुसुमावचयव्यग्रहस्ता–*Śakuntala*, Act IV. 2. सकरुण etc.—करुणा sorrow. Her sorrow strengthens because she hears Vāsantī, her dear friend, speak. "स्वजनस्य हि दुःखमग्रती विवतद्वारमित्रोपजायते" । औत्मुक्य eagerness. This is to know the details of the mishap to which Vāsantī refers. 3. पुनर्नेपथ्ये–The पुनर is useless. The simple नेपथ्ये is enough. In fact one of Vidyāsāgara's manuscripts omits पुनर । 4. स्वकर etc.—कलित *plucked*—Vidyāsāgara. Vīrarāghava says 'offered'. But plucked implies more concern for the little one than *offered*, and is to be preferred. 5. लोलः–लोलः restless. The restlessness is usually explained as due to his longing for the twigs in Sītā's hand. It seems better to attribute it to the playfulness of childhood. In "येनोट्गच्छद्दिस-

किलयसस्निग्धदन्ताङ्कुरेण व्याकृष्टस्ते सुतनु लवली पल्लवः कर्णमूलात्'' (sl. 15, below) Rāma refers to लोलत्व in connection with the childhood of this elephant. 6. करि etc.—करभ a young elephant, camel or horse. Here a young animal in general. स एव करभकः। करो चासौ करभक्रश्च or करिणः करभकः। 7. बध्वा etc.—This means that he is a grown up elephant now. 8. उद्दामेन–दामन् chain, curb. In the feminine it becomes दासन्+डाप् दामा। उद्धती दामाया, उद्दाभः प्रादितत्–। तेन। There is nothing to curb him; he is irresistible. 6. etc.—द्वौ रदौ दन्ती एवं द्विरदाः elephants. This is a misnomer. Only two of the teeth are *visible,* but there are others also—the grinders द्विरदाना पतिः। Hence the प्रमाद (danger). He is quite young while his assailant is a mighty leader of tuskers. 10. सन्निपत्य–सम्+नि+पत+ल्यप्। Both सम् and नि are intensive. Together they imply a *defiant trespass.* Compare ''किमुक्तैः सन्निपत्यैव पताकां वो हराम्यहम्''–Act IV, sl. 26. There defiance is obvious. Hence, we take सन्निपत्य here as implying a wanton attack, a supposition which दर्पात् confirms.

(*xiii*) सीता (ससम्भमं कतिचित् पदानि दधती)–अज्जउत्त परित्ताहि परित्ताहि मम तं पुत्तअं [आर्यपुत्र, परित्रायस्व परित्रायस्व मम तं पुत्रकम्]। (स्मृतिमभिनीय सवैल्कव्यम्) हद्धी हद्धी एव चिरपरिचिदाइं अक्खराइं पञ्चवटीदंसणेण पुणो वि मं मन्दभाइणिं अणुरुन्धन्ति। हा अज्जउत्त [हा धिक् हा धिक्, तान्येव चिरपरिचितानि अक्षराणि पञ्चवटीदर्शनेन पुनरपि मां मन्दभागिनीमनुरुन्धन्ति। हा आर्यपुत्र]। (इति मूर्च्छति)।

(प्रविश्य) तमसा–वत्से समाश्वसिहि समाश्वसिहि।

Sītā (*Taking a few steps in alarm*)— Save, my husband, save that poor darling of mine. (*Acting recollection—In despair*) Alas! Alas ! Those very letters, long familiar, come up to my ill-fated self once again at the sight of the Pañcavaṭī, Ah ! My husband ! (Faints away).

(Entering) Tamasā—Cheer up, my child, cheer up.

मित–।'सम्भ्रमेण' आवेगेन सह 'ससम्भ्रमम्'।'कतिचित्' कानिचित्।'पदानि दधती' पदक्षेपान् केर्वती। 'पुत्रकम्' दत्यनुकम्पायां ह्रस्वे वा कन्। 'स्मृति' परित्यागवृत्तान्त स्मरणम् 'अभिनीय' अभिनयेन दर्शयित्वा। 'वैल्कव्यम्' अवसादः

तेन सह।' चिरं दीर्घकालं ' परिचितानि अभ्यस्तानि ' अक्षराणि वणां आर्य्यपुत्रशब्दघटका वर्णाः।' अनुसरन्ति पूर्वसंस्कारवशादुततिष्ठन्ते।।

Notes. 1. कति etc.—काः संख्या एषाम् इति किम्+इति कति in the Ist case plural. चित् is an अव्यय adding indefiniteness to the word preceding. No समास, two distinct words. कतिचित् कियन्ति अपि। 2. स्मृतिम्–Her appeal to her आर्यपुत्र was due to forgetfulness of the present. After having uttered the word आर्यपुत्र she recollects (स्मृति) that neither is her आर्यपुत्र with her at the time, nor is she entitled to appeal to him. Hence the वैल्कव्य। 3. सवैल्कव्यम्–ल्कव literally is भय, hence despair. विशिष्टः ल्कवः अस्याः विल्कवा। तस्या भावः इति विल्कवा+घञ् वैल्कव्यम्। तेन सह। 4. हव धिक् etc.—She explains how she forget the presents. It is पञ्चवटीदर्शनेन। The sight of पञ्चवटी brings the past vividly before her and she forgets the present.

(*xiv*) **नेपथ्ये–विमानराज, अत्रैव स्थीयताम्।**

(In the Tiring Room)—O the best of ballons, stop just here.

सीता (आश्वस्य सप्ताध्वसोल्लासम्)–अम्महे जलभरिद-मेहत्थणिदगम्भीरमंसलो कुदोणु एसो भारदीणिग्घोसो भरिज्जमाण-कणविवरं मं वि मन्दभाइणिं झत्ति उस्मावेदि [अहो जलभरितमेघ-स्तनितगन्भीरमांसलः कुतो नु एष भारतीनिर्घोषो भ्रियमाणकर्णाविवरां मामपि मन्दभागिनीं झटिति उच्छ्वासयति]?

Sītā (*coming round—with joy and agitation*)—Ha ! Whence deos this pronunciation of speech, deep and full like and rumble of a water-laden cloud, quickly revive even me the ill-fated whose ear-holes are becoming full of it?

तमसा (सस्नेहास्त्रम्)–अयि वत्से

Tam. (*With tears of offection*)—O my child,—

किमव्यक्तेऽसि निनदे कुतस्त्येऽपि त्वमोदृशो।
स्तनयिन्तोर्मयूरीव चकितोत्कण्टितं स्थिता।। 7।।

Why do you, thus placed, stand startled and uneasy even at anuncomprehended and un-located sound like a pea-hen at that of a cloud ? (7).

मित–।'विमानराज' इति पुष्पकं प्रति' रामस्य कण्ठ एषः। 'साध्वसं' भयम्। कृत इह रामस्य कण्ठः, भ्रमोऽयं मे स्यात् इति भयम्। ततो रामस्यैव इति निश्चयः तेन च उल्लासः'। 'जलेन भरितः' सञ्जातभरः यो 'मेघः' तस्य 'स्तनितं ध्वनिः तथाविधो 'गम्भीरः' गाम्भीर्यपुर्णः मासलः' विपुलश्च। 'भारत्याः' वाणयाः 'निर्घोषः' ध्वनिः। 'भ्रियमानम्' आपूर्यमाणं 'कर्णविवरं' यस्याः तथाविधां कुर्वन् 'उच्छासयति' उज्जीवयति।। किमिति।।

अन्वयः–ईदृशी त्वम् अवाक्ते कुतस्त्ये अपि निनदे स्तनयित्रोः मयूरीव किं चकितोत्कण्ठितं स्थिता असि।

व्याख्या–'ईदृशी' एवंविधा मोहमापन्ना इत्यर्थः त्वम् अवाक्ते, अपरिस्फटै 'कुतस्त्ये' अविज्ञातकण्ठादागते 'अपि निनदे' ध्वनी 'स्तनयित्लोः' मेघस्य निनदे 'मयूरी इव किं' कथं 'चकितं' त्रस्तं यथा तथा 'उत्कण्ठितं' यथा तथा च 'स्थिता असि। किमुच्यते को वा वक्ता न ज्ञातं तथापि मूर्च्छिताया अपि ते चकितता उत्कण्ठा च इति किम् इत्यर्थः।।

Notes. 1. जलभरित etc.—भर+इतच् (तारकादि) भरितः laden. Now see *Mitabh*—गम्भीर deep; मांसल full. It is difficult to distinguish between the two. The full is usually deep and *vice versa*. 2. अव्यक्ते–वि+अञ्ज+क्त कर्मकर्त्तरि व्यक्त clear परिस्फुट। न व्यक्तः अव्यक्तः, पस्मिन्। The import of the words is not clear. Here some have अपरिस्फट टनिक्वाणे for the first quarter. This seems preferable (see next para). Explain thus—'ईदृशी त्वम् कुतस्तो अपि अपरिस्फट टे' अव्यक्ते निक्वाणो' ध्वनी etc. as before. 3. निनदे–नि+नद+अप् कर्म्मणि निनद or घञ् कर्म्मणि निनाद। घञ् alternates with अप् by "नौ गदनद–"। 4. कुतस्त्रे–किम+ङसि (5मी)+तसि स्वार्थे कुतः। This is an अव्यय। Next कुत आगत इति कुतस्+त्यप् कुतस्त्रः। अव्यय words with तसि take त्यप् by the Vārttika "अमेहकृतसित्रेभ्यस्त्यवविधिर्योऽव्ययात् स्मृतः"। The source of the words is unknown. 5. ईदृशी–Thus circumstanced, *i.e.*, in a swoon. From the character of the sound as described (अव्यक्त, कुतस्त्य), even one wide awake ought not to be impressed, yet you were affected even in your swoon. 6. स्तनयित्लोः–स्तन् to utter the rumble of a cloud (अदन्तचुरादि)+णिच् स्वार्थे+इत्नु कर्त्तरि ताच्छील्येस्तनयित्नुः। तस्य। 7. चकित etc.—चकितश्च तत् उत्कण्ठितश्च, कर्मधा–। तत् यथ तथा। The reading चकितोत्कण्ठितार is perhaps better.

(*xv*) सीता–भअवदि किं भणासि अपरिप्फुडंत्ति ? मए उण

सरसंजोएण पच्चभिआणिदं अज्जउत्त एव वाहरदि [भगवति, किं भणसि अपरिस्फुटमिति ? मया पुनः स्वरसंयोगेन प्रत्यभिज्ञातम् आर्यपुत्र एव व्याहरति]।

Sītā—My worshipful friend, do you say indistinct ? I again recognise from the modulation of the voice that it is my husband himself that speaks.

तमसा–श्रूयते तपस्यतः शूद्रस्य दण्डधारणार्थम् ऐक्ष्वाको राजा जनस्थानमागत इति।

Tam.—We hear that the king, the descendat of Ikṣvaku, has come to Janasthana to inflict punishment on a Śūdra practising prenance.

सीता–दिट्ठिआ अपरिहीणराअधम्मो क्खु सो राआ [दिष्ट्या अपरिहीणराजधर्मः खलु स राजा]।

Sītā—O joy, that king is indeed without lapse in his kingly duties. (Lit.—has his kingly duties unneglected).

नेपथ्ये–

यत्र द्रुमा अपि मृगा अपि बन्धवो मे
यानि प्रियासहचरश्चिरमध्यवात्सम्।
एतानि तानिबहुनिर्झरकन्दराणि
गोदावरीपरिसरस्य गिरेस्तटानि।।8।।

(In the Tiring Room)—These are those slopes, with numerous streams and caves, of the hill that has the Godāvarī at its skirts (hill Prāsravaṇa), slopes which I long occupied in company with my darling, where even the deer (nay) even the trees are like friends to me.

मित–। 'भगवति' महिममयि तमसे 'अपरिस्फुटमिति भणसि किम्' ? भण। अपरिस्फुटमेव ते भवतु न मे काचित् क्षतिः। 'मया पुनः' पक्षान्तरे स्वरस्य संयोगेन' उच्चारणप्रकारेण भया 'प्रत्यभिज्ञातम्' अवधारितम् 'आर्यपुत्र एव व्याहरति' भाषते। एतत्तु 'किमव्यक्तेऽपि निनदे'' इति पाठोन सद्धच्छते, तन्मन्ये ''अपरिस्फुटनिक्काणे'' इत्येव तत्रत्यः पाठः।। 'तपस्तयः' तपश्चरतः 'शूद्रस्य' सम्बन्धे 'दण्डधारणार्थ'

राजशासननिर्वाहार्थं 'जनस्थानमागतः'। कुतस्तस्य तत्राग्रहः इत्याह–'राजा' सः, प्रजास अपचारप्रशमनं राजधर्मः, तत् अपचारप्रवृत्तस्य शूद्रस्य दमनार्थमागतः। भवतु कः अन्यो राजा एवं करोति इत्याह 'ऐक्ष्वाको राजा' इति। राजधर्म्मपालनमिक्ष्वाकूणां कुलव्रतं तदिह दण्डस्य स्याद्वा इति भर्त्तृसमागमे अभिमुखीकरणं सीतायाः।। 'दिष्ट्या' इति हषे अव्ययम्। 'अपरिहीणः अव्याहतः राजधर्मः' यस्य तादृशो 'राजा'। अक्षतो राजधर्म इत्यन्वर्थसंज्ञः स राजा, स च ममैव भर्त्रा इत्यानन्दः। एवं राजधर्मकुलधर्मयोः परिपालने यद्यहं त्यक्ता, शोच्यः स न निन्दाः, इति समर्थनमुखेन समाश्वासनमपि वैदेह्या ध्वन्यते।। यत्रेति।

अन्वयः–तानि तटानि 'प्रियासहचरः' सीतासमेतः सन् 'चिरम् अध्ववात्सम्' दीर्घनिवासेन समभाजयम् 'यत्र' चिरवासादेव 'मृगा अपि द्रुमा अपि' वृक्षाश्च 'मे बन्धवः' बन्धुतुल्या अजायन्त 'तानि' चिरपरितानि 'बहवो निर्झराः' जलप्रवाहः 'कन्दरा' गह्वराणि यषु तानि 'गोदावरी परिसरः' प्रान्तभूमिः यस्य तादृशस्य 'गिरेः' 'तटानि' साननि 'एतानि' दृश्यन्ते।।

Notes. 1. अपरिस्फटम् etc.—you may call it अपरिस्फुट। To me it is unnecessary to know that the voice announces (अपरिस्फुट) or whence the voice proceeds (कुतस्त्थ); the modulation of the voice (स्वरसंयोग) is enough for me for indentification as the voice of my husband, and that is all that I care for, 2. तपस्यतः–तपश्चरति इति तपस्+क्यङ् (नाम धातु)+शत्रु तपस्यन्। तस्य। क्यङ् usually gives the आत्मनेपद, but तपस् has परस्मैपद by the Vārttika "तपसः परस्मैपदञ्च"। 5. ऐक्ष्वाकः–इक्ष्वाकोर्गोत्रापत्यम् इति इक्ष्वाकु+अञ् ऐक्ष्वाकः, the उ dissappearing by निपातन in the rule "दाण्डिनायनहास्तिनायन–"। She says ऐक्ष्वाको राजा avoiding the familiar रामभद्रः। The reason is she wants to emphasise Rāma's duty as राजा and also the faithful observance of those duties by kings of the line of इक्ष्वाकु। Hence both kingly duty and family tradition make it imperative on Rāma's part to come out personally and chastise the Śūdra 4. दिष्ट्या etc.—His kingly (राजा) duties are unimpaired (अपरिहीण) and this is a matter for joy to her (दिष्ट्या) because this dutiful king (राजा) is her own husband. In his terrible bereavement it would not be surprising if there were lapses in the discharge of his arduous duties. But स्त्रिया विरहो राजधर्मात् प्रच्यावयति इत्यह्यमेतत्। Luckily he has escaped this scandal, O joy (दिष्ट्या) ! Hence the surmise that from his point of view perhaps she judges Rāma leniently in the matter of her own abandonment. 5. मृगाः–This may also mean all the animals there. 6. बन्धवः–बन्धु Friend. By transference of epithets like *friends*. 7. यानि (The आधार of अध्यवात्सम् appearing as कर्म by "उपान्वध्याङ्वसः"। 8. बहु etc.—There are springs for the thirsty and caves for the homeless, hence a suitable place for residence. 9. गोदावरी etc.—परि+मृ+घ संज्ञायां परिसरः outskirts. गोदावरी परिसरो यस्य। Refers to the hill प्रस्रवसण। Comp" ......स्निग्धनीलपरिसरारण्यपरिणद्धगोदावरीमुखरकन्दर......गिरिः प्रस्रवणो नाम" Act I. ante.

(*xvi*) **सीता (दृष्ट्वा)–हा कहं। पहादचन्दमण्डलावण्डुरपरिक्षाम-दुबलेण आआरेण अअं सोम्मगम्भीराणुभावमेत्तपञ्चमिआणिदो अज्जउत्तो एब्ब। ता मं धारेहि धारेहि [हा कथम् ! प्रभातचन्द्रमण्डलापाण्डुरपरिक्षाम-दुर्बलेन आकारेण अयं सौम्यगम्भीरानुभावमात्रप्रत्यभिज्ञात आर्यपुत्र एव। तत् मां धारय धारय]। (इति तमसामाश्लिष्य मूर्च्छति)।**

Sītā. (Spying)—Ha ! How so ! This one with a frame pale and wan and weak like the lunar or bat dawn is indeed my husband recognised by his grave and attractive majesty alone. Then hold me, (*faints having embraced Tamasā*).

तमसा (धारयन्ती)–वत्से समाश्वसिहि समाश्वसिहि।

Tam. (*Holding*)—Courage, my child, courage.

नेपेथ्ये–अनेन पञ्चवटीदर्शनेन–

अन्तर्लीनस्य दुःखाग्नेरद्योद्दामं ज्वलिष्यतः।
उत्पीड़ इव धूमस्य मोहः प्रगावृणोति माम्।। ९।।

(In the Tiring Room)—At this sight of the Panchvati—Stupor shroudus me first like a column of smoke from the fire of grief lurks within and will blaze unchecked to-day.

हा प्रिये जानकि।

Alas ! Janakī, my darling.

मित–। 'कथम्' इत्याश्चर्यें 'प्रभाते' यत् चन्द्रमण्डलं' तदिव 'आपण्डरः' विवर्णः किञ्च 'परिक्षामा' ल्कशः 'दुर्बलश्च' य आकारः' देह तेन परिलक्षितः 'अयं सौम्यः' मनोरमः 'गम्भीरः' अप्रधृष्यश्च यः 'अनुभावः' प्रभावः तन्मात्रेण प्रत्यभिज्ञातः' परिचितः 'आर्य्यपुत्र एव'। एतद्दर्शनेन शोकविह्वला पतामि 'धारय मां'।। अन्तरिति।

अन्वयः–अद्य उद्दामं ज्वलिष्यतः अन्तर्लीनस्य दुःखाग्रेः धूमस्य उत्पीड़ इव मौहः प्राक माम् आवृणोति।

व्याख्या–'अद्य उद्दामम्' अनियन्त्रितं यथा तथा 'ज्वलिष्यतः' दौपिष्यमाणास्य अन्र्लीनस्य' हदि गूढ़स्य 'दुखाग्रेः' अग्नितुल्यस्य शोकस्य धूमस्य उत्पीड़ इव' धूमरशितुल्यो 'मोहः प्राक्' प्रथमं 'माम् आवृणोति' प्रच्छायति। अच शोकभिभवात् पूर्वे मोहः परं वा इति चिन्तनीयम्, किञ्च दुःखस्य ज्वलनं मोहस्य च आवरकता रुपके युज्यते न उपमायाम्।।

Notes. 1. प्रभात etc.—The resemblance with चन्द्रमण्डल lies in the आपाण्डरता only; क्षामता and दुर्बलता have nothing to do with it. Expound प्रभातचन्द्रण्डलमिव आपण्डरम्। तथा च प्ररिक्षामश्च etc. 2. आकरिण–उपलक्षणे३या। Or—better सहार्थे३या। 3. धारय etc.—आवेगे द्विरुक्तिः। The reading here is adopted from Vidyāsāgara's manuscript No. 4. Vidyāsāgara himself prefers तत् धारय तु मां प्रियसखी of No 3. But तमसा replies वत्से etc. वत्से does not seem to come well from a प्रियसखी। 4. दुःखाग्रेः–दुःखम् अग्निरिव, उपमित कर्मधा–। The रूपक, viz, दुःखरूपः अग्निः has to be avoided. because in the next half we have उपमा in उत्पीड़ इव etc. See under ज्वलिष्यतः below. 5. उद्दामम्–see sl. 6. उद्दामेन। Apte takes उद्दामम् as a मकारान्त अव्यय। But उद्धतं दामायाः etc. as in sl. 6 is available here also, while the indeclinable does not suit sl.6. 6. ज्वलिष्यतः–In दुःखाग्नि we have दुःखत्व prominent not अग्नित्व, so ज्वलिष्यतः is out of place. ज्वलन of दुःख is possible through a रूपक only. Hence, say ज्वलिष्यतः प्रकीपिष्यतः प्रकटीभविष्यतः etc. (धातूनामनेकार्थत्वात्)। 7. प्राक्–Here a difference of opinion is possible. Some might think that the shock of grief comes first an;d the the swoon as the consequence. We may defend saying that ज्वलन here is manifestation to outside people through lamentation etc. The shock may be so intense that swoon occurs first and lamentation follows after consciousness is regained. 8. आवृणोति–Here again मोहत्व is prominent, not धूमातृपीड़त्व। Hence आवरण is unsuitable. Say आवृणोति अभिभवति (धातूनामनेकार्थत्वात्)।

(*xvii*) **तमसा (स्वगतम्)–इदं तदाशङ्कितं गुरुजनेनापि।**

Tam. (*To herself*)—This is what the superiors too apprehended.

सीता–(समाश्वस्य)–हा कहं एदं [हा कथमेतत्]।

Sītā. (*Having recovered*)—Ha ! How is this ?

नेपथ्ये–हा देवि दण्डकारण्यवासप्रियसखि, हा देवि विदेहराजपुत्रि। (इति मूर्च्छति)।

(In the Tiring Room)—Ah ! Queen, my dear companion during my stay in the Daṇḍaka. Alas ! My queen the daughter of the king of Videha. (*Faints away*).

सीता–हद्धी हद्धी मं मन्दभाइणिं वाहरिअ आमीलन्तणेतणीलुप्पलो मुच्छिदो एब्ब अज्जउत्तो। हा कहं धरणीवट्टे निरुस्माहणीसहं विपलहत्थों। भअवदि तमसे परित्ताहि परित्ताहि जीवावेहि अज्जउत्तं [हा धिक् हा धिक्! मां मन्दभागिनीं ब्याहृत्य आमीलन्नेत्रनीलोत्पलः मूर्च्छित एव आर्यपुत्रः। हा कथं धरणीपृष्टे निरुत्साहनिः सहं विपर्यस्तः! भगवति तसमे परित्रायस्व परित्रायस्व, जीवय आर्यपुत्रम्]।

Sītā—Fie on me ! Naming me, the ill-fated, my husband has indeed fainted away with the blue-lotus of his eyes closing up. How so ! Alas ! He lies on his face spiritless and powerless, on the surface of the ground. Help ! Worshipful Tamasā, help ! Save my husband. (*Falls at her feet*).

तमसा–

त्वमेन ननु कल्याणि सञ्जीवय जगत्पतिम्।
प्रियस्पर्शो हि पाणिस्ते तत्रैव नियतो भवः।।10।।

Tam.—Do you yourself revive the lord of the earth, of blessed one. The touch of your hand is indeed dear to him; theirin alone lies weal.

मित–। 'इदं तत्' इति रामण्य गुरुशोकाभिवः।। 'कथमेतत्' इत्यपि शोकाभिभवमेव लक्षयति विशेषतश्च मोहावरणम्।। 'मां मन्दभागिनीं व्याहृत्य' इति अहमेव मोहकारणम्। 'आमीलन्नेत्र' निमीलन्नेत्र। 'निरुत्साह' निश्चेष्ट। 'निःसह' दुर्बल। 'पिपर्यस्तः' विपर्यासेन पतितः अधोमुखः पतित इत्यर्थः। 'परित्रायस्व' मामित्यर्थः। कथं तत् इत्याह 'जीवय आर्यपुत्रम्' आर्यपुत्रस्य उज्जीवनेन मामपि मरणाद्रक्षस्व इति भावः। त्वमेति।

अन्वयः–ननु कल्याणि त्वमेव जगत्पतिं जीवय। पाणिस्ते प्रियस्पर्शो हि। तत्रैव भवः नियतः।

व्याख्या–'ननु' आक्षेपे। यद्वा–अनुजानामि त्वां हे 'कल्याणि' रावणवधात्

जगन्मङ्गलदायिनि सीते जगत्यतेर्मोहात् भूयोऽपि दुःस्थितं जगत् तत् 'तमेव जगत्पतिं जीवय' मोहावरणात् मोचय तेन च न केवलं तव अपि तु कृत्स्नस्यापि जगतः परित्राणं भवति। मा मामाक्रन्द परिचायस्वेति। कथं स मया जीवनीय इत्याह–'पाणिस्ते' तव करः 'प्रियस्पर्शो हि' रामस्य सम्बन्धे तव करस्य स्पर्शः सुतरां प्रियः। भवतु किं ततः ? 'तत्र एव' तव करस्पर्शो एव रामस्य 'भवः' मङ्गलं मोहापगमः 'नियतः' निश्चितत्वेन अवधारितः। तत् पाणिना स्पर्शेनम् अपय।तु मोहः जगच्च स्वस्थं भवतु।।

Notes. I. कथमेतत्–Sītā had heard Rāma say मोहः आवृणीति and the intensity of Rāma's grief surprises her. 2. निरुत्साह etc,—सहते इति सहः strenght, पचाघच। उत्साह Stir. निरुत्साह still. निःसह powerless. निरुत्साहश्च निःसहश्च यथा तथा। Qual त्रिपर्य्यस्त। निरुत्साह alone is enough to give the required impression of helpness. 3. विपर्यस्तः–वि+परि+अस+क्त कर्मणि। वि and परि give in the idea of विपरीतता। He was lying on his stomach, not on his back. 4. परित्रायस्व–The appeal is for herself. The swoon of her husband is sure to kill her. 5. त्वमेव–एव implies—you do it yourself, why call on me? 6. ननु–आक्षेपे or अनुज्ञायाम्। The एव seems to declare for आक्षेप (contradiction)। अनुज्ञा also give good sense—I perimt you to touch Rāma. 7. कल्याणि–कल्याण is मङ्गल ; by transferance of epithets मङ्गलकर। स्त्रियां कल्याण+ङीष् कल्याणी, also कल्याण with टाप् (बह्वादि)। For force see Tika. 8. जगत्पतिम्–This particular epithet is chosen to show that the whole world is in jeopardy, so be quick with the rescue. 9. तत्रैव–तत्र तस्मिन् पाणी। How ? प्रियस्पर्शो हि पाणिः। Hence apply पाणिस्पर्शं The एव implies अवधारण (अन्ययोगव्यवच्छेद)। There is no other alternative. Hence I permit परिस्पर्श (ननु अनुज्ञायाम्) ''नन्वाक्षेपे परिप्रश्ने प्रत्युक्तावववधारणे। वाक्यारम्भेऽप्यनुनयामन्त्रणानुज्ञयोरपि'' इति हैमः।

(*xviii*) **सीता–जं होदु तं होदु जहा भअवदी भणादि [यद्भवतु तद्भवतु, यथा भगवती भणति]।**

Sītā—Come what may, I do as your worshipful self says.

(इति ससम्भ्रमं निष्क्रान्ता)

(*Exit hurriedly*).

(ततः प्रविशति भूमी निपतितः सास्त्रया सीतया स्पृश्यमानः साहलदोच्छ्वासो रामभद्रः)।

(*Then enters Rāmabhadra stretcheed on the ground in joyful consciousness being rubbed gently by Sītā in tears*).

सीता (किञ्चिचत् सहर्षं स्वगतम्)–जाणो पुणो हि पञ्चाअदं विअ जीविदं तुल्लोअणाहस्म [जाने पुनरपि प्रत्यागतमिव जीवितं त्रिलोकनाथस्य]।

Sītā (*To herself with slight satisfaction*)—Methinks, it looks like life come back to the lord of the three worlds.

रामः–हन्त भोः किमेतत्?

Rāma—O joy ! what is this ?

प्रश्चोतनं नु हरिचन्दनपल्लवानां
निष्पीड़ितेन्दुकरकन्दलजो नु सेकः
आतप्तजीविततरोः परितर्पणो मे
सञ्जीवणौषधिरसो नु हृदि प्रसिक्तः ।।11।।(रा–)

Is it the dripping of the leaves of the Harichandana (nectar) that is poured into my heart ? Or the juice of the pressed sprouts of moon-beams ? Or the juice of the herb that vivifies—the refresher of the scorched tree of my life ?

(R.—)

मित–।'यथा भगवती भणति' तथैव करोमि इति वाक्यशेषः। अत्रान्तरे आर्यपुत्रस्य स्पर्शः युक्तो वा अयुक्तो यथैवास्ते तथैव आस्ताम्, मया तु तत् नय विचार्यते। भगवती तमसा स्पर्शमिच्छति इत्येव मे पर्य्याप्तम् इत्यर्थः।।'आह्लादः' आनन्दः।'उच्छ्वासः' पुनरुज्जीवनम्। ताभ्यां सह वर्त्तमानः।। व्यवयवो लोकः 'त्रिलोकः' त्रिभुवनम्। तस्य 'नाथः'। तस्य।। प्रश्च्योतनमिति।

अन्वयः–हदि मे हरिचन्दनपल्लवानां प्रश्च्योतनं नु, निष्पीड़ितेन्दुकरकन्दलजः सेको नु, आतप्तजीविततरोः परितर्पणः सञ्जीवनीषधिरमः प्रसिक्तो नु।

व्याख्या–'हृदि मे मदीये हृदये 'हरिचन्दनस्य' देवतरुविशेषस्य यानि 'पल्लवानि नवपत्राणि नवपत्राणि तेषां 'प्रश्च्योतनं नु' रसस्त्रावः किं पतितः ? 'निष्पीड़िताः' निष्पिष्टाः ये 'इन्दुकरकन्दलाः' चन्द्रकिरणाङ्कुराः तेभ्यो 'जातः सेको नु' प्रोक्षणं किम् ?'आप्यायन 'सञ्जजीवन्याः' प्राणप्रदाया 'ओषधेः' लताविशेषस्यः रसः प्रसिक्तो नु' वृष्टः किम्। मूर्च्छिते मयि कृपालुना केनचिन्महापुरुषेण प्रश्च्येतनं सेको वा कृतः नो चत् कथं झटिति प्रत्युज्जीवनम्, उज्जीवितस्य च एतावान् आन्दः इत्यर्थः।।

Notes, 1. सास्त्रया–अस्त्र tears. अस्त्रेण सह वर्तमान सास्त्रा। तया। She was weeping at Rāma's plight. 2. साह्लाद etc.—उच्छ्वास breath. आह्लादश्च उच्छ्वासश्च। ताभ्यां सह। He had come back to sense and was feeling joyful. 3. त्रिलोक etc.—त्रात्रयवी लोकः त्रिलोकः, शाकपर्थिवादि। तस्य नाथः। Avoid त्रयाणं लोकाणां नाथः। Such a तत्पुरुष is irregular. Usually तत्पुरुष compounds are of two words only. Sītā is still thinking of the worlds—Should anything happen to Rāma how would the worlds bear it ? 4.किमेतत्–A question to which he canot find a definite answer. The verse following suggests three likely answers. 5. प्रश्च्योतनम्–प्र+श्च्यत to drip+ल्युट भावे। The drippings are nectar. 6. हरिचन्दन etc.—हरिचन्दन is one of the five divine tress that drip nectar. These are "मन्दारः पारिजातश्च। सन्तानः कल्पवृक्षश्च पुंसि वा हरिचन्दनम्।।" Comp. "श्रीरेषा पाणिरप्यस्याः। पारिजातस्य पल्लवः। किमन्यथा स्नवत्येष स्वेदच्छद्मामृतद्रवम्।।"–*Ratnāvali.* 7. निष्पीड़ित etc.—कन्दल is young shoot. निष्पीड़ित pressed. 8. आतप्त etc.—जीव+क्त भावे जीवित life. जीवितं जोविततः। आ सम्यक् तप्तः आतप्तः। Next कर्मधा–। Wr avoid जीवितरूपतरुः because this makes तरुत्व prominent. But सञ्जीवनौषधिरस is never applied to a tree. 9. सञ्जीवन etc.—सञ्जीवयति अनया इति सम्+जीव+णिच्+ल्युट् करणे स्त्रियाम् सञ्जीवनी vivifying. ओषधि herb. सञ्जीवनी औषधिः कर्मधा–। 10. *Remark*—The verse leaves Rāma in doubt as to the correct answer to his question हन्त भोः किमेतत्। But he is sure that it must be one of the three enumerated in the verse.

(*xix*) **(रा)–**

स्पर्शः पुरा परिचितो नियतं स एष
सञ्जीवनश्च मनसः परिमोहनश्च।
सन्तापजां सपदि यः प्रतिहत्य मूर्च्छा-
मानन्दनेन जड़तां पुनरातनोति।। 12।।

(R.—) Surely it is that touch—the same touch, familiar of old,the reviver as well as the stupefier of the mind, which, having instantly dispelled the swoon arising from grief, develops stupor again by causing delight.

मित–। स्पर्श इति।

अन्वय:–नियतं स्पर्श एष:। स पुरा परिचित: मनस: सञ्जीवनश्च परिमोहनश्च (स्पर्श:) य: सपदि सन्तापजां मूर्च्छा प्रतिहत्य आनन्दनेन पुन: जड़ताम आतनोति।

व्याख्या–एवं पूर्वत्र वितर्कमारूढ़े रामे सहसा स्मृतिरायाता, दृष्टश्च पूर्वोक्तेषु विष्वपि पक्षेषु भ्रम:। तत: पक्षान्तरेण चतुर्थेन निश्चयमाह–'नियतं स्पर्श एष:' न प्रश्च्योतने नापि सेक:। न हि य: कथित् स्पर्श: किन्तु 'स पुर परिचित:' प्राक: नित्यमनुभूत: 'मनस: सञ्जीवनश्च' समाश्वसनश्च 'परिमोहनश्च' अवसादनश्च स्पर्शे: 'य: सपदि' अनुभवक्षणे एव 'सन्तापजां' दु:खकृतां 'मूर्च्छाम्' अचेतनतां 'प्रतिहत्य' सञ्जीवनधर्मेण विधूय 'आन्दनेन' प्रहर्षजननेन 'पुन:' भूयोऽपि 'जड़ताम आतनोति' परिमोहनधर्मेण मोहमादधाति। नूनमिह सीता प्राप्ता अयञ्च स्पर्श स्तस्या: नान्यत् किञ्चित् इति निश्चय:।।

Notes. 1. पुरा–अव्यय। In the days before Sītā's exile. 2. परिचित:–I know it, hence I can unerringly identify it. This is the basis of the निश्चय। 3. सञ्जीवनश्च etc.—This characteristic is pecliar to Sītā's touch with regard to Rāma, and distinguishes her touch from that of any other woman. Comp. ''तव स्पर्शे मम च परिमूढ़ेन्द्रियगणो विकारश्चैतन्यं भ्रमयति समुन्मीलयति च''–I, sl 36.7. Both परिमोहन and परिमोहण are correct. 4. सन्तापजाम् etc.—The touch does it because it is मनस: सञ्जीवन:। 5. आनन्देन etc—This also it can do because it is मनस: परिमोहन:। But this with a difference. The previous मोह (मूर्च्छन्) was सन्तापज (सन्तापजाम्) and the मोह (जड़ताम्) now overtaking me is from excess of delight (आनन्देन)। 6. *Remark*—Some editions introduce this verse with अपि च। This entirely misses the connection of the two verses. अपि च adds something similar to what has gone before; the verse following, however, contradicts the conclusion of the preceding verse.

(*xx*) **सीता (ससाध्वसकरुणं किञ्चिदपमृत्य)–एत्तिअं एब्ब दानीं मे बहुदरं [एतावदेव इदानीं मे बहुतरम्]।**

Sītā (*Falling back slightly in alram and grieg*)—This much indeed is enough for me now.

राम: (उपविश्य)–न खलु वत्सलया सीतादेव्या अभ्युपपन्नोऽस्मि ?

Rāma (*Sitting up*)—Have I not been favoured by my affectionate queen Sītā ?

सीता–हद्धी हद्धी किं त्ति मं अज्जउत्तो मग्गिस्सदि [हा धिक् हा धिक् किमिति माम् आर्यपुत्रो मार्गिष्यति]?

Sītā—O fie ! O fie! Would my husband search for me ?

राम–भवतु पश्यामि।

Rāma—Well I will see.

सीता–भअवदि तमसे आसरम्ह, जइ दाव मं पेक्खिस्सादि तदो अणव्भणुस्णादसणिधाणेण अहिअदरं मम महाराओ कुविस्सादि [भगवति तमसे, अपसराव:, यदि तावत् मां प्रेक्षिष्यते ततः अनभ्यनुज्ञातसन्निधानेन अधिकतरं मम महाराजः कोपिष्यति]।

Sītā—Worshipful Tamasā, I will fall back; if indeed he sees me, the great king will be very angry with me for unauthorised presence.

तमसा–अयि वम्से, भागीरथीवरप्रभावात् वनदेवतानामप्यदृश्या संवृत्तासि।

Rāma—Dear Child, under the influence of Bhāgirathī's boon, you have become invisible to the forest-deities even.

सीता–आम् अस्ति एतत्।

Sītā—So it is indeed.

मित–।'साध्वसं' भयम् 'करुणं दुःखम्। राभेण प्रत्यमिज्ञाता इति साध्वसम्। 'अपसरणम्' इति करुणम्। मुहूर्त्तमामि यस्य अदर्श नमसह्यमासीत् ततोऽप्यद्य अपसरणम् अहो दैवम् ! साध्वकरुणाभ्यां सह। अपसरणिक्रियाविशेषणमेतत्। प्रत्यागतप्राण: त्रिलोकनाथः तत्र च अहमेव हेतुः इति 'एतादेव इदार्नीं' वियोगकाले 'मे बहुतरम् एतेनैव मया अद्य सन्तोष्टव्यम्। जीवत्यार्यपुत्रः जीवति भुवनेश इत्येव पर्याप्त मे। तत् अद्य अपसरणं दुःखं न मया मन्तव्यम्, इति ससाध्वसकरुणमित्यस्य पाक्षिक आक्षेपः।। उपविश्य' पार्श्वं' शून्यं विलोक्य विस्मित आह–'सीतादेव्या अभ्युपपन्नः' अनुगृहीताः 'न खलु' न किम्। मम तु स एवासीत् निश्चयः सा च नेह दृश्यते, किमेतत् ? हा धिगिति–'''किमिति' हद वितर्कें रामस्य आकारं दृष्ट्वा सन्दिग्धा सीता आह 'मां मार्गिष्यति' विचेष्यति न वा।। भगवतीति–' अपसराव:' दूरं गच्छाव:। प्राक् तु किञ्चिदपसृता दूरतरं यातुमिच्छति। कारणमाह 'यदि तावत्' इत्यादिना।

'अनभ्यनुज्ञातम्' अननुमोदितं यत् 'सन्निधानं' समीपागमनं तेन। जना जानन्ति भवत्या सामगमः परिहृतो मय, स एव समागमस्त्वया घटितः। राजभवश्च मे विघ्नित इति कोपकारणम् अतएव च महाराज इत्युक्तिः। राजत्वपुरस्कारेणैव दर्शनम् न भर्तृत्वपुरस्कारेण।। आमित्यादि। 'आम्' इति मकारात्मव्ययम् अवधारणार्थकम्। सत्यम् ईदृश्येव जाताहम् इत्यर्थः।।

Notes 1. समाध्वस etc.—We may take करुण or करुण as the word here. Both can mean 'grief' by transference of epitlhets. साध्वसश्च करुणश्च or करुणा च साध्वसकरुणे। ताभ्यां सह। करुण because it breaks her heart to think that she has to be at a distance (अपमृत्य) From Rāma. 2. एतादेव etc.—The usual interpretation is that she deems it reward enough that even now Rāma remembers her touch. We explain differently (see Ṭīkā). Henceforth whatever Rāma says is heard by Sītā and Tamasā but the talk of these two is जनान्तिक (aside) to Rāma. 3. न खलु etc.—Rāma expected to see Sītā by his side. But on not seeing her he question within himself "Have I not been really touched by Sītā". 4. हा धिक् etc.—Rāma's remark raises suspicious in Sītā that he would search for her. 5. भवतु etc.—Sītā's suspicion is confirmed. 6. भगवति etc.—Sītā has in her excitement forgotten the fact that she has become invisible to Rāma by Bhāgīrathī's boon. 7. महाराजः–For propreity see Ṭīkā. 8. आम्–This implies अवधारण। Comp "आम्–स्निग्धश्यामाः क्वचिदपरती भीषणभोगवृक्षाः" etc. II, sl. 14. She actually sees that Rāma cannot see her. Hence the अवधारण।

(*xxi*) रामः–प्रिये जानकि।

Rāma—Jānakī, my darling.

सीता (समन्यु गद्गदम्)–अज्जउत्त असरिसं क्ख एदं वअणं इमस्स वुत्तान्तस्स [आर्यपुत्र, असदृशं खलु एतत् वचनम् अस्य वृत्तान्तस्य]। (सास्रम्) अहवा किं त्ति वज्जमई जन्मनतरेसु वि पुणो असम्भाविद-दुल्लहदंसणस्स मं एब्ब मन्दभाइणिं उद्दिशिअ वच्छलस्स एवंवादिणो अज्जउत्तस्स उवरि णिरणुक्कोसा भविस्स। अहं एदस्स हिअअं आणामि मम एसोत्ति [अथवा किमिति वज्रमयी जन्मान्तरेष्वपि पुनरसम्भावित-दुर्लभदर्शनस्य मामेब मन्दभागिनीमुद्दिश्य वत्सलस्य एवंवादिन आर्य्यपुत्र उपरि निरनुक्रोशा भविष्यामि। अहमेतस्य हृदयं जानामि मम एष इति]?

Sītā (*In a voice sobbing with pique*)—My husband, these words are indeed inconsistent with this state of things. *(with tears)* Or, I know his hart, he mine; then why should I. becoming adamantine, be unkind towards my husband of whom I can hardly get a glimpse even in other births, and who, with a foundness; or my own ill-fasted self is talking thus ?

रामः–(सर्वतोविलोक्य सनिर्वेदम्)–हा ! कथम्! अत्र न कश्चिदपि।

Rāma (*Looking round—In despair*)—Alas ! Strage ! There is no one here.

मित– । प्रिये इत्यादि । 'यत्तु प्रागुक्तं' "भवतु पश्यामि" इति तस्यैवायमनुबन्धः। पार्श्वे तास्तामपश्यन् समीपे क्वापि तिरोहिता अस्ति न वा सीता इति परिज्ञानार्थं' क्रोशति "प्रिये जानकि इति।। समन्यु इति। 'मन्युः' प्रणयकोपः। तेन 'गद्गदम्' अव्यक्तकण्ठध्वनिविशिष्टं यथा तथा आहै। 'एतत् वचनम्' प्रिये जानकि इत्युक्तिः अस्यवृत्तान्तस्य' परित्यागरुपस्य व्यापारस्य' असदृशम्' अननुरुपम्। न हि प्रिया केनचित् त्यज्यते इत्यर्थः। 'वज्रकठिना सती। 'असम्भावितम् अचिन्तितम्' असम्भवम् 'दुर्लभं' दुर्घटं 'दर्शनं' यस्य तथाविधस्य। 'निरनुक्रोशा' अकरुण 'किमिति भविष्यामि कथं स्याम्? नैव स्याम् इत्यर्थः। प्रकृष्टतरं कारणमाह–' अहमेतस्य' इत्यादिना। अहं जानाभि मयि वत्सल आर्यपुत्रः, एषोऽपि जानाति वत्सलाहमस्मिन्निति। 'निर्वेदः' दैन्यम्।

Notes. 1, प्रिये etc.—Rāma has made up his mind to make a search (भवतु पश्यामि) and accordingly he is now shouting for her (प्रिये जानकि)। The reading हा प्रिये जानकि seems out of place in a search. The हा makes it a mere moan not a shout. 2. असदृशम् etc.—The address प्रिये has piqued her and she points out its inconsistency with what has traspired (see *Mitabh*—). 3. अथवा Here she corrects herself. I should not be so petulant towards him, because—(i) Even if he is inconsistent, the fact remains that I never expected (असम्भावित) to meet him in this birth or in future births either. If then chance has brought about a meeting, this is not the time for me to become unkind, (ii) There is no longer any inconsistency now. He has become actually वत्सल towards me and is openly declaring (बवं वादिनः) his वत्सलता। The declaration is sincere, for in spite of all that has happened, I know his heart just as he knows mine. 4. सर्वतः etc.—He was sure that Sītā had touched him and was expecting a reponse to his shout प्रिये जानकि। Not receiving one he knew Sita was not there, and this threw him into dispair. But why did he not notice

तमसा there ? The poet has not prepared us sufficiently to expect that तमसा also should remain invisible to राम। She was visible to मुरला who certainly is not as high a personage as राम।

(*xxii*) सीता–भअवति तसमे तहा निक्कारणपरिच्चाइणो वि एदस्स एवंविहेण दंसणेण केरिसो विअ मे हिअआणुवन्धी त्तिण आणामि [भगवति तमसे, तथा निष्कारणपरित्यागिनोऽपि एतस्य एवंविधेन दर्शनेन कीदृश इव मे हृदयानुबन्ध इति न जानामि]।

तमसा–जानामि वत्से जानामि।

तटस्थं नैराश्यादपि च कलुषं विप्रियवशा-
द्वियोगे दीर्घेऽस्मिन् झटितिघटनोत्तम्भितमिव।
प्रसन्नं सौजन्याद्दयितकरुणैर्गाढकरुणं
द्रवीभूतं प्रेम्ना तव हृदयमस्मिन् क्षण इव।।13।।

Sītā—Worshipful Tamasā, on seeking him thus, though he abandoned me in that fashion without cause, I do not know what the inclination of my heart is.

Tam.—I know it, my child I know it.

Your heart, paralysed as it were at the unexpected meeting after his long separation, then in different through despair, next offended by reason of wrong done, afterwards appeased through his goodness, thereafter deeply grieved at the grief of your darling, has at this moment turned liquid as it were through love (Or—through his love).

मित–। 'तथा' तेन प्रकारेण निर्द्रयमित्यर्थः। इति कोपकाणम्। 'निष्कारणं' कारणं विनैव 'परित्यागिनः' त्यक्तवतः। एतदपि कोपकारणम्। द्वाभ्यामप्येताभ्यां स्थिरकोपं प्रति हृदवानुबन्धी युक्तः। तथा 'अपि सत्यपि चिररोषकारणे 'एतस्य एवंविधेन' अचिन्तितेन करुणीद्दीपकेन च 'दर्शनेन मे हृदयस्य' मनसः 'अनुबन्धः' पश्चात्ताप दर्शनजनितावस्था 'कोदृशः न जानामि'।। तटस्थमिति।

अन्वयः–दीर्घे अस्मिन् वियोगे झटितिघटनोत्तस्मितमिव तव हृदयं नैराश्यात् तटस्थम्, अपि च विप्रियवशात् कलुषम्, सौजन्यात् प्रसन्नम्, दयितकरुणैः गाढ़करुणम्, प्रेम्ना अस्मिन् क्षणो द्रवी भूतमिव–।

व्याख्या–'दीर्घे अस्मिन् वियोगे' चिरसन्तते विरहे। प्राक्तु लङ्कायां वर्षादप्यूनं

कालं विरह आसीत्, अघ पुनः द्वादशेवर्षेभ्योऽधिकम्। 'झटितिघटनयां अक्षिन्तितसमागमेन 'उत्तम्भितमिव' जड़ीभूतमिव 'तव हृदयं नैराश्यात् पुनः समागमाशाविरहात् 'तटस्थम्' उदासीनम्, 'अपि च' किञ्च विप्रियवशात्' निष्कारणपरित्यागात् 'कलुषम्' अप्रसन्नम्, 'सौजन्यात्' दयितस्य सदाशयतया 'प्रसन्न' विमलम्' 'दयितस्य' प्रियस्य रामस्य 'करुणैः' दुःखै 'गाढ़करुणं' गुरुशोकम्, 'प्रेम्ना' भर्तुः त्वदाश्रयया प्रीत्या 'अस्मिन् क्षणे' एतन्मुहूर्ते 'द्रवीभूतमिव' रसमयमिव। एवं क्रमेण अनुबन्धात् अनुबन्धान्तरं भजमानं ते हृदयम् इति न त्वया ज्ञायते मया तु बुध्यते एव।।

Notes.— Remark—Here तमसा points out the different stages through which Sītā's heart has passed. There are expressed in order of succession by the epithets उत्तम्भित, तटस्थ, कलुष, प्रसन्न, गाढकरुणा and द्रवीभूत। The grounds for this statement are given below. 2. झटिति etc.— उद्+स्तम्भ+णिच् कर्मणि उत्तम्भित paralysed. Comp. "हा कथम्......आर्यपुत्र एव। तत् मां धारय धारय"–Para xvi. The order of succession of the stages is not observed in the first two lines of the verse. It becomes all right if the lines change places. 3. तटस्थम् etc.—तटे तिष्ठति इति तट+स्था+क कर्त्तरि। Lit. on sitting at the margin and and not touching the water; hence indifferent. Comp. "जाने पुनरपि....त्रिलोकनाथस्य–Para *xviii.* Here सीता thinks not of herself but of what the worlds gain if राम lives. Also compare "एतादेव इदानीं मे बहुतरम्"–Paraxx. 4. कलुषम् etc. Compare "आर्यपुत्र असदृशं खलु एतत् वचनमस्य"–Para xxi. 5. प्रसन्नम् etc. Compare "अथवा किमिति वज्रमयी etc.—Para xxi. 6. दयित etc. करुण is शोक। गाढं करुणां यस्य यस्मिन् वा गाढकरुणाम् of a deep pathos. Comp "हा धिक्...जीवग आर्यपुत्रम्"–Para xvii, also "अहमेतस्य...मम एषः"–Para xxi. 7. द्रवीभूतम् etc— Comp. "एतस्य एवंविधेन दर्शनेन....न जानामि"। This will appear more clearly in the parts that follow.

(*xxiii*) **रामः–देवि,**

Rāma—My queen.

प्रसाद इव मूर्त्तस्ते स्पर्शः स्नेहार्द्रशीतलः।
अद्याप्यानन्दयति मां त्वं पुनः क्वासि नन्दिनि।। 14।।

Thy touch, wet and cool through affection, as if favour incarnate, even at this moment is delighting me; but where art thou the delighter ?

सीता–एदे क्खु दे अगाधदंसिदसिणेहसम्भारा आणन्दणिस्मन्दिणो

सुहामआ अज्जउत्तस्प्त उल्लावा जाणं पच्चएण निक्कारणपरिच्चा-असल्लिदो वि बहुमदो मे जन्मलाहो [एते खलु ते अगाधदर्शितस्नेहसम्भारा आनन्दनिस्यन्दिनः सुधामया आर्यपुत्रस्य उल्लापा येषां प्रत्ययेन निष्कारणपरित्यागशल्यितोऽपि बहुमतो मे जन्मलाभः]।

Sītā—These are really the same ambrosial words of my husband, pouring joy, that disclose carefully cherished love of bottomless depth, through trust in which my coming into being, though beset with the thorn of causeless abandonment, is hightly esteemed by me.

रामः–अथवा कुतः प्रियतमा ? नूनं सङ्कल्पाभ्यासपाटवोत्पाद एष रामभद्रस्य भ्रमः।

Rāma—Or, whence could my darling (be here)? Surely this is a delusion of Rāmabhadra arising from a predisposition (proneness) created by the frequency of thought.

मित–। प्रसाद इति।

अन्वयः–स्नेहार्द्रशीतलः ते स्पर्श मूर्त्तः प्रसाद इव अद्यापि माम् आन्दयति। नन्दिनि, त्वं पुनः क्वासि।

व्याख्या–'स्नेहेन' प्रीत्या 'आर्द्रः' सरसः 'शीतश्च 'ते स्पर्शः मूर्त्तः' मूर्त्तिमान् 'प्रसाद इव' अनुग्रह इव 'अद्यापि' अस्मिन् क्षणे अपि स्पर्श विरहे अपि 'माम् आनन्दयति' आनन्देन योजयति। स्पर्श जानेत आन्दो मापुज्जीव्य नाद्यापि विरमति किन्तु हे 'नन्दिनि' तस्य आन्नदस्य कर्त्री 'त्वं पुनः क्व असि'। त्वतृकृत आन्नदः अनुभूयते त्वं तु न दृश्यसे इति किम् ? इत्यर्थः।। 'अगाधः' अति गभीरश्च 'दर्शितः' प्रकटितश्च 'स्नेहसम्भारः चिरसञ्चितः स्नेहः येषु अतएव 'आनन्दनिस्यन्दिनः' हर्षस्त्राविणः आनन्दल्पावितां मां कुर्वन्तः इत्यर्थः 'आर्यपुत्रस्य सुधामया उल्लापाः' विलापवचनानि। 'येषां' येषु इत्यर्थः। सप्तमी तु युक्ता। 'प्रत्यनेन' विश्वासेन। 'निष्कारणपिरत्यागरूपं' यत् 'शङ्कः तत् जातं यस्य तथाविधः 'अपि जन्मलाभः' लब्धं जनम मे बहुमतः' सार्थको 'मे जन्मलाभः इत्यर्थः।। 'अथवा' इति प्रागुक्तस्य आक्षेपः। "त्वं पुनः क्वासि" इत्यनेन स्थितामपि त्वां न पश्यामि इत्यच्युते। एतदयुक्तम् 'कुतः' इह 'प्रियतमा 'सीता मे ? नास्त्येव सा। यदि नास्ति कुतः स्पर्शः ? उच्यते–'एष रामभद्रस्य भ्रमः'। किमस्ति भ्रमकारणम्?–सीतया पुनः समागमो भवतु इति यः

'सङ्कल्पः' या चिन्ता तस्य यः अभ्यासः' पुनः पुनरावृत्तिः तस्मात् जातं यत् 'पाठवं' पटुता, इयं सीता आगच्छति अयं तस्याः स्पर्शः इत्यादिद परिकल्पननैपुण्य, तस्मात् 'उत्पादः' उत्पत्तिर्यस्य तादृशोऽयं 'भ्रमः'। निरन्तरं भया सीता एव ध्यायते, तेन ध्यानांनुरूपवस्तुकल्पनाप्रवणोऽहं जातः, कल्पनागता च सीता मया तात्विकौति मन्यते, नेह वस्तुतः सीता अस्ति इत्यर्थः।।

Notes—1. प्रसाद etc.—मूर्च्छ+क्त कर्त्तरि मूर्त्तः embodied. You have touched me. That is a favour done—favour personified in the touch. 2. स्नेह etc.—It was an affectionate touch (स्नेहार्द्र) that cooled down (शीतल) my heated heart. 4. अद्यापि etc. You have withdrawn, but the pleasure of the touch thrills me still. 4. त्वं पुनः–नन्दयति इति नन्द+णिच्+णिनि कर्त्तरि ताच्छील्ये स्त्रियाम् नन्दिनी। You cannot be very far away, then why do you not respond to my call ? 5. अगाध etc.—Your affection is fathomless (अगाध); It is openly declared (दर्शित) and not left to me to infer; it is not a momentary display but affection cherished for years together (सम्भार)। सम्+भृ+घञ् भावे सम्भार collection. स्नेहस्य सम्भारः स्नेहसम्भारः *i.e.,* सम्भृतः स्नेहः by the dictum "भावानये द्रव्यानयनम्"। Such being the character of the affection, there must be प्रत्यय in it (येषां प्रत्यनेन)। 6. निष्कारण etc.—Only the thought that I was abandoned without cause still ranks within me. I regret the past only, I am reconlised with the present. 7. सङ्कल्प etc.—I picture to myself lots of things about Sītā. One such picture (that she touched me) I have taken as a reality—Sītā cannot be here, ro she would have answered.

(*xxiv*) **नेपथ्ये–प्रमादः प्रमादः। ("सीतादेव्या स्वकरकलितैः इत्यर्द्धं पठ्यते)।**

(In the Tiring Room)—Mishap ! Mishap ! The half "सीतादेव्या स्वरकलितैः" etc. is repeated)

रामः–(सकरुणौत्सुक्यम्)–क्रिं तस्य?

Rāma *(With sorrow and anxiety)*—What of him?

नेपथ्ये–("वध्वा सार्द्धम्" इत्युत्तारार्द्धं पठ्यते)।

(In the Tiring Room)—*(The latter half* "बध्वा सार्द्धम्" etc. *is repeated).*

सीता–को दाणिं अहिउज्जिस्मदि [क इदानीम् अभियोक्ष्यते]।

Sītā—Who now will set about it?

रामः–क्वासौ क्वासौ दुरात्मा यः प्रियायाः पुत्रकं बधूद्वितीयमभिभवति? (इत्युत्तिष्ठति)।

Rāma—Where is he ? Where is that vile-hearted wretch that troubless my darling's adopted son accupained by his mate ? *(Gets up).*

(प्रविश्य सम्भ्रान्ता) वासन्ती–कथं देवो रघुनन्दनः।

(Enterring in a hurry) Vāsantī—What ! King Raghunandana !

सीता–कहं प्रिअसही मे वसन्ती [कथं प्रियसखी मे वासन्ती]!

Sītā—What ! My dear friend Vāsantī !

मित–।'अभियोक्ष्यते' द्विरदपतेः प्रतिभटो भविष्यति।। कृत्रिमः पुत्रः 'पुत्रकः' 'कथं' प्रियसखी' इत्यादिक न श्रूयते, नापि सीता दृश्यते वासन्त्या रामेण वा।।

Notes. 1. अभियोक्ष्यते–will fight. अभि+युज+लृट् स्यते कर्त्तरि। 2. पुत्रकम्–The affix is कम् by the गणसूत्र "पुत्र कृत्रिमे"। 3. कथं प्रियसखी etc.—Even वासन्ती does not see सीता or hear her. (because the speech is जनान्तिके) Comp. "न च त्वाम्....वनदेवता अपि द्रक्ष्यन्ति" etc. ante.

(xxv) **वासन्ती–जयति जयति देवः।**

Vāsantī—Prosper, let Sire prosper.

रामः–कथं देव्याः प्रियसखी वासन्ती !

Rāma (Marking)—What ! The queen's dear friends Vāsantī.

वासन्ती–देव त्वर्य्यतां त्यर्य्यताम्। इतो जटायुगिरिशिखरस्य दक्षिणेन सीतातीर्थेन गोदावरीमवतीर्थ सम्भायतु देव्याः पुत्रकं देवः।

Vāsantī—Quick, Sire quick. Having gone down to the Godāvarī from here by Sītā's landing place (Ghāṭa) to the right of the peak of Jaṭāyu's hill let Sire greet (help) the queen's adopted son.

सीता–हा ताद जटाओ अज्ज सुणां तुए विणा जणठ्ठाणं [हा तात जटायो, अद्य शून्यं त्वया विना जनस्थानम्]।

Sītā—Alas ! Father Jaṭāyu, without thee Janasthāna is a void to-day.

रामः—अहह हृदयमर्मच्छिदः खल्वमी कथोद्धाताः।

Rāma—Ah ! These allusions to old stories indeed pierce the vitals of the heart.

वासन्ती—इत इतो देवः।

Vāsantī—This way, sire, this way.

मित—।'जटायोगिरिः जठायुगिरिः जटायुना अध्य षित्रो गिरित्यर्थः। तस्य 'शिखरं' शृङ्गम्। तस्य 'दक्षिणेन' [एनपा षष्ठी अपि इष्यते]। 'सम्भावयत्' सम्प्नानयतु साहायकेन इत्यर्थः।'उद्घातः' आरम्भः प्रसङ्गः। हृदयमर्मच्छिदः' प्राग्व त्तस्मरणात्।।

Notes 1. कथम्–Implies surprise. 2. त्वर्यताम्–सम्भ्रमे द्विरुक्तिः। त्वर्यतां त्वया इति वाक्यशेषः।3. इतः–This seems superflouous. 3. दक्षिणेन–दक्षिणा+एनप् दक्षिणेन। The एनप् usually gives द्वितीयां as in "दक्षिणेन वृक्षवाटिकाम्" –*Śakuntala*. But by योगाविभाग of एनपा in "एनपा द्वितीया" we get षष्ठी also. 4. जटायु etc.—The word is spelt जटायुम् also जटायु। "जटायुषा जटायुश्च चिद्यादायुं तथायुषा"। Comp. "तस्य स प्रवयसो जटायुषः" "जटायोर्जन्मेदं विफलमग–मद्भाग्यरहितम्" etc. Also see sl, 43. The reading जटायुगिरिशिखरस्य occurs in Vidyāsāgara's manuscripts Nos. 1 and 4.5 कथोद्घाताः–उद्+हन+घञ् भावे उद्घात् commencement, introduction, allusion etc. कथानाम् उद्घाताः। उद्घात in the sense of आरम्भ occurs in "उद्घातः प्रणवी यासाम्"–*Kumāra*. They hurt because they remind him of all the old incidents. 6. *Remark*.—जटायुगिरि etc. des. cribes the route. This is quite useless because वासन्ती herself is leading. The poet is on the look out for an opportunity to introduce the name of जटायु, hence जटायुगिरि etc. though superfluous.

(*xxvi*) **सीता—भअवदि सच्चअं एब्ब वणदेवता वि मं ण पेक्खदि [भगवति सत्यमेव वनदेवतापि मां न प्रेक्षते] ?**

Sītā—Worshipful Lady, is it really ture that even forestdeities do not see me ?

तमसा—अयि वत्से सर्वदेवताभ्यः प्रकृष्टमैश्वर्यं भागीरथीदेव्याः तत् किमित्याशङ्कसे ?

Tam.—Dear child, the power of the goddess Bhāgirathī is higher than that of all other deities. Then why do you hesitate ?

सीता–तदो अणुसरम्ह [तत् अनुसरावः]। (इति परिक्रामतः)।

Sītā—Then we follow. *(They go round the stage).*

रामः–(परिक्रम्य)–भगवति गोदावरि नमस्ते।

Rāma *(Going round the stage)*—Worshipful Godāvarī salutation to thee.

वासन्ती (निरूप्य)–देव देव मोदस्व विजयिना बधद्वितीयेन देव्याः पुत्रकेण।

Vāsantī (Marking)—Sire, Sire, rejoice at the victory of the queen's adopted child accompained by his mate.

रामः–विजयतामायुष्मान्।

Rāma—Let the long-lived one prosper.

सीता–अम्महे एरिसो एस सो संवुत्तो [अहो ईदृश एष स संवृत्तः]।

Sītā—Ha! He has grown to this one of such size !

मित–। 'सत्यमेव' इति प्रश्नकाकुः।। 'सर्वदेवताभ्यः' इति लक्षणया 'सर्यदेवतैश्वर्य्येभ्यः' इत्यर्थे वर्त्तते। 'आशङ्कसे' वासन्ती मां पश्येदिति।। 'गोदावरि नमस्ते' इति तु जाते गोदवरीदर्शने।। 'निरूप्य' निपुणं दृष्टा। 'पुत्रकेण' इति हेती तृतीया।। 'सः' बालः 'ईदृशः' प्रतापवान् महाकायः 'एष संवृत्तः'।।

Notes. 1. अनुसराव:–She assumes that तमसा also remains invisible. We have to assume that this was through Tamasā's own power. She chooses to remain invisible to Vāsantī, so Vāsantī cannot see her. To मुरला She wanted to reveal herself and मुरला saw her. 2. विजयताम्–आत्मनेपद by "विपराभ्यां जेः"। This refers to the future and expresses a hope. Let him live long (आयुष्मान्) and be victorious (विजयताम्) in his encounters. (Or—prosperous).

(*xxvii*) **रामः–देवि दिष्ट्या वर्द्धसे।**

Rāma—You prosper, my queen ! O joy !

येनोद्गच्छद्बिसकिसलयस्निग्धदन्ताङ्कुरेण
व्याकृष्टस्ते सुतनु लवलीपल्लवः कर्णमूलात्।
सोऽयं पुत्रस्व मदमुचां वारणानां विजेता
यत् कल्याणं वयसि तरुणे भाजनं तस्य जातः ।।15।।

O fair limbed lady, he by whom the stalk of the *Lavalī* creeper used to be pulled off the root of thy ear with the shoot of his tusk that looked smooth like a sprout of lotus growth, the same son of thine, now the vanquisher of tuskers. shedding ichor, has become the recipient of blessing that unfold in youth.

सीता—अविउत्तो दाणीं अअं दोहाउ इमाए सोम्मदंसणाए समं होदु [अवियुक्त इदानीमयं दीर्घायुः अनया सौम्यदर्शनया समं भवतु]।

Sītā—May this long-lived one now countinue unseparated from this his good-looking mate.

मित–। 'दिष्टिः' भाग्यम्। तथा। यद्वा–'दिष्ट्या इत्यव्ययम् हर्षे भाग्य च। 'वर्द्धसे' त्वम् अहो हर्षः भाग्यं वा।। हर्षकारणमाह येनेति।

अन्वयः–सुतनु, येन उद्गच्छद्बिसकिसलयस्निग्धदन्ताङ्कुरेण ते कर्णभूलात् लवलीपल्लवो व्याकृष्टः स अयं तव पुत्रः मदमुचां वारणानां विजेता (सन्) तरुणे वयसि यत् कल्याण तस्य भाजनं जातः।

व्याख्या–हे 'सुतनु' चारुगात्रि देवि सीते 'येन' बालेन नव पुत्रेण 'उद्गच्छत्' भूमिं भित्वा ऊर्ध्वं गच्छत् यत् 'विसकिसलयं' मृणालाङ्कुरः तदिव स्निग्धेन' कोमलेन 'दन्ताङ्कुरेण' अचिरोद्गतेन दन्तेन 'ते कर्णमूलात् लवलीपल्लवः' अवसंतभूत इति शेषः 'व्याकृष्टः' वालचापलात् आकृष्य पातितः 'सः अयं तव पुत्रः 'मदमुचां' दानस्त्राविणाम् उदयग्राणमित्यर्थः 'वारणानां' करिणां विजेता' सन् 'तरुणे वयसि' यौवने 'यत् कल्याणं' यत् भद्रभुपजायते 'तस्य भाजनं' पात्रं 'जातः' तत् सर्वभनुभवति इत्यर्थः।। 'अवियुक्तः' वियोगरहितः।।

Notes. 1. दिष्ट्या–दिष्टि means हर्ष, rarely भाग्य। तथा। हर्षेण or भाग्येन इत्यर्थः। हेती 3या। Or दिष्ट्या is an अव्यय implying भाग्य or हर्षं It is an exclamation—what luck! or O joy! "दिष्टिरानन्दे माने च" इति हैमः।"दिष्ट्या हर्षे मङ्गले च" इति मेदिनी। 2. उद्गच्छत् etc.—For समाप्त see Tika. Elephants often drag things with their tooth. 3या करणो। Vidyāsāgara makes a बहुव्रीहि of it qualifying येन, thus—उद्गच्छत् यत् विसकिसलयं तदिव स्निग्धः

दन्ताङ्कुरो यस्य तेन। 5. व्याकृष्टः–सीता used tc feed it with शल्लकीपल्लवाग्र While eating these he with one of his newly acdquired teeth playfully removed the लवलीपल्लव from her ear ! 5a. सुतनु–सम्बोधन of सुतनु। तनू शब्दोऽत्रकान्तावाची। Then by कर्मधा we get सु शोभनः तनुः इति सुतनुः। Adding उङ् by "ऊङुतः the form is सुतनू (like वधू) । If we make a बहु–of सु and तनु (short उ) then the सम्बोधन form will be भुतनो। बहु–of मु and तनु (long) will give सुतनूक। Hence to recourse to कर्मधा– । cp. "वरतनुरिति बहुव्रीही यदि ह्रस्वान्तस्तनुशब्दस्ततः 'सम्बुद्धीच' इति गुणप्रसङ्गः। दीर्घान्तेतु नदीलक्षणः कप् प्राशेति। केचिदाहुः तनुशब्दः स्त्रोजाती कविभिः प्रयुज्यते। तस्मात् 'उङुतः' इति ऊङि कृते कर्मधारयः अयम्।"—*Haradatta*. "सुतनु प्रत्यादेशब्यलीकमुपैतु ते"—Śak. 4. भाजनम्–भाजन is नित्यक्लीव। We left him quite a child, he is now a full-grown young tusker ! 5. अवियुक्त etc.,—Let him enjoy life and not pine away in solitude like myself.

(*xxviii*) **रामः–सखि वासन्ति, पश्य पश्य कान्तानुवृत्तिचातुर्यमपि शिक्षितं वत्सेन।**

Rāma—Behold, friend Vāsantī, behold; cleverness in humouring his beloved has also been acquired by our child.

लीलोत्खातमृणालकाण्डकवलच्छेदेषु सम्पादिताः
पुष्ट्यत्पुष्करवासितस्य पयसो गण्डूषसंक्रान्तयः।
सेकः शीकरिणा करेण विहितः कामं विरामे पुन–
र्यत् स्नेहादनरालनालनलिनीपत्रातपत्रं घृतम्।।16।।

For, through affections, trasference of sips of water, scented with blooming lotuses, ahs been executed at intervals between mouthfuls of lotus-shoots dus up with ease; through sprinkling has been done with his trunk ful of spray; at the end of it again, is now held and umbrella of a lotus-leaf with a straight stalk.

सीतां–भअवदि तमसे अअं दाव एरिसो जादो दे उण ण आणामि कुसलवा एत्तिएव कालेण कीदिसा विअ होन्ति [भगवति तमसे अयं तावदीदृशो जातः तौ पुनर्न जानामि कुशलवौ एतावता कालेन कीदृशौ इव भवतः]।

Sītā—Worshipful Tamasā, this one has grown thus; I do not know how they again, Kuśa and Lava, look like by this time.

तमसा–यादृशोऽयं यतादृशौ तावपि।

Tamasā—As this one is so too are they.

मित–'कान्तायाः' प्रियाया या 'अनुवृर्त्तिः आनुगुणयम् अनुरञ्जनं तत्र यत् 'चातुर्य' पठुता तत्।। तदेव दर्शयति लीलेति।

अन्वयः–यत् स्नेहात् लीलोत्खातमृणाल- काण्डकवलच्छेदेषु पुष्यत्पुष्करवासितस्य पयसो गण्डूषसंक्रान्तयः सम्पादितः, शौकरिण करेण कामं सेको विहितः, विरामे पुनः अनरालनालनलिनीपचातपत्रं धृतम्।

व्याख्या–'यत्' यस्मात् 'स्नेहात्' प्रीतिवशात् 'लीलया' अनायासेन 'उत्खाताः' दन्ताग्रेण भूमिं विदार्य्य उत्पाटिता ये 'मृणालकाण्डाः' विसस्तम्बाः त एव ये 'कवलाः' प्रियायै दत्ता ग्रासाः तेषां 'छेदेषु' विरामेषु 'पुष्यद्धि' विकसद्धिः 'पुष्करैः- पद्मैः 'वासितस्य' आभोदितस्य 'पयसः' जलस्य 'गण्डूषसंक्रान्तयः' स्वमुखात् उद्धृत्य मुखपूरणादानानि 'सम्पादिताः' अनुष्ठिताः। सुखरोचकं भक्ष्यं दत्तम्, क्षणी क्षणी सुवासितञ्च पेयम् इति भावः। ततः आतपखेदनोदनाय 'शोकरिणा' जलकणापूर्णेन 'करेण' शुण्डेन 'सेको विहितः' वर्षणं कृतम्। 'विरामे पुनः' वर्षणान्ते तु 'अनरालम्' अवक्रं 'नालं' दण्डो यस्य तादृशं यत् 'नलिनीपत्रं' पद्मपत्रं तद्रूपम् 'आतपत्रं' छत्रं 'धृतम्' ऊढ़म्।। भगवतीति। 'ईदृशः महाबल इत्यर्थः। 'एतावता कालेन दृादशवर्षमितेनय कालेन।। यादृश इत्यादि। तावपि महाबली जाती इत्याशयः।।

Notes. 1. लीला etc.—His mate showing an inclination to eat, he himself finds food for her sparing her the trouble to procure it herself. This he does easily (लीला) with his powerful tusks. For समाप्त see Ṭīkā. छेद is troublesome here. Vidyāsāgara takes it as खण्ड, अंश etc.—"कवलच्छेदेषु ग्रासांशेषु। The idea is that he digs up the lotus-shoot, reserves a share for himself and offers the rest to his mate. We interpret छेद as विराम। The plural is natural, because after a few mouthfuls of food the desire for drink arises. Forwith he drags water with his trunk and transfers (संक्रान्ति)it to the mouth of his mate. This is done *several times* until she has her fill of food and drink. विरामे पुनः in the third line seems to support this sense. 2. पुष्यत् etc.—This time was summer (see II, sl. 9). The blooming of lotuses in profusion so as to scent the water of the river sounds odd. 3. सेक etc.—They were out in the sun, and, meal over, left the heat. The second half of the verse describes what the elephants does not allay the heat of his mate. One is apt to think that a dip in the water and retreat to some shady place would be the best for it. 4. कालेन–अपवर्गे 3या।

(*xxix*) **सीता–एरिसी अहं मन्दभाइणी जाए ण केअलं णिरन्तरं अज्जउत्तविरहो, पुत्रविरहो वि [ईदृशी अहं मन्दमागिनी यस्या न केवलं निरन्तरम् आर्य्यपुत्रविरहः पुत्रविरहोऽपि]।**

Sītā—Such am I the ill-fated of whom there is ceaseless sepration not from husband alone but from sons too.

तमसा–भवितव्यतेयमीदृशी।

Tam.—Such is your fate.

सीता–किं वा मए पसूदाप जेण तारिसाणं मम पुत्तकाणं ईसिविरल-कोमलधअलदसणुज्जलकवोलं अणुवद्धमुद्धकाअलिविहसितं णिवद्धकाअसिहण्डअं अमलमुहपुण्डरीअजुअलं णा परिचुम्बिदं अज्जउत्तण [किं वा मया प्रसूतया येन तादृशयोर्मम पुत्रकयोः ईषद्विरल-कोमलधवलदशनोज्जवलकपोलम् अनुबद्धमुग्धकाकलिविहसितं निबद्धकाकशिखण्डकम् अमलमुखपुण्डरीकयुगलं न परिचुम्बित-मार्यपुत्रेण]।

Sītā—What was the good of my lying in? For of such boys of mine, the spotless pair of lotus-faces, with hair made up into side locks, wiht bright cheeks and soft white teeth that are slightly, with laughter followed by a charming lisp, were not kissed by my husband.

तमसा–अस्तु देवताप्रसादात्।

Tam.—Be it so (kissed) through the grace of God.

मित– ।'निरन्तम्' अविच्छेदं यथा तथा वर्त्तते, 'आर्यपुत्रेण विरहः पुत्राभ्यां' च विरहः'।। 'भवितव्यं' भावी। तस्य भावः 'भविव्यता' अवश्यम्भावः। भाग्यमिति फलितम्। 'इयम् एषा त्वदीया 'भवितव्यता' नियतिः ईदृशो' एवंविधा, अत्र मानुषः प्रतीकारो नास्ति।।'प्रसूतया' प्रजातया जातापत्यया इत्यर्थः 'किं' किं कृतं न किमपि। कारणमाह 'येन' यतः 'मम पुत्रकयोः अमलमुखपुण्डरीकयुगलं न परिचुम्बितमार्य-

पुत्रेण'। 'ईषद्विरला:' अनतिनिविड़ाः अचिरोन्द्गत्वात् 'कोमला: धवला:' शुभ्रा ये 'दशनाः तै उज्जवलौ' भ्राजमानौ 'कपोलौ' गण्डौ यस्मिन् तत्। 'अनुबद्धा ' अनुगता 'मुग्धा' मनोहरा 'काकलि:' अव्यक्तध्वनिः यत्र तथाविधं 'विहसितं' हासो यस्मिन् तत्। प्रथमं हासः पश्चात् काकलिरित्यर्थः। 'निबद्धाः काकशिखण्डकाः' काकपक्षाः यस्मिन् तत्।। 'अस्तु' परिचुम्बितमस्तु।।

Notes. 1. भवितव्यता–भू+तव्य कर्त्तरि बाहुलकात् भवितव्यम् that which has to be. तस्य भवः। Refers to Sītā's luck. 2. प्रसूतया —For प्रसूता see दारकद्वयं प्रसूता, para v, ante. 3. अनुबद्ध etc.—कलि sound शब्द। ईषन् कलिः इति कुशब्देन समाप्तः।"ईषदर्थे च" इति कुशब्दस्य कोर्दशे काकलिः low sound. ङीप् is optional in the feminine by "कृदिकारदक्तिनः"। Hence both काकलिः and काकली। For समाप्त see Ṭīkā. 4. निबद्ध etc.—Tufuts of hair at the sides, and here and there on the head, left after shaving, are called काकपक्ष or शिखण्डक। काकशिखण्डक is unusual. 5. *Remark*—This para is an - adaption of Kalidasa's "आलक्ष्यदन्तसुकुलाननिमित्तहासैरव्यक्तवर्णरमणीय-वचःप्रवृत्तीत्। अङ्काश्रयप्रणयिनस्तनयान् वहन्तो धन्यास्तदङ्गरजसा मलिनीभवन्ति।।" 6. अस्तु etc.—The तमसा flows close by Vālmīki's hermitage. Hence perhaps she was aware of the preparations that were in progress at the hermitage to bring about the re-union of Rāma and Sītā, and here she hints at them (see Act VII).

(*xxx*) सीता–भअवदि तमसे एदिणा अवञ्चसंसुमरणेण उस्सपिद-पह्नुदत्थणी ताणं च पिदुणो सन्निधाणेण खणमेत्तं संसारिणी म्हि संवुत्ता [भगवति तमसे, एतेन अपत्यसंस्मरणेन उच्छ्वसितप्रस्नुतस्तनी तयोश्च पितुः सन्निधानेन क्षणमात्रं संसारिणै अस्मि संवृत्ता]।

Sītā—Worshipful Tamasā, I have just for a moment turned a householder with my breasts throbbing and dripping at this recollection of my children and owing to the presence of their father.

तमसा–किमत्रोच्यते। प्रसवः खलु प्रकर्षपर्यन्तः स्नेहस्य। परमश्चैतदन्योन्यसंश्लेषणं पित्रोः।

Tam.—What are you talking about it? Offspring is indeed the limit of the intensity of affection; it is really the most powerful source of the mutual attachment of the parents.

अन्तः करणातत्वस्य दम्पत्योः स्नेहसंश्रयात्।
आनन्दग्रन्थिरेकोऽयमपत्यमिति बध्यते।।17।।

This, what is called offspring, is, through the centerning of affection in it, a strange delightful knot tied of the mental entities of the parents.

मित–। भगवतीति–'उच्छ्वसितौ' कम्पमानौ 'प्रस्तुतौ' क्षीरनिष्यन्दिनौ च 'स्तनौ यस्याः सा। 'संसारः' गार्हस्थ्यम् य तदस्त्यस्या इति। यस्मिन् क्षणे मन्ये पतिपुत्रवती संसारधर्मं चरन्ती एवाहम् न तु भर्त्रा परित्यक्ता पुत्राभ्याञ्च वियुक्ता मन्दभागिनी सीता इत्यर्थः।। किमिति–'प्रसवः' अपत्यम्। 'स्नेहस्य' यः 'प्रकर्षः' आतिशय्यं तस्य पर्यन्तः' सीमा। अपत्यं एवं स्नेहस्य परा काष्ठा दृश्यते इत्यर्थः। 'एतत् प्रसवरूपंवस्तु 'पित्रोः परमं सातिशयम्' अन्योऽन्यस्य' परम्परस्य 'संश्लेषणं' मेलनसाधनम्। अतएव अपत्यसंस्मरणात् स्नेहातिशयस्ते, भर्तृदर्शनात् भर्त्रा सङ्गतमेवात्मनं मन्यसे तेन चोच्यते "संसारिणी अस्मि संवृत्ता" इति।। अन्तरेति।

अन्वयः–अपत्यमित्ययं स्नेहसंश्रयात् दम्पत्योः अन्तःकरणतत्त्वस्य एकः आनन्दग्रन्थिः बध्यते।

व्याख्या–'अपत्यम् इति अयं स्नेहस्य' पित्रोः प्रीतेः 'संश्रयात्' सामश्रयणात् हेतोः 'दम्पत्यो' जायापत्योः अन्तःकरणारूपस्य तत्त्वस्य' मनोरूपस्य पदार्थस्य 'एकः' अनिर्वचनीयः 'आनन्दमयो ग्रन्थिः परम्परबन्धनं 'बध्यते' ग्रथ्यते। उभयोरपि एकस्मिनन्नपत्ये स्निह्याति मनः इति मनसोर्बन्धनमेव तदपत्यम्। इतरविलक्षणञ्च तत् बन्धनम्, यतः प्राकृतं बन्धनं क्लेशकरं भवति इदञ्च आनन्दकरम् इति।।

Notes 1. संसारिणी etc.—संसरण is पुनर्जन्मग्रहण। संसरत्यस्मिन् इति सम्+मृ+घञ् अधिकरणे संसारः the world. सः अस्ति अस्या इति संसार+इति मत्वर्थे स्त्रियाम् संसारिणी। I am no longer a woman of the world, yet for the time being I feel like one. 2. किमत्र etc.—अत्र in the matter of your feeling just now. What you say is superflous. 3. प्रसवः–प्र+सू+अप् कर्मणि प्रसवः offspring. 4. प्रकर्ष etc.—The extreme limit of excess. "offspring is the highest grade of affection" is intended to mean "The highest grade of affection is centered in offspring", 5. अन्योऽनय etc.—अन्यस्य अन्यस्य अन्योऽन्यस्य by "कर्मव्यतिहारे सर्वनाम्नोः–" etc. (see ante). सम्+शिलष्+णिच्+ल्युद् करणे संश्लेषणम् that which unites, *i.e.*, a knot (as in the verse below). अन्योऽन्यस्य सश्लेषणम्। 6. पित्रोः–माता चपिता च पितरौ। तथोः। 7. अनतः etc.—करण is दन्द्रिय। अन्तःस्थितं करणम् अन्तःकरणम् the inner sense, *i.e.*, the mind. तत्व is पदार्थ principle, entity. अन्तःकरणारूपंतत्त्वतम्। तस्य। शेषे षष्ठी, related to आनन्दग्रन्थिः।8. दम्पत्योः–जाया च पतिश्च जायापती, जम्पती, दम्पती। The प्रातिपदिक

is दम्पति। तथोः। शेषे, षष्ठी, related to अन्तःकरणतत्व। दम्पत्योः अन्तःकरणतत्वस्य आनन्दग्रन्थिः is the same as अन्योऽन्यसंश्लेषणं पित्रोः of the prose above. 9. स्नेह etc.—संश्रयणाम् इति सम्+अच भावें संश्वयः सम्यगबलम्बनम्। स्नेहस्य संश्रयः स्नेहसंश्रयः the through centering of affection. तस्मात्। The अपत्य is the स्नेहसंश्रय। For this reason it is दम्पत्योः अन्तःकरणतत्वस्य आनन्दग्रन्थिः। Remembering that सम् in संश्रय is intensive, we see that अपत्यं स्नेहसंश्रयः is the same as प्रसवः खलु प्रकर्षपर्य्यन्तः स्नेहस्य as in the prose above. आनन्दग्रन्थिः-ग्रन्थि is the same as संश्लेषण above. 11. एक-Unique. Its distinction from an ordinary ग्रन्थि lies in the fact that is it blissful while any other ग्रन्थि is painful. 12. *Remark*—The verse is an exact translation of the foregoing prose.

(*xxxi*) **वासन्ती–इतोऽपि देवः पश्यतु।**

Vāsantī—Let Sire look this way too.

अत रूणमदताण्डवोत्सवान्ते-
ष्वयमचिरोगटतमुग्धलोलवर्हः।
मणिमुकुट इवोच्छिखः कदम्बे
नदति स एष बधूसखः शिखण्डी।।18।।

Here is the same peacock, with a tuft grown on his crest and with a fine not-long fledged sweeping tail, crowing in company with his mate, at the end of every festive farmantic dance, through great hilarity, on the Kadamba as if on a crown of gems.

मित–। अतरुणेति।

अन्वयः–एष सः अयम् उच्छिखः अचिरोग्दतमुग्धलोलवर्हः शिखण्डी बधूसखः (सन्) अतरुणमदताण्डवोत्सवान्तेषु मणिमुकुटे इव कदम्बे नदति।

व्याख्या–'एष' दृश्यमानः सीतया परिवर्द्धितः शिशुः 'सः अयम्' सम्प्रति तरूणे वयसि 'उच्छिखः' उगटतया शिखया मण्डितः 'अचिरोद्गतं' नवोद्भिनं' 'मुग्धं' मनोहरं 'लोलं' चञ्चलं खेलत् इत्यर्थः 'वर्हं' चिच्छं यस्य तादृशः 'शिखण्डी' मयूरः 'बधूसखः' सन् करिकरभक इव वध्वा सार्द्धम् 'अतरूणः' प्रौढ़ यः 'मदः' आनन्दः तेन हेतुना ये 'ताण्डवीत्सवाः' उद्धतनृत्तामोदाः तेषाम् 'अन्तेषु' विरामेषे 'मणिमुकुटे इव कदम्बे' पुष्पिते अधो विस्तारवति उर्ध्वञ्च आनुपूर्व्या सङ्कुचिते अतएव मणिमये मुकुटे इव अस्मिन् सीतया एव परिवर्द्धिते कदम्बे 'नदति' आरटति। करिकरभक इव एष शिखण्डी अयञ्च कदम्बः "यत् कल्याणं वयसि तरुणे भाजनं तस्य जा" इति भावः।।

Notes 1. अतरुण etc.—The plural show that several times in the day he enjoys such bouts of merry dance on the top of the कदम्ब and crows at its end at the top of his voice. Comp. the plural in कवलच्छेदेषु, sl. 16. This is the reading in three of Vidyāsāgara's four manuscripts. The fourth has अन्ते in the singular and then स्वयम् etc. स्वयम् does not give good sense. अन्तेषु अयम् (अन्तेष्वयम्) does not offend against the metre; Comp. "उपान्तवानीरवनोपगूढ़ान्यालक्ष्यपारिल्पवसारसानि" –*Raghu*. 2. अचिर etc.—लोलता of the वर्ह lies in the fact that the वर्ह can be turned any way and it was being so turned. 3. मणिमुकुट इव–this is usually taken as मणिमुकुटः इव qualifying शिखण्डी which overlooks the fact that मुकुट is neuter. We take it as coming from मणिमुकुटे इव by सन्धि। A well-grown कदम्ब tree is broadest where it branches off, the branches growing almost horizontally all round. It then tapers to a point at the top and looks from a distance like a cone placed vertex upwards which is just the appearance of a मुकुट। Besides even to this day a मुकुट is never made without a peacock at its crest. 4. वधूसखः–Thus both the elephant-calf and peacock are prospering well.

(*xxxii*) **सीता (सकौतुकास्त्रम्)–एसो सो।**

Sītā—(*With interest and tears*)—It is he !

रामः–मोदस्व वत्स मोदस्व।

Rāma—Enjoy it, darling, enjoy it.

सीता–एवं होदु [एवं भवतु]।

Sītā—So be it.

रामः– भ्रमिषु कृतपुटान्तर्मण्डलावृत्ति चक्षुः
प्रचलितचतुरभ्रूताण्डवैर्मण्डयन्त्या।
करकिसलयतालैर्मुग्धया नर्त्त्यमानं
सुतमिव मनसा त्वां वत्सलेन स्मरामि।।18।।

Rāma—With a loving heart I remember you—as though my own son—being danced by the charming (Or-artless) girl, with the clapping of her leaf-like plams at each whirl adding grace, with the play of her gracefully moving eyebrows, to the eyes that turned in a circle their sockets.

मित– । भ्रमिष्विति ।

अन्वयः–भ्रमिषु कृतपुटान्तर्मण्डलावृत्ति चक्षुः प्रचलित- चतुरभ्रूताण्डवैः मण्डयन्त्या मुग्धया करकिसलयतालैः नर्त्त्य मानं त्वां वत्सेन वत्सलेन मनसा स्मरामि।

व्याख्या–'भ्रमिषु' देव्याः परितो त्वदीयेषु मण्डलशो भ्रमणेषु 'कृता पुटान्तः' अक्षिरकोटराभ्यन्तरे 'मण्डलावृत्तिः' तनवानुवृत्तैः' चक्रभ्रमणं येन तथाविधं 'चक्षुः प्रचलितयोः' प्रकम्पितयोः 'चतुरयोः' लीलानिपुणयोः सुन्दरयावां 'भ्रुवोः ताण्डवैः' नृत्तैः मण्डयत्या' भूषयन्त्या 'मुग्धया' मनोहारिण्या सरलया वा सीतया 'करकिसलययोः' पाणिपल्लवयोः 'तालैः' कालमानार्थं दत्ताभिः करतालिकाभिः 'नर्त्त्यमानं त्वां सुतमिव' निजमिव पुत्रं 'वत्सेन स्निग्धेन 'मनसा स्मरामि'। यद्वा 'सुतामिव' सीतया आत्मतनयमिव 'नर्त्त्यमानं त्वां स्मरामि' इत्यर्थः।।

Notes. 1. प्रचलित etc.—चतुर may also be rendered सुन्दर, सुभग etc. Mallinātha under तां बीक्ष्य लीलाचतुरमनङ्गः expounds लीलाचतुरां विलाससुभागाम्। ताण्डव here is quick motion right and left or up and down. 2. मण्डयन्त्या–मण्ड+णिच् स्वार्थे+शतृ स्त्रियाम् मण्डयन्ती। तया। The eyes were beautiful but their beauty was enchanced by the play of her eye-brows. 3. करकिसलय etc.—करौ किसलयमिव करकिसलयौ उपभितकर्मधा–। The comparison with किसलय is to add grace to the poems. This act of keeping time was specially beautiful. 4. नर्त्त्यमानं स्मरामि–I can picture before me the whole scene. She, in the perfection of her beauty, standing at the centre you going round her in a circle, her beautiful eyes looking still more beautiful through the play of her restless eye-brows, and her graceful hands keeping time in a charming manner.

(*xxxiii*) (रा–) हन्त तिर्यञ्चोऽपि परिचयमनुरुध्यन्ते।

(R—) Ha! Even the lower order of beings respect acquaintanceship !

कपितयकुसुमोद्गमः कदम्बः
प्रियतमया परिवर्द्धितो या आसीत्। (20–)

The Kadamba has now a show of a few flowers—the Kadamba that was reared by my darling.

सीता (निरूप्य सास्त्रम्)–सुठ्ठु, पच्चहिआणिदं अज्जउत्तेन [सुष्ठ प्रत्यभिज्ञातमार्यपुत्रेण]।

Sītā (Marking—With tears) —My husband has well recongnised it.

रामः– स्मरति गिरिमयूर एष देव्याः
स्वजन इवात्र यतः प्रमोदमेति।। 20।।

Rāma—The queen's hill-peacock remembers it [Or—This hill-peacock remembers the queen]; for, he feels joy here a with a kinsman.

मित–।'हन्त' इति विषादे।'तिर्य्यञ्च' पशुपक्षिणो नीचा जातयः'अपि परिचयं' पूर्वानुभूतं प्रणयम् 'अनुरुध्यन्ते' सम्मानयन्ति। तिर्यञ्चोऽपि अनुरुध्यन्ते मयाः पुनर्मानुषजात्यभिमानिना अननुरुध्यैव परिचयं त्यक्ता प्रियतमा इति सविषादमात्माधिक्षेपः। कतिपयेति।

अन्वयः–कदम्बः कतिपयकुसुमोगटमः यः प्रियतमया परिवर्द्धित आसीत्।

व्याख्या–'कदम्बः' एष दृश्यमानो नीपः 'कतिपयकुसुमोद्गमः स्वल्पैरेव कुममैरलङ्कृतः 'यः' कदम्बः 'प्रियतमा' सीतया 'परिवर्द्धित आसीत्'।। स्मरतीति।

अन्वयः–एष गिरिमयूरः देव्याः स्मरति' यतः स्वजने इव अत्र प्रमोदमीति।

व्याख्या–स्वल्पेऽपि कुसुमे बहुकुसुमान् अपरान् वृक्षान् परिहृत्य इहैवायंमोदते मयूर इत्येतावता मन्ये 'एष गिरिमयूरः देव्याः स्मरति' सोतागतं ध्यायति, प्रियायाः परिचयम् अनुरुध्यते, तेनैव 'स्वजने इव' सीतासम्पर्कात् निजे इव भ्रातरि 'अत्र' अस्मिन् कदम्बे 'प्रमोदम् इति' आनन्दमनुभवति। द्वयोरपि आवयोः पोषणात् एकैव माता सीता तेन भ्रातायं मे इति सीतासम्पर्कं स्मृत्वा इहैवायं मोदते।।

Notes. 1. तिर्यञ्चः–तिरः वक्रम् अञ्चन्ति इति तिरस्+अञ्च+क्विन् कर्त्तरि birds and beasts. 2. अपि–Even the lower creation, not I. This is a self-condemention (see Ṭīkā). 3. कपितय etc.—कुसुमानाम् उन्दमाः कुसुमोद्गमाः which means उन्द्गतानि कुसुमानि by the dictum "भावानयने द्रव्यानयनम्"। कतिपया कुसुमोद्गमाः अस्य, बहु–। Avoid कपितयानि कुसुमानि, तेषाम् उद्गमः अस्मिन्। In the first place कपितयानि कुसुमानि gives कुसुमकतिपयानि by the rule "पोटायुवति–"। Secondly, the अधिकरण बहु–with षष्ठी in the पूर्वपद is objectionable. 4. प्रिय etc.—Vāsantī has not identified the कदम्ब, but Rāma has reconised it. 5. देव्याः–Construe देव्या स्मरति remembers of the queen (without कर्मविवक्षा of देवी)। षष्ठी शेषे। The construction देव्या गिरिमयूरः ignores the drift of the speech and omits the कर्म of स्मरति। 6.

Remark—It is summer-time and Kadambas are not expected to bloom. This seems to be an anomaly.

(*xxxiv*) **वासन्ती–अत्र तावदासनपरिग्रहं करोतु देवः।**

Vāsantī—Meanwhile let Sire take his seat here.

एतत्तदेव कदलीवनमध्ववर्त्ति
कान्तासखस्य शनीयशिलातलं ते।
अत्र स्थिता तृणमदाद्बहुशो यदेभ्यः
सीता ततो हरिणकैर्न विमच्यते स्म।। 21।।

This is the very same stone-slab which was your bed inside the plantain-grove when accompanied by your beloved. It has not deserted by the deer yonder because, seated here, Sītā often offered grass to them.

मित–'अत्र' इति वक्ष्यमाणं शिलातलं निर्दिशति।। एतदिति

अन्वयः–एतत् तदेव ते कान्तासुखस्य कदलीवनमध्यवर्त्ति शयनीयशिलातलम्। यत् सीता बहुशः अत्र स्थिता एभ्यः तृणमदात् हरिणकैः न विमुच्यते स्म।

व्याख्या–एतत्' दृश्यमानं 'तदेव ते कान्तासस्वस्य' वधुद्वितीयस्य 'कदलीवनमध्यवर्त्ति' सावरणमित्यर्थः 'शयनीयं शिलातलम्'। 'यत्' 'सीता वहुशः अत्र' अस्मिन् शिलातले 'स्थिता' सती 'एभ्यः' पुरोवर्त्तिभ्यः हरिणेभ्यः 'तृणाम् अदात् ततः' एभिः 'हरिणकैः' मृगैः 'न विमुच्यते' न त्यज्यते। 'स्म' इति पादपूरणे। असत्यपि अधुना इह भोज्ये सीतायाः स्मरन्त इसे आगत्यात्र विश्राभ्यन्ति। यथा अयं मयूरः तथा इसे मृगाः। तत सत्यमेवोक्तं देवेन परिचयमनुरुध्यन्ते तिर्यञ्च इति।।

Notes. 1. कान्तासखस्य–कान्तायाः सखा इहति कान्ता सखि+टच् समासान्त। 2. हरिणकैः–Some thirteen years have passed since these enjoyed Sītā's company here. The deerlings are now more than full grown deer. Hence, the क cannot be अल्पे or ह्रस्वे। Take it as स्वार्थे 2. स्म–An अव्यय here पादपूरणे। We cannot take it as giving a past sense to विमुच्यते। For that would mean that in the past the deer did not leave it i.e., they continued to come here for some time after Sītā had left and then ceased to come. But this contradicts एभ्यः which shows that the deer present there at the time. Vidyāsāgara has rightly taken स्म as पादपूरणे। We think the text is corrupt. The correct reading is perhaps something else. पादपूरण is for people who do not know how to make up a verse and is not desirable in भवभूति। Besides the कर्म of विमुच्यते has to be grathered with some effort. विमुच्यतेऽदः meets all these objections. The objection, that अदस् speaks of some विप्रकृष्ट object and therefore अदः is inadmissible, is immaterial. Poets sometime do use अदः to point out something close by. Compare "अदश्वरावर"–*Kumāra*. We therefore propose to read "सीता ततो हरिणकैर्न विमुच्यतेऽदः"। 3. *Remark*—Vāsantī here endorses Rāma's remark "तिर्यञ्चोऽपि परिचयमनुरुध्यन्ते"। तिर्य्यञ्चः includes birds and beasts. Birds are represented by the मयूरः of which Rāma has spoken; Vāsantī points out the beasts here in हरिणकैः। The deer too remember सीता–"परिचयमनुरुध्यन्ते"।

(*xxxv*) **रामः–इदं तावदशक्यमेव द्रष्टुम्। (इत्यन्यतो रुदन्नु पविशति)।**

Rāma—It is indeed impossible for me to lcok as it. *(Sits elsewhere weeping).*

सीता–सहि वासन्दि किं तुए कअं अज्जउत्तस्स मम अ एदं दंसअन्तीए। हद्धी ! हद्धी ! सो एव अज्जउत्तो, तं एव पञ्चवटी वणां, सा एव पिअसही वासन्दी, तं एव विविहवीसम्भसाक्खिणो गोदावरीकाणणुद्देसा, ते एव्व जाननिविसेसा मिअपक्खिपादवा, सा एव चाहं, मम उण मन्दभाइणीए दीसमाणं वि सव्वं एव एदं णत्थित्ति। ता एरिसो जीअलोअस्स परिवत्तो [सखि वासन्ति, किं त्वया कृतामर्यपुत्रस्य मम च एतत् दर्शयन्त्या ? हा धिक् ! हा धिक् ! स एब आर्यपुत्रः, तदेब पञ्चबटीबनम्, सा एव प्रियसखी वासन्ती, ते एव विविधविस्त्रम्भसाक्षिणो गोदावरीकाननोद्देशाः, ते एव जातनिर्विशेषा मृगपक्षिपादपाः, सा एव चाहम्; मम पुनर्मन्दभागिन्याः दृश्यमानमपि सर्वमेवैतन्नास्तीति। तत् ईदृशो जीवलोकस्य परिवर्त्तः]।

Sītā—Friend Vāsantī, in showing this, what have you done unto me or my husband ? Alas ! Here is my husband as before : the very same forest of Pañcavaṭī ; the very same Vāsantī my dear friend ; the very same forest tracts of the Godāvarī, witnesses to our various confidences ; the same indeed the deer, the birds, and the trees, not at all different from our children (*i.e.,* looked upon as our children); and I am the same to be sure. But to me, the ill fated, the whole of it, though being seen, is as if non-existent ! Such then has been the change in the land of the living !

मित– ।'विविधविस्रम्भसाक्षिणः' व्याख्यातं प्राक्।'गोदावरीश्लिष्टं' वत्'काननं' तस्य 'उद्देशाः।'जातम्' अपत्यम्।'जीतेभ्यो निर्विशेषाः' अभिन्ना। अपत्यवल्ललिता इत्यर्थः। 'मृगाः शिलातलसपीपस्थिता हरिणाः। 'पक्षी' मयूरः। 'पादपः' कदम्बः। 'जीवानां' 'लोकः 'भुवनम्। 'परिवर्त्तः अवस्थान्तरम्। एकस्थामवस्थायां सर्वमस्ति अवस्थान्तरे सर्वमेव नास्ति।।

Notes. 1. किं त्वया etc.—What have you done ? You have done a disservice to both of us. We suffer by seeing it. 2. दृश्यमानपमपि etc.—They exist, yet to me they are non-existent. I have changed (परिवर्त्तः) and in consequence these have changed (परिवर्त्तः) from existent to non-existent.

(*xxxvi*) **वासन्ती–सखि सीते, कथं न पश्यामि रामस्यावस्थाम् ?**

Vāsantī—Friend Sītā, why don't you notice Rāma's plight ?

कुवलदलस्निग्धैरङ्गैर्ददौ नयनोत्सवं
सततमपि ते स्वेच्छादृश्यो नवं नवमेव यः।
विकलकरणः पाण्डुः सोऽयं शुचा परिदुर्बलः
कथमपि स इत्युन्नेतव्यस्तथापि दृशां प्रियः ।। 22 ।।

He the same who, though to be always seen at will, gave fresh and fresh joy indeed to your eyes with limbs pleasing like the petals of the blue lotus is, now through grief—wan greatly weakened, with senses failing, yet delighter of the eyes—hardly recongnisable he.

सीता–पेक्खामि सहि पेक्खामि [प्रेक्षे सखि प्रेक्षे]।

Sītā—I see it, friend, I see it.

तमसा–पश्यन्ती प्रियं भूयाः।

Tam.—May thou be seeing thy beloved (at your will as before) !

मित– । कुवलयेति।

अन्वयः–सततं स्वेच्छादृश्यः अपि यः कुवलनयदलस्निग्धैः अङ्गैः नवं नवमेव ते नयनोत्सवं ददौ, शुचा पाण्डुः विकलकरणः परिदुर्बलः तथापि दृशां प्रियः सः अयं कथमपि स इत्युन्नेतव्यः।

व्याख्या–'सततं' सदा स्वेच्छया दृश्यः अपि' अनियन्त्रितदर्शनोऽपि 'यः कुवलयदलैः' नीलोत्पलपत्रैः इव 'स्निग्धैः' नेत्रतर्पणैः अङ्गैः नव नवमेव' नवप्रकारमेव 'ते नयानोत्सवं' नेत्रान्दं 'ददौ' पुरा इति शेषः सम्प्रति 'शुचा' शोकेन त्वद्विरहजनितेन इति शेषः 'पाण्डुः' अपरक्तः 'विकलकरणः' क्षीणेन्द्रियः 'परिदुर्बलः बलहीनः तथापि दृशां प्रियः लोचनाह्लादनः 'स अयं कथमपि' अतिकृच्छ्रेण 'सः' एवायम्' इति उन्नेतव्यः' प्रत्यभिज्ञातव्यः। कृच्छ्रेणौवायं रामि इति ज्ञायते ईदृशो शोचनीया अस्य अवस्था जाता कि न पश्यसि सखि सीते। नह्येत् सीतां प्रति। मृता सीता इत्येव वासन्ती जानाति, परलोकस्थां तां प्रत्येतत्।। 'पश्यन्ती भूयाः' इत्याशीः।। अचिरणैव प्रियस्य दर्शनम् अविघ्नं तेऽस्तु।।

Notes 1. नवं नवम्–The repetition is प्रकारे। Like new. The विभक्ति should have disappeared yielding नवनवम् as in "नवनवा वनवायवः"। But भवभूति has a will, comapare "मन्दं मन्दमासत्तियोगात्" (I. 27). 2, शुचा–This goes with all the three विकलकरणाः, पाण्डुः, परिदुर्बलः। 3. *Remark*—In the explanation usually given दृशां प्रियः is the predicate. This draws attention to Rāma's प्रियदर्शनता which cannot excite pity. In her apeal कथं न पश्यासि etc. Vāsantī means to say that Rāma is in a pitiable plight—"Friend Sītā, you do not notice Rāma's plight or you would have come down to him from heaven out of compassion." This is Vāsantī's thought, hence he is दृशां प्रियः is inadmissible as a predicate. We have therefore made कथमपि च इत्युन्नतेव्यः as the predicate. This serves Vāsantī's purpose. 4. भूयाः–आशिषि लिङ्। Tamasā hopes for a reunion of the pair.

(*xxxvi*) **सीता–हा देव एसो मए विणा, अहं ऐदण विणात्ति केण सम्भाविदं आसी। ता मुहुत्तअं वि जन्मन्तरादो विअ लद्धदंसणं वाहसलिलन्तरेसु पेक्खामि दाव वच्छलं अज्जउत्तं [हा दैव, एष मया विना अहमेतेन विना इति केन सम्भावितामासीत्। तत् मुहूर्त्तकमपि जन्मान्तरादिव लब्धदर्शनं वाष्पसलिलान्तरेषु प्रेक्षे तावत् वत्सलमार्यपुत्रम्]। (इति सतृष्णं पश्यति)।**

Sītā— O Fate ! By whom could it be imagined that he would be parted from me or I from him ? So I will see, even though for a moment, at intervals between floods of tears, my loving husband whose sight has been obtained as if through re-birth. *(Looks wistfully).*

तमसा (सस्नेहास्रं परिष्वज्य)–

Tam. *(Embracing with tears of affection)*—

विलुलितमतिपूरैर्वाष्पमानन्दशोक-
प्रभवमवसृजन्ती तृष्णयोत्तानदीर्घा
स्नपयति हृदयेशं स्नेहनिस्यन्दिनी ते
धवलबहलमुग्धा दुग्धकुल्येव दृष्टिः ।। 23 ।।

Your eye, wide and long through ardour, mainly white yet charming, pouring love and shedding tears that are caused by joy and grief and flowing in great profusion, bathes the lord of your heart like a stream of milk.

मित– । 'सम्भावितं' चिन्तितम्। 'मुहूर्त्तकम्' इति स्वार्थे कन्। 'अन्मानतरात्' हेतोः 'लब्धं' दर्शनं' यस्य तादृशम् आर्यपुत्रम्'। इह जन्मनि दर्शनमसम्भावितमेव, तन्मन्ये जन्मान्तरमेवाद्य मे जातं ततो लब्धमार्यपुत्रस्य दर्शनम् इत्यर्थः।'वाष्पसलिलानाम्' अश्रुजलानाम् अन्तरेषु' अवकाशेषु, यदा यदा अश्रुललानाम् एकः प्रवाहो निवृत्तः द्वितीयश्च न तावदुट्गतः तदा तदा। 'वत्सलं' मय्येव सस्नेहम्।। विलुलितेति।

अन्वयः–अतिपूरैः विलुलितम् आनन्दशोकप्रभवं वाष्पम् अवसृजन्ती तृष्णाया उत्तानदीर्घा धवलवहलमुग्धा दुग्धाकुल्येव ते दृष्टिः स्नेहनिस्यन्दिनी (सती) हृदयेशं स्नपयति।

व्याख्या–'अतिपूरैः महद्भिः प्रवाहै 'विलुलितं विगलितम्, भर्त्तृदर्शनात् यः 'आनन्दः' भर्त्तुरवस्थादर्शनाच्च यः 'शोकः' तत्–'प्रभवं' तज्जनितं 'वाष्पम्' अश्रु 'अवसृजन्ती पातयन्ती, 'तृष्णाया' दर्शनात्कण्ठया 'उत्ताना' विस्फारिता 'दीर्घा' कर्णानतलम्बिनी च परित्यागरोषापगमात् 'धवलबहला' अतिशुभ्रा 'मुग्धा' प्रकृत्या मनोहरा च अतएव स्फारत्वदीर्घत्वधवलत्वादिभिः पयःप्रवाहेण च 'दुग्धकुल्येव' दुग्धपूर्णा कृत्रिमसरिदिव लक्ष्यमाणा 'ते दृष्टिः' चक्षुः स्नेहनिस्यन्दिनी' प्रीतिवषिणी सती 'हृदयेशं प्राणेश्वरं रामं 'स्नपयति स्नातवत् करोति। चक्षुषः क्षरिता स्नेहधाग भर्त्तरि पतति मन्ये तथा तस्य स्नानमेव भवति इत्यर्थः।।

Notes. 1. आनन्द etc.—आनन्दश्च शोकश्च आनन्दशोकौ। तौ प्रभवः कारणं यस्य तम्। आनन्द because she has met her lord and the lord is वत्सल। शोक because she has met him in this plight also because the meeting brings back to memory the incidents that cause the almost unbelievable separation (Comp. हादैव, एष भया विना etc.) 2. उत्तानदीर्घा–Bhavabhūti believes that eagerness to see not only widens the eye but lengthens it also. Comp. "तृष्णादीर्घस्य चक्षुषः–III, sl 46. 9. स्नपयति–The मित्व of स्ना is optionaly by "गलास्नावनुंवमां च"। Hence स्ना+णिच्=स्नापि or स्नपि and स्नापयति also is correct. Here there is no actual स्नानः, hence, though स्नपयति means स्नातं करोति we render it as स्नातवत् करोति। 3. स्नेह etc.—स्नेहं निस्यन्दयतीति स्नेह+नि+स्यन्द+णिच्+णिनि साधुकारिणि कर्त्तरि स्त्रियाम्। The derivation स्नेहनिस्यन्दः अस्ति अस्याम् (इनि मत्वर्थे) puts the कर्त्तृता of दृष्टि in the back-ground which is not desirable. In our derivation दृष्टि is the हेतुकर्त्ता. The reading स्नेहनिष्यन्दिनी is derived with इनिय भत्वर्थे and is therefore avoided. If we attach णिच् the rule "अनुविपर्यभिनिभ्यः स्यन्दतेरप्राणिषु" does not apply because, as a rule, the enunciation of a root does not cover its णिजन्त form also. We have therefore rejected निष्यन्दिनी। The reading however becomes available if we suppose that स्यन्द in निष्पन्दिनी is अन्तर्मावितण्यर्थं

(*xxxviii*) **वासन्ती–**

ददतु तरवः पुष्पैरर्घ्यं फलैश्च मधुश्च्युतः
स्फुटितकमलामोदप्रायाः प्रावन्तु वनानिलाः।
कलमविरलं रज्यत्कणठाः क्वणन्तु शकुन्तयः
पुनरिदमयं देवो रामः स्वयं वनमागतः।। 24।।

Vāsantī—Here, Sire Rāma has of his own accord cone to this forest again; let treeses shedding honey offer *Arghya* with and flowers ; let forest breezes blow, rich in fragrance of full-blown lotuses; let birds having a voice tuned to music sung sweetly and uninetrruptedly.

मित–ददत्विति।

अन्वयः–मधुश्च्युतः तरवः पुष्पैः फलैश्च अर्घ्यं ददतु। स्फटितकमलामोदप्रायाः वनानिलाः प्रवान्तु। रज्जत्कण्ठाः शकुन्तयः अविरलकलं कृणन्तु। अयं देवो रामः स्वयम इदं वनं पुनरागतः।

व्याख्या–येषां पुष्पाणि सुरभीणि फलानि न सुरसानि तादृशाः 'मधुश्च्युतः' मधुवर्षिणः 'तरवः' पुष्पैः फलैश्च अर्ध्य" पुजोपहारं 'ददतु'। अनादेयं पुष्पं वा फलं वा इह मास्तु। ये च 'स्फुटितकमलामोदप्रायाः' विकसितपद्मगन्धबहुलाः तादृशाः

'वनानिला:' वनवाताः 'प्रवान्तु' वहन्तु। पूतिगन्धयो वायव इह मा चरन्तु। ये पुनः 'रज्यन्' सरागः 'कण्ठी' येषां तादृशाः मधुरभाषिणः 'शकुन्तयः' पक्षिणः ते एव 'अविरलम्' अजस्रं 'कलं' मधुरं 'कूणन्तु' गायन्तु। कट रवाः काकादय इह मा रटन्तु। कारणमाह–'अयं देवो रामः स्वयम्' स्वेच्छया एव, प्राक् तु पित्राज्ञया परवशः अद्य युष्मत्प्रीत्या 'इदं वनं पुनरागतः' तन्मोदध्वं सर्वे यूयम्।।

Notes. 1. मधुश्च्युतः–श्च्युत (श्च्युतिर्) means क्षरण to trickle down, and is usually अकर्मक। Comp. "एतास्ता मधुनो धाराश्च्योतन्ति साविषास्त्वयि"–sl. 34. Hence say श्च्युत here is अन्तर्भावितण्यर्थं मधु+श्च्युत्+क्विप् कर्त्तरि। 2. स्फुटित etc.—स्फुटितकमलानाम् आमोदः स्फुटितकमलाभोदः। स्फुटितकलामोदस्य प्रायः बाहुल्यम् एषु। "प्रायश्चानशने मृत्यौ तुल्यबाहुल्योरपि।" इति विश्वः। Here स्फुटितकमल is a bit tautolgous, for कमल itself is a full-blown lotus. 3. रज्यत्कण्ठाः–रज्यत् (रञ्ज of the दिवादि class+शतृ) is राजयुक्त tuned. She wants the sweet-throated birds only to sing. The reading रत्युत्कण्ठाः means रामे या 'रतिः' प्रीतिः तया 'तत्कण्ठाः' उद्ग्रीवाः। In that case the statement of the reason in the fourth line becomes superfluous. Besides, it does not fit in with the epithets मधुश्च्युत् and स्फुटितकमलमोदप्रायाः which exclude undersirables. रत्युत्कण्ठाः excludes no bird. 4. *Remark*—Here again we must remember that the time being summer स्फुटितकमल is hardly availble in quantity.

(*xxxix*) **रामः–एहि सखि वासन्ति, नन्वितः स्थोयताम्।।**

Rāma—Come, friend Vāsantī, do sit down here.

वासन्ती (उपविश्य सास्त्रम्)–महाराज, अपि कुशलं कुमारलक्ष्मण-स्य ?

Vāsantī (*Sitting down—With tears*)—O mighty king, is it all right with Prince Lakṣmaṇa ?

रामः–(अश्रुतिमभिनीय)–

Rāma, (*Acting as if not listening)*—

करकमलवितीर्णैरम्बनीवारशष्पै-
स्तरुशकुनिकुरङ्गान् मैथिली यानपुष्यत्।
भवति मम विकारस्तेषु दृष्टेषु कोऽपि
द्रव इव हृदयस्य प्रस्तरोद्भेदयोग्यः।। 25।।

On seeing the trees, birds and deer which Maithili tended with water, wild grain and fresh shoots of grass, distributed with her lotus-hand, a strange change overtakes me as if there was a rush of the melted heart capable of bursting rocks.

मित–'ननु' इत्यनुनये।। करकमलेति।

अन्वयः– यान् तरुशकुनिकुरङ्गान् मैथिली करकमलवितीर्णैः अम्बुनीवारशष्पैः अपुष्यत् तेषु दृष्टेषु मम प्रस्तरोद्भेदयोग्यः हृदयस्य द्रव इव कोऽपि विकारो भवति।

व्याख्या–सुगमा। 'तरुशकुनिकुरङ्गान् अम्बुनीवारशष्पैः' इति यथाक्रमं नेयम्। 'अम्बुना तरुं' कदम्बम् अपुष्यत्, 'नीवारेण शकुनिं' मयूरमपुष्यत्, 'शष्पेणा कुरङ्गान्' अपुष्यत् इति। 'प्रस्तरस्य उद्भेदे' दारणे 'योग्यः' समर्थः हृदयस्य द्रवः इव विकारः। मन्ये हृदयं मे द्रवीभवति स च द्रवः आत्मप्रवाहेण प्रस्तरमपि भिन्द्यात् मनोविकारश्च प्रकटीभवेत्।

Notes. 1. करकमल etc. —वि+तु+क्त कर्मपि वितीर्ण offered. This applies to अम्बु, नीवार and शष्प all these were वितीर्ण। विकारः–Consture मम विकारः or हृदयस्य विकारः। 3. प्रस्तर etc—Hence the द्रव will come out. *i.e.*, my lamenations will be unchecked to-day.

(*xl*) **वासन्ती–महाराज, ननु पृच्छामि अपि कुशलं कुमारलक्ष्मणस्य ?**

Vāsantī—Well, Mahārāja, I ask, is it well with Prince Lakṣmaṇa ?

रामः (स्वागतम्)–अये महराजेति निष्प्रणयमामन्त्रणपदं सौमित्रिमात्रे च वाष्पस्खलिताक्षरः कुशलप्रश्नः। तथा मन्ये विदितसीतावृत्तान्तेयमिति। (प्रकाशम्) आं कुशलं कुमारस्य। (इति रोदिति)।

Rāma (*To himself*)—Ha ! The word of address is "Mahārāja" which is colourless (indifferent); the enquiry after welfare is about Saumitri alone and in accents faltering with tears ; I think she is informed of the facts about Sītā.

(*Aloud*) Yes, the prince is well. (*Weeps*).

वासन्ती–अयि देव, किमिति दारुणः खल्वसि?

Vāsantī—O Sire, why indeed hast thou become so cruel ?

सीता–सहि वासन्दि किं तुमं सि एवंवादिणी ? पिआरुहो क्खु

सवस्प्त अज्जउत्तो विसेसदो मम पिअसहीए [सखि वासन्ति, किं त्वमसि एवंवादिनी ? प्रियार्हः खलु सर्वस्य आर्यपुत्रो विशेषतो मम प्रियसख्याः]।

Sītā—Friend Vāsantī, why dost thou speak thus ? My husband deserves kind words of all, especially of my dear friend.

मित–'महाराज' इति सखिभावं परिहृत्य राजभावमात्रमादृत्य उक्तम् अतो निष्प्रणायम् आमन्त्रणापदं' सम्बोधनपदम्। 'सौ.मित्रिमात्रे' सौमित्रावेव न तु सीतायामपि 'कुशलप्रश्नः'। किञ्च 'वाष्पेणा' कण्ठवर्त्तिन उष्मणा 'स्खलितानि' गद्गदानि 'अक्षराणि' यस्मिन् तथाविधः कुशलप्रश्नः। त्रिभिरेभिर्निमितैर्मन्ये 'विदितः सीतावृत्तान्तो' यस्या तादृशो 'इयम्'। 'आम्' इत्यव्ययमिह प्रतिवचने। "आमिति प्रतिवचनावधारणयोः" इति वर्द्धमानः। 'प्रियार्हः प्रियवचनार्हं।

Notes. 1. ननु–Implies अनुनय। 2. आम्–In the sense of अवधारण, compare "आम्–स्निग्धश्यामाः क्वचिदपरतो–" (II, sl. 14), आम् अस्त्येतत्" (III, para 2a). 3. प्रियार्हः–प्रियं प्रियवचनम् अर्हति इति प्रिय+अर्ह+अण् कर्त्तरि।

(*xli*) **वासन्ती–**

त्वं जीवितं त्वमसि मे हृदयं द्वितीयं
त्वं कौमुदी नयनयोरमृतं त्वमङ्गे।
इत्यादिभिः प्रियशतैरनुरुध्य मुग्धां
तामेव–शान्तमथवा किमिहोत्तरेण।।26।।

(इति मूर्च्छिति)।

Vāsantī—"To me, thou art life, thou a art a second heart, thou art moon-light to the eyes, thou art ambrosia to the body"—with hundreds of such endearments, having indeed won over that artless one—. Or peace, why (refer to the sequal in this matter) ?

(*Faints away*).

रामः–स्थाने खलु वाक्यनिबृत्तिर्मोहश्च। सखि समाश्वसिहि समाश्वसिहि।

Rāma—The break in the speech and the swoon are right (Or—are in the right place) indeed. Take courage, friend, take courage.

वासन्ती (समाश्वस्य)–तत् किमिदमकार्यमनुष्टितं देवेन ?

Vāsantī—(*Coming round*)—Well then, why was this misdeed done by Sire ?

मित–। त्वमिति।

अन्वयः–जीवितम्, त्वं मे द्वितीय हृदयमसि, त्वं नघनयोः कौमुदी, त्वम् अङ्गे अमृतम्। इत्यादिभिः प्रियशतैः तां मुग्धाम् अनुरुध्य एव–अथवा शान्तम्। इह उत्तेरण किम् ?

व्याख्या–'त्वं' सम 'जीवितं प्राणा असि। त्वामन्तरेण नाहं जीवामि। 'त्वं मे द्वितीयं हृदयमसि' हृदयं यथा भावं जानाति तथा त्वमपि मे सर्वं जानासि किञ्चिदपि त्वतो गोपितं नास्ति मे। 'त्वं' मे 'नयनयोः कौमुदी' असि ज्योत्स्नेव मे नेत्रानन्दकरी त्वम्। त्वं' मे 'अङ्गे अमृतम्' असि स्पर्शस्तव मां जीवयति। 'इत्यादिभिः एवम्प्रकारकैः' 'प्रियशतैः चाटुपरम्पराभिः 'तां मुग्धां' सरलाम् अनुरुध्य' वशीकृत्य 'एव' प्रतारितवानसि इति उपालम्भगर्भो वाक्यशेषः। 'अथवा शान्तम्' यातु तत्। 'इह अस्मिन्' कितव्यवहारे 'उत्तरेणा' परवर्त्तिना व्यापारेण प्रातरणारुपव्यापारोल्लेखेन 'किम्' फलं स्यात् फलं नास्त्येव। कितवे प्रत्यय एवमेव परिणमति इति प्रसिद्धम्, निष्फला तदालोचना निष्फलश्च तदाश्रय उपालभ्यः इत्यर्थः।। 'स्थाने' इत्यव्ययं युक्तार्थे प्रतारक एवाहम् उचितश्च मदुपालम्भ इत्यर्थः।।

Notes. 1. अनुरुध्य–अनुरुध् is literally to ply with importunities; here to win over. 2. एव–We have taken it with अनुरुध्य। अनुरुध्य एव having indeed gained her confidence. Or consture मुग्धाम् अनुरुध्य तामेव अनुरोधवशीभूतामेव etc. 3. स्थाने–This may also be treated as the सप्तमी of स्थान which means here यथास्थान the right place. 5. अकार्यम्–कृ+णयत् कर्मणि कार्य करणीयम्। तद्विरुद्धम् अकार्यम् a wrong.

(*xlii*) **सीता–सहि वासन्दि विरम विरम [सखि वासन्ति, विरम विरम]।**

Sītā—Cease, friend Vāsantī. cease.

रामः–लोको न मृष्यतीति।

Rāma—Because the people are intolerant.

वासन्ती–तत् कस्य हेतोः ?

Vāsantī—What for is that ?

रामः–स एव जानाति किमपि।

Rāma—They alone know whatever it is.

तमसा–उचितस्तदुपालभ्वः।

Tamasā—The censure then is merited [Or—A rebuke is the right think for them].

वासन्ती– अयि कठोर यशः किल ते प्रियं
किमयशो ननु घोरमतः परम्।
किमभवद्विपिने हरिणीदृशः
कथय नाथ कथं वत मन्यसे।।27।।

Vāsantī—It is really fame that is dear to thee, O hard hearted one ? Well, infamy could be more dire than this ? What befell to the fawn-eyed one in the woods ? Tell me alas ! my lord, how you take it.

मित–।'लोको न मृष्यति' न सहते सीताया गृहे वासम् इति शेषः।।'तत् अमर्षं कस्य हेतोः' किं निमित्तम्।। 'सः' लोकः एव जानाति किमपि' मया तु कारणं न दृश्यते।। 'तत्' तस्मात् यदि कारणमविज्ञायैव न्यक्तवानसि पत्रीं तदा 'उपालम्भः' वासन्त्या कृत उचितः' युक्त एव। यद्वा–'तस्य' लोकस्य 'उपालम्भः' तिरस्कारः 'उचितः' आसीत् न वैदेह्याः परित्यागः।। अयीति।

अन्वयः–अयि कठोर यशः किल ते प्रियम् ? ननु अतः परं घोरम् अयशः किम ? नाथ, कथय विपिने हरिणीदृशः किमभवत् कथं वत मन्यसे।

व्याख्या–'अयि' भोः 'कठोरः' निर्दय 'यशः' किल ते प्रियम्' इति काकुः। 'ननु' आक्षेपे 'अतः परं' तथाविधायाः सीतायाः तादृशात् परित्यागात् अधिकं 'घोरम् अयशः' अयशस्करं 'किं' स्यात्। हे 'नाथ' प्रमो 'कथयविपिने' असहायायाः 'हरिणीदृशः' मृगलोचनायाः सीतायाः 'किमभवत्' इत्यत्र 'कथं वत' खेदे 'मन्यसे' तर्कयसि।।

Notes. 1. कस्य हेतोः–"षष्ठी हेतुप्रयोगे" इति षष्ठी। 2. अयि–The tone is of the censure. 3. किल–Implies अरुचि disapproval, disbelief etc. You say fame is dear to you, I do not believe it. There is an intonation here which makes it question. You love fame ? I do not believe it. 4. परम्–पर means अधिक। परं घोरम् is घोरतरम्। Hence the तरप् is dispensed with—वाक्येन प्रात्ययार्थस्य उक्तत्वात्। 5. वत–Implies खेद।

(xliii) **सीता–तुमं एव सहि वासन्दि दारुणा कठोरा अ जा एवं**

अज्जउत्तं पदीत्तं पदीवेसि [त्वमेव सखि वासन्ति दारुणा कठोरा च या एवमार्यपुत्रं प्रदीप्तं प्रदीपयसि]।

तमसा—प्रणय एवं व्याहरति शोकश्च।

रामः—सखि किमत्र मन्तव्यम् ?

त्रस्तैकहायनकुरङ्गविलोलदृष्टे-
स्तस्याः परिस्फुरितगर्भभरालसायाः।
ज्योत्स्नामयीव मृदुबालमृणालकल्पा
क्रव्याद्भिरङ्गलतिका नियतं विलुप्ता।।18।।

Sītā—Hard-hearted art thou rather, Vāsantī, and fierce too, as thou art inflaming my husband who is already in falmes.

Tamasā—It is love that speaks thus, and grief too.

Rāma—Friend, what is there to think of in this matter ?

The twig of her body, like a soft young shoot of the lotus, as if made of moon-beams, and weary with the weight of her quivering womb, was surely destroyed by eaters of raw meat as her wandering eyes rolled like those of a one-year old fawn frightened.

मित—। त्वमिति। स्वयं प्रदीप्तं' शोकेन दुर्वचोभिः भूयोऽपि 'प्रदीपयसि' तापयसि।। प्रणय इति। वयस्ये रामे यः 'प्रणयः' प्रश्रयः तेन राजोचितं समुदाचारं परित्यज्य 'व्याहरति'। किं पुनर्व्याहारकारणमित्याह 'शोकश्च' तवावस्थां विचिन्त्य शोकतप्ता वयस्यं रामं निर्मर्य्यादमुपालभते इत्यर्थः।। त्रस्तेति।

अन्वयः—नियतं परिस्फुरितगर्भभरालसायाः त्रस्तैकहायनकुरङ्गविलोलदृष्टेः तस्याः मृदुबालमृणालकल्पा ज्योत्स्नामयीव अङ्गलतिका क्रव्याद्भिः विलुप्ता।

व्याख्या—'नियतं' नूनं तदानीं विपिने हिंस्त्रेभ्यः पलायनोद्यतायाः तस्याः प्रयत्नवशात् 'परिस्फुरितः' कम्पितः यः 'गर्भः' तस्य 'भरेण' भारेण 'अलसायाः' मन्थरायाः धावनविरतायाः इत्यर्थः अतएव निश्चितं ग्रहणं मृत्युश्च इति हेतोः 'त्रस्तः' चकितः यः 'एकहायनकुरङ्गः' वर्षमात्रवयस्को हरिणशिशुः तस्य इव 'विलोला' चञ्चल शरणमन्विष्यन्ती इत्यर्थः दृष्टि' यस्याः तथाविधायाः तस्याः' सीतायाः 'मृदु' कोमलं यत् बालमृणालं' विसकिसलयं तत्तुल्या सुखभक्ष्वा इति शेषः 'ज्योत्स्नामयीव' ज्योत्स्नागठितेव 'अङ्गलतिका' देहलता 'क्रव्याद्भिः श्वापदैः 'विलुप्ता क्लिोप' गमिता भक्षिता इत्यर्थः।।

Notes. 1. त्रस्त etc.—For समास see Ṭīkā. Or say she was त्रस्ता, hence एकाहायनकुरङ्गविलोलदृष्टिः। त्रस्ता because she saw there was no escape. विलोल in search of help. त्रस्ता चासौ एकहायनकुरङ्गविलोलदृष्टिश्च। दृष्टि eye. She lost hope because she could not run. 2. परिस्फुरित etc.—That was the day of delivery. The womb quivered at the slighest effort. Comp. "परिस्फुरतीव मे गर्भभारः तत् शिथिलं गच्छामि"–I, para lxziv. 3. ज्योत्स्नामयीव–ज्योत्स्ना प्रकृतिरस्या इति ज्योत्स्ना+मयट्+स्त्रियाम् ज्योत्सामयी made of moon light. The इव implies a mere surmise (उत्प्रेक्षा)। See next. 4. मृदु etc.—मृणाल is white and tender. मृदु and बाल are to intensify the whiteness and tenderness. ईषदसमाप्तं मृदुबालसमृणालम् इति मृदुबालमृणाल+कल्पप् स्त्रियाम्। Such being the character, the surmise follows ज्योत्स्नामयीव। 5. क्रव्याद्भिः–For क्रव्याद see I, sl. 50 ("क्रव्याङ्गयोवलिमिव निर्घृणः क्षिपामि")। 6. विलुप्ता–लुप सकर्मक when meaning छेदन। (तुदादि) वि+लुप+क्त कर्मणि स्त्रियाम् विलुप्ता quartered, *i.e.*, eaten up. Or take the अकर्मलुप meaning अदर्शन and assume it to be अन्तर्भावितण्यर्थं।

7. *Remark*—The thought is the same as in Act. I. sl. 50.

(*xliv*) **सीता–अज्जउत्त धरामि एसा धरामि [आर्यपुत्रध्रिये, एषा ध्रिये] !**

Sītā—I live, my husband. I live.

राम–हा प्रिये जानकि क्वासि।

Rāma—O dear Jānakī. where are you ?

सीता–हद्धी हद्धी अज्जउत्तो वि पमुक्ककण्ठं रुणो [हा धिक्, हा धिक् आर्यपुत्रोऽपि प्रमुक्तकण्ठं रुदितः]।

Sītā—Alas ! Alas ! My husband too is weeping at the top of voice.

तमसा–वत्से साम्प्रतिकमेवैतत्। कर्त्तव्यानि दुःखितै-र्दुःखनिर्वापणानि। यतः–

Tamasā—child, this is right indeed. The relief of their affliction has to be achieved by the afflicted ; for—

पूरोत्पीड़े तड़ागस्य परीवाहः प्रतिक्रिया।
शोकक्षोभे च हृदयं प्रलापैरेव धार्यते।। 28।। (तम–)

When there is pressure of flood in a tank, the remedy is a drain ; and when there is shock of grief, the heart is steadied by wails aone. (29). (Tam.—)

मिति–। 'ध्रियये' जीवामि।। साम्प्रतम् इत्यव्ययं युक्तार्थें साम्प्रतमेव इति 'साम्प्रतिक्रम्'। ठक् स्वार्थें 'निर्वापनानि' प्रशमनानि। पूरेति।

अन्वयः–तड़ागस्य पूरीतपीड़े परीवाहः प्रतिक्रिया। हृदयञ्च शोकक्षोभे प्रलापैरेव धार्य्यते।

व्याख्या– 'तड़ागस्य' जलाशयस्य 'पूरकर्त्तृके' जलवृद्धिजनिते 'उत्पीड़े' विमर्दे सति 'परीवाहः पयः प्रणाल्या जलनिर्गमः एव 'प्रतिक्रिया' प्रतीकारः अन्यथा जलभरेण तड़ागतटं मिद्यते। एवं 'हृदयञ्च' हृदयमपि 'शोककृते क्षोभे' संबाधे सति 'प्रलापैरेव' रोदनैरेव 'धार्यते' रक्ष्यते अन्यथा शोकभरेण भिद्येत हृदयम्।।

Notes. 1. आर्यपुत्र etc.—Of course this is not heard by Rāma. 2. रुदितः–कर्त्तरि क्तः। 3. साम्प्रतिकम्–साम्प्रातम् is an अव्यय meaning युक्त। साम्प्रतमेव इति साम्प्रतम्+ठक् स्वार्थें विनयादि is आकृतिगण and साम्प्रतम् is supposed to belong to this class. 4. दुःख etc.— निर्+वा+णिच्+ल्यट् करणे निर्वापणानि the means to allay. दुःखस्य निर्वापणानि। 5. पूर flood. उद्+पीड़+घञ् भावे उत्पीड़ pressure. परूस्य उत्पीड़ः। Here तड़ाग is the कर्म and पूर the कर्त्ता of उत्पीड़नक्रिया। Both take षष्ठी by the Varttika "शेषद्विभाषा"। 6. परीवाहः– परिवाह्यते अनेन इति परि+वह+घञ् करणे परिवाहः or परीवाहः the ई being optional by "उपसर्गस्य घञि अमनुष्ये बहुलम्"। 7. प्रतिक्रिया–प्रति+कृ+श करणे the remedy. Cut a drain, let out the surplus water and the tank is saved. 8. शोकक्षोभे–शोक is the counterpart of पूर and क्षोभ of उत्पीड़। 9. प्रलापैः–प्रलाप is the counterpart of परीवाह। प्रलाप lets out some शोक and the heart is steadied. Hence प्रलाप is a दुःखनिर्वापण and becomes कर्त्तव्य।

(*xlv*) **(तम–) विशेषतो बहुतरप्रकारकष्टो रामभद्रस्य जीवलोकः।**

Tam—To Rāmabhadra especially the land of the living is beset with troubles of many sorts.

इदं विश्वं पाल्यं विधिवदभियुक्तेन मनसा
प्रियाशोको जीवं कुसुममिव धर्म्मः क्लमयति।
स्वयं कृत्वा त्यागं विलपनविनोदोऽप्यसुलभ-
स्तदद्याप्युच्छ्वासो भवति ननु लाभो हि रुदितम्।।30।।

This world has to be duly guraded with a mind fully applied; (on the other hand) grief for his darling is oppressing his soul as the heat does a flower. The relief of laments is not availalble to him he having himself (*i.e.* of his own accord) adopted the abandonment ; hence, even now, but bursts do occur. Verily, weeping is a boon to him.

मित– । 'बहुतरा:' विविधा: 'प्रकारा:' भेदा: येषां तादृशानि 'कष्टानि' यस्मिन् तादृशो 'जीवलोक:' संसार:।। कष्टबाहुल्यमेव दर्शयति इदमिति।

अन्वय:–अभियुक्तेन मनसा इदं विश्वं विधिवतम् पाल्वम्। प्रियाशोक: घर्म: कुसुममिव जीवं क्लयति। स्वयं त्यागं कृत्वा् विलपनविनोदोऽपि असुलभ: तत् अद्यापि उच्छासो भवति। ननु रुदितं लाभो हि।

व्याख्या–'अभियुक्तेन मनसा' अवहितेन चेतसा 'इदं विश्वं' कृतस्नमेव जगत् 'विधिवत्' यथाशास्त्र 'पाल्यम् राज्ञ: कर्त्तव्यतया रक्षणीयम्। कृतस्त्रं विश्वं तेन हि न सुकरा रक्षा। विधिवत् रक्ष्यमिति परमदुष्करता रक्षाया:। अत: अभियुक्तेन मनसा पाल्यम् इत्येकं कष्टम्। 'प्रियाशोक:' सीताविरहसन्ताप: 'धर्म्म:' आतप: 'कुसुमभिव जीवं'' प्राणान् 'क्लमयति' ग्लपयति। तेन हि मनस: अभियुक्ता दु:साध्या इति कष्टं द्वितीयम्। एचच्च न स्यात् यदि ''पूरीत्पीड़े तड़ागस्य परीवाह:'' इव विलाप: सुलभ: स्यात् किन्तु 'स्वयं' स्वेच्छया 'त्यागं कृत्वा' सीतां परित्यज्य स्थितस्य तस्य 'विलपनं' विलाप: तद्रपो विनोद:' शोकप्रशनमनोपाय: 'असुलभ:' दुर्लभ:। यत् स्वच्छेया त्यज्यते तस्यार्थे विलापो न सङ्गच्छते इति भाव:। इति कष्टं तृतीयं बहुत्वञ्च कष्टस्य। अत उच्यते ''बहुतरप्रकारकष्टो जीवलोक:'' इति। 'तत्' तस्मात् इत्थं प्रतिक्रियाविरहात्, अप्रशमिते हृदयस्य शोकक्षोभे 'अद्यापि' द्वादशवर्षाधिककाले व्यतीतेऽहिप 'उच्छ्वास:' शोकोच्छ्वास: 'भवति' जायते। तत् किमुच्यते ''हा धिक्'' इत्रि, 'ननु रुदितं' रामस्य विलाप: 'लाभो हि' लाभाय एव। इयन्तं कालम् असुलभेन अद्य तु लब्धेन विलापेन हृदयं तस्य धार्य्यते एव, मा त्वं व्यथिष्ठा:।।

Notes. 1. विधिवत्–विधि is शास्त्रविधि। विधिम् अर्हति। इति विधि+वति। An अव्यय। 2. अभियुक्तेन etc.—the sphere of operation is vast (विश्व) and the quality of the work is to be high (विधिवत्) hence the necessity of supreme attention (अभियुक्तेन मनसा) । This is trouble No. 1. 3. प्रियाशोक: etc.—The thought is the same as in ''किसलयमिव मुग्धम् etc.'' (sl. 5) This is trouble No. 2. It interferes with the work ''इदं विश्वम्'' etc. The necessary attention cannot be given to the work. 4. स्वयं कृत्वा etc.—This introduces trouble No. 3. The heart cannot be relieved because the only relief is lamentation (''प्रलापैरेव धार्यते'') and lamentation is not available to him. This establishes बहुत्व of कष्ट and justifies the remark "बहुतरप्रकारकष्टः"। Here note the grammar—असुलभः has तेन for its nominative understood. The खल् in सुलभ bars the षष्ठी in the कर्त्ता. Or we may say स्वयं त्यागं कृत्वा स्थितस्य तस्य असुलभः with शेषे षष्ठी in तस्य not कर्त्तरि षष्ठी। 5. तदद्यापि etc.—उद्+श्वस्+घञ् भावे उच्छ्वास outburst. The pent up grief has at last found a vent. This is well benefit him. 6. ननु–Implies आक्षेप। Why exclaim हा धिक् at his wails ? You are wrong. Hail this outburst with joy, it will steady his heart.

(*xlvi*) **रामः–कष्टं कष्टम् !**

Rāma—Misery ! O misery !

दलति हृदयं गाढ़ोद्वेगं द्विधा तु न भिद्यते
वहति विकलः कायो मोहं न मुञ्चति चेतनाम्।
ज्वलयति तनूमन्तर्दाहः करोति न भस्मज्ञामात्
प्रहरति विधिर्मर्मच्छेदी न कृन्ताति जीवितम्।।31।।

The heart, with deep agitation, becomes pounded but does not cleave into two. The frame, unnerved, develops a swoon but does not renounce consciousness. The internal heat burns the body (Or—The heat burns the body within) but does not reduce it to ashes. Fate piercing the vitals, strikes, but does not sever life.

सीता–एवणेदं [एवमेतत्]।

Sītā—So it is.

मित–। दलतीति।

अन्वयः–गाढ़ोदेदं हृदयं दलति द्विधा तु न भिद्यते। विकलः कायः मोहं वहति चेतनां न मुञ्चति। अन्तर्दाहः तनूं ज्वलयति भस्मसात् न करोति। विधिः मर्मच्छेदी (सन्) प्रहरति जीवितं न कृन्तति।

व्याख्या–'गाढ़' प्रबलः 'उद्वेगः' विचलितता यस्या तादृशं मम 'हृदयं दलति' निष्पिष्टं भवति 'द्विधा तु' किन्तु इयोर्भागयोः 'नः भिद्यते' भिन्नं न भवति। यदि तथा स्यात् मृत एव स्यां दुःखानुभवश्च न स्यात्। किञ्च 'विकलः कायः' असारो मे देहः 'मोहं वहति' मूर्च्छां तनोति किन्तु 'चेतनां न मुञ्चति' चैतन्यस्वरूपं तत्त्वतो न जहाति। अथ जह्यात् चिरमेव अचेतनः स्यां दुःखानुभवो न स्यात्। अपि च 'अन्तर्दाहः' मनस्तापः 'तनूं ज्वलयति' देहं दहति 'भस्मसात् न करोति' भस्मीभूतं न करोति। कुर्य्यात् चेत् मृतः स्यां दुःखानुभवश्च न स्यात्। "कष्टं भोः कष्टम् !" मन्ये विरुपो मे 'विधिः' दुःखसंवेदनं स्यात् इति 'मर्मच्छेदी' मर्माणि छित्वा 'प्रहरति' किन्तु 'जीवितं

न कलन्तति' प्राणान् न छिनति। "दुःखसंवेदनायैव रामे चैतन्यमाहितम्। ममोपघातिभिः प्राणीर्वज्रक्रीलायितं स्थिरैः।।" इति भावः।। 'एवमेतत्' ममापि एवमेवानुभवः इति रामेण आत्मनस्तुल्यावस्था विज्ञाप्यते।।

Notes. 1. दलति–दल implies भेदन and is usually सकर्मक। Here the sense is altered and it means भिन्नीभवन। 2. गाढ़ etc.—उद्+विज+घञ् भावे करणो वा उद्वेग shock (करणो), agitation (भावे)। Prefer करणो। 3. भिद्यते–भिद+लट् ते कर्मकर्त्तरि। 4. विकलः–कला is कलना any movement or imaginative work ; hence सामर्थ्य strenght. "कलनाकालयोः कला" इति विश्वः। विगता कला अस्य। 5. ज्वलयति–ज्वल+णिच्=ज्वलि or ज्वालि optionally by "ज्वलहव्लह्मलनमाम् अनुपसर्गात् वा"। Hence ज्वालयति is also correct. 6. अन्तर्दाहः–Here we may also take अन्तः as uncompounded and construe दाहः तनूम् अन्तः ज्वलयति–the burn of grief inflames the body within. If cc mpounded, say अन्तः मध्ये दाहः अन्तर्दाहः internal heat, सुप्सुपा। 7. भस्मसात्–ञाकल्येन भस्म इति भस्म+साति completely reduced to ashes. An अव्यय। 8. प्रहरति etc.—This sums up the matter of the preceding three lines, The heart aches etc., hence infer that the Ordainer (or fate) strikes and at the same time purposely preserves life so as to make me feel the pain in full. The verse is an amplification of दुःखसेवेदनायैव etc." (Act I, sl, 47). 9. एवमेतत्–Sītā endorses Rāma's view. I too feel it thus; I suffer unspeakable misery yet life persists in me.

(*xlvii*) **रामः–हे भवन्तः पौरजानपदाः,**

Rāma—O ye citizen and villagers.

न किल भक्तां स्थानं देव्या गृहेऽभिमतं तत-
स्तृणमिव वने शून्ये त्यक्ता न चाप्यनुशोचिता।
चिरपरिचितास्ते ते भावाः परिभ्रमयन्ति मा-
मिदमशरणैरद्याप्येवं प्रसीदत रुद्यते।। 32।।

The queen's stay at home, I was told, was not to your liking; so, like straw, she was abandoned in the lonely forest ahnd not mourned even. Even now helpless I weep thus ; all those long familiar objects bewilder me. O pardone me.

मित–। न किलेति।

अन्वयः–देव्याः गृहे स्थानं भवतां न अभिमतं किल ततः (सा) तृणमिव शून्ये वने त्यक्ता न च अनुशोचिता अपि। अद्य अपि चिरपरिचिताः ते ते भावा मां परिभ्रमयन्ति, अशरणैः इदम् एवं रुद्यते, प्रसीदत्।

व्याख्या–'देव्याः' सीतायाः 'गृहे' राजभवने 'स्थानं' स्थितिः निवासः 'भवतां न अभिमतं' सस्मतः 'किलं' इति श्रुतं मया 'ततः' तस्मात् सा देवी 'तृणमित्र' अकिञ्चित्करमिव किञ्चित् वस्तु 'शून्ये वने' विजने कानने 'त्यक्ता' निर्वासिता। 'इत्यं' मृत्यवे दत्ता सा 'न च' नैव 'अनुशोचिता अपि' पश्चात्तापेनापि सम्भाविता। 'अद्य अपि' अधुना च तस्या अर्थे यो विलापः तत्र ब्रवीमि 'चिरपरिचिताः' दीर्घं कालं सीतया सह अनुभूताः 'ते ते भावाः' तरुशकुनिकुरङ्गादयः गिरिकाननादयश्च पदार्थाः अद्य दृष्टाः सन्तः 'मां परिभ्रमयन्ति' त्रिकलयन्ति, तेन च 'अशरणैः निरुपायैः अस्माभिः 'इदम्' एतत् 'एवम्' अन्येन प्रकारेण उच्चैरिति शेषः 'रुद्यते' विलप्यते। अत्र मे अनिच्छकृतरोदने 'प्रसीदत, प्रसन्ना भवत मा कुप्यत इत्यर्थः।।

Notes. 1. किल–अव्यय implying ऐतिह्य reported matter. I heard it from my man दुर्मुख। 2. भवताम्–कर्त्तरि षष्ठी in connection with अभिमत (which see) 3. अभिमतम्–अभि+मन+क्त कर्मणि वर्त्तमाने। This gives षष्ठी in the कर्त्ता by "क्तस्य च वर्त्तमाने"।4. परिभ्रमयन्ति–भ्रम+णिच्=भ्रमि not भ्रामि because the root is मित। परिभ्रमयन्ति bewilder. 5. इदम्–Take this with रुद्यते। इदम् points at the क्रिया, *i.e.*, रोदनक्रिया। Comp. "इदं रक्षोभिर्वृत्तम्" (I. sl. 28). 6. अशरणैः–शरण is रक्षण help. "शरणं रक्षणे गृहे" इति विश्वः। अविद्यमानं शरणमेषाम्। तैः। Refers to himself चनुक्ते कर्त्तरि ३या। He has spoken above of himself in the singular (माम्), hence it would have been more natural to say अशरणेन मसर रुद्यते।7. प्रसीदत–Weeping is an offence against you. Excuse me (प्रसीदत) I am helpless in the matter.

(*xlviii*) **तमसा–अतिगम्भीरमवगूरणं शोकसागरस्य।**

Tamasā—A very deep whirl-pool of the sea of sorrow !

वासन्ती–अतिक्रान्ते धैर्य्यमवलम्ब्यतां देवेन।

Vāsantī—Let Sire have patience in the matter of what is past.

रा–सखि किमत्रोच्यते धैर्यमिति ?

Rāma—Friend, do you cry 'patience' in this matter ? This is the twelth year of the world bereft of the queen.

Even the name 'Sītā' is forgotten, but it is not that Rāma does not live.

मित–। 'अवगूरणम्' आवर्त्तइति विद्यासागरपादाः।। 'अतिक्रान्ते' विगते सीताविनाशविषये।। 'अत्र'' अतिक्रान्ते इत्यर्थः। अकाण्डे त्वया उक्तं धैर्य्यमिति।। अवलग्वितमेव मया धैर्य्यमित्याह देव्या इति।

अन्वयः–सुगमः।

व्याख्या–'देव्या' सीतया 'शून्यस्य' विरहितस्य 'जगतः' अद्य 'द्वादशः परिवर्तेसरः' वर्षं वर्त्तते। इतः प्राक् द्वादशे वत्सरे मृता सीता। [द्वादश इति भ्रमः त्रयोदश इति युक्तम्]। 'सीता इति नाम अपि लुप्तं" तिरोहितं जगति। कोऽपि नाद्य सीतेति नाम स्मरति। किन्तु 'रामः न च' नैव 'न जीवति' जीवत्येव वज्रमयो रामः। किमतः पुरमच्यते धैर्यमिति।।

Notes. 1. अवगूरणम्–The root गूर means गति। अव means निम्र अवगूर्यते (दिवादि आत्मनेपदी) अधो गच्छति अस्मिन् इति अव+गूर+ल्युट् अधिकरणे अवगूरणाम् a place where the motion is down-wards. But at every whirl-pool there is a strong downward suction. Hence अवगूरण is आवर्त्त whirl-pool. 2. द्वादशः–This is a miscalculation. Sītā was abandoned on or about the day अष्यशृङ्ग commenced his यज्ञ। The यज्ञ lasted 12 years and was finished a day or two before राम came to पञ्चवटी। Hence it was the thirteenth year of her exile then running. But तमसा gives us (para ix) a contradictry report. She says that very day the twelfth year was completed. Any way राम perhaps should have said त्रयोदशः परिवत्सरः। 3. न च–च implies अवधारण। 4. न न–The two nagatives make a strong affirmative rendering च wellnigh superfluous.

(*xlix*) **सीता–मोहिद म्हि एदेहिं अज्जउत्तवअणेहिं [मोहितास्मि एतैरार्यपुत्रवचनैः]।**

Sītā—I am dazed by these words of my husband.

तमसा–एवं वत्से,

Tamasā—Just so, my child.

नैताः प्रियतमा वाचः स्नेहार्द्राः शोकदारुणाः।
एतास्ता मधुनो धाराःश्च्योतन्ति सविषास्त्वयि।। 34।।

These words, tender with love, terrible with grief, are not very pleasent to you. These are streams of honey pouring on you mixed with poison. [Or—These, as they are, pour on you streams of honey mixed with poison].

मिति–'मोहिता' मोहमापादिता। मोहः विकलता। 'आर्यपुत्रस्य, शोकोद्गारिभिर्वचनैः अहमपि शोकेन विवशा जाता।। 'एवं' युक्तमेवैतत्। रामस्य वचनानि दुःखकरिण्येवते। कारणमाह नैता इति।

अन्वयः–स्नेहार्द्रा शोकदारूणा एता वाचः प्रियतमा न। ता एताः सविषा मधुनो धाराः त्वयिश्च्योतन्ति।

व्याख्या–स्नेहेन' वात्सव्येन 'आद्राः' कोमला इत्यर्थः किन्तु 'शोकेन' भर्त्तुः शोकेन दारुणाः' कठोराः दुःसहा इति यावत 'एता वाचः' रामोक्तानि वचनानि 'प्रियतमाः न त्वत्सम्बन्धे नितरां प्रीतिप्रदा नैव भवन्ति। 'ताः' तथाविधाः स्नेहार्द्रासः शोकदारूणाः 'एता' वाचः न हि मन्ये वाच एव किन्तु 'सविषाः' विषसंमृष्टः 'मधुनः धाराः' मधुप्रवाहाः 'त्वयि श्चोतन्ति' क्षरन्ति। श्च्युतिर् क्षरणे अकर्मकः। सकर्मकपक्षे–'ता एताः' रामवाचः 'सविषा' विषमिश्राः मधुनो धाराः मधुप्रतापान् 'त्वथि क्षरन्ति वर्षन्ति। स्नेहार्द्रत्वात् मधुतुल्या शोकदिग्धत्वात् विषकल्पाः, विषसाम्याच्च मोहजनन्यः। तत् युक्तमुच्यत "मोहितास्मि" इति।।

Notes. 1. मोहिता–मुह+णिच्+क्त कर्मणि स्त्रियाम्। 2. प्रियतमाः–No comparison is implied, तमप् expresses आतिशय्यमात्र here. 3. श्क्योतन्ति–For a सकर्मक use compare मधुश्चश्च्यतः (sl. 24). Those who do not admit the सकर्म्मक sense, have to suppose श्च्युतिर to be अन्तर्भावितरणयर्थ in such instances.

(*l*) रामः–अयि वासन्ति, मया खलु–

Rāma—O Vasantī by me, indeed,—

यथा तिरश्चीनमलातशस्यं प्रत्युल्पमन्तः सविषश्च दंशः।
तथैव तीव्रो हृदि शोकशङ्कुर्मर्माणि कृन्तन्नपि किं न सोढ़।। 34।।

Is not the keen shaft of grief being borne in the heart though rending the vitals like a bent spike of glowing coal driven in or like the bite of some venomous snake.

सीता–एवं म्हि मन्दभाइणो पुणो वि आआसआरिणी अज्जउत्तस्स [एवमस्मि मन्दभागिनी पुनरपि आयासकारिणी आर्यपुत्रस्य]।

[N. B.—The verse is obscure].

Sītā— Thus have I, the ill-starred, become again an afflicter of my husband.

मित–।'मया खलु' इति परिवर्तना श्लोकेन अन्वितम्।। यथेति।

अन्वयः– यथा अन्तः प्रत्युपतं तिरश्चीनम! अलातशल्यं सविषः दंशश्च तथैव मर्माणि कृन्तन्नपि तीव्रः शोकशङ्कः हृदि भया खलु सोढ़ः न किम् ?

व्याख्या–'यथा' यद्वत् 'अन्तः' मध्ये 'प्रत्युप्तं' निखातं 'तिरश्चीनं' वक्रम् 'अलातम्' अङ्गार एव 'शल्यं' कीलकः 'सविषः' गरलसंयुतः 'दंशश्च' सर्पदंशं वा 'तथैव' तद्वदेव 'मर्माणि' जीवनस्थानानि 'कृन्तन्नपि छिन्दन्नपि 'तीव्रः' 'शोकशङ्कुः' शोकरूपः कीलकः 'हृदि' हृदये 'मया खलु नूनं 'सोढ़ः न किम्' सोढ़ एव। इदमपि न किं धैर्यमिति त्वया सम्भाव्यते? एवमिति।'एवम्' अनेन प्रकारेण 'पुनरपि' प्राक् रावण्यता अद्यतु परित्यक्ता 'आयासकारिणी' दुःखदायिनी।।

Notes. 1. तिरश्चीनम्–तिरस् means वक्र। तिर्यच् is a प्रातिपदिक also meaning वक्र। This is an अव्यय and different from the तिर्यच् derived from तिरस्। "तिर्यक् तिरोऽर्थे वक्रे च विहङ्गादी त्वनव्ययम्" —*Viśva and Medini*. तिर्यगेव इति तिर्यच्+ख स्वार्थे तिरश्चीनम् by the rule "विभाषाञ्चेरदिक्स्त्रियाम्"। 2. अलात etc.—अलात is a fire brand. अलातरूपं शल्यम्, कर्मधा–of the शाकपार्थिवादि class. 3. च–This means वा here, i.e., it implies पक्षान्तर। "च पादपूरणो पक्षान्तरे हेती विनिश्चये" इति त्रिकाण्ड शेषः !"च पादपूरणो पक्षान्तरे हेतौ विनिश्चये" इति त्रिकाण्ड शेषः! 4. दंश–Snake-bite सर्पक्षत। "दंशो वर्मणि....भुजगक्षते" इति हैमः।

(*li*) **रामः–एवम् अतिनिष्कम्पस्तम्भितान्तःकरणस्यापि मम संस्तुततत्तत्प्रियवस्तुदर्शनात् उद्दामोऽयमावेगः। तथाहि–**

Rāma—To me, even with the heart thus steadied so as not to waver in the least, this agitation has become uncontrollable at the sight of all those familiar objects. Thus—

लोलोल्लोलक्षुभितकरुणोज्जृम्भणस्तम्भनार्थं
यो यो यत्नः कथमपि मयाधीयते तं तमन्तः।
भित्वा भित्वा प्रसरति वलात् कोऽपि चेतोविकार-
स्तोयस्थेवाप्रतिहतरयः सैकतं सेतुमोघः।। 36।।

An indescribabie agitation of the mind prevails forcibly nipping up in the interval (अन्तः) whatever efforts I somehow make to check the outburst of the heart (करुण) excited like a surging blllow [Or—outburst of the heart (करुणा) so agitated as to become fickler than the ficklest, just as the current of water with its force unchecked does a sandy dam.

सीता–एदिणा अज्जउत्तस्म दुवारदारुणारम्भेण दुक्खसंक्षोहेण पप्फरिदणिअदुक्खं विअ आकम्पिदं मे हिअअं [एतेन आर्य्यपुत्रस्य दुर्वारदारूणारम्भेण दुःखसंक्षोभेण प्रस्फुरितनिजदुःखमिव आकम्पितं मे हृदयम्]।

Sītā—My heart shudders as if with its own grief awakended by my husband's shocks of grief the grim progress of which is uncontrollable.

मित–। एवमिति। 'अतिनिष्कस्पं' सुनिश्चलं यथा तथा 'स्तम्भितं' स्थिरीकृतम् 'अन्तःकरणं' मानसं येन तथाविधस्य 'अपि मम संस्तुतस्य' पूर्वपरिचितस्य 'तस्य तस्य प्रियवस्तुनः' करियमयूरादेः 'दर्शनात् उद्दामः' उच्छृङ्खलः दुर्दम इत्यर्थः 'अयम् आवेगः विकारः।। उद्दामतामेव दर्शयति लोलेति।

अन्वयः–लोलोल्लोलक्षुभित- करुणोज्जृम्भणास्तम्भणार्थं मया यो यो यत्नः कथमपि आधीयते तं तम् अप्रतिहतरयः तोयस्य ओघः सैकतं सेतुमिव अन्तः बलात् भित्त्वा भित्त्वा कोऽपि चेतोविकारः प्रसरति।

व्याख्या–'लोलः' धावन् यः उल्लोलः' महोर्भिः स इव क्षुभितः' संस्तुतवस्तुदर्शनात् प्राप्तसंक्षोभः यः 'करुणः' करुणोरसः लक्षणया शोकः तस्य यत् 'उज्जृम्भणं' परिव्यक्तिः तस्य 'स्तम्भनार्थं' निरोधार्थं 'मया यो यो यत्नः कथमपि' अतिकृच्छ्रेण 'आधीयते' अवलम्ब्यते 'तं यत्नम् अप्रतिहतः' अनिरुद्धः 'दयः' वेगो यस्य तथाविधः 'तोयस्य ओघः' जलप्रवाहः 'सैकतं' बालुकामयं 'सेतुमिव' बन्धं यथा करोति तथा 'अन्तः' मध्ये आधानस्तम्भनयोरन्तराले 'बलात्' उद्दामताहेतुकरभसेन 'भित्त्वा भित्त्वा' विधूय विधूय 'कोऽपि' अननुभूतपूर्वः 'चेताविकारः' चित्तविक्षोभः 'प्रसरति' प्रवर्त्तते। 'क्षुभित करणं' इति पाठे 'लोलात्' चञ्चलादपि 'उल्लोलं' चञ्चलं यथा यथा 'क्षुभितं' यत् 'करणाम्' अन्तःकरणं हृदयमित्यर्थः इत्यादि कथञ्चित् व्यख्येयम्।। एतेनेति–'हृदयं मे आकस्पितं ' कम्पते। किम्भूतं हृदयम् ?–'प्रस्फुरितम्' आविर्भूतं 'निजदुःखम्' आत्मशोकः यस्मिन् तथाविधमिव हृदयम्। आर्यपुत्रस्या-निष्टशङ्कया एवं नाम कम्पते मे हृदयं येन मन्ये हदयस्यैव गुरुदुःखं किमप्यापतितमद्य। कुतः शङ्का ?–'दुःख संक्षोभेण शोकाभिघातेन। ननु निग्रहीष्यते शोकः–'दुर्वारः' दुर्निग्रहः 'दारुणः' विषमः 'आरम्भः' प्रवृत्तिः यस्य तथाविधेन दुःखसंक्षोभेण। अनिवार्या अस्य संक्षोभस्य क्रिया तत् न जाने किमत्याहितं तस्य स्यादिति शङ्का।।

Notes. 1. अतिनिष्कम्प etc.—निर्गतः कम्पः अस्मात् निष्कम्पम्, बहु– । The निर् is privative, but often, instead of indicating complete privation, it implies scarcity only. In such cases अति is added to indicate entire absence. Comp. "अतिनिष्करुणस्य शुद्धशीला"–*Śakuntala*. अतिशयेन निष्कम्पम् अतिनिष्कम्पम् । 2. संस्तुत etc.—सम्+स्त+क्त कर्म्मणि संस्तुत known. तानि च तानि च तत्तानि those there and those yonder. द्वन्द्व । प्रियाणि वस्तूनि प्रियवस्तूनि । तत्तानि प्रियवस्तूनि तत्तत् प्रियवस्तूनि । संस्तुतानि तत्तत्प्रियवस्तूनि । तेषां दर्शनम् । तस्मात् । 3. उद्दामः–see उद्दामेन, sl. 6. Vidyāsāgara reads अघायमावेगः which is almost as good. Our reading occurs in Vīrarāghava and three of Vidyāsāgara's manuscripts. The verse suggests उद्दामता and seems to support our reading. 4. लोल etc.—उल्लोल billow. "अथोर्भिषु । महत्सूल्लोलकल्लोलौ" इत्यमरः । क्षुभ+णिच्+क्त कर्मणि क्षुभित or क्षुब्ध । For समास see Ṭikā. With the reading करण say करणा is अन्तःकरण, thence by लक्षणा it is हृदयावेग । 5. यः यः तम्–वीष्सायां द्विरुक्तिः । *All my efforts*. 6. अन्तः–अन्तर् is an अव्यय meaning मध्ये । Vidyāsāgara constures अन्तः प्रसरति । 7. भित्वा etc.—The repetition implies frequency (नित्यता) । भित्वा itself shows उद्दामता । 8. बलात्–Another indication of उद्दामता । बलमवलम्बा इति लयब्लोपे 5मी । 9. सैकतम्–सिकता is बालुका । It is usually in the feminine plural. "आपः समनसो वर्षा अष्मरःसिकताः मुमाः । एते स्त्रियां बहुत्वे स्यरेक त्वेऽप्य त्तरत्रम् ।।" सिकतानामयम् इति सिकता+अण् सैकतः । तम् । 10. दुर्बार etc.—दुर+वारि+खल् कर्मणि दुर्वारः irresistible. क्षिपद बहु–(See Ṭikā). II. प्रष्फुरित etc.—निज here refers to the pang of the heart itself. 12. हृदयम्–The heart is personified. She does not say *my* grief but the *heart's* grief.

(*lii*) वासन्ती (स्वागतम्)—कष्ट मभ्यापन्नो देवः, तदन्यतः क्षिपामि तावत् । (प्राकशम्) चिरपरिचितानामिदानीं जनस्थानभागानामावलोकनेन आत्मानमानन्दयतु देवः ।

Vāsantī (*To herself*)—Sire is in a sad plight, so I will draw him elsewhere. (*Aloud*) Let Sire now divert himself with a sight of these long familiar sites of Janasthāna.

राम–एवमस्तु । (इत्युत्थाय परिक्रामति) ।

Rāma—So be it. (*Rises and goes round the stage*).

सीता–सन्दीवणाइं एव दुक्खस्स पिअसही विणोदणोवायो त्ति मस्णेदि [सन्दीपनान्येव दुःखस्य प्रियसखी विनोदनोपाय इति मन्यते]।

Sītā—My dear friend deems as sources of diversion the very things that are inciters of grief.

वासन्ती– देव देव,

Vāsantī—Sire, Sire,

अस्मिन्नेव लतागृहे त्वभभवस्तमार्गदत्तेक्षणः
सा हंसैः कृतकौतुका चिरमभूद्गोदावरीसैकते।
आयान्त्या परिदुर्मनायितमिव त्वां वीक्ष्य बद्धस्तया
कातर्यादरविन्दकुड्मलनिभो मुग्धः प्रणामाञ्जलिः।। 37।।

In this very bower of creepers you stood with your eyes fixed on her track, while she tarried long on the sand-banks of the Godāvarī making fun with the swans. While approaching, seeing you as if, annoyed, she, in distress, made in supplication a charming fold of the plams like a lotus-bud.

मित–। 'देवः' राजा रामः 'कष्टं' सङ्कटं शोच्यामवस्थामित्यर्थः 'अभ्यापन्नः' प्राप्तः। 'तत् अन्यतः अन्यस्मिन् हृद्यतरे विषये 'क्षिपामि' प्रेरयामि।। 'सन्दीपनानि' उज्जृम्मणानि।। असमन्निति।

अन्वयः–अस्मिन्नेव लतागृहे त्वं तन्मार्गदत्तेक्षणः अभवः, सा हंसैः कृतकौतुका (सती) गोदावरीकसैकते चिरम् अभूत्। आयान्तया तया त्वां परिदुर्मनायितमिव वीक्ष्य कातर्यात् अरविन्दकुड्मलनिभः मुग्धः प्रणामाञ्जलिः बद्धः।

व्याख्या–अस्मिन्नेव' पुरोवर्त्तिनि 'लतागृहे' कुञ्जे 'त्वं तस्थाः' सीतायाः 'मार्गे वर्त्मनि 'दत्ते' स्थापिते 'ईक्षणे' लोचने येन तथाविधः सन् 'अभवः' अस्थाः, 'सा' सीता पुनः 'हंसैः कृतं कौतुकं' क्रीड़ामोदः यया तादृशी सती गोदावर्याः सैकते' पुलिने 'चिरम् अभूतं व्यलम्बयत्। इतस्त्वं तस्यां सोत्कणठः ततः सा क्रीड़ापरा इति कोपहेतुः।'आयान्त्या' गोदावर्या लतागृहं प्रत्यावर्त्तमानया 'तया त्वां परिदुर्मनायितामिव' अप्रसन्नचेतसमिव 'वीक्ष्य' दृष्टा ममवात्रापराधः इति 'कातर्यात्' दुःखात् पुनःप्रसन्नताविधानार्थ तव 'अरविन्दकुड्मलनिभः कमलकोरकोपमः अतएव 'मुग्धं' मनोहरः 'प्रणामाञ्जलि' प्रणिपातसूचकः करपुटः 'बद्धः' रचितः।।

Notes. 1, चिरपरिचितानाम् etc.—This reading occurs in three of Vidyāsāgara's manuscripts. The fourth has "चिरपरिचितान् एतान् जनस्थनभागान् अवलोकयतु देवः"। But Sītā's remark "प्रियसखी विनोदनोपाय

इति मन्यते'' requires the direct mention of विनोदन or आनन्दन in Vāsantī's speech. Hence, we reject the reading of the fourth manuscript thought supported by the weighty authonity of Vidyāsāgara. 2. देव देव–सम्भ्रमे विरुक्तिः। सम्भ्रम is त्वरा। Perhaps they were passing by without noticing the bower when suddenly वासन्ती drew Rāma's attention to it. Here three of Vidyāsāgara's manuscripts have ''(सकरुणम्) देव देव''। But a piteous appeal (सकरुणम्) like that is bound to affect Rāma the more; hence this is inconsistent with Vāsantī's determination to divert Rāma's attention (अन्यतः क्षिपामि) and to give him some sort of joy (आनन्दयतु)। Hence सकरुणम् is rejected. 3. सा हंसैः etc.—She was playing with the swans. Usually this is taken to mean—her curiosity was roused at the sight of the swans. But why? The sight was before her the whole day every day. So, there can be no room for curiosity. Play with the swan is always possible like one's play with one's own dog. 4. आयान्त्या–आ+ या+शतृ स्त्रियाम् आयान्ती or आयाती। तया। Note the शतृ। आयान्त्या not आयातया। She had not yet entered the bower but from a distance, or her way to it, she noticed that Rāma sat morose. 5. परिदर्मनायितम्–परिदुर्मनाय+क्त कर्त्तरि पदुर्म नायितः looking very moody. 6. अरविन्द etc.—अरविन्दकुट्नल, 6तत्–। अरविन्दकुट्नलेन तुल्य इत्यर्थे नित्यसमास of अरविन्दकुट्नल and निभ। निभ means तुल्य only when it is an उत्तरपद in a समाप्त। Consequently no वाक्य with निभ can be given and we have an अस्वपदविग्रह–a नित्यमास। 7. कातर्यात्–कातर is दुःखित sorry, तस्या भाव इति कातरा+ष्यञ् कातर्यम्। कातरा need not become कातरा here by पुंवद्भाव, the आ will disapper by ''यस्येति च''। The पुंवद्भाव is however available by ''भस्य अठे तद्धिते''। 8. *Remark*—This incident occured in privacy; but Vāsantī being a deity nothing could be hidden from her.

(*liii*) सीता–दारुणा सि सहि वासन्दि दारुणा सि जा एदेहिं हिअअमम्मगूढसल्लघट्टणेहिं पुणो पुणो मां मन्दभाइणिं अज्जउत्तं अ सन्दावेसि [दारुणासि सखि वासन्ति दारुणासि या एतैः हृदयमर्मगूढ शल्यघट्टनैः पुनः पुनर्मां मन्दभागिनीम् आर्यपुत्रञ्च सन्तापयसि]

Sītā—Cruel, you are, friend Vāsantī, cruel you are, who, as if with snakes of the shaft buried in the vitals of the heart, again and again torture my ill-fated self and my husband.

रामः–चण्डि जानकि, इतस्ततो दृश्यसे इव न चानुकम्पसे।

Rāma—Jānakī, O Fury, you are as if seen here and there but you do not pity me.

हा हा देवि स्फुटति हृदयं ध्वंसते देहबन्धः
शून्यं मन्ये जगदविरतज्वालमन्तर्ज्वलामि।
सीदन्नन्धे तमसि विधुरो मज्जतीवान्तरात्मा
विष्वङ्मोहः स्थगयति कथं मन्दभाग्यः करोमि।। 38।।

(इति मूर्च्छति)

Alas ! Alas ! my queen, my heart bursts ; my bondage to the body ceases ; the world I deem a void ; within I burn in a ceaseless fire ; my in-most self, helpless and despairing, sinks in blinding gloom ; stupor veils me all roud ; ill fated as I am, what can I do ?

मित–। दारुणेति–'या' त्वं हृदयस्य मर्मणि' जीवस्थले 'गूढं' तावता निखातं घत्'शन्त्यं' शङ्कुः तस्य 'घटनैः सञ्चलनैः तत्तुल्यैरित्यर्थः 'एतैः' लतागृहप्रदर्शनादिभिः कार्यैः। हृदयमर्मगूढ़दशल्यघट्टनमिव रुजारकरमेतत् लतागृहप्रदर्शनम् इति भावः। चण्डीति–'दृश्यसे इव' त्वट्नतया भावनया निर्माय इव पुरो निधीयसे। भागीरथीवर-प्रभावात् वस्तुतदर्शनं तत्कथाश्रवणञ्ञ न सम्भावयते। हाहेति।

अन्वयः–हा हा देवि हृदयं स्फुटति, देहबन्धः ध्वंसते, जगत् शून्यं मन्ये, अन्तः अविरतज्वालम्, ज्वलामि सीदन् विधुरः अन्तरात्मा अन्धे तमसि सज्जतीव, मोहः विष्वक् स्थगयति। मन्दभाग्यः (अहम्) कथं करोमि।

व्याख्या–'हा हा' अहो खेदः 'देविः' सीते 'हृदयं स्फुटित' विदीर्यते 'देहबन्धः' आत्मनः शरीरेण योगः 'ध्वंसते' नश्यति, मन्ये दैहत्याग एव में भवति इत्यर्थ; 'जगत्' संसारं शून्यम्' असारं मन्ये 'अन्तः' मध्ये 'अविरतज्वाल' सन्ततवेदन यथा तथा 'ज्वलामि' दह्ये ; सीदन्' अवसन्नो भवन् 'विधुरः' विकलः 'अन्तरात्मा' देहमध्यस्थश्चिन्मयः पुरुषः 'अन्धे' दृष्टिरोधकरे 'तमसि' ध्वान्ते 'मज्जति इव' अवतरतीव; 'मोहः' विचेतना 'विष्वक्' समन्तात् 'स्थगयति' निरुणादि। 'मन्दभाग्यः' भाग्यहीनः अहं 'कथं करोमि' केन प्रकारेण प्रतिविधास्येयं।

Notes 1. हृदय etc.—There was actually no shaft embedded in the heart of राम or सीता to which वासन्ती was now and then giving a snake. सीता means that by drawing attention to the मयूर, the marble slab, the bower etc. वासन्ती was distressing her and राम, and the pain they were feeling was like that felt when a shaft of that kind is shaken. Hence explain '–शल्यइघट्टनैः'–शल्यघट्टनतुल्यैः। 2. दृश्यसे–This is only Rāma's imagination; actual sight was impossible because of Bhāgirathī's boon. 3. देहबन्धः–देहेन बन्धः the tie with the body. सुप् सुपा। 4. अन्धे–अन्धं करोति इति अन्ध+णिच् (नामधातु)+अच् कर्त्तरि अन्धम् that which blinds. 5. अन्तरात्मा–अन्तःस्थः आत्मा the self within, कर्मधा–।6. विष्वक्–विषु is an अव्यय implying सर्वतोभाव। विषु अञ्चतीति विषु+अञ्च+क्विन कर्त्तरि विष्वक् that which goes all round. तत् यथा तथा। Qual. स्थगयति। Or qualifies मोहः। विष्वङ् मोहः (a pervading stupor) may be: compouded or uncompounded. 7. स्थगयति–स्थग also means "to fill up" Comp. "रव श्रवणाभैरवः स्थगितरोदसीकन्दरः"–*Veṇīsaṁhāra*. 8. कथं करोमि–Vidyāsāgara explains कसुपायमवलम्बे।

(*liv*) **सीता–हद्दी हद्दी पुणो विपमूढ़ो अज्जउत्तो [हा धिक्, हा धिक्, पुनरपि प्रमूढ़आर्यपुत्रः]।**

Sītā—Alas ! Alas ! my husband has fainted again.

वासन्ती–देव समाश्वसिहि ससाश्वसिहि।

Vāsantī—Take courage, Sire, take courage.

सीता–हा अज्जउत्त मं मन्दभाइणीं उद्दिमिअ सअलजीअ लोअमङ्गलाधारास्स दे वारं वारं संसयिदजीविददारुणो दसापरिणामो। हा हदम्हि [हा आर्यपुत्रम मां मन्दभागिनीमुद्दिश्य सकलजीवलोक-मङ्गलाधारस्य ते वारं वारं संशयितजीवितदारुणो दशापरिणामः हा हतास्मि]। (इति मूर्च्छति)।

Sītā—Alas ! My husband ! With reference to me, the ill starred, is over and over coming unto you, the abode of blessing for the whole living world, this terrible change of condition in which life is endangered. Alas ; I am lost.

(*Faints away*).

तमसा–वत्से सामश्वसिहि समाश्वसिहि। पुनस्त्वत्पाणिस्पर्श एव जीवनोपायो रामभद्रस्य।

Tamasā—Take courage, child, take courage. Again the touch of your hand alone is the means for the reviving of Rāmabhadra.

वासन्ती–कथमद्यापि नोच्छ्वसिति ! हा प्रियसखि सीते, क्वासि ? सम्भाबय आत्मनो जीवितेश्वरम्।

Vāsantī—How so ! Even now he does not recover ! Alas ! Dear friend Sītā, Where are you ? Do resusciate the lord of your life.

मित–। 'सकलस्य' कृत्स्नस्य जीवलोकस्य' प्राणिजगतः यत् 'मङ्गलं' कल्याणं तस्य 'आधारः' निलयः यदधीनं विश्वस्य शुभं तस्य 'ते'। 'वारं वारं' पुनः पुनः। 'संशयितं सङ्कटापन्नं 'जीवितं' प्राणाः यस्मिन् अतएव 'दारुणः' घोरः 'दशायाः' अवस्थायाः 'परिणामः' परिवर्त्तः।। 'जीवनस्य पुनर्जीवनस्य 'उपायः' पन्थाः।। 'उच्छ्वसिति' प्रत्युज्जीवति।'सम्भावय सम्यक् भावय प्रकृतिस्थं कुरु। यद्वा–'सम्मावय' सम्भानय आत्मोपस्थिता तर्पय।।

Notes 1. हा धिक् etc.—She blames her own luck. 2. प्रसूढ़ः–प्र+मुह+क्त कर्त्तरि has fainted. 3. वारं वारम्–वार is क्षण् opportunity, interval, अत्यन्तसंयोगे द्वितीया the क्रिया being भवति understood. वारं वारं दशापरिणामो भवति means अनेकवारं दशापरिणामो भवति। Duplication by "स्वार्थे अवधार्य्यमाणे–" (See under स्थाने स्त्याने, Act II, sl. 14). 4. सम्भावय–सम्+भू+णिच्+लोट् हि। In the sense to succour' comp. "सम्भावयतु देव्याः पुत्रकम्"–Para xxv. Or here as well as there we apply लक्षणा and have वीप्सायां द्विर्वचनम्। Thus वार is अवसुर occasion *i.e.*, the right occasion. वारं वारम् at every right occasion. Similarly स्थान place *i.e.*, the right place, स्थाने स्थाने at every suitable place.

(*lv*) **सीता–(ससम्भ्रममुपसृत्य हृदि ललाटे च स्पृशति)।**

Sītā—(*Hastily advancing touches him on the heart and forehead*).

वासन्ती–दिष्ट्या प्रत्यापन्नचेतेनो रामभद्रः।

Vāsantī—Luckily Rāmabhadra has his conciousness restored to him.

राम– आलिम्पन्नमृतयैरिव प्रलेपै-
रन्तर्वा बहिरपि वा शरीरधातून।
सं स्पर्शः पुनरपि जीवयन्नकस्मा-
दानन्दादपरंविधं तनोति मोहम्।। 38।।

Rāma—Unexpectedly, yet again the touch, as if smearing, with ambrosial ointments, the constituents of my body within and without, revies me and, through joy, promotes stupor of a different kind.

(आनन्दमिमीलिताक्ष एव) सखि वासन्ति, दिष्ट्या वर्द्धसे।

(*Countinuing with eyes closed in joy*) Friend Vāsantī, luckily you are blessed.

मित– । 'प्रत्यापन्ना' पुनरागता 'चेतना' यस्य सः।। आलिम्पन्निति।

अन्वयः– अकस्मात् पुनरपि संस्पर्शः अन्तर्वा वहिरपि वा शरीरधातून् असतमयैः प्रलेपैः आलिम्प्रन्निव जीवयन् आनन्दात् अपरविधं मोहं तनोति।

व्याख्या–'अकस्मात्' सहसा 'पुनरपि संस्पर्शः' पूर्वानुभूतः सीतापाणिस्पर्शः 'अन्तर्वा' मध्ये च 'बहिरपि वा' वहिश्च देहस्य 'शरीरधातून' शरीरोपादानानि त्वङ् मांस प्रभूतीनि 'अमृतमयैः' सुधा–प्रकृतिकैः 'प्रलेपैः' विलेपनैः 'आलिम्पन्निव' सम्यक् लिम्पन्निव 'जीवयन्' लपनेनैव माम् उच्छ्वासयन् लेपनजनितात् 'आनन्दात् अपरविधं' पूर्वानुभूतात् मोहात् विलक्षणं 'मो' विसुग्धतां 'तनोति' विस्तारयति।।

Notes. 1. प्रत्यापन्न etc.—पद means 'to go'. आ+पद means 'to come.' Comapre याति means 'goes', आयाति means 'comes.' Hence प्रत्यापन्ना *has come back*. 2. अमृतमयैः–अमृतस्य विकारा इति अमृत+मयट् अमृतयाः made of nectar. तैः। 3. अश्चर्वा etc. वा implies समुञ्चच as in "सा वा शम्भोस्तदीया वा मूर्त्तिर्जलमयी मम"। Also comp. "अतोर्हसि चन्तुमसाधु साधु वा"–*Kirat*. I. Here Malli says "वा शब्दोऽप्यर्थे" 4. अपरविधम्–अपरा विधा अस्य etc. comp. "तव स्पर्शे स्पर्शे मम च परिमूढ़ेन्द्रियगणो विकारश्चैतन्यं भ्रमयति समुन्मीलयति च"–Act I, sl. 36; also "सन्तापजां सपदि यः प्रतिहत्य मूर्च्छामानन्देन जड़तां पुनरातनोति"–Act III. sl, 12. 5. आनन्दनिमीलिताक्षः–निमोलिते अक्षिणीऽस्य निमीलिताक्षि+षच् समासान्त निमीलिताक्षः by "बहुव्रीहौ सक् त्यक्ष्णोः स्वाङ्गात् षच्"।

(*lvi*) **वासन्ती–देव कथमिव ?**

Vāsantī—How so, sire ?

रामः–सखि किमन्यत्, पुनः प्राप्ता जानकी।

Rāma—What else, friend ? Jānakī has come back.

वासन्ती–अयि देव क्व सा ?

Vāsantī—Well, Where is she, O Sire.

रामः–(स्पर्शसुखमभिनीय)–पश्य नन्वियं पुरत एव।

Rāma—(Acting the joy of toch)—Why, look, here she is, just in form of you.

वासन्ती–अयि किमिति मर्मच्छेददारुणैरेभिः प्रलापैः प्रियसखीदुःख-दग्धामपि पुनर्मन्दभागिनीं दहसि माम् ?

Vāsantī—Why O with these ravings, frightful because piercing the vitals, do you again burn me, the ill-fated, though burnt alrady with sorrow for my dear friend ?

सीता–ओसरिदुं इच्छामि एसो उण चिरसब्भावसोम्नोसौअलेन अज्जउत्तप्फंसेण दीहदारुणं वि मन्दाबं इति हरन्तेण वज्जलेबोवणाद्धो विअ सिज्जन्तणोसहविवल्हत्थो वेवादि अवसो विअ मे हत्था [अपसुर्त्तमिच्छामि एष पुनश्चिरसद्भावसौम्यशीतलेन आर्यपुत्रस्पर्शो दीर्घदारुणमपि सन्तापं झटिति हरता वज्रलेपोनद्ध इव स्विघन्निः-सहविपर्यस्तो वेपते अवश इव मे हस्तः]।

Sītā—I wish to withdraw, but this my hand—as if cemented with Vajralepa by the touch of my husband which is cool and pleasing through lasting good-will and is quickly removing my long and terrible anguish—is seating, languid, supine and trembling like one paralysed.

मित–।'कथमिव' कथं वर्द्धे इत्यर्थः।।'किमन्यत्' उच्यताम् इति वाक्यशेषः।। 'पुरत एव' तव पुरोवर्त्तिनी एव सा।।'मर्मणाः' जीवस्थानस्य ये 'छेदाः' कर्त्तनानि ते इव 'दारूणाः' घोराः। तैः प्रलापैः असम्बद्धभाषितैः 'प्रियसख्याः' सीतायाः एते यत् 'दुःखं तेन 'दुग्धां' तापिताम्। 'दहसि' इति रामस्यार्थे एव शोकः तेन च दाहः। प्रलापैर्ज्ञायते आगत उन्माद इति। ततो मूर्च्छा तदनु मरणां स्यात् इति हि दशाक्रमो विरहिणाम्। तत् रामस्य विपदमाशङ्कमाना दह्यते वासन्ती।। 'अपसुर्त्तुं दूरे यातुम् 'इच्छामि' किन्तु 'हस्तो मे अवश इव वेपते' तेन अपसुर्त्तुन शक्नोमि। कथमवशः?– 'स्विद्यन्' सखेदः 'निःसहः' विकलश्च 'विपर्यस्तः 'उत्तानश्च हस्तः। भवतु' प्रधाव्य अपसर पादौ तु न अवशौ–'वज्रलेपः' इति प्रसिद्धेन सुदृढ़ेन प्रलेपेन 'उपनहः' आर्यपुत्रस्य शरीरेण सह वद्ध 'इव' जातो मे हस्तः तत् कथमपस्त्रियाम् ? तदपि कथम्– 'आर्यपुत्रस्पर्शेन। किम्भूतेन स्पर्शेन एवमपनद्धो हस्तः ?–'दीर्घदारुणामपि' मे 'सन्तापं' झटिति हरता' स्पर्शेन। कथञ्चत तत् ?–'चिरसद्भावेन' स्थायिन्या प्रीत्या यः स्पर्शः 'सौम्यशीतलः' सुखशीतलः न वा उष्णाः त चातिशीतलः तेन। मयि अद्यापि स्नेहवान् आर्य्यपुत्र इति तस्य स्पर्शो मां सखयति, तेन नापसराभि इति सरलार्थः।

Notes. 1. पुरत:–This is ambigous. It may mean before *you* or before *me*. But पश्य suggests facility for वासन्ती to see. Now if सीता is in front of राम, it does not necessarily follow that she is visible to वासन्ती। Hence we prefer 'before *you*'. 2. मर्म etc.—मर्मच्छेदा इव दारुणा:, उपमानकर्मधा–Here वासन्ती takes Rāma's talk as the ravings of a mad man, because through Bhāgirathī's boon she cannot see सीता। The thought rends her vitals (मर्मच्छेद) as it were because the last three stages of विरह are उन्माद, मूर्च्छा and मरण। She has noticed the first two in Rāma already and now apprehends the last. Comp. *Vidūṣaka's* "गृहीतोनेन पन्था उन्मत्तानाम्" in *Śakuntala*, Act VI. 3. प्रियसखी etc.—प्रियसख्या: दु:खम् the grief caused by Sītā, तेन दग्धा। Sītā has already given me a shock and you are now going to cause another. 4. चिरसद्भाव etc.—सन् भाव: सद्भाव: good-will, *i.e.*, love. चिर is चिरस्थायी। चिर: सद्भाव: lasting, unshaken love. सौम्य is सुमग pleasing. सौम्यश्चायी। शीतलश्च। तेन। 5. दीर्घ etc.—दीर्घश्चासौ दारुणाद्भ, तम्। 6. वज्र etc.—वज्रलेप is a kind of cement of a very firm grip. तेन उपनद्ध्व:। My hand has stuck fast on my husband's person, I cannot remove it; hence it is impossible for me to recede. 7. स्विद्यन् etc,—The whole may be taken as a compound. स्विद्यन् perspiring; नि:सह powerless; विपर्यस्त up-turned. स्विद्यंश्च नि:सहश्च स्विद्यन्नि: सह:। तथा चासौ विपर्यस्तश्च। Or नि:सहं यथा तथा विपर्यस्त: नि:सहविपर्यस्त:। स्विद्यंश्चासौ नि:सहविपर्यस्तश्च। Also compare "निरुंत्साहनि: सहं विपर्यस्त:"।

(*lvii*) **राम:–सखि कुत: प्रलाप: ?**

Rāma—Friend, how ravings' ?

गृहीतो य: पूर्वं परिणयविधौ कङ्कणाधर-

श्चिरं स्वेच्छास्पर्शेरमृतशिशिरैर्य: परिचित:।–

The one carrying the nuptial-thread that was accepted by me at the wedding ceremony ; the one long known by its cool nectar-like touch obainted at will ;—

सीता–अज्जउत्त सो एव्व दाणिं सि तुम [आर्यपुत्र, स एव इदानीमसि त्वम्]।

Sītā—That is just what you are my husband.

रामः–

स एवायं तस्यास्तुहिननिकारौपम्यसुभगो

मया लब्धपाणिर्ललितलवलीकन्दलनिभः ।। स० ।।

(इति गृह्णाति)।

Rāma—Here has been found by me the very same hand of hers agreeble through resemblance with a lump of ice and like the soft shoot of the Lavali. (Seizes it).

मित– । गृहीत इति।

अन्वयः–पूर्व परिणयविधौ कङ्कणाधरः य गृहीतः, अमृतशिशिरैः स्वेच्छास्पर्शोः यः चिरं परिचितः– ।

व्याख्या–'पूर्वं' प्राक् जनकभवने 'परिणायविधौ' विवाहनुष्ठाने 'कङ्कणाधरः' धृतोद्वाहसूत्रः 'यः' पाणिः 'गृहीतः' आसीत् ततः परम् 'अमृतम्' इव 'शिशिरैः' शीतलेः सन्तापहरैरिति याक्त्'स्वेच्छास्पर्शैः इच्छामात्रलब्धम्स्पर्शैः सुलभस्पर्शैं रित्यर्थः 'यः चिरं' बहुकालं 'परिचितः' अनुभूतः– ।। आर्यपुत्रेति– । पूर्ववर्त्तिना श्लोकार्द्धेन अन्वितमिदम्।

अन्वयः–पूर्वं परिणायविधौ कङ्कणधरः यः गृहीतः अमृतशिशिरैः स्वेच्छास्पर्शैः यः चिरं परिचितः स एव इदानीं त्वमसि।

व्याख्या–'पूर्वं परिणायविधौ कङ्कणधरः' विवाहमूत्रमण्डितकरः यः गृहीतः भर्त्तृत्वेन मया लब्धः ततः परम् 'अमृतशिशिरैः स्वेच्छास्पर्शैः यः चिरं परिचितः स एव इदानीम् इति वाक्यालङ्कारे 'त्वमसि'। यत्तु सोतायाः पाणिं प्रति वक्तमिष्यते रामेण तदेव इव सीतया वाग्भङ्ग्या रामं प्रति समर्प्यते "आर्यपुत्र" इत्यादिभिः।। स एवेति।

अन्वयः–तुहिननिकरौपम्यसुभगः ललितलवलीकन्दलनिभः स एव अयं तस्याः पाणिः मया लब्धः।

व्याख्या–'तुहिननिकरेण' तुषारराशिना सह यत्'औपम्यं' सादृश्यं स्पर्शविषयते इति शेषः तेन 'सुभगः' हृद्यः किञ्च ललितं कोमलं मनोहरं वा यत् 'लवलीकन्दलं' लवलीलताया अङ्कुरः तत्तुल्यः 'स एव अयं तस्याः पाणिः' हस्तः 'मया लब्धः' प्राप्तः। तत् कुतः प्रलापाः।

Notes. 1. कङ्कणधरः–कङ्कण is मङ्गलमूत्र tied on the hand of both bride and bridegroom at marriage. In the case of the bride, comp. "अयुमन्दृहीतकमनीयकङ्कणस्तव मूर्त्तिमानिव महोत्सवः करः" —Act I, sl. 18. For the bridegroom "देव्यः कङ्कणमोक्षणाय मिलित राजन् वरः प्रेष्यताम्"– *Viracarita*. This refers to पाणि in Rāma's speech and to राम himself in what सीता

says below, 2. अमृतशिशिरैः–Here शिशिर is not शीतल for अमृत is not known as a particulary cool substance. Hence we render it as सन्तापहर। 3. स एव etc.—To Sītā राम was precisely of that character. For इदानीम् implying वाक्याङ्कार Comp. ''कं इदानीमुष्णोदकेन नवमालिकां सिञ्चति''–*Śakuntala*. Or say इदानीम् अस्मित् क्षणो। 4. तुहिन etc.—उपमाया भाव इति उपमा+ष्यञ् औपम्यम् similarity. The similarlity is in temperature. The low temperature revives my heated frame. The word औपम्य seems superfluous तुहिनिकरसुभगः serves equally well. निकर occurs in three in Vidyāsāgara's manuscripts. The fourth has करका instead. But तुहिनकरका sounds tautologous. करका (hail) *is* of तुहिन। ''वर्षोले स्त्री करका'' इति त्रितकाण्डशेः। If तुहिन means शीतल same difficulty arises, for करका as a matter of course is शीतल। Hence prefer निकर। 5. ललित etc.—नित्यसमाप्त with निभ as in अरविन्दकुट्मलनिभः, sl. 37. The resemblance here is in :he consistency. It was soft like the लवली कन्दल। तुहिन etc. and ललित etc. both refer to the sense of touch. The first makes it *cool*, the second *soft*.

(*lviii*) **सीता–हद्दी हद्दी अज्जउत्तप्फं समोहिदाए पमादे क्खु मे संवुत्तो [हा धिक्, हा धिक् ! आर्यपुत्रस्पर्शमोहितायाः प्रमादः खलु मे संवृत्तः]।**

Sītā—Alas ! Alas ! Carelessness has indeed occured on my part infatuated as I was with the touch of my husband.

रामः–सखि वसन्ति, आनन्दनिमीलितेन्द्रियः साध्वसेन परवानन्मि। तत् त्वं तावदेनां धारय।

Rāma—Friend Vāsantī with the sense deadened through joy I am overcome by agitation, so do you take hold of her.

वासन्ती–कष्टमुन्माद एव।

Vāsantī—O misery ! Madness indeed !

सीता–(ससम्भ्रमं हस्तमाक्षिप्य अपसर्पति)।

Sītā—(*Hastily releases her hand and retires*).

रामः–हा धिक् प्रमादः।

Rāma—O fie, a mishap !

करपल्लवः स तस्याः सहसैव जड़ाज्जड़ः परिभ्रष्टः।
परिकम्पिनः प्रकम्पी करान्मत स्विघतः स्विघन्।। 41।।

The spring-like hand of hers has suddenly slipped out

of my hand—the benumbed out of the benumbed, the trembling out of the trembling, the seating out of the sweating.

मित–।'आर्यपुत्रस्य स्पर्शेन मोहिता' कर्त्तव्यविमूढा।'प्रमादः' अनवधानता। कर्त्तव्यविमूढा सती अनवधाना जाता' चिरमार्यपुत्र समीपे स्थिता, अतएव गृहीतम्। सावधाना चेत् अभविष्यं नाग्रहीष्यत् माम्। 'हा धिक्' माम् 'हा धिक्' माम् इत्यात्मनिन्दा।। सीताया पुनःप्राप्तिजनितेन 'आनन्देन निमीलितानि' मुद्रितानि स्फुरणाहीनानि इत्यर्थः 'इन्द्रियाणि' यस्य तादृशोऽहं सम्भ्रमेणा साध्वसेन भूयो वा नश्यत् इत्यावेगेन इत्यर्थः 'परवान्' परतन्त्र अभिभूत इत्यर्थः।।'उन्मादः' उन्मत्तता।। 'ससम्भ्रमं' सत्वरं 'हस्तम् आक्षिप्यं' रामस्य हस्तादाकृष्य 'अपसर्पति' दूरे याति।। 'प्रमादः' अनवधानता, तज्जनिता विपत्तिरति यावत्। तामेव विपत्तिं विवृणोति करेति।

अन्वयः–स्विद्यन् प्रकम्पी जड़ः स तस्याः करपल्लवः स्विद्यतः परिकम्पिनः जड़ात् मम करात् सहसा एव परिभ्रष्टः।

व्याख्या–'स्विद्यन्' सस्वेदः 'प्रकम्पी' सवेपधुः 'जड़ः' विवशः 'सः मया गृहीतः 'यस्याः' सीतायाः 'करपल्लवः' किसलयसदृशः करः 'स्विद्यतः' स्वेदं प्रकटयतः 'परिकम्पिनः' वेपथयुमतः 'जड़ात्' अवशात् 'मम करात् सहसा' अतर्कितम् 'एव परिभ्रष्टः' विच्युतः। इति महान् प्रमादः।।

Notes. 1. प्रमादः etc —I should have avoided being caught. But I was not sufficiently careful (प्रमाद) because I was मोहिता by touch of my husband. 2. आनन्द etc.—निमीलितः is मुद्रित closed. My senses are not awake hence a fear (साध्वस) has seized me (परवानप्) that she might escape. 3. साध्वसेन etc.—पर master. परवान् one having a master. I have become परवान् by साध्वस, *i.e.*, साध्वस is my master. साध्वसेन has अभेदे करणे 3या, पर and साध्वस being indenfied (अभेद)। 4. प्रमादः–This is in secondary sense, *i.e.*, mishap. 5. करपल्लवः–करपल्लष इव। उपमित कर्मधा–। 6. सः–प्रक्रान्तार्थत्वात् न यच्छब्द्व्यपेक्षा। The hand that was मया लब्धः (sl. 40). 7. जड़ात etc.—Both of us were showing सात्त्विकभाव। जड़ is स्तम्भ is a सात्त्विकभाव। 8. परिकम्पिनः–परि+कम्प+णिनि साधुकारिणि कर्त्तरि परिकम्पी। तस्मात्। No णा because "इजादेश्च सनुभः" is restrictive prohibiting णत्व with roots that have नुम् but to not begin with इच्। कम्प is another सात्त्विकभाव। 9. स्विद्यतः–स्वेद too is a सात्त्विक भाव। It is not neccasary that the same भाव should appear in both male and female or that certain भावः are resticted to males and certain to females. Compare—"आसीद्वरः

कण्टकितप्रकोष्टः खिन्नाङ्गलिः संववृत्ते कुमारी" "रोमोद्गमः प्रादुरभूदुमायाः खिन्नाङ्गुलिः पुङ्गवकेतुरासीत्" etc.,

(*lix*) **सीता–हद्धी हद्धी अज्ज वि अणवत्थिसिदमूढ़धूमन्तअणो ण पज्जवत्थावेदि अत्तणाअं [हा धिक् हा धिक् अद्यापि अनवस्थित-स्त्रिमितमूढ़घूर्णन्नयनो न पर्यवस्थापयत्यात्मान्]।**

Sītā—Alas ! Alas ! With eyes now restless again still, now dull agian rolling, he is even now unable to collect himself.

तमसा–(सस्नेहहासकौतुकं निर्वर्ण्य)–

Tamasā (*Marking with a loving and curiosity*)—

सस्वेदरोमाञ्चिकम्पिताङ्गी जाता प्रियस्पर्शमुखेन वत्साः।
मरुन्नवाम्भःप्रविधूतसिक्ता कदम्बयष्टिः स्फुटकोरकेव।। 42।।

With her person sweaty, trembling and having the hairs on end, though joy from the touch of her beloved, my darling has become like a Kadamba twig with the buds blown and shaken and wetted by the wind and the first shower of the season.

मित– ।'अद्यापि' अस्मिन्नपि मुहूर्ते 'अनवस्थिते' अस्थिरे च ते स्तिमिते' निश्चले च 'अनवस्थितस्तिमिते'। 'मूढ़े' जड़े रूपहणाविकले च ते 'घूर्णती' रूपग्रहणाय मण्डलशो भ्रमन्ती च 'मूढ़घूर्णती'। 'अनवस्थितस्तिमिते मूढ़घूर्णती नयने यस्य। एवं नयनयोर्विरुद्धधर्मदर्शनात् मन्ये 'अद्यापि' अयम् 'आत्मानं न पर्यवस्थापयति' न प्रकृती पुनः स्थापयति।। स्नेहपूर्णः हासः 'स्नेहहासः'। 'कौतुकं' कौतुहलम्। ताभ्यां सह। सखेदेति।

अन्वयः–प्रियस्पर्शमुखेन वत्सा मरुन्नवाम्भःप्रतिधूतसिक्ता स्फुटकोरका कदम्बयष्टिरिव सस्वेदरोमाञ्चितकम्पिताङ्गी जाता।

व्याख्या–'प्रियस्य' भर्त्तुः रामस्य 'स्पर्शात् यत् मुखं' तेन 'वत्सा' सीता 'मरुता' वायुना 'नवाम्भसा' प्रथमेन वर्षेण च यथाक्रमं 'प्रविधूता' कम्पिता 'सिक्ता' अभिवृष्या च 'स्फुटकोरका' प्रफुल्लकुद्मला 'कदम्बयष्टिरिव' कदम्बशाखा इव 'सस्वेदं' धर्माद्रं 'रोमाञ्चित' पुलकितं 'कम्पितं' वेपथु मत् च 'अङ्गं' तथाविधा जाता। अतःपरं किमेषा करोति इति कौतुकम्।। स्वगतमेतत्तमसायाः, अनयथा "जाता वत्सा" इति न सङ्गच्छते।।

Notes. 1. अनवस्थित etc.—For समाप्त see Tika. We may also expound thus—मूढ़ यथा तथा घूर्णात् मूढ़घूर्णात् rolling meaninglessly. अनवस्थितंस्तिभितं

मूढ़घर्णात् नयनं यस्य। 2. सस्नेह etc.—For समाप्त see टीका। कौतुक is curiosity. She is currious to see what follows this. 3. सस्वेद etc.—स्वेद, रोमाञ्च, कम्प are सात्त्विक भाव। A चतुष्पद बहु-। The ङीष् is optional by "अङ्गगात्रकण्ठेभ्य इति वक्तव्यम्"। 4. मरुन्नवाम्भः etc.—नवाम्भः refers to the first few showers at the begining of the rains. प्रविधूत goes with कम्पित of सीता, सिक्त with सस्वेद, स्फुटकीरक with रोमाञ्चित। 5. कदम्बयष्टिः–यष्टि is a twig Females are often compared to twing to trees. Thus—"सञ्चारिणी पल्लविनी लतेव" "इमां तटाकशोकलताञ्च तन्वीम्" etc. 6. स्फुट etc.—स्फुट is विकशित। A full—blown flower of the कदम्ब has its filamants placed all round like hairs on end.

(*lx*) सीता (स्वगतम्) अम्महे अवसेण एदेण अत्ताणएण लज्जाविद म्हि भअवदीए तमसाए। किं त्ति किल एसा मणिस्मदि एसो परिच्चाओ एसो ए हिअआसङ्गो त्ति [अहो अवशेन एतेन आत्मना लज्जापितास्मि भगवत्याः तमसायाः। किमिति किल एषा मंस्यते एष परित्यागः एष च हृदयासङ्ग इति]।

Sītā—(*To herself*)—O I am shamed before the worshipful Tamasā by this uncontrolled self of mine. Such being the renunciation and such the attachement of the heart, what would she think ?

रामः–(सर्वतोऽवलोक्य)–हा कथं नास्त्येव। नन्वकरणे वैदेहि–

Rāma—(*Looking all round*)—Alas ! How is this ? Not here indeed. O pitiless Vaidehi,—

सीता–सच्चं अकरुणम्हि जा एबंविधं तुमं पेक्खन्ती णं धरासि एव जीविदं [सत्यमकरुणास्मि या एवंविधं त्वां प्रेक्षमाणा ननु धराम्येव जीवितम्]।

Sītā—Truly I am pitiless who, O fie, seeing you in this plight, does preserve life.

रामः–क्वासि। देवि प्रसीद। न मामेवंविधं परित्युक्तुमर्हसि।

Rāma—Where are thou ? Be gracious my queen. It behovee thee not to fosake me in this plight.

मित–।'अवशेन' अनायत्तेन 'एतेन आत्मना' प्रयोजकेन कर्त्ता अहं 'भगवत्यसः

तमसायाः सम्बन्धे 'लज्जपिता' लज्जया योजिता अस्मि। अधुना भगवतीं वीक्ष्य अहं लज्जे इति भावः। लज्जाकारणमाह–'एषः' ईदृशः अभावनीयः 'परित्यागः, भर्त्रा 'एषं च' ईदृशः पुनः 'हृदस्य आसङ्ग' पक्षपातो मे भर्त्तरि 'इति' एतत् असदृशं वीक्ष्य किमिति किल एषां भगवती 'मंस्यते' सम्भावयिष्यति। अपदार्थः सीता इति मंस्यते ततो मे लज्जा।। अत्रान्तरे रामः 'सर्वतोऽवलोक्य' सीतामपश्यन् सखेदमाह 'हा कथं नास्त्येव'। 'ननु' इत्यनुनये। हे 'अकरुणे' निर्दये 'वैदेहि' इत्यद्धोक्ते तदेव अनुमीदमाना सीता प्राह 'सत्यमकरुणास्मि'। 'ननु धरामि' इत्यत्र आक्षेपे ननु।

Notes. 1. लज्जापिता–लज्जा shame. लज्जया योजिता इति लज्जा+णिच् (नाम धातु)+क्त कर्मणि लज्जापिता put to shame. This is by the Vārttika "प्रातिपदिकात् धात्वर्थे"। 2. भगवत्याः तमसायाः–This is usually rendered भगवत्या तमसाया in the तृतीया। The sense then becomes—I have been put to shame by तमसा। Reference is of course to Tamasā's remark "सस्वेद–"etc. in the verse above. But then that verse is स्वगत (See Ṭīkā on that verse), so सीता cannot already made by तमसा then मंस्यते in the future is unsuitable, because तमसा must have first drawn her conclusion and then made the remark. मंस्यते should then be altered into अमंस्त। Hence भगवत्याः तमसायाः is preferable, both forms being available from the प्राकृत। 3. नन्वकरुणे etc.—सीता does not let him finish his sentence. She hastily interrupts and confirms Rāma's remark. ननु implies अनुनय entreaty (see also note 5). 4. ननु धरामि–Here ननु implies आक्षेप censure. I ought to be ashamed (निन्दा–censure) that I am still alive (धरामि जीवितम्)। 5. क्वासि—This completes Ramas sentence –नन्वकरुणे वैदेहि क्वासि O pitiless वैदेहि whither are thou. I entreat (ननु) you let me have a sight to you. Or say ननु आक्षेपे–It is cruel (अकरुणे वैदेहि) of you to remain invisible. 6. एवंविधम्–In this pitiable plight ईदृशं शोकविह्वलम्।

(*lxi*) **सीता–अइ अज्जउत्त विवरीदं विअ एदं [अयि आर्यपुत्रस्य विपरीतमिवैतत्]।**

Sītā—O my husband, this seems contrary to facts.

वासन्ती–देव प्रसीद प्रसीद। स्वैनैव लोकोत्तरेण धैर्येण संस्तम्भय अतिभुमिगतविप्रलम्भमात्मानं कुतोऽत्र मे प्रियसखी ?

Vāsantī—Excuse me Sire excuse me. By your

superhuman firmness itself do steady your self of which the delusion has transcended its bounds. Whence could my dear friend be here ?

रामः–व्यक्तं नास्ति। कथमन्यथा वासन्त्यपि तां न पश्येत् ? अपि खलु स्वप्न एषः ? न चास्मि सुप्तः कुतो रामस्य निद्रा। सर्वथा स एव भगवान् अनेकवारपरिकल्पनानिर्मितो विप्रलम्भः पुनः पनुरनुबध्नाति माम्।

Rāma—Evidently she is not here ; or, why sould not even Vāsantī see her ? It is really a dream. But am not asleep, whence is sleep for Rāma ? Verily it is the very same mighty delusion, built by imgination many times indulged in, that time and agian follows me.

सीता–मए एव दारुणाए विप्पलद्धो अज्जउत्तो [मया एव दारुणया विप्रलब्ध आर्यपुत्रः]।

Sītā—My husband has been deluded by my cruel self itself.

मित–।'विपरीतं' तत्त्वतो विरुद्धम्। त्वयाहं परित्यक्ता इति हि तत्वम्।।'लोकोत्तरं व्याख्यातं प्राक्।'संस्तम्भय' धारय स्थिरीकुरु। अत्युच्चा भूमिः'अतिभूमिः' ऊर्ध्वतमं तलम्। तां 'गतः' प्राप्तः तत्रारूढ़ इत्यर्थः। तथाविधो 'विप्रलम्भः' भ्रमः प्रणष्टप्रियजनस्य भावनाजनिता वञ्चना इति यावत् तस्य तादृशम्।।'व्यक्तं' स्फुटम् असंशयम्।'भगवान्' महाप्रभावः। 'परिकल्पनया' सङ्कल्पेन 'निर्मितः' जनितः। 'अनेकवारं' बहुशः 'परिकल्पनानिर्मितः मनः कल्पितः 'विप्रलम्भः' वञ्चना काल्पनिके सीतासमागमे परमार्थबोधः इत्यर्थः 'पुनः पुनः माम् अनुवध्नाति' अनुसरति। अनिशं सीतासमागमनुचिन्तयतो मे "पुनः प्राप्ता जानकी" इति महानभूद्भ्रमः इति भावः।। 'विप्रलब्धः' प्रतारितः। अद्य तु योऽयमस्य विप्रलम्भः नह्येव परिकल्पनानिर्मितः किन्तु 'मया एव' अदृश्यरूपया जनितः।।

Notes. 1. विपरीतम्–वि implies opposition. परि is सर्वतो भावे। वि+परि+इ+क्त कर्त्तरि विपरीत altogether opposite, just the reverse. You discarded me, not I you. 2. प्रसीद–She is going to contradict Rāma and hence begs his pardon. 3. अतिभूमि etc.—भूमि is तल storey. अतिभूमि the topmost storey. Or भूमि station. भूमिम् अतिक्रान्तः अतिभूमिः outside the station. New see टीका। 4. सर्वथा etc.—He is now reconciled to his fate with the conviction that सीता is lost to him for ever.

(*lxii*) **वासन्ती–देव पश्य पश्य–**

Vāsantī—Look, Sire look.

पौलस्त्यस्य जटायुषा विघटितः कार्ष्णायसोऽयं रथः
पश्यैते पुरतः पिशाचवदनाः कङ्कालशेषाः खराः।
खड्गच्छिन्नजटायुपक्षतिरितः सीतां ज्वलन्तीं वहन्
अन्तर्व्याकुलविद्युदम्बुद इव द्यामभ्यदस्थादरिः ॥ 43 ॥

Here is Paalastya's car of steel smashed by Jaṭāyu. Behold in front of you these demon-faced mules of which the skeletons now remain. From here, the enemy, with the roots of Jaṭāyu's wings chopped off with the sword, lifting the glowing Sītā ascended the sky like a cloud with lightning playing within.

मित–। 'देव' इत्यादि परवर्त्तिना श्लोकेन अन्वितम्। पौलस्तस्येति–।

अन्वयः–देव पश्य पश्य अयं जटायुषा विघटितः पौलस्त्यस्य कर्ष्णायसः रथः। पश्य पुरते एते कङ्कालशेषाः पिशाचवदनाः खराः। इतः खड्गच्छिन्नजटायुपक्षतिः अरिः ज्वलन्तीं सीतां वहन् अन्तवर्याकुत्मविद्युत् अम्बद इव द्याम् अभि उदस्थात्।

व्याख्या–हे 'देव' रामभद्र 'पश्य पश्य' द्रष्टव्यमस्ति। 'अयम्' एष 'जटायुषा' गरुड़ात्मजेन विघटितः' भग्नः 'पौलस्त्यस्य' 'पुलस्त्यौत्रस्य रावणस्य 'कार्ष्णायसः लौहरचितः रथः'। 'पश्य पुरतः' अग्रे स्थिता 'एते कङ्कालशेषाः' अस्त्यिपञ्जरावशिष्टाः 'पिशाचवनदनाः' राक्षमुखाः 'स्वरा जटायुषैव निहता अश्वतराः रथवाहा इत्यर्थः। 'इतः' अस्मात् प्रदेशात् खड्गेन छिन्ने जटायोः पक्षती' पक्षमूले येन तथाविधः 'अरिः' रिपुः रावणः 'ज्वलन्ती' दीष्यमानां अनसूयाप्रदत्तेन अङ्गरागेण स्फुरत्प्रभामण्डला-मित्यर्थः 'सीतां वहन्' रथनाशात् हस्ताभ्यामेव धारयन् 'अन्तः' अभ्यन्तरे 'व्याकुला' चञ्चला 'विद्युत्' यस्य तादृशः 'अम्बुद इव' मेघ इव 'धाम्' आकाशम् 'अभि' अभिलक्ष्य 'उदस्थात्' उत्पपात॥

Notes, 1. पौलस्त्यस्य–पुलस्त्य was Brahman's son, one of the Saptarṣis. His son was विश्रवस् who agian had रावण, कुम्भकर्ण and विभीषण for sons. पुलस्त्वस्व गोत्रापत्यं पुमान् इति पुलस्त्व+अण् पौलस्त्यः॥ Some read

पुलस्ति for पुलस्त्य। In that case say पुलस्तेर्गोत्रापत्यं पुमान्+इति पुलस्ति+यञ् (गर्गादि) पौलस्त्य etc. 2. कार्ष्णायसः–अयस् is लौह। कृष्णम् अयः इति कृणा+अयस्+टच् समासान्त कृष्णांसयम् a variety (जाति) of iron *i.e.,* steel. This is by "अनोऽश्यायस्मरसां जातिसंज्ञयोः"। Next कृष्णायसस्य विकारः इति कृष्णायस्य+अण् or मयट् कर्णायसः or कृष्णायसमयः। It was a steel car, very hard to break. Yet it was samshed to pieces, so fierce was Jaṭāyu's onslaught. 3. पिशाचवदनाः–पिशित is आममांस raw meat. पिशितम् अश्नातीति पिशित+अश+अण् कर्त्तरि पिशाच where पिशित has become पिश and आश becomes आच the word being of the पृषोदरादि class. पिशाचस्य वदनं पिशाचवदनम्। तदिव वदनभेषाम्। 4. ज्वलन्तीम्–This was due to the glitter of the permanent unguent given her by अनसूया the Wife of the sage अत्रि। Comp. "स्फुरत्प्रभामण्डल-मानसूयं सा विभ्रती शाश्वतमङ्गरागम्। रराज शुद्धेति पुनः सवपुर्यै सन्दर्शिता वह्निगतेव भर्त्रा।" *Raghu.* 5. खड्ग etc.—पक्ष+ति पक्षति which means पक्षमूल। Both जटायु and जटायुस् are correct. 6. अन्तः etc.—ज्वलन्ती सीता compare with व्याकुलविद्युत् and the swarthy रावण with the dak अम्बुद। 7. द्याम्–द्यो is आकाश and is fem. अभियोगे (कर्मप्रवचनीय) द्वितीया।

(*lxiii*) **सीता–(सभयम्)–अज्जउत्त तादो वावादीअदि अहं अ अवहरीआमि परित्ताहि परित्ताहि [आर्यपुत्र, तातो व्यापाद्यते अहञ्च अपह्रिये, परित्रायस्व परित्रायस्व]।**

Sītā—(*In fright*) My husband, father is being killed and I am being carried off. Save us ! Save us !

रामः–(सवेगमुत्थाय)–आः पाप तातप्राणसीतापहारिन् क्व यासि?

Rāma—(*Hastily sitting up*)Ha ! Villian, that takes off father's life and Sītā, whither are you going ?

वासन्ती–अयि देव राक्षसकुलप्रलयधूमकेतो अद्यापि ते मन्युविषयः ?

Vāsantī—O Sire, the comet of destruction to the race of the Rakshasas, does the object of your wrath exist even now?

सीता–अम्मो उन्मत्तिअ म्हि संवुत्ता। [अहो उन्मत्तिकास्मि संवृत्ता]।

Sītā—Ha ! I have become insane !

मित–।'तातो व्यापाद्यते' इत्यादि पूर्ववृत्तान्तस्मरणम्।। 'राक्षसकुलस्य प्रलये'

प्रलयविषये 'धूमकेतो' यथा धूमकेतोरुदये कस्यचित् राजवंशस्यप्रलयः सूच्यते तथ्रा तवाप्युदये राक्षसवंशस्य। मन्यीः कोपस्य विषयः पात्रं 'मन्युविषयः' रावण इति काकुः। मन्युविषयो निराकृतस्त्वया।। 'उन्मत्तिका' असम्बद्धभाषणात्।।

Notes. 1. व्यापाद्यते–वि+आ+पद+णिच्+लट् ते कर्मणि। The past in mistaken for the present. 2. सवेगम् etc.—Rāma also forgests that it is a past affair to which वासन्ती refers and takes it as present. Here राम does not act on hearing Sītā's exclamation. As already remarked तमसा and सीता speak जनान्तिके (beside) respect to राम and वासन्ती, so राम is supposed as not to have heard Sītā's call for help at all. Vāsantī's speech affects both सीता and राम exactly in the same manner and they act in a like fashion accordingly. 3. राक्षसकुल etc.—Comp पौलस्त्यकुल- धूमकेतोः, Act, I, para iv. 4. उन्मत्तिका etc.—She sees the absurdity of her fright.

(*lxiv*) **रामः–अन्वर्थ एवायमधुना प्रलापो वर्त्तते।**

Rāma—This raving has indeed become full of meaning now.

उपायानां भावादविरतविनोदव्यतिकरै-
र्विमर्दैर्वीराणां जगति जनितात्यद्भुतरसः।
वियोगे मुग्धाक्ष्याः स खलु रिपुघातावधिरभूत्।
कथं तूष्णीं सह्यो निरवधिरयं त्वप्रतिविधः ।। 44 ।।

That loss of the lovely-eyed which by encounters of heroes had provided the world with a taste of the supremely mavellous—encounters which from the existence of remedies were attended by steady relief [*Or,*—ceaseless diversion] had indeed its end in the slaying of the enemy. But how is this irremediable and unending one to be borne in silence ?

सीता–णिरवधि त्ति हा हदम्हि मन्दभाइणी [निरवधिरिति हा हतास्मि मन्दभागिनी]। (इति रोदिति)।

Sītā—He says "Unending" ! Ha ! Ha ! I am lost, ill-fated as I am. *(Weeps).*

मित–। अर्थम् अनुगत: अन्वर्थ:' युक्त इत्यर्थ:। अयं प्रलाप:' अद्य यत् रोदनादिकं मया कृतं तत् युक्तमेव।। अनवर्थतां दर्शयति उपायानामिति।

अन्वय:–उपायानां भावात् अविरतविनोदव्यतिकरै: वीराणां विमर्द्दै : जगति जनितात्यद्भु तरस: मुग्धाक्ष्या: स वियोग: रिपुघातावधि: खलु अभूत्। (किं) तु अप्रतिविध: निरवधि: अयं कथं तुष्णीं सह्य:।

व्याख्या–'उपायानां' प्रतीकाराणां 'भावात्' वर्त्तमानत्वात् लभ्यत्वा दित्यर्थ: प्रतीकारा: सन्ति इति हेतो: 'अविरत:' अविच्छिन्न: 'विनोदव्यतिकर:' दु:खलाघसम्पर्क: येषु तादृशै: 'वीराणां' कपिराक्षसभटानां 'विमर्द्दै: सम्प्रहारे: 'जगति' भुवने 'जनित:' उत्पादित: 'अत्यद्भुतस्य' परमविस्वप्नयस्य 'रस:' स्वाद: येन तथाविध: 'मुग्धाक्ष्या:' सुलोचनाया: सीताया: 'स वियोग:' असौ रावणकृत: पूर्वविरह: 'रिपुघात:' शत्रुनिपात: 'अवधि' सीमा यद्वा 'रिपुघाते अवधि:' अन्त: यस्य तथाविध: 'खलु' तादृश एव 'अभूत' रावणनाशेन सहैव तस्य पर्यवसानमभूत। किं 'तु' पक्षान्तरे अप्रतिविध: प्रतीकारहित: अतएव 'निरवधि:' अनन्त: 'अयम्' एष वर्त्तमानो विरह: 'कथं तूष्णीं' निर्वत्रनं 'सह्य:' सोढुं शक्य: न कथमपि शक्य: अत: अन्वर्थ अधुना प्रलाप:''।। 'निरवधि: इति' आह इति वाक्यशेष:।।

Notes. 1. अयम् etc.—प्रलाप is असम्बद्धभाषण as in ''सखि कुत: प्रलापा:'' (para lvii), also विलाप as in ''शीकक्षोभे च हृदयं प्रलापैरेव धार्यते'' (sl. 29). Here both are intended. अयम् refers to all the occurrences of the day. 2. उपायानाम् etc.—उप समीपे फलस्य समीपे अयते एभि: इति उप+अय+घञ् करणे उपाया: means adopted to a certain end. Here the steps taken to remove the वियोग। भावात् has हेतौ 5मी–because (हेतु) there were remedies. The existence of उपाय was the reason whence विनोदव्यतिकर was possible. 3. अविरत etc.—विनोद relief also diversion. वि+अति+कृ+अप् भावे व्यतिकर concurrence, hence *presence*. For समास see टीका। Qual. विमर्द्दै:। The encounters kept me incessantly occupied (विनोद= diversion). Or—the encounters gave me steady relief (विनोद=relief) ''Steady relief' implies that each single विमर्द ended in victory of Rāma's party. 4. जनित etc.—रस is खाद taste. "पारदखादो रस:" इत्यादि त्रिकाण्डशेष:। विमर्द is the प्रयोजक and रस the प्रयोज्य। रसो जात:=विमर्दै: रसो जनित:। The world for the first time then knew what the अत्यद्भुत् was. 5. रिपु etc.—अवधि a time limit. The वियोग was attended by विनोद; it also had an अवधि। 6. तूष्णीम्–A मकारान्त अव्यय meaning silently'. The implication is that refers is no विनोदव्यतिकर। 7. निवधिः–Why so ? Because अप्रतिविधः–प्रति+वि+धा+अङ् भावे प्रतिविधा remedy. अविद्यमाना प्रतिविधा अस्मिन्। Contrast this with उपायानां भावात्। The previous वियोग was attended with विनोदव्यतिकर, this has to be suffered तूष्णीम्। The other was रिपुघातावधिः, this is निरवधिः।

(*lxv*) **रामः–हा कष्टम् !**

Rāma—O woe !

व्यर्थं यत्र कपीन्द्रसख्यमपि मे वीर्य्यं हरीणां बृथा
प्रज्ञा जाम्बवतोऽपि यत्र न गतिः पुत्रस्य वायोरपि।
मार्गं यत्र न विश्वकर्मतनयः कर्त्तुं नलोऽपि क्षमः
सौमित्रेरपि पत्रिणामविषये तत्र प्रिये क्वासि मे ।। 45 ।।

In what place, not within reach of Saumitri's arrows too, are you, my darling, with regard to which my friendship with the monkey-chief is useless to me, towards which the prowess of the monkeys as well as the wisdon of Jāmbavat is futile, where there is no access for the son of the wind-god too, to which Nala too the son of Viśvakarman is unable to make a track ?

सीता–बहु मणाविद म्हि पुवविरहम् [बहु मानितस्मि पूर्वविरहम्]।

Sītā—I am led to think better of the former separation.

मित–। अप्रतिविधत्वं वर्तमानवियोगस्य निवधित्वे हेतुरुक्तम्। तत् अप्रतिविधित्वं परिष्कुर्वन् पूर्वविरहे ये उपाया तेषां वर्त्तमाने निष्फलतां दर्शयति व्यर्थमिति।

अन्वयः–प्रिये मे सौमित्रेरपि पत्रिणामविषये क्व तत्र असि यत्र मे कपीन्द्रसख्यमपि व्यर्थम्, हरीणां वीर्य्य जाम्बवतः प्रज्ञा अपि वृथा, यत्र वायोः पुत्रस्य अपि गतिः न यत्र विश्वकर्मतनयः नलः अपि मार्ग कत्रकु न क्षमः।

व्याख्या–हे –'प्रिये मे मदीये दयिते जानकि 'सौमित्रेरपि' एकधनुर्द्धरस्य लक्ष्मणस्य च 'पत्रिणां' वाणानाम् 'अविषये' अगोचरे 'क्द तत्र असि' कस्मिन् देशे वर्त्तसे 'यत्र मे' मत्सम्बन्धे 'कपीन्देण' वानरराजेन सुग्रीवेण यत् 'सख्यं' मिचता तत् 'अपि व्यर्थं' विफलम्, हरीणां वानराणां नलनीलादीनां 'वीर्यं' पराक्रमः 'जाम्बवतः प्रज्ञा अपि' ऋक्षराजस्य बुद्धिरपि 'वृथा' विफला 'यत्र वायोः पुत्रस्य अपिं मारुतेश्च 'गति न' प्रवेशो न विद्यते 'यत्र विश्वकर्मतनयः' विश्वकर्मणः पुत्रः 'नलः' अपि मार्गं' द्वारं

'कर्त्तुं' न क्षमः' असमर्थः एवम् उपायानामत्यन्ताभावे सति अप्रतिविध एष वियोगः।। 'पूर्वविरहं बहु' यथा तथा 'मानिता' बोधिता 'अस्मि'। पूर्वविरहो वरमासीत् इति मे बोधो जातः।।

Notes. 1. कपीन्द्र etc.—कपीन्द्र is सुग्रीव। He was Rāma's कृत्रिममित्र–friend by deed. It was he who collected the army of monkeys. 2. प्रज्ञा etc.—जाम्बवत् was the bear prince. He was a veritable repository of the word's wisdom and had twice saved the brothers from peril, once when they were fettered with नागपाश and again when लक्ष्मण was pierced with the शक्ति by रावण। 3. न गतिः etc.—Refers to हनुमान्। It was he who crossed the sea and traced सीता to the अशोकवन। He again brought the द्रोणाद्रि to लङ्का and saved लक्ष्मण। 4. मार्गम् etc.—नल was the architect to bridge the sea and let the monkey host cross over to लङ्का। 5. सौमित्रेः etc.—As his brother, he was Rāma's सहजमित्र। To his arrows Rāma owed victory over इन्द्रजित् the redoubtable son of रावण। Thus, backed by सहजमित्र, कृत्रिममित्र, a vast army, a capable general (सुग्रीव), perfect counsel (जाम्बवत्, विभीषण etc.) and a host of invincible fighters (हनुमत,अङ्गद etc.). राम was fully equipped to fight the first वियोग (उपायानां भावात्)। 6. मानिता–मन is बुद्ध्यर्थ, hence the अणिकर्त्ता becomes कर्म, thus—अहं पूर्वविरहं बहु मन्ये, एव मां पूर्वविरहं बहु मानयति। Changing the voice एतेन अहं पूर्वविरह बहु मान्ये (बहु मानिता)।

(*lxvi*) रामः–सखि वासन्ति, दुःखायैवेदानीं रामस्य दर्शनं सुहृदाम्। कियच्चिरं त्वां रोदयिष्यामि ? तदनुजानीहि मां गमनाय ।–

Rāma—Friend Vāsantī, Rāma's sight is now only for the sorrow of friends. How long shall I make you weep ? So permit me to return.—

सीता (साद्वेगमोहं तमसामवलम्ब्य)–भअवदि तमसे कधं गच्छदि एव अज्जउत्तो [भगवति तमसे कथं गच्छत्येव आर्यपुत्रः]।

Sītā—(*With alarm and bewilderment leaning on Tamasā*)—Worshipful Tamasā, how is this? My husband is indeed going !

तमसा–वत्से समाश्वसिहि समाश्लिहि। ननु आवामपि आयुष्मतोः कुशलयोवर्षग्रन्थिमङ्गलं सम्पादयितुं भागीरथीपादान्तिकमेव गच्छावः।

Tamasā—Cheer up, my child, cheer up. Why, we too are really going to the neighbouhood of the feet of Bhāgīrathī (Or—near honoured Bhāgīrathī) to perform the auspicious ceremony of tying the anniversary knot of long-lived Kuśa and Lava.

सीता–भअवति पसीद खणमेत्तं वि दाव दुल्लहं जणं पेक्खामि [भगवति प्रसीद क्षणमात्रमपि तावत् दुर्लभं जनं प्रेक्षे]।

Sītā—Be pleased worshipful lady, even but for a moment let me see this person whose sight is hardly available (to me).

मित–।'दुःखाय' इत्रि चतुर्थी। असमाप्ते एव रामवाक्ये आक्षिष्यते तत् सीतया भगवतीति।।'वर्षाणां' ग्रन्थिः' ग्रन्थिवन्धनम्। तस्य 'मङ्गलं' मङ्गलकर्म 'भागीरथ्याः पादयोः अन्तिकं' समीपम्। यद्वा–पूजा भागीरथीपादाः'। तेषामन्तिकम्।।

Notes. 1. रामस्य etc.—रामस्य has अनुक्ते कर्मणि and सुहृदाम् has अनुक्ते कर्त्तरि षष्ठी owing to the कृत in दर्शनम्। The रामं पश्यन्ति सुहृदः (तिङ् योगे)=रामस्य दर्शनं सुहृदाम्। This is by the Vārttika "शेषे विभाषा"। 2. कियत् etc.—किं परिमाणामस्य इति किम्+वतु कियत् how much. चिर is long time. कियत् qualifies. चिरम् and demands the measures of the lenght of time. I have grieved you petty long, and do not want to grieve you longer. 3. गमनाय–"तुमर्थाच्च–" इति चतुर्थी गनतुमनुजानिहि is the sense. Rāma has not finished yet ; सीता hastily interrupts on hearing him speak of going. Speech ends with चक्षुर्विनोदयामि (next para). The interruption extends from सीता (सोद्वेगमोहम्) to दुर्लभं जनं प्रेक्षे।

(*lxvii*) **रामः–......अस्ति चेदानीमश्वमेधाय सहधर्मचारिणी मे–**

Rāma—...And now for purpose of the Aśvamedha, my coworker in the rites is—

सीता(सोत्कम्पम्)—अज्जउत्त का सा [आर्यपुत्र का सा] ?

Sītā—(*With trepidation*)—Who is she, my husband ?

रामः–....हिरणमयी सीताप्रतिकृतिः।

Rāma—....a golden image of Sītā.

सीता (सोच्छ्वासं सास्त्रम्)–अज्जउत्तो दाणिं सि तुमं ! अम्महे

उक्खाणिदं मे दाणिं परिच्चाअलज्जासल्लं अज्जउत्तेण [आर्यपुत्र इदानीमसि त्वम् ! अहो उत्खातं मे इदानीं परित्यागलज्जाशल्य-मार्यपुत्रेण]।

Sītā—(*With a sigh of relief and with tears*)—What a specimen of a husband you have now become ! Ha ! my shaft of shame from renunciation has now been extracted by my husband.

रामः–.....तत्रापि तावद्बाष्पदिग्धं चक्षुर्विनोदयामि।

Rāma—...Even there I shall regale my tear—soiled eyes.

सीता–धणा सा जा अज्जउत्तेण बहु मणाअदि, जा अ अज्जउत्तं विणोदअन्ती आसाणिबन्धणं जादा जीअलोअस्म [धन्या सा या आर्यपुत्रेण वहु मन्यते, या च आर्यपुत्रं विनोदयन्ती आशानिबन्धनं जाता जीवलोकस्य]।

Sītā—Worthy is she who is highly prized by my husband, and who, by diverting my husband, has become the peg of hope for the land of the living.

मित–। 'अस्ति' इत्यादि आतस्य वाक्यस्य अनुबन्धः। 'सहधर्मचारिणी मे' इत्यत्रापि असमाप्तं वाक्यम्।।'सीता (सोत्कम्पम्) 'इति भूयोऽप्याक्षेपः।।''हिरण्मयी' इति व्याख्यातं प्राक्। अयमपि तस्यैव वाक्यस्य अनुबन्धः।। 'सीता (सोच्छ्वासम्)' इति पुनराक्षेपः। 'इदानीम्' एतत् कृत्वा 'आर्यपुत्रः' आर्यपुत्रनिदर्शनम् 'असि त्वं' जगताम्। 'परित्यागस्य' या 'लज्जा' सा एव 'शल्यम्'।। यथ इह पञ्चवट्यां तथा 'तत्रं' सीतापतिकृतौ 'अपि' प्राग्वृतस्मरणात् 'वाष्पदिग्धं' जलपूर्णं 'चक्षर्विनोदयामि'। तत् भाभूत सुहृदामपि रोदनम्। म तुं यथाकथञ्चित् विनोदो भविष्यति, अनुजानीहि मां गमनाय इति वाक्यशेषः। इदन्तु पूर्णं वाक्यम्–रामः–''सखि वासन्ति, दुःखार्यवेदानीं रामस्य दर्शनं सहृदाम्। कियच्चिरं त्वां रोदयिष्यामि। तदनुजानीहि मा गमनाथ। अस्ति चेदानीमश्वमेधाय सहधर्मचारिणी मे हिरण्मयी सीताप्रतिकृतिः। तत्रापि तावद्बाष्पदिग्धं चक्षुर्विभोदयामि''।।'' आशाया निबन्धनं समाश्रयः अवलम्वनम् आशास्थलमित्यर्थः। यद्वा–'आशाया निबन्धनं' कारणम्। आशा–रामः स्वस्थो भवतु इत्याशा 'जीवलोकस्य' इयञ्च प्रतिकृतिर्विनोद हेतुः रामस्य इत्याशास्थलं भुवनवासिनाम्, अनया जीवति रामे सनाथा वयमिति।।

Notes. 1. अस्ति etc.—This is continuation of Rāma's speech which is again interrupted at मे। As a beginning of a fresh speech it is extremely awkward, because there is no occasion to refer to the subject. 2. का सा—Here we have the jealousy of a co-wife which causes the interruption. 3. हिरण्मयी etc.—See Act II. The speech continues to be again interupted at प्रतिकृतिः। This connot be a fresh speech in reply to Sita's का सा for the simple reason that Rāma cannot her Sītā. 4. आर्यपुत्र इदानीम् etc.—You are a model of a husband now. 5. उत्खातम् etc.—This indicates complete reconciliation. 6. तत्रापि etc.—This concludes Rāma's speech. Here I seek solace in the sight of familiar objects. But the memory is painful and my eyes water. This causes you also to weep (रोदयिष्यामि) which is an additional source of pain to me. Let me suffer alone, retiring to my capital (अनुजानीह etc.). There I have a golden image of Sītā to keep me compamy at the अश्वमेध। In it I shall find what diversion is possible to wretched me. विनोदयामि इति भविष्यत्सामीप्ये वर्त्तमान। 7. धन्या–Blessed. The reasons follow—(1) आर्यपुत्रेण बहु मन्यते–My husband prizes it ; (2) आशानिबन्धनं जाता जीवलोकस्य–It raises hopes in the mind of the entire creation. निबध्यते अस्मिन् इति नि बन्ध+ल्युट् अधिकरणे निवन्धनम् tying post, a peg. Hopes rest in it, because it comforts my husband.

(*lxviii*) **तमसा (सस्मितस्नेहास्त्रं परिष्वज्य)–अयि वत्से एवमात्मा स्तूयते !**

Tamasā *(Embracing with a smile and tears of affection)*—O child, thus is self being praised !

सीता–(सलज्जमधोमुखी स्वगतम्)–परिहसिदम्हि भअवदीए [परिहसितास्मि भगवत्या]।

Sītā—(*Becoming crest-fallen and bashful—Aside*)—I have been laughed at by her worshipful self.

वासन्ती–महानयं व्वतिकरोऽस्माकं प्रसादः। गमनं प्रति पुनर्यथा कार्य्यहानिर्न भवति तथास्ताम्।

Vāsantī—This meeting is a great favour unto me. But, as to your leaving, be it so that no neglect of duty may result.

सीता–पड़िउला दाणिं मे वासन्ती संवुत्ता [प्रतिकूला इदानीं मे वासन्ती संबृत्ता]।

Sītā—Vāsantī has now become adverse to me.

तमसा–एहि वत्से गच्छाव:।

Tamasā—Come child, we go.

सीता (सकष्टम्)–एवं करेम्ह [एवं कुर्वः]।

Sītā—(*Woefully*)—So do we.

तमसा–कथं वा गम्यते यस्यास्तव–

Tamasā—Or how could leave be taken by you, by whose—

प्रत्युप्तस्येव दयिते तृष्णादीर्घस्य चक्षुषः।
मर्मच्छेपरैर्यन्तैराकर्षो न समाप्यते ।। 46 ।।

Efforts that are bent upon rending the vitals, the drag is not being finished on eyes that have become wide (*lit*-long) through longing and implanted as it were on the beloved.

मित–।'स्मितेन' ईषद्धासेन 'स्नेहास्रेण' वात्सल्यजनितेन वाष्पेण च 'सह'। 'एवम्' अनेन प्रकारेण प्रतिकृतेः स्तवेन 'आत्मा' स्वयं त्वमेव 'स्तूयते'। आत्मप्रशंसा इयं ते इति परिहासः।। 'अयं व्यतिकारः'एष आवयोः समागमः 'अस्माकं' मम सम्बन्धे 'महान् प्रमादः' परमः अनुग्रहः। इति गमनं ते अनीप्सितं मम। 'पुनः' पक्षान्तरे 'गमनं प्रति' ब्रवीमि 'यथा कार्यहानिः न भवति तथा आस्तां' तथैव भवतु। विलम्बे चेत् कार्यातिपातः मा मूद्दिलम्बः गमनमेव भवतु।।'प्रतिकूला' गमनानुमोदनात् विरुद्धा।। कयं वा गम्यते त्वया। 'यस्यास्तव' इति श्लोकेन अन्वितम्। प्रत्युप्तेति।

अन्वयः–यस्यास्त्व मर्म्मच्छेदपरैः यत्नैः तृष्णादीर्घस्य दयिते प्रत्यप्तस्येव चक्षुषः आकर्षो न समाप्यते।

व्याख्या–'यस्याः तव मर्मच्छेदपरैः' मर्मच्छेदे प्रवृत्तैरिव 'यत्नैः' चेष्टाभिः 'तृषाया' प्रियदर्शनवाञ्छया 'दीर्घस्य' व्यातस्य विस्तारितस्य इत्यर्थः अपि च 'दयिते' प्रिये रामे 'प्रत्युप्तस्य इव' निखातस्येव अतएव झटिति प्रत्यानयनायोग्यस्य 'चक्षुषः' नेत्रस्य [कृद्योगा कर्मणि षष्ठी] 'आकर्षः' उद्धाराकर्षणं न समाप्यते न विरतिं नीयते। सतृष्णं ते चक्षुर्गाढ़ निखातं दयिते, तददुद्दारार्यं महानप्यस्ति ते प्रयासः किन्तु अनिच्छाकृतः सः, तेन हि मन्ये हृदयग्रन्थिस्तेत छिद्यते इव तथापि चक्षुर्निवर्त्तयितुं न शक्नोषि, तत् कथं वा त्वया गम्यताम् ?

Notes. 1. आत्मा–Your own self. 2. परिहसिता–परि+हस is सकर्मक owing to the उपसर्ग 3. व्यक्तिकरः–Coming together, a chance meeting. 4. अस्माकम्–मम। 5. प्रसादः–A favour. Hence, it is not to my interest to let you go. 6. यथा कार्यहानिः etc.—But I am not so selfish as to stand in the way of business. If a longer stay interferes with state affairs then go by all means. Vāsantī did not say this immediately after Rāma's अनुजानीहि मां गमनाय (para lxvi) because राम had not then finished his speech. This is an additional proof that we have a single speech from सखी वासन्ती (para lxvi) to चक्षुर्विनोदयामि (para lxvii). 7. आकर्ष–आ+कृष+घञ् भावे आकर्ष pull. The construction is यत्नैः चक्षुः आकर्षन्ति with तिङ् becomes यत्नैः चक्षुषः आकर्षः with कृत by the rule "उभयप्राप्तौ कर्मणि"। 8. *Remark*—Tamasā means to say—your eye has sunk deep (प्रत्युप्त) in the body of your दयित। You must first pull it out and then go. But your efforts to extract the eye seem futile and only hurt you to the quick. You cannot go you are tied here to your दयित through your eye. In plain words—The very thought of separation pains you.

(*lxix*) **सीता–णमो णमो अपुव्वपुणजणिददंसणाणां अज्जउत्तक्षरण-कमलाणं [नमो नमः अपूर्वपुण्यजनितदर्शनानामार्यपुत्र चरण-कमलानाम्]। (इति मूर्च्छति)।**

Sītā—I bow, I bow unto the lotus-feet of my husband sight of which has been procured by merit recently accured. *(Faints away)*.

तमसा–वत्से समाश्वसिहि समाश्वसिहि।

Tamasā—Cheer up, my child cheer up.

सीता (समाश्वस्य)–किअच्चिरं वा मेहन्तरेण पुणिमाचन्दस्स दंसणं [कियच्चिरं वा मेघान्तरेण पूर्णिमाचन्द्रस्य दर्शनम्]।

Sītā *(Recovering)*—Well, how long can the sight of the full-moon be had through an opening in the clouds ?

तमसा–अहो संविधानकम्।

Tamasā—O the metamorphosis !

एको रसः करुण एव निमित्तभेदाद्-
भिन्नः पृथक्पृथगिवाश्रयते विवर्त्तान्।
आवर्त्तवुद्ध, दतरङ्गमयान् विकारान्
अम्भो यथा सलिलमेव तु तत् समग्रम ।।47।।

The one sentiment of sorrow indeed, varied through variety in the cause, undergoes changes as though they were different entities ; just as water assumes transformations in the shape of whirls, bubbles and billows, while all these are but water to be sure.

मित–। 'अपूर्वेण' नवेन 'पुण्येन' सुकृतेन 'जनितं' निर्वाहितं 'दर्शनं' येषाम्। प्राक् क्षीणे पुण्ये परित्यक्ता अभवम्। त्यागात् परं पनुः किञ्चिदर्जितं पुण्यं तेनैव नवेन पुण्येन आर्यपुत्रचरणदर्शनं मे जातिमित्यर्थः। 'चरणामनाम्' इति गौरवे बहुवचनम्। नमस्शब्दयोगे चतुर्थी युक्ता।। 'मेघानाम् अन्तरेण' अवकाशेन 'पूर्णिमायां चन्द्रस्य दर्शनं कियच्चिरं भवति। क्षणिकमेव तत् भवति, ममापि आर्यपुत्रचरणादर्श नं क्षणितकमेव जातम्। तदलं परितापेन।। संविधीयते इति 'संविधानक' रचना। स्वार्थे कन्। एक इति।

अन्वयः–एक एव करुणो रसः निमित्तभेदात् भिन्नः (सन्) पृथक् पृथक् इव विवर्त्तान् आश्रयते, यथा अम्भः आवर्त्तवुद्वुदतरङ्गमयान् विकारान्। तत् समग्रं तुं सलिलमेव।

व्याख्या– 'एक एवं स एव अभिन्नः 'करुणो रसः' शोकरूपो भावः निर्मित्ते' कारणे उद्दीपके इत्यर्थः यो 'भेदः' पृथकत्वं तस्मात् भिन्नः रूपान्तरितः सन् 'पृथक् पृथक् इवं नवान् इव 'विवर्त्तान परिणामान् आश्रयते' भजते, 'यथा अम्भः' जलम् 'आवर्त्तमयान्' भ्रमिरूपान् 'वुद्वदमयान्' वुद्वदरूपान् 'तरङ्गमयान्' तरङ्गरूपान् 'विकारान्' आपाततो भिन्नान् परिणामान् आश्रयते। 'तत् समग्रं तु' वस्तुतः पुनः आवर्त्तादिकं सलिलमेव' जलमेव। कारणभेदात् एक जलमेव आवर्त्तरूपेण वुद्वदरूपेण तरङ्गरूपेण च परिणमति, एवं शोक एव सीतायाः नैराश्यात् नैराश्यात् तटस्थता विप्रियवशात् कलुषता इत्यादि प्रागुक्तक्रमेण विवर्त्तते।।

Notes. 1. अपूर्व etc.—अपूर्व is नूतन। Usually it is taken to mean उत्कट। 2. पूर्णिमा etc.—पूर+क्त भावे पूर्णम् fullness पूर्णता। पूर्णेन निर्वृत्ता इति पूर्ण+इमप् स्त्रियाम् पूर्णिमा the night when the moon is full. etc. 3. संविधानकम्–सम्+वि+धा+ल्युट् भाने संविनम् change, creation etc. तदेव इति स्वार्थे कन्। 4. निमित्त etc.—निमित्त is हेतु cause, निमित्ते भेदः निमित्तभेदः a difference in the cause सुप्सुपा। तस्मात्। 5. पृथक् etc.—The remark is perfectly general.

In the special case of सीता, sl. 13. ("तटस्थ नैराश्यादपि च कलुषं विप्रियवशात् etc.") very well summarises the different विवर्त्तs of करुण (i.e., तटस्थता कलुषता, etc.) owing to a difference in the निमित्त (i.e., नैराश्य, विप्रिय etc.) Act. III. pp. 41-3.

(*lxx*) **रामः–विमानराज इत इतः। (इति सर्वे उत्तिष्ठन्ति)।**

Rāma—This way, O the best of baloons, this way. (*All get up*).

तमसावासन्त्यौ (सीतारामौ प्रति)–

Tamasā and Vāsantī (To Sītā and Rāma)—

अवनिरमरसिन्धुः सार्द्धमस्मद्विधाभिः
स च कुलपतिराद्यश्छन्दसां यः प्रयोक्ता।
स च मुनिरनुयातारून्धतीको वशिष्ठ-
स्त्वयि वितरतु भद्रं भूयसे मङ्गलाय।। 48।।

(इति निष्क्रान्ताः सर्वे)।

May the earth, the stream of the gods along with those of our stamp, that Kulpati too the first user of metres, also Vasiṣṭha that sage whom Arundhatī follows, shower blessings upon you for abudant bliss. (*Exeunt all*)

इति छाया नाम तृतीयोऽङ्कः

This is the Third Act named Shadow.

मित–। अवनिरिति।

अन्वयः–अवभिः, अस्मद्दिधामिः सार्द्धम, अमरसिन्धुः, य छन्दसाम् आद्यः प्रयोक्ता स कुलपतिश्च, अनुयातारुन्धतीकः स सुनिः वशिष्ठश्च, भूयसे मङ्गलाय त्वयि भद्रं वितरतु।

व्याख्या–'अवनिः' देवी पृथिवी 'अस्मद्विधाभिः' माद्वशोभिः 'सार्द्धं' 'अमरसिन्धुः सुरसरित् गङ्गा यः छन्दसां' वेदवहिर्मूतानां छन्दसाम् 'आघः प्रयोक्ता' प्रथम उदाहर्त्ता 'स कुलपतिश्च' सुनिकुलपोषको वान्मीकिश्च 'अनुयाता' अनुगता अरुन्धती' यं 'स मुनिः वशिष्ठश्च भूयसे मङ्गलाय' महते शुभाय 'त्वयि' विषये 'भद्रं' वितरतु' कल्यानं दिशतु।।

Notes. 1. तमसा etc.—Th e stage direction creates an unnatural situation. It is inconceivable that तमसा and वासन्ती would utter the same words in the same order without collusion. 2. अवनिः–The ङीप् is optional, hence अवनी also. 3. सार्द्धम् etc.—This suits तमसा because she too is a सिन्धु (river—"सिन्धुर्ता सरिति स्त्रियाम्") thought only a मरसिन्धु not अमरसिन्धु। But it seems misplaced with वासन्ती who has no right to class herself with गङ्गा। 4. कुलपतिः–This is the designation of a मुनि who lodges, feeds and educates 10,000 disciples. The reference is to वाल्मीकि। 5. अनुयाता etc.—Indicates constant companionship. In the constellaction of the सप्तर्षि Arundhatī is seen seated behind वशिष्ठ। Here the implication is that अरुन्धती also त्वयि वितरतु भद्रम्। 6. त्वयि–विषयाधिकरणविवक्षया सप्तमी।

Chapter - 4

(i) (ततः प्रविशतस्तापसौ)।

(*Then enter two hermits*)

एकः–सौधातके, दृश्यतामद्य भूयिष्ठसन्निधापितातिथिजनस्य समधिकाम्भरमणीयता भगवतो वाल्मीकेराश्रमपदस्य। तथाहि–

First—Saudhataki, observe the attractiveness to-day, due to elaborate preparations, of the site of the hermitage of worshipful Vālmīki where guests have been brought together in large number. Thus—

नीवारौदनमण्डमुष्णामधुरं सद्यः प्रसूताप्रिया–
पीतादभ्यधिकं तपोवनमृगः पर्याप्तमाचामति।
गन्धेन स्फुरता मनागनुसृतो भक्तस्य सर्पिष्मतः
कर्कन्धूफलमिश्रशाकपचनामोदः पस्तिीर्यते ।।1।।

This deer of the hermitage drinks to his fill the warm and sweet water of the boiled wild-rice—residue after his just-then-calaved mate had her drink. The aroma of vegetables cooked along with the fruit of the *Jujube* is being diffused all round attended slightly by the spreading fragrance of rice boiled with *ghi*.

मित–। सुधातुरपत्यं पुमान् सौधातकिः तत्संबुद्धौ 'सौधातके'। 'अद्य भगवतो वाल्मीकेः आश्रमपदस्य' आश्रमस्थानस्य 'समधिकैः विशिष्टैः आरम्भैः' अनुष्ठानैः या 'रमणीयता रुचिता जाता सा 'दृश्यतां' त्वया। कुतोऽयं समाधिकारम्भ इत्याह 'भूयिष्टं' अतिबहुलं यथा तथा 'सन्निधापिताः' समानीताः 'अतिथिजनाः' अतिथयः यस्मिन् तथाविधस्य आश्रमपदस्य। अद्य बहवः प्राप्ता अतिथयः, तेषां परिचर्यार्थं विशिष्या ओदनाः पच्यन्ते, तेन च रमणीयतरमद्य आश्रमपमिति भावः।। नीवारेति।

अन्वयः–तपोबनमृगः सद्यःप्रसूताप्रियापीतात् अभ्यधिकम् उष्णमधुरं नीवारौदनमण्डं पर्याप्तम् आचामति। सर्पिष्मतः भक्तस्य स्फुरता गन्धेन मनाक् अनुसृतः कर्कन्धूकलमिश्रशाकपचनामोदः परिस्तीर्यते।

व्याख्या–'तपोवनमृगः एष आश्रममृगः 'सद्यःप्रसूता' तत्क्षणाकृतगर्भविमोचना अतएव अतितृषिता या '-प्रिया' मृगी तया यत् 'पीतं' ततः 'अभ्यधिकं' शेषम् 'उष्णं' सधोनिगालितं न पर्युषितम् अतो 'मधुरं' स्वादु 'नीवारौदनस्य' नीवारसाधितभक्तस्य 'मण्डं' फेन 'पर्याप्तं' प्रचुरं यथा 'आचामति' पिवति। प्रभूता नीवाराः सधिताः इति समधिकारम्भः। किञ्च 'सर्पिष्मतः भक्तस्य' घृतसाधितस्य अन्नस्य 'स्फुरता' आविर्भवता 'गन्धेन मनाक्': ईषत् 'अनुसृतः अनुयातः लेशेन तन्मिश्र इत्यर्थः 'कर्कन्धूफलैः' वदरैः 'मिश्रः' समेतः यः' 'शाकः' तस्य यत् 'पचनं' पाकः तस्य आमोदः' गन्धः पक्वशाकगन्ध इत्यर्थः 'परिस्तीर्यते' वायुना समन्ततो बाह्यते। एतदपि नूतनमिति समधिकारम्भ एव।।

Notes. 1. सौधातके–सुधातुर्गोत्रापत्यं पुमान् इति सुधातृ+इञ्। The ॠ of सुधातृ now changes into अक and we get सुधातक+इञ्=सौधातकिः etc. 2. भूयिष्ट etc.—सम्+नि+धा+णिच+क्त कर्मणि सन्निघापित made of assemble, invited, अतिश्रय एव जनाः अतिथिजनाः etc. 3. समाधिक etc.—रम+अनीयर् कर्त्तरि बाहुलकात् रमणीयः that which pleases. तस्य भावः etc. 4. आश्रम etc.—आश्रमस्य पदं स्थानम् etc. 5. नीवार etc.—नीवार is wild rice, ओदन food. नावारसधितः औदनः etc. 6. उष्णा etc.—उष्ण warm, i.e., the rice water was fresh ; hence it was मधुर। 7. सद्यः etc.—For समाप्त see *Mitabh.*—सद्यःप्रसूता implies that the doe was very thirsty, hence she took in a big draught. The कर्मधा–in सधः प्रसूता प्रिया gives the form सघः प्रसूतिया with पुंवद्भाव by the rule 'पुं वत् कर्मधारयजातीयदेशीयेषु''। The excepting अपूरणीप्रियादिषु does not affect कर्मधा–compounds. Also सधःप्रसूतिया preserves the metre. It is very likely the poet did write प्रसूत but the scribes have made it. प्रसूता। 8. पर्य्याप्तम्–Enough. The hermits are poor eaters. Comp. नीवारमुष्टिपचना गृहिणो गृहाणि'' (Act I, sl. 25.). Usually the daily collection of rice water in a hermitage is small. Today however not only was there enough of it for the thirsty doe, but there was left after she had her fill, an ample supply for the buck to drink to his heart's content (पर्याप्त)। Really then there was समधिकारम्भ। 9. कर्कन्धू etc.—शाकपचनामोदः is पक्वशाकामोदः, by the maxim ''भावानयने द्रव्यानयनम्,'। पचन is a क्रिया, it can have no आमोद। 10. परिस्तीर्यते–परि+स्तॄ-लट्ते कर्मणि। The nominative is वायुना understood. It is not possible for the flavour to scent the surroundings unless a large quantity is cooked. Hence also समधिकारम्भ।

(*ii*) **सौधातकिः–साअदं अणीअपियाराणं जिणकुच्चाणं अणज्झाअकालणाणं [स्वागतम् अनेकप्रकाराणां जीर्णा कूर्च्चानाम् अनध्यायकारणानाम्]।**

Saudhataki—Welcome to these grey-beards of various types who have caused a break in our studies (*i.e.* have given us a holiday).

प्रथमः–(बिहस्य)–अपूर्वः कोऽपि ते बहुमानहेतुर्गुरुषु सौधातके।

First *(Laughing)*—The reason for your regard for the elders, Saudhataki, is novel and peculiar.

सौधातकिः–भो भाण्डाअण किणामघेओ एसो महन्तस्म दूविरसत्थस्स धुरन्धरो अज्ज चीरधारओ अदिधी आअदो [भो भाण्डायन किंनामधेय एष महतः स्थविरसार्थस्य धुरन्धरः अघ चीरधारकः अतिथिरागतः]।

Saudhataki—Ho ! Bhāṇḍāyana, of what name is this guest in rags that has come at the head of a big caravan of old people to-day ?

भाण्डायनः–धिक् प्रहसनम्। नन्वयमृष्यशृङ्गाश्रमादरुन्धतोपुरस्क्तान् महाराजदशरथस्य दारानधिष्ठाय भगवान् वशिष्ठः प्राप्तः। तत् किमेवं प्रलपसि?

Bhāṇḍāyanai—A curse on your joking ! (Or- Fie ! Joking?) Why, this is worshipful Vaśiṣṭha come from the hermitage of Ṛṣyaśṛṅga leading the queens of the great king Daśaratha with Arundhatī at their head. Why then dost thou rave thus ?

मित–। भूयिष्टसन्निधापितातिथिजनेत्युच्यते, तत् 'अनेकप्रकाराणां' नानाविधानां 'जीर्णाकूर्च्चानां' पक्वशमश्रूणाम् 'अनध्यायस्य' अध्ययनविरामस्य 'कारणानां' हेतुभूतानां तेषाम् अतिथीनां सम्बन्धे यो मे बहुमानः तेन तेभ्यः 'स्वागतम्' उच्चारयामि।। 'गुरुषु बहुमानस्य अपूर्वः' नूतनः 'कोऽपि ते हेतुः' दृश्यते यत् त्वं तान् अनध्यायकारणारूपेण वर्णयसि।। भाण्डस्य गोत्रापत्यं पुमान् 'भाण्डःयनः'। 'किन्नामधेयः' व्याख्यातं प्राक्। 'स्थविराणां' बृद्धानां 'सार्थः' समूहः तस्य। 'धुरन्धरः' व्याख्यातं प्राक्। चीरं धरतीति

चीरधारः। कुत्सितश्चीरधारः 'चीरधारकः'।। 'प्रसहसनं' प्रहासः।। 'ननु' आक्षेपे। 'अरून्धती पुरस्कृता' अग्रे स्थापिता याभिः ताः। 'अधिष्ठाय' नेतृत्वेन सम्भाव्य।।

Notes. 1. जीर्णकुर्चानाम्–जीर्ण कूर्चं श्मश्रु येषां ते जीर्णकूर्चाः gay-beards. तेषाम्। There were only two greay-beards there, *viz.*, वशिष्ठ and जनक। But by transference of epithets it stands here for the *aged* in general. This justifies the plural. This is the विशेष्य। सम्बन्धसामान्ये षष्ठी। 2. अनध्याय etc. अधि+इ+घञ् भावे अध्याय study. न अध्यायः No study (no lecture). तस्य कारणानि। सीधातकि appreciates ths attribute of the guests. Hence his reverence for these guests. Our text here is from कीरराघव। Vidyāsāgara reads "आगतम्अनध्यायकारणं सविशेषभूतम् अद्य जीर्णकूर्चानाम्"। Explain 'अद्य' जीर्ण कूर्चानाम् आगतम् आगमनं 'सविशेषभूतं' विशिष्ठप्रकारकम् 'अनध्यायकारणम्'। Translate "To-day the arrival of the grey-beards is a special reason for no-lecture'! This does not declare बहुमान for the grey-beards and the next speaker's remark becomes irrelevant (see note 5). Hence prefer वीरराघव। 3. अपूर्वः–न पूर्वः new, novel etc. 4. कोऽपि ते–There of Vidyāsāgara's manuscripts omit ते which is not desirable, 5. बहुमानहेतुः–बहुमान repect. The respect is expressed by स्वागतम् in Saudhataki's speech. Hence the reading स्वागतम् etc. is to be preferred. धीधातकि thinks highly of the guests because they have given him a holiday !! This appreciation of the guests is novel (अपूर्व)। It is peculiar (कोऽपि) i.e., I condemn it. 6. चीरधारकः–चीर+धृ+अण् कर्त्तरि चीरधारः one clad in rags. चीरधार+क चौरधारकः a fellow rage. "कुत्सिते" इति कः। 7. अधिष्ठाय–Comp. "वशिष्ठाधिष्ठिताः etc."—I, sl. 3. 8. प्रलपसि–Such disrepectful talk regarding वशिष्ठ is indeed प्रलाप।

(*iii*) **सौधातकिः–हुं वसिठ्ठो [हुं वशिष्ठः]?**

Saud.— Hey ! Vaśiṣṭha ?

भाण्डायनः–अथ किम् ?

Bhāṇḍ.—Who else ?

सौधातकिः–मए उण जाणिदं वग्घो वा विओ वा एसो त्ति [मया पुनर्ज्ञातं व्याघ्रा वा वृको वा एष इति]।

Saud.—But I thought he was a tiger or a wolf.

भाण्डायनः– आः किमुक्तं भवति ?

Bhāṇḍ.—Avaunt ! What is being insinuated ?

सौधातकिः–तेण परावड़िदेण एव्व सा वराइआ कल्लाणिआ मड़मड़ाइदा [तेन परापतितेन एवसा वराकिका कल्याणिका मड़मड़ायिता]।

Saud.—No sooner he came, the poor little heifer uttered the sound मड़ (*i.e.* was killed).

भाण्डायनः–समांसो मधुपर्क इत्याम्नायं बहु मन्यमानाः श्रोत्रियाभ्यागताय वत्सतरीं महोक्षं वा महाजं वा निर्वपन्ति गृहमेधिनः इति हि धर्मसूत्रकाराः समामनन्ति।

Bhāṇḍ.—Authors of the Law-codes, respecting the Vedic text that Madhuparka should go with meat, say that house holders have to offer a heifer or a big bull or a bing goat to a Brāhmaṇa guest versed in the Vedas.

मित– ।'हुम्' इति अनिच्छायाम्।।'पुनः' पक्षान्तरे 'मया ज्ञातम्' अव धारितम्। 'वृकः' तरक्षुरिति व्याघ्रभेदः।। 'परापतितेन' सम्प्राप्तेन 'ए वतेन'। हेतौ दृतीया। 'कल्याणी' वत्सरी। कन् स्वार्थे। 'वराकिका' दीना 'कल्याणिका' वत्सरी 'मड़मड़ायिता' ''मड़'' इति अव्यक्तशब्दं' कृतवती, प्राणान् अत्याक्षीतत् इति यावत्। वलिदानार्थं पातिते खड्गे भिन्नः स्कन्धसन्धिः ''मड़'' इति च शब्दो जातः। स च इह शब्द उपचारात् वत्सतर्या एव कृत इत्युच्यते।।'मधुपर्कः' मधुमिश्रा दधिघृतादिसम्भारः' समांस मासेन सह दातव्यः 'इति आम्नायम्' एतत् श्रुतिवचनं 'बहुमन्यमानाः' आद्रियमाणाः 'धर्मसूत्रकाराः' मन्वादयः 'श्रोत्रियाभ्यागताय' गृहागताय श्रोत्रियाय 'वत्सतरीं तरुर्णीं गोवत्सां' महोवक्षं वा' वृषम वा 'महाजं वा' वृहन्तं छागं वा 'गृहमेधिनः' गृहस्थाः 'निर्वपन्ति' ददति''इति हि' इत्येव 'समामनन्ति' संस्मरन्ति। तत् वशिष्ठस्यार्थे वत्सतरीविशसनं शास्त्रसमतमेव, किमेव' प्रलपसि ?

Notes. 1. हुम्–An अव्यय here implying अनिच्छा unwillingness to admit. ''हुम् इत्यनिच्छाभयस्मरणकोपेषु'' इति वर्द्धमानः।2.ज्ञातम्–ज्ञा+क्त कर्मणि अतीते। The क्त not being in the वर्त्तमानकाल the अनुक्तकर्त्ता does not take षष्ठी and we get मया not मम्। 3. वराकिका–वराकी is दीना। सा एव इति वराकी+कन् स्वार्थे वराकिका। This expresses pity for poor thing. 4. कल्याणिका–कल्याणी heifer वत्सतरी। अल्पा कल्याणी इति कल्याणी+कन् अल्पे कल्याणिका the little heifer. Here we cannot have अनुकम्पायां becuse अनुकम्पा is alrady expressed by वराकिका। 5. मड़मड़ायिता–मड़ is an imitation of the sound with which something breaks. These imitative words have to take the affix डाच् by "अव्यक्तानुकरणात् द्वजवरार्द्धात् अनितौ डाच्" when इति is not attached to them. Again the word has to be doubled first and then डाच् added. ("डाचि द्वे भवतः")। Thus in the sense मड़ इति शब्दं कृतवती we have मड़मड़+डाच्+क्यष् (नामधातु)+क्त कर्त्तरि मड़मड़ायिता uttered the sound मड़, *i.e.,* the sound of the neck-bone breaking. In other words, the sacrificial knife fell on her neck and servered her head. क्त is atached कर्त्तरि because the root मड़ामड़ाय is अकर्मक the कर्म (मड़मड़ा) being included in the धात्वर्थ ("धात्वर्थेनोपसंग्रहात्")। Comp. "धातोरर्थान्तरे वृतेर्धात्वर्थेनोपसंग्रहात्। प्रसिद्धेरविवक्षातः कर्मणोऽकर्मिका क्रिया।।" मड़मड़ायिता is usually explained as भक्षिता। This requires the क्त to be in the कर्मवाच्य which is not available after अकर्मक roots. Besides भाण्डायन defends the *killing* and does not at all refer to eating. Comp. "वत्सतरीं.... निर्वपन्ति", "वत्सतरीं विशसिता"। 6. मधुपर्कः–मधुना पृच्यते इति मधु+पृच+घञ् कर्मणि। A kind of *sherbet* made of curd, honey ghi, sugar and water constituting the first offer of welcome to a guests. 7. श्रोत्रिय etc.—छन्दः अधीते इति छन्दम्+घन् श्रोत्रियः a Brāhmaṇa versed in the Vedas. छन्दस् because श्रोत्र optionally by निपातन is the rule "श्रोत्रियंश्छन्दोऽधीते"। श्रोत्रियश्चासौ अभ्यागतश्च श्रोत्रियाभ्यागतः। तस्मै। 8. महोक्षम्–महान् उक्षा इत्रि महा उक्षन्+अचमसासान्त=महोक्षः। तम्।

(*iv*) **सौधातकि–भो णिगिहीदो सि [भोः निगृहीतोऽसि]।**

Saud.—Ha! You are taken (or—worsted, disgraced etc.).

भाण्डायनः–कथमिव ?

Bhāṇḍ, How so?

सौभातकिः–जेण आअदेसु वसिठ्ठमिस्सेसु वच्छदरी विससिदा अज्ज एव्व पज्जाआदस्म राएसिणी जणअस्स भअवदा वमीएण दहिमहुहिं एब णिवतिदों महुवक्को वच्छदरी उण विसज्जिदा [येन आगतेषु वशिष्ठमिश्रेषु वत्सतरी विशसिता अद्यैव पर्यागतस्य राजर्षेर्जनकस्य भगवता वाल्मीकिना दधिमधुभिरेव निर्वर्त्तितो मधुपर्कः वत्सतरौ पुनिर्विसृष्टा]।

Saud.—For the very day, revered Vaśiṣṭha coming, the heifer was killed, but unto the Royal sage Janaka, who had returned, the Madhuparka was gone through by worshipful Vālmīki with curd, honey, etc. only while the heifer was let loose.

भाण्डायनः–अनिवृत्तमांसानामेवं कल्पमृषयो मन्यन्ते निवृत्तमांसस्तु तत्रभवान् जनकः।

Bhāṇḍ.—The sages approve of this practice for those (guests) who have not renounced meat ; but hououred. Janaka has renounced meat.

मित–।'निगृहीतः' पराजितः। मान्यो वशिष्ठः 'वशिष्ठमिश्राः'। गौरवे बहुवचनम्। 'विसृष्टा' विमोचिता बन्धनात्। समानार्थं समानीता एव वासतरी परं तां तस्मै प्रदर्श्य एवं बन्धनात् मुमोच न तु जघान।। अनिवृत्तं मांसमेषाम् 'अनिवृत्तमांसाः' अपरित्यक्तमांसभोजनाः। तेषाम्। 'कल्पः' शास्त्रविधिः।।

Notes : 1. निगृहीतः–निग्रहः often means लाञ्छना disgrace. निग्रहीतः disgraced, worsted. 2. विशसिता–वि+शम to kill+क्त कर्मणि। 3. दधि. etc.—The plural implies that the other three ingredients were also there. 4. अनिवृत्त etc.—Bhandayana could have easily silenced Saudhataki saying that Janaka was not a श्रोत्रिय। "जन्मना ब्राह्मणः प्रोक्तः संस्कारैर्द्विज उच्यते। विद्यया याति विप्रत्वं त्रिभिः श्रोत्रिय इष्यते।।" Bhāṇḍāyana, had said श्रोत्रियाभ्यगताय, so Saudhataki's retort is irrelevant.

(*v*) **सीधा–किं णिमित्तं [किं निमित्तम्] ?**

Saud.—For what reson ?

भाण्डा–स तदैव सीतादेव्यास्तादृशं दैवदुर्विपाकमुपश्रुत्य वैखानसः संवृत्तः। तथास्य कतिपये संवत्सराश्चन्द्रद्वीपतपोवने तपस्तप्यमानस्य।

Bhāṇḍ.—He having heard of such an evil turn of fate of queen Sītā that very moment became an anchorite. It is now some years since he has been as such practising penance in the penance-grove of Candra-dvīpa.

सौधा–तदो किं त्ति आअदो [ततः किमिति आगतः]।

Saud.—Then why has he come ?

भाण्डा–चिरन्तनप्रियसुहृदं प्राचेतसं द्रष्टुम्।

Bhāṇḍ—To see his dear old friend Prāchetasa.

सौधा–अवि अज्ज सम्बन्धिनोभिः समं संबुत्तं से दंसणं ण व त्ति [अपि अध सम्बन्धिनीभिः समं संवृत्तमस्य दर्शनं न वा इति] ?

Saud.—Has an interview taken place or not to-day between him and his female relatives by marrige ?

भाण्डा–सम्प्रत्येव भगवता वशिष्ठेन देव्याः कौसल्यायाः सकाशं भगवत्यरुन्धती प्रहिता यत् स्वयम् उपेत्य वैदेहो द्रष्ठव्य इति।

Bhāṇḍ.—Just now worshipful Arundhatī has been sent by mighty Vaśiṣṭha to queen Kausalyā saying "The king of the Videhas has to be personally approached and seen by you."

मित–।'किं निमित्तं' निवृत्तमांसो जनकः इति पूरणीयम्।। 'तदेव' सीतापरित्याग-काले एव।'देवस्य दुष्टं विपाकं विषमां परिणतिम्।' तथा' तेन प्रकारेण वैखानसरूपेण इत्यर्थः।'संवत्सराः' अतीताः इति शेषः।'तपः तप्यमानस्य' तपः अर्जयतः।। चिरं भवः 'चिरन्तनः'।।

Notes. 1. स तदैव etc.—Till then he was all along an आहिताग्नि गृहस्थ। "सङ्कटा ह्याहिताग्नीनाम्" etc, I. Sl. 8. वैखानसः–He has left his home and become an anchorite. Hence meat has been renounced, 2. तप्यमानस्य–तप+शानच् कर्मकर्त्तरि। 3. चिरन्तन etc.—चिरम् is an अव्यय meaning "a lone time." चिरम्+ट्युल् चिरन्तनः। स चासौ प्रियसुहृच्च। तम। 4. सम्बन्धिनीभिः–Refers to the queens.

(*vi*) सौधा–जधा एदे सब्बे त्थविरा परप्परं मिलिदा तधा अम्हे विवडुएहिं समं मिलिअ अणज् झाअमहूसवं खेलन्ता सम्भावेम्ह [यथा एते सर्वे स्थाविराः परस्परं मिलिताः तथा आवामपि वटुकैः समं मिलित्वा अनध्यायमहोत्सवं खेलन्तौ सम्भावयाव:]। (इति परिक्रामतः)।

Saud.—As all these old people have met one another, so we too meeting with the scholars will celebrate, by playing the great festival of break in study. (*They go round the stage*).

भाण्डा–तदयं ब्रह्मवादी पुराणराजर्षिर्जनकः प्राचेतसवशिष्ठावुपास्य सम्प्रति आश्रमबहिर्वृक्षमूलमधितिष्ठति। य एषः–

Bhāṇḍ.—Here now the old royal sage Janaka, the discourser on Brahman, having paid his repects to Prāhetasa and Vaśiṣṭha, sits at the foot of a tree outside the hermitage. He it is who—

हृदि नित्यानुषक्तेन सीताशोकेन तप्यते।
अन्तः प्रसुप्तदहनो ज्वलन्निव वनस्पतिः ।।2।।

(इति निष्क्रान्तौ)।

Like the tree (Sami) burning within with fire lurking therein is being tortured at heart by grief for Sītā ever clinging there. *(Exeunt).*

विष्कम्भकः

Here ends Viṣkambhaka.

मित–। 'अनध्यायरूपं महोत्सवम्' क्रीड़ाभिः 'समावयावः' सम्मानयावः। क्रीड़ाभिरेव अस्य महोत्सवस्य अनुरूपा समानना भवति।। 'पुराणश्चासौ राजर्षिश्च'। हृदीति।

अन्वयः–यः णषः अन्तः प्रसुप्तदहनः ज्वलन् वनस्पतिरिव हृदि नित्यानुषक्तेन सीताशोकेन तप्यते।

व्याख्या–'यः' एषः अन्तः' मध्ये 'प्रसुप्तः' लीनः 'दहनः' अग्निर्यस्य तादृशः अतएव 'ज्वलन्' दह्यमानः 'वनस्पतिः' शमीवृक्ष 'इव हृदि' अन्तः 'नित्यानुशक्तेन' चिरलग्नेन 'सीताशोकेन तप्यते' दह्यते।।

Notes. 1. आवाम्–भाण्डायन also was one of the puplis of Vālmīki. 2. वटुकैः–वटु is a Brahman boy. स्वार्थे क। 3. तत्–अव्यय implying हेतु। Because he has renounced the world through grief, *therefor* (तत्) he avoids company and is now sitting alone at the root of yonder tree to brood over his misfortune. 4. नित्य etc.—अनु+सञ्ज+क्त कर्मणि वा अनुषक्त। नित्यम् अनुषक्तः सुत्सुपा। 5. अन्तः etc.—Usually the whole is treated as a compound. But as हृदि in the first line stands separate, it is better to take अन्तः as uncompounded. 6. विषम्भकः–Already explained.

(vii) **(ततः प्रविशति जनकः)**

(Then enters Janaka)

जनकः–

अपत्येयत् तादृगदुरितमभवत्तेन महता
विषक्तस्तीव्रेण व्रणितहृदयेन व्यथयता
पटुर्धारावाही नव इव चिरेणापि हि न मे
निकृन्तन् मर्माणि क्रकच इव मन्युर्विरमति।।3।।

Janaka—Impressed by that great and peculiar mishap which befell my child, and which, keen as it was, had pierced my heart and is torturing me, my grief, continuing unceasingly, deep like a fresh one, cutting my vitals like a saw, does not indeed cease even after this long time. (Jan—).

मित–। अपत्ये इति।

अन्वयः–अपत्ये यत् तादृक दुरितम् अभवत् महता तीव्रेण व्रणितहृदयेन व्यथयता तेन विषक्तः धारावही नव इव पटुः क्रकच इव मर्माणि निकृन्तन् मे मन्युः चिरेणापि न हि विरमति।

व्याख्या–'अपत्ये' सन्ततौ सीतायां 'यत् तादृक्' तथाविधं धोरमित्यर्थः 'दुरितं' दुर्ब्यापारः सापवादपरित्यागरुपः 'अभवत् महता' विपुलेन 'तीव्रंण' दारुणेन तीक्ष्णेन इत्यर्थः अतएव 'व्रणितं' भिन्नं 'हृदयं' येन यथाविधेन अतश्च 'व्यथयता' क्लिश्नता 'तेन' दुरितेन 'विषक्तः' दृढ़मारोपितः 'धारावाही' सततं प्रवर्त्तमानः 'नव इव पटुः' अचिरजात इव तीव्रः 'क्रकच इव' करपत्रमिव 'मर्माणि निकृन्तन्' जीवस्थानानि दारयन् 'मे मन्युः' शोकः 'चिरेणापि कालात्ययेऽपि 'न हि विरमति' नैव शाम्यति।।

Notes. 1. दुरितम्–दुष्टम् इतं प्राप्तम् an ugly situation, hence a disaster or disservice. 2. विषक्तः–विशेषेण सक्तः लग्नः। सन्ज+क्त कर्मणि सक्तः attached, implanted. This supposes that तेन has अनुक्ते कर्त्तरि 3या। 3. व्रणित etc.—व्रण to pound+णिच् स्वार्थे (चुरादि)+क्त कर्मणि व्रणितम् pounded ; hence *pierced*. The root is व्रण गात्रविचूर्णने। This is a bit awkward in the case of the heart, hence we change the meaning to भेदने। But विचूर्णातं हृदयम् does not sound mere harsh than "दलति हृदयं गाढ़ोद्वेगम्" (III, sl 31). 4. चिरेण–चिर a long time. तेन। अपवर्गे 3या। We have taken this with विरमति। चिरेणापि इव is also good and is supported by अनेकसंवत्सरातिक्रमेऽपि.... प्रत्यग्र इव of the next para. 5. विरमति–"व्याङ् परिम्यो रमः" इति परस्मैपदम्। It has to be seen if नव इव and न विरमति are not tautologous.

(*viii*) **कष्टम् ! एवं नाम जरसा, दुःखेन च दुरासदेन, भूयः पराकसान्तपनप्रभृतिभिस्तपोभिरात्तरसधातुः अनुपयुज्यमानो नाद्यापि मे दग्धदेहः पतति। अन्धतामिस्त्रा ह्यसूर्या नाम ते लोकास्तेभ्यः प्रतिविधीयन्ते ये आत्मघातिनः, इत्येवमृषयो मन्यन्ते। अनेकसंवत्सरातिक्रमेऽपि च प्रतिक्षणपरिभावनया स्पष्टनिर्भासः प्रत्यग्र इव दारुणो न मे दुःखसंवेगः प्रशाम्यति। अयि मातर्देवयजनसम्भवे देवि सोते, ईदृशस्ते निर्माणभागः परिणतो येन लज्जया स्वच्छन्दमाक्रन्दितुमपि न शक्यते। (ज–)।**

Jan—O woe ! My cursed frame, with sap and substance dried up to such extent indeed by age and unspeakable grief then again by austerities such as Parāka, Santapana etc. and partaking of no food; even no food, even now does not drop down dead. Those regions, sunless and of blinding gloom. Or—named Asūryā with nights of bliding gloom, art indeed allotted to those who kill themselves—Go say the Ṛṣis. With a vivid perception through ceaseless brooding, the shock of my grief, unbearable like new, does not abate even after the expiry of many years. O mother, O divine Sītā sprung from the sacrificial ground of the Gods, thy lot at creation has taken such a trun that, through shame, it is not possible even to weep freely. (Jan—)

मित–। 'कष्टम्' अहो दुखम् ! 'अद्यापि मे दग्धदेहः' हतशरीरं 'न पतति' विनिपातं न गच्छति न नश्यति इत्यर्थः। किमस्ति पातकारणम् इत्याह–'जरसा' वार्द्धकेन 'एवं नाम' ईदृशम् अतिमात्रमिति यावत् 'आत्तः' गृहीतः शोषित इत्यर्थः 'रसः' शोणितादिद्रवपदार्थः 'धातुः' मांसादिघनपदार्थश्च यस्य अतएव पतितुं योग्गः दग्धदेहः। जराजीर्णोऽपि क्वचित् चिरं जीवति–न केवलं जराजीर्णः 'दुरासदेन' दुःसहेन 'दुःखेन च आत्तरसधातुः तथापि 'न पतति'। चित्रमेतत्–'भूवः' पुनश्च 'पराकसान्तपनप्रभृतिभिः' कष्टभोजनविधायकैः 'तपोभिः व्रतैः 'आत्तरसधातुः' शोषितशरीरोपादानः तथापि 'न पतति'। मन्ये भगवान् ब्रतादीनाम् अवकाशेषु प्रचुरं भुङ्क्ते ततो न देहः पतति–'अनुपयुज्यमानः' अभोजनमाचरन्नपि न पतति। यद्येवम् आत्मानं पातयतु भवान्–'ये' जनाः 'आत्मघातिनः तेभ्यः' देहपातात् परम् 'अन्धा' दृष्टिविधातिका 'तामिश्रा' रात्रि येषु तादृशाः 'असूर्याः' सूर्यसञ्चारशून्याः 'नाम लोकाः प्रतिविधीयन्ते' वासत्वेन निरुप्यन्ते 'इत्येयम् ऋषयो मन्यन्ते' अतो नात्मानं पातयामि। 'अनेकसंवत्सरातिक्रमेऽपि च' चिरेणापि 'प्रतिक्षणं' निरन्तरम् 'परिभावनया' अनुध्यानेन

'स्पष्टः' स्फुटः 'निर्भासः' दीप्तिः यस्य तादृशः धारावाही इति यावत् प्रत्यग्र इव दारुणः' नव इव पुटः 'मे दुःखसंवेगः न प्रशाम्यति' न विरमति। 'निर्माण भागः' सृष्टिकाले विधात्रा विहितं भाग्यम्। 'इदृशः परिणतः' एवं जुगुप्सितेन परिणामेन योजितः अपवादकलङ्कित इत्यर्थः।।

Notes. 1. दुरासेन–दुखेन आसद्यते इति दुर्+आ+सद+खल् कर्मणि दुरासन्दम् unapproachable, unbearable. 2. पराक etc.—पराक is a fast for 12 days. "द्वादशाहोपवासेन पराकः परिकीर्त्तितः।" सान्तपन in thus defined "गोमूत्रं गोमयं क्षीरं दधि सर्पिः कुशोदकम्। एकरात्रोपवासश्च कृच्छ्रं सान्तपनं विदुः।।" 3. अन्ध etc.—अन्धयति इति अन्ध+णिच् स्वार्थे+अच कर्त्तरि अन्ध bliding. तमः अस्ति अस्याम् इति तमस्+र मत्वर्षे तमिस्त्रा night रात्रिः। तमिस्त्रा एव इति तमिस्वा+अण् स्वार्थे प्रज्ञादि तामिस्वा। अन्धा तामिस्वा येषु ते having one continuous night of a blinding gloom. 4. असूर्याः–This is perhaps better taken as the proper name of the regions. They are known as (नाम) असूर्य and are ever peravaded by a blinding gloom. 5. प्रतिविधीयन्ते–दीयन्ते। 6. अनेक etc.—This is a paraphrase of the second half of sl. 3. Thus अनेक etc. corresponds to चिरेणापि ; प्रतिक्षण etc. to धारावाहौ; प्रत्यग्र etc. to नव इव पटुः। 6. निर्माणभागः–Explained. I am ashamed to weep because of the scandal attached to your banishment.

(*ix*) **(ज–) हा हा पुत्रि,**

Jan—Alas ! Alas ! My daughter.

अनियतरुदितस्मितं विराजत्-
क्रतिपयकोमलदन्तकुड्मलाग्रम्।
वदनकमलकं शिशोः स्मरामि
स्खलदसमञ्जसमुग्धजल्पितं ते ।।4।। (ज–)।

I constantly recall the little lotus-face of thine as a child, with causeless cry and laughter, with the tips of few soft bud-like visible and with a lisping, incoherent and charming prattle.

मित–। अनियतेति।

अन्वयः–शिशोः ते अनियतरुदितस्मितं विराजत्कपितय- कोमलदन्तकुट्नलाग्रं स्खलदसमञ्जसमुग्धजल्पितं वदनकमलकं स्मरामि।

व्याख्या–'शिशोः' बालिकायाः तव 'अनियतं' नियमरहितम् अहेतुकमित्यर्थः 'रुदितं' रोदनं 'स्मितं' हासश्च यस्मिन् तथाविधम्, किञ्च 'विराजन्ति, शोभमानानि

'कपितयानि' कियन्ति 'कोमलानि दन्तकुट्नलाग्राणि' दशनसकुलाग्राणि यस्मिन् तत, पुनश्च 'स्खलत्' अविस्पष्टम् 'असमञ्जसम्' असंलग्नं 'मुग्धं' मधुरं 'जल्पितं' भाषितं यस्मिन् तथाविधं 'वदनकमलकं' मुखपद्मं 'स्मरामि'।।

Notes. 1. अनियत etc.—नि+यम+क्त कर्मणि नियत restricted. न नियते अनियते unrestricted, *i.e.*, fitful. Vidyāsāgara has *causeless*. रुदितञ्च स्मितञ्च रुदिर्स्मिते। अनियते रुदितस्मिते यस्मिन्। 2. विराजत् etc.—दन्ताः कुद्मला इव दन्तकुट्नलाः। तेषाम् अग्नाणि only the tips are visible. The laugh and the cry expose the tips. 3. स्मरामि–I remember. It constantly comes up before my vision and the memory pains me. 4. स्खलत् etc.—One of Vidyāsāgara's manuscripts reads मञ्जु for मुग्ध। Remembering Bhavabl ūti's preference for alliteration I am inclined to prefer मञ्जु।

(*x*) **(ज–) भगवति वसुन्धरे, सत्यतिदृढ़ासि।**

Jan.—O mighty Earth, you are really very hard-hearted.

त्वं वह्निर्मुनयो वशिष्ठगृहिणी च यस्या विदु-
र्माहात्म्यं यदि वा रघोः कुलगुरुर्देवः स्वयं भास्करः।
विघां वागिव यामसूत भवती तद्वत्त या दैवतं
तस्यास्त्वं दुहितुस्तथा विशसनं किं दारुणेऽमृष्यष्थाः।।5।।

Why did you allow, O crnel one, the immolation, in that fashion, of that daughter of yours whose greatness yourself, Fire, the sages, Vaśiṣṭha's wife, and Gaṅgā too know, though certainly god Bhāskara himself, the ancestor of Raghu's race, knows ; whom you brought forth as the goddess of learning does knowledge and who was indeed a divinity like herself ?

मित–। त्वमिति।

अन्वयः–दारुणे, यस्या माहात्म्यं यदि वा रघोः कुल गुरुः स्वयं देवः भास्करः (वेत्ति), त्वं वक्तिः सुनयः वशिष्ठगृहिणौ गङ्गा च विदुः ; यां भवतौ विद्यां वागिव असूत ; या तु तद्वत् दैवतम् ; तस्याः दुहितुः तथा विशसनं किं त्वम् अमृष्यथाः।

व्याख्या–हे 'दारुणे' कठिने 'यस्याः' सीतायाः 'महात्मयं' महिमानं 'यदि वा यदि च रघोः कुलगुरुः' वंशकर्त्ता 'स्वयं देवो भास्करः' सूर्यः वेत्ति अधस्तनेषु पुनः 'त्वं वहिः मुनयः वशिष्ठगृहिणौ- अरुन्धती 'गङ्गा च विदुः' जानन्ति [वित्थ इति न्यार्य्यम्] 'यां' सीतां 'भवतो' त्वं विद्या देवी 'वागिव' सरस्वतीव 'अमूत' सूतवती

या तु तद्वत् सरस्वतीव 'दैवतं' देवता 'तस्याः दुहितुः' सीतायाः 'तथा' तेन प्रकारेण धीरेण विधिना 'विशसनं' मारण 'किं त्वम् अमृष्यथाः' सीढ़वती ।।

Notes. I. Remark—Here those who are aware of Sita's greatness are divided into two classes. In one class is Sun himself the worshipped of all, who transcends all else,. In the other class are lesser beings Earth (त्वम्), Fire, the sages, Vasistha's wife and गङ्गा । I. विदुः-विद+लट् अन्ति (उस्) । This is irregular. The rule "युष्मद्युपपदे समानाधिकरणे स्थानिन्यपि मध्यमः" requires the मध्यमपुरुष here because we have युष्मद् as उपपद here. वित्थ the correct form, does not preserve the metre, so it cannot be taken as copyists' slip. Call it a poetical license. 3. रथीः etc.—It is curious वशिष्ठ is omitted from the list though वशिष्ठगृहिणौ is there. We therefore suggest that the list of higher personages contain *two* names, viz, रथीः कुलगुरुः *i.e.,* वशिष्ठ and भास्करः। Consture—'यदि रथोः कुलगुरुः' वशिष्ठः 'स्वयं देवो भास्करी वा' सविता च। वा is often used in the sense of च। 4. तद्वत्- तया तुल्य वर्त्तते। इति तद्+वति। तद् here refers to वाच्। 'तद्वत्' वाग्देवतातुल्या। 5. दैवतम्-देवता एव इति देवताः देवता+अण्। "क्वचित् स्वार्थिकाः प्रकृतितो लिङ्गवचनान्यतिवर्त्तन्ते" इति क्लीवत्वम्।

नेपथ्ये-इत इतो भगवतीमहादेवौ।

(In the Dressing Room)—This way, worshipful lady and great queen, this way.

जनकः (दृष्ट्वा)-अये! गुष्टिनोपदिश्यमानमार्गा भगवत्यरून्धती। (उत्थाय) कां पुनर्महादेवीत्याह? (निरूप्य) हा कथं: महाराजदशरथस्य धर्म्मदाराः प्रियसखो मे कौसल्या! क एतत् प्रत्येति सैवेयमिति?

Janaka *(Espying)*—Hey ! Worshipful Arundhati with the way being shown her by Grishti. *(Rising)* Whom again does he address as Madadevi? *(Noticing)* Alas! Strange! my dear friend Kausalya the lawfully wedded wife of the great king Dasaratha! Who can believe that this is the herself?

आसीदियं दशरसीस्य गृहे यथा श्रौः
श्रीरेव वा मिुपमानपदेन सैषा।
कष्टं वातान्यदिव दैववशेन जाता
दुःखात्मकं किमपि भूतमहो विपाकः ।। 6 ।।

In the house of Dasaratha this one was like the goddess

of fortune ; or the goddess of fortune herself, why the epithet of comparison? O pity! This one, the same Kausalya, Alas ! has become some strange creature with grief for its body. What a change ! (6) (Jan—)

मित–।'गृष्टिः' कञ्चुकिनो नाम।'उपदिश्यमानः' निर्दिश्यमानः 'मार्गः' पन्थाः यस्याः सा। धर्मार्या दाराः 'धर्मदाराः' पत्नी।। असीदिति।

अन्वयः–दशरथस्य गृहे यथा श्रौः इयम् आसीत्। श्रीः एव वाए उपमानपदेन किम् ? कष्टं वत ! सा एषा दैव- वशेन अन्यत् किमपि दुःखात्मकं भूतं जात इव। अहो विपाकः!

व्याख्या–'दशरथस्य गृहे यथा श्रीः' लक्ष्मीः आसीत् तथा 'इयं कौसल्या' 'आसीत्' द्वितीया श्रीरिव इयं तत्र अलक्ष्यत। 'श्रीः एव वा' अथवा इयं कौसल्या एव तत्र श्रीः आसीत् न हि श्रीरिव इयम्। 'उपामानम्' उपमा। तस्य 'पदेन' तद्वोधकेन यथाशब्देन 'किम्' ? निष्प्रयोजनो यथाशब्दः। ''आसीदियं दशरथस्य गृहे श्रीः'' इत्येवोच्यताम्। 'कष्टं वत्' अहो कष्टम् ! 'सा एषा' कौसल्या 'दैववशेन' दुरदृष्टप्रभावात् 'अन्यत् किमपि' अपरम् अविज्ञातं किञ्चित् 'दुःखात्मकं' दुःखस्वरूपं दुःखोपादानकल्पितं 'भूवं' सत्वं 'जाता इव' तद्रूपेण इव। 'अहो विपाकः हा विपरिणतिः !

Notes. 1. अरुन्धती–He recognized अरुन्धती but not कौसल्या though दृष्ट्वा implies that both were seen. 2. कां पुनः etc.—He is now looking at कौसल्या alone, yet he cannot make her out. Hence the query—"Why is this other one addressed as महादेवी" ? 3. निरुप्य–निरूपण is careful scrutiny. Recognition has now come and he exclaims हा कथम् etc. 4. धर्मदाराः–धर्म is धर्मकर्म। These have to be performed in company with a lawfutly wedded wife. Hence expound धर्मार्था, धर्मप्रयोजना etc. दाराः, शाकपाथिवादिः। Malli expounds such compounds as धर्मस्य दाराः etc. like अश्वघासः। 4. उपमान etc. उप+मा+ल्युट् भावे उपमानम् comparison उपमा। It is different from उपमान–the standard of comparison—which is got with ल्युट् करणे।5. दुःखात्मकम्–आत्मन् here is स्वरूप। दुःखम् आत्मा स्वरूपम् अस्य whose essence is दुःख, *i.e.,* which is दुःखमय।

(*xii*) **(ज–) अयमपरः पापो दशाविपर्यासः।**

(Jan—) Here is another vile reversal of attitude (mental condition).

य एव मे जनः पूर्वमासीन्मूर्त्तौ महोत्सवः।
क्षते क्षारमिवासह्यं जातं तस्यैव दर्शनम्।। 7।।

Of that very person who was formely high restivity incarnate to me, the sight has now become unbearable like salt in an ulcer.

मित– । 'पाप:' पापी, लक्षणया अनभिप्रेत: । 'दशाया:' मनोगतस्य भावस्य विपर्यास:' परिवर्त्तनम् ।। य इति ।

अन्वय:–य एव जन: पूर्वं मे मूर्तो महोत्सव आसीत् तस्यैव दर्शनं क्षते क्षारमिव असह्यं जातम् ।

व्याख्या–सुगमा । 'पूर्वं' सीताविवासनात् पूर्वम् । 'मूर्त्त:' मूर्त्तिमान् । 'क्षाणं' लवणम् ।

Notes. 1. दशा etc.—दशा is अवस्था which may be mental also. विपर्यास *reversal* as in "विपर्यासं यातो घनविरलभाव: क्षितिरुहाम्" (II, sl. 27). 2. मूर्त्त:–मूर्च्छ+क्त कर्त्तरि मूर्त: embodied. 3. महोत् सव:–महान् उत्सव: । Hence her sight was very much अभिप्रेत । 4. क्षारम्–क्षार salt. The neuter use of क्षार is against पाणिनि । The rule "रोपध:" makes it masucline. 5. असह्यम्–सोढुं शक्यम इति सह+यत् कर्मणि सह्यम् bearable. न सह्यम् । Hence her sight has become अनभिप्रेत । The change from अभिप्रेत to अनभिप्रेत is a complete reversal (दशाविपर्यास) ।

(*xiii*) **(तत: प्रविशति अरुन्धती कौसल्या कञ्चुकी च)**

(*Then enter Arundhatī, Kausalyā and Kañcukī*)

अरुन्धती–ननु ब्रवामि "द्रष्टव्य: स्वयमुपेत्य वैदेह:" इत्येष व: कुलगुरोरादेश:, अत एवाहं प्रेषिता । तत् कोऽयं पदे पदे महाननध्यवसाय: ?

Arundhatī—Well, I tell you. The king of the Videhas has to be personally approached and seen by you" this is the command of your family-preceptor; for that very reason I have been sent here. Then what towering irresolution is this at every step ?

कञ्चुकी–देवि संस्तम्भयात्मानम्, अनुरुध्यस्व भगवतो वशिष्ठस्यादेशम्, इति विज्ञापयामि ।।

Kañcukī—Queen, I submit that you should steady yourself and respect the command of mighty Vaśiṣṭha.

कौसल्या–एरिसे काले मिहिलाधिदेवो दट्ठब्बो त्ति समं एब्ब

सब्बदुक्खाइं समुव्भवन्ति, ण सक्कणोमि उद्घट्टमाणमूलबन्धणं हिअअं अवत्थाविदुं [ईदृशे काले मिथिलाधिदेवो द्रष्टव्य इति सममेव सर्वदुःखानि समुद्भवन्ति, न शक्नोमि उद्घट्टमानमूलबन्धनं हृदयमवस्थापियतुम्]

Kausalyā—My sorrows, all of them indeed, reappear simultaneously at (the thought) that the lord of Mithilā has to be seen at such a time. I cannot steady my heart the ligatures of the very bottom of which are being snapped.

मित–। 'ननु' आक्षेपे। 'उपेत्य समीपे गत्वा। 'अध्यवसायः' आग्रहः। 'अनध्यवसायः' अनिच्छा। 'पदे पदे' प्रतिपदक्षेपम्। 'कोऽयम् अनध्यवसायः निन्द्रोऽयमनध्यवसायः। गुरोरादेशः तथापि नेच्छसि द्रष्टुमित्यनुचितम्।। 'संस्तम्भय' स्थिरीरकुरु। 'अनुरुध्यस्व' सम्मानय।। 'ईदृशे काले' सति सर्वनाशे, यदा तस्य कन्यारत्नं विहापितं तदा इत्यर्थः। मन्ये 'सर्वाणि दुःखानि सममेव' युगपदेव 'समुद्भवन्ति' पुनरुपजायन्ते। शोक क्षोभाच्च 'उद्वट्टमानम्' उन्मथ्यमानं मूलबन्धनम्' अन्तस्तलग्रन्थिः यस्य तादृशं 'हृदयं अवस्थापयितुं' स्थिरीकर्तुं 'न शक्नोमि"।।

Notes. 1. ननु etc.—Evidently अरुन्धती has been remonstrating with कौसल्या all the way for her unwillingness to see जनक। 2. तत् कोऽयम् etc.—Since the कुलगुरु commands, it does not look well for you to heasitate. 3. संस्तम्भय–The Kañcukī has noticed her emotion. It is not perverseness that keeps her away from जनक, but, as she explains, at the thought of seeing him all the miseries of her life do as if come up simultaneously to her.

(*xiv*) **अरुन्धती–अत्र कः सन्देहः?**

Arun—What doubt can there be in it ?

सन्तानवाहीन्यपि मानुषाणां दुःखानि सद्बन्धुवियोगजानि।
दृष्टे जने प्रेयसि दुःसहानि स्त्रोतः सहस्त्रैरिव संप्लवन्ते।। ४।।

Man's sorrows arising from the loss of good friends throught flowing continuously, become unbearable on some dear one being seen and gush forth as if in thousands of streams.

मित–। 'अत्र' अस्मिन् विषये "सर्वदुःखानि समुद्भवन्ति" इत्येतत्प्रति।। सन्तानेति।

अन्वयः–मानुषाणां सद्बन्धुवियोगजानि दुःखानि सन्तानवाहीन्यपि प्रेयसि जने दृष्टे दुःसहानि (सन्ति) स्रोतः सहस्रैरिव संपल्लवन्ते।

व्याख्या–'मानुषाणां सद्बन्धूनां सुहृद्रत्नानां' वियोगात्' विनाशात्' जातानि दुःखानि 'सन्तानेन' अविच्छेदेन 'वहन्ति' प्रवर्त्त मानानि अपि 'प्रेयसि प्रियतरे' जने दृष्टे दुःसहानि' सोढ़ मशक्यानि 'स्रोतसहस्रैरिव' संख्यातीतधाराभिरिव 'संपल्लवन्ते' समुच्छलन्ति।।

Notes. 1. सन्तान etc,—सम्+तन+घञ् भावे सन्तानः continuity. सन्तानेन वोढुं शीलमेषाम् इति सन्तान+वह+णिनि कर्त्तरि ताच्छील्ये। Flowring continuously, *i.e.*, they are being borne in silence. 2. सद्बन्धु etc.—सन् बन्धुः सद्बन्धः। वि+युज+घञ् भावे वियोगः loss. etc. 3. प्रेयसि–अतिशयेन प्रियः इति प्रिय+ईयसुम् प्रेयान्। तस्मिन्। No comparison is implied. 4. दुःसहानि–दुर्+सह+खल् कर्मणि दुःसह। They were bearable so long, but the sight of some dear one makes them unbearable. cp. "स्वजनस्थ हि दुःखमग्रतो विवृतद्वारमिवोपजायते"–Kālidāsa. 5. स्रोतः सहस्रैः–सहस्र is not actually a thousand, but merely a large. स्रोतसां सहस्राणि। तैः। 3या करणे।

(*xv*) **कोसल्या–कहं बच्छाए वहूए एब्वं गदे तस्म राएसोण मुहं दंसेम्ह [कथं वत्साया बध्वा एवं गते तस्य राजर्षेर्मुखं दर्शयामः] ?**

Kaus.—Such a fate having befallen our dear daughter-in-law can I show my face to that royal sage ?

अरुन्धती–

एष वः श्लाघ्यसम्बन्धी जनकानां कुलोद्वहः !
याज्ञवल्क्यो मनिर्यस्मै ब्रह्मपारायणं जगौ।। 8।।

Arun.—Here is your worthy relation, the maiastay of the house of Janaka, unto whom the *sage* Jainyavalkya sang the Vedas in their totality.

मित–।'एवं गते' ईदृशे प्राप्ते, धीरे विशसने जाते इत्यर्थः।'राजवर्षेः' जनकस्य। सम्बन्धमात्रविवक्षया षष्ठी।। एष इति।

अन्वयः–एष वधः श्लाघ्यसम्बन्धी जनकानां कुलोद्दहः यस्म मुनिः याज्ञवल्क्यो ब्रह्मपारायणं जगौ।

व्याख्या–'एषः' दृश्यमानः'वः श्लाघ्यः सम्बन्धी, स्तुत्यो वैवाहिकः जनकानां' 'जनकवंशीयानां' कुलोद्वहः' कुलधुरन्धरो राजर्षिर्जनकः 'यस्मै' यमभिप्रेत्यस 'मुनिः

यज्ञवल्क्यः ब्रह्मणो' वेदस्य 'पारायणं' पारगमनं साकल्येन पाठमित्यर्थः 'जगौ' गौतवान्। यं मुनिर्याज्ञवल्क्यो आदित आरभ्य अन्तं यावत् वेदानध्यापयामास इत्यर्थः।।

Notes. 1. मुखं etc.—I am ashamed to show my face to him. 2. एष वः etc.—They have now come up to Janaka. This is an introduction—अरुन्धती introduces जनक to कौसल्या–not a reply to Kausalyā's remark above. 3. श्लाघ्य–etc.—श्लाघ+णयत् कर्मणि श्लाघ्यः one to be proud of. etc. 4. जनकानाम–जनक here stands for all the followers of जनक। 5. यस्मै–चतुर्थी सम्प्रदाने by the rule "कर्मणा यमभिप्रैति स सम्प्रमानम्"। 6. ब्रह्मपारायणम्–पारस्य अयनं पारायणम् reaching of the other end. But it has a technical sense. Crossing a river, or a country is not पारायणम्। It is restricted to mean the reading of a book from first to last. Hence it is a संज्ञाशब्द। न becomes ण by the rule 'पूर्वपदात् संज्ञायामगः"। 7. जगौ–he sang. Reading is here singing. याज्ञवल्क्य read with him the entire Vedas. याज्ञवल्क्य got the Vedas from the Sun himself and he communicated his knowledge to जनक। The fact is a point of no small honour to जनक। Hence श्लाघ्यसम्बन्धी।

(*xvi*) कौसल्या–एसो सो महाराअस्स हि अहआणन्दो वच्छाए बहूए पिदा राएसी। हद्दी हद्दी सम्भाविद म्हि अणुवत्थिदमहूसवे दिअहे। हा देब्ब सव्वं एब्बं तं णत्थि [एष स महाराजस्य हृदयानन्दः वत्साया बध्वाः पिता राजर्षिः। हा धिक् हा धिक्, सम्भावितास्मि अनुपस्थितमहोत्सवे दिवसे। हा दैव सर्वमेव तत् नास्ति]।

Kaus.—Here is he, royal sage, the heart's delight of the great king, the father of our dear daughter-in-law. Alas ! Alas ! I am honoured on a day when no great joy has come up to me. O fate, all that indeed exists no longer.

जनकः–(उपसृत्य)–भगवत्यरुन्धति वैदेहः सीरध्वजोऽभिवादयते।

Jan. *(Approaching)*—Worshipful Arundhatī , Sīradhvaja the king of Videha salutes you.

यया पूतम्मन्यो निधिरपि पवित्रस्य महसः।
पतिस्ते पूर्वेषामपि खलु गुरुणां गुरुतमः।
त्रिलोकौमङ्गल्यामवदितललोलेन शिरसा
जगद्वन्ध्यां देवीकमुषसिव वन्दे भगवतीम् ।। 10।।

With my head going down to the earth's suface I salute your worshipful self, adorable of the worlds like divine Usas, the benefactor of the three worlds, by whom your husband cosiders himself sanctified though he is an abode of holy light and is the great preceptor of even the old preceptors.

मित– । 'हृदयस्य आनन्दः' आनन्दकरः। 'सम्भाविता' समानिता दर्शनदानेन इति शेषः।'अनुपस्थितः' अनागतः 'महोत्सवः' परमानन्दः यस्मिन् तस्मिन् 'दिवसे' काले। दृष्टेऽस्मिन् आनन्दमनुभवति स्म महाराजः, मया पुनरद्यायं दृष्टः आनन्दस्तु नागतो मे इत्यर्थः।'सर्वमेव तत्' पूर्वानुभूतं 'नास्ति सर्वं विपरीतमधुना जातामित्यर्थः।। 'शैहेदः' विदेहानां राजा 'सीरध्वजः' जनकः।। यत्रेति।

अन्वयः–अवनितललोलेन शिरसा त्रिलोकीमङ्गल्यां देवीम् उषसमिव जगद्वन्दयां भगवतीं वन्दे यया पवित्रस्य महसः निधिरपि पूर्वेषां गुरुणां गुरुतमः अपि ते पतिः पूतमन्यः खलु।

व्याख्या–'अव नितले' भूपृष्ठे 'लोलेन' चलितेन 'शिरसा त्रिलोक्याः' त्रिभुवनस्य 'मङ्गल्यां' प्रवोधविधानेन मङ्गलकरीं 'देवीम् उषसमिव' प्रातःसन्ध्यामिव 'जगद्वन्द्रयां' सर्वलोकपूज्यां 'भगवतीं' समग्रमहात्म्यामयीं त्वां 'वन्दे' नमामि 'यया' भगवत्या स्वयं 'पवित्रस्य महसः' पूतस्य तेजसः 'निधि अपि' आस्पदमपि 'पूर्वेषां' प्राचीनानां 'गुरुणां' याज्ञवाल्क्यप्रभृतीनां 'गुरुतमः अपि' पूज्यतमः अपि 'ते पतिः' भर्त्ता वशिष्ठः 'पूतन्मन्यः खलु' आत्मानं पवित्रमेव मन्यते। ब्रह्मपुत्रः स्वयं वशिष्ठोऽपि भवत्या पूतः तद्भवतीं वन्दे इत्यर्थः।।

Notes. 1. हृदयानन्दः–हृदयम् आनन्दयति इति हृदय+आ+नन्द+णिच्+अण् कर्त्तरि। 2. सम्भाविता etc.—I am honoured by his sight, but no joy greets me. The reason follows 3. सर्वमेव etc.—This is because the old state of things (सर्वमेव तत्) has changed. 4. पूतम्मन्यः–पूतमात्मानं मन्य ते इति पूत+मन+खश् कर्त्तरि। 5. त्रिलोकी etc.—मङ्गले साध्वी इति मङ्गल+यत् मङ्गल्या benefactress. त्रयाणां लोकानां समाहारः त्रिलोकी। त्रिलोक्या, ताम्। Or त्रिलोकीमङ्गले साध्वी। ताम्। This is taken with both उषसम् and भगवतीम्। It seems better to make it qualify उषसम् only. उषम् is त्रिलोकीमङ्गल्या because she rouses people from the stupor of sleep. 6. उषसम्–उषस् here is the presiding deity of the dawn called पितृप्रसू। It is then feminine. "उषः प्रत्युषसि क्लीवं पितृप्रस्वाञ्च योषिति" इति मेदिनी।

(*xvii*) **अरुन्धती–परं ज्योतिस्ते प्रकाशताम्, अयं त्वां पुनातु देवः परोजयाः य एष तपति।**

Arun—-May the light Supreme appear unto you ; may the god that transcends *Rajas*—this one that shines—sanctify you.

जनकः–आर्य गृष्टे अपि कुशलमस्याः प्रजापालमातुः।

Jan.—Noble Gṛṣṭī, is it all well with this mother of the guardian of his subjects ?

कञ्चुकी (स्वगतम्)–निरवशेषमतिनिष्ठुरमुपालब्धाः स्मः।

Kañch. (*To himself*)—We have been soundly and most cruelly rebuked.

(प्रकाशम्) राजर्षे अनेनैव मन्युना चिरपरित्यक्तरामभद्रमुखचन्द्रदर्शनां नार्हसि त्वं दुःखयितुमतिदुःखितां देवीम्। रामभद्रस्यापि दैवदुर्नियोगः कोऽपि यत् किल समन्तात् प्रवृत्तबीभत्स किं वदन्तीकाः पौरजानपदा नाग्निशुद्धिम् अल्पकाः प्रतिपद्यन्ते इत्यतो दारुणमनुष्ठितम्।

(*Aloud*) O royal sage, it behoves you not to grieve the much-grieved queen by whom from this very grief, the sight of the moon-face of Rāmabhadra has been long shunned. Of Rāmabhadra again it was an inconceivable misdirection by destiny that this curel deed was done because the mean townsmen and villagers, through whom disgusting slander spread all round, would not accept the purification by Fire.

मित–।'परं' सर्वोत्तम 'ज्योतिः' तेजः परब्रह्म इत्यर्थः।'प्रकाशताम्' आविर्भवतु। ब्रह्मदर्शनं ते भवतु इत्यर्थः।'रजसः' रजोगुणस्य 'परः' दूरवर्ती 'परोरजाः' रजोव्यतिरिक्तः इत्यर्थः।'य एष तपति' इति देवः सवित लक्ष्यते।।'प्रजापालस्य' प्रजारञ्जनतत्परस्य रामस्य। प्रजारञ्जनार्थं साध्वीं पत्नीं व्यक्तवतः इत्याक्षेपः। कौसल्यां प्रति साक्षात् कुशलप्रश्नः परिहतः इति कुषलता हृदयस्य।। 'निरवशेषं' यथा तथा 'उपालब्धाः' तिरस्कृताः। ''प्रजापाल'' इत्यनेन तिरस्कारस्य विषयः समग्र एव उक्तः कोऽपि नावशिष्यते। 'अतिनिष्ठुरं यथा तथा 'उपालब्धाः'। उक्तिप्रकारश्च कौसल्याया इति वक्तव्ये प्रजापालमातुरिति नितरां कर्कश इत्यर्थः।'अनेनैव' सीताविवासनकृतेन 'मन्युना' शोकेन 'चिरं' दीर्घकालं 'परित्यक्तं' रामभद्रस्य मुखचन्द्रदर्शनं' यया तादृशीम्।

'समन्तात्' सर्वासु दिक्षु 'प्रवृत्ता' प्रचरिता 'बीभत्सा' जुगुप्सिता 'किंवदन्ती' अपवादः येभ्यः ते 'अल्पका' क्षुद्राः 'पौरजानपदाः अग्निशुद्धिं न प्रतिपद्यन्ते' नाङ्गीकुर्वन्ति 'इत्यतः' एतस्मात् हेतोः 'दारुणं' सीतापरित्यागरूपं घोरं कार्यम् 'अनुष्ठितम्'। एष च 'रामभद्रस्य कोऽपि' अचिन्तनीयः 'दैवकृतो दुर्नियोगः दुर्व्यापारः। दैवेन परतन्त्रो राम एवमकरोत्, मृष्यतां तस्य तत्।।

Notes. 1. परोरजाः–See परःसहस्राः, I, sl. 15. 2. प्रजापालमातुः–प्रजाः पालयतीति–प्रजा+पा+णिच्+अण् कर्त्तरि प्रजापालः। Refers to राम्। तस्यमाता। तस्याः। He does not address कौसल्या directly which shows estrangement. This is a rubuke (see next). 3. निरवशेषम्–अवशिष्यते इति अव+शिष+घञ् कर्मणि अवशेषः remainder. निगतः अवशेषः, अस्मात्। तत् यथा तथा। All has been siad that could be said against us, nothing left unsaid. That single word प्रजापाल instead of रामभद्र includes all manner of उपालम्भ। "He tha cared for प्रज्ञा alone" is a censure that cannot be improved upon. 4. अतिनिष्ठुरम्–प्रजापालमातृ in place of कौसल्या is extremely cruel. The tree is known by its fruit. The considerateness of प्रजापाल's mother can be gauged from that of the प्रजापाल himself. Next look at the reference in third person to one who at one time was amongst his dearest. What can be more cruel than this ? 5. चिर etc,—For समास see मित–। Here चिर is a misrepresentation. It is true she has not been seeing Rāma's face since her departure from अयोध्या 12 years ago. But that was because of Ṛṣyaśṛṅga's याग not अनेनैव मन्धुना। InAct II we are told that the याग is finished and only 2 or 3 days have elapsed since then. So Kausalyā's avoidance of Rāma's sight on account of this मन्यु is only of 2 or 3 day's duration. The old man deliberately exaggerates to produce some impression on Janaka's mind. 6. समन्तात्–etc.—बीभत्स explained (I, para lxvii). For किंवदन्ती see I, sl. 42. गौरादित्वात् ङीष्। The कप् is by "नद्यृतश्च"।

(*xviii*) जनकः–आः कोऽयमग्निर्नाम अस्मत्प्रसूतिपरिशोधने ? कष्टम् ! एवंवादिना जनेन रामपरिभूता अयि वयं पुनः परिभूयामहे।

Jan.—Ah ! who, pray is this Fire in the purification of my child ? O woe ! Insulted by Rāma, I am again being insulted by one talking thus.

अरुन्धती (निःश्वस्य)—एवमेतत्। अग्निरिति वत्सां प्रति परिलघून्यक्षराणि, सीता इत्येव पर्याप्तम्। हा वत्से,

Arun. (*Sighing*)—So it is. The word 'Fire' sounds small by the side of our child ; (the word) 'Sītā' is indeed enough. Alas ! my child.

शिशुर्वा शिष्या वा यदसि मम तत् तिष्ठतु तथा
विशुद्धेरुत्कर्षस्त्वयि तु मम भक्तिं जनयति।
शिशुत्वं स्त्रैणं वा भवतु ननु वन्द्यासि जगतां
गुणाः पूजास्थानं गुणिषु न च लिङ्गं न च वयः ।।11।।

Whether child or pupil, whatever you are to me, let that stand as it is ; but the climax of purity rouses in me a sense of reverence for you. Childhood or womanhood let there be, you are surely to be adored by all the worlds. Virtues are the objects of worshipful the virtuous, neither sex nor age.

मित– ।'आः' इति सकारान्तमव्ययम् इह कोपे। कञ्चुकिना अग्नेः प्रमङ्गः कृतः इति कोपः। 'नाम' इति इह कुत्सायामव्ययम्। सीतयाः परिशोधने अग्निः प्रसरति, अहो अनात्मज्ञता ! इत्यग्रेः कुत्सा। 'प्रसूतिः' सन्ततिः सीता। 'जनेन' कञ्चुकिना। 'रामेण परिभूताः' विमानिताः। प्राक् सीतामग्निप्रवेशं कारयित्वा विमानना मे कृता रामेण, अद्य पुनस्तदेव समर्थयमानेन गृष्टिना इत्यर्थः।। 'एवमेतत्' अग्निर्न कोऽपि इति सत्यमेव। 'वत्सां प्रति' वत्सापेक्षया। 'परिलघूनिं' सर्वथा हीनानि। परस्परापेक्षया सीता इति महत्तरम् अग्निरिति लघुरतम् इत्यर्थः। 'पर्याप्तम्' परिपूर्णम्, न हि किञ्चिदपि इह असम्पूर्णम।। शिशुरिति।

अन्वयः–मम शिशुर्वा शिष्या वा यत् असि तत् तथा तिष्ठतु। विशुद्धेः उत्कर्षस्तु त्वयि मम भक्तिं जनयति। ननु शिशुत्वं स्त्रैणां वा भवतु जगतां वन्द्या असि। गुणिषु गुणाः पूजास्थानं न च लिङ्गं न च वयः।

व्याख्या–'मम' सम्बन्धे त्वं शिशुर्वा' बालिका वा 'शिष्या वा' उपेदश्या वा 'यत् असि तत् तथा तिष्ठतु' आस्ताम् त्वमपिरणतवयाः अपरिपक्वबुद्धिश्चेति। 'विशुद्धेः' पवित्रतायाः 'उत्कर्षस्तु' आतिशयं पुनः 'त्वयि मम भक्तिं जनयति, मन्ये मम वन्द्या असि। अत्यल्पमिदमुच्यते मया 'ननु' असंशयं शिशुत्वं असि' किं पुनमर्म। तत्र कारणमाह–'गुणिषु' विषये 'गुणाः पूजास्थानं' वन्दनपात्रं 'न च लिङ्गं नैव पुंस्त्वादिकं

'न च वय:' नैव वृद्धत्वादिकम्। गुणा: सन्ति त्वयि इति जगतां तत: अग्नेरपि वन्द्रयासि त्वं, तत् नूनम् अग्निरिति त्वां प्रति परिलघून्यक्षराणि।

Notes. 1. अस्मत् etc.—विषयाधिकरणे 7मी। प्रसूयते इति प्र+सू+क्तिन् कर्मणि प्रसूति: offspring. 2. परिलघूनि–The न does not become ण because परि is not an उपसर्ग here. The exposition is परितो लघूनि परिलघूनि, inferior every way, प्रादितत्–।3. शिशुर्वा etc.—The first half of the verse speaks of सीता with reference to अरुन्धती। सीता was शिशु by the side of अरुन्धती and she was actually her शिष्या। From both these considerations it is अरुन्धती who should be वन्द्य of सीता। But no, mark the difference (तु–भेदे) अरुन्धती is prompted to adore सीता। 4. शिशुत्वम् etc.— This is not at all derogatory to अरुन्धती, for the whole universe has to bow down to सीता though with respect to the universe सीता is शिशु and only a स्त्री। स्त्रिया भाव इति स्त्री+अञ् स्त्रैणम्। गुणा: etc.—This is an adaptation of Kālidāsa's "तामगौरवभेदेन सुर्नीश्चापश्यदीश्वर:। स्त्री पुमाननित्यनास्थैषा वृत्तं हि महितं सताम्।।" "गुणा: पूजास्थानम्–" and 'वृत्त हि माहितं सताम्" both are familiar quotations.

(*xix*) **कौसल्या–अमो उमीलन्ति वेअणाओ [अहो उन्मीलन्ति वेदना:]। (इति मूर्च्छति)।**

Kaus.—O my sores re-open ! (*faints away*).

जनक:–हा कष्टम् ! किमेतत् ?

Jan.—O woe ! What is this ?

अरुन्धती–राजर्षे किमन्यत् ?

Arun.—What else, O royal sage ?

स राजा तत् सौख्यं स च शिशुजनस्ते च दिवसा:
स्मृतावाविर्भूतं त्वयि सुहृदि दृष्टे तदखिलम् !
विपाके घोरेऽस्मिन्नथ खलु विमूढा तव सखी
पुरन्ध्रीणां चेत: कुसुमसुकुमारं हि भवति ।।12।।

That king, that happiness, those young people and those days, all this has reappeared to her memory on seeing you her friend; and then, at this terrible pass, your friend has indeed fainted away. [Or—at this terrible pass, on seeing you her friend, that king...fainted away]. Verily, the heart of matrons is tender as a flower.

मित– ।'उन्मीलन्ति' आविर्भन्ति 'वेदना:' व्यथा:। भूयोऽपि दुःखवेगमनुभवामि इत्यर्थ:।। स इति।

अन्वय:–सुहृदि त्वयि दृष्टे स राजा, तत् सौख्यम्, स च शिशुजन: ते च दिवसा: अखिलं तत् स्मृती आविर्भतम्। अथ अस्मिन् घोरे विपाके तव सखी विमूढ़ा खलु। [यद्वा–घोरे विपाके सुहृदि त्वयि दृष्टें स राजा इत्यादि]। पुरन्ध्रीणां चेत: कुसुमकुसुमा भवति हि।

व्याख्या–'सुहृदि' मित्रोत्तमे 'त्वयि दृष्टे स राजा' दशरथ:' तत् सौख्यं' राजचक्रवर्त्तिनो महिषीत्वेन अनुभूतानि सुखानि तत: कृतदारे तनये 'स च शिशुजन:' सीतारामादि: 'ते च' नयैर्वधूभिरुत्सवपूर्णा दिवसा:' इति 'अखिलं' सर्वं 'तत् स्मतौ आविर्भूतम्' उदितम्। 'अथ' अनन्तरम् आविर्भावात् परम् 'अस्मिन् घोरे विपाके' सर्वेषां दु:खानां युगपदुदयरूपे दु:सहे व्यक्तिरे 'तव सखी' कौसल्या दु:खभरम् असहमाना 'विमूढ़ा खलु' मूर्च्छिता एव। [यद्वा–'घोरे अस्मिन् विपाके' दु:सहे एतस्मिन् दशाविपर्यासे 'सुहृदि त्वयि दृष्टे स राजा' इत्यादि। प्राग्वत्]। कथमेतन्न सोढ़म् अनया इत्याह 'पुरन्ध्रीणां' पतिपुत्रवतीनां स्त्रीणां 'चेत: कुसुमम्' इव 'सुकुमारं' कोमलं 'भवति हि' भवत्येव।।

Notes. 1. अखिलम्–Here इति is understood referring to all those that are enumerated, इति अखिलं तत् etc. Hence तत् is singular because a single group is intended. 2. विपाके–वि+पच+घञ् भावे विपाक: विषम: परिणाम:। We have suggested two ways of viewing the विपाक। (i) The simultaneous recollection of all is a विपाक। (ii) The altered circumstances now prevailing are a विपाक। The second view seems more natural.

(*xx*) **जनक:–हन्त हन्त सर्वथा नृशंसोऽस्मि संवृत्त: स: चिरस्य दृष्टान् प्रियसुहृद: प्रियान् दारान् न स्निग्ध पश्यामि।**

Jan.—Alas ! Alas ! I have turned altogether heartless as I do not look kindly upon the beloved wife of my dear friend seen after (such) a long time.

स सम्बन्धो श्लाघ्य: प्रियसुहृदसी तञ्च हृदयं
स चानन्द: साक्षादपि च निखिलं जीवितफलम्।

शरीरं जीवो वा यदधिकमतो वा प्रियतरं
महाराजः श्रीमान् किमिव मम नासीद्दशरथः ।।13।।(ज–)

What was he not to me, the great and illustrious king Daśaratha? He was an estimble connection ; he was a dear friend ; he was my very heart ; (to me) he was joy incarnate and indeed the entire object of life, be it the body or soul, or what is higher and dearer than either of these two. Jan.—)

मित– ।'नृशंसः' निष्ठुरः।'चिरस्य' इत्यव्ययम्। चिरेण कालेन इत्यर्थः।'स्निग्धं' सस्नेहम्।। स इति।

अन्वयः–श्रीमान् महाराजो दशरथः मम किमिव न आसीत् ? स श्लाघ्यः सम्बन्धी असौ प्रियसुहृत्, तत् हृदयञ्च, साक्षात् आनन्दश्च सः, अपि च निखिलं जीवितफलं शरीरं जीवो वा अतो वा अधिकं प्रियतरं तत्।

व्याख्या–'श्रीमान्' श्रिया लीलाभूमिः 'महाराजः' राजचक्रवर्ती 'दशरथः मम किमिव न आसीत्' सर्वमेव मम सः। तथा च 'स श्लाघ्यः' स्तुत्यः 'सम्बन्धी' वैवाहिको मे।'असौ' मम 'प्रियसुहृत्' प्रेयान् सखा।'तत्' हृदयञ्च'। विधेयप्राधान्यात् क्लीवत्वम्।'साक्षात्' मूर्तिमान् 'आनन्दश्च सः' मे।'अपि च' स मे 'निखिलं' समग्रं 'जीवितस्य' जीवनधारणास्य 'फलं–तत् फलं शरीरं' देहो वा भवतु देहव्यक्तिरिक्तः 'जीवो वा' जीवात्मा वा भवतु 'अतो वा' अथवा अस्मात् शरीरात् जीवात् वा 'अधिकं' प्रशस्यम् अतएव 'प्रियतरं यत्' परमात्मा इति तदपि मे दशरथ एव।।

Notes. 1. नृशंसः–See I, sl. 45. 2. जीवितफलम्–जीव+क्त भावे जीवितम् living. तस्य फलम्। But what is this फल of life? Those, who hold that beyond the body nothing exists, will answer—it is शरीरम्। Other will say it is जीवः the occupier of the body. Yet a different class will deem ब्रह्म (ब्रह्मप्राप्ति) as the aim of life. These different views are taken up in शरीरं जीवो वा etc.

(*xxi*) **(ज–) कष्टम् ! इयमेव सा कौसल्या।**

(Jan—) O woe ! This very one is the same Kausalyā.

यदस्याः पत्युर्वा रहसि परमं दूषितमभू-
दभूवं दम्पत्योः पृथगहमुपालम्भविषयः।
प्रसादे कोपे वा तदनु मदधीनो विधिरभू-
दलं वा तत् स्मृत्वा दहति यदवस्कन्द्य हृदयम्।।14।।

Whatever serious annoyance occurred unto this one or her husband in secret, I used to become the recipient of the complaint of the couple separately ; and then regarding the pacification as well as (for the cause) for the irritation, the steps were under my control. Or, away with recalling that which overhelms and consumes the heart.

मित–। 'इयमेव' विपाके प्रत्यभिज्ञातुशक्या 'सा' मे प्रियसखी 'कौसल्या'।। यदिति। अन्वयः–अस्याः पत्युर्वा रहसि यत् परमं दूषितमभूत (तत्र) अहं दम्पत्योः पृथक् उपालम्भविषयः अभूवम्। तदनु कोपे प्रसादे वा विधिः मदधीनः अभूत। (अथ) वा यत् हृदयम् अवस्कन्द्य दहति तत् स्मृत्वा अलम्। व्याख्या–'अस्याः' कौसल्यायाः पत्युर्वा' भत्तुर्दशरथस्य वा 'रहसि' मिथः 'यत्' यदेव 'परमं गुरु 'दूषितं' दोषः प्रणयापराधः 'अभूत' तत्र 'अहं दम्पत्योः' जायापत्योः कौसल्यादशरथयोः 'पृथक्' विभिन्ने काले 'उपालम्भस्य' तिरस्कारस्य अन्योऽन्यगर्हायाः 'विषयः' आधारः 'अभूवम्' मय्येव परस्परोपालम्भः निवदितः। 'तदनु' उपालम्भनिवेदनात् परं 'कीपे कोपकाले' यावत् कोपो न प्रशान्तः तावत् 'प्रसादे वा' यदा प्रसन्नता पुनरागता तदा 'विधिः' परस्परव्यवहारः 'मदधीनः' यथा भया उपदिष्टः तथैव 'अभूत्'।'वा अथवा 'यत्' वस्तु 'हृदयम् अवस्कन्द्य' आक्रम्य 'दहति' तापयति 'तत् स्मृत्वा अलम् निष्प्रयोजनं तत्स्मरणम्।।

Notes. 1. कष्टम्–He deplores the change, 2. यत्–The correlative तत्र is understood. Or take it as in अव्यय implying हेतु। अहम् उपालम्भविषयः अभूवम् because (यत्) दूषितमभूत। 3. परमम्–Grave. They did not approach me at evey slight ruffle, but only when greatly (परम) annoyed. 4. दम्पत्यौः–जाया च पतिश्च दम्पती, जम्पती जायापती। तयोः। 5. उपालम्भ etc.—विषय is used here in a peculiar sense. Usually one complained against is called the विषय of the complaint. Here it is one with whom the complaint is lodged. 6. प्रसादे etc.—So long as the कोप lasted and also when reconciliation. (प्रसाद) came. 7. महधीनः–मयि अधि इति मदघि+ख (ईन) by the rule "–अध्युत्तरपदात् खः"। सप्तमी तत्–अधि being of the शौण्डादि class. 8. अलं वा etc.—No use calling back all this to mind, it only pains.

(*xxii*) अरुन्धती–हा कष्टम् ! चिरनिरुद्धनिःश्वासनिष्ठुरं हृदयमस्याः।

Arun.—O woe ! Her heart has become still from breath held very long.

जनकः–हा प्रियसखि। (इति कमण्डलदकेन सिञ्चति)।

Jan.—Alas ! My dear friend. (*Sprinkles with water from his jug*).

कञ्चुकी–सुहृदिव प्रकटय सुखप्रदः
प्रथममेकरसामनुकूलताम्।
पुनकाण्डविवर्त्तनदारुणो
विधिरहो विशिनष्टि मनोरुजम्।।15।।

Kañc.—Alas ! Fate at first having shown concord of uniform flavour, offers comforts like a friend ; again, becoming discordant with an unexpected turn, heightens the pang of the heart.

मित–।'चिरनिरुद्धः' यः 'निःश्वासः' तेन 'नष्ठुरं' निश्चलम्।। सुहृदिति।

अन्वयः–अहो विधिः प्रथमम् एकरसाम् अनुकूलतां प्रकटय सुहदिव सुखप्रदः, पुनः अकाण्डविवर्त्तनदारुणः (सन्) मनोरुजं विशिनष्टि।

व्याख्या–'अहो' खेद एष यत् 'विधिः' देवं 'प्रथसं' पूर्वम् 'एकरसाम्' अभिन्नप्रकृतिकाम् अविच्छिन्नामित्यर्थः 'अनुकूलतां सहायतां 'प्रकटयं दर्शयित्वा सततमनुकूलो भवन्नित्यर्थः 'सुहविदव' मित्रवत् 'सुखप्रदः' आनन्दवर्द्धनः। आदौ प्रसन्ने विधौ राजचक्रवर्त्तिना भर्त्रा, पुरुषसिंहेन पुत्रेणा, रमणीरत्नेन च स्नुषया सुखसन्तानवती इयमासीत् कौसल्या इत्याशयः।'पुनः' पश्चात् 'अकाण्डे' असमये यत्'विवर्त्तनं' अन्यथाभवनं तेन 'दारूणः निष्ठुरः सन्' मनोरुजं' हृदयवेदनां 'विशिनष्टि' विशेषयति वर्द्धयति। सम्प्रति तु विधुरे विधौ दुःखमयं सर्वमस्याः इति स्वेदः।।

Notes. 1. चिर etc.—निष्ठुर obdurate, hence motionless. The heart has stopped throbbing. 2. प्रकटय–प्र+कट+णिच्+ल्यप् Having disclosed. 3. सुखप्रदः–सुखं प्रददाति इति सुख+प्र+दा+क कर्त्तरि। Usually this is taken to qualify सुहृत्। We predicate this of विधि। प्रथमम् and पुनः favour our interpretation. Two different stages are contemplated here with a separate assertion suiting each stage. प्रथमं सुखप्रदः, पश्चात् दुःखायी (मनोरुजं विशिनष्टि) etc, see Ṭikā. 4. एकरसाम्–रस is स्वाद। एकः रसः अस्याम् एकरसा of uniform flavour, ताम्। 5. अनुकूलात्–अनुगतः कूलम् अनुकूलः favourable, प्रादितत्–। तस्य भावः, ताम्। एकरसा अनुकूलता is अविमिश्रा अनुकूलता, *i.e.*, not at times अनुकूल and again प्रतिकूल but uniformly अनुकूल। 6. अकाण्ड etc.—

काण्ड occasion. अकाण्ड an awkward moment. वि+वृदुत+ल्यु् भावे विवर्त्तन lit. turning back, hence change. Now see Ṭīka 7. *Remark*—The sense becomes more clear if the first two lines change position.

(*xxiii*) **कौसल्या (संज्ञां लब्ध्वा)–हा वच्छे जाणइ कहिं सि। सुमरामि दे विआहलच्छीपरिग्गहेक्कमण्डणं पप्फुरन्तसुद्धविहसिदं मुद्धमुहपुण्डरीअं। आप्फुरन्तचन्दिआसुनदरेहिं अङ्गेहि पुणो वि मे जादे उज्जीएहि उच्छङ्गं। सब्बदा महाराओ भणादि एसा रहुउलमहत्तराणं वहू, अम्हाणं उण जणअसम्बन्धेण दुहिदिआ एब्ब [हा वत्से जानकि, कस्मिन्नसि। स्मरामि ते विवाहलक्ष्मीपरिग्रहैकमण्डणं प्रस्फुरच्छुद्धविहसितं मुग्धमुखपुण्डरीकम्। आस्फुरच्चन्द्रचन्द्रिकासुन्दरैरङ्गैः पुनरपि मे जाते उद्द्योतय उत्सङ्गम्। सर्वदा महाराजो भणति एषा रघुकुलमहत्तराणां वधः, अस्माकं पुनर्जनकसम्बन्धेन दुहिता एव]।**

Kaus. (*Recovering consciousness*)—Alas ! Child Jānakī, where are you ? I recall your charming lotus-face (with an artless laugh sparkling on it) which had the assumption of the grace of wedding for its best decoration. My child light up my lap once again with your limbs lovely like the beams of a brightly shining moon. The great king always used to say—This is the daughter-in-law of the mightier ones of the race of Raghu, but of us through our tie with Janaka, she is a daughter indeed.

मित–। 'विवाहजनिता' या 'लक्ष्मीः' शोभा तस्याः 'परिग्रहः' धारणमेव 'एकं मुख्यं 'मण्डनं' भूषणं यस्य तत्। 'प्रस्फुरत्' शोभमानं 'शुद्ध 'सरलं 'विहसितं' हासः यस्मिन् तत्। 'जाते' वत्से 'आ' सम्यक् 'स्फुरत्' विभ्राजमानः यः 'चन्द्रः विमले गगने यः पूर्णचन्द्रः तस्य या 'चन्द्रिका' ज्योत्सना तया इव 'सुन्दरैः अङ्गैः उत्सङ्गं' क्रीड़म् 'उद्धोतय' भूषय। 'रघुकुलस्य 'ये 'महत्तराः' प्रधानपुरुषाः पूर्वपुरुषा इत्यर्थः तेषाम् 'एषा वधूः अस्माकं पुनः' आवयोस्तु 'जनकेन' यः 'सम्बन्धः' परमः सखिभावः तेन 'दुहिता एवं इयं जानकी।।

Notes. 1. विाहलक्ष्मी etc.—It is supposed that marrige adds fresh grace to a newly wedded couple. एक is best. 2. प्रस्फुरत etc.—शुद्ध artless. 3. मुग्धमुख etc. मुग्ध charming. 4. आस्फुरत् etc.—आस्फुरच्चन्द्र

excludes on ordinary चन्द्र। We want a चन्द्र which is shining at its best, *i.e.,* the sky must be perfectly clear and the moon full. 5. भणति–She here transfers herself to that time and imagines the same as present to her. Hence वर्त्तमाने लट्।

(*xxiv*) **कञ्चुकी–यथाह देवी।**

Kañc.—It is as the queen says.

पञ्चप्रसूतेरपि राज्ञ आसीत् प्रियो विशेषण सुबाहुशत्रुः।
बधूचतुष्केऽपि यथा हि शान्ता प्रिया तनूजास्य तथैव सीता।।16।।

To the king, though with five children, the slayer of Sabāhu was especially dear. Among the four daughter-in-law again Sītā was as dear to him as was his daughter Śāntā.

मित–। पञ्चेति।

अन्वयः–पञ्चप्रसूतेः अपि राज्ञः सुबाहुशत्रुः विशेषेण प्रियः आसीत्। बधूचतुष्केऽपि सीता तथैव अस्य प्रिया यथा हि तनूजा शान्ता।

व्याख्या–सुगमा।'सुबाहुः' मारीचसहचरः कश्चित् राक्षसः। तस्य 'शत्रुः' निहन्ता। "मारीचशुत्रुः" इति छन्दोभङ्गभयात् अप्रधानेनापि सुबाहुना निर्देशः। 'बधूनां चतुष्के' चतुअरिमाणे सङ्घे।।

Notes. 1. पञ्च etc.—The five were the 4 brothers and शान्ता 2. सुबाहु etc.—He speaks with reference to Daśaratha's knowledge. दशरथ knew राम as ताड़काशत्रु, सुबाहुशत्रु, मारीचशत्रु भार्गवविजेता। Of thesse सुबाहुशत्रु suits the metre. 3. बधू etc—चत्वारि परिमाणमस्य इति चतुर+कन् चतुष्कः a group of four. The rule for कन् is "संख्याया अतिशदन्तायाः कन्"। बधूनां चतुष्कः। तस्मिन् अधिकरणे 7मी। सीता was as dear as शान्ता, but राम was dearer.

(*xxv*) **जनकः–हा प्रियसख महाराज दशरथ, एवमसि सर्वप्रकार-हृदयङ्गमः। कथं विस्मर्थसे ?**

Jan.—Alas ! Dear friend, great king Daśaratha, thus, are you in every way heart-reaching. How can you be forgotten ?

कन्यायाः किल पूजयन्ति पितरो जामातुराप्तं जनं
सम्बन्धे विपरीतमेव तदभूदाराधनं ते मयि।
त्वं कालेन तथाविधोऽस्यपहृतः सम्बन्धवीजञ्च तदु-
घोरेऽस्मिन् मम जीवलोकनरके पापस्य धिग्जीवितम्।।17।।

In a connection by marriage, surely it is the parents of the bride that adore the bridegroom's own men. The attentions which you always bestowed on me were just the reverse. Such as you were, you have been carried away by Death, as also the source of our tie. Fie upon the life of me, a sinner in this horrible of the land of the living.

मित– । 'सर्वप्रकारेण हृदयङ्गमः' हृदयप्रियः । कन्याया इति ।

अन्वयः–सम्बन्धे कन्यायाः पितरः किल जामातुः आप्तं जनं पूजयन्ति । मयि ते तत् आराधनं विपरीतमेव अभूत् । तथाविधः त्वं कालेन अपहृतः असि, तत् सम्बन्धवीजञ्च (अपहृतम्) । घोरे अस्मिन् जीवलोकनरके पापस्य मम जीवितं धिक् ।

व्याख्या–'सम्बन्धे वैवाहिके सम्बन्धे जाते 'कन्यायाः पितरः' पित्रादयो गुरुवः 'किलं ते एव 'जामातुः' आप्तं' निजं 'जनं पूजयन्ति अर्चयन्ति । कन्यावर्गीया एव विशिष्टामर्चनां कुर्वन्ति न तु वरवर्गीयाः । 'मयि' कन्यापितरि ते' वरपितुस्तव 'तत् आराधनं पूजनं 'विपरीतमेव अभूत' मद्दत्तेभ्यः त्वद्दता एव विशिष्टा अभूवन्नु पहाराः । 'तथाविधः' तादृशः प्रियसुहृत 'त्वं कालेन' दैवेन 'अपहतः असि' चोरितः लोकादस्मान्नीतोऽमि । 'तत्' कन्यारूपं 'सम्बन्धवीजञ्च सम्बन्धहेतुरपि अपहतम् । तत् 'घोरे' भीमे अस्मिन् जीवलोकरूपे नरके पापस्य' पापिनः 'मम जीवितं' जीवनं 'धिक्' गर्ह्यम् ।।

Notes. 1. सर्वप्रकार etc—हृदयं गच्छतीति हृदय+गम+खच् कर्त्तरि हृदयङ्गमः । "खच्प्रकरणे गमेः सुप्युपसंख्यानम्" इति खच् । 2. किल–अव्यय in the sense of अवधारण । कन्यायाः पितर एव not the reverse. 3. पितरः–पितरौ seems better. Or पितरः पितृपर्याया such as father, uncle etc.

(*xxvi*) **कौसल्या–जादे जानइ किं करेमि दिढ़वज्जलेवघड़िअ बन्धणिच्चलं हदजीविदं मं मन्दभाइणिं ण परिच्चअइ [जाते जानकि किं करोमि ? दृढ़वज्रलेपघटितबन्धनिश्चलं हतजीवितं मां मन्दभागिनीं न परित्यजति]।**

Kaus—Child Jānakī, what shall I do ? This cursed life, firm (as if) with fastenings made of the tough Vajralepa, does not quit me the ill-fated.

अरुन्धती–आश्वसिहि राजपुत्रि, वाष्पविश्रामोऽप्यन्तरे कर्त्तव्य एव।

अन्यच्च किं न स्मरसि यदवोचदृष्यशृङ्गाश्रमे युष्माकं कुलगुरुः "तदुपजातमेव, किन्तु कल्याणोदर्कं भविष्यति ?

Arun.—Cheer up, Daughter of a king. Cessation of tears too has indeed to be allowed at times. Besides, do you not remember what your family-preceptor said in the hermitage of Ṛṣyaśṛṅga—"It is a misfortune indeed, but it will have a happy end"?

कौसल्या–भअबदि अदिक्कन्तो मणोरहो [भगवती अति क्रान्तो मनोरथः]।

Kaus.—Worshipful Lady, the object of my desire has passed away [Or—my desire has vanished].

अरुन्धती–तत् किं मन्यसे राजपुत्रि मृषोधं तदिति ? नहौदं सुक्षत्रिये अन्यथा मन्तव्यम् ! भवितव्यमेव तेन।

Arun.—Do you then think, O daughter of a king, that those were false words ? Good Kṣattriya Lady, it should not be taken otherwise. It has to be indeed.

आर्विर्भुतज्योतिषां ब्राह्मणानां ये व्याहारास्तेषु मा संशयो भूत्।
भद्रा ह्येषां बाचि लक्ष्मीर्निषक्ता नैते बाचं विलुप्तां व्याहरन्ति ।।18।।

Let not doubt attach to those that are the declarations of Brāhmaṇas unto whom the Light has appeared. A happy felicity attends upon their speech. They do not utter unture words.

मित–'दृढः' 'वज्रलेपः' सौधविलेपनविशेषः तेन 'घटितः' रचितः यो 'बन्धः' संश्लेषः तेन 'निश्चलं' स्थिरम्।। वाष्पमोचनमेव कुरूषे 'वाष्पविश्रामः अपि अन्तरे' अवकाशे 'कर्त्तव्य एव' तत् सम्प्रति वाष्पविरामं कुरू। 'अन्यच्च' वाष्पविरामे कारणमस्ति–'युष्माकं' कुलगुरुः वशिष्ठः 'ऋष्यशृङ्गाश्रमे' सीताविवासनवार्त्तां श्रुत्वा 'अवोचत्'–"'उपजातं' दुर्जातम् 'एव तत्' सीताविवासनम् 'किन्तु कल्याणोदर्क' परिणामशुभं 'भविष्यति'। तदद्ब्रवीमि आशां पुषाण वाष्पं स्तम्भय।। 'मनोरथः' मनोरथविषयीभूतं वस्तु सीता इत्यर्थः 'अतिक्रान्तः' इहलोकं परित्यज्य गतः। यद्वा–'मनोरथः अभिलाषः सीतायाः पुनदर्शनरूपः 'अतिक्रान्तः' गतः। नाहं सीताया पुनदर्शनमाशंसे तत् किमुच्यते आशां पुषाण इति।। 'तत्' वशिष्ठवचनं 'सृषोद्यं'

मिथ्यावचनं 'मन्यसे किम्' ? 'इदं' वशिष्ठोक्तम् 'अन्यथा' अर्थातिक्रमेण भिथ्या इत्यर्थकः 'न मन्तव्यम्'। 'तेनं वचसा 'भवितव्यमेव' अवश्यम् अर्थानुक्रमेण एव भाव्यं न हि अर्थातिक्रमेण।। आविर्भूतेति।

अन्वयः–आविर्भतज्योतिषां ब्राह्मणानां ये व्याहाराः तेषु संशयो मा भूत्। एषां वाचि भद्रा लक्ष्मीः निषक्ता हि, एते विप्लुतां वाचं न व्याहरन्ति।

व्याख्या–'आविर्भतं' प्रकटीभूतं 'ज्योतिः' शब्दब्रह्मप्रकाशः येभ्यः तथा विधानां वशिष्ठ वाल्मीकिप्रमुखानां ब्राह्मणानां ये व्याहाराः' उक्तयः 'तेषु संशयो मा भूत् तेषु श्रद्धेहि। 'एषां वाचि भद्रा' शोभना 'लक्ष्मी' सुभगता 'निषक्ता हि' संलग्ना एव, तत्प्रभावात् 'एते विप्लुताम्' अन्यर्थाथां 'वाचं न व्याहरन्ति' न उच्चारयन्ति। तन्मात्यज्यतामाशा इति सप्तमाङ्कप्रतिबिम्बनम्।।

Notes. 1. कर्त्तव्य एव–This points to the physical impossibility of weeping without a stop and doing nothing else. 2. अन्यच्च–Here she offers a better reason to cease weeping. The reason Vaśiṣtha himself has declared by तदुपजातम् etc. 3. उपजातम्–उप here declares दोष। दुष्टं जातम् इत्यर्थे उप+जन+क्त कर्त्तरि उपजातम् a bad trun, a misfortune. This must have been when the news of Sītā's exile reached them there. "उप सामर्थ्य दाक्षिण्यदोषाख्यानात्ययेषु चं" इत्यादि विश्वः। 4. कल्याणोदर्कम्–उदर्क is भाविफल। कल्याण उदर्कः अस्य। Hence, there are grounds for hope, weeping is undesirable. So stop the flow of tears. 5. अतिक्रान्तः etc.— I have given up all hopes. 12 years have passed and no signs of returning happiness ! 6. मृषोद्यम्–मृषा+वद+क्यप् कर्मणि भावे वा। With कर्मणि the meanning is *that which is falsely uttered* ; भावे giving the sense *utterance to an untruth*. Bhaṭṭoji prefers भावे। 7. सुक्षत्रिये–क्षत्रस्य अपत्यं जातिः इति क्षत+घ+स्त्रियाम् टाप् क्षत्रिया a woman of the warrior class. शोभना क्षत्रिया सुक्षत्रिया, प्रादि तत्–। Here क्षत्रिया alternates with क्षत्रियाणी by the Varttika "अर्यक्षत्रियाभ्यां वा"। But when meaning "wife of some क्षत्रिय the only form is क्षत्रियी by the rule "पुंयोगादाख्यायाम्"। 8. आविर्भूत etc— This is the same as आविर्भूतशब्दब्रह्मप्रकाशम् of act II. with शब्दब्रह्मप्रकाश replaced by ज्योतिस्। 9. भद्रा etc—This line is in imitation of the Vedic line "भद्रेषां लक्ष्मीर्निहिताधिवाचि" quoted in the महाभाष्य। There लक्ष्मी is explained by कैयट as "या लक्ष्मीर्वेदान्तेषु परमार्थविल्लक्षणा उक्ता सा"–लक्ष्मी is the same as is described in the वेदान्त as परमार्थसंविद् (knowledge of the Supreme Truth). With the possession of such knowledge नेते वाचं विपल्लुतां व्याहरन्ति–they cannot utter an untruth. So do cherish hope. Refers to the denoument brought about by Vālmīki in Act. VII. अरुन्धती was denouement brought about by Vālmīki in Act VII. अरुन्धती was aware of the facts regarding सीता and her children (see भागीरथीनिवेदितरहस्यम्, para xxviii).

(*xxvii*) **नेपथ्ये–(कलकलः–सर्वे आकर्णयन्ति)।**

In the Tiring Room—(A hum—All listen).

जनकः–अद्य शिष्टानध्याय इति उद्धतं खेलतां वटूनां कलकलः।

Jan.—The hum is of scholars sporting boisterously because today is a holiday (No-study) in honour of distinguished visitors.

कौसल्या–सुलहसोक्खं दाए वालत्तणं होदि [सुलभसौख्यं तापद्बलत्वं भवति]। (निरूप्य) अम्महे एदाणं मज्झे को एसो रामभद्दलच्छी-परिसोहिदेहिं सावट्टम्भमुद्धललिदेहिं अङ्गेहिं अम्हाणं लोअणाइं सीदलावेदि [अहो एतेषां मध्ये क एष रामभद्रलक्ष्मीपरिशोभितः सावष्टम्भमुग्ध-ललितैरङ्गैः आस्माकं लोचनानि शीतलयति]।

Kaus.—Childhood indeed has pleasures easily accessible. *(Marking)* Ha ! Who is this in their midst that soothes my eyes with limbs firm, handsome and lovely and adorned with the grace of Rāmabhadra ?

मित– 'शिष्टाः' विशिष्टा अतिशयं प्राप्ता महान्त इति। तदर्थः 'अनध्यायः' अध्ययनविरतिः।। अवष्टम्भेन आलम्बनेन सह 'सावष्टभानि' दृढ़ानि इत्यर्थः। तादृशैः 'मुग्धैः' मनोहरैः 'ललितैः' लावण्यमयैः 'अङ्गैः'।।

Notes. 1. शिष्ट etc.—अधि+इ or अय+घञ् भावे अध्यायः study. शस+क्त कर्मणि शिष्ट trained, *'i. e.'* a sage. शिष्टार्थः अनध्यायः, शाकपार्थिवादि कर्मधा–। 2. सुलभ etc—सुखमेव सौख्यम्। सुलभ। सौख्यं यस्मिन्। Boys are always happy. Miserable are the old !! 3. रामभद्र etc.—रामभद्रस्य लक्ष्मीः the grace of Rāmabhadra. तया परिशोभितानि etc. 4. मावष्टम्भम् etc.—मुग्ध charming. ललित lovely. मुग्धानि च तानि ललितानि च मुग्धललितानि lovely and charming. Lovely limbs do not always charm. In a boy, beauty going with strength becomes charming. The strength is supplied by the epithet सावष्टम्भ। अव+स्तम्भ+घञ् भावे अवष्टम्भ the स becoming ष by the rule 'अवाच्च आलम्बनाविदूर्ययो:''। Here अवष्टम्भ means आलम्बन support. तेन सह सावष्टम्भानि supported. 'i. e. strong (becuause it is strength that supports). सावष्टम्भानि अतएव मुग्धललितानि। तै:। The first distant glimmer of आशा comes to कौसल्या almost with the very words of hope spoken by अरुन्धती।

(*xxviii*) **अरुन्धती (अपवार्य महर्षबाष्पम्)–इदं नाम तत् भागीरथीनिवेदितरहस्यं कर्णामृतम्। नत्वेवं बिद्म: कतरोऽयमायुष्मतो: कुशलबयोरिति।**

Arun. (*Aside—With tears of joy*)—Surely this is that nectar to the ears the secret of which was divulged by Bhāgīrathī. But I cannot make out which one is this of Kuśa and Lava, the long-lived.

जनक:–

कुबलयदलस्निग्धश्याम: शिखण्डकमण्डनो
बटुपरिषदं पुण्यश्रीक: श्रियेव सभाजयन्।
पुनरिव शिशुर्भूतो बत्स: स मे रघुनन्दनो
झटिति कुरुते दृष्ट: कोऽयं दृशोरमृताञ्जनम् ।।19।।

Jan.—Soft-blue like the petals of a blue-lotus, adorned with youthful locks, of a holy grace, and adorming as it were with his grace the whole assembly of the scholars, looking as if he was that child of mine the delighter of the race of Raghu turned boy again who is this that on being seen forwith applies as it were an unguent of nectar to my eyes ?

मित–। 'अपवार्य' आच्छाद्य। पारिभाषिमेतत् अन्यैरश्रुतस्य अनुच्चसुक्तस्य। 'सहर्षवाष्पम्' हर्षाश्रुणा सह। 'भागीरथ्या निवेदितम्' ऋष्यशृङ्गाश्रममागत्य विज्ञापितं 'रहस्यं जन्मादिगूढ़वृत्तान्त: यस्य 'तत् कर्णामृतम्' आत्मवृत्तान्तेन कर्णयोर मृततुल्यम्। 'कतरोऽयं' कुशो वा लवो सा इति तु न विद्म:'।। कुवलयेति।

अन्वय:– कुवलयदलस्निग्धश्याम: शिखण्डकमण्डन: पुण्यश्रीक: श्रिथा

वटुपरिषदं सभाजयन्निव पुनः शिशुर्भूतः स मे वत्सो रघुनन्दन इव क अयं दृष्टः झटिति दृशोः अमृताञ्जनं कुरुते।

व्याख्या–'कुवलयदलमिव नीलोत्पलपत्रभिव 'स्निग्धश्यामः मनोहरश्यामलः 'शिखण्डकमण्डनः' काकपक्षभूषणः 'पुण्यश्रीकः' प्रशान्तकान्तिः 'श्रिया' देहशोभया 'विटुपरिषर्द' छात्रसमाजं 'सभाजयन्निव' अलङ्कुर्वन्निव 'पुनः शिशुर्भूतः' भूयः शैशवमापन्नः 'स मे वत्सो रघुनन्दन इव' रामभद्र इव 'कः अयं' बालः 'दृष्टः' बालः 'दृष्टः' सन् 'झटिति' तत्क्षणमेव दृशोः' नयनयोः 'अमृताञ्जन' सुधाविलेपनं कुरुते तापिते नेत्रे शीत लयति।।

Notes. 1. अपवार्य–अप+वृ+णिच्+ल्यप्। The definition of अपवारण is "तद्भवेदपवारितम्, रहस्यं तु यदन्यस्य परावृत्य प्रकाश्यते।।" 2. कर्णामृतम्–अमृत *is like* अमृत, *i.e.*, gratifying. कर्णयोः अमृतम्। But the body cannot be called "gratifying to the ears" (कर्णामृत) It is the narration of Bhāgīrathī that was gratifying. The body (इदम्) is indentified with the communication of his secret by लक्षणा। 3. पुण्यश्रीकः–श्रयति पुरुषम् इति श्रि+क्विप श्रीः। The ई is not ङीष्। The समसान्त affix कप् is optionalby "शेषाद्विभाषा"। In सुन्दरश्रीः (I, para xxvi) there is no कप्। 4. अमृताञ्जनम्–अञ्ज+ल्युट् भावे अञ्जन painting अमृतेन अञ्जनम्। Here again no actual painting is done, but the result of the painting—relief of wariness etc.—is there. Hence अमृताञ्जनं करुते is only a surmise from the likeness in the result.

(*xxix*) **कञ्चुकी–क्षत्रियब्रह्मचारी दारकोऽयमिति मन्ये।**

Kañch.—I guess thus boy is Kṣattriya studying the Vedas.

जनकः–एवमेतत्। तथाहि–

Jan.—So it is.

चूड़ाचुम्बितकङ्कपत्रमभितस्तूणोद्वयं पृष्ठतो
भस्मस्तोमपवित्रलाञ्छनमुरो धत्ते त्वचं रौरवीम्।
मौर्व्या मेखलया नियन्त्रितमधो वासश्च माञ्जिष्ठिकं
पाणौ कार्मुकमक्षसूत्रवलयं दण्डं तथा पैष्पलम् ।। 20 ।।

Thus—He carries at his back quivers the heron feathers in which are kissed at the sides by the tuft of hair of his crest;

a chest, with the holy imprint of a little ash ; the skin of a deer; in the lower half the madderdyed garment held fast with a gridle of the *Murva* grass ; in the hand a bow (left), bracelet of a string of rosaries (right) and a staff of the *Pippala besides* (right).

भगवत्यरुन्धति किमत्पेक्षसे कुतस्त्योऽयमिति।

Worshipful Arundhatī, can you guess whence he comes ?

मित–। ब्रह्म वेदः लक्षणया वेदाध्ययनार्थं व्रतम्। तत् व्रतं क्षरतीति 'ब्रह्मचारी'। क्षत्रियश्चासौ ब्रह्मचारी च 'क्षत्रियब्रह्मचारी' जात्या क्षत्रियः असमाप्तविद्यः कश्चित् बाल्मीकिशिष्यः।। चूडेति।

अन्वयः–(अयम्) पृष्ठतः अभितः चूडाचुम्बितकङ्कपत्रं तूणीद्वयम्, भस्मस्तोमपवित्रलाञ्छनम् उरः, रौरवीं त्वचम्, अधः मौर्व्या मेखलया नियन्त्रितं माञ्जिष्ठिकं वासः, पाणी कार्मुकम् अक्षसूत्रवलयं तथा पैप्पलं दण्डं धत्ते।

व्याख्या–अयं बालः 'पृष्ठतः' पृष्ठे 'तूणीद्वयम्' इषुधियुगलं 'धत्ते' इत्यन्वयः। किम्भूतम् तूणीद्वयमित्याह 'अभितः' उभयतः पार्श्वयोरित्यर्थः चूड़या' शिखया' शिरःस्थया 'चुम्बितानि गतिवशात् स्पृष्टानि 'कङ्कपत्राणि वाणपुङ्खस्थिताः गृध्रविशेषपक्षाः यस्य तथाविधं तूणीद्वयम्। क्षत्रियलक्षणमेतत्। 'भस्मनां स्तोभः' समूह एव 'पवित्रं लाञ्छनं' यस्य तथाविधम् उरः वक्षः धत्त इत्युरेण सम्बन्धः। एतत्तु ब्रह्मचारिलक्षणम्। 'रौरवीं' रुरुमृगादागतां 'त्वचम्' उत्तरीयरुपेण धत्ते। एतत् पुनर्ब्रह्मचारिलक्षणं क्षत्रियलक्षणञ्च। त्वचं धत्ते इति ब्रह्मचर्य रौरवीं त्वचमिति क्षत्रियत्वं कथ्यते। 'अधः' नाभेरधः मौव्यां गृणतृणनिर्मितया 'मेखलया' कटिबन्धेन 'नियन्त्रितं नियमितं 'माञ्जिष्ठिकं' मञ्जिष्ठारञ्जितं 'वासः' वस्त्र धत्ते। एतदपि उभयलक्षणम् वाससा ब्रह्मचारी मौर्व्या मेखलया च क्षत्रिय इति ज्ञायते। 'पाणौ' हस्ते 'कार्मुकं' धनुः 'अक्षसूत्रस्य' जपमालिकाया 'वलयं' वलयाकरेण जपमालिकामित्यर्थः 'तथा पैप्पलम्' अश्वत्थशाखानिर्मितं 'दण्डं' लगुड़ 'धत्ते'। अत्र कार्मुकमिति क्षत्रियः अक्षसूत्रमितति दण्ड इति च ब्रह्मचारी, पैप्पलं इति चु क्षत्रियः।। 'उत्प्रेक्षसे' तर्कयसि अनुमन्यसे। 'कुतस्त्या' कस्माद्देशात् आगतः।।

Notes. 1. चूडा etc.—कङ्क is an aquatic bird looking like a very big heron ; it is commonly known as काक। Its feathers are placed at the root of the arrow in the belief that this improves the flight of the arrow. The body playing, and the dangling tuft of hair on his crest, thrown by the body's movements now this side and again that side of the neck, each time touched the feathers in the arrows in its oscilations. 2. अभितः–अभि here means उभय। तस्मिन् इति अभि+ङि+तासि। Consture अभित चूड़ाचुम्बित–। 3. पृष्ठतः–पृष्ठ+ङि+तासि स्वार्थे। Consture पृष्ठती धत्ते on his back he carries etc. 4. मौर्व्या–मूर्वा is a king of tough grass which supplies the bowstring. सूर्वाया इयम् इति मूर्वा+अण् स्त्रियाम् मौर्वी, तया। 5. माञ्चिष्ठिकम्–माञ्जिष्ठिकम्। This is irrugular, the correct affix being अण् giving माञ्जिष्ठम्।

(*xxx*) **अरुन्धती–अद्यैवागता वयम्।**

Arun.—We have come but today.

जनकः–आर्य गृष्टे, अतीव मे कौतुकं वर्त्तते, तत् भगवन्तं वाल्मीकिमेव गत्वा पृच्छ। इमञ्च दारकं बूहि केऽप्येते प्रवयसस्त्वां दिदृक्षव इति।

Jan.—Noble Gṛṣṭī, great indeed is my curiosity, so go and ask worshipful Vālmīki himself ; also tell his boy "Certain old people here are desirous of seeing you".

कञ्चकी–यथाज्ञापयसि। (इति निष्क्रान्तः)।

Kañch.—As you command. *(Exit).*

कौसल्या–किं भणध एवं भणिदो आगमिस्सदि ति [किं भणथ एवं भणित आगमिष्यतीति] ?

Kaus.—Do you say he would come thus told ?

अरुन्धती–भिद्येत वा सद्वृत्तमीदृशस्य निर्माणस्य ?

Arun.—Would good manners fail in such a from ?

कौसल्या (निरूप्य)–कधं सविणयं णिसामिदगिट्ठिवअणो विसज्जिदइसिदारओ इदो अहिमुहं पसरिदो एव सो वच्छो [कथम् ! सविनयं निशामितगृष्टिवचनी विसृष्टर्षिदारक इतोऽभिमुखं प्रसृत एव स वत्सः]।

Kaus.—*(Marking)*—Ha ! That dear one is indeed coming

this way having listened meekly to Gṛṣṭī's words and dismissed [Or—left] the ascetic boys.

मित– ।'अद्यैव' इत्यादिभिः परिहतमुत्तरं जनकस्य।'प्रवयसः' बृद्धाः।।'भिद्येत' भिन्न भवेत् ईदृशनिर्माणविरोधि भवेदित्यर्थः। 'सदवृत' साधुशीलम्। 'ईदृशस्य' एवंविधस्य अलौकिकस्य 'निर्माणस्य' सृष्टेः। यथा हारिणीयं विधातु सृष्टिः तथा वृत्तमपि हारि एव स्यात्, नूनमयमागच्छेत् इति भावः।।'निशामितं श्रुतं 'गृष्टिवचनं' येन तादृशः।'विसृष्टाः' परित्यक्ता 'ऋषिदारकाः' येन सः।।

Notes. 1. अद्यैव etc.—This is a fact but is avoids a reply to Janaka's query. Arundhatī knows all, perhaps even the arrangements made Vālmīki and prefers to maintain silence lest the sage's plans are frustrated. 2. प्रवयसः–प्रकृष्टं क्यो येषां ते। The respect due to age will attract the boy thither. 3. भिद्येत etc.—भिद+लिङ् ईत कर्मकर्त्तरि कर्मणि वा। Comp ''न तादृश आकृतिविशेषा गुणविरोधिनो भवन्ति–*Śakuntala*. 4. निशामित etc.—शम+णिच् स्वार्थे (चुरादि)+क्त कर्मणि। The चुरादि root is not मित् hence वृद्धि with णिच्। 5. विसृष्ट etc.—विसृष्ट is ambiguous ; it may mean "dismissed" or "left" both."Left" seems better. He left the company of the other boys, and proceeded towards the old people.

(*xxxi*) **जनकः (चिरं निर्वर्ण्य)–भोः किमप्येतत् ?**

Jan. (*Nothing long*). Ho ! What is this again ?

महिम्नामेतस्मिन् विनयशिशुतामौग्ध्यमसृणो
विदग्धैर्निर्ग्राह्या न पुनरदिवग्धैरतिशयः।
मनो मे सम्मोह स्थिरमपि हरत्येष बलव।न्
अयोधातुं यद्वत् परिलघुरयस्कान्तशकलः ।।21।।

In this boy there is a preponderance of grandeur, softened by childhood, modesty and simplicity, perceptible to the adept but not to the inept. He attracts my mind though firm against infatuation just a very small bit of a magnet, possessing the power, does metallic iron.

मित– ।'एतदपि' इदञ्च 'किम्' अनुभवामि ? महिम्नामिति।

अन्वयः–एतस्मिन् विनयशिशुतामौग्धामसृणः (अतएव) विदग्धैः न पुनरविदग्धैः निर्ग्राह्यः महिम्नाम् अतिशयः। एष समोहस्थिरमपि मे मनः हरति यद्वत् परिलघुः बलवान् अयस्कान्तशकलः अयोधातुम्।

व्याख्या–'एतस्मिन्' शिशी 'विनयेन, नम्रतया 'शिशु तया' बालत्वेन 'मौग्ध्येन' सरलतया च मसृण:' अनुदग्र: अतएव 'विदग्धै:' निपुणै: 'न पुन: अविदग्धै:' अनिपुणैस्तु न 'निर्गाह्य:' अनुमेय: 'महिम्नां' प्रभावनां तेजसामित्यर्थ: 'अतिशय:' आधिक्यं लक्ष्यन्ते। सुदु:सहमस्मिन् तेजो वर्त्तते, तच्च बालत्वात् सहजेन विनयेन सारल्येन च मन्दीभूतमिति दुर्लक्ष्यम्, मया पुनर्निपुणमीक्षमानेन ज्ञातं तत्। किं क्रियते महिमातिशयेन इत्याह 'एष:' बाल: 'सम्मोहे' रूपादिकृतमोहविषये स्थिरमपि अविचलितमपि 'मे मन: हरति' आकृष्य आत्मानं प्रति नयति 'यद्वत्' यथा 'परिलघु:' क्षद्रु: [इदं बालं प्रत्यपि नेयं विशेषणम्] 'बलवान्' महिम्नामतिशयवान् शक्तिमान: इत्यर्थ: अयस्कान्तशकल:' चुम्बकमणिखण्ड: 'अयोधातुं' लोहं हरति त्रथा। तत् पृच्छामि "भो: किमप्येतत्"।।

Notes. 1. चिरं निर्वर्ण्य–Having watched the boy for some time. 2. भो: etc.—He notices something going on within him and is surprised. 3. महिम्नाम्–महतो भाव इति महत्+इमणिच् महिमा greatness. Related to अतिशय:। 4. विनय etc.—मसृण is *smooth*, hence *subdued*. If there is an excess of greateness it must be apparent to all. But no, the excess is subdued (मसृण) by his meekness (विनय) etc. 5. विदग्धै: etc.—विदग्ध clever ; derivation uncertain. Only the clever can detect it because it is subdued. 6. समोह etc.—मोह is विषयमोह the longing felt for external objects. समोहे स्थिरम्, सुप्सुपा। This is the reading in Vidyāsāgara's manuscript No. 3. My mind is indifferent to external impressions, yet this boy interests me, what is this ("भो: किमप्येतत्")? Vidyāsāgara himself rejects the readings of all his four manuscripts and proposes to read सम्मोद:। समोदो हरति joy overpowers. This seems to disconnect the two halves of the verse and to render the simile in the 4th line less attractive (see below). 7. हरत्येष:–Vidyāsāgara's manuscripts 1 and 2 read हरत्येव। But if समोहस्थिरम् is preferred, हरत्येव has to go being without a nominative. Manuscript No.3. has हरत्येष:। 8. बलवान्–Qual. अयस्कान्तशकल:। Contrast with महिम्नामतिशय: in the boy. One is महिम्नामतिशयवान् the other is बलवान्। This strenghtens the simile. 9. यद्वत्–No तच्छव्द is necessary because the यच्छन्द is in a subsequent clause (उत्तरवाक्यगत)। 10. परिलघु:–Both the boy and the अयस्कान्त are *small* in size.

(*xxxii*) (प्रविश्य) लव: (स्वगतम्)–अज्ञातनामक्रमाभिजनान्

पूज्यानपि नः स्वतः कथमभिवादयिष्ये। (विचिन्त्य) अयं पुनरविरुद्धः प्रकार इति वृद्धेभ्यः श्रूयते। (सविनयमुपसृत्य) एष वो लवस्य मूर्द्धा प्रणमपर्यायः।

(*Entering*) Lava (To himself)—Though worthy of respect how shall, I guided by my own wit only, salute these people whose name, precedence and lineage are unknown to me ?

(*Reflecting*) This, however, is being heard from our superiors as not an inconsistent form. (*Approaching with humility*). Here is unto you Lava's succession of bows with his head.

अरुन्धतीजनकौ–कल्याणिन्नायुष्मान् भूयाः।

Arun. and Jan.—O blessed one, may you have long life !

कौसल्या–जाद चिरं जीव।

Kaus.—Child, my you live long !

अरुन्धती–एहि वत्स। (लवमृत्सङ्गे कृत्वा अपवार्य) दिष्ट्या न केवलमुत्सङ्गः चिरामनोथोऽपि मे सम्पूर्णः।

Arun.—Come my child. (*Having Lava on her lap Aside*) O joy ! Not only the lap, but after long, my desire also has filled.

मित– ।'अज्ञातं नाम' आख्या 'क्रमः' पौर्वापर्यं मानव्यवस्था इत्यर्थः 'आभजनः' कुलञ्च येषां तान् 'स्वतः' सुबुद्ध्या। कः एतेषां पूर्वमभिवाद्यः कश्च पश्चात् इति न जनामि तत् कथमभिवादनं स्यादित्यर्थः। 'अविरुद्धः' शास्त्रेण आचारेण च सङ्गतः। 'प्रणामानां पर्यायः' परम्परा पूज्यानुक्रमेण प्रणामाः।। 'उत्सङ्गः' अङ्कः 'सम्पूर्णः सुगठितेन बालेन परिव्याप्तः'। मनोरथः अभिलाषः कुशलवी क्रीड़े कर्याम् इत्येवंरूपः 'सम्पूर्णः' संसिद्धः।।

Notes. 1. लवः–The boy is not yet intorduced by name. Hence it seems better to say प्रविश्य दारकः। Next, after the दारक himself has announced his name saying एष वी लवस्य etc. the name लव may be used in the stage direction. 2. अविरुद्धः–वि+रुध+क्त कर्त्तरि विरुद्ध inconsistent. न विरुद्धः consistent, *i.e.,* consistent with law (शास्त्र) and practise (आचार)। 3. प्रकारः–Style. 4. मूर्द्धा–This is conected with प्रणाम in प्रणामपर्यायः। सापेक्षत्वेऽपि गमकत्वात् समासः। 5. सम्पूर्ण–सम+पूर+णिच्+क्त कर्मणि

सम्पूर्ण or सम्प्रूरित। This has a double meaning. Taken with उत्सङ्ग it means "filled up". The well-developed boy has taken up all the room in my lap. In connection with मनेरथ the sense is "fulfilled"—at last I have been longing for—I have placed Rāma's progeny on my lap !

(*xxxiii*) **कौसल्या–जाद इदो वि दाव एहि [जात इतोऽपि तावदेहि]। (क्रोड़े कृत्वा) अम्महे ण केअलं दरविसन्तणीलुप्पलदामसामलुज्ज्वलेण देहबन्धेण कवलिदारविन्दकेसरकसाअकण्ठकलहंसणिददीहरदीहरेण सरेण अ रामभद्दं अणुहरदि। णं कठोरकमलगब् भपक्खलो सरीरीप्फंसो वि तारिसो एवच्छस्म। जाद पेक्खामि दे मुहचन्दं [अहो न केवलं दरविकसन्नीलोप्तदामश्यामलोज्जलेन देहबन्धेन, कवलितार विन्दकेशर-कषायकण्ठकलहंसनिनाददीर्घदीर्घेण स्वरेण च राम भद्रमनुहरति, ननु कठोरकमलगर्भपक्ष्मलः शरौरस्पर्शोऽपि तादृश एव वत्मस्य। जात प्रेक्षे ते मुखचन्द्रम्]। (चित्रुकमुन्नमय निरूप्यं च साष्पाकूतम्) राएसि किं ण पेक्खसि णिउणं णिरु विज्जमाणं से मुहं वच्छाए वहूए मुहचन्देण संवददि एब्ब [राजर्षे किं न प्रेक्षसे निपुणं निरूप्यमाणमस्य मुखं वत्साया बध्वा मुखचन्द्रेण संवदति एव]।**

Kaus.—Child come this way too. (*Placing him on lap*) Ha! He takes after Rāmabhadra not only in the build of his body which is blue and glossy like a string (?) of slightly opening blue-lotuses, and in his voice which is rather long-drawn like the note of a swan whose throat has become sweet from eating lotus-filaments, but even the touch of body of the dear one, is like that of his (Rāma's) velvety as of the core of a full grown lotus. Child, let me (I will) see your man-like face. (*Raising his chin and nothing—With tears and meaningly*) O royal, sage, do you not notice that his face, closely observed tallies indeed with the lotus-face of our daughter-in-law ?

मित–।'रामभद्रम अनुहरति' अनुकरोति। कथमित्याह कथमित्याह 'देहबन्धेन' वद्धेन देहेन इत्यर्थः [''भावनयेन द्रव्यानयनम्'']। कीदृशेन देहेन ? 'दरविकसन्ति' ईषदुन्मीलन्ति यानि 'नीलोप्लानि' कुवलयानि तेषां यत् 'दाम्' माला तदिव श्यामलः उज्जलश्च' देहः। तेन अनुहरति। पुनश्च केन अनुहरति ?'स्वेरण'। कथम् ?'कवलिताः

भक्षिता ये 'अरविन्दकेशरा: कमलकिञ्जल्का: तै: 'कषायकण्ठ:' मधुरकण्ठ: य: 'कलहंस:' राजहंस: तस्य 'निनाद:' ध्वनिरिव ' दीर्घदीर्घ: दीर्घ इव प्रतीयमान: स्वर:। तेन च अनुहरति। द्वयमप्येतत् ज्ञातं भवद्भि, मया तु तृतीयमपि सादृश्य मनुभूतम् किमित्याह–'शरीरस्पर्श: अपि तादृश:' रामशरीरस्पर्श इव। किम्भूत: स स्पर्श: ? –'कठोरं' परिणतं यत् 'कमलं 'पद्म' तस्य 'गर्भ:' अन्त:कीलक इव 'पक्ष्मल:' मनोरम: (?) स्पर्श:। 'वाष्पेण' नेत्रजलेन 'आकूतेन' अभिप्रायेण मनोगतं ज्ञायतां जनकेन इत्यभिप्रायेण 'सह'। 'संबदति तुलामारोहति।।

Notes. 1. दर etc.,—दर is अव्यय when meaning ईषत्। "ईषदर्थे दराव्ययम्" इति विश्व:। दामन् in the compound serves no purpose and is confusing. It is better omitted. 2. देह etc.—देहस्य बन्ध:, तेन। But बन्ध is a भाव action. It cannot be called श्यामल or उज्जवल which are द्रव्यधर्म। Hence देहबन्ध=बद्धो देह:। The देहबन्ध is before the eyes of all present there and forms no part of Kausalyā's special experience. 3. कवलित etc.—कषायकण्ठ sweet throated. Compare—"चूताङ्कुरास्वादकषायकण्ठ: पुंस्कोकिलो यन्मधुरं चुकूज"—*Kumāra*, दीर्घप्रकार: इति दीर्घदीर्य:। प्रकारे द्विर्वचनम्। The doubled form is treated as a कर्मधारय compound by "कर्मधारयवदुत्तरेषु"। The voice is sweet and does not stop abruptly, *i.e.*, it has a resonance (दीर्घदीर्घ)। This also has been noticed by all present when लव announced himself saying "एष वो etc." 4. कठोर etc.—This is her own experience. पक्ष्मल is a troublesome word here. From the comparison with the core of the lotus, the idea appears to be that of a *soft yet from* substance. The derivation is पक्ष्माणि नेत्रलोमानि लक्षणया तत्तुल्यस्पर्शं लातीति पक्ष्मल (क: प्रत्यय:), or तत्तुल्यस्पर्श: अस्ति अस्य पक्ष्मल: (लच् प्रत्यय:)। Hence I have rendered it 'velvety' Vidyāsāgara read कोमल:। उन्नमय–उद्+नम+णिच् ल्यप्। 5. सवाष्प etc.—आकूत is अभिप्राय meaning Kausalyā speaks meaningly, i.e., she wants Janaka to understad that the suspects the boy to be her पौत्र and Janaka's दौहित्र–Sītā's boy.

(*xxxiv*) **जनक:–पश्यामि सखि पश्यामि।**

Jan.—I see it friend, I see it.

कौसल्या–अम्मा उन्मतीभूदं विअ मे हिअअं किं वि चिन्तअन्तो बहु विप्पलवदि [अहो उन्मत्तीभूतमिव मे हृदयं किमपि चिन्तयत् बहु विप्रलपति]।

Kaus.—Ha ! My mind, gone and mad as it were, raves much with something absurd in view.

जनकः–

वत्सायाश्च रघूद्वहस्य च शिशावस्मिन्नभिव्यज्यते
सम्पूर्णप्रतिबिम्बतेव निखिला सैवाकृतिः सा द्युतिः।
सा वाणी विनयः स एव सहजः पुण्यानुभावोऽप्यसौ
हा हा दैव किमुत्पथैर्मम मनः पारिल्पवं धावति ।।22।।

Jan.—In this boy appear, as it were, the characteristics of a perfect image of my child and of the upholder of the race of Raghu—the features are all the very same, the same complexion, the voice the same, just the same natural humility even the same pleasing majesty Alas ! Alas ! O destiny, why does my restless mind run along wrong tracks ?

मित– 'किमपि' असम्भाव्यं 'चिन्तयत्' सीतासूतोऽयमिति मन्यमानमित्यर्थः। 'बहु विप्रलयति' असम्बद्धं प्रस्तौति।। वत्साया इति।

अन्वयः–अस्मिन् शिशौ वत्सायाश्च रघूद्वहस्य च सम्पूर्णप्रतिबिम्बता अभिव्यज्यते इव। सा इव निखिला आकृतिः, साद्युतिः, सा वाणी, स एव सहजो विनयाः, असौ पुणयानुभावः अपि। हा हा दैव मम पारिल्पवं मनः किम उत्पथैः धावति।

व्याख्या–'अस्मिन् शिशौ' बालके लवे 'वत्सायाश्च' सीताया अपि 'रघूद्वहस्य च' रघुधुर्यस्य रामस्य 'सम्पूर्णप्रतिबिम्बता' छयासमगता 'अभिव्यज्यते इव' अभिव्यक्ता भवतीव प्रतिभासते इव। कीदृशी सम्पूर्णता इत्याह–'सा एव' सौतारामगता एव 'निखिला आकृतिः' सर्वावयवविन्यासः, 'सा द्युतिः' रामस्येव कान्तिः, 'सा वाणी' रामस्येव कण्ठः स एव' रामनिष्ठः 'सहजो विनयः' नैसर्गिकी नम्रता 'असौ पुण्यानुभावः अपि' रामस्येव च पावनं तेज' । तत् किमयं सीताया एव तनजः ? न हि नहि असम्भवं तत्। 'हा हा' अहो खेदः 'दैव' भो नियते 'मम पारिल्पवं' चञ्चलं 'मनः किं' कथम् 'उत्पथैः' विभार्गैः 'धावति' प्रसरति। यद्वा–'मनः पारिपल्वं सत् इत्यादि।।

Notes. 1. उन्मतीभूतम्–अनुन्मत्तम् उन्मतं भूतम् इति उन्मत+च्वि+भू+क्त कर्त्तरि। I have been suffering it is true, my mind. however, has been clear so long. But now it is inclined to take this boy as Sītā's son. This is so absurd that I well might doubt my sanity. 2. सम्पूर्ण etc.—प्रतिगतं बिम्बं प्रतिबिम्बम् reflection. सम्पूर्ण प्रतिबिम्बम् perfect reflection. तस्य भावः। 3

निखिला: etc.—He places the premises before him without drawing the conclusion. The inference however is irresistible, *viz.*, this is Sītā's boy. No sooner the inference is seen that he also sees the absurdity of it. Sītā must have died the very day she was banished. The wild beasts (क्रव्याद्) that ate her up had certainly not spared the progeny in her womb. The thought is then a delusion with which his mind has run away. So he exclaims pathetically हा हा etc. 4. उत्पथै:–उत्क्रान्ता: पथ: उत्पथा: with the समासान्त affix टच्। उत्पथ is विभार्ग wrong track. 5. पारिप्लवम्–परित: ल्पवते इति परि+ल्पु+अच् कर्त्तरि परिप्लवम् restless. परिप्लवमेव पारिप्लवत्। प्रज्ञाद्यण् स्वार्थे। This takes away from he force of his appeal to दैव। He himself has answered his question किमुत्पथैर्मनो धावति। Thus उत्पर्थर्धावति because मन: is पारिप्लव। Hence, the appeal to दैव for an answer is needless. So better consture मन: पारिप्लवं सत् etc.

(xxxv) **कौसल्या–जाद अत्थि दे मादा सुमरसि वा तादं [जात, अस्ति ते माता, स्मरमि वा तातम्]।**

Kaus.—Child, is your mother alive and do you remember you father ?

लव:–न हि।

Lava.—No.

कौसल्या–तदो कस्स तुमं [तत: कस्य त्वम्] ?

Kaus.—Whose are you then ?

लव:–भगवती वाल्मीके:।

Lava.—Of worshipful Vālmīki.

कौसल्या–अइ जाद कधिदब्वं कधेहि [अयि जात कथयितव्यं कथय]।

Kaus.—Child, say what ought to be sold.

लव:–एतदेव जानामि।

Lava.—This is just what I know.

मित–। सुगमा।

(xxxvi) नेपथ्ये—भोः भोः सैनिकाः एष खलु कुमारश्चन्द्रकेतु-राज्ञापयति न केनचिदाश्रमाभ्यर्णभूमिक्रमितव्येति।

(In the Tiring Room)—Ho ! Ho ! Soldiers, Prince Candraketu hereby commands, that the outskirts of the hermitage must not be trespassed into by any one.

अरुन्धतीजनकौ—अये मेध्याश्वरक्षाप्रसङ्गादुपागतो वत्सश्चन्द्रकेतुरद्य द्रष्टव्यः अहो सुदिवसः।

Arun. and Jan.—Ha ! Child Candraketu who has approached in course of guarding the sacrificial horse is to be seen today. What a lucky day !

कौसल्या—वच्छलक्खणस्स पुत्तओ आणवेदि ति अमिअविन्दुसुन्दराइँ अक्खराइँ सुणीयन्ति [वत्सलक्ष्मणस्यपुत्रक आज्ञापयति इत्यमृत-विन्दुसुन्दराणि अक्षराणि श्रूयन्ते]।

Kaus.—The son of child Lakṣmaṇa commands—these words heard are as agreeble as drops to nectar.

लवः—आर्य क एष चन्द्रकेतुर्नाम ?

Lava.—Noble Sir, who indeed is this Candraketu ?

जनकः—जानासि रामलक्ष्मणौ दाशरथी ?

Jan.—Do you know of Rāma and Lakṣmaṇa the sons of Daśaratha ?

लवः—ताबेव रामायणकथापुरुषौ ।

Lava.—The very same are the heroes of the story of the Rāmāyaṇa.

जनकः—तत् कथं न जानासि तस्य लक्ष्मणस्यायमात्मजश्चन्द्रकेतुः ?

Jan.—Then how is it you do not know that this Candraketu is the son of that Lakṣmaṇa ?

लवः—उर्मिलापुत्रस्तर्हि मैथिलस्य राजर्षेदौहित्र :।

Lava.—He is then Urmilā's son and daughter's son to the royal sage the king of Mithilā.

मित—।'आश्रमस्य अभ्यर्णा' अदूरवर्तिनी 'भूमिः न आक्रमितव्या' न पीड़नीया।।

'मेध्याश्वस्य' यज्ञियाश्वस्य 'रक्षाप्रसङ्गात्' रक्षणानुरोधात् 'उपागतः' इह प्राप्तः। 'सुदिवसः' शुभदिनम्। अद्यैव प्रथमदर्शनम् इति सुदिवस एवायम्।। कर्णयोः सम्बन्धे 'अमृतविन्दुः' इव 'सुन्दराणि' सुभगानि। एतत्त स्वगतमिव प्रतिभाति। अन्यथा लवस्य "क एषः" इत्यादि न सङ्गच्छते।। 'रामायणम्' इत्याख्या यस्याः 'कथायाः' तस्याः 'पुरुषौ' नायकौ। रामायणपाठात् जानाम्येव तौ इत्यर्थः।।

Notes. 1. आश्रम etc.—अभि+अर्द+क्त कर्तरि अभ्यर्ण close by. अभ्यर्णा भूमिः अभ्यर्णभूमिः। आश्रमस्य अभ्यर्णभूमिः। 2. अद्य द्रष्टव्यः —This is to be the first sight. 3. अमृत etc.—The words pour nectar into my ears. 4. तत् कथम् etc.—Janaka has not seen the Rāmāyaṇa, hence the query ; the Rāmāyaṇa doers not refer to the children. 5. *Remark*—Lava's question is uncalled for Kausalyā has already said "वत्सलक्ष्मणस्य पुत्रकः etc. Janaka's answer is not fuller than this. I suspect Kausalyā's वत्सलक्ष्मणस्य etc." is स्वगत।

(xxxvii) **अरुन्धती (विहस्य)–आविष्कृतं कथाप्रावीण्यं कुमारेण।**

Arun (*Laughing*)—Mastery of the stroy has been shown by the boy.

जनकः–यदि त्वामीदृशः कथायामभिज्ञः तत् ब्रूहि तावत् पृच्छामः तेषां दशरथात्मजानां किन्नामधेयान्यपत्यानि केषु दारेषु प्रसूतानि।

Jan.—If you are so well-informed in the story, then tell me, I say, of the sons of Daśaratha, how named are the children and born unto which of the wives ?

लवः–नायं कथाप्रविभागः अस्माभिरन्येन वा श्रुतपूर्वः।

Lava.—This part of the story has not been heard yet by me or any one else.

जनकः–किं न प्रणीतः कविना ?

Jan.—Has it not been composed by the poet ?

लवः–प्रणीतो न प्रकाशितः। तस्यैव कोऽप्येकदेशः सन्दर्भान्तरेण रसवानभिनेयार्थः कृतः। तञ्च स्वहस्तलिखितं मुनिर्भगवान् व्यसृजत् भरतस्य मुनेस्तीर्यत्रिकसूत्रकारस्य।

Lava.—Composed but not published. A certain highly emotional portion of the very same has been rendered capable of stage-representation by a different composition ; and that, written out with his own hand, the mighty sage has sent over to sage Bharata the author of the rules of dramaturgy.

जनकः—किमर्थम् ?

Jan.—What for ?

लवः—स किल भगवान् तमप्सरोभिः प्रयोजयिष्यतीति।

Lava—So that he the worshipful (Bharata) might have it staged by celestial nymphs.

जनकः—सर्वमिदमस्माकमाकूतकरम्।

Jan.—All this rouses our curiosity.

मित—।'कथायां' रामायणे 'प्रावीण्य'' निपुणता अभिज्ञता।।'प्रस्तानि' जातानि।। 'कथायाः प्रविभागः' अंशविशेषः। पूर्वं श्रुतः' श्रुतपूर्वः।।'प्रकाशितः प्रचारितो लोके। यत्र कथाप्रविभागे दाशरथीनामपत्योत्पतिर्वर्णिता 'तस्यैव रसवान्' भावप्रधानः करुणादिरसाढ्यः 'कोऽपि एकदेशः सन्दर्भान्तरेण अन्येन सन्दर्भेण प्रबन्धेन 'अभिनेयः' अभिनययोग्यः 'अर्थः' वस्तु यस्य तादृशः 'कृतः' नाटकरूपेण रक्षितः। अनवसरे अन्येन एतदर्थी मा विज्ञायि इति 'सहस्तेन लिखितम्'। 'तौर्यत्रिकसूत्रकारस्य' नाट्यसूत्रकारस्य [शेषे षष्ठी]। 'आकूतकरम्' अभिप्रायजननं कौतूहलौद्दीपकम् ।।

Notes. 1. कथाप्रावीण्यम्—प्रकृष्टा वीणा अस्य प्रवीणः an expert in the lyre; hence, except in general. तस्य भाव इति प्रवीण+ष्यञ् प्रावीण्यम् etc. 2. कुमारेण—कुमार a boy. तेन। 3. किन्नाम etc.—नाम एव इति नामन्+धेय स्वार्थे नामधेयम् name. किं नामधेयमेषाम् etc. 4. कथाप्रविभागः—प्रविभाग section etc. 5. तौर्यत्रिक etc.—तूर्य is पटह। तुर्यस्य इदम् इति तूर्य+अण् तौर्यम् related to the drum, i.e., any thing to the accompaniment of the drum. त्रीणि एव इति चि+कन् स्वार्थे त्रिकम्। Singular because the स्वार्थ of a संख्या is संख्या in the abstract. तौर्याणं त्रिकम् the triad related to the drum. This is नृत्यगीतवाद्य or नाट्य। ''तौर्यत्रिकं नृत्यगीतबाद्यं नाट्यमित्रयम्'' इत्यमरः। सूत्र and principles, the canons. सूत्रं कृतवान् इति सूत्र+कृ+अण कर्त्तरि सूत्रकारः। तौर्यत्रिकस्य सूत्रकारः the author of the principles of dramaturgy. 6. अप्सरोभिः etc.—प्र+युज means here 'to stage' अभियनम्। अप्सरसः प्रयोक्ष्यन्ति=भगवान् अप्सरोभिः प्रयोजयिष्यन्ति with णिच्। This refers to Act VII. 7. आकूत etc.—The secrecy observed by the sage rouses our curiosity.

(xxxviii) लवः—महती पुनस्तस्मिन् भववतो बाल्मीकेरास्था। केषाञ्चिदन्तेवासिनां हस्तेन तत् पुस्तकं भरताश्रमं प्रेषितम्। तेषामानुयात्रिकश्चापपाणिः प्रमादापनोदनार्थम् अस्मद्भ्राता प्रेषितः।

Lava.—Great, however, is mighty Vālmīki's concern for it ; the book has been sent to the hermitage of Bharata through the hand of certain pupils ; my brother has been sent bow in hand as their attendant to avert accidents.

कौसल्या—जाद भादा विदेअत्थि [जात, भ्रातापि ते अस्ति]।

Kaus.—Is there a brother to you too, dear boy ?

लवः—अस्त्वार्यः कुशो नाम।

Lava—There is noble Kuśa by name.

कौसल्या—जेठ्ठो त्ति भणिदं होदि [ज्येष्ठ इति भणितं भवति]।

Kaus.—It is implied that he is the elder.

लवः—एवमेतत्। प्रसवक्रमेण स किल ज्यायान्।

Lava.—So it is. He is my senior in order of delivery.

जनकः—यमजावायुष्मतौ ?

Jan.—Are your long-lived selves twins ?

लवः—अथ किम् ?

Lava—What else ? (Yes).

मित—। 'आस्था आग्रहः'। 'अन्तेवासिनां' शिष्याणाम्। 'प्रेषितः' गमितः। 'आनुयाचिकः' अनुचरः।'प्रमादानोदनार्थं' विपन्निवारणार्थम्।।'प्रसवस्य' यः'क्रमः' परिपाटी आनुपूर्वी इत्यर्थः तेन हेतुना। 'ज्यायान्' वृद्धतरः। अगजः सः अनुजोऽहम् इति भावः। 'यमजौ' युग्मजातौ।।

Notes. 1. हस्तेन etc.—प्रेषित has इष गती दिवादि। Thus पुस्तकं भरताश्रमं प्रेषितवत् गतवत्=वाल्मीकिः पुस्तकं (अणिकर्तृकम्–प्रयोज्यकर्म) भरताश्रमं प्रेषितवान् गमितवान्। Changing voice वाल्मीकिना पुस्तकम् (उक्त प्रयोज्यकर्म) भरताश्रमं प्रेषितम्। 2. आनुयात्रिकः–अनु पश्चात् यात्रा अनुयात्रा following. अनुयात्रा प्रयोजनमस्य इति अनुयात्रा+ठञ् आनुयात्रिकः a follower. 3. चाप etc.—चापः पाणी अस्य। The परनिपात of सप्तमी is by "प्रहरणार्थेभ्यश्च'। The bow shows that Vālmīki apprehended an attack from some hostile party. This seems absurd. 4. प्रमाद etc.—प्रमाद is अनवधानता carelessness ; hence, accident arising from carelessness, a disaster. The disaster is such as can be removed by an armed guard (चापपाणि) । 5. जात etc.—कौसल्या asks this question in despair. A mother with *two* children must be some one other than सीता । 6. प्रसवक्रमेण etc.—This again revives hope. If these are twins, it is not unlikely that सीता gave birth to them before she perished.

(xxxix) **जनकः—कथय कथाप्रबन्धस्य कीदृशः पर्यन्तः।**

Jan.—Tell me, of what kind the last stage of the composition of the story is.

लवः—अलीकपौरप्रवोदोद्विग्नेन राज्ञा निर्वासितां देवयजनसम्भवां सीतादेवीम् आसन्नप्रसववेदनाम् एकाकिनोमरण्ये परित्यज्य लक्ष्मणः प्रतिनिवृत्त इति।

Lava—This (is what it is)—Lakṣmaṇa returned, having left alone, in the forest, queen Sītā with labour pains imminent—Sītā, sprung from the sacrificial ground of the gods, who was banished by the king annoyed by the unfounded slander of the citizens.

कौसल्या—हा वच्छे मुद्धचन्दमुहि को दाणीं दे सरीरकुसुमस्स देब्बदुव्विलासपरिणामो एअलिआए णिवड़िदो [हा वत्से मुग्धचन्द्रमुखि क इदानीं ते शरीरकुसुमस्य दैवदुर्विलासपरिणाम एकाकिन्या निपतितः]।

Kaus.—Ah ! my artless child with a moon-like face, what kind of an end, by evil trun of fate, befell your flower-like frame when alone ?

जनकः—हा वत्से,

Jan.—Alas ! Child,

नूनं त्वया परिभवश्च नवश्च घोरं
ताञ्च व्यथां प्रसवकालकृतामवाप्य।
क्रव्यान्दणेषु परितः परिवारयत्सु
सन्त्रस्तया शरणमित्यसकृत् स्मतोऽस्मि ।। 23 ।।

I was surely more than once invoked by you as protector when you felt that fresh and deep insult and that pain brought on by the hour of delivery and got frightened, groups of beasts of prey crowding all round.

मित– । 'कथाया: प्रबन्ध: ग्रन्थनम्। पर्यन्त:' प्रान्तभाग: अवसानमित्यर्थ:।। 'अलीक:' असत्य: य: 'पौरप्रवाद:' लोकनिन्दा तेन 'उद्विग्नेनं' विचलितेन।। 'मुग्धा' सरला 'चन्द्रमुखी' विधुवदना, तत्संबुद्धौ। 'दैवस्य' भाग्यस्य 'दुर्विलासात्' दुर्व्यापारात् 'परिणाम:' दशाविपाक:।। नूनमिति।

अन्वय:–नूनं नवञ्च धोरञ्च परिभवम्, प्रसवकालकृतां तां व्यथाञ्च, अवाप्य परित: क्रव्याद्गणेषु परिवारयत्सु सन्त्रस्तया त्वया असकृत शरणमिति स्मृतोऽस्मि।

व्याख्या–'नूनं निश्चितं 'नवञ्च अपूर्वञ्च 'धोरञ्च' दारुणञ्च 'पराभवम्' अपमानम्, 'प्रसवकालेन कृतां' जनितां 'तां व्यथाञ्च' भुवनविदितां वेदनामपि 'आवाप्य' प्राप्य 'परित:' समन्तात् 'क्रव्याद्गणेषु' आममांसाशनेषु हिंस्रेषु इत्यर्थ:। 'परिवारयत्सु' वेष्टमानेषु सत्सु 'सन्तस्त्या' भीतया 'त्वया असकृत्' वहुश 'शरणम् इति' त्रायस्व तात शरणं गतास्मि इत्येवंरूपेण 'स्मृतोऽस्मि आकन्दितोऽस्मि।।

Notes. 1. अलीक etc.—The narration incites their grief, and कौसल्या is the first to give expression to it. 2. मुग्ध etc.—मुग्ध is here सरल। मुग्धा चासौ चन्द्रमुखी च। 3. इदानीम्–This is an expletive here (वाक्याङ्कारे)। 4. शरीर etc.—शरीरं कुसुममिव etc. The comparison is in सौकुमार्य tenderness. 5. एकाकिन्या:–Expresses helpness. Hence जनक says सन्त्रस्तया शरणमित्यसकृत् स्मृतोऽस्मि। 6. नवम्–A new and unheard of insult. 7. घोरम्–A deep insult.

(xl) **लव: (अरुन्धती प्रति)–आर्य कावेतौ ?**

Lava (To Arundhatī)—Noble Lady, who are these two ?

अरुन्धती–इयं कौसल्या अयं जनक:।

Arun.—This is Kausaly, this is Janaka.

लव:–(सबहुमानखेदकौतुकं पश्यति)।

Lava—(*Eyes them with respect, sympathy and curiosity*).

जनक:–अहो दुर्मर्यादाता पौराणाम्, अहो रामस्य राज्ञ: क्षिप्रकारिता।

Jan.—O the impudence of the citizen ! O the rashness of king Rāma !

एतद्वैशरघोरवज्रपतनं शश्वन्ममोत्पश्यत:
क्रोधस्य ज्वलितु धगित्यवसरश्चापेन शापेन वा ! (24)

Of me ever brooding over this terrible thunderstroke of a butchery, this is the time for wrath of blaze forth, sounding धक्, with the bow or a curse.

कौसल्या–भअवदि परित्ताहि पारित्ताहि। पसादेहि रुसिदं राएमिं [भगवति परित्रायस्व पिरत्रायस्व। प्रसादय रुषितं राजर्षिम्]।

Kaus—Save us, O worshipful (Arundhati)] save us. Pacify the enraged royal sage.

अरुन्धती–

एतद्धि परिभूतानां प्रायश्चित्तं मनस्विनाम्।
राजन्नपत्यं रामस्ते पाल्याश्च कृपणाः प्रजाः।। 25।।

Arun.—This is indeed usually the reslove of the spirited when insulted. Rāma is your child, O king and the poor subjects have to be spared.

जनकः–

शान्तं वा रघुनन्दने तदुभयं तत् पुत्रभीण्डं हि मे।
भूयिष्ठद्विजबालवृद्धविकलस्त्रैणश्च पौरो जनः।। 26।।

Jan.—O let both these desist (lit—both have been quieted) in the case of Raghunandana ; he is my treasure of a son. The crowd of citizens again is mostly one of Brāhmaṇas, the aged, the deformed and women.

मित–। 'बहुमानः' गौरवं 'खेदः' समवेदना 'कौतुकं' कौतूहलम्। तैः सह। कथमिहागतौ इति कौतूहलम्।। "मर्यादा' सीमा करणीयस्य अवधिः। दुःस्थिता मर्यादा एषां दुर्मर्यादाः। तेषां भावः। क्षिप्रं द्रुतं करोति इति क्षिप्रकारी। तस्य भावः अविमृश्यकारिता ।। एतदिति।

अन्वयः–एतत् वैशसघोरवज्रपतनं शश्वत् उत्पश्यतः मम क्रौधस्य चापेन शापेन वा 'धक्' इति ज्वलितुम् अवसरः (अध प्राप्तः)।

व्याख्या–'एतत् इदं 'वैशसरूपं' दीनाया सीताया विहननरूपं 'घोरं' दारुणं यत् 'वज्रपतनम्' अशनिसन्पातः तत् 'शश्वत्' सदा 'उत्पश्यतः' ध्यायतः 'मम क्रोधस्य' कोपाग्नेः 'क्षापेन' धनुषा 'शापेन वा' करणेन 'धक् इति' शब्देन सह 'ज्वलितुम् अवसरः' समयः अद्य प्राप्तः इति वाक्यशेषः।। एतद्धीति।

अन्वयः–परिभूतानां मनस्विनां चितं प्रायः एतत् हि। राजन्, रामः ते अपत्यं कृपणाः प्रजाश्च पाल्याः।

व्याख्या–'परिभूतानां' विमानितानां 'मनस्विनां' दृढ़वितानां तेजस्विनामित्यर्थः 'चित्तं' चेतः सङ्कल्पः इत्यर्थः 'प्रायः' बाहुल्येन 'एतत् हि' ईदृशमेव चापेन शापेन वा प्रतिकर्त्तुमनस एव ते भवन्ति। किन्तु हे 'राजन्' मिथिलेश उभयमेव परिहर्त्तव्यं ते, यतः 'रामः ते अपत्यं' सन्ततिसदृशः तत् क्षिप्रकारित्वेऽपि तं प्रति कुतश्चापस्त शापस्य वा प्रयोगः। 'कृपणाः' दीनाः 'प्रजाश्च पौरा अपि 'पाल्याः' पालनमेव अर्हन्ति दुर्मर्यादत्वेऽपि ते चापस्य शापस्य वा विषयो भावतु नार्हन्ति।। शान्तमिति।

अन्वयः–(अथ) वा रघुनन्दने तत् उभयं शान्तम्, तत् मे पुत्रभाण्डं हि। पौरो जनश्च भूयिष्ठद्विजवालवृद्धविकलस्त्रैणः।

व्याख्या–अथ 'वा' पक्षान्तरे 'रघुनन्दने' रामे 'तत्' चापरूपम् शापरूपम् 'उभयं शान्तं' निष्क्रियं तिष्ठतु 'तत्' रघुनन्दनरूपं वस्तु 'मे पुत्रभाण्डं हि' पुत्ररूपं नहि चापो वा शापो वा तस्मिन् युज्यते। 'पौरो जनश्च' पुरवासिनः अपि 'भूयिष्ठः' बहवो 'द्विजाः' ब्राह्मणः 'बालाः शिशवः 'वृद्धा विकलाः' भग्नाङ्गाः 'स्त्रैणं' स्त्रीसमूहश्च यस्मित् तादृशः तत् दर्मर्यादत्वेऽपित तस्मिन्नयोग्यो दण्डः। तदेष प्रशान्तोऽस्मि।।

Notes. 1. दुर्मर्यता–मर्यादा here it limit, limit of the liberty that may be allowed. दुःस्थिता मर्यादा is *misplaced*, limit, *i.e.'* transgression of the limit. 2. वैशस etc.—विशसति हिनस्ति इति वि+शस+अच् कर्त्तरि विशसः a murderer. तस्य कर्म इति विशस+अण् वैशसम् murder. etc 3. ज्वलितुम्–To become manifest. We do not say 'to burn', for then क्रोध becomes identified with fire and शापेन ज्वलितुम् is then incongruous. 4. धगिति–A man in anger often shouts. The noise made is here referred to by the familiar sound धिक् which a fire makes when kindled. Hence there is an implied comparison of क्रोध with fire. 5. चापेन etc.—3या करणे। 6. रुषितम्–रष+क्त कर्त्तरि रुषित or रुष्ट। This exhibition is inconsistent with Janaka's character as a sage. 7.शान्तम्–शम्+णिच्+क्त कर्मणि शान्त or शमित quelled. 8. पुत्रभाण्डम्–भाण्ड funds treasure. तत् here is in the neuter because भाण्ड is neuter and भाण्ड is the विधेय here. "भाण्डं मूलवणिग्धेन" इति विश्वः। 9. भूयिष्ठ etc.—अतिशयेन बहव इति बहु+इष्ठन् भूयिष्ठाः numerous. स्त्रीणां समूहः इति स्त्री+नञ् स्त्रैणम् a group of women. etc.

(*xli*) (प्रविश्य) सम्भ्रान्ता वटवः–कुमार अश्वः अश्वः इति कोऽपि भूतविशेषो जनपदेषु श्रूयते। सोऽयमधुना अस्माभिः प्रत्यक्षीकृतः।

(*Entering*) Excited Scholar—O youth, we hear there is a certain kind of animal in the provinces called 'Horse.' Here is that one just now seen by us.

लवः—अश्व इति पशुसमाम्नाये सांग्रामिके च पठ्यते। तद्ब्रूत कीदृशः।

Lava—'Horse' is mentioned in the enumeration (list) of animals also in works on warfare. So tell me how it looks.

वटवः—श्रूयताम्।

Scholars—Listen.

पश्चात् पुच्छं वहति विपुलं तच्च धूनोत्यजस्रं
दीर्घग्रीवः स भवति खुरास्तस्य चत्वार एव।
शष्पाण्यत्ति प्रकिरति शकृत्पिण्डकानाम्रमात्रान्
किं वाख्यातैर्ब्रजति स पुनर्दूरमेह्येहि यामः ।। 26 ।।

Behind, it carries a big tail and waves it ceaselessly ; it is long-necked ; its hoofs are but four ; it eats grass and drops lumps of dung of the size of a mango. Or, away with descriptions ; come, come, we go ; it will move far away.

(इत्य पसृत्य अजिने हस्तयोश्चापकर्षन्ति)।

(*Adavancing they drag him by the deer-skin and the hands*).

मित–। 'सम्भ्रान्ताः' जातसम्भ्रमाः।। 'पशूनां सामस्नायः' नामसंग्रह तस्मिन्। 'संग्रामं युद्धम् अर्हति इत 'साग्रामिकः' युद्धोपयोगी पदार्थः। लक्षणया तत्पदार्थः—नामसंग्रहः। तस्मिन्।। पश्चादिति।

अन्वयः—पश्चात् विपुलं पुच्छं वहति तच्च अजस्नं धूनोति। स दीर्घग्रीवो भवति। तस्य चत्वार एव खुराः। शष्पाणि अत्ति, आम्रमात्रान् शकृपिण्डकान् प्रकिरति। आख्यातैः कि वा, स पुनर्दूरं ब्रजति, एहि एहि यामः।

व्याख्या–'पश्चात्' कटिप्रान्ते 'विपुलं पुच्छं' बृहल्लाङ्गलं 'वहति' धत्ते। 'तच्च' पुच्छं पुनः 'अजस्रं धूनोति' सततं चलयति। 'सः' पशुः 'दीर्घा ग्रीवा' यस्य तादृशो 'भवति'। 'तस्य चत्वार एव खुराः' अभिन्नास्तस्य शफाः। सः 'शष्पाणि अत्ति' तृणभोजी किल सः 'आम्रमात्रान् आम्वप्रमाणान् 'शकृत्पिण्डकान्' पुरीषपिण्डान्, प्रकिरति' त्यजति। 'आख्यानैः' आख्यातैः वर्णनाभिः 'कित्वां स्यात् 'स पुनर्दूरं ब्रजति' यावद्वर्णायामः तावत् स दृष्टिविषमत्येति तत् 'एहि एहि यामः' यत्र स आस्तेतत्रैव। स्वयं दृष्ट्वा ज्ञास्यसि कीदृशः सः इति।।

Notes. !. भूत etc.–भूतानां विशेषः भेदः a kind of animal. 2. जनपदेषु etc.—Construe भूतविशेषो जनपदेषु (अस्ति इति) श्रूयते। 3. प्रत्यक्षीकृतः–अक्ष्णः प्रति इति प्रति+अक्षि+टच् समासान्त प्रत्यक्षम् cognition of the eye. An अव्ययी– । तत् अस्ति इति प्रत्यक्ष+ अच् मत्वर्थे प्रत्यक्षः visible. अप्रत्यक्षः प्रत्यक्षः सम्पद्यमानः कृतः इति प्रत्यक्ष+च्वि+कृ+क्त कर्मणि प्रत्यक्षीकृतः rendered visible. 4. पशुसमाम्नाये–सम्यक् आम्नायते अस्मिन् इति सम्+आ+स्ना+घञ् अधिकरणे समास्नायः a list. पशूनां समाम्नायः। 5. सांग्रामिके–संग्राम war. संग्रामम् अर्हति इति संग्राम+ठञ् सांग्रामिकः anything having a place in war. By transference of epithets it means here the list containing enumeration of war meterials. 6. अजस्रम्–न जस्यति मुञ्चति इयि नञ्+जस+र कर्त्तरि अजस्रम् ceaselessness. तत् यथा तथा। Qual. धूनोति। 7. आम्रमात्रान्–आम्रं मात्रा परिमाणमेषाम् आम्रमात्राः। तान्। 8. आख्यातैः–आ+ख्या+क्त भावे आख्यातम् description. 7. अजिने etc. They catch hold of लव, some by the garment some by his hands. etc.

(*xlii*) **लवः (सकौतुकोपरोधविनयम्)–आर्याः पश्यत पश्यत एभिर्नीतोऽस्मि। (इति त्वरितं परिक्रामति)**

Lava (*With humility and pressure of curiosity*)—Behold. Noble Sirs, behold, I am being led away by these (boys) (*Goes round the stage quick*).

अरुन्धतीजनकौ–पूरयतु कौतुकं वत्सः।

Arun. and Jan.—Let the dear child satisfy his curiosity.

कौसल्या–भअवदि जाणामि एदं अणलोअन्ती ण जीआमि विअ। अदो अणदो भविअ पेक्खम्ह दाव गच्छमाणं दीहाउं [भगवति जानामि एतम् अनालीकयन्ती न जीवामि इव। अतः अन्यतो भूत्वा प्रेक्षे ताबद्गच्छन्तं दीर्घायुषम्)।

Kaus.—Worshipful lady, I feel as if I shall not live on not seeing this boy. So, shifting elsewere, let us see the long-lived one go.

अरुन्धती–दूरमतिक्रान्तः स चपलः कथं दृश्यते !

Arun.—Far has the nimble boy gone, how can he be seen.

(प्रविश्य) कञ्चुकी–भगवान् वाल्मीकिराह ज्ञातव्यमेतदवसरे भवद्भिरिति।

(Entering) Kañch.—Mighty Vālmīki says that you will know it at its time.

जनकः—अतिगम्भीरमेतत् किमपि भविष्यति। भगवत्यरुन्धति सखि कौसल्ये आर्य गृष्टे स्वयमेव भगवन्तं प्राचेतसं पश्यामः। (इति निष्क्रान्तो वृद्धवर्गः)।

Jan.—This must be something very deep. Worshipful Arundhatī, friend, noble Gṛṣṭī, we shall go ourselves and see the mighty Prcetasa. (*Exeunt the group of elders*).

मित–। 'कौतुकस्य' अश्वदर्शनकुतूहलस्य यः 'उपरोधः' नियन्त्रणं तेन सह 'विनयेन' नम्रतया च सह।। 'अवसरे' यथासमये।। 'अतिशयेन गम्भीरं गूह्यम्।।

Notes. 1. सकौतुक etc.—उपरोध importunity here, urging, etc. कौतुकोपरोध the urging of curiosity. He was unable to resist it but he though it would be rude to leave the elders abruptly and he meekly blurts out something like an apology—What can I do sirs, these people are dragging me away !

(xliii) **वटवः—पश्यतु कुमारस्तदाश्चर्यम् ।**

Scholars—Let our young friend see that wonder.

लवः—दृष्टम् अवगतञ्च । नूनमाश्वमेधिकोऽयमश्व इति।

Lava—It is seen and known. Surely it is a horse for the Aśvamedha sacrifice.

वटवः—कथं ज्ञायते ?

Scholars—How is that known ?

लवः—ननु मूर्खाः पठितमेव युष्माभिस्तत्काण्डे किं न पश्यथ। प्रत्येक शतसंख्याः कवचिनो दण्डिनो निषङ्गिणश्च रक्षितारः। तत्प्रायमेव बलमिदं दृश्यते। यदीह न प्रत्ययः तत् गत्वा पृच्छत ।

Lava—Why idiots ! why do you not see what has been acually read by you in that section ? The gurads have to be armour-bearers, mace-holders, quiver-carriers, each a hundred in number. This force indeed seems to be about that much. If you do not believe in it, then go and ask.

वटवः—भोः भोः किम्प्रयोजनोऽयमश्वः परिवृतः पर्यटति ?

Scholars—Ho ! Ho ! For what purpose does this horse roam guarded ?

लवः–(सस्पृहमात्मगतम्)–अये अश्वमेध इति विश्वविजयिनां क्षत्रियाणाम् ऊर्जस्वलः सर्वक्षत्रियपरिभावी महानुत्कर्षनिष्कर्षः।

Lava (*Longingly to himself*)—Ha ! Of Kṣattriyas that have conquered the world, this Aśvamedha is the mighty and pre-eminent emblem (Lit essence) of ascendancy disgracing all other Kṣattriyas.

नेपथ्ये– अयमश्वः पताकेयमथवा वीरघोषुणा।
सप्तलोकैककवीरस्य दशकण्ठकुलद्विषः ।। 27 ।।

In the Tiring Room—This horse is—Or rather his valour proclaming banner is one of the matchless hero of the seven worlds, the slayers of the race of the ten-necked monster.

मित–। 'आश्चर्यम्' अद्भुतं वस्त अश्वमित्यर्थः।। 'आश्वमेधिकः' अश्वमेध–प्रयोजनः।। 'तत्काण्डे' अश्वमेधप्रकरणे। 'कवचिनः' वर्मधारिणः' 'दण्डिनः' लगुड़हस्वाः, 'निषङ्गिणाः' तूणीरवन्तः।'प्रायेणा' बाहुल्येन 'तत्' तथाविधं 'तत्प्रायम्' [''एकविभक्ति चापूर्वनिपाते'' इति प्रायशदस्य परनिपातः]। 'इह' मदुक्तौ। 'किं प्रयोजनम्' अस्य।। 'स्पृहया' आत्मनस्तदस्तु इति वाञ्छया। 'ऊर्जो बलम् अस्ति अस्मिन् 'ऊर्जस्वलः' तेजोमयः।'सर्वेषां क्षत्रियाणां परिभावी' अपमानकरः।'उत्कर्षस्य प्राधान्यस्य 'निष्कर्षः' सारोद्धारः।। अयमिति।

अन्वयः–अयम् अश्वः–। अथवा सप्तलोकैककवीरस्य दशकण्ठकुदद्विषः इयं वीरघोषण्णा पताका।

व्याख्या–'अयम् अश्वः'। 'रामाश्वमेधप्रयोजनः' इत्युत्तरमिष्टं वटूनां प्रश्नस्य। असमाप्ते वाक्ये स्वयमेवाच्छि प्राह 'अथवा' नायमश्वः, किन्तु 'सप्तसु लोकेषु 'यः 'एकवीरः' वीराग्रणीः तस्य 'दशकण्ठकुलस्य' रावणवंशस्य द्विषः' निहन्तुः रामस्य राज्ञः 'इयं वीरघोषणा' वीर्यविज्ञापनी 'पताका' वैजयन्ती। पताकेयं न अश्वः तत् किं पृच्छसि ''किम्प्रयोजनोऽयमश्वः'' इति।।

Notes. 1. वटवः–But the scholars have left the stage. Comp. ''दूरमतिक्रान्तः etc.'' above. Better say ''(ततः प्रविशति लवः वटवश्च)। वटवः''। 2. आश्चर्यम्–आ+चर+यत् कर्मणि आचर्य practicable ; but आश्चर्य with सुट् by the rule ''आश्चर्यमनित्ये'' when meaning something very rare, *'i.e.'* not of everyday occurrence (अनित्य)। 3. आश्वमेधिकः–अश्वमेधः प्रयोजनयमस्य

इति अश्वमेध+ठञ्। 4. मूर्खाः–पठितमेव न पश्यथ, hence मूर्खाः। 5. तत्प्रायम्–For परनिपात of प्राय Comp. "प्रबलतमसामेवन्प्रायाः शुभेषु हि वृत्तयः"–*Śakuntala*. 6. सस्पृहम्–स्पृहा longing May I become such a क्षत्रिय some day ; this is the longing. 7. विश्व etc.—विश्वं साधु विजितवन्तः इति विश्व+वि+जि+इनि कर्त्तरि साधुकारिणि। तेषाम्। 7. ऊर्जस्वलः–ऊर्जस्+वलच् मत्वर्थे by निपातन in the rule "ज्योत्स्नातमिस्रा–"। निपातन does not bar the regular विनि, hence ऊर्जस्वी is also available. 8. सर्व etc.—सर्वक्षत्रिय+परि+भू+णिनि कर्त्तरि। ताच्छील्ये। 9. उत्कर्ष etc.—निष्कर्ष is सार extract. उत्कर्ष excellence, ascendancy, महान् उत्कर्षनिष्कर्षः the quintessence of excellence of ascendancy. 10. अयमश्वः etc.—This is in reply to the scholars' "किन्प्रयोजनोऽयमश्वः"। The reply means to say—This horse in meant for Rāma's Aśvamedha ; अयमश्वः is only the beginning of the reply. The speaker, however, does not complete the reply. When only half-uttered, he changes his mind and treats the horse not as a horrse but as an ensign. Accordingly the wording of the answer is altered into पताकेयम् etc. It is usual to treat the अश्व and the पताका as two distinct things here. But then why does the answer speak of the पताका at all ? The question does not refer to it. Besides लव himself treats the horse as पताका। To the guards he says below "पताकां वो हराम्यहम्" and forthwith asks the scholars to lead the horse to the hermitage—"लोष्टैर्घ्नन्तः परावर्त्त यतैनमश्वम्"। The scholars again in reply say "कृतमनेन अश्वेन" not "कृतमनया पताकया"। 11. वीरघोषणा–वीराणां घोषणा proclamation which heores usually make. Or वीर stands for वीर्य। वीरस्य घोषणा। 12. सप्त etc.—सप्तावयवो लोकः सप्तलोकः the seven-limbed universe. एकेषु मुख्येषु वीरयते इति एक+वीर (अदन्त चुरादि आत्मनेपदी)+णिच् अच् कर्त्तरि। Or—एकः वीरः इति एक वीरः। वीरैकः was expected by" पूर्वापर प्रथम–"। This is irregularly formed (बाहुलकात्) ; cp "कथमेकवीर इति ?" "पूर्वकालैक–" इति वाधित्वा परत्वादनेन ("पूर्वापर" इति सूत्रेण) समासे वीरैक इति हि स्यात्। बहुलग्रहणात् भविष्यति।"–*Bhaṭṭoji*. Also comp. "शरवर्षमनेकमेकवीर"–Śiśu. सप्तलोकस्य or सप्तलोके एकवीरः। तस्य। 15. दशकण्ठ etc.—दशकण्ठकुलं द्वेष्टि इति दशकण्ठकुल+द्विष+क्विप् कर्त्तरि। तस्य।

(xliv) **लवः (सव्यथमिव)–अहो सन्दीपनान्यक्षराणि।**

Lava (*Showing as if pained*)—Ah ! What provoking words!

वटवः–किमुच्यते, प्राज्ञः खलु कुमारः।

Scholars—What say you ? Our young friend is indeed well-informed.

लवः—भोः भोः, तत् किमक्षत्रिया पृथ्वी यदेवमुदीर्यते।

Lava.—Ho ! Ho ! Is then the world devoid of Kṣattriyas that you speak thus ?

नेपथ्ये—अरे, महाराजं प्रति कुतः क्षत्रियाः ?

In the Tiring Room—Sirrah [Or—Aha]! Where are Kṣattriyas to vie with our great king?

लवः—धिग् जाल्मान्।

Lava—Fire, idiots !

यदि ते सन्ति सत्त्वेव केयमन्या बिभीषिका।

विभुक्तैः सन्निपत्यैब पताकां वो हराम्यहम् ।।28।।

If there are so, let them be so ; what again is this terrorising. Away with words ; I will even fall upon you and carry away your 'banner'.

भो वटवः, लोष्टैर्घ्नन्तः परावर्त्तयतैनमश्वम्। एष रोहितानां मध्ये वराकश्चरतु।

Ho ! Scholars, trun this horse back hitting him with clods. Let this poor thing graze among the deer.

मित—। एतदुक्तानि 'अक्षराणि' अयमश्व इत्यादीनि 'सन्दीपनानि' तेजःसन्धुक्षणानि। श्रुत्वा दीप्यते मदीयं तेजः।। 'किमुच्यते' भवद्भिः मम तु मतं 'प्राज्ञः खलु' सम्यक् ज्ञाता एव 'कुमारः' यतः सत्यमूहितं तेन।। 'अक्षत्रिया अविद्यमानाः' क्षत्रिया वीरा इत्यर्थः यस्यां तथाविधा। अस्ति चेत् वीरः कश्चित् न स नूनं भृष्यति। 'उदीर्यते' उच्चैरुच्यते।। 'महाराजं प्रति' रामं प्रत्यर्थ्य स्थिताः, रामस्य प्रतिभटा इत्यर्थः। 'जाल्मान्' मूर्खान्। यदीति।

अन्वयः—यदि ते सन्ति सन्तु एव। इयम् अन्या विभषीका का ? उक्तैः किम् ? सन्निपत्य एव अहं वः पताकां हरामि।

व्याख्या—'यदि ते' राजानः [गौरवे बहुवचनम्] रामः इत्यर्थः 'सन्ति' सर्वातिशायित्वेन 'सन्ति' वर्त्तन्ते 'सन्तु एवा' तत्र कः कस्य मत्सरः ? 'इयं युष्मदुक्ता ' अन्या' अपरा, तेषां सत्ताया इतरा, अयमश्व इत्यादिना उक्त्वा 'विभीषिका' भयप्रदर्शनं 'का' अयुक्ता किल सा। राजा प्रवीरः इत्येव पर्याप्तं प्रजानां संयमे, तस्य वीरत्वमुद्घोष्य भयप्रदर्शनमयुक्त मित्यर्थः। यद्वा—'इयम् अन्या' अभिनवा 'का विभीषिका' भयहेतुः

न कापि, वीराः सन्ति इति नाहं विभेभि इत्यर्थः। अथवा 'उक्तैः' वाक्यव्ययेन 'किम्' अलम्। कर्मणा वः प्रत्याययामि–'सन्निपत्य एव' युष्मन्मध्ये पतित्वा एव 'अहं वः पताकां' इममश्वं यः पताका इति युष्माभिवर्ण्यते 'हरामि' रक्षतैनं यदि शक्ताः। 'परावर्त्तयत विवृत्तमुखं वाहयत। 'रोहितानां' मृगाणाम्। 'वराकः' दीनः।

Notes. I. सन्दीपनानि–सम्+दीप्+णिच्+ल्युट् करणे। 2. वटवः–Evidently the scholars did not speak out all together. One of them is the speaker, and he addresses the rest. 3. प्राज्ञः–प्रजानाति इति प्र+ज्ञा+क कर्त्तरि प्रज्ञः well informed. स एव इति प्रज्ञ+अण् स्वार्थे प्राज्ञः। 4. महाराजं प्रति–कर्मप्रवचनीययोगे 2या। 5. विभीषिका–वि+भी+णिच्+ण्वुल् भावे धात्वर्थनिर्देशे विभीषिका frightening. कैयम् etc. implies that it is bad policy to frighten people in the name of the king, be he ever so powerful. That he is king is enough to extort loyalty. Intimidation only stiffens the back of the people, and if any of them has any spirit in him (क्षत्रियः) he will resist, not because he thinks he can overcome the king, but because it is the nature of a क्षत्रिय not to tolerate intimidation, and he will gladly come out to get crushed. 6. सन्निपत्य–Comp. "उद्दामेन द्विरदपतिना सन्निपत्याभियुक्तः"।

(xlv) **(प्रविश्य) सक्रोधदर्पः पुरुषः–धिक्, चापलम् ! किमुक्तवानसि ? तीक्ष्णानीरसा ह्यायुधायश्रेणयः शिशोरपि दृप्तां वाचं न सहन्ते। राजपुत्रश्चन्द्रकेतुरिविमर्दनः सौम्यपूर्वारण्यदर्शनकुतूहलाक्षिप्तहृदया न यावदायाति तावत् त्वरितमनेन तरुगहनेन अपसर्पत।**

(Entering) A man in anger and hauteur—A curse on your rashness ! What did you say ? Ranks of warriors are rough and ruthless indeed and do not tolerate insolent speech even in a child. Slink away quickly by this thicket of trees by the time Prince Candraketu, the slayer of enemies who now has his mind allured by the pleasures of seeing the charming eastern woods, does not return.

वटवः–कुमार, कृतमनेनाश्वेन। तर्जयन्ति विस्फुरितशस्त्राः कुमारम् आयुधीयश्रेणयः, दूरे चाश्रमपदमितः तदेहि हरिणल्पुतैः पलायामहे।

Scholars—Young friend, no use of this horse. The ranks of warriors whose weapons have flared up are threatening you, our young friend. and the site of the hermitage is far from here ; so come, we scamper off with the bound of the deer.

मित– । 'चापलं' चपलता । तत् । 'तीक्ष्णा सुलभकोपा: 'नीरसा:' अकरुणाश्च । 'आयुधीया:' शस्त्रजीविन: । तेषां 'श्रेणय:' राजय: । 'दृप्तां' दर्पसंस्पृष्टाम् । 'अरीणां विमर्दन: रिपुदलन: ! 'सौम्यस्य' सुदर्शनस्य 'पूर्वारण्यस्य दर्शनकुतूहलेन आक्षिप्तं' व्यासक्तं 'हृदयं' यस्य स: ! 'तरुभि: गहन:' दुर्गम: । तादृशेन पथा । विशेश्यमात्रप्रयोगो विशेष्यप्रतिपत्तौ ।। कृतम्' अलम् । मुच्यताम् अश्व इत्यर्थ: । 'विस्फुरितानि' प्रदीप्तानि 'शस्त्राणि' यासां ता: । 'हरिणानां प्लुतानि' उत्प्लवनानि, तै: ।।

Notes. 1. धिक् etc.—We may take धिक् by itself as an exclamation of reproof of लव । In that case चापलम् also has to be taken by itself with an intonation—चापलम् ? चापलं क्रियते किम् ? 2. अरि etc.—That shows his prowess, you have sinned against no ordinary fighter. 3. सौम्य etc.—-You are lucky that he is not here now. 4. तरु etc.—The road being a rought one you will easily escape. 5. कृतम्–मान्त अव्यय implying prohibition (निषेध) ।

(xlvi) लव: (विहस्य)–किं नाम विस्फुरन्ति शस्त्राणि ?

Lava (Laughing loudly)—What ! Do weapons flare up ?

(धनुरारोपयन)

(*Stringing the bow*)

ज्याजिह्वया वलयितोत्कटकोटिदंष्ट्र-
मुद्नारि घोरघनर्घरघोषमेतत् ।
ग्रासप्रसक्तहसदन्तकवक्त्रयन्त्र–
जम्भाविड़म्बि विकटोदरमस्तु चापम् ।।28।।

Let this bow has encircled its sharp teeth-like tips with its tongue-like string, (the bow) that will be uttering an awful growling roar like that of a cloud, become, with its deep concavity, a copy, of the chasm of the machine of a mouth of Death when inten upon swallowing (the Universe) hence grinning (with delight). (*Exceunt all suitably going round the stage*).

(इति यथोचितं परिक्रम्य निष्क्रान्ता: सर्वे) ।

कौसल्याजनकयोगो नाम चतुर्थोऽङ्क: ।

This is the Fourth Act called the meeting of Kausalyā and Janaka.

मित–। 'आरोपयन्' आरोहयन्' ज्यां धनुषि योजयन् इत्यर्थः। ज्येति।

अन्वयः–ज्याजिह्वया वलयितोत्कटकोटिद्रंष्ट्रं विकटोदरम् एतत् चापं घोरघनघर्घरघोषम् उद्गारि (सत्) ग्रासप्रसक्तहसदन्तकवक्तव्यन्त्रजृम्भविड़म्बि अस्तु।

व्याख्या– 'ज्याजिह्वया जिह्वातुल्यया ज्यया गुणेन 'वलयिता' वेष्टिता 'उत्कटा' तीक्ष्णा 'कोटिदंष्ट्रां' दुंष्ट्रातुल्या कोटिः अग्रभागः यस्य अतएव 'विकटं' महत् 'उदरं' गह्वरं यस्य तादृशन् 'एतत् चापम्' इदं धनुः आसन्ने अस्मिन् रणव्यापारे 'घोरं' भीमं 'घनस्य' इव 'घर्घरघोषं' घर्घरशब्दम् 'एद्गरि' डद्गोषयत् सत् 'ग्रासे' जगद्ग्रासे 'प्रसक्तः' व्यापृतः अतएव सुमचितभोज्यलाभेन आनन्दात् 'हसन्'यः' अन्तकः' यमः तस्य 'वक्त्रव्यन्त्रस्य' यन्त्ररूपस्य वक्तस्य मुखस्य या 'जृम्भा' व्यादानं 'तद्विडिम्बि' तदनुकारि 'अस्तु' भवतु स्वयं यमेन गिलितमिव धनुषा विलयं यातु बलमिदम् इत्यर्थः।।

Notes. 1. किं नाम etc.—नाम implies क्रोध rising anger. 2. धनुः etc. आ+रुह+णिच्+शतृ आरोपयम् or आरोहयत् causing to mount. The sentence is eiliptical ज्यां आरोपयन् is the complete form. The string usually lies relaxed on the bow and does not reach the tip. When strung the string rises (आरोहति) to the tip. Hence ज्या धनुः आरोहति–the string climbs up the bow. With णिच्, धन्वी ज्यां धनुः आरोहयति or आरोपयति the अणिकर्त्ता becoming कर्म because the root is गत्यर्थक। 3. ज्याजिह्वया–ज्या जिह्वा इव ज्याजिह्वा etc. 4. वलयित etc.—वलय braclet. वलयेन योजिता इति वलय+णिच् (नाम धातु)+क्त कर्मणि वलयिता provided with a bracelet. कोटि दंष्ट्राइव कोटिदंष्ट्रा। Now see टीका। 5. उद्गारि–साधु उद्गिरति इति उद्+ग+णिनि साधुकारिणि कर्त्तरि। 6. घोर etc. 'घर्घर is an अनुकरणशब्द। घर्घर घोषः a gurgling sound. घनस्य घर्घरघोषः घनघर्घरघोषः gurgling sound of a cloud. By transference of epithets this means *like* the gurgling sound of a cloud. घोरः घनघर्घरघोषः etc. 7. ग्रास etc.—For समास see टीका। This alludes to the प्रलय when everything prishes—अन्तक swallows up all. हसन् laughing ; the laugh is one of glee. Ha ! Ha ! I can fill my maw today !! 8. विकट etc.—When strung, the bow is bent. This creates a cavity bounded by the curve of the bow and the staight string, 9. यथोचितम्–उचितस्य अनतिक्रमः यथोचितम् as suited. The परिक्रमण was different with लव and the वटुs। In the case of लव, say त्वरितोद्धतक्रमं निष्क्रान्तः ; the scholars were of course हरिणप्लुतैर्निष्क्रान्ताः।

Chapter - 5

(*i*) **नेपथ्ये–भो भोः सैनिकाः, जातं जातमवलम्वनमस्माकम्।**

In the Tiring Room—Ho ! Ho ! Soldiers, help has come, helop has come unto us.

नन्वेष त्वरितसुमन्त्रनुद्यमानव्यावल्मत्प्रजवनवाजिना रथेन।

उद्घातवप्रचलितकोविदारकेतुः श्रुत्वा नः प्रधनभुपैति चन्द्रकेतुः ।।1।।

Having heard of our fight, here indeed comes Candraketu is his car of which the fleet steeds, urged on by hurrying Sumantra, are galloping and his falgstaff of Kovidara wood shaking throught impacts (against the uneven ground).

(ततः प्रविशति सुमन्त्रसारथिना रथेन धनुष्पाणिः साद्भतहर्षसम्भ-मश्चन्द्रकेतुः)

(*Then enters Candraketu bow in hand in wonder, haste and joy in a car with Sumantra as the charioteer*).

मित–'अवलम्बनं शरणम्। लवेन प्रपीड़ितानाम्'अस्माकं' शरणं समागतम्।। नन्विति।

अन्वयः–ननु एष चन्द्रकेतुः न प्रधनं श्रुत्वा त्वरितसुमन्त्रनुदामानव्यावल्ग-त्प्रजवनवाजिना रथेन उद्घातप्रचलितकोविदारकेतुः (सन्) उपैति।

व्याख्या–'ननु' निश्चितम्'एष चन्द्रकेतुः नः प्रधं' युद्धं' श्रुत्वा त्वरितः' त्वरावान् यः 'सुमन्त्रः' रघुकुलसारथिः तेन 'नुद्यमानाः' प्रयुज्यमानाः अतएव 'व्यावल्गन्तः' धावन्तः 'प्रजवनाः' वेगवन्तः 'वाजिनः' अश्वा यस्मिन् तादृशेन 'रथेन' रथवेगाच्च विषमासु भूमिषु ये 'उद्घाता' गतिप्रतिबन्धाः तैः 'प्रचलितः' कम्पमानः 'कोविदारकेतुः' कोविदारकाष्ठ निर्मितो रथध्वजः यस्य तथाविधः 'उपैति' आगच्छति।। 'सुमन्त्रः सारथिः' यस्मिन् तथाविधेन।'अद्भुतेन' आश्चर्येणा 'हर्षेण' आनन्देन 'सम्भ्रमेण त्वरया च 'सह' ।।

Notes. 1. जातम् etc.—सम्भ्रमे द्विरुक्ति। 2. अवलम्बनम्–अवलम्बते अस्मिन् इति अव+लम्ब+ल्युट् अधिकरणे अवलम्बनम् support. 3. ननु–अवधारणे अव्ययम्। 4. त्वरित etc.—वरा सञ्जाता अस्य इति त्वरा+इतच् त्वरितः hurrying. प्रजवति इति प्र+ज

वेगमने+युच् कर्त्तरि ताच्छील्ये प्रजवनाः speedy. The steeds were naturally speedy, yet Sumantra was in such a hurry that he thought it was necessary to urge them to faster motion. 5. उद्घात etc. उद्+हन+घञ् भावे उद्घात an upward shock. प्र+चल+णिच्+क्त कर्मणि or प्र+चल+क्त कर्त्तरि प्रचलित the क्त being वर्त्तमाने। 6. साद्भ त etc.—अद्भत because of the magnitude of Lava't feat ; हर्ष at the sight of a real hero ; सम्भ्रम for the safety of his own men.

(*ii*) **चन्द्रकेतुः–आर्य सुमन्त्र पश्य पश्च,**

Candraketu—Look, noble Sumantra, look, !

किरति कलितकिञ्चत्कोपरज्यन्मुश्वश्री-
रनवरतनिगुञ्जत्कोटिनाकार्मकेण।
समरशिसि चञ्चत्पञ्चचूड़श्चमूना-
मुपरि शरतुषारं कोऽप्ययं वीरपोतः ।। 2 ।। (चन्द्र–)

This hero of a boy, whoever he is, with his five tufts of hair darling about in from of battle, with the beauty of his face tinged from some anger displayed, spreads over the troops a mist of arrows with his bow the horns of which are twanging ceaselessly.

मित–। किरतीति।

अन्वयः–कलितकिश्चित्कोपरज्यन्मुखश्रीः समरशिसि चञ्चत्पञ्चचूड़ः अयं कोऽपि, वीरपोतः अनवरतनिगुञ्जत्कोटिना कार्मुकेण चमूनाम् उपरि शरतुषारं किरति।

व्याख्या–'कलितेन' दर्शितेन 'किञ्चित्कोपेन' ईषत्क्रोधेन 'रज्यन्ती' लोहितायमाना 'सुखश्री' वदनप्रभा यस्य तादृशः किञ्च 'समरशिरसि रणमुखे 'चञ्चन्त्यः' दोदुल्यमानाः 'पञ्चचूड़ाः' शिखाः यस्य तादृशः अयं कोऽपिं अज्ञातः 'वीरपोतः' शूरो बालकः 'अनवरतम्' अजस्त्रं यथा तथा 'निगुञ्जत्यौ' नदन्तयौ 'कौटी' शृङ्गे यस्य तथाविधेन 'कार्मुकेण' धनुषा 'चमूनां' बलानाम् 'उपरिशरतुषारं' तुषारपात- कल्पं शरपातं 'किरति' तनोति। यथा पौषे भासि प्रातस्तुषारपातेत समन्तात् सर्वमदृश्यं भवति तथा अस्य शरतापेन अद्य मदीया सेना इत्यर्थः।

Notes. 1. किरति–कृ ordinarily means विक्षेप। Here we have it in a slightly altered sense—to spread. He spreads mist of arrows etc. 2. कलित etc.—See टीका। कल+णिच् स्वार्थे (चुरादि)+क्त कर्मणि कलित worked up. रञ्ज (दिवादि)+शतृ रज्यत्, स्त्रियां ङीप् रज्यन्ती becoming tinged. In the final बहु–the कप् is not obligatory because the ई in श्री is not ङी। However, we may have कप् *optionally* as in पुण्यश्रीकः IV, sl. 19. 3. चञ्चत् etc.—He was constantly on the move, hence the tufts the tufts or hair oscillated. 4. शरतुषारम्–तुषार mist. शरः तुषारः इव शरतुषार mistlike arrow, *i.e.*, so many arrows were shot that the army appeared as if in a mist. 5. वीरपोतः–पोत boy. वीरश्चासौ पोतश्च the पूर्वनिपात of वीर being compulsory by "प्रथमचरम–"।

(*iii*) **(चन्द्र–) आश्चर्यम् !**

(Can—) Worshipful !

मुनिजनशिशुरेकः सर्वतः सैन्यकाये
नव इव रघुवंशस्याप्रसिद्धः प्ररोहः।
दलितकरिकपोलग्रन्थिटङ्कारघोरं
ज्वलितशरहस्त्रः कौतुकं मे करोति ।। 3 ।।

This ascetic boy, (who appears) like a new unseen shoot of the race of Raghu, rouses my curiosity having all alone set, on the boy of the army all round, thousands of arrows ablaze in manner that is frightful from the cracklilng of the smashed joints of elephants' jaws.

मित– । मुनीति।

अन्वयः–रघुवंशस्य नवः अप्रसिद्धः प्ररोह इव मुनिजनशिशुः एकः सर्वतः सैन्यकाये दलितकरिकपालग्रन्थिटङ्कारघोरं ज्वलितशरहस्त्रः (सन्) मे कौतुकं करोति।

व्याख्या–'रघोः वंशस्य नवः' नूतनः लक्ष्मणादीनलामपत्येभ्यो भिन्नः 'अप्रसिद्धः' रघुवंशभवत्वेन लोके अविदितः 'प्ररोह इव' अङ्कुर इव एष 'मुनिजनशिशुः' तापसवेषः कुमारः 'एकः' असहाय एव 'सर्वतः' सर्वत्रसैन्यकाये, 'सैन्यशरीरे सेनाङ्गे पादातेषु अश्वेषु हस्तिषु रथेषु च इत्यर्थः दलितः' विमर्दितः यः 'करिकपोलग्रन्थिः' गजगण्डसन्धिः तस्य 'टङ्कारेण' भङ्गजनितेन टम् इति शब्देन 'घोरं भीषणं यथा तथा 'ज्वलितं' प्रदीप्त 'शरसहस्त्रं' असंख्या बाणाः यस्य तादृशः सन् 'मे कौतुकं करोति' कुतूहलं जनयति। कुतोऽयं कस्यामद्भुतकर्मा कुमारः इत्यादि ज्ञातुम् उत्कण्ठा इत्यर्थः।।

Notes. 1. मुनिजनशिशुः–मुनिश्चासी जनश्च मुनिजनः hermit folk. तस्य शिशुः। This is how the compound is usually dissolved. Against this we obeserve that there is no reason to suppose that the boy's father is an ascetic. On the contary with evident signs of a क्षत्रियब्रह्मचारी it is natural to take him otherwise. Hence say मुनिजनश्चासौ शिशुश्च, कर्मधा–। 2. एकः–Alone. This is a ground for curiosity. 3. सर्वतः–सर्वस्मिन् इति सर्व+ङि (7मी)+तसि स्वार्थे। This is another reason for being curious. Alone he is everywhere. 4. सैन्यकाये–सेनां समवेता इति सेना+ण्य सैन्याः forces. सेन्यानां कायः अङ्गम् तस्मिन्। "हस्त्यश्वरथपादातं सेनाङ्गस्याच्चतुष्टयम्"। 5. नव इव etc.—This is the strongest factor to rouse curiosity. 6. दलित etc.—Qualifies ज्वलनक्रिया in ज्वलितशरसहस्रः। Not only is he everywhere but his presence is unbearably felt everywhere—another reason for curiosity.

(*iv*) **सुमन्त्रः–आयुष्मन्,**

Sumantra—O long-lived one,

अतिशयितसुरासुरप्रभावं शिशुमवलोक्य तवैव तुल्यरूपम्।
कुशिकसुतमखद्विषां प्रमाथे धृतधनुषं रघुनन्दनं स्मरामि ।। 4 ।।

On seeing this child that has excelled the might of gods and demons and is of similar with thy own self, I recall to mind the delight-of-the-race-of-Raghu with his bow taken up at the extirpation of the obstructors of the sacrifice of the son of Kuśika.

मित–। अतीति।

अन्वयः–अतिशयितसुरासुरप्रभावं तवैव तुल्यरूपं शिशुम् अवलोक्य कुशिकसुतमखद्विषां प्रमाथे धृधनुषं रघुनन्दनं स्मरामि।

व्याख्या– 'अतिशयितः' अतिक्रान्तः 'सुरासुराणां' देवदानवानां 'प्रभावं' वीर्यं येन तादृशं 'तवैव तुल्यरूपं' सच्छायं शिशुम्' इमं बालम् अवलोक्य कुशिकसुतस्यं विश्वमित्रस्य 'मखद्विषां यागविघ्नानां राक्षसानां 'प्रमाथे' विनाशे अन्तकर्मणि 'धृतनधनुषं' आत्तशरासनं 'रघुनन्दनं रामभद्रं 'स्मरामि'। कार्मुकेण सव्यापारमेनं दृष्ट्वा रूपसादृश्यात् कर्मसादृश्याच्च प्राक् मारीचादीन् प्रति धनुर्व्यापारायन्तं राममेत्र स्मरामि।।

Notes. 1. अतिशति etc.–अति+शी means to transcend. सुराश्च असुराश्च सुरासुराः। No एकवद्भाव because the विरोध is not शाश्वतिक but कारणकृत। Comp. "देवासरैरमृतमन्बनिधिर्ममन्थे"। 2. प्रमाथे–प्र+मथ+घञ् भावे प्रमाथ destruction. अधि 7मी। मन्थ is a different root. 3. धृत etc.—धृतं धनुर्येन स धृतधनुः। तम्। The समासान्त affix अनङ् is absent because these affixes are sometimes treated as optional. Compare "स्वलावणयाशंसा धृतधनुशमह्णाय तृणवत्"। 4. स्मरामि–The boy reminds me of राम dispersing the obstructors of Viśvāmitra's sacrifice. Now स्मृति is always of a past experience. No स्मृति if there is no actual experience. सुमन्त्र did not accompany राम when the latter went to guard the sacrifice. He did not see Rākṣasas dispersed. Hence, it is incongruous for him to say "कुशिक....स्मरामि"।

(v) **चन्द्रकेतुः—इममेकमुद्दिश्य भूयसामारम्भ इति हृदयमपत्रपते।**

Candra—My heart shames that preparations of so many are directed against the single one.

अयं हि शिशुरेककः समरभारभूरिस्फुरत्-
करालकरकन्दलीकलितशस्त्रजालैर्बलैः।
क्वणत् कनककिङ्किणीझनझनायितस्यन्दनै-
रमन्दमददुर्दिनद्विरदवारिदैरावृतः ॥5॥

Alone indeed is this boy surrounded by troops with weapons of sorts displayed in sprout-like hand that are uplifited and excessively busy [Or—troops whose grim weapons of sorts wieded with sprout-like hands are incessantly flashing], in the thick of fight,—troops among which chariots rattle and the golden bells in them tinkle—troops in which are cloud-like elephants whose profuse flow of ichor resembles a heavy down-pour.

मित—।'उद्दिश्य' लक्ष्यीकृत्य।'भूयसां' बहूनाम्।'आरम्भ' व्यापारः।'अपत्रपते' लज्जते।। अयमिति।

अन्वयः—समरभारभूरिस्फुरत्करालकरकन्दलीकलितशस्त्रजालैः क्वणत्कनककिङ्किणीझनझनायितस्यन्दनैः अमन्द्रमददुर्दिनद्विरदवारिदैः क्लैः एकको हि अयं शिशुः आवृतः।

व्याख्या—'समरभारे' रणमूर्द्धनि महाहवकेन्द्रे इत्यर्थः 'भूरिस्फुरन्ति' सातिशयदीप्यमानानि 'करालकरकन्दलीकलितानि' उच्छ्रितबाहुशाखा- प्रयुक्तानि 'शस्त्रजालानि' अश्वारोहिणाम् आयुधसमूहाः येषु तादृशैः किञ्च समरकेन्द्रभभिलक्ष्य त्वरमाणेषु रथिषु 'क्वणान्त्यः' मधुरं रुवन्त्यः 'कनककिङ्किण्यः रथस्थाः सुवर्णघण्टिका येषु तादृशाः 'झनझनायिताः' झनत् इत्यव्य शब्दं कुर्वन्तः 'स्यन्दनाः' रथा येषु तथाविधैः अपि च 'असमन्दमददुर्दिनाः' अमन्दं मददुर्दिनं प्रभूतं मदवर्षणां येषां तादृशाः 'द्विरदवारिदाः' मेघतुल्या गजाः येषु तादृशैः बलैः एकको हि' असहाय एव 'अयं शिशुः आवृतः वेष्टितः इति महती मे हृदये लज्जा अनुकम्पा च शिशौ इत्यर्थः।

Notes. 1. एकक:–अनुकम्पित एकः इति एक+कन् अनुकम्पायाम्। He pities the boy at his plight, also censures his opponents for this cowardly attack. 2. समर etc.—भार weight, brunt. समरभार the brunt of the battle. thick of the fight etc. कराल is तुङ्ग high ; hence *up-lifted*. "करालो दन्तुरे तुङ्गे" इति विश्वमेदिन्यौ। कन्दली is द्रुम a tree ; hence a branch of tree. ''कन्दली द्रुमे'' इति हेमः। कराः कन्दल्य इव। Now see टीका। Or dissolve thus—समरभारे भूरिस्फुरन्तीषु (excessively busy) करालासु (up-lifted) करकन्दलीषु कलितानि (displayed) शस्त्रजालानि येषु। Or thus—समरभारे भूरिस्फु- रन्तीभिः करालाभिः करकन्दलीभिः कलितानि (wielded) etc.—Or again thus—सरभारे भूरिस्फुरन्ति etc.—The epithet seems to refer to the cavalry. These were the first to draw weapon. The entire cavalry force became engaged simultaneously. The chariots and elephants were but coming up and were not yet in the mist of the fight. 3. क्वणात् etc.—The chariots are hastening to the scene. झनझनायति etc. refers to the rattle of the wheels. कृणत् etc. to the jingle of the bells. If we intend to express झनत् इति अव्यक्तः शब्दः कृतो यैः by means of affixes etc. we shall have to (*i*) attach डाच् to झनत् with the consequent doubling of झनत्, (*ii*) add क्यष् to obtain a root (नाम धातु), (iii) attach क्त to this root. Hence झनत् झनत्+डाच्+क्यष् क्त कर्त्तरि (झनत् झनत् becoming झनझनत् by पररूप) झनझनायिताः, गतित्–। The क्त is वर्त्तमाने। The final compound is a त्रिपदबहु–(see टीका)। 4. अमन्द etc.—दुर्दिन shower. Comp. द्विषां विषस्थ काकुतस्थस्तत्र नाराचदुर्द्दिनम्''–*Raghu*. मदस्य दुर्दिनं मददुर्दिनम्। अमन्दं मददुर्दिनं येषाम्। द्विरदा वारिदा इव द्विरदवारिदाः। Now see टीका।

(*vi*) **सुमन्त्रः–वत्स एभिः समस्तैरपि किमस्य, किं पनुर्व्यस्तैः ?**

Sum.—Child, what matters to him even with all these jointly ? Much less agin severally.

चन्द्रकेतुः–आर्य त्वर्यतां त्वर्यताम्, अनेन हि महान् आश्रितजन-प्रमाथः अस्माकमारब्धः। तथाहि–

Chand.—Hasten, noble Sir, hasten. By this one is indeed commenced a great slaughter of our dependent people Thus—

आगुञ्जद्गिरिकुञ्जकुञ्जरघटाविस्तीर्णकर्णज्वरं
ज्यानिर्घोषममन्ददुन्दुभिरवैराध्मातमुज्जृम्भयन्।

वेल्लद्भैरवरुणमुण्डनिकरैर्वीरो विधत्ते भुव-
स्तृप्यत्कालकरालवक्त्रविघसव्याकीर्यमाणा इव ।।6।।

The hero, sending forth the twang of his bow-string which is swelled by the loud note of drums and spreads ear-ache among [Or—and gives an ache to the big ears of] the rows of our shricking hill-roving tuskers [Lit.—Shrieking tuskers born in mountain caves] renders the grounds, with the heads of the hideous headless trunks tottering about, as if being strewn with the leavings of the frightful mouth of Death that is getting cloyed.

मित–।'समस्तैः' मिलितैः युगपत्कृतव्यापारैः अपि अश्वैः रथैः गजैश्च 'अस्य किं' क्रियताम्। 'व्यस्तैः पृथग्व्यापृतः एकदा अश्वैः अन्यदा रथैर्गजैर्वा पुनः किम्' न किमपि। एक एवायं सर्वेभ्योऽपि पर्याप्तः इत्यर्थः। तदलमनुकम्पया।। 'अनेन हि' वीरेण 'अस्माकम् आश्रितजनानां प्रमाथ' वधः 'आरब्धः' तत् 'त्वर्यतां' योद्धव्यं मयैव।। आगुञ्जदिति।

अन्वयः–अमन्ददुन्दुभिरवैः आध्मातम् आगुञ्जद्गिरिकुञ्ज-कुञ्जरघटाविस्तीर्णकर्णज्वरं ज्यानिर्घोषम् उज्ज्म्भयन् वीरः वेल्लद्भैवरुण्डमुण्डनिकरैः भुवः तृप्यत्कालकरालवक्त्रविघसव्याकीर्यमाण इव विधत्ते।

व्याख्या–'अमन्दैः' गुरुभिः 'दुन्दुभिरवैः' सैनिककृतैः पटहध्वनिभिः 'आध्मातं' वर्द्धितम् 'आगुञ्जन्तीषु' चीत्कारवतीषु 'गिरिकुञ्जरघटासु' सैन्यस्थासु गिरिगुहाजातानां निर्भीकाणामपि गजानां श्रेणिषु 'विस्तीर्णः प्रसारितः 'कर्णज्वरः' श्रोत्रपीड़ा येन तादृशं 'ज्यानिर्घोषं धनुर्गुणागञ्जनम् 'उज्जृम्भयन्' उच्चारचन् 'वीरः' शूर एष बालः 'वेल्लतां रणाङ्गने धावतां 'भैरवरुण्डनां' भीमकबन्धानां 'मुण्डनिकरै' शिरःसमूहैः 'भूवः रणभूमीः 'तृप्यतः तृप्तिं भजमानस्य 'कालस्य' यमस्य 'करालवक्त्रस्य' भीषणमुखस्य 'विघसैः भुक्तशेषैः 'व्याकीर्यमाणा इव आस्तीर्यमाणा इव 'विधत्ते करोति।।

Notes. 1. एभिः etc.,—This is said to allay Candraketu's apprehensions. Do you think the boy will be crushed by your cavarly, or chariots or elephants ? Not at all. Separately, none of the three classes are a match for him ; this is evident. Even united, they will go down before him. 2. आगुञ्जत् etc.—Usually this is taken to refer to some hill in the neighbourhood which is a resort of elephants which elephants are annoyed by the noise. But there is no mention of such a hill near the hermitage of Vālmīki. Besides, no कुञ्ज–a den or thicket—can possibly accommodate a whole घटा of elephants. It seems batter to refer to the elephants in the army itself. गिरिकुञ्जकुञ्जर then means "elephants born in caves of hills" which are expected to be a hardy lot not to be frightened easily. 3. ज्यानिर्घोषम्– Refers to Lava's bow. 4. अमन्द etc.— दुन्दुभि drum, refer to the drums in the army. 5. वेल्लत्–etc. वेल्लत् swinging towards a fall. रुण्ड a headless trunk कबन्ध। मुण्ड head "मुण्डो मुण्डितशीर्षयोः" इति हैमः। The head is cut down and brought to the ground while the trunk is tottering (वेल्लत्) । 6. तृप्यत् etc.—कराल dreadful भीषण। "करालो भीषणेऽन्यवत्" इति विश्वः। वि+अद+अप् कर्मणि विघस leavings of the table भुक्तावशेष। The अप् is by "उपसर्गे अदः" and घस is subtituted by "घञपोश्च"। 7. *Remark*—The idea is taken from—"शिलीमुखोत्कृत्तशिरः फलाढ्या च्युतैः शिरस्त्रैषकोत्तरेव। रणक्षितिः शोणितमद्यकुल्या रराज मृत्योरिव पानभूमिः।।"–*Raghu*.

(*vii*) **सुमन्तः (स्वगतम्)–कथमीदृशेन सह वत्सस्य चन्द्रकेतोर्द्वन्द्व-सम्प्रहारमनुजानीयाम् ? (विचिन्त्य) अथवा इक्ष्वाकुगृहबृद्धाः खलु वयम्, प्रत्यपस्थिते च का गतिः ?**

Sum. *(To himself)*—How can I permit the single combat of child Candraketu with such a one ? (*Reflecting*) Or indeed I have grown grey in the house of Ikṣvāku ; and what is the (alternative) way out in what has turned up ?

चन्द्रकेतुः (सविस्मयलज्जासम्भ्रमम्)–धिक्, प्रतिनिबृत्तानि सर्वतः सैन्यानि मम।

Cand. (*With wonder, shame and agitation*)—Fie ! My troops have fallen back on all sides !

सुमन्त्रः (रथवेगमभिनीय)–आयुष्मान् एष वाग्विषयीभूतः स वीरः।

Sum. (*Acting the speed of the car*)—O long-lived one, the hero is now within talking distance.

चन्द्रकेतुः (विस्मृतिमभिनीय)–आर्य, किमस्य नामधेयमाख्यात-माख्यापकैः ?

Cand. (*Acting foretfulness*)—Noble Sir, what was his name given by the messengers ?

सुमन्त्रः–लव इति।

Sum.—Lava it was.

चन्द्रकेतुः—

भो भो लव महाबाहो किमेभिस्तव सैनिकैः।
एषोऽहमेहि मामेव तेजस्तेजसि शाम्यतु ।। 7 ।।

Chand.—Ho ! Ho ! mighty-armed Lava, what have you got to do with these soldiers ? Here I am, go at myself ; let might (Or—spirit) subside in might (Or—spirit).

मित—। 'इदृशेन' एवं विधेन वीरेण। 'द्वन्द्वसम्प्रहारं' द्वयोर्द्वयोयुद्दम्। सति युद्धे चन्द्रकेतोः पराजयमुत्पश्यामि इत्यर्थः। 'इक्ष्वाकोः गृहे वृद्धाः स्वलु वयम्' वीरव्रतं जानीमः। 'प्रत्युपस्थिते च' सम्प्राप्ते वियये पुनः 'का गतिः' अन्यः कः पन्था वर्त्तते ? न कोऽपि, तत् अगतिके द्वन्द्वसम्प्रहार एव भवतु।। बालेन प्रौढ़ानां पराजय इति 'विस्मयः'। ईदृशानामसाराणां नेता अहमिति 'लज्जा'। झटिति उपायः कर्त्तव्य इति 'सम्भ्रमः।। वाचां विषयः गोचरः 'वाग्विषयः'। अवग्विषयः वाग्विषयः सम्पद्यमानो 'भूतः'। सम्प्रति समीपे एव वर्त्तते स तत् कथां गुरु इत्यर्थः।। 'आख्यायकैः' वार्त्ताहरैः। स्थानदस्मात् मदन्तिकं गत्वा ये प्रधनं निवेदयामासुः तैः।। भो इति।

अन्वयः—भो भोः महाबाहो लव एभिः सैनिकैस्तव किम् ? एषः अहम्। मामेव एहि। तेजः तेजसि शाम्यतु।

व्याख्या—'भोः भोः महाबाहो' विशालभुज 'लव एभिः सैनिकैः तव किं' प्रयोजनम् ? किमपि प्रयोजनं नास्ति। 'एषः अहम्' स्थितः 'मामेव एहि' अभिगच्छ। 'तेजः पराक्रमः 'तेजसि' पराक्रमान्तरे 'शाम्यतु' विलयं यातु। आवयोर्द्वन्द्वद्धमस्त यावदेको न जीयते इत्यर्थः।।

Notes. I. द्वन्द्व etc.—द्वयोः द्वयोः इति द्वन्द्वम् निपातनात्। The double in treated as a कर्मधा-, द्वि becomes द्व and the विभक्ति in the second become अम्। सम्प्रहरन्ते अस्मिन् इति सम्+प्र+ह+घञ् अधिकरणे सम्प्रहारः fight. द्वन्द्व सम्प्रहारः द्वन्द्वसम्प्रहारः सुप्सुपा। तम्। 2. भो भोः etc.—This is a graceful challenge. तेजस्तेजसि शाम्यतु is purposely vague. It does not mean I will humble thy pride or you mine. The plain meaning is—let one spirit (तेजस्)–subside (शाम्यतु) in another (तेजसि), *i.e.*, let there be a fight until one is conquered.

(*viii*) **सुमन्त्रः—कुमार, पश्य पश्य—**

व्यपवर्त्तत एष बालवीरः पृतनामिर्मथनात् त्वयोपहूतः।
स्तनयित्न रवादिभावलीनामवमर्दादिव दृल्पसिंहशावः ।। 8 ।।

(ततः प्रविशति त्वरितोद्धतकमो लवः)

लवः–साधु, राजपुत्र, साधु ! सत्यमैक्ष्वाकः खल्वसि। तदयं परागत एवास्मि।

(नेपथ्ये महान् कलकलः)।

Sum—Behold, Prince, behold !

This boy-hero turns round giving up the slaughter of troops on being challenged by you, like an enraged lion-cut leaving the killing of crowds of elephants from the roar of clouds.

(*Then Lava enters in quick and haughty steps*).

Lava—Bravo ! Prince, bravo ! Verily you are a true descendant of Ikṣvāku. So here I am come indeed.

(*A great hubbub in the Tiring room*).

मित– । व्यपवर्त्तत इति।

अन्वयः–दृप्तसिंहशावः स्तनयित्नुरवात् इभालीनाम् अवमर्दादिव एष बालवीरः त्वया उपहूतः पृतनानिर्भथनात् व्यपवर्त्तते।

व्याख्या–'दृप्तः' बलगर्वितः 'सिंहशावः' हरिपोतकः 'स्तनयित्नुरवात्' मेघगर्जनात् 'इभावलीनां गजघटानाम् 'अवमर्दात् इव' हननात् इव 'एष बालवीरः' शूरः कुमारः 'त्वया उपहूतः' द्वन्द्वयुद्धाय आहूतः सन् 'पृथनामिर्मथनात् 'व्यपवर्त्तते' निवृत्य परावर्त्तते।।'त्वरितः' द्रुतः 'उद्धतः' गर्वितः क्रमः' पादक्षेपो यस्य तथाविधः। 'एक्ष्वाकः' इक्ष्वाकुकुल- नन्दनः। 'परागतः' प्राप्तः उपस्थितः इत्यर्थः।।

Notes. 1. व्यपवर्त्तते–विवर्त्तन is truning round, desisting. अपवर्तन is receding. Hence, the sense is—He desists from the carnage and moves away from the scence. He stops because you say किमेभिस्तव सैनिकैः। He comes owing to your call अहि मामेव। 2. पृतना etc. पृतना army, पृतनाया निर्मथमन्। तस्मात्। अपादाने 5मी। अपाय is implied by व्यपवर्त्तते। 3. उपहूतः–उप+ह्वे+क्त कर्मणि। Challenged आहूत is more common in this sense. 4. स्तनयित्र etc.—हेतौ 5मी। This is something like a challenge to the lion-cub. 5. इभ etc.—इभ elephant. इभानाम् आवलयः इभावलयः rows of elephants. तासाम्। 6. ऐक्ष्वाकः–इक्ष्वाकोर्गोत्रापत्यं पुमान् इति इक्ष्वाकु+अञ् ऐक्ष्वाकः with the elision of उ by निपातन in the rule "दाण्डिनायन–"।

(*ix*) लवः (सावेगं परावृत्य)—आः कथमिदानीं भग्ना अपि प्रतिनिबृत्य युद्धाभिसारिणः पर्यवष्टभ्य निन्घन्तित मां चमूपतयः ! धिग्जल्मान्।

Lava (*Turning round excitedly*)—How is it that the leaders of army, though repulsed, have returned seeking battle and are hitting me having come up quite close ? Fie on the idiots.

अयं शैलाघातक्षुभितवड़वावक्त्वहुतभुक्-
प्रचण्डक्रोधार्चिर्निचयकवलत्वं व्रजतु मे।
समन्तादुत्सर्पन् घनतुमुलसेनाकलकलः
पयोराशेरोघः प्रलयपबनास्फालित इव ।। 8 ।।

Let this deep and tumultous hubbub of the army, swelling on every side like the tide of the ocean lashed up by the wind on the day of destruction, attain the state of food (*i.e.*, become food) to the array of flames of my fury which is as frightful as the fire from the mouth of the mare provoked by blows of rocks.

(इति परिक्रामति)।

(*Goes round the stage*).

मित–। 'आवेगेन' सम्भ्रेण सह 'परावृत्य' विवृतवदनो भूत्वा। 'भग्नाः' पलायिताः। 'युद्धाभिसारिणः' रणकामाः। 'पर्यवष्टभ्य' विशेषेण समन्ताद्वा अदूरे स्थित्वा। 'निघ्नन्ति' ताड़यन्ति आयुधैः। 'चमूपतयः' सेनानायकाः।। अयमिति।

अन्वयः–प्रलयपवनास्फालितः पयोराशेः ओघ इव समन्तात् उप्सर्पन् अयं घनतुमुलसेनाकलकलः मे शैलाघातक्षुभितवड़वक्त्रहुतभुक् प्रचणडक्रोधिार्चिर्निचयकवलत्वं व्रजतु।

व्याख्या–'प्रलयपवनेन' युगान्तवातेन 'आस्फालितः' विताड़ितः 'पयोराशेः' सागरस्य 'ओघ इव' प्रवाह इव 'समन्तात्' सर्वत 'उप्सर्पन्' विवर्द्धमानः 'अयं धनः' गभीरः 'तुमुलः' सङ्कुलः विमिश्र इत्यर्थः 'सेनाकलकलः' सैन्थकोलाहलः 'मे' मम 'शैलानां' गिरीणां सागरगर्भस्थानमिति शेषः यः 'आघातः' तेन 'क्षुभितः' समुद्दीपितः यः 'वड़वावक्त्रहुतभुक्' अश्विनीवदनानलः वाड़वानल इत्यर्थः स इव 'प्रचण्डः' करालः यः क्रोधः' तस्य 'अर्चिर्निचयस्य' शिखासमूहस्य 'कवलत्वं' ग्रासत्वं 'व्रजतु' गच्छतु। मदीयः क्रोधः कोलाहलमिमं शमयतु इत्यर्थः।।

Notes. 1. युद्ध etc.—युद्धम् अभिसरन्ति अभिलक्ष्य धावन्ति इति युद्ध+अभि+मृ+णिनि

साधुकारिणि कर्त्तरि seeking battle. 2. पर्यवष्टभ्य–परि+अव+स्तम्भ+ल्यप्। Having come up close. स becomes ष by "अवाच्चालम्बनाविदूर्ययोः"। Here आविदुर्य (nearness) is implied. 3. निघ्ननित–नि+हन+ल्युट् अन्ति hitting me. Hence there is कर्मविवक्षा, "जासिनिप्रहण–" does not apply, and we have माम् not मम। 4. शैलाघात etc.—वड़वावबत्रहुभुक् refers to the fire of Aurva's wrath which that stage discharged into the sea. It assumed the shape of a horse's head and continued there consuming sea-water. Comp."ततस्तं क्रोधजं तात और्वोऽग्निं वरुणालये। उत्ससर्ज स चैवाप उपयुङ्क्ते महोदधौ। महद्धयशिरो भूत्वा यत्तद्वेदविदोविदुः।।" 5. समन्तात्–All round. An अव्यय। This is an exaggeration. लव was facing चन्द्रकेतु at the time ; the army was behind लव, so the noise could not actually proceed from *all sides.* That the army was behind him is openly stated in sl. II. below–"पश्चाद्बलैरनुमृतोऽयमुदीर्णधन्वा"। 6. घन etc.—तमुल refers to a state in which every things has got mixed up. A state of consfusion. The idea is well expressed by the English word *tumult*. The cry of the soldier, the horse, the elephant etc. could not be caught separately; only a confused hubbub reached the ear. 7. प्रलय etc.—आ+स्फल सञ्चलने+ णिच्+क्त कर्मणि आस्फालित। It is supposed that at the time of universal destruction there are high winds which drive the sea out of its bed and cause a deluge.

(*x*) चन्द्रकेतुः–भो भोः कुमार,

Candra.—Ho ! Ho ! Youth,

अत्यद्भुतादसि गुणातिशयात् प्रियो मे
तस्मात् सखा त्वमसि यन्मम तत् तवैव।
तत् किं निजे परिजने कदनं करोषि
नन्वेष दर्पनिकषस्तव चन्द्रकेतुः ।।10।।

You are dear to me from the highly wonderful profusion of your merits, so you are my friend ; what is mine is yours indeed. Why then play havoc with your own attendants ? Well, here is Candraketu, the touch-stone of your valour.

लवः–(सहर्षसम्भ्रमं परावृत्य)–अहो महानुभावस्य प्रसन्नकर्कशा वीरवचनप्रयुक्तिर्विकर्त्तनकुलकुमारस्य। तत् किमेभिः एनमेव तावत् सम्भावयामि।

Lava (*Turning back with joy and regard*)—O the gracious

and yet grim application of heroic words by the magnanimous prince of the solar race ! Then what is the use of these ? Him I will honour.

मित– । अत्यद्भुतादिति ।

अन्वयः–अत्यद्भुतात् गुणतिशयात् मे प्रियः असि, तस्मात् त्वं सखा असि । यत् मम तत् तव एव । तत् निजे परिजने किं कदनं करोषि ? ननु एष चन्द्रकेतुः तव दर्पनिकषः ।

व्याख्या–'अत्यद्भुतात्' परमविस्मयकरात् 'गुणातिशयात्' गुणप्रकर्षात् 'मे प्रियः असि' मां प्रीणयसि । एवंविधस्य तव दर्शनात् मे प्रीतिर्जाता 'तस्मात्' प्रीतिजननात् 'त्वं' सखा असि' मे । 'यत्' वस्तु 'मम तत्' वस्तु 'तव' एव । 'तत्' तस्मात् निजे परिजने मत्सम्पर्कात् आत्मपरिजने किं कदनं करोषि' कथं घातं विदधासि । न हि युक्तं तत् । 'ननु एष चन्द्रकेतुः तव दर्पनिकषः' बलपरीक्षापाषाणो वर्त्तते तस्मिन्नेव विक्रमस्व ।। 'परावृत्य' मुखं व्यावर्त्त्य । 'प्रसन्ना' कोमला 'कर्कशा' कठोरा च । 'वीरस्य वचनं' तस्य 'प्रयुक्तिः' प्रयोगः उच्चारणम् । 'विकर्त्तनः सूर्यः । 'सम्भावयामि' समानयोमि द्वन्द्वयुद्धदानेन ।।

Notes. 1. गुण etc.–अति+शी+अच् भावे अतिशय excess. गुणनाम् अतिशयः । तस्मात् । हेतौ 5मी । 2. प्रियः–प्रीणति इति प्री+क कर्त्तरि प्रियः । You please me. I feel attracted towards you. 3. तस्मात् etc.—Hence you are my friend. 4. परिजने–परिगतो जनः परिजनः attendant. Refers to the army.

(*xi*) (पुनर्नेपथ्ये कलकलः)

(*A hubbub again in the dressing room*)

लवः (सक्रोधनिर्वेदम्)–आः कदर्थितोऽहमेभिर्वीरसंवादविघ्नकारिभिः पापैः । (इति तदभिमुखं परिक्रामति) ।

Lava (*With anger and disgust*)—O I am insulted by these wretches who are causing interruption to my conversation with his hero. (*Steps towards them*).

चन्द्रकेतुः–आर्य दृश्यताम्, दृष्टव्यमेतत् ।

Cand.—Noble Sir, behold ; it is worth beholding.

दर्पेण कौतुकवता मयि बद्धलक्ष्यः
पश्चालद्बलैरनुसृतोऽयमुदीर्णधन्वा ।
द्वेधासमुद्धतमरुत्तरलस्य धत्ते
मेघस्य माधवतचापधरस्य लक्ष्मीम् ।।11।।

This one, with his bow up-lifted, having his attention fixed upon me with hauteur and curiosity, followed behind by the troops, exhibits the beauty of a cloud that wears Indra's bow and wavers on account of wind blowing in two ways.

मित–। 'निर्वेदः वैराग्यम्, घृणा। कुत्सितः अर्थः 'कदर्थः' निन्द्यो विषयः, विमानना इत्यर्थः। स सञ्जातः अस्य 'कदर्थितः' विमानितः। 'वीरण संवादः' सम्भाषणम् मेलं वा। तत्र 'विघ्नम्' बाधां 'कुर्वन्ति' जनयन्ति ये तैः। तदभिमुखं' बलाभिसुखम्।। दर्पेणेति। **अन्वयः**–कौतुकवता दर्पेण मयि बद्धलक्ष्यः पश्चात् बलैः अनुसृतः उदीर्णधन्व अयं द्वेधासमुद्धतमरुत्तरलस्य माधवतचापधरस्य मेघस्व लक्ष्मीं धत्ते। **व्याख्या**–'कौतुकवता' सकौतुकेन' दर्पेण' कौतुकमिश्रेण गर्वेण सह इत्यर्थः। युद्धाय आह्वानम् इति दर्पः। भग्नेषु प्रवीरेषु मम तुल्यरूपेण बालेनैवाह्वानम् इति कौतुकम्। 'मयि बद्धलक्ष्यः' दत्तदृष्टि 'पश्चात् 'बलैः अनुमृतः' सैन्यैः अभिद्रुतः इति तत्रापि कृतलक्ष्य 'उदीर्णधन्तवा' उच्छ्रितकार्मुकः 'अयम्' एष वीरः 'द्वेधा' द्विप्रकारेण 'समुद्धतः' समुच्चलितः यो मरुत्' वायुः तेन 'तरलस्य' अस्थिरस्य क्षणमितः क्षणं ततश्च 'माघवतचापधरस्यं इन्द्रधनुर्द्धरस्य 'मेघस्य लक्ष्मीं धत्ते, शोभां विभर्त्ति।।

Notes. 1. कदर्थितः–अथ is विषय matter. कुत्सितः अर्थः कदर्थः disgraceful matter. स सञ्जातः अस्येति कदर्थ+इतच् कदर्थितः disgraced, insulted—तारकादि। 2. वीर etc.—सम्+वद+घञ् भावे संवाद interview Comp. "यदृच्छासंवादः किमु किमु गुणनामतिशयः–" sl. 16. साधुकारिणि कर्त्तरि णिनि (see टीका)। 3. तदभिमुखम्–He was coming towards चन्द्रकेतु and is now going towards the army. Hence the comparison below. 4. उदीर्णधन्वा–उद्+ऋ (गतौ)+क्त कर्त्तरि उदीर्ण gong up, *i.e.*, up-lifted. उदीर्णा धनुर्यस्य इति उदीर्णा+धनुस् अनङ् समासान्त उदीर्णाधन्वा। Now and then the समासान्त is not added as in "धृतधनुषं रघुनन्दनं स्मरामि", sl. 4. 5. द्वेधा etc.—द्विप्रकारेण इति द्वि+एधाच् द्वेधा in now ways. सम्+उद्+हन (गतौ)+क्त कर्त्तरि समुद्धत arisen. तरल is opposed to स्थिर steady. For समाप्त see टीका। 6. माधवत etc.—मधवन् is इन्द्र। मघोन इदम् इति मधवन्+अण् माधवनम् or माधवतम् the stem irregularly changing into मधवत् by "मधवा बहुलम्"। For absence to change compare "न वनी माधवनी विनोदहेतुः" and "विजानात्ववर्नी वर्ली माघवनीम्–*Rasagaṅgā*. 7. *Remark*—It is not possible for wind to blow *simultaneously* in two directions. We have to suppose that the wind is unsteady and makes the cloud also unsteady.

(*xii*) **सुमन्त्रः–कुमार एवैनं दृष्टुमपि जानाति, वयन्तु केवलं परवन्तो विस्मयेन।**

चन्द्रकेतुः–भो भो राजानः,

संख्यातीतैर्द्विरदतुरगस्यन्दनस्थैः पदाता-
वत्रैकस्मिन् कवचनिचितैर्मेध्यचर्मोत्तरीये।
कालज्येष्ठैरभिनववयःकाम्यकाये भवद्भि-
र्योऽयं बद्धो युधि परिकरस्तेन वो धिग् धिगस्मान् ।।12।।

Sum.—Even to mark him the prince alone is able ; we are simply overpowered by wonder.

Candra—Ho ! Ho ! Kings,

Shame to you and shame to me for this attempt that is being made by you on this one at fight—attempt by you senior in age, on one this with a body tender by young age ; by you m ail-coated, on this with a wrap of holy skin ; by you beyond number, on this one alone ; by you on elephants, horses and cars, on this one on foot.

मित–। 'द्रष्टुमपि इत्यत्र–अनेन योर्द्धुं कोऽपि इह बले न जानाति। आस्तां युद्धम् एवं द्रष्टुमपि न जानाति।–इत्यपेरर्थः।'परवन्तः' पराधीनाः अभिभूता इत्यर्थः।। संख्येति।

अन्वयः–संख्यातीतैः द्विरदतुरगस्यन्दनस्थैः कवचनिचितैः कालज्येष्ठैः भवद्भिः एकस्मित् पदातौ मेध्यचर्मोत्तरीये अभिनवयः काम्यकाये अत्र यः अयं युधि परिकरः बद्धः तेन वः धिक् अस्मान् धिक्।

व्याख्या–:सरव्यातीतैः' असंख्यैः द्विरदस्थैः गजारूढ़ैः 'तुरगस्थैः, अश्वारूढ़ैः 'स्यन्दनस्थै' रथारूढ़ैश्च 'कवचनिचितैः वर्मावृतैः 'कालज्येष्ठैः' वयोधिकैः ' भवद्भिः एकस्मिन्' एकाकिनि 'पदातौ' पादचारिणि 'मेध्यचर्मोतरीये' मृगाजिनोत्तरासङ्गे 'अभिनववयसा' शैशवेन 'काम्यकाये' कमनीयगात्रे कोमलाङ्गे 'अत्र' अस्मिन् बाले विषये 'यः अयं युधि' युद्धे 'परिकरः' सज्जा 'बद्धः' कृतः 'तेन' अधर्मयुद्धपरिकरेण 'वः धिक्' युष्मान् गर्हे अस्मान् धिक्' ईदृशबलनायकस्य ममापि गर्हा।।

Notes. 1. संख्यातीतैः–Contrast with एकस्मिन्। You are so many and he alone. It is an unequal fight. संख्यामतीताः, तैः। 2. द्विरह etc.—द्विरदाश्च तुरागाश्च स्यन्दनाश्च द्विरदतुरगस्यन्दनम्। Neuter singular by "द्वन्द्वश्च प्रार्णितूर्य-सेनाङ्गानाम्"। तत्र तिष्ठन्ति इति क प्रत्ययः कर्त्तरि। This contrasts with पदातौ। No fair fight between mounted and unmounted. 3. कवच etc.—नि+चि+क्त कर्मणि निचित covered. कवचेन निचिताः। Contrast with मेध्यचर्मोत्तरीये। You are well guarded while the boy has but a wrap of deer skin on his upper half, the lower being altogether uncovered. 4. कालज्येष्ठैः-अतिशयेन वृद्धा इति वृद्ध+इष्ठन् ज्येष्ठाः। कालेन ज्येष्ठाः। Hence your muscles are firm and you can bear hard knocks. Contrast with अभिनववयः काम्यकाये। The pity of it you do not see the unfairness. Fie on you ! On me too because such a lot I am leading.

(*xiii*) **लवः (सोन्माथम्)—कथम्, अनुकम्पते नाम ? (विचिन्त्य) भवतु कालहरणप्रतिषेधाय जृम्भकास्त्रेण तावत् सैन्यानि संस्तम्भयामि। (इति ध्यानं नाटयति)।**

Lava (*With annoyance*)—What ! Does he pity me ? *(Reflecting)* well, I will paralyse the troops with the Jṛmbhaka weapon to prevent the loss of time. *(Acts meditation.)*

सुमन्त्रः–तत् किमकस्मादस्मत्सैन्यघोषः प्रशाम्यति ?

Sum.—Well, why does the din of our army stop suddenly ?

लवः–पश्याम्येनमधुना सप्रगल्भम्।

Lava—Well, now see this spirited one.

सुमन्त्रः–वत्स मन्ये कुमारकेणानेन जृम्भकास्त्रमामन्त्रितम्।

Sum.—Child, I think the Jṛmbhaka weapon has been invoked by this boy.

चन्द्रकेतुः–अत्र कः सन्देहः ?

Cand.—What doubt can there be in it ?

व्यतिकर इव भीमस्तामसो वैद्युतश्च
प्रणिहितमपि चक्षुर्ग्रस्तमुक्तं हिनस्ति।
अथ लिखितमिवैतत्सैन्यमस्पन्मास्ते
नियतममितवीर्यं जृम्भते जृम्भकास्त्रम् ।।13।।

Surely the Jṛmbhaka weapon of matchless might have appeared on the scene. An intermixture terrible like that of gloom and lightning hurts even the eye that is directed with care but which is shrouded and then freed [Lit.—swallowed up and then disgorged]. Besides, this army stands motionless like one painted. (Chand.—)

मित–। 'उन्माथः' पीड़ा। तेन सह। 'अनकम्पते' इति पीड़ाः। 'नाम' इति कुत्सा। समर्थोऽहम् एष वा एषां प्रमामाय, नाहं विपन्नः तत् कुत्सिता इयमनुकम्पा। 'तावत्' इत्यवधारणे। 'संस्तम्भयामि तावत्' इत्यन्वयः।। प्रगल्भनं स्वच्छन्दवाम्व्यहारः 'प्रगल्भः'। तेन सह। 'सप्रगल्भमेनं पश्यामि' इति 'एनं सप्रगल्भं यथा तथा पश्यामि' इति वा अन्वयः। वीरसंवादविघ्नाभवात् 'अधुना' स्वच्छदवाग्व्यवहारं कुर्वन् 'पश्यामि'।। 'आमन्त्रितः' आवाहितः व्यापारित इत्यर्थः।। व्यतिकर इति।

अन्वयः–तामसः वैद्युतश्च व्यतिकरः इव भीमः (व्यतिकरः) प्रणिहितमपि ग्रस्तमुक्तं चक्षुः हिनस्ति। अथ एतत् सैन्यं लिखितमिव अस्पन्दमास्ते। नियतम् अमितवीर्यं जृम्भकास्त्रं जृम्भते।

व्याख्या–'तामसः' तमसां 'वैद्यतश्च' विद्युताञ्च यः 'व्यक्तिकरः' समागमः युगपत्प्राप्तिः स 'इव भीमः' भयानकः व्यतिकरः 'प्रणिहितमपि' प्रणिधानपरमपि पूर्वं 'ग्रस्तम्' आवृतं पश्चात् 'मुक्तम्' अपावृतं 'चक्षुः हिनस्ति' क्लिश्नाति, रूपग्रहो न जायते। 'अथ' क्रिञ्च 'एतत् सैन्यं लिखितमिव चित्रार्पितमिव 'अस्पन्दं' निश्चलं यथा तथा 'आस्ते अवतिष्ठते। तस्मात् 'नियतं' नूनम्, 'अभितवीर्यम्' अतुलपभावं 'जृम्भकास्त्रं जृम्भते आविर्भवति।।

Notes. 1. नाम–अव्यय implying कुत्सा (see टीका)। "नाम आकाश्यकुत्सयोः" इत्यादि हेमः। 2. संस्तम्भयामि–I will paralyse जड़ीकरोमि। 3. व्यतिकरः–वि+अति+कृ+अप् भावे। Meeting, coming together etc. as in "महानश्चं व्यतिकरोऽस्माकं प्रसादः"–Act III. 4. ग्रस्तमुक्तम्–ग्रस्तश्च मुक्तश्च। The समाप्त is by "पूर्वकालैकसर्व–" which restricts the lead to the word that refers to पूर्वकाल (prior time). The obstruction comes first, hence ग्रस्त leads. This sorts of व्यक्तिकर is not seen with any weapon except the जृम्भक। 5. अथ–अव्यय implying समुच्चय, *i.e.,* introduces an additional reason why it must be the जृम्भक weapon and no other. "अयोऽथ स्यातां समुच्चये" इत्यादि हैमः। अमित etc.—मा+क्त भावे मित measure मान। न मितम् अमितम् measureless, matchless. अमितं वीर्यमस्य। अमित is the reading of वीरराघव and Vidyasagara's manuscripts 1 and 2.

(*xiv*) **(च–) आश्चर्यमाश्चर्यम्।**

(Cand.—) Wonder ! Wonder !

पातालोदरकुञ्जपुञ्जिततमः श्यामैर्नभो जृम्भकै-
रुत्तप्तस्फुरदारकूटकपिलज्योतिर्ज्वलद्दीप्तिभिः।
कल्पाक्षेपकठोरभैरवमरुद्व्यस्तैरवस्तीर्यते
मीलन्मेघतड़ितकड़ारकुहरैर्विन्ध्याद्रिकूटैरिव ।।14।।

The sky is being overcast by the Jṛmbhaka weapons that are dark like the gloom massed in the pit of the nether regions and have flashing like the purple glow of molten and running brass, as if by the peaks of the Vindhya hill driven by high and terrific gales at the end of *Kalpa* with their caverns made purple by the lightning of colliding clouds.

मित–पातालेति।

अन्वयः–कल्पाक्षेपकठोरभैरवमरुधस्तैः मीलन्मेघतड़ित्कड़ार- कुहरैः विन्ध्याद्रिकूटैः इव पातालोदरकुञ्जिततमः श्यामैः उत्तप्रस्फ रदारकूटकपिलज्योति-जर्वलद्दीप्तिभिः जृम्भकैः नभः अवस्तीर्यते।

व्याख्या–'कलपस्य' ब्रह्मणो दिनस्य 'आक्षेपे' अवसाने युगान्ते इन्तर्थः ये 'कठोराः' प्रवृद्धा 'भैरवाः' भीमाश्च 'मरुतः' वायवः प्रलयपवना इत्यर्थः तैः 'व्यस्तैः विक्षिप्तैः किञ्च 'मीलन्तः' गतिवशात् समापतन्तः ये मेघाः' तेषां याः 'तड़ितः' विद्युतः ताभिः 'कड़ाराणि' पिङ्गलानि 'कुहराणि' गह्वराणि येषां तादृशैः 'विन्ध्याद्रिकूटैः विन्ध्यगिरिशृङ्गैः 'इव पातालस्य उदरकुञ्जे कुक्षिगह्वरे 'पुञ्जितं पिण्डीभूतं यत् 'तमः' तदिव 'श्याभैः' किञ्च 'उत्तप्तः' अतएव 'स्फुरन्' चञ्चलः यः आरकूटः' पित्तलराशिः तस्य तत् 'कपिलं' पिङ्गलं 'ज्योतिः' प्रभा तदिव 'ज्वलन्ती' 'दीप्ति' प्रभा तथाविधैः 'जृम्भकैः नभः' आकाशम् 'अवस्तीर्यते व्याप्यते।।

Notes. 1. पाताल etc.—पुञ्ज a heap. पुञ्जः सञ्जातः अस्य इति पुञ्ज+इतच् पुञ्जितम् heaped. Now see टीका। This epithet secures resemblance in *colour* with the Vindhya peaks, also justifies तामसो व्यतिकरः of sl. 13. 2. उत्तप्त etc.—आरकूट is explained as रीति। "रीतिः स्त्रियामारकूटः" इत्यमरः। रीति again is a synoym for पित्तल brass. "रीतिस्तु पित्तले" इत्यादि हेमः। This furnishes another point of resemblance with the कड़ारकुहर of विन्ध्याद्रिकूट and explains how वैद्युतश्च व्यतिकरः। 3. कल्पाक्षेप। 3. कल्पाक्षेप etc.—Kalpa is a day of Brahman. At the end of it everything perishes. High gales prevail and masses of ominous clouds appear. The peaks of the the Vindhya are supposed by the poet to have been uprooted by the wind and sent hurting along to collide with some of the namerous masses of clouds that are floarting about. Thus this epithet justifies

मीलन्मेघ in the next. 4. मीलन्मेघ etc.—The previous epithet has explained how the peaks and the clouds meet. Then the lightning in the clouds flashes and empurples the crevices in the peaks. It is not clear why the peaks of the Vindhya are singled out. Like those of the Vindhya it is natural to suppose that the peaks of the other mountaints are also in motion. Why then विन्ध्याद्रिकूटैः ? Possibility the poet lived close by the Vindhya. That hill was always before his eyes and when thinkinig of a mountain his thought inevitably turned to the Vindhya.

(*xv*) **सुमन्त्रः–कुतः पुनरस्य जृम्भकाणामागमः स्यात् ?**

Sum—But whence could a knowledge of the Jṛmbhakas come to him ?

चन्द्रकेतुः–भगवतः प्राचेतसादिति मन्यामहे।

Cand.—I think, from the worshipful, Prāchetasa.

सुमन्त्रः–वत्स नास्य व्यवहारोऽस्त्रेषु विशेषतो जृम्भकेषु। यतः,

Sum.—Child he has no experience of weapons especially of the Jṛmbhaka weapons. For,

कृशाश्वतनया ह्येते कृशाश्वात् कौशिकं गताः।
अथ तत्सम्प्रदायेन रामभद्रे व्यवस्थिताः ।।15।।

Verily these are Kṛśāśvas children. From Kṛśāśva they passed on to Kauśika ; then through initiation by him they rest now with Rāmabhadra.

चन्द्रकेतुः–अपरेऽपि परमोपचीयमानसत्वप्रकाशाः स्वयं हि मन्त्रदृशः पश्यन्ति।

Cand—Other seers of mantras too themselves see (such secrets) with the light of the *Sattva guṇa* greatly strengthening (within them).

मित–। 'आगमः' आगमनं लाभः इत्यर्थः। 'अस्त्रेषु' विषये 'अस्यं भगवतः प्राचेतसस्य 'व्यवहारः' चर्चा 'न' नास्ति। सामान्यतः अयमस्त्राणि जानाति सत्यं किन्तु न व्यहरति, जृम्भकास्त्राणि तु नैव जानाति। अज्ञानकारणमाह 'यतः' इति। कृशाश्वेति।

अन्वयः–एते कृशाश्वतनया हि। कृशाश्वात् कौशिकं गताः। अथ तत्सम्प्रदायेन रामभद्रे व्यवस्थिताः।

व्याख्या–'एते कृशाश्वस्य तनया हि' तनया एव न तु अस्त्रमात्रम्। 'कृशाश्वात् कौशिकं' कुशिकतनयं विश्वामित्रं 'गताः' संक्रान्ताः।'अथ' अनन्तरं 'तस्य' विश्वामित्रस्य यः 'सम्प्रदायः' नियमपूर्व कप्रदानं तेन हेतुना सम्प्रति 'रामभद्रे व्यवस्थिताः' नियताः नान्यगामिन एते तत् कुतोऽस्य आगमः स्यात्।।'परमं' प्रभूतं यथा तथा 'उपचीयमानः' वर्द्धमानः' सत्त्वस्य' सत्त्वगुणस्य 'प्रकाशः' आविर्भावः येषु तादृशाः अतएव सत्त्वगुणस्य उद्भासकत्वात् गुहायां निहितमपि दुष्टुं समर्थाः 'मन्त्रदृशः' मन्त्रद्रष्टारः 'अपरे अपि' कृशाश्वव्यतिरिक्ता अन्ये च गुरुपदेशं विनैव 'स्वयं हि' मन्त्रात् 'पश्यन्ति'। तादृशं वा भगवती वाल्मीकेर्ज्ञानं जृम्भकेषु स्यात् ।।

Notes. 1. व्यवहारः–वि+अव+ह+घञ् भावे practice, experience 2. एते–The तनयत्व is emphasised, hence masucline. 3. तत्–सम्प्रदायेन–सम्+प्र+दा+घञ् भावे सम्प्रदाय a gift by formal initiation. हेतौ 3या। 4. रामभद्रे etc.—The Vīracarita imparts the knowledge to लक्ष्मण also. 5. परम etc.—The सत्वगुण is described as प्रकाशक, *i.e.*, lights up dark corners. "सत्त्वं लघु प्रकाशकम्"–*Tattva-kaumudī*. Hence it reveals secrets. Consequently when सत्त्वगुण has sufficiently developed in a person he can see the प्रयोग and संहार mantras of any weapon and therefore of the Jṛmbhakas also. So even if कृशाश्व had seen before, it is not unlikely वाल्मीकि also saw them independently through the development of सत्त्वगुण with him.

(*xvi*) सुमन्त्रः–वत्स, सावधानो भव परागतः प्रवीरः।

Sum.—Be careful, child, the great her has come.

कुमारी (अन्योऽन्यं प्रति)—अहो प्रियदर्शनः कुमारः।

(सस्नेहानुराग निर्वर्ण्य)

The Youths. (*With reference to each other*)—Ha ! Pleasing is the sight of this youth ! (*Marking with love and affection*).

चदृच्छासंवादः किमु किमु गुणानामतिशयः
पुराणो वा जम्भान्तरनिविड़बन्धः परिचयः।
निजो वा सम्बन्धः किमु विधिवशात् कोऽप्यविदितो
ममैतस्मिन् दृष्टे हृदयमवधानं रचयति ।।16।।

Is it this chance meeting, (or) is it the profusion of merit, (is it) again old acquaintance with a firm attachment in a prior birth, or close ralationship unknown through the influence of fate, that this one being seen, froces the heart to close attention.

मित– ।'अवधानम्' एकाग्रता। तेन सह 'सावधानः'। प्रकृष्टो वीरः 'प्रवीरः'।। 'अन्योऽन्यं प्रति अन्योऽन्यमुद्दिश्य। लवस्य स्वगतम् चन्द्रकेतोस्तु सुमन्त्रं प्रति जनान्तिके। यदृच्छेति।

अन्वयः–एतस्मिन् दृष्टे किसु यदृच्छासंवादः किसु गुणानाम् अतिशयः, किमु जन्मान्तरनिविड़बन्धः पुराणः परिचयो वा, विधिवशात् अविदितः कोऽपि निजः सम्बन्धो वा मम हृदयम् अवधानं रचयति।

व्याख्या–'एतस्मिन्, अस्मिन् कुमारे 'दृष्टे सति 'किम' किंस्वित् यदृच्छासंवादः' एष आकस्मिकः समागम, 'किमु' किंस्वित् एतस्य 'गुणानाम् अतिशयः' गुणप्रकर्ष' 'किमु' किंस्वित् 'जन्मान्तरे' पूर्वस्मिन् कस्मिंश्चित् जन्मनि 'निविड़ः' दृढ़ः बन्धः' बन्धनं यस्य तादृशः 'पुराणः' प्राक्तनः परिचयो वा' सम्बन्धो वा, विधिवशात् दैवगत्या 'अविदितः परस्परस्य अविज्ञातः 'कोऽपि निजः सम्बन्धो वा' आत्मीया बान्धवता वा ''मम हृदयं' चेतः 'अवधानम्' एकाग्रतां 'रचयति' गमयति।।

Notes. 1. प्रियदर्शनः–प्रीणातीति प्री+क कर्त्तरि प्रियम् pleasing. प्रियं दर्शनमस्य। 2. यदृच्छा etc.—ऋच्छा is गति course of events. या ऋच्छायदृच्छा। तया संवादः, a casual meeting. 3. किमु–An अव्यय implying वितर्क deliberation. Each notices his heart being attracted towards the other and he then deliberates as to its cause. Three explanations occur—(a) It is pure chance (यदृच्छासंवादः) ; (b) It is the endowments of the other (गुणानामतिशयः) ; (c) It is the existence of some sort of relationship. The last again falls under two heads—(i) Relationship in a prior life (जन्मान्तरनिविड़बन्धः परिचयः) ; (ii) Present relationship accidentally remaining unknown (निजो वा सम्बन्धकः etc.) 4. हृदयम्–अणिकर्त्तृकर्म of रचयति। Thus हृदयम् अवधानं रचयति–the heart adots attention. Attaching णिच् again (This time हेतुमणिच्) यदृच्छासंवादः (प्रयोजक) हृदयम् (प्रयोज्य) अवधानं रचयति by the rule "गतिबुद्धि–" because रच has become here गत्यर्थक। 5. रचयति–We have singular because the nominatives यदृच्छासंवाद etc. exclude one another. If any one of them is adopted, the rest must be dropped. Hence with only one nominative we have the singular. 6. *Remark*—As already remarked this sort of अनुयोऽन्यभाषण is extremely unnatural. Again it seems the correct reading of the verse has escaped us. We have explained अवधानं रचयति

as अवधानं गमयति। In that case it is difficult to see why the poet rejects the plain गययति and prefers the awkward रचयति। Both suit the metre.

(*xvii*) **सुमन्त्रः–भूयसा जीविधर्मं एष यत् रसमयी कस्यचित् क्वचित् प्रीतिः यत्र लोकिकानां व्याहारः तारामैत्रकं चक्षूराग इति। तमप्रतिसंख्येयम् अनिबन्थनं प्रमाणमामनन्ति।**

Sum. It is mostly the way of the living that some one's friendliness for some one else is full of affection, for which the designation of the wordly people is 'pupil-friendship'. 'eye-delight' etc. That inconceivable and causeless something they call 'love'.

अहेतुः पक्षपातो यस्तस्य नास्ति प्रतिक्रिया।
स हि स्नेहात्मकस्तन्तुरन्तर्मर्माणि सीव्यति ।।17।।

There is no counter-action to the leaning that is causeless. That thread in the shape of affection stitches up indeed the vitals of the heart.

मित–'भूयसा' प्रायेण 'जीविधर्मः' प्राणिस्वभाव 'एष यत् कस्यचित् प्रीतिः' आनन्दः क्वचित्' क्वापि जने 'रसमयी' प्रेमपूर्णा भवति 'यत्र' यस्यां रसमयां प्रीतौ 'लौकिकानां' लोकानां 'तारामैवकं' कणीनिकासख्यं 'चक्षूरागः' नयनरञ्जनम् 'इति' च 'व्याहार' उक्तिः। तामेव प्रीतिं लोकाः केचित् तारभैत्रकमाहुः केचित् पुनश्चक्षूराग इति।'अप्रतिसंख्येम्'अनिर्वचनीयम्' अनिबन्धनम्' अहेतुकं 'तुं प्रेमाणम् आमनन्ति' प्रेमशब्देन निर्दिशन्ति लोका इति शेषः। यत् वस्तु तारमैचकिमिति चक्षूराग इति च कथ्यते तत् किमाक्तं कुत उत्पद्यते इति ज्ञातुमशक्यम्, परं तस्य प्रेम इति संज्ञा लोके। अहेतुरिति।

अन्वयः–य पक्षपातः अहेतुः तस्य प्रतिक्रिया नास्ति। स हि स्नेहात्मकः तन्तुः अन्तर्ममाणि सौव्यति।

व्याख्या–'यः पक्षपातः अभिसमाश्रयः पक्षावलम्बन- मित्यर्थः। सेहकृतः पक्षपातः इति उपचारात् पक्षपातः स्नेहः। यः स्नेहः' अहेतुः' निष्कारणः 'तस्य प्रतिक्रिया' प्रतिविधा नं नास्तिं। 'स हि' न स्नेहः किन्तु 'स्नेहात्मकः' स्नेहरूपः 'तन्तुः' सूत्रम्। किं क्रियते तेन सूत्रेण इत्याह–'अन्तर्ममाणि' आभ्यराणि मर्मस्थानानि स 'सीव्यति' योजयति। तन्नाशे हृदयमेव भिद्यते इत्यर्थः। प्रेमा ते अस्मिन् लवे जातः, अनुवर्त्तस्व तमहेतुकं प्रेमाणम् इत्याशयः।।

Notes. 1. भूयससा–प्रकृत्यादि 3या। 2. जीविधर्मः–जीवः जीवनम्। स अस्ति एषाम् जीव+इनि जीविनः the animate world. तेषां धर्मः। 3. तारा etc.—तारा pupil of the eye. मैत्र friendship. तदेव मैत्रकम् ताराणं मैत्रकम्। 4. चक्षूरागः–राग affection.

चक्षुषां रागः। 5. अप्रति etc.—प्रतिसंख्या is *enumeration* after the manner of the सांख्य system of philosophy, *i.e.*, enumeration as प्रकृति or as महत्, अहङ्कार etc. प्रतिसंख्यातुमशक्यम् अप्रतिसंख्येयम् incapable of being classed by प्रकृति महत् etc. Hence *inconceivable*, 6. अनिबन्धनम्– निबध्यते नियम्यते अनेन इति नि+बन्ध+ल्युट् करणे निबन्धनम् that with which restrained, cause. अविद्यमानं निबन्धनमस्य।7. प्रेमाणाम्–प्रियस्य भाव इति प्रिय+इमनिच् प्रेमन् (प्रातिपदिक)। This is often used in the neuter ; here it is masucline. 8. अहेतुः–etc.—पक्षपात preference. Here सुमन्त्र declares for यदृच्छासंवादः in Candraketu's speech above. गुणनामतिशयः etc. are evidently cited as हेतु for the preference. यदृच्छसंवादः furnishes the only instance where the preference is अहेतु।

(*xviii*) **कुमारी (अन्योऽन्यं प्रति)–**

एतस्मिन् मसृणितराजपट्टकान्ते
मोक्तव्याः कथमिव सायकाः शरीरे।
यत्प्राप्तौ मम परिरम्भणभिलाषा-
दुन्मीलत्पुलककदम्बमङ्गमास्ते ।।18।। (कु–)

The Youths (*With reference to each other*)—How indeed are arrows to be shot at this body that is lovely like a polished Rājapaṭṭa gem and at the arrival of which (Or—sight of which) my body stands with hairs on end through a desire to embrace. (The Youths—)

मित–एतस्मिन्निति।

अन्वयः–मसृणितराजपट्टकान्ते एतस्मिन् शरीरे कथमिव सायका मोक्तव्याः यप्प्राप्तौ परिरम्भणभिलाषात् मम उन्मीलत् पुलककदम्बम् आस्ते।

व्याख्या–'मसृणः कृतः' यः 'राजपट्टः' इन्द्रनीलो (?) मणिः तस्मिन्निव 'कान्त' कमनीये सुन्दरे इत्यर्थः एतस्मिन् शरीरे कथमिवं केन वा प्रकारेण 'सायका मोक्तव्याः' वाणः पात्रयितव्याः न कथमपि इत्यर्थः। अस्य शरीरस्य सौष्ठवहानिर्वाणपातेन न कर्त्तव्या इति भावः। न केवललमनौचित्यम्, अप्रसङ्गश्च बाणपातस्य इत्याह–'यत्प्राप्ती यस्य शरीरस्य 'प्राप्तौ' समागमे इति यद्दशने जाते इत्यर्थः परिरम्भणस्य' आलिङ्गनस्य 'अभिलाषात्' इच्छया 'मम अङ्गम् उन्मीलत्' आविर्भवत् 'पुलककदम्बं' रोमाञ्चसमूहः यस्मिन् तथाविधं सत् 'आस्ते' वर्त्तते। अङ्गे रोमाञ्चः कृतो नु करे बाणस्य प्रसङ्गः इति भावः।।

Notes. 1. अन्योऽयम् etc.—Unnaturalness is already noted. 2. मसृणित etc.—मसृण smooth. मसृणः कृत इति मसृण+णिच् (नाम धातु)+कतकर्मणि मसृणितः polished. राजपट्ट is some gem, which gem it is not clear. But the boys were कुवलयदलस्निग्धश्याम् (IV, sl. 19). इन्द्रनीलमणिमेचकच्छवि (VI, sl. 17), etc. So possibly राजपट्ट is an *emerald*. 3. कथमिव etc.—The first half of the verse shows the undesirability of shooting. It is sheer vandalism to spoil the beauty of it with arrow-marks. 4. यत्प्राप्तौ etc.—The second half states the fighter's inability to shoot. Love rules supreme, how can there be a fight ?

(*xix*) (**कु–**)

किन्त्वाक्रान्तकठोरतेजसि गतिः का नाम शस्त्रं विना
शस्त्रेणापि हि तेन किं न विषयो जायेत यस्येदृशः ।
किं वक्ष्यत्ययमेव युद्धविमुखं मामुद्यतेऽप्यायुधे
वीराणां समयो हि दारुणरसः स्नेहक्रमं बाधते ।।19।।

(The Youths)—But in the matter of one who has resorted to stern mettle, what other source of help exists but weapons ? What again is really the use of the weapon of which such a one may not become the mark ? What will this very one think of (lit.—say to) me if I turn back from the fray even when the bow is raised ? Verily the horrid-flavour ways of warriors (Or—the ways of warriors are horrid-flavoured and) check the course of affection.

मित– । किन्विति ।

अन्वयः–किन्तु आक्रान्तकठोरतेजसि शस्त्रं विना का नाम गतिः। यस्य ईदृशः विषयो न जायेत तेन शस्त्रेण अपि किम्। आयुधे उद्यते अपि युद्धविमुखं माम् अयमेव किं वक्ष्यति। दारुणरसः वीराणं समयः स्नेहक्रमं बाधते हि।

व्याख्या–'किन्तु' अनुचितेऽपि वाणपते 'आक्रान्तम्' अधिकृतं 'कठोरं' प्रौढं 'तेजः' शौर्यं येन तथाविधे जने विषये 'शस्त्रं विना का नाम गतिः' उपायः स्यात्। उद्यतायुधे अस्मिन् ममापि आयुधमेव शरणं न किञ्चिदन्यत् इत्यर्थः। 'यस्य' शस्त्रस्य 'ईदृशः' एव विधः शरः 'विषयो न जायेत' पात्रं न स्यात् 'तेनं अपात्रे प्रयुक्तेन 'शस्त्रेण अपि किं प्रयोजनं न किमपि। अतः पातीनीयो वाणः। अन्यथा 'आयुधे' धनुषि 'उद्यते अपि' मयि अहर्त्तुम् उत्तोलिते अपि 'युद्धविमुखं रणपराङ्मुखं 'माम् अयमेव किं वक्ष्यति' स्नेहपात्रम् एष व मत्सम्बन्धे किं संस्यते कापुरुषं मां मंस्यते

इत्यर्थः। तत् प्रवर्त्ततां रणाः।'दारुणरसः' क्रूरास्वादः 'वीराणां समयः' आचारः 'स्नेहस्य क्रमं' प्रसरं बाधते हि' वारयत्येव।।

Notes. 1. आक्रान्त etc.—आक्रान्त is आरूढ़। कठोर is प्रवृद्ध। Now see टीका। Lit.—He has mounted fully developed mettle, *i.e.,* He has adopted a stern course in the matter of myself. We have to suppose that each of the youths assumes the other to be in a stern mood while he himself is afffectionate. 2. जायेत–"हेतुहेतुमतोर्लिङ्" इति लिङ्। The sense is शस्त्रेण किमपि न स्यात् यदि विषयो न जायेत। The कार्यकारणभाव is obvious. 3. आयुधे–आ+युध+क करणे घञर्थे आयुधम् the bow. In this sense compare "तन्मदीयभिदमायुधं ज्यया संगमय सशरं विकृष्यताम्"–*Raghu*. 4. दारुणरसः–दारुण bitter. रस taste स्वाद। दारुणः रसो यस्य of a bitter taste.

(*xx*) सुमन्त्रः–(लवं निर्वर्ण्य साश्रमात्मगतम्)–हृदय किमन्यथा परिकल्पसे ?

Sum. (*Having marked Lava—To himself with tears*)—O heart, why do you build perversely ?

मनोरथस्य यद्वीजं तद्दैवेनादितो हतम्।
लतायां पूर्वलूनायां प्रसूनस्यागमः कुतः ।। 20 ।।

What was the source of my desire had long before been demolished by fate. The twig being first clipped whence is the show of flower ?

चन्द्रकेतुः–अवतराम्यार्य स्यन्दनात्।

Cand.—Noble Sumantra, I alight from the car.

सुमन्त्रः–तत् कस्य हेतोः ?

Sum.—And that for what reason ?

चन्द्रकेतुः–यतस्तावदयं वीरपुरूषः पूजितो भवति, अपि खलु आर्य क्षात्रधर्मश्चानुगृहीतो भवति रथिनः पादचारमायोधयन्ति इति शास्त्रविदः परिभाषन्ते।

Cand.—For then this mighty soul becomes honoured, besides, noble Sir, the duty of the military caste is observed too ; Charioteers do not fight those that are o foot" so do say those that are versed in the Śāstras.

मित– 'लवं निर्वर्ण्य' निपुणं दृष्ट्वा ''सीतासुतोऽयं वा स्यात्'' इति सन्दिह्यमानः, तत्क्षणमेव ''मृता सीता असम्भवमेतत्'' इति समादधानः 'सास्त्रं' रुदन् स्वगतमाह–'हृदय अन्यथा' अन्यप्रकारेण मिथ्या इत्यर्थः 'किं परिकल्पसे' परिकल्पयसि। अन्तर्भावितण्यर्थः कल्पतिः।। मनोरथस्येति।

अन्वयः–मनोरथस्य यत् वीजं तत् आदितः दैवेन हतम्। लतायां पूर्व लूनायां कुतः प्रसूनस्य आगमः।

व्याख्या– 'मनोरथस्य' सीतासुतोऽयं भवेत् इत्येवंरूपस्य अभिलाषस्य 'यत् वीजं' मूलकारणं सीतारूपं 'तत् आदितः' पूर्वमेव 'दैवेन हतम्' तत् असङ्गतो मे मनोरथः।'लतायां पूर्वलूनायां प्रसूनागमकालात् प्रागेव छिन्नायां' कुतः प्रसूनस्य आगमः' पुष्पोदमो भवेत्।'पूजितः' आदृतः।'क्षात्रधर्मः' क्षत्रियाचारः।'अनुगृहीतः अनुसृतः। प्रकृते तमेव आचारं वर्णयति न रथिनः इति।'पादचारं' पदातिम्।'परिभाषन्ते' वदन्ति।।

Notes. 1. परिकल्पसे–For similar use with the *sense* of णिच् compare ''श्रेयसे शाश्वतो देवो पराहः परिकल्पताम्''—sl. 27 below. Some read परिप्लवसे for परिकल्पसे। With this transtale—Why do you rush perversely ? Also compare ''अयञ्च संप्लवमानमात्मानम् etc.''—VI, xxx; again ''परिल्पवमानहृदयः संप्रमुग्धोऽस्मि''–VII, xv. 2. क्षात्र etc.—क्षत्रस्य अयम् इति क्षत्र+अण् क्षात्रः। क्षात्रः धर्मः। पादचारम्–पादेन चारः अस्य, तम्। आयोधयन्ति–आ+युध+णिच्+लट् अन्ति cause to fight.

(*xxi*) **सुमन्त्रः–(स्वगतम्)–कष्टं वतानुप्रपन्नोऽस्मि।**

Sum. (*To himself*)—Alas ! I am in a fix.

कथं न्यायमनुष्ठानं मादृशः प्रतिषेधतु।
कथं वाभ्यनुजानातु साहसैकरसां क्रियाम् ।। 21 ।।

How can one like me either disapprove a just course of action or approve a step that savours solely of rashness ?

चन्द्रकेतुः–यदा तातमिश्रा अपि पितुः प्रियं सखायं धर्मसंशयेषु आर्यमेव पृच्छन्ति तत् किमार्यो विमृशति ?

Cand.—As our revered elders too refer to your noble self, their father's dear friend, in conficts of duty, then why does the noble one hesitate ?

सुमन्त्रः–आयुष्मन् एवं यथाधर्ममभिमन्यसे।

Sum.—O long-lived one, law is as you take it (lit.—You take it in accordance with the law).

एष सांग्रमिको न्याय एषध धर्मः सनातनः।
इयं हि रघुसिंहानां वीरचारित्रपद्धतिः ।। 22।।

This is the rule of battle ; this is the ancient usage ; this indeed is the source of heroic conduct of the lions of Raghu's race.

मित–।'कष्टं' सङ्कटम् 'अनुप्रपन्नः' प्राप्तः।'वत्' अहो खेदः।। कथमिति।

अन्वयः–मादृशः कथं न्यायमनुष्ठानं प्रतिधेतु कथं वा साहसैकरसां क्रियाम् अभ्युनजानातु।

व्याख्या–'मादृशः' वीराचारभिज्ञः 'कथं न्यायम्' समुचितं युक्तम् 'अनुष्ठानम्' आचरणं 'प्रतिषेधतुं निषेधतु। रथादवतरणम् अनमोदनीयं मे इत्यर्थः।'कथं वा' पक्षान्तरे केन प्रकारेण 'साहसम्' अविमृश्यकारिता एव 'एकः रसः' स्वाद यस्यास तादृशीं 'क्रियाम्' अनुष्ठानम् 'अभ्यनुजातु' अनुमोदतम्। इह रथादवतरणे अविमृश्यकारितामात्रं पश्यामि तदेतदपि नानुमन्तुमुत्सहे। एवं कार्यनिर्णयकष्टे पतितोऽस्मि।। 'तातभिश्राः' पूज्यास्ताता रामादयः। 'पितुः' तेषां जनकस्य दशरथस्य। 'धर्मेषु' कर्त्तव्येषु कर्मसु 'संशयाः' इदं वा कर्त्तव्यमिदं वा इत्येव रूपाः सन्देहाः' तेषु विषये। 'विमृशति' विचारयति।। 'एवम्' अनेन प्रकारेण 'यथाधर्मं धर्ममनतिक्रम्य एव 'अभिमन्यसे' कर्त्तव्यमवगच्छसि। रथादवतरणं युक्तमेव ते इत्यर्थः।। एष इति।

अन्वयः–एष सांग्रामिको न्यायः, एष सनातनो धर्मः, इयं हि रघुसिंहाना वीरचारित्रपद्धतिः।

व्याख्या–'एष सांग्रामिकः' संग्रामप्रयोजनः 'न्यायः' धर्मः। अनेनैव धर्मेण संग्रामः प्रयोक्त्वा इत्यर्थः। नायमिदानीन्तनो धर्मः किन्तु 'एष सनातनः। चिरन्तनो 'धर्म':। सनातनतामेव दर्शयति–इयं हि रघुसिंहानां मनुप्रभृतीनां रघुकुलतिलकानां 'वीरचारित्रस्य' वीरोचिताचारस्य 'पद्धतिः' मार्गः। अनेनैव पथा रघुवृद्धा वीरपदवीमारूढ़ाः। यं धर्मं कुलपुरुषा अन्ववर्त्तन्त तमेवानुवर्त्तस्व इति भावः।

Notes. 1. कष्टम्–कष्ट here is dilemma. 2. कथम् etc,—This presents the two horns of the dilemma. I can neither approve nor disapprove. Sumantra is hesitating. 3. विमृशति–Deliberates, *i.e.*, hesitates. "वितर्कः स्यात् उन्नयनं परामर्शो विमर्शनम्।"–हेमचन्द्रः In this sense, cp. "रामप्रवासे व्यमृशन् दोषम्"–*Bhaṭṭi*. 4. सांग्रामिक–संग्राम war, battle. संग्राम प्रयोजनमस्य इति संग्राम+ठञ् सांग्रामिकः the object of which is a fight, see next. 5. न्यायः–नितराम् अयते अनेन इति नि+अय+घञ् करणे न्यायः guide, code, rule etc. 6. सनातनः–सना is सदा always. It is an अव्यय। सना भव इति तना+ट्युल् सनातनः eternal. 7. इयं हि etc.—This shows that the code or rule has long been observed in the family. चारित्र is the same as चरित्र। अण् स्वार्थे, प्रजादि। पादाभ्यां हन्यते इति पाद+हन+क्तिन् कर्मणि पद्धतिः track, पाद becomes पद् by "हिमकाषिहतिषु च"।

(*xxii*) **चन्द्रकेतुः–प्रतिरूपं वचनमार्यस्य।**

Chand.—A declaration worthy of the noble one !

इतिहासं पुराणञ्च धर्मप्रवचनानि च।
भवन्त एव जानन्ति रघूणाञ्च कुलस्थितिम् ।। 23 ।।

You alone know history, mythology, the techings of law and the observances of the race of the Raghus.

सुमन्त्रः–(स्नेहाश्नं परिष्वज्य)—

Sum. (*Embracing with tears of effection*)—

जातस्य ते पितुरपीन्द्रजितो विजेतु-
र्वत्सस्य वत्स कति नाम दिनान्यमूनि।
तस्याप्यपत्यमनुगच्छति वीरवृतं
दिष्ट्या गतं दशरथस्य कुलं प्रतिष्ठाम् ।।24 ।।

Well, how many, O child, are the days passed since even that dear boy, your father, the slayer of Indrajīt, was born ? Even this child follows the course of heroes. Luckily (Or—O joy !) the house of Daśaratha has attained stability.

मित–"एष सांग्रामिको न्यायः" इत्यादि 'वचनम् आर्यस्य प्रतिरुपम्' अनुरुपम्। कोऽन्य एवं ब्रवीतु।। इतिहासमित्यादि।

अन्वयः–इतिहासं पुराणञ्च धर्मप्रवचनानि न रघूणां कुलस्थितिञ्च भवन्त एव जानन्ति।

व्याख्या–'इतिहासं' पुरावृत्तं 'पुराणञ्च' सृष्टिस्थितिप्रलयादिविवरणग्रन्थांश्च 'धर्मस्य' कर्त्तव्याकर्त्तव्यस्य 'प्रवचनानि च' अनुशासनानि च 'रघूणां कुलस्थितिञ्च' कुलप्रतिष्ठापकमाचारञ्च 'भवन्त एव जानन्ति'। इतिहासज्ञाः पुराणज्ञाः, धर्मप्रवचनज्ञा स्यितिज्ञाश्च सन्त्येव, परं चत्वारि इतिहासदीनि समुदितानि आर्ये एव भवति सन्ति न्यायस्मिन् इत्यर्थः।। जातस्येति।

अन्वयः–वत्स इन्द्रजितो विजेतुः पितुरपि ते जातस्य अमूनि कति नाम दिनानि तस्य अपत्यमपि वीरवृतम् अनुगच्छति। दिष्ट्या दशरथस्य कुलं प्रतिष्ठां गतम्।

व्याख्या–हे 'वत्स' तात 'इन्द्रजितो विजेतुः' दमयितुः 'पितुरपि ते' लक्ष्मणस्यापि 'जातस्य अमूनि कति नाम दिनानि' स्यल्पान्येव दिनानि। 'तस्य' अनतिचिरजातस्य

'अपत्यमपि' तनयोऽपि 'वीरवृत्तं' वीराणं चरितम् 'अनुगच्छति' अनुकरोति। 'दिष्ट्या अहो हर्षः 'दशरथस्य कुलं प्रतिष्ठां गतं' कुलस्थितं प्राप्तम्।।

Notes. 1. इतिहासम्–इतिह is an अव्यय meaning traditional knowledge. इतिह आस्ते इति इतिह+आस+घञ् अधिकरणे इतिहासः history. 2. पुराणम्–पुरा is an अव्यय meaning *prior time*. पुरा भवम् इति पुरा+ट्युल् पुरातनम् or पुराणम्। The latter form is by निपातन। But पुराण has a technical meaning, *viz.*, works describing creation, destruction, etc. "सर्गश्च प्रतिसर्गश्च वंशो मन्वन्तराणि च। भूम्यादेश्चैव संस्थानं (वंशानुचरितञ्चैव) पुराणं पञ्चलक्षणम्।।" This is a sort of mythology. A knowledge of इतिहास and पुराण entitles one to say "एष सांग्रामिको न्यायः"। 3. धर्म etc.—प्रोच्यते एभिः इति प्र+वच+ल्यट् करणे प्रवचनानि discourses. धर्मस्य प्रवचनानि। Knowing these one can say "एष धर्मः सनातनः। 4. भवन्त एव–You alone know all the four, so it befits you alone to say "एष सांग्रामिको न्यायः" etc, 5. कुलस्थितिम्–तिष्ठन्यनया इति स्था+क्तिन् करणो स्थितिः measures which secure stability. कुलस्य स्थितिः etc. Without knowing this you could not have said "इयं हि रघुसिंहानाम् etc." 6. पितुरपि etc.—You are boy ; even your father is a boy. This is the force of अपि। 7. इन्द्रजितो विजेतुः–पितुः alone leaves it in doubt wheter राम, लक्ष्मण, भरत वा शत्रुघ्न is meant. इन्द्रजितो विजेतुः specifies लक्ष्मण। The epithet is for identification. दिष्ट्या–An अव्यय implying joy or luck. 8. प्रतिष्ठाम्–प्रतितिष्ठति अनया इति प्रति+स्था+अङ् भावे प्रतिष्ठा preservation, stability. Unless the young generation knows how to behave, the race is as good as extinct. Fortunately Candraketu's chivalry shows that Daśaratha's race has escaped that danger.

(*xxiii*) चन्द्रकेतुः (सकष्टम्)—

अप्रतिष्ठे रघुज्येष्ठे का प्रतिष्ठा कुलस्य नः।
इति दुःखेन तप्यन्ते त्रयो नः पितरोऽपरे ।। 25।।

Candra. (*In anguish*)—"What is the stability of our race the eldest of the descendants of Raghu going unrepresented"—With this greif our other three elders are being consumed.

सुमन्त्रः–अहह हृदयमर्मदारणानि एतानि चन्द्रकेतोर्वचनानि।

Sum.—Ah ! These words of Candraketu rend the vitals of the heart.

लव–हन्त मिश्रीकृतोरसो वर्त्तते।

Lava.—Alas ! The feelings have become mingled.

यथेन्दावानन्दं ब्रजति समुपोढ़े कुमुदिनी
तथैवास्मिन् दृष्टिर्मम कलहकामः पुनरयम्।
झनत्कारक्रूरक्वाणितगुणगुञ्जन्दुरुधनु-
र्घृतप्रेमा बाहुर्विकचविकरालोल्वणरसः ।। 26 ।।

On this one coming to view, my sight feels joy like the lily when the moon has come in sight ; while my arm has the grim heroic sentiment clearly betrayed and courts fight with its love fixed upon the mighty bow that hums in its string and the tinkle (of whose bells) are sharp like a rarttle.

मित– । अप्रतिष्ठे इति।

अन्वयः–'रघुज्येष्ठे अप्रतिष्ठे नः कुलस्य का प्रतिष्ठा'' इति दुःखेन नः अपरे त्रयः पितरः तप्यन्ते।

व्याख्या–'रघुषुज्येष्ठे' रामे 'अप्रतिष्ठे' प्रतिष्ठाविरहिते अपत्यलोपात् वंशस्थितिशून्ये सति 'नः कुलस्यं रघुवंशस्य 'का प्रतिष्ठा' प्रतिष्ठा नास्ति। 'इति' अनेन दुःखेन नः अपरे त्रयः पितरः' लक्ष्मणभरत- शत्रुघ्नाः 'तप्यन्ते' तापमनुभवन्ति।। 'हृदयस्य' यत् 'मर्म' जीवस्थानं तस्य 'दारुणानि' भेदनानि। हृदयमर्म एभिश्छिद्यते इव इत्यर्थः।। 'रसः' एकाधिको रसः 'मिश्रीकृतः' परम्परसंमिश्रो 'वर्त्तते' जातः।। तदेव दर्शयति यथेति।

अन्वयः–यथा इन्दी समुपोढ़े कुमुदिनी आनन्दं व्रजति तथा अस्मिन् (समुपोढ़े) मम दृष्टिः। अयं पुनः विकचकवि- करालोल्वणरसो बाहुः झनत्कारक्रूरक्कणितगुणगुञ्जदगुधरुधनुर्धृतप्रेमा (सन्) कलह कामः।

व्याख्या–'यथा इन्द्री' चन्द्रे 'समुपीढे' उपस्थिते 'कुसुदिनी आनन्दं ब्रजति' प्रीतिं लभते 'तथा अस्मिन्' कुमारे समुपोढ़े 'मम दृष्टिः' आनन्द ब्रजति। 'अयं पुनः पक्षान्तरे एषः 'विकचः' परिव्यक्तः 'विकरालः' अतीभीषणः 'उल्वणरसः' वीरो रसः यस्य तथाविधः मम 'बाहुः भुजः 'झनत्कारः' इव 'क्रूरं' कठोरं 'क्वणितं' किङ्किणीध्वनिः यस्य तादृशं 'गुणेन' मौर्व्या 'गुञ्जत्' ध्वनत् यत् 'गुरु' महत् 'धनुः' तस्मिन् 'धृतं' बद्धं 'प्रेम' प्रीतिः यस्य तादृशः सन् 'कलहकामः' युद्धार्थी संवृतः। दृष्टी शान्तः वाही वीरः इति मिश्रीकृतो रसो वर्त्तते इत्यर्थः।।

Notes. 1. दुःखेन etc.—अनुक्ते कर्त्तरि तृतीया and कर्मणि ल। 2. समुपोढ़े–सम्+उप+वह+क्त कर्मणि समुपोढ़ brought close. 3. कलहकामः–कलहं कामयते इति

कलह+कामि+ण कर्त्तरि। 4. झनत्कार etc.—झनत् here has to be taken as an original शब्द not a mere अनुकरणशब्द। If treated as an अनुकरणशब्द then डाच् becomes compulsory giving द्वित्व etc. as in झनतझनायितस्यन्दनैः, sl. 5. झनत्+कृ+घञ् भावे झनत्कार a rattle, उपपदतत्–। अनुकरणशब्द gives झनझनाकार, a गति तत्–क्वण+क्त भावे क्वणित् a tinkle. These are from small bells (किङ्किणी) attached to the horns of the bow. Comp. "झनज्झनितकङ्कक्वणितकिङ्किणीकं धनुः", VI, 1. Now see टीका।

(*xxv*) चन्द्रकेतुः (अवतरन्)–आर्य सावित्रश्चन्द्रकेतुरभिवादयते।

सुमन्त्रः–

अजितं पुण्यमूर्जस्वि ककुत्स्थस्येव ते महः।
श्रेयसे शाश्वतो देवो वराहः पकिल्पताम् ।। 27।।

अपिच

देवस्त्वां सविता धिनोतु समरे गोत्रस्य यस्ते पिता
त्वां मैत्रावरुणोऽभिनन्दतु गुरुर्यस्ते गुरुणामपि !
ऐन्द्रं वेष्णवमाग्निमारुतमथो सौपर्णमोजोऽस्तु ते
देयादेव च रामलक्ष्मणधनुर्ज्याघोषमन्त्रो जयम् ।। 28।।

Candra. (*Alighting*)—Noble Sir, Candraketu of the Solar race salutes you.

Sum.—May the eternal god Varāha grant you, for safety holy, mighty, unbeaten majesty as of Kakutstha.

Moreover, in the fight, may the sun, the god that is the father of your race, cheer you on ; may the son of Mitra and Varuṇa who is the preceptor of even your seniors, bless you ; may you have the valour of Indra, Viṣṇu, Fire nad Wind as well as of Garuḍa ; may the charm of the twang of the string of the bows of Rāma and Lakṣmaṇa unfailingly grant you seuccess.

मित– । अजितमिति।

अन्वयः–शाश्वतो देवा वराहः ते श्रेयसे ककुत्स्थस्येव पुण्यम् ऊर्जस्वि अजितं महः परिकल्पताम्।

व्याख्या–'शाश्वतः सनातनः 'देवो वराहः' आदिवराहरूपो नारायणः 'ते' तव 'श्रेयसे' मङ्गलाय 'ककुत्स्थस्येव' राज्ञः पुरञ्जयस्य इव 'पुण्यं' पवित्रम् 'ऊर्जस्वि' वीर्यवत् 'अजतम्' अपराहतं 'महः' तेजः 'पारिकल्पताम्' परिकल्पयतु। अन्तर्भावितण्यर्थः।। देव इति।

अन्वयः–देवः सविता यः ते गोत्रस्य पिता, त्वां समरे धिनोतु मैत्रावरुणः, यः ते गुरुणामपि गुरुः त्वाम् अभिनन्दतु। ऐन्दं वैष्णावम् आग्निमारुतम् अथो सौपर्णम् ओजेः ते अस्तः। रामलक्ष्मणधनुर्ज्याघोषमन्त्रश्च जयं देयादेव।

व्याख्या–'देवः सविताः' सूर्यः 'यः ते गोत्रस्य पिता' वंशस्य प्रवर्त्तकः 'त्वां समरे' अस्मिन् युद्धे 'धिनोतु' प्रीणयतु शङ्कां निरस्य मनसः प्रसादमादधातु। मित्रारुणयोः अयं 'मैत्रावरुणः' वशिष्ठः 'यः ते गुरुणां' रामादीनाम् 'अपि गुरुः' आचार्यः 'त्वाम् अभिनन्दतु' युद्धाय सन्नद्धं प्रशंसतु। 'ऐन्द्रम्' इन्द्रसम्बन्धि, 'वैष्णव विष्णुसम्बन्धि 'आग्निमारुतम्' अग्निसहकृतपवनसम्बन्धि 'अथो सौपर्णम्' गरुड़ सम्बन्धि च 'ओजः' तेजः 'ते अस्तु'।'रामलक्ष्मणयोः धनुषोः' याभ्यां त्वं युध्यसे तयोः 'ज्याघोषः गुणञ्जनमेव यो 'मन्त्रः' स 'च' ते 'जयं देयात् एवं' अनन्यथाभावेन ददातु।।

Notes. 1. ककुन्तस्थस्य–ककुदि तिष्ठति इति ककुद्+स्था+क कर्त्तरि ककुत्स्थः one mounted on the hump of a bull. तस्य। ककुत्स्थ is the name given to पुरञ्जय the grandson of इक्ष्वाकु, because thus mounted he fought demons on behalf of Indra who had assumed the form of a bull. Comp. "पुरञ्जयस्तस्थ सुत इन्द्रवाह्य इतीरितः। वाहनत्वे वृतस्तस्य बभूवेन्द्रो महावृषः।.. स्तूयमानस्तमारुह्य युयुत्सुः ककुदि स्यितः। तेजसप्यायितो विष्णोः पुरुषस्य परात्मनः।।" Also "महेन्द्रमास्थाय महोक्षरूपं यः संयति प्राप्तपिणाकिलीलं। चकार वाणीरसुराङ्गानानां गुण्डस्थलीः प्रोषितपत्रलेखाः।।" etc. 2. परिकल्पताम्–For a similar use of क्लृप compare "किमन्यथा परिकल्पसे", para xx. 2.a. धिनोतु–धिन्वि+ लोट तु। cp. "धिनोति हव्येन हिरणयरेतसम्"–*Kirāt* I. 3. मैत्रावरुणयोः अयम् इति मित्रावरुण+अण्। 4. आग्निमारुतम्–अग्निश्च मरुञ्च अग्नामरुतौः। The इ of अग्नि becomingआ by "देवताद्वन्द्वे च"। अग्नामरुतोः इदम् इति अग्नामरुत्+अण् अग्निमारुतम्। Here the आ of अग्ना is ousted by इ by the rule "इद्वृद्धौ"–when the उत्तरपद has वृद्धि the आ and ई of अग्नि make way for इ। The उत्तरपद also takes वृद्धि by the rule "देवताद्वन्द्वे च" which occurs again in connection with उभयपदवृद्धि। आग्निमारुतम् ओजः does not mean the ओज of अग्नि and मरुत् *separately*, but of the two working together. Fire is irrestisible when it is urged on by wind. 5. रामलक्ष्मण etc.—चन्द्रकेतु had both the bows with him.

(*xxvi*) **लवः–कुमार, अति हि नाम शोभसे रथस्य एव, कृतं कृतमत्यादरेण।**

Lava—Prince, staying on the car you are really showing off to great advantage. Away, with over attention.

चन्द्रकेतुः–तर्हि महाभागोऽप्यन्यं रथमलङ्करोतु।

Chand.—Then let your highly talented self also grace a chariot.

लवः–आर्य प्रत्यारोपय रथोपरि राजपुत्रम्।

Lava—Noble Sir, take the prince back on the car.

सुमन्त्रः–त्वमप्यनुरुध्यस्व चन्द्रकेतोर्वचनम्।

Sum.—Do you too repect Candraketu's request.

लवः–को विचारः स्वेषूर्णकरणेषु ? किन्तु अरण्यसदो वयमनभ्यस्तरथचर्या।

Lava—What is the hesitation about one's own things ? But we the denizens of the wood are unpractised in the movements of cars.

मित–। 'नाम' इत्यव्ययम् अभ्युपगमे। 'कृतम्' इति मान्तमव्ययं निषेधे।। 'अलङ्करोतु' आरोहणेन इति शेषः।। 'प्रत्यारीपय' प्रयतवस्थापय।। अनुरुध्यस्व' समानय।।'विचारः' पर्यालोचना गृह्णामि न वा इत्याकारा।'स्वेषु' निजेषु 'उपकरणषु' सामग्रीषु। निजं द्रव्यम् अविचार्यैव ग्राह्यं तत् भवदुपस्थापितं रथम् आरोहामि इत्यत्र कः सन्देहः। 'किन्तु अरण्यसदः' वनवासिनो 'वयम् अनभ्यस्ता' अननुशीलिता 'रथचर्या' रथेन योधनं यैः तादृशाः। रथे स्थित्वा युद्धं गलग्रहो मे इत्यापाततः, वस्तुतस्तु पदातिरति रथिनं त्वां जेष्वाम्येव इति हृदयम्।।

Notes. 1. कृतम्–सम्भ्रमे द्विर्वचनम्। 2. प्रत्यारोपय–प्रत्यारोहय is the alternative form. This is to सुमन्त्र। 3. स्वेषु–This is in accordance with Candraketu's offer "यन्मम तत् तवैव", sl. 9. Hence your chariot is my chariot, so there can be no hesitation (विचार) in using it. 4. उपकरणेषु–उपक्रियते एभिः इति उप+कृ+ल्युट् करणे उपकरणनि things that minister to one's comfort. तेषु विषयाधिकरण 7मी। 5.अनभ्यस्त etc.—चरणम् इति चर+यत् भावे स्त्रियां चर्या movement. रथस्य चर्या रथचर्या movement of the chariot. Now see Ṭīkā

This does not mean that Lava pleads his inability to drive a car. The offer of a chariot includes that of a qualified drivers also. But accurate shooting from a moving chariot comes from practice alone. Hence the car would be, at this stage, a hadicap to Lava : this is what Lava apparently means to stage, to say. But he really feels that though on foot he is more than a match for Candraketu on a chariot.

(*xxvii*) **सुमन्त्रः–जानासि वत्स दर्पसौजन्ययोर्यथोचितमाचरितुम्। यदि पुनरत्वामीदृशमैत्र्क्षाको राजा रामभद्रः पश्येत् तदास्य स्नेहेन हृदयमभिस्यन्देत।**

Sum.—My child, you know how to behave befitting pride and courtesy. As you are, if Rāmabhadra, the king of the race of Ikṣvāku, sees you, then his heart will melt with affection.

लवः–आर्य सुजनः न राजर्षिः श्रूयते। (सलज्जमिव)–

Lava—Noble Sir, that royal sage is said to be a good man. (*As if with shame*)—

वयमपि न खल्वेवंप्राया: क्रतुप्रतिघातिनः
क इह च गुणैस्तं राजानं न वा बहु मन्यते।
तदपि खलु मे स व्याहारस्तुरङ्गमरक्षिणं
विकृतिमखिलक्षत्राक्षेपप्रचण्डतयाकरोत् ।। 27 ।।

We too are not indeed usually like this the obstructors of sacrifices. Who ever again does not in the world think highly of that king for his virtues ? Even thus, that proclamation of the guards of the horse really caused me annoyance by its bitterness as an insult to the whole Kṣattriya race.

मित–। 'दर्पस्य सौजन्यस्य' च 'यथा उचितं' भवति तथा आचरितुं जानासि'। अस्मिन् रथप्रत्याख्याने परमा त्वया विदग्धता प्रकटीकृता, दर्पश्च दर्शितः सौजन्यञ्च अव्याहतमेव। 'ईदृशम्' एवंविधम्, वाचि कर्मणि च प्रवीणमित्यर्थः। 'अभिस्यन्देत' द्रवीभवेत्।। वयमिति।

अन्वयः–वयमपि न खलु एवंप्रायाः क्रतुप्रतिघातिनः। कः वा इह तां राजानं गुणैः न च बहुमन्यते। तदपि तुरङ्गमरक्षिणां स व्याहारः अस्विलक्षत्राक्षेपप्रचण्डतयां मे विकृतिम् अकरोत् खलु।

व्याख्या–'वयमपि न खलुं नैव 'एवंप्रायाः' प्रायेण ईदृशाः 'क्रतुप्रतिघातिनः'

यज्ञविघातकाः। सुजनः न राजर्षिः, वयमपि न दुर्जनाः इत्यर्थः। 'कः वा' पक्षान्तरे कः 'इहं' जगति 'तं राजानं गुणैः न च' नैव 'बहुमन्यते' पूजयति। सर्व एव बहुमन्यते वयञ्च इति भावः। 'तदपि एवं सत्यपि 'तुरङ्गमरक्षिणाम् अश्वरक्षकाणाम्' स व्यवहारः' अयमश्वः पताकेयम् इत्यादिघोषणा 'अखिलक्षत्रस्य' निखिलक्षत्रि जातेः 'आक्षेपात्' अवमाननात् या 'प्रचण्डता' दुःसहता तया 'मे विकृतिं' मनोविकारम् अकरोत् 'खलु' अकरोदेव।।

Notes. 1. ऐक्ष्वाकः–Explained (See para viii). 2. अभिस्यन्देत–Also अभिष्यन्देत। 3. तदपि–तद् is an अव्ययः implying निर्देश–pointing at. The निर्देश is two facts—(i) We are not disposed to obstruct. (ii) We respect the king. In spite of these facts I was annoyed.

(*xxviii*) **चन्द्रकेतुः–(सस्मितम्)–किं नु भवतस्तातप्रतापोत्कर्षेऽप्यमर्षः ?**

Chand. (*With a smile*)—Do you forsooth cherish intolerance at the excess of even father's majesty ?

लवः–अस्त्विहामर्षो मा भूद्वा। एतत्तु पृच्छामि–दान्तं हि राजानं राघवं शृणुमः, स किल नात्मना दृप्यति नाप्यस्य प्रजासु दृप्तत्वं जायते। तत् किं मनुष्यास्तस्य राक्षसीं वाचमुदीरयन्ति ? (ल–)

Lava—Be there intolerance or be not ; this, however, I ask—We hear that king Rāghava is self-restrained ; he himself does not surely show pride nor again can pride find footing among his subjects. Why then do his men utter fiendish language ? (L.—)

मित–। 'तातस्य प्रतापः'। तस्य 'उत्कर्षः' अतिशयः। तस्मिन् विषये 'अमर्षः' असहनम्।। 'दान्तं' दमसम्पन्नं क्रोधिदिदमनशीलम्। 'राक्षसी' राक्षसोचितां दृप्तामित्यर्थः।

Notes. 1. दान्तम्–दम+णिच्=क्त कर्मणि दान्त or दमित। तम्। 2. राक्षसीम्–रक्षस इयम् इति रक्षस्+अण स्त्रियाम् राक्षसी suiting a demon ताम्।

(*xxix*) **(ल–)–**

ऋषयो राक्षसीमाहुर्वाचमुन्मत्तदृप्तयोः।
सा योनिः सर्ववैराणं सा हि लोकस्य निर्ऋतिः ।। 30 ।।

(L.—) The language of the wild and the haughty the

sage's call fiendish [Or—a demoness]. That is the root of all enmities ; it is indeed the bane of the world.

इति ह स्म तां निन्दन्ति, अथ इतरामभिष्टुवन्ति।

For this very reason they condemn it while they extol its opposite.

कामान् दुग्धे विप्रकर्षत्यलक्ष्मीं
कीर्त्तिं सूते दुष्कृतं या हिनस्ति।
ताञ्चाप्येतां मातरं मङ्गलानां
धेनुं धीराः सूनृतां वाचमाहुः ।। 31।।

And a true and agreeable speech, the mother of blessings, the wise call a cow—the speech that milks desires, keeps ill luck at a distance, yields fame, kills demerit.

मित–। ऋषय इति।

अन्वयः–ऋषयः उन्मत्तदृप्तयोः वाचम् राक्षसीमाहुः। सा सर्ववैराणां योनिः। सा लोकस्य निर्ऋतिः हि।

व्याख्या–ऋषयः उन्मत्तस्यं सुराविह्वलस्य 'दृप्तस्य' बलगर्वि तस्य च 'वाचं राक्षसीम् आहुः'। 'सा' राक्षसी 'सर्ववैराणां जगति वैरप्रपञ्चानां 'योनिः' कारणम्। 'सा लोकस्य' जगतः 'निर्ऋतिर्हि' अलक्ष्मीरेव।। 'ह' इति 'स्म' इति च वाक्यपूरणे अव्ययम्।। कामानिति।

अन्वयः–या कामान् दुग्धे अलक्ष्मीं विप्रकर्षति कीर्तिं सूते दुष्कृतं हिनस्ति ताम् एतां मङ्गलानां मातरं सूनृतां वाचं धीराः धेनुम् आहुरपि च।

व्याख्या–'या' इतरा वाक् 'कामान्' मनीषितान् 'दुग्धे' सम्पादयति 'अलक्ष्मीं' दुर्भाग्यं विप्रकर्षति' दूरीकरोति 'कीर्त्तिं सूते' यश आवहति 'दुष्कृतं हिनस्ति' पापं नाशयति 'ताम् एतां मङ्गलानां मातरम्' इत्थ कल्याणानां निदानं तां 'सुनृतां वाचं' सत्यप्रियभाषणं 'धीराः' ऋषयः 'धेनुम् आहुरपि च'। एकां राक्षसीमाहुः अपराञ्च धेनुम्।।

Notes. 1. राक्षसीम्–रक्षः एव इति रक्षस्+अण् स्वार्थे स्त्रियाम् राक्षसी (demoness) is the name given to it by sages in contradistinction from the other kind of speech which receives from them the name धेनु (milch-cow). 2. ह स्म–Bath ह and ण्म are अव्ययs used as expletives (वाक्यपूरणे)। 3. अभिष्टुवन्ति–अभि+स्तु+ल्युट् अन्ति। स becomes ष by "उपसर्गात् सुनोति–"।4. च अपि–Both imply समुच्चय। The context is राक्षसीम् आहुः घेनुम् आहुरपि च। Or was may take च as implying पक्षान्तर–the other side. "च पादपूरणे पक्षान्तरे हेतौ विनिश्चये" इति त्रिकाण्डशेषः।

(*xxx*) **सुमन्त्रः–परिपूतस्वभावोऽयं कुमारः प्राचेतसान्तेवासी। वदत्ययमभिसम्पन्नमार्षेण संस्कारेण।**

Sum.—This boy, the pupil of Prāchetasa, is of a thoroughly pure character. What he say is replete with Vedic conceptions (or conceptions befitting a sage) [Or—is endowed with Vedic refinement (or refinement befitting a sage)].

लवः–यत् पुनश्चन्द्रकेतो वदसि 'किं नु भवतस्तातप्रतापोत्कर्षेऽप्यमर्षः'' इति तत् पृच्छामि किं व्यवस्थितविषयाः क्षत्रधर्मा इति।

Lava—Again, Candraketu, as you say ''Do you forsooth cherish intolerance at the excess of even father's majesty''. so I ask ''Are the virtues of the Kṣattriya caste of a restricted sphere ?''

सुमन्त्रः–नैव खलु जानासि देवमैक्ष्वाकम्। तद्विरम विरमातिप्रसङ्गात्।

Sum.—Surely you know not Sire of Ikṣavāku's race, so cease, O cease from over-reaching.

सैनिकानां प्रमाथेन सत्यमोजायितं त्वया।
जामदग्न्यस्य दमने नैवं निर्वक्तुमर्हसि ।। 32 ।।

True, herison been shown by you by the slaughter of troops. It behoves you not to talk thus of the vanquisher of Jamadagnya.

मित–। 'अन्ते' समीपे 'वमति' इति अन्तेवासी' शिष्यः। 'अयम् आर्षेण संस्कारेण' श्रौतेन शोधनेन यद्वा ऋषिजनोचितेन ज्ञानेन 'अभिसम्पन्नं' युक्तं वच 'वदति' युक्तं यथा तथा वदति वा।।'व्यवस्थितः' नियतः 'विषयः' येषां तादृशाः। 'आत्रधर्माः' शौर्यादयः इहैव सन्ति नान्यत्र इत्यस्ति काचित् व्यवस्था? अतिशयितः प्रसङ्गः 'अतिप्रसङ्गः' अनविकारचर्चा। तस्मात्।। सैनिकानामिति।

अन्वयः–सैनिकानां प्रमाथेन त्वया ओजायितं सत्यम्। जामदग्न्यस्य दमने एवं निवर्क्तुन अर्हसि।

व्याख्या– 'सैनिकानाम्' अस्मत्पक्षीयाणां बलानां 'प्रमाथेन' हननेन 'त्वया ओजायितम्' ओजस्विना बलवता इव आचरितं 'सत्यम्'। तथापि 'जामदग्न्यस्य' जमदग्निसुतस्यभृगुपतेः 'दमने' विजेवरि विषये रामे इत्यर्थः 'एवम्' अनेन प्रकारेण

अनादरेण इत्यर्थः। 'निर्वक्तुं' निर्देष्टं 'न अर्हसि' न युज्यसे। जामदग्न्यदमने रामे क्षात्रधर्मा व्यवस्थितविषया एव इति भावः ।।

Notes. 1. आर्षेण etc.—ऋषि sage or Veda. "ऋषिर्वेदे वशिष्ठदौ" इत्यादि विश्वमेदिन्धौ। तस्य अयम् इति ऋषि+अण् आर्षः belonging to a sage or Vedic. सम्+कृ+घञ् करणे संस्कार purification ; or घञ कर्मणि संस्कार conception. 2. यत् तद् imply हेतु। Because (यत्) you ask me a question, so (तत्) I reply with another question, *viz.*, किं व्यवस्थित etc. 3. व्यवस्थित etc.—वि+अव+स्था+क्त कर्त्तरि व्यवस्थित restricted. विषय is the subject to which क्षत्रधर्म attaches. Lava asks—Are we to understand that क्षत्रधर्म adheres to a certain particular object (राम) and is to be found no where else ? Of course the drift is that it is possible that there are other Kshattriyas quite as valorous as राम। Who knows that I myself am not a match for him ? 4. अतिप्रसङ्गात्–प्र+सञ्ज+घञ् भावे प्रसङ्ग context, अतिप्रसृतः प्रसङ्गः अतिप्रसङ्गः carrying of point beyond its limit, rushing in where angels fear to tread ! 5. ओजायितम्–ओजस् here means ओजस्वि powerful. ओजसा, *i.e.*, ओजस्विना इव आचरितम् इति औजस्+क्यङ् (नाम धातु)+क्त भावे ओजायितम् played the hero. The स of ओजस् disappears by "कर्त्तुः क्यङ् स लोपश्च"।6. जामदग्न्यस्य–जमदग्नेर्गोत्रपत्यं पुमान् इति जमदग्नि+यञ् जामदग्न्यः a desecendent of जमदग्नि। Here the *son* is treated as a mere descendant. If the son is taken as a *son*, affix is अण् giving जामदग्नः। 7. नैवम् etc.—If you do speak thus, it becomes अति प्रसङ्ग on your part and I say विरम विरमातिप्रसङ्गात्।

(*xxxi*) लवः (सहासम्)–आर्य जामदग्न्यस्य दमनः स राजा इति कोऽयमुच्चैर्वादः ?

Lava *(With a laugh)*—Noble Sir, what high praise is this that king is the subduer of Jamadagnya ?

सिद्धं ह्येतद्वाचि वीर्यं द्विजानां
वोह्वोर्वीर्यं यत्तु तत् क्षत्रियाणाम्।
शस्त्रग्राही ब्राह्मणो जादग्न्यस्तस्मिन्।
दान्ते का स्तुतिस्तस्य राज्ञः ।।33।।

It is surely an established fact that the strength of Brāhmaṇas is in speech while the stength that is in the arms lies with the Kshattriyas. Jamadagnya, a Brāhmaṇa, took to arms. He being subded, what credit goes to that king ?

मित–'उच्चैः' ऊर्जितः 'वादः' उक्तिः इति कर्मधारयः। महती कथा इति विद्यासागरः।। सिद्धमिति।

अन्वयः–द्विजानां वीर्यं वाचि, यतु वीर्यं वाह्वोः तद् क्षत्रियणाम्, एतत् सिद्धं हि। जामदग्न्यः शस्त्रग्राही ब्राह्मणः। तस्मिन् दान्ते तस्य राज्ञः का स्तुतिः।

व्याख्या–'द्विजानां' ब्राह्मणानां 'वीर्यं' प्रतापः 'वाचि' तिष्ठति, 'यत् तु' यन् पुनः 'वीर्यं' बाह्वोः' भुजयोः 'तत् क्षत्रियाणाम्' अस्ति न तु ब्राह्मणानाम् 'एतत् सिद्धं हि' सर्वजनविदितमेव। 'जामदग्न्यः शस्त्रग्राही' अस्त्रधारी 'ब्राह्मणः' शस्त्रग्रहणे अनधिकारी इत्यर्थः स कथं क्षत्रियवत् निपुणमस्त्राणि प्रयुञ्जीत। तत् 'तस्मिन्' कुत्सित–शस्त्रधारिणि 'दान्ते' विजिते 'तस्य राज्ञः' रामस्य 'का स्तुतिः' कोऽयमुच्चैर्वादः।।

Notes. 1. सिद्धम्–Well-known. Comp. "नैसर्गिकी सुरभिणः कुसुमभ्य सिद्धा etc."—I, sl. 14. 2. द्विजानाम्–द्वि here means not two but twice. द्विः जाता इति द्वि+जन+ड कर्त्तरि द्विजाः Brāhmanas. तेषाम्। strictly speaking ब्राह्मण, क्षत्रिय, वैश्य are all द्विज but the poet restricts the word here to Brāhmaṇas only. Comp. "क्षात्रं द्विजत्वञ्च परम्परार्थम्।"–*Bhaṭṭi*. 5. शस्त्रग्राही–शस्त्रं गृह्णाति इति शस्त्र+ग्रह+णिनि कर्त्तरि साधुकारिणि। But lding of weapons requires strength of arms which Brāhmaṇas do not possess. Hence Jamadagnya must have been a feeble fighter. 4. दान्ते–इम+णिच्+क्त कर्मणि दान्त or दमित। भावे 7मी।

(*xxxii*) **चन्द्रकेतुः–(सोन्माथमिव) –आर्य आर्य कृतं कृतमुत्तरोत्तरेण।**

Cand. (*As if with great pain*)—Noble Sir, Noble Sir, away with more and more discussions.

कोऽप्येष सम्प्रतिः नवः पुरुषावतारो
वीरो न यस्य भगवान् भृगुनन्दनोऽपि।
पर्याल्पसभुवनाभयदक्षिणानि
पुण्यानि तातचरितानि च यो न वेद ।। 34।।

This now is some fresh incarnation of the Soul Supreme to whom even the mighty delighter of the race of Bhṛgu is no hero and who does not know of the holy deeds of father through which was obtained the grant of safety to the seven worlds.

मित–।'उन्माथः पीड़ा। तेन सह यथा तथा।'आर्य' इत्यत्र सम्भ्रमे द्विरुक्तिः। 'कृतम्' इति निषेधे अव्ययम्। सम्भ्रमे द्विरूक्तिः। 'उत्तरम्' प्रत्यक्तिः। 'उतरञ्च प्रतिवादिकृतम्'उतरञ्च' वादिकृतम्'उतरीतरम्'।'सर्वो द्वन्द्वो विभाषया एकवद्भवतीति वक्तव्यम्'' इति द्वन्द्वै कत्वम्। यद्वा 'उत्तरस्य' प्रतिवादिकृतस्य 'उत्तरं' वाश्किृता प्रत्युक्तिः उत्तरोत्तरम्' उक्तिप्रत्युक्तिपरम्परा। तेन 'कृतम्' अलम्।। कोऽपीति।

अन्वयः–एष सम्पति नवः कोऽपि पुरुषावतारः यस्य भगवान् भृगुनन्दनः अपि न वीरः, यश्च पर्याप्तसप्तभुवनाभदक्षिणानि पुण्यानि तातचरितानि न वेद।

व्याख्या–'एष सम्प्रति' इदानीन्तने काले 'नवः कोऽपि' अचित्यस्वरूपः 'पुरुषावतारः' पुरूषस्य भगवतो नारायणस्य अवतारविशेषः 'यस्य' समचं 'भगवान् भृगुनन्दनः' एकविंशति- वारक्षत्रियान्तकरणेन भृगुवं शीयानां नन्दयिता जामदग्न्योऽपि 'न वीरः'।'यश्च' यः पुनः 'पर्याप्ता' साकल्येनप्राप्ता 'सप्तभवुनस्य अभयदक्षिणा' अभयदानं येभ्यः अतएव 'पुण्यानि' पावनानि तादृशानि 'तातसा' रामसा 'चरितानि' कर्माणि 'न वेद' न जानाति। इदानीन्तनया एष भृगुपतिचरि तातचरितञ्च न जानाति, ईदृशेन अज्ञन सह का उक्तिप्रत्युक्तिः। तत् विरमतां भवान् इति सुमन्त्रं प्रति चन्द्रकेतोरुक्तिः।।

Notes. 1. सोन्माथम्–उद्+मथ+घञ् भावे उन्माथः pain पीड़ा। तेन सह यथा तथा। See para xiii. 2. पुरुष etc.—पुरुष is नारायण। अवतरत्यनेन इति अव+तृ+घञ् करणे अवतारः incarnation. पुरुषस्य अवतारः।3. यस्य–सम्बन्ध सामान्ये षष्ठी। यस्य सम्बन्धे न वीरः।3. पर्याप्त etc.—परि+आप+क्त कर्मणि पर्याप्त fully attained. परि implies सर्वतोभाव। दक्षिणा gift दान।''दक्षिणा दिशि दाने च'' इति त्रिकाण्डशेषः। Now see टीका।

(*xxxiii*) **लवः–को हि रघुपतेश्चरितं महिमानञ्च न जानाति ? यदि नाम किञ्चिद्वक्तब्यमस्ति–अथवा शान्तम्।**

Lava—Who ever does not know of the deeds and greatness of the lord of the Raghus ? If there is something to be criticised—Or peace !

वृद्धास्ते न विचारणीयचरितास्तिष्ठन्तु किं वर्ण्यते
सुन्दस्त्रीदमनेऽप्यण्डयशसो लोके महान्तो हि ते।
यानि त्रीण्यपराङ्मुखान्यपि पदान्यसन् खरायोधने
यद्वा कौशलमिन्द्रसूनुनिधने तत्राप्यभिज्ञो जनः ।। 35।।

Why discussed ? He is our senior, his deeds are not for scrutiny. Leave him alone. He is indeed great in the world with fame unimpaired even in the killing of the wife of Sunda. Also the three steps, with the face not turned back, that were taken in the fight with Khara; or again the skill (strategy ?) displayed in killing of the son of Indra—in all these the people are well informed !

मित– । 'चरितं' तत्तदद्भुतं कार्यजातम् । 'महिमानस्' महत्त्वम् । 'यदि नाम' इति सम्भावनायाम् । 'वक्तव्यं' विचार्यं सत् वा असत् वा इति चिन्तनीयम् । 'अववा शान्तम्' इति परवर्त्तिना श्लोकेन अन्वितम् ।। वृद्धा इति ।

अन्वयः–अथवा शान्तम्, किं वर्र्यते । वृद्धाः ते विचारणीयचरिता नु, तिष्ठन्तु । सुन्दस्त्रीदमने अपि अखण्डयशसः ते लोके महान्तो हि । यानि खरायोधने अपराङ्सुखानि त्रीणि पदानि आसन् अपि, यत् इन्द्रसूनुनिधने कौशलं वा, तत्रापि जनः अभिज्ञः ।

व्याख्या–'अथवा' पक्षान्तरे 'शान्तम्' मास्तु वक्तव्यम्, 'किं वर्ण्यते' चरितस्य महिम्नश्च वर्णनया अलम् । कारणमाह–'वृद्धाः' वयोज्येष्ठाः 'ते स रामः [गौरवे बहुवचनमिह सोत्प्रासम्] । 'विचरणीयं' समालोहचनार्हिं 'चरितं कार्यं येषां तथाविधा 'न' भवन्ति, तत् तिष्ठन्तु' ते । एतत्तु चरितं प्रति । महिमानं प्रत्याह–'सुन्दस्त्री' ताड़का तस्या 'दमने' निधने 'अपि' स्त्रीवधे कृतेऽपि 'अखण्डम्' अविकलं 'यशो' येषां तथाविधाः 'ते' स रामः 'लोके' जगति 'महान्तो हि' लोकोत्तरा एव । यदि महान्तो न स्युःस्त्रीवधात् अयशो जायेत लोकोत्वरत्वादेव न जातम् । 'यानि खरेण' सह यत् 'आयोधनं' युद्धमभूत् तस्मिन् 'अपराङ्मुखानि' अपरावृत्तानि अविवृत्तवदं यथा तथा पश्चात् निहितानि इत्यर्थः । 'त्रीणि पदानि' पदपेक्षाः 'आसन् अपि' अभवंश्च, 'यत् इन्द्रसूनोः' इन्द्रपुत्रस्य बालिनः 'निधने' प्रमाथे 'कौशलं वा' निपुणता च [वा इति समुच्चये] 'तत्र अपि' तेषु सर्वेषु च 'जनः अभिज्ञः' लोको विज्ञानवान् । सर्व विदि लोकस्य ।।

Notes. 1. यदि नाम etc.—यदि and नाम are अव्यय, both implying सम्भावना । Comp. "न त्रस्तं यदि नाम भूतकरुणासन्तानशान्तात्मनः" etc. *Vīracarita*. He was going to criticise, but he checks himself with 'अथवा शान्तम्'। 2. शान्तम्–An अव्यय (मकारान्त) implying prohibition. Away with criticism. 3. महान्तः–This is said tauntingly. महत् great, super-human. स्त्रीवध ruins the fame of ordinary men ; it did not affect Rāma because Rāma is super-human ! ! 4 यानि etc.—Rāma had to fall back three steps though all the while facing (अपराङ्मुखानि) खर । Here विद्यासागर quotes from the रामायण–"विकलः स कृतो बाणौः खरो रामेण संयुगे । मत्तो रुधिरगन्धेन तमेवभ्यद्रवद् द्रुतम् ।। तमापतन्तं संक्रुद्धं कृतास्त्रो रुधिराप्लुतम् । अपासर्पद्द्वित्रिपदं

किञ्चित्वरितविक्रमः।।" 5. अपराङ्मुखानि–पराक् विवृतं मुखमेष पराङ् मुखानि with face turned back. न पराङ्मुखाति। No ण because a पद intervenes (परा+अच्+मुख)। The prohibition is by 'पदव्यवायेऽपि"। The अपि here and the वा in यद्वा imply समुच्चय of पदानि and कौशलम्। See टीका। 6. तत्र–This is the correlative of यानि and यत्। 7. अभिज्ञो जनः–This is in support of को हि....न जानाति।

(*xxxiv*) **चन्द्रकेतुः–आः ! तातापवादभिन्नमर्याद, अति हि नाम प्रगल्भसे।**

Cand.—Ah' You, that have broken the bounds of decorum by denouncing father, you are rattling on a bit too much.

लवः–अये ! मयेव भ्रकुटीधरः संवृत्तः।

Lava—Ha ! He has worked up a frown, at myself.

सुमन्त्रः–स्फरितमनयोः क्रोधेन। तथाहि–

Sum.—Their ire is up. Thus—

चूड़ामण्डलबन्धनं तरलयत्याकूतजो वेपथुः
किञ्चित् कोकनदच्छदस्य सदृशे नेत्रे स्वयं रज्यतः।
धत्ते कान्तिमकाण्डताण्डवितयोभेङ्गेन वक्त्रं भ्रुवो-
श्चन्द्रस्योत्कटलाञ्छनस्य कमलस्यासेद्भ्रान्तभृङ्गस्य च ।।36।।

The nodding resulting from emotion shakes the knot of the tufts of hair ; the eyes, that by nature slightly resemble the petals of the red-lotus, are becoming deep red ; the face, by the knitting of the eye-brows that are giving sudden jumps, shows the beauty of the moon when the stain is prominent and of the lotus when black-bees hover above.

कुमारौ–तदितो विमर्दक्षमां भूमिमवतरावः।(इति निष्क्रान्ताः सर्वे)।

The Youths—Then let us repair hence to ground suitable for fighting. *(Exeunt all).*

इति कुमारविक्रमो नाम पञ्चमोऽङ्कः।

This is the Fifth Act named The Valour of the Youths.

मित–'आः' इत्यव्ययं कोपे। 'तातस्य' रामस्य अपवादने' निन्दया 'भिन्ना' भग्ना 'मर्यादा' सत्कारक्रमकः येन तत्संबुद्धिः। 'प्रगलभसे' वाक्चापलं कुरुषे।। 'कुटी' भङ्गः वक्रता।' भुत्रोः कुटी' भूभङ्गः। ["इको ह्रस्वः–" इति ह्रस्वविकल्पः]। भ्र कुट्या धरः।। 'स्फरितं' प्रकठीभूतम्। भावे क्तः।। चूड़ेति।

अन्वयः–आकूतजो वेपथः चूड़ामण्डलबन्धनं तरलयति। स्वयं कोकनदच्छदस्य किञ्चित् सदृशे नेत्रे रज्यतः। अकाण्डताण्डवितयोः भ्र वोः भङ्गेन वक्त्रं उत्कटलाञ्छनस्य चन्द्रस्य उरुभ्रान्तभृङ्गस्य कमलस्य च कान्तिं धत्ते।

व्याख्या–'आकूतात्' अभिप्रायात् आवेगात् इत्यर्थः 'जातः' यः 'वेपथः' कस्पः शिरः कम्प इति यावत् 'स चूड़ामण्डलस्य' शिखासमूहस्य 'बन्धनं' ग्रन्थिं 'तरलयति' दोलयति। 'स्वयम्' आत्मना स्वभावादित्यर्थः 'कोकनदच्छस्य' रक्तोत्पलपत्रस्य 'किञ्चित् सदृशे' ईषत्तल्ये 'नेत्रे' नयने 'रज्यतः' लोहिते भवतः।' आकाण्डे' अनवसरे 'ताण्डवितयोः' कृतोद्धतनृत्ययोः 'भ्र वोः भङ्गेनः' कौटिल्येन हेतुना 'वक्त्रं' मुखम् 'उत्कटलाञ्छनस्य' परिस्फटकलङ्कस्य 'चन्द्रस्य' एवम् 'उद्भ्रान्ताः' परिपतन्तः 'भृङ्गाः' भ्रमराः यस्मिन् तादृशस्य 'कमलस्य च प्रफल्लपद्मस्यापि 'कान्तिं धत्ते' शोभां विभर्त्ति।। 'तत् तस्मात् विमर्दः कर्त्तव्य इति हेतोः 'इतः' अस्मात् रणकर्मणः अयोग्यात् स्थानात् 'विमर्द क्षमां' युद्धयोग्यां 'भूमिम् अवतरावः' यावः।।

Notes. 1. तात etc.—For समाप्त see टीका। मर्यादा here *is the respect due* स्थिति। Observance of स्थिति is a high virtue always. Hence "न मर्यादाभङ्गः क्षणमपि न नीचेष्वभिरुचिः", स्थितेरभेत्ता स्थितिमन्तमन्वयम् etc. 2. भ्रुकुटी etc.—भ्रू becomes optionally भ्रु or भ्र। Hence there forms—भ्रूकुटी, भ्रुकुटी, भ्रकुटी। Some add yet a forth form भृकुटि। cp. the rule ईको ह्रस्वोऽङ्यो गालवस्य" and the *Vārttika* "अभ्रुकुंसादीनामिति वक्त्रव्यम्"। Some also wish अ to come in place of the vowel of भ्रू। "अकारोऽनेन विधोयते इति व्याख्यानान्तरम्"–*Bhaṭṭoji.* Thus 3 forms. 3. तरलयति–तरल is चञ्चल। तरलं करोति इति; तरल+णिच् (नाम धातु)+लटति। 4. आकूतजः–आकूत is usually अभिप्राय hence आवेग eagerness. 5. अकाण्ड etc.—काण्ड is अवसर occasion. अकाण्ड no occasion, off season. ताण्डव is उद्धतनृत्य, here quick movement. ताण्डवः सञ्जातः अनयाः इति ताण्डव+इतच्। Now see टीका। 6. चन्द्रस्य etc.—It seems difficult to realise comparison here. Is the comparison with चन्द्र and कमल separately or with the two combined ? Either way the idea seems hazy. चन्द्र is *white*, कमल is *purple* while the faces of the boys are blue! ! Separate comparison, so far as *appearance* (धत्ते कान्तिम्) is concerned, is a hazardous matter. If चन्द्र and कमल be taken, combined, the concept well-nigh escapes comprehension. 7. विमर्द-etc.—विमर्दं क्षमते इति विमर्द+क्षम+ण कर्त्तरि स्त्रियाम् विमर्दक्षमा allowing a combat, ताम्। The place they they were was not unsuitable, as is obvious from the fact that लव was fighting the soldiery (बल) there. The object is to remove them from the stage, because actual fighting must not be staged—this is against is rules of dramaturgy. 8. निष्क्रान्ताः सर्वे-Remember चन्द्रकेतु is not foot, he has not yet remounted his chariot.

Chapter - 6

(i) (ततः प्रविशति विमानेनोज्ज्वलेन विद्याधरमिथनम्)

(*Then enter a pair of Vidyādharas is a bright balloon*)

विद्याधरः–अहो खलु अनयोर्विकर्त्तनकुलकुमारयोरकाण्ड प्रचण्डकलहयोः उद्योतितक्षात्रलक्ष्मीकयोरद्भतोद्भ्रान्तदेवासुराणि विक्रान्त चरितानि। तथाहि प्रिये पश्य पश्य–

Male Vidyādhara—O the deeds of valour—deeds with gods and demons bewildered at the marvels—of the two youths of the race of the Sun who are suddenly enagaged in a fierce fight and by whom lustre has been added to the virtues of the Kṣattriya tribe. Thus behold, darling behold—

झनज्झनितकङ्कणक्वणितकिङ्किणीकं धनु-
र्ध्वनद्गुरु गुणटनीक्तकरालकोलाहलम्।
वितत्य किरतोः शरानविरतस्फुरच्चूड़यो-
र्विचित्रमभिवर्द्धते भुवनभीममायोधनम् ।।1।।

(वि–)

A wondrous fight, awful to the universe, waxes between these two who with tufts of hair dangling incessantly, are showering arrows, having drawn the bow that is twanging deeply with a fierce tumult raised by the string and the horns and with the bells souding like jingling bracelets. (Male).

मित–। 'विद्याधरयोः मिथुनम्' कश्चित्! विद्याधरः तत्पत्नी च इत्यर्थः। 'अहो खलु अनयोः विक्रान्तचरितानि'। 'विक्रान्तं' विक्रमः। भावे क्तः। तस्य 'चरितानि' कर्माणि विक्रमकृतानि कर्माणि इत्यर्थः। अनयोः कयोः ?–'अकाण्डे' अप्रसङ्गे अकस्मात् इत्यर्थः 'प्रचण्डः कलहो' ययोः तादृशयोः 'विकर्त्तनकुलकुमारयोः' सूर्यवंशप्रभवयासेः बालयोः। पुनः किम्भूतयोः ?–'उद्योतिता' उद्भासिता' निजकर्मभिः इति शेषः 'क्षात्रलक्ष्मीः' क्षत्रकुलश्रीः याभ्यां तयोः। ययोरेभिः चरितैः क्षात्रलक्ष्मीः

अलङ्कृता भवति तयोः इत्यर्थः। किम्भूतानि चरितानि ?–'अद्भुतेन' आर्येण 'उद्भ्रान्ताः' विचलिताः 'देवासुराः' सुरदावनाः येषु तथाविधानि चरितानि।। झनजझनितेति।

अन्वयः–झनज्झनितकङ्कणक्वणितकिङ्किणीकं गुणाटनीकृतकरालकोलाहलम् (अतएव) गुरु ध्वनत् धुनः वितत्य शरान् किरतोः अविरतस्फुरच्चूड़योः भुवभीमं विचित्रम् आयोधनम् अभिवर्द्धते।

व्याख्या–'झनज्झनितं' झनज्झनशब्दं कुर्वत् यत् 'कङ्कणं' करभूषणं तस्य 'क्वणितं' शब्द इव 'क्वणितं' यासां तादृश्यः 'किङ्किण्यः' क्षुद्रघण्टिकाः यस्मिन् तथाविधं किञ्च 'गुणेन अटनीभ्यां कोटिभ्याञ्च 'कृतः करालः' भीमः 'कोलाहलः' शब्दः यस्मिन् तथाविधं अतएव 'गुरु' 'गभीरं यथा तथा 'ध्वनत्' गर्जत्' 'धनुः वितत्य' आकृष्य 'शरान् किरतोः वर्षतोः 'अविरतम्' अविश्रान्तं यथा तथा 'स्फुरन्ती' दोलायमाना 'चूड़ा' बद्धं चूड़ामण्डलं ययोः तादृशयोः अनयोः 'भुवनानां' सम्बन्धे 'भीमं' भयावह 'विचित्रम्' अत्यद्भकुतम्' आयोधनं' युद्धम् 'अभिवर्द्धते' भृशायते।।

Notes. I. विद्याधर etc.—विद्याधर is a kind of demi-gods. मिथुन a couple. विद्याधरयोः मिथुनम्। 2. उद्योतित etc.—उद्+द्युत+णिच्+कर्मणि उद्योतित illumined. क्षत्र the warrior class. क्षत्रस्य इयम् इति क्षत्र+अण्+ङीप् क्षात्री belonging to the warror class. लक्ष्मी wealth, virtues etc. क्षात्री लक्ष्मीः क्षात्रलक्ष्मीः the natural endowments of the military class, *i.e.*, strength, courage, martial training etc. Next बहु–with कप् added as समासान्त। 4. विक्रान्त etc.—see टीका। Vidyasagara takes विक्रान्त as विक्रमपरिचायक the क्त being कर्त्तरि। 4. झनज्झनित etc.—झनज्झन is a व्यक्त word, not an अव्यक्तानुकरण as in झनझनायित (V, sl. 4). In झनझनायित the word is झनत् which is double ; hence the whole of झनज्झन is the word and no doubling. झनज् झनः सञ्जातः अस्य इति झनजझन+इतच् झनज् झनितम्। क्वण+क्त भावे कणितम् sound. Now see टीका।

(ii) **(बि–)** **बिजृम्भितञ्च दिव्यस्य मङ्गलाय द्वयोरपि।**
स्तनयिन्तोरिवामन्द्रं दुन्दुभेर्दन्दुमायितम् ।। 2 ।।

(Male—) And the dum-dum-ing of the divine drum deep like that of cloud has begun for the safety of both.

तन्प्रबर्त्थतामनयोः प्रवीरयोग्नवरतम् अविरलललितबिकचकनक-कमलकमनीयसन्ततिः अमरतरुतरुणमणिमुकुलनिकरमकरन्दसुन्दरः पुष्पनिपातः।

So let there be commenced unto these mighty heroes an incessant shower of flowers that is pleasant from the honey of a mass of gem-like fresh buds of the celestial tree— shower, the flow of which is made charming by lovely full—blown golden lotuses strewn thick.

विद्याधरो–ता किं त्ति उण अआण्डबिप्फुरिदतड़िच्छड़ाकड़ारं बिअ अम्बरं झत्ति संवुत्तुं (तत् किमिति पुनः अकाण्डविस्फुरिततड़िचछटा-कड़ारमिव अम्बरं झटिति संवृत्तम्) !

Female Vid.—Well then, why again has the sky suddenly become yellow as if with an unseasonably flashed array of lightning ?

मित– । विजृम्भितेति । अन्वयः–द्वयोरपि मङ्गलाय दिव्यस्य दुन्दुभेः स्तनयित्रोरिव आमन्द्रं दुन्दु मसायितं विजृम्भितञ्च। व्याख्या–'द्वयोरपि' कुमारयोः 'मङ्गलाय' अक्षतदेहत्वाय 'दिव्यस्य दुन्दभेः' स्वर्गीयपटहस्य 'स्तणयित्नोरिव' मेधस्येव 'आमन्द्रं' अतिगभीरं 'दु·दुभायितं दुम् इति शब्दः 'विजृन्मितञ्च' आर्विभूतमपि ।। 'तत् तस्मात् । यतो देवा मङ्गलमाचरन्ति अतो वयमपि पुष्पवर्षणेन मङ्गलं कुर्मः । ' अविरलैः अनल्पैः 'ललितैः' सुन्दरैः 'विकचैः' प्रफुल्लैः 'कनककमलैः' सुवर्णपद्मैः 'कमनीयां हृद्या 'सन्ततिः' प्रवाहो यस्य तादृशः, किञ्च 'अमरतरुणां' सुरपादपानां पारिजातादीनां यः 'तरुणः' अपर्युषितः 'मणितुल्यानां मुकुलानां निकरः' समूहः तस्य 'मकरन्देन' मधुना 'सुन्दरः' सुभगः 'पुष्पनिपातः' कुसुमवर्षं 'प्रवर्त्यताम्' आरभ्यताम् ।। ' अकाण्डे अनवसरे अकस्मादित्यर्थः 'विस्फुरिता' विजृम्भिता या 'विजृम्भिता या 'तड़िच्छटा' विद्युच्छिखा तया 'कड़ारं' पिङ्गलम् ।।

Notes. 1. स्तनयित्नीः—स्तन to rumble+इत्नुच् कर्त्तरि (उणादि) cloud. तस्य। 2. दुन्दुमायितम्–दुम is an imitation of sound of a drum (अव्यक्तानुकरण) । दुम् इति शब्दकरणम् इत्यर्थः दुम्+डाच्+क्यष्+क्त भावे (see झनझनायित, Act V, sl. 5). 3. प्रवीरयोः–सम्बन्धसामान्ये षष्ठी । 4. प्रवर्त्त्यताम्–Now. is आवाभ्याम् understood. Flowers are showered when some noble deed is done. Sometime the gods sometime the demi-gods shower them. Comp. 'अवाङ्मुखस्योपरि पुष्पवृष्टिः पपात विद्याधरहस्तमुक्ता'' also ''सुरभि सुरविभुक्तं पुष्पवर्षं पपात''।

(*iii*) **विद्याधरः–तत् किं नु खल्वद्य–**

Male V.—Can it then be that just now—

त्वाष्ट्रयन्त्रभ्रमिभ्रान्तमार्त्तण्डज्योतिरुज्ज्वलः।
पुटभेदो ललाटस्थनीललोहितचक्षुषः ।। 3 ।।

Has happened the parting of the lids of the eye of Nīlalohita that is on his forehead—the parting which is dazzling like the brilliancy of the sun turned in the whirl of Tvāṣṭri's lathe ?

(विचिन्त्य) आं ज्ञातम्। वत्सेन चन्द्रकेतुना प्रयुक्तमस्त्रमाग्नेयम्। तस्यायमग्निच्छटासम्पातः। सम्प्रति हि–अवदग्धकर्वुरितकेतुचामरैरपयातमेव हि विमानमण्डलैः।

(*Reflecting*) Ah ! I see ! The fire-weapon has been invoked by dear Candraketu ; of that is this concentration of the glow of fire. Verily now—

दधति ध्वजाङ्कुशपटाञ्चलेष्विमाः क्षणकुङ्कमच्छरणविभ्रमं शिखाः ।।4।। (व–)

The hosts of balloons, the flage and *chowries* of which have become scorched and spotted have indeed retreated to a distance ; and these flames display at the wraps of the falgstaffs the sppearance of a momentary paint of saffron. (Male).

मित–।'तत्' इत्यादि परिवर्त्तिना श्लोकेन अन्वितम्।'तत् किं खल्वद्य–नील-लोहितचक्षुषः पुटभेदो' जातः इत्यन्वयः।। त्वाष्ट्रेति।

अन्वयः–तत् किं न खलु ललाटस्थनीललोहितचक्षुषः त्वाट्रयन्त्रभ्रमिभ्रान्तमार्त्तमण्डयोतिरुज्ज्वलः पुटभेदः। अद्य (जातः)।

व्याख्या–'तत्' तस्मात् यतः कड़ारमम्बरं तत इत्यर्थः।'किं' प्रश्ने 'नु' वितर्के, 'खलु' जिज्ञासायाम्। तत्वपरिज्ञानार्थं वितर्कगर्भः प्रश्नः इति भावः।'ललाटस्थं' यत् 'नीललोहितस्य' रुद्रस्य 'चक्षुः' हरस्य तृतीयं नयनं तस्य 'त्वाष्ट्रं' विश्वकसस्वामिकं यत् 'यन्त्रं' शाणयन्त्रं तस्य 'भ्रमिभिः' आवर्त्तनैः 'भ्रान्तस्य' आर्त्तितस्य 'मार्त्तण्डस्य' सूर्यस्य 'ज्योतिरिव उज्जवलः पुटभोदः आवरणमोचनम् 'अद्य' जातः किम् इति पृच्छामि।। 'आम्' इत्यवधारणे। संशयो मे अपयातः इत्यर्थः। 'अग्निच्छटानाम्' अग्निशिखानां 'सम्पातः' राशीभवनम्।। अवदग्धेति।

अन्वयः–अवदग्धककुर्वरित– केतुचामरैः विमानमण्डलैः अपयातमेव हि। इमाः शिखाः ध्वजाङ्कुशपटाञ्चलेषु क्षणकुङ्कमच्छुरणविभ्रमं दधति।

व्याख्या–'अवदग्धाः' ईषत् प्लुष्टा अतएव 'कुर्वरिताः' शवलीकृताः 'केतवः' पताकाः 'क्षामराणि' च येषां येषु वा तादृशैः 'विमानमण्डलैः' व्योमयानसमूहैः

'अपायतम् एव हि' दाहविषयात् दूरे एव गतम्। दूरगमनाच्च 'इमा:शिखा:' आग्नेयास्त्रस्य ज्वाला: 'ध्वजानां' विमानगतपताकानां ये 'अङ्कुशा:' अङ्कुशाकारदण्डा: तेषां ये आवरका: 'पटा:' वसानि तेषाम् 'अञ्चलेषु' प्रान्तेषु 'क्षणं' मुहूर्त व्याप्य यत् 'कुङ्कुमच्छ्रणं' कुङ्कुमानुलेप: तस्य 'विभ्रमं' शोभां दधति' धारयन्ति। पटाञ्चलेषु पतिता: शिखाभास: कुङ्कु मानुलेप इव प्रतीयन्ते इत्यर्थ:।।

Notes. 1. तत् किं etc.—नु implies deliberation., doubt etc. वितर्क। ''वितर्कावमानयो: इत्यादि मेदिनी। खलु implies जिज्ञासा a desire to know facts. ''खलु स्याद्वाक्यभूषायां जिज्ञासायाञ्च सान्त्वने'' इत्यादि मेदिनी। 2. त्वाष्ट्र etc.—त्वष्टृ is विश्वकर्मन्। तस्य इदम् इति त्वष्ट्र+अण् त्वाष्ट्रम्। The allusion is to the story that संज्ञा, the wife of the Sun and daughter of त्वष्टृ, was unable to approach her husband on account of his heat. Viśvakarman, with the Sun's permission, sliced down the solar sphere with his lathe. This reduced the heat though brillinacy was enchanced (उज्जवल:) and made him approachable. मार्त्तण्ड sun. मृतस्य अण्डस्य अयम् इति मृत+अण्ड+अण्=मृतण्ड+अण्=मार्त्तण्ड:। Here मृत+अण्ड gives मृतण्ड just as शक+अन्धु yields शकन्धु by पररूप। The पररूप is allowed only when अण् has to be attached. Otherwise मृत+अण्ड=मृताण्ड। 3. पुटभेद:–पुट is a close holder. The third eye of Śiva, usually remains closed. The lids are opened to destroy, for fire issues from it forthwith. Here the Vidyādhara surmises if Śiva has opended his third eye. This is at this stage a mere suspicion on his part. Now पुटभेद is a क्रिया (a भाव)—the act of opening. As such it cannot be called उज्जवल। Hence चक्षुष: पुटभेद: means भिन्नपुटं चक्षु: by the maxim 'भावानयने द्रव्यानयनम्''। The उज्ज्वलता is of the चक्षु:। 4. ललाट etc.—नीलश्चासौ लोहितश्च नीललोहित: a name if Sixa. He was नील in the throat and लोहित in his matted locks. This is also explained differently by Rāyamukuṭa, thus—''नीलं येन ममाङ्गं तु रसात्कं लोहितं त्विषा। नीलालोहत इत्येव ततोऽहं परिकर्त्तित:।।'' इति वा। This is from the स्कन्दपुराण। The god paints his body blue while his lustre is red. 5. आम्–This implies अवधारण। The suspicion is removed and is replaced by certainty. No पुटभेद but आग्नेयास्त्रप्रयोग। 6. अवदग्ध etc.—अव here is ईषदर्थ as in ब्राहीन् अवहन्ति। Thus अवदग्ध means *slightly burnt*. केतु is ध्वज banner. कर्वुर spotted. कर्वुराणि कृतानि इति कर्वुर+णिच् (नामधातु)+क्त कर्मणि कुर्वुरितानि। केतवश्च चामराणि च केतुचामाराणि। अवदग्धानि कर्वुरितानि केतुचामराणि

येषाम्।5. ध्वजाङ्कुश etc.—ध्वाजङ्कुश is the flag-staff. It is wrapped in fancy cloth (पट) for the sake of appearance.

(iv) (वि–) आश्चर्यम् ! प्रवृत्त एवायम् उच्चण्डवज्रखण्डावस्फोटपटुरस्फुलिङ्गविकृतिः उत्तालतुमुललेलिहानज्वालासम्भारभैरवो भगवान् उषर्बुधः। प्रचण्डश्चास्य सर्वतः सन्तापः। तत् प्रियामङ्गेनाच्छाद्य दूरमपसारामि। (इति तथा करोति)।

Male—Wonderful ! The mighty fire is indeed spreading—fire, the outburst of whose sparks is mightier than the terrific bursting of fragments of the thunderbolt—fire, in its towering and tumultuous mass of flickering flames. And intense is its heat all round. So I will move away screeing my darling with my own body. (*Does so*).

विद्याधरो–दिट्ठिआ एदेण विमलोत्तिअसीदलमसिणमंसलेन णहदेहप्फंसेन आनन्दमन्दमुउलिदघुम्मन्तलोअणाए अन्दरिदो एब्ब सन्दाबो [दिष्ट्या एतेन विमलमौक्तिकसरशीतलमसृण मांसलेन नाथदेहस्पर्शेन आनन्दमन्दमुकुलितघूर्णल्लोचनाया अन्तरिव एव सन्तापः]।

Fem.—Luckily the heat is indeed at a distance from me (Or—my heat is indeed relieved) whose eyes are rolling and slightly closed through joy from the cool, smooth and solid touch of my lord's person as of that of a string of spotless pearls.

मित–।'प्रवृत्त एवायं भगवान् उषर्बुंधः' अग्निः। किम्भूत उषर्बुधः ?'उच्चण्डः' यः 'वज्रखण्डस्य' वज्रांशस्य 'अवस्फोटः' स्फोटनः ततोऽपि 'पटुतरः' प्रवलतरः 'स्फुलिङ्गानाम्' अग्निकाणानां 'विकृतिः' विकारः अवस्फोट इति यावत् यस्य तथाविधः। पुनः कोदृशः ? 'उत्तालां' अत्युच्चाः 'तुसुलाः' सङ्कुलाः' 'लेलिहानाः प्रसारणशीलाः याः 'ज्वालाः' शिखाः तासां 'सम्भारेण' राशिना 'भैरवः' भीमः।। 'दिष्ट्या' अहो हर्षः 'सन्तापः' अग्निकृतो गात्रदाहः 'अन्तरित एव' अपयात एव। कस्य सन्तापः ?–'आनन्देन मन्दम्' ईषत् 'मुकुलितं' निमीलिते 'घूर्णती' आवर्त्तमाने च 'लोचने यस्याः तथाविधाया मम। कुत आनन्दः ?'विमलः' अनवद्यः यः 'मौक्तिसरः' मुक्ताहारः तस्य इव 'शीतलः मसृणः' अपरुषः' 'मासलः' धनः स्पष्टानुभूत इति यावत् यः 'नाथदेहस्य स्पर्शः' तेन आनन्दः।।

Notes. 1. उच्चण्ड etc.—वज्रखण्ड is rather awkward. The idea of the breaking up a single piece of thunder into parts, each part being a वज्रखण्ड seems outrageous. The तद्धित affix. खण्डच् in the sense तस्य समूहः is perhaps equally bad. अवस्फोट is brusting. विकृति is transformation, which is here *bursting*. Now see टीका। 2. उत्ताल etc.—उद्गता तालेभ्यः इति उत्तालाः taller than a Tala tree. By transference of epithets उत्ताल is *very high*. पुनः पुनः लिहन्ति इति लिह+यङ्+शानच् लेलिहानाः making constant attempt to lick, i.e., flickering. Now see Tika. उषर्बुधः–उषसि सन्ध्यायां बुध्यते प्रकाशते इति उषस्+बुध+क कर्त्तरि उषर्बुधः fire. 4. अन्तरितः–अन्तरं सञ्जातमस्य इति अन्तर+इतच् अन्तरितः। Now अन्तरः means *distance* also *screen*. Hence the sense *relieved*.

(v) **विद्याधरः–अयि किमत्र मया कृतम् ? अथवा–**

Male—What is done by me in this matter, eh ! Or—

अकिञ्चिदपि कुर्वाणः सौख्यैर्दुःखान्यपोहति।
तत्तस्य किमपि द्रव्यं यो हि यस्य प्रियो जनः ॥ 5 ॥

Without doing anything he banishes sorrow through joy. What a treasure to him is he who is his beloved !

विद्याधरी–कहं अविरलविलोलघुमन्तविज्जुल्लदाविलासमण्डिदेहिं मत्तमोरकण्ठसामलेहिं ओत्थरीअदि नहत्थलं जलहरेहिं [कथम्, अविरलविलोलघूर्णद्विद्युल्लताविलासमण्डितैः मत्तमयूरकण्ठश्यामलैः अवस्तीर्यते नभस्तलं जलधरैः]।

Fem.—Why is the bottom of the sky being overcast with clouds that are dark like the throat of a giddy peacock adorned with the frequent play of transient, wandering streaks of lightning ?

विद्याधरः–अयि कुमारलवप्रयुक्तावारुणास्त्रप्रभावः खल्वेषः। कथम्, अविरलप्रवृत्तवारिधारासहस्त्रसम्पातैः प्रशान्तमेव पावकास्त्रम् !

Male—Well this is surely the majesty of the Varuna weapon invoked by prince Lava. Hullo ! The fire weapon is indeed quenched by the showering of thousands of streams of warer flowing incessantly !

विद्याधरी–पिअ मे [प्रियं मे]।

Fem.—Joy to me !

मित–।'अत्र' अस्मिन् तापप्रशमे 'मया किं कृतं' न किमपि। दूरगमनात् अन्तरितः सन्तापः' न हि मत्कृतात् कस्मादपि कर्मणाः।। अकिञ्चिदिति। व्याख्यातं द्वितीयाङ्के।। 'अविरलः' निरन्तरः यः 'विलोलानां' चपलानां 'घूर्णन्तीनां' मेघात् मेघान्तरं गच्छन्तीनां 'विद्यूल्लतानां' तड़िल्लेखानां 'विलासः' स्फुरणं तेन 'मण्डितैः' भूषितैः। 'मत्तः' सञ्जातमदः यः 'मयूरः' तस्य 'कण्ठः' इव 'श्यामलैः'। 'अवस्तीर्यते' व्याप्यते। 'नभसः' आकाशस्य 'तलम्' तिम्नपृष्ठम्।। 'कथम्' इत्याश्चर्ये। 'अविरलं' निरन्तरं यथा तथा 'प्रवृत्तानि' प्रसृतानि यानि 'वारिधारासहस्राणि' असंख्या जलधाराः तेषां 'सम्पातैः' प्रपतनैः 'प्रशान्तं' लब्धप्रशमम्।

Notes. 1. अत्र—In this matter, *i.e.,* in the matter of allaying your heat. 2. अविरल etc.—न विरलः not rare, *i.e.,* ceaseless. This qualifies विलास। विलोल implies that the flashes were transitory. घुर्णत् implies that the streaks passed from cloud to cloud. Now see Ṭīkā for समास।

(vi) **बिद्याधरः–हन्त हन्त सर्वमतिमात्रं दोषाय। यत्प्रबलवाताबलिक्षोभगम्भीरगुनगुनायमानमेदुरान्धकारनीरन्ध्रनिरुद्धम्। एकवारविश्वग्रसनविकचविकरालकालकण्ठकण्ठकन्दरविवर्त्तमानमिब युगान्तयोगनिद्रानिरुद्धसर्वद्वारनारायणोदरनिविष्टमिव भूतयातं प्रवेपते।**

Male.—Alas ! Alas ! Everything beyond measure is for evil. For, the the entire creation, enclosed, without a loophole, in drakness made denser by clouds that are booming deep from shocks of terrific typhoons, is trembling as when sprawling in the awful abyss of Nīlakaṇṭha's throat opened to swallow up the universe at one gulp, or when placed in the maw of Nārāyaṇa with all his outlets closed by the sleep of trance at the end of *Yuga*. Bravo Child Candraketu, bravo ! Just in time has the Wind-weapon been invoked. For—

साधु ! वत्स चन्द्रकेतो साधु ! स्थाने वायव्यास्त्रमोरितम् यतः–

विद्याकल्पेन मरुता मेघानां भूयसामपि।
ब्रह्मणीव विवर्त्तानां क्वापि विप्रलयः कृतः ।। 6 ।।

By a gale resembling knowledge has been achieved the

regression of all the numerous clouds has been something inscrutable as of manifestations into Brahman.

मित– । 'मात्राम्' उचितं परिमाणम् 'अतिक्रान्तम्' व्यतीत्य स्थितम् 'अतिमात्रम्'। असह्यो जातो वारूणास्तस्य प्रभाव इति भावः। 'यत्' यस्मात् 'भूतयातं प्रवेपते' निखिलं जगत् कम्पते। किम्भतं सत् प्रवेपते ?–'प्रबलाभिः वातावलिभिः'–कृतो यः 'क्षोभः' प्रतिघातः तेत 'गम्भीरं' यथा तथा 'गुनगुनायमानैः' गुन इत्यव्यक्तं गर्जद्भिः 'मेघैः मेदुरं' सान्द्रीकृतं यत् 'अन्धकारं' तेन 'नीरन्ध्रं' निरवकाशं' यथा तथा 'निरुद्धं' परिव्याप्तं भूतजातम्। किमिव प्रवेपते ? 'एकेन वारेण' सकृत्कृतेनैव प्रयत्रेन 'विश्वस्य' भूतजातस्य यत् 'ग्रसनं ग्रासः तत्र 'विकचः' व्यात्तः अतएव 'विकरालः' अतिभीषणः यः 'कालकण्ठस्य' नीलकण्ठस्य प्रलये संहारमूर्तेर्हरस्य 'कण्ठकन्दरं' वदनविवरं तत्र 'विवर्त्तमानं' विचेष्टमानमिव भूतजातं प्रवेपते। पुनः किमिव ? 'युगान्ते' कल्पक्षये प्रलये 'या 'योगरूपा निद्रा' तया 'निरुद्धानि सर्वाणि द्वाराणि' रन्ध्राणि चक्षुरादीनिरा यस्य तादृशस्य 'नारायणस्य उदरे' कुक्षी 'निविष्टम्' अवस्थितमिव भूतजातम्।। विद्येति।

अन्वयः–विद्याकल्पेन मरुता भूयसामपि मेघानां विवर्त्तानां ब्रह्मणि इव क्वापि विप्रलयकः कृतः।

व्याख्या–'विद्या' तत्त्वज्ञानम्। तत्सदृशेन 'मरुता' वायव्यास्त्र- प्रयुक्तेन वायुना 'भूयसामपि' अप्रमेणामपि 'मेघानां विवर्त्तानां भेदबुद्धिकल्पितानां पदार्थानां 'ब्रह्मणि' अभेदबुद्धिदर्शिते एकस्मिन् तस्मिन् सति 'इव क्वापि' अविज्ञाते देशे 'विप्रलयः कृतः' अदर्शनं नीतः।।

Notes. 1. प्रवल etc.—गुन इत्यव्यक्तं शब्दं कुर्वन्त इत्यर्थे गुन+डाच्+क्यच् (नाम धातु)+शानच् कर्त्तरि गुनगुनायमानाः as in झनझनायित (V, sl. 5). 2. एकवार etc.—This is in accordance with the theory that final dissolution comes through Śiva who destroys the entire creation. 3. युगान्त etc.—This follows the belief that at dissolution नारायण withdraws the creation within himself and then lies in a trance (योगनिद्रा)floating in water. Comp. ''अमु युगान्तोचितयोगनिद्रः संहृत्य लोकान् पुरुषोऽधिशेते''–Raghu. 3. ब्रह्मणि etc.—ब्रह्मन् alone is *Existent*, the rest are like apparitions.वि+वृत+घञ् कर्मणि विवर्त्त, the root being अन्तर्भावितण्यर्थ ; this stands for the creation, Comp. 'एकस्य सतो विवर्त्तः कार्यजाताम्''।

(*vii*) **विद्याधरी–णाह को दाणिं एसो ससम्भमुक्खित्तकरवृभमिद-पठ्ठकञ्चलो दूरदो एव महुरवअणपड़िसिद्धजुज्झवावारो एदाणं कुमाराणं मज्झे विमाणं ओदरावेदि [नाथ क इदानीमेष ससम्भ्रमोत्क्षिप्तकर-**

भ्रमितपट्टकाञ्चलो दूरत एव मधुरवचनप्रतिषिद्धयुद्धव्यापार एतयोः कुमारयोर्मध्ये विमानमवतारयति] ?

Fem.—My husband, who now is this who, waving the skirt of his upper garment in his hand up-lifted in haste, has, even from afar, prohibited the battle-struggle in sweet words and is causing his balloon to descend between the princes ?

विद्याधरः (दृष्ट्वा)–एष शम्वूकवधात् प्रतिनिवृतो रघुपतिः

Male (*Observing*)—This is the head of the house of Raghu returning after the killing of Śambūka.

शब्दं महापुरुषसंबिहितं निशभ्य
तद्गौरवात् समुपसंहृतसम्प्रहारः ।
शान्तो लवः प्रणत एब च चन्द्रकेतुः
कल्याणमस्तु सुतमङ्गमनेन राज्ञः ।। 7 ।।

Having heard the shout uttered by this great personage and with fight stopped in deference to it, Lava has calmed down and Candraketu has indeed prostrated himself. May good come unto the king through union with his sons.

तदितस्तावन्निर्गच्छावः । (इति निष्क्रान्तौ)।

So we retire hence. (*Exeunt*).

विष्कम्भकः ।

(*Here end the Viṣkambhaka*).

मित– । सम्भ्रमेण' त्वरया सह 'उत्क्षिप्तः' उत्तोलितः यः 'करः' दक्षिणो हस्तः तेन 'भ्रमितः' आवर्त्तितः 'पट्टकाञ्चलः' उत्तरीयप्रान्तः येन तादृशः ।। शब्दमिति ।

अन्वयः–महापुरुषसंविहितं शब्दं निशम्य तद्गौवात् समुपसंहृतसम्प्रहारः लवः शान्तः चन्द्रकेतुः प्रणत एव च । सुतसङ्गमनेन राज्ञः कल्याणम् अस्तु ।

व्याख्या–'महापुरुषेण' पुरुषप्रकाण्डेन रामेण 'संविहितं' ससभ्रममुच्चारितं 'शब्दं' निषेधवाक्यं 'निशम्य श्रुत्वा 'तद्गौरवात्' तस्मिन् निषेधवाक्ये आदरात् हेतोः 'समुपसंहृतः' परित्यक्तः 'सम्प्रहारः' युद्धं येन तादृशः सन् 'लवः शान्तः' यातः 'चन्द्रकेतुः प्रणत एव' कृतताताभिन्दन एव । 'सुताभ्यां' सङ्गमनेन' सह मेलनेन 'राज्ञः कल्याणं' भद्रम् 'अस्तु' इति सुप्तमाङ्क्च्छाया ।।

Notes. 1. ससम्भ्रम etc.—He noticed the fight from above on his way back to Ayodhyā. Of course he could not recognise लव but could know that his own army was engaged. It was in the neighbourhood of Vālmīki's hermitage almost in the hermitage itself ; and evidently it was not an ordinary fight ; Hence Rāma's anxiety to stop the fight—आश्रमबाधा मा भूत् इति। The hand was uplifted and the skirts waved to draw attention. 2. शम्बू कवधात्–शम्बू कवधं विधाय इति ल्यब्लोपे कर्मणि भूमौ। 3. महापुरुष etc.—लव did not know that it was राम himself. But as he was descending from above in a विमान he know for certain that he was some महापुरुष। 4. निशम्य–शम of the दिवादि class means 'to hear'. 5. तद्गौरवात्–The तद् here refers to the शब्द। Or we may तद् refer to the महापुरुष in महापुरुषसंविहित। लव obeyed because he saw that the speaker was some महापुरुष। 6. सुत etc.—सुत refers to both लव and चन्द्रकेतु। Or better to लव and कुश। The विद्याधर being a demi-god was aware of the facts relating to लव and कुश।

(*viii*) (ततः प्रविशति रामो लवः प्रणतश्चन्द्रकेतुश्च)।

(*Then enter Rāma, Lava and Candraketu prostrate.*)

रामः (पुष्पकादवतरन्)–

Rāma (*Alighting from the Puṣpaka*)—

दिनकरकुलचन्द्रकेतो सरभसमेहि दृढं परिष्वजस्व।
तुहिनशकशीतलैस्तवाङ्गैः शममुपयातु ममापि चित्तदाहः ।। 8।।

Come quick and embrace me close, O Candraketu, the gladdener of the race of Raghu. May the burning of the heart of even me undergo abatement from your limbs that are cool like lumps of snow.

(उत्थाप्य सस्नेहास्त्रं परिष्वज्य) अपि नाम कुशलं तव दिव्यास्त्रधरदेहस्य ?

(*Raising and embracing with tears offection*) Is it all well with your person carrying the divine weapons ?

मित–। दिकरेति।

अन्वयः–दिनकरकुलचन्द्र चन्द्रकेतो सरभसम् एहि, दृढं परिष्वजस्व। तव तुहिनशकलयशीतलैः अङ्गैः मम अपि चित्तदाहः शमम् उदपयातु।

व्याख्या–हे 'दिनकरकुलस्य चन्द्र' आनन्दन 'चन्द्रकेतो सरभसं' द्रुतम् 'एहि' मत्पमीपमागच्छ 'दृढ़ं' परिष्वजस्व' गाढ़म् माम् आलिङ्ग माम्। 'तव तुहिनशकलैः' हिमखण्डैः इव 'शीतलैः अङ्गैः' हेतुभिः 'मम अपि' निरन्तरं दाहमनुभवतो रामस्य 'चित्तदाहः' मनःसन्ताप 'शमं' लाघवम् 'उपयातु लभताम्।। 'दिव्यास्त्राणां धरः' यो 'देहः' तस्य। अक्षतः किं ते देहः इति प्रश्नः।।

Notes. 1. प्रविशति–प्रवेश is not possible for one lying prostate (प्रणत)। Hence प्रविशति=is discovered. 2. दिनकर etc.—चन्दति आह्लादयति इति चन्द+रक् कर्त्तरि चन्दः gladdener. This is used here as an ordinary attributive. Rāma being childless, the hopes of the race naturally contered in चन्द्रकेतु। 3. सरभसम–रभस is वेग। ''रभसौ हर्षवेगयोः'' इति मैदिनी। 4. दिव्यास्त्र etc.—दिव्यास्त्राणं धरः दिव्यास्त्रधरः। तादृशो देहः। तस्य। Rāma noticed from above that the going on with divine weapons. The opponent was thus a hero, the query.

(*ii*) **चन्द्रकेतुः–कुशलमत्यद्भुतक्रियस्य प्रियदर्शनस्य लवस्य लाभाभ्युदयेन। तद्विज्ञापयामिमामिव विशेषेण वा मत्तः शिवेन चक्षुषा पश्यत्वमुं महाबीरप्रकाण्डं तातः।**

Cand.—All well through the fortunate acquisition of Lava of pleasing looks and highly wonderful deeds. So I pray may Sire eye this best of mighty heroes with as gracious a look as when eying me or surpassing that.

रामः (लवं निरूप्य)–दिष्ट्या अतिगम्भीरमधुरकल्याणाकृतिरयं वयस्यी वत्सस्य !

Rāma (*Marking Lava*)—Luckily this friend of my child is of a highly serene, charming and auspicious mien.

त्रातुं लोकानिव परिणतः कायबानस्त्रवेदः
क्षात्रो धर्मः श्रित इव तनुं ब्रह्मकोषस्य गुप्त्यै।
सामर्थ्यानामिब समुदयः सञ्चयो वा गुणाना–
माविर्भूय स्थित इव जगत्पुण्यनिर्माणराशिः ।। 8 ।।

Methinks the science of Arms has become incarnate to save the worlds ; (or) Military Virtue has taken form for guarding the treasure of the Vedas ; (or there has been) a concurrence of all powers or an assemblage of all virtues ;

(or again) the heap of materials for the making of all that is holy in the universe is standing manifest.

मित–। 'अत्यद्भुता' अत्याश्चर्या 'क्रिया' कर्म यस्य तस्य। 'लाभः' मित्रत्वेन प्राप्तिरेव 'अभ्युदयः' मङ्गलं तेन 'कुशलम्'। 'मामिव असुं' प्रशस्तं महावीरं 'महावीरप्रकाण्डं शिवेन चक्षुषा' प्रसन्नेन नयनेन न तु युद्धव्यापारात् सकोपेन 'पश्यतु तातः'। अथ 'वा मतः विशेषेण' आधिक्येन पश्यतु। अधिकार्थविशेषशब्दयोगे मत्त इति पञ्चमी।।'अतिगम्भीरा' अक्षोभ्या 'मधुरा' कल्याणी शुभा 'आकृतिः यस्य सः।। त्रातुमिति।

अन्वयः–लोकान् धातुम् अस्त्रवेदः कायवान् परिणत् इव। ब्रह्मकोषस्य गुप्तौ क्षात्रो धर्मः तनु श्रित इव। सामर्थ्यानां समुदयः गुणानां सञ्चय इव वा। जगत्पुण्यनिर्माणराशिः आविर्भूय स्थित इव।

व्याख्या–लोकान् त्रातुं' विश्वस्य रक्षायै 'अस्त्रवेदः' धनुर्वेदः 'कायवान्' मूर्त्तिमान 'परिणतः इव' संवृतः इति मन्ये अथवा 'ब्रह्मकोषस्य' वेदरूपस्य रत्नभाण्डस्य 'गुप्त्यै' रक्षायै 'क्षात्रो धर्मः' क्षत्रिगुणराशिः 'तुनं श्रित इव' धृतदेहः संवृत इति मन्ये। अथवा 'सामर्थ्यानां' साफल्यानां जगति भिन्नाधारे स्थितायाः कृतकृत्यतायाः 'समुदयः' एकाधारे आविर्भावः 'गुणनाम्' भिन्नाधारस्थानाम् उत्कर्षाणां 'सञ्चय इव वा' एकाधारे धृतो राशिर्वा इति मन्ये।'जगति' यानि 'पुण्यानि' पायनानि वस्तूनि सन्ति तेषां यत् 'निर्माणाम्' उपादानम् [ल्युट् करणे] तस्य 'राशिः' पुञ्जः 'आविर्भूय' मूर्त्तिमाश्रित्य 'स्थित इव' बालरूपेण अवस्थित इति मन्ये ।।

Notes. 1. विशेषण etc.,—वि+शिष+घञ् भावे विशेषः अधिक्यम् excess. In this sense compare "असीद्विशेषा फलपुष्पबृद्धिः"–*Raghu* सहार्थे 3या। मत्तः has पञ्चमी because विशेष has अधकार्थ included in it. Comp. "यस्मादधिकम्" *(Pāṇini)*. 2. महावीर etc.—प्रकाण्ड is प्रशंसावचन and नित्यक्लीव।'प्रशस्तो महावीरः महावीरप्रकाण्डम्, नित्यसमास by प्रशंसावचनैश्चं"। 3. अतिगम्भीर etc.—गम्भीरा चासौ मधुरा च गम्भीरमधुरा। गम्भीरमधुरा चासौ कल्याणी च गम्भीरमधुरकल्याणी। तादृशी अकृतिर्यस्य गम्भीरमधुरकल्याणकृतिः। अतिशयेन तादृशः। The कर्मधारय in stages as above is a necessity because otherwise पुंवद्भाव is not available and the बहु–yields the form गम्भीरामधुराकल्याणाकृतिः with पुंवद्भाव of कल्याणी only. 4. सामर्थ्यानाम्–सङ्गतः अर्थेन समर्थः one with the end (अर्थ) achieved, *i.e*, successful. तस्य भावः इति समर्थ+व्यञ् सामर्थ्यम् success, etc. It is usual to take सामर्थ्य here as *power* such as शौर्य etc. But then these are गुण and सामर्थ्यानामिव समुदयः becomes included in सञ्चयौ वा गुणानाम् thus leading to tautology. We have therefore explained differently as above.

(x) **लवः—अहो पुण्यानुभावदर्शनोऽयं महापुरुषः—**

Lava—O this great soul of saintly majesty and presence is—

आश्वासस्नेहभक्तीनामेकमालम्बनं महत्।
प्रकृष्टस्येव धर्मस्य प्रसादो मूर्त्तिसञ्चरः ॥ 10 ॥

A mighty common resort of consolation, affection and devotion, the favour as it were of supreme virtue moving embodied.

आश्चर्यम् !

O marvel !

विरोधी विश्रान्तः प्रसरति रसो निर्वृतिघन-
स्तदौद्धत्यं क्वापि व्रजति विनयः प्रह्वयति मामः।
झटित्यस्मिन् दृष्टे किमिब परवानस्मि यदि वा
महार्घस्तीर्थनामिव हि महतां कोऽप्यतिशयः ॥ 11 ॥

Discord had ended ; a sentiment rich in pleasure is developing ; that haughtiness departs who knows where ; modesty bends me down. This one being seen I have somehow become forthwith enslaved ; or, of the great, like that of holy places, there is an inexplicable and highly adorable ascendancy (that extorts homage).

मित–।'अहो' इत्यादि परिवर्त्तिना श्लोकेन अन्वितम्।। आश्वास इति।

अन्वयः– अहो पुण्यानुभावदर्शनः अयं महापुरुषः आश्वासस्नेहभक्तीनां महत् एकम् आलम्बनम्– प्रकृष्टस्य धर्मस्य मूर्त्तिसञ्चरः प्रसाद इव। यद्वा–अहो आश्वासस्नेहभक्तीनां महत् एकम् आलम्बनम अयं पुण्यानुभावदर्शनो महापुरुषः प्रकष्टस्य धर्मस्य मूर्त्तिसञ्चरः प्रसाद इव।

व्याख्या–'अहो' आश्चर्यम् !'पुण्यः' पवित्रः 'आनुभावः' प्रभावः 'दर्शनम्' आकृतिश्च यस्य तादृशः 'अयं महापुरूषः आश्वासस्य' सान्त्वनायाः 'स्नेहम्य' वात्सल्यस्य 'भक्तेः' पूजकगतस्य अनुरागस्य च 'महत्' विपुलम् 'एकं' साधारणम् 'आलम्बनं' समाश्रयः, किं बहुना मन्ये अयं 'प्रकृष्टस्य धर्मस्य' प्रभूतस्य पुनराशेः 'मूर्त्तिसञ्चरः' देहेन विहरन् 'प्रसाद इव' प्रसन्नता इव। धर्मस्य प्रसादः' प्रसन्नो धर्म इत्यर्थः। भावानयने द्रव्यानयनम्। ममैव पुण्यराशिः प्रसन्नो सूत्वा अग्रतो मे अनया महापुरुषमूर्त्या वर्त्तते इव इत्यर्थः।। विरोध इति।

अन्वयः–विरोधी विश्रान्तः। निर्वृतिघनः रसः प्रसरति। तत् औद्धत्यं क्वापि ब्रजति। विनयः मां प्रह्वयति। अस्मिन् दृष्टे किमिव झुटिति परवान् अस्मि। यदि वा तीर्थानामिव महतां कोऽपि महार्घः अतिशयो हि।

व्याख्या–विरोधः' वैरं 'विश्रान्तः' निवृत्तः। 'निर्वृत्या' आनन्देन 'घनः' सान्द्रः 'रसः प्रसरति' भावो विवर्द्धते। अपगतं रौद्रं शान्तिरुज्जृम्भते इत्यर्थः। 'तत् औद्धत्यं' दृप्तता 'क्वापि व्रजति' विलीयते' विनयः' नम्रता 'मां प्रह्वयति' आनतशिरसं करोति। 'अस्मिन्' महापुरुषे 'दृष्टे किमिवं न जाने कुतो हेतौः 'परवान् अस्मि' आत्मनः अनीशोऽहं जातः। 'यदिवा' अथवा अस्त्येवात्र हेतुः–'तीर्थानामिव' पुण्यक्षेत्रणामिव 'महतां' महापुरुषाणां 'कोऽपि' अनिर्वचनीयः 'महार्घः' महामूल्यः परमपूज्यो वा 'अतिशयो हि' माहत्म्यं वर्त्तते इव, तैनैवास्मि परवान् ।।

Notes. 1. आश्वास etc.—आश्वास consolation. This gentleman's sight seems to console me. स्नेह affection. This gentleman seems to be affectionately disposed towards me. भक्ति devotion. My devotion seems spontaneously to go towards this gentleman. 2. एकम्–Common. All the three are centered in this person so far as I am concerned. 3. मूर्त्ति etc.—मूर्त्या सञ्चरते इति मूर्त्ति+सम्+चर कर्त्तरि। My merits have taken shape and come up to me in the person of this gentleman. 4. निर्वृति etc.—हन+अप् भावे घनः solidity. By transference of epithets this means here 'solid.' निर्वृत्या घनः। रस, the sentiment, is a solid one, solid with joy. In other words, a deep sense of joy prevails. 6. प्रह्वयति–प्रह्व is नम्र। प्रह्वं करोति इति प्रह्व+णिच् (नाम धातु)+लट ति। 7. यदि वा–This may be taken as a compound अव्यय meaning अथवा। For a different sense compare "यदि वा रघोः 'कुलगुरुः', Act IV, sl. 5. There too the sense अथवा is not unsuitable. 8. महार्घः–अर्घ is मूल्य, also पूजा or पूजाविधि। महान् अर्घः अस्य। 9. अतिशयः–अति+शी+अच् भावे करणे वा। Grandeur. 10. *Remark*—In the second half लव is at first surprised that he is so much overcome that he does not know why (किमिव) ।But presently he sees the reason—It is the natural majesty of the great that extorts homage.

(*xi*) रामः–तत् किमयमेकपदे एब मे दुःखविश्रामं ददाति उपस्नेहयति च कुतोऽपि निमित्तादन्तरात्मानम्। अथवा स्नेहश्च निमित्तसव्यपेक्ष इति विप्रतिषिद्धमेतत्। तथाहि–

Rāma—Well, why does he forthwith procure cessation of my misery and for some reason or other melts my inner self with affection ? Or—"Affection yet dependent upon external reason" is self-contradictory, For—

व्यतिषजति पदार्थानान्तरः कोऽपि हेतु-
न खलु बहिरुपाधीन् प्रीतयः संश्रयन्ते।
विकसित हि पतङ्गस्योदये पुण्डरीकं
द्रवति च हिमरश्मावुद्गते चन्द्रकान्तः ।। 12 ।।

Affection certainly does not cling to external circumstances ; some inexplicable internal reason connects things together. The lotus invariably opens at the rise of the sun ; the moon having risen the moon—gem runs (melts) undoubtedly.

मित–एकं पदं पदोच्चारणकालः 'एकपदं' मुहूर्त्तमात्रमित्यर्थः। तस्मिन्। क्षणेन इति यावत्। 'उपस्नेहयति' स्नेहेन योजयति। 'कुतोऽपि' अविज्ञातात् 'निमित्तात्'। अथवा' नास्त्यच निमित्तस्य प्रसङ्गः।'निमित्तेन' ब्राह्येन हेतुना 'सव्यपेक्षः' व्यपेक्षायुक्तः हेत्वधीनमिति च 'स्नेहश्च' एतत् द्वयं 'विप्रतिषिद्ध' परस्परविरुद्धम्। यदि स्नेहः, बाह्यं निमित्तं नापेक्षते। अथ बाह्यनिमित्तापेक्षः, नासौ स्नेहः। इति भावः। कुतस्तर्हि स्नैह इति चेत् तत्राह व्यतिषजतीति।

अन्वयः–आन्तरः कोऽपि हेतुः पदार्थान् व्यतिषजति, प्रीतयः खलु बहिरुपाधीन् न हि संश्रयन्ते। पतङ्गस्य उदये पुण्डरीकं विकसति हि, हिमरश्मौ उद्गते चन्द्रकान्तः द्रवति च।

व्याख्या–'आन्तरः' आभ्यन्तरः पदार्थस्य स्वभावप्रतिवद्ध इत्यर्थः 'कोऽपि' अनिर्वचनीयः 'हेतुः' निमित्तं 'पदार्थान्' वस्तूनि 'व्यतिषजति' व्यतिषञ्जयति मिथो मेलयति, 'प्रोतयः खलु' स्नेहादयः किल 'वहिरुपाधीन्' वाह्यानि निमित्तानि हि संश्रयन्ते' नैव आलम्बन्ते।'पतङ्गस्य' सूर्यस्य 'उदये पुण्डरीकं' पद्मं 'विकसति हि' उन्मीलत्येव, 'हिमरश्मो' शीताशी चन्द्रे उद्गते सति 'चन्द्रकान्तः' मणिभेदः 'द्रवति च' आर्द्रीभवत्येव तत्रतु नमितं प्रकृतिः न हि बाह्यं किञ्चित्।।

Notes. 1. एकपदे–For समास see टीका। Instantly. Comp. "निहन्त्यरीन् एकपदे"–*Śiśupāla*. "कथमेकपदे निरागसम्"–*Raghu*, etc. 2. स्नेहश्च etc.—The two epithets स्नेह and निमित्तसव्यपेक्ष are contradictory (विप्रतिषिद्ध), hence my search for an external reason (कुतोऽपि निमित्तात्) must be futile. 3.

व्यतिषजति–सज्ज is usually अकर्मक। The present seems to be a सकर्मक use. Compare "मृतं स्कन्धे समासजत्"–*Mahābhārata*, "भूयः स भूमेर्धुरमाससज्ज"—*Raghu*. Or say these are instances of अन्तर्भावितणयर्थ use of सज्ज (see Tika). 4. आन्तरः—Internal, i.e., something depending on the nature of the things (पदार्थ); more than this we cannot say (कोऽपि), we do not know the character of the dependence. 5. बहिः etc.—बहिस् exterior, outside, is an अव्यय। उपाधीयन्ते इपि उप+आ+धा+कि कर्मणि उपाधयः conditions, cicumstance, accident etc. बहिर्भूता बाह्या इत्यर्थः उपाधयः बहिरुपाधयः। तान्। 6. हि, च–Both are अवधारणे। विकसति हि–Opens without fail ; द्रवति च–Surely melts. These are facts ; there is some mysterious connection between the nature of the sun and the lotus on the one hand, and of the moon and the moon-gem on the other, the nature of which we do not know.

(xii) **लवः–चन्द्रकेतो क एते ?**

Lava—Candraketu who are these (who is he)?

चन्द्रकेतुः–प्रियवयस्य ननु तातापादाः।

Cand—Dear friend, revered father assuredly.

लवः–ममापि तर्हि धर्मतस्तथैव यतः प्रियवयस्य इत्यात्थ, किन्तु चत्वारः खलु भवतामेवव्यं पदेशभगिनस्तत्रभवन्तो रामायणकथापुरुषाः, तत् विशेषं ब्रूहि।

Lava—Then by custom (Or—in law) he is the same to me also as you call me 'Dear friend'. But all the four illustrious heroes of the story of the Rāmāyaṇa enjoy the designation from you. So give me particulars (distinctive details).

चन्द्रकेतुः–ननु ज्येष्ठतातपादा इत्यवेहि।

Cand.—Well, take him as the eldest father.

लवः–(सोल्लसम्)–कथं रघुनाथः ! दिष्ट्या सुप्रभातमद्य यदयं दृष्टो देवः। (सविनयकौतुकं निर्वर्ण्य) तात प्राचेतसान्तेवासी लवोऽभिवादयते।

Lava. (*With joy*)—What ! The lord of the Raghus ! Luckily it is a happy dawn to-day,for this, king is seen. (*Observing with humility and curiosity*). Father, Lava, a pupil of Prācetasa, bows to you.

मित–।'एते' इति गौरवे बहुवचनम्।।'धर्मतः आचारात् शास्त्रात् वा।'भवतां' तव। गौरवे भवच्छब्दप्रयोगे बहुवचनञ्च। 'एवम्' ईदृशो 'व्यपदेशः' अभिधानम् 'एवंव्यपदेशः' तातपादाभिधानमिति यावत्। तं भजन्ते इति 'एवव्यपदेशभागिनः' 'विशेषं' भेदम् भेदम् विस्तरमित्यर्थः। शोभनं प्रभातं 'सुप्रभातम्'।।

Notes. 1. धर्मतः–धर्म is here आचार।" धर्मोऽस्त्री पुण्य आचारे" इत्यादि मेदिनी। Or say धर्म stands for धर्मशास्त्र। धर्मात् इति धर्म+ङसि (5मी)+तसि स्वार्थे धर्मतः। हेतौ 5मी। 2. एवं etc.—एवंव्यपदेश+भज+णिनि कर्त्तरि। 3. विशेषम्–विशेष्यते अनेन इति वि+शिष+णिच्+घञ् करणे विशेषः distinctive character.

(*xiii*) रामः–आयुष्मान् एह्येहि। (स्नेहमालिङ्ग्य) अयि कृतं कृतमतिविनयेन। अनेकवारमपरिश्लथं परिष्वजस्व।

Rāma.—Come long-lived one, come. (*Embracing him affectionately*). Darling, away, away with modesty ; embrace me more than once and close.

परिणतकठोरपुष्करगर्भच्छदपीनमसृणसुकुमारः।
नन्दयति चन्द्रचन्दननिस्यन्दजड़स्तव स्पर्शः ।।13।।

Your touch, full smooth soft like that of the inner leaves of a mature and full-blown lotus and cool like the moon-beam or sandal paste, delights me.

लवः (स्वागतम्)–ईदृशो मां प्रत्यमीषाकारणस्नेहः, मया पुनरेभ्यः एवाविदुग्धमज्ञेन यदायुधपरिग्रहं यावदध्यारूढ़ो दुर्योगः। (प्रकाशम्) मृष्यन्त्विदानीं लवस्य वालिशतां तात्पादाः।

Lava. *(To himself)*—Such is his spontaneous affection for me ! But I, a fool even upon him have warred, for the mishap culminated in the taking up of arms. (*Aloud*) Now let my revered father pardon Lava's stupidity.

मित–। आलिङ्गितेन प्रत्यालिङ्गनमाचारः। विनयेन तद्विमुखे लवे राम आह 'अयि कृतम्' इत्यादि। प्रत्यालिङ्गनं सकृदेव क्रियते, तत्तु नालं मम तोषाय, तत् 'अनेकवारम् अपरिश्लथं गाढ़ं च 'परिष्वजस्व' आलिङ्ग माम्। तथा करणे कारणमाहपरिणतेति।

अन्वयः–परिणतकठोरपुष्करगर्भकच्छदपीनमसृणसुकुमारः चन्द्रचन्दननिस्यन्दजड़ः तव स्पर्शः नन्दयति।

व्याख्या–'परिणतं' विकसितं तत् 'कठोरं' पूर्णावयवं 'पुष्करं' पद्मं तस्य 'गर्भच्छः' अन्तःपलाशम् 'इव पीनः' स्थूलः 'मसृणः' अकर्कशः 'सुकुमारः' मृदुश्च 'चन्द्रचन्दनयोः' यः 'निस्यन्दः' क्षरणं चन्द्रिका घृष्टचन्दनञ्च स इव 'जड़ः' शीतलः 'तवः स्पर्शः' मां 'नन्दयति' आह्लादयति। तत् "अनेकवारम्" इत्यादि। 'आपीषाम्' अमुष्य रामस्य। गौरवे बहुवचनम्। 'एभ्यः' एनान् पराजेतुम् 'अज्ञेन मया अभिद्रुग्धं' वैरायतिम्। अभिद्रुग्धं मया इति संशयः 'यत्' यस्मात् 'आयुधपरिग्रहं यावत्' अस्त्रग्रहणपर्यन्तं 'दुर्योगः' अपव्यवहारः 'अध्यारूढ़ः' प्रसृतः। 'वालिशतां मूर्खताम्।

Notes. 1. परिणत etc.—परिणाम final stage. The final stage of flower is its विकास। Hence परिणत is विकसित। कठोर is fully developed as in कठोरगर्भा (Act I, para xviii). छद+णिच्+घ करणे छद leaf. गर्भस्था छदाः गर्भच्छदाः। प्याय+क्त कर्त्तरि पीन stout. The idea in पीनः स्पर्शः is similar to that in मांसल देहसौभाग्यम् (Act I. para xxvi). For a similar idea compare "कठोरकमलगर्भ पक्ष्मलः शरीरस्पर्शः" (Act IV, para xxxiii). 2. चन्द्र etc.—निस्यन्द and निष्यन्द are optional forms meaning *oozings*. The moon beams are here supposed to be oozings of the moon. जड़ is हिमग्रस्त benumbed by cold. "जड़ो मूर्खे हिमग्रस्ते विश्वः। Hencd *cool*. 3. मया etc.—मया अभिद्रुग्धम् is in the भाववाच्य। Hence अभि+द्रुह is here अकर्मक। As such it cannot have a कोपतात। Thus the rule 'क्रधुद्रहोरुपसृष्टयोः कर्म" has no scope here, and एभ्यः take the चतुर्थी विभक्ति by the rule "क्रियार्थोपपदस्य च कर्मणि स्थानिनः" the sense being एनान् विजेतु मया अभिद्रुग्धम्। 4. अध्यारूढ़ः–अधि+आ+रुह+ क्त कर्त्तरि अध्यारूढ़ lit, gone up, hence proceeded, reached etc- 5. दुर्योगः–दुष्टो योगः a had bad move, and evil or unhappy step.

(xiv) **राम–किमपराद्धं वत्सेन ?**

Rāma—Has any wrong been done by my child ?

चन्द्रकेतुः–अश्वानुयात्रिकेभ्यस्तातप्रतापाविष्करणमुपश्रुत्य वीरायितमनेन।

Cand.—He played the hero on hearing the proclamation of Sire's prowess from the followers of the horse.

रामः–नन्वयमलङ्कारः क्षत्रस्य।

Rāma.—Well, that is an adornment of a Kṣattriya.

न तेजस्तेजस्वी प्रमृतमपरेषां प्रसहते
स तस्य स्वो भावः प्रकृतिनियतत्वादकृतकः।
मयूखैरश्रान्तं तपति यदि देवो दिनकरः
किमाग्नेयो ग्रावा निकृत इव तेजांसि वमति ।।14।।

The spirited (one) does not brook the spirit radiated from others; that is his own character, not assumed because as singed by name (Or—inherent in his elements). Why does the fire-stone, like one insulted, emit flames if the god, the day-maker steadily heats it with his rays ?

मित–। 'वत्सेन' अपराद्धं किम अपराधः कश्चित् कृतः किम् ? 'तातस्य' भवतः 'प्रतापस्य आविष्करणम्' उद्घोषणम्। 'अनेन वीरायितं' वीरेण इव आचरितम्।। न तेज इति।

अन्वयः–तेजस्वी प्रसृतम् अपरेषां तेजेकः न प्रहसते। स तस्य प्रकृतिनियत्वात् आकृतकः स्वः भावः। देवो दिनकरः यदि मयूखैः अश्रान्तं तपति आग्रेयो ग्रावा निकृत इव किं तेजांसि वमति।

व्याख्या– 'तेजस्वी' महातेजा जनः 'प्रसृतं' प्रकटितम् 'अपरेषाम्' अन्येषां 'तेजः' प्रतापं 'न प्रसहते' न मृष्यति। 'सः' अमर्षः 'तस्य तेजस्विनः' 'प्रकृत्या' स्वाभावेन 'नियत्वात्' आबद्धत्वात् [यद्वा–'प्रकृतौ' उपादाने 'नियत्वात्' सम्बद्धवात्] 'अकृतकः' अकृत्रिमः 'स्व भावः' निजो धर्मः। अतश्च 'परवृद्धिमत्सरि मनो हि मानिनाम्'। दृष्टान्तमाह–'देवो दिनकरः' भगवान् आदित्यः ययिद मयूखैः किरणैः 'अश्रान्तं तपति' अविरामं दहति तदा 'आग्नेयो ग्रावा' अग्न्युपादिका शिला 'निकृतं इव' अपमानित इव 'किं तेजांसि वमति' कथम् आत्ममयूखान् प्रकट्यति। तत्प्रकटनं तस्य निजो धर्म इत्येव। एवम् अनेनापि स्वधर्ममाश्रित्य वीरायितं कस्तत्र मर्षणप्रसङ्गः।।

Notes. 1. अपराद्धम्–अप+राध+क्त भावे। 2. वीरायितम्–वीरेण इव आचरितम् इति वीर+क्यङ् (नामधातु)+क्त भावे। 3. अयम्–This refers to वीरायण (वीराचण) and is masucline because the निधेय, i.e., अलङ्कार is prominent here and is masucline (निधेयप्राधान्यात्)। 4. आग्नेयः–आग्नेयम् इति अग्नि+ढक् आग्नेयः belonging to fire, connected with fire etc. 5. निकृतः–निकार is अवमानना। निकृतः अवमानितः। *c.p.* "प्राप्यनिकारमीदृशम्"–*Kirat*.

(xv) चन्द्रकेतुः–अमर्षोऽप्यस्यैव शोभते वीरस्य। पश्यतु हि तातः प्रियवस्यविनियुक्तजृम्भकास्त्रनिष्कम्पस्तम्भितानि सर्वतः सैन्यानि।

Cand.—This intolerance again befits this hero alone. For,

behold Father, the forces all round are motinelessly fixed by the Jṛmbhaka weapon employed by my dear friend.

रामः–(विलोक्य)—वत्स लव संह्रियतामस्त्रम्। त्वमपि चन्द्रकेतो निर्व्यापारविलक्षितानि सान्त्वय सैन्यानि।

Rāma (*observing*)—Lava, my child, let the weapon be withdrawn. You too Candraketu cheer up the forces that are bewildered because powerless.

लवः–यथाज्ञापयति तातः। (इति प्रणिधानं नाटयति)।

Lava—As father commands. (*Acts maditation*).

चन्द्रकेतुः–यथादिष्टम् (इति निष्क्रान्तः)।

Cand—As commanded (by father). (*Exit*).

लवः–प्रशान्तमस्त्रम्।

Lava—The weapon has quited down.

मित–'अमर्षः' तातप्रतापविष्करणे अक्षमा। अस्यैव शोभते' नान्यस्य। यद्वा–'अस्य शोभते एव' यतः 'प्रियवयस्येनं अनेन 'विनियुक्तेन जृम्भकास्त्रेण निष्कम्पं' यथा तथा 'स्ताम्भितानि बलानि'। नान्यः कश्चिदीदृशः अस्त्रवेदाभिज्ञः।।'संह्रियताम्' प्रशम्यताम्।'निर्वापाराणि' निरुद्धक्रियाणि अतएव 'विलक्षितानि' विमूढ़ानि।'सान्त्वय' समाश्वासय।।

Notes. 1. अमर्षः etc.—He is such a hero, he can afford to be intolerant. He is master of the जृम्भक weapons ; no one else is, except Sire. Hence no wonder he resented the procalmation. 2. संह्रियताम्–The संहार of a weapon is its withdrawal from action. 3. निर्व्यापार etc.—निर्गतः व्यापारः एभ्यः निव्यापाराणि motionless स्तम्भितानि। विलक्षित is rendered "विस्मयान्वित by वीर राघव। वि+लक्ष (आलोचने चुरादि)+णिच् स्वार्थे+क कर्मणि विलक्षित bewildered, वि being a *privative* here. Comp. विलक्ष in "गोत्रेषु स्खलितः.....भवति च व्रीड़ाविलक्षश्चिरम्"–*Śakuntala*. 4. प्रणिधानम्–ध्यानम् meditation. He meditates upon the charm (मन्त्र) that withdraws the weapon.

(xvi) **रामः–वत्स सरहस्यप्रयोगसंहरणान्यस्त्राणि आम्नायवन्ति।**

Rāma—My child, weapons wiht a secret charm for their

employment and withdrawal have a (are handed down by—*Tawney*) tradition.

ब्रह्मादयो ब्रह्महिताय तप्त्वा परःसहस्राः शरदस्तपांसि।
एतान्यपश्यन् गुरवः पुराणाः स्वान्येव तेजांसि तपोमयानि ।। 15 ।।

(As to the Jṛmbhakas), the old masters, headed by Brāhmaṇa, having practised penance for over a thousand years, for the good of the Vedas, saw these, the very fire of their austerities.

अथैतन्मन्त्रपारायणोपनिषदं भगवान् कृशाश्वः परसहस्रपरिवत्-सरान्तेवासिने कौशिकाय विश्वामित्राय प्रोवाच। स तु भगवान् मह्यम्। इत्येव क्रमः। कुमारस्य तु कः सम्प्रदाय इति पृच्छामि।

Next the secret of the complete mastery of the charms of these weapons the worshipful Kṛśāśva revealed unto Viśvāmitra the son of Kuśika who had been his pupil for over a thousand years ; he again, the worshipful, unto me ; this is the succession. I ask this—What is the tradition in my child's case ?

मित– ।'सरहस्ये समन्त्रके प्रयोगसंहरणे' येषां तादृशानि 'अस्त्राणि आम्नायवन्ति' उपदेशवन्ति गुरुपदेशेनैव सिध्यन्ति। एवं सामान्यत उपदेशसापेक्षातामुक्ता जृम्भकाणां विशेषमाह ब्रह्मेति। व्याख्यातं प्राक्।। 'एतेषां' जृम्भकास्त्रणां यत् 'मन्त्रपारायणं' साकल्येन मन्त्रावृत्तिः तद्रूपा या 'उपनिषत्' गुह्यविद्या तां 'परःसहस्रपरिवत्सरान्' सहस्रादप्यधिकानि वर्षाणि व्याप्य 'अन्तेवासिने शिष्याय।'क्रमः' गुरुपम्परा मत्सम्बन्धे। 'कुमारस्य ते 'कः सम्प्रदायः का गुरुपरम्परा।।

Notes. 1. आम्नायवन्ति–आ+म्ना+घञ् भावे आम्नाय instruction, initiation. आम्नायः अस्ति एषाम् इति आम्नाय+मतुप। Require initation. This is a general remark true of all weapons that are invoked and dismissed by secret charms. 2. एतन्मन्त्र etc.—For समास see टीका। मन्त्राणं पारायणम् अन्तगमनम् मन्त्रपारायणम् complete pronouncement of the charm. उपनिषद्यते समीपे स्थीयते अस्याम् इति उप+नि+सद+क्विप् अधिकरणे उपनिषत् secret knowledge. 3. क्रमः—Order पौर्वापर्यम, succession of teachers. 4. सम्प्रदायः– सम्प्रदीयते अस्मिन् इति सम्+प्र+दा+घञ् अधिकरणे a succession of teachers, a school.

(xvii) **लवः–स्वतःप्रकाशान्यावयोरस्त्राणि।**

Lava—The weapons stood self-revealed unto us two.

रामः (विचिन्त्य)–किं न सम्भाव्यते ? कोऽपि प्रकृष्टपुण्य-परियाकोपादानो महिमा स्यात्। द्विवचनन्तु कथम् ?

Rāma—(Reflecting)—What is not possible ? There might be merit. But why the dual ?

लवः–भ्रातरावावां यमजी।

Lava—We are brothers, twins.

रामः–तर्हि द्वितीयः कः ?

Rāma—Who then is the other ?

नेपथ्ये–भाण्डायन भाण्डायन,

In the Tiring Room—Bhāṇḍayana, Bhāṇḍayana,

आपुष्मतः किल लवस्य नरेन्द्रसैन्यै-
रायोध्नं ननु किमात्थ सखे तथेति।
अद्यास्तमेतु भुवनेष्वधिराजशब्दः
क्षत्रस्य शस्त्रशिखिनः शममद्य यान्तु ॥ 16 ॥

They say there is a fight of Lava the long-lived with the king's forces. Well, do you say, friend, "Yes". To-day let the tittle "Lord Paramount" suffer extinction in the wrolds. Let the flames of the weapons of the Kṣattriyas be quenched to-day.

मित– 'आवयोः' सम्बन्धे गुरुपदेशं विनेव 'स्वतः' अयत्नेनैव 'प्रकाशानि' प्रकटानि' बभूवुः 'अस्त्राणि' जृम्भकाणि।। 'किं न सम्भाव्यते' जगति असम्भवं किमपि नास्ति 'प्रकष्टस्य' महतः 'पुणयस्य परिपाकः' विपरिणामः एव 'उपादानं' कारणं यस्य तथाविधः 'कोऽपि महिमा' माहात्म्य स्यात् तव। प्रभूतस्य पुण्यस्य फलंकिमपि माहात्म्य ते जातं, ततः एव विनापि गुरुपदेशम् अस्त्राणि अद्राक्षीः इति भावः। परम् 'आवयोः' इति द्विवचनेन कथमुच्यते ? आयुष्मत इति।

अन्वयः–आयुष्मतः लवस्य नरेन्द्रसेन्यैः आयोधनं किल। ननु सखे किं "तथा" इति आत्थ। अद्य भुवनेषु अधिराजशब्दः अस्तम् एतु। अद्य क्षत्रस्य शस्तशिखिनः शमं यान्तु।

व्याख्या– 'आयुष्मतः लवस्य नरेन्द्रसैन्यैः' राजवलैः सह 'आयोधनं' युद्धं 'किल' इति वार्त्ता श्रूयते। 'ननु सखे किं' त्वं 'तथा' सत्यमेव तत् 'इति आत्थ' ब्रवीषि? यद्येवम् 'अद्य भुवनेषु अधिराजः इति 'शब्दः अस्तम् एतु' विलयं गच्छतु। एष मया हन्यतेस अधिराज इत्यर्थः। 'अद्य क्षत्रस्य' क्षत्रि जातेः 'शस्त्रशिखिनः' बाणानलः 'शमं यान्तु' निर्वाणं लभन्ताम्। तेन सह अद्य अस्य सैन्यानि अपि नाशयमि इति भावः।।

Notes. 1. स्वतः etc.—प्रकाशन्ते इति प्र+काश-अच् कर्त्तरि प्रकाशानि manifest. स्वतः and प्रकाशानि may be taken as compounded or uncompounded. 2. प्रकृष्ट etc.—उपादीयते अनेन इति उप+आ+दा-ल्युत् मरणे उपादानम् material. प्रकष्टं पुण्यं प्रकृष्टपुण्यम्। तस्यपरिपाकः प्रकृश्चपुण्यपरिपाकः। This means परिपक्वं प्रकृष्टपुण्यम्। by the maxim "भावनयने द्रव्यमानयम्"। But परिपक्वपुण्य is the फल of that पुण्य। That फल is taken as the उपादान of a cetain महिमा–It is identified as the महिमा। In other words the महिमा is the फल of that पुण्य। This is an iinstance of Bhavabūti's preference for a bombast and the round about. प्रकृष्टपुण्यकृतो महिना would have served the purpose equally well. 3. किल–Implies वार्त्ता rumour, report etc. 4. ननु–Implies प्रश्न।

(xviii) **रामः**–

अथ कोऽयमिन्द्रमणिमेचकच्छवि-
र्ध्वनिनैव दत्तपुलकं करोति माम्।
नवनीलनीरधरधीरगर्जित-
क्षणबद्धकुड्मलकदम्वडम्वरम् ।।17।।

Rāma—Well who is this one of a blue complexion like a sapphire that makes me, with horripilation imparted by his mere voice, look a Kadamba that has budded blossoms at the very moment of the deep rumble of a dark early cloud ?

लवः–अयमसौ मम ज्यायान् आर्यः कुशो नाम भरताश्रमात् प्रतिनिवृत्तः।

Lava—This is he, my noble senior known as Kuśa, come back from the hermitage of Bharata.

रामः (सकौतुकम्)–वत्स इत आह्वयैनमायुष्मन्तम्।

Rāma (*With eagerness*)—My child, you call hither this long-lived one.

लवः–एवम्। (इति परिक्रमति)।

Lava—So be it. *(Goes round the stage).*

मित–। अथेति।

अन्वयः–अथ इन्द्रमणिमेचकच्छविः कः अयं ध्वनिनैव दत्तपुलकं मां नवनीलनीरधरगर्जितक्षणबद्धकदम्बडम्बरं करोति।

व्याख्या–'अथ' ननु पृच्छामि 'इन्द्रः' इन्दनीलाख्यः यो 'मणिः' स इव 'मेचकच्छविः' नीलद्युतिः 'कः अयं' क एष बालः 'ध्वनिना इव' कण्ठस्वरेणेव 'दत्तः पुलको' यस्मै तथाविधं जनितरोमाञ्चं 'मां नुतनः वर्षारम्भे प्रादुर्भूत इत्यर्थः यः 'नीलनीधरः' श्यामाम्बुदः तस्य यत् 'धीरगर्जितं' चन्द्रध्वनिः तस्य 'क्षणे' तन्मुहूर्ते इव [यद्वा–तस्मात् यः 'क्षणः' उत्सवः स एव यः 'क्षणः' इति वा, तेन] 'बद्धकुड्मलः' उद्भिन्नमुकुलः यः 'कदम्बः' तस्य 'डम्बरः' विलास इव 'डम्बरी' यस्य तादृशं 'करोति'। सञ्जातपुलकः सन् उद्भिन्नसकलः कदम्ब इव भवामि इत्यर्थः।।

Notes. 1. इन्द्रमणि etc.—मेचक is blue श्यामलं। "मेचकः श्यामलेऽपि च" इति विश्वः 2. ध्वनिनैव–एव is आधारणे and implies that the पुलक appears *instantaneously* with the ध्वनि। Hence, we have interpreted क्षण below as काल the instant of the गर्जित। If however, it be argued that the instantaneous show of पुलक was due to the thrill of joy that ध्वनि gave, then क्षण may be interpreted as उत्सव। 3. नवनील–etc.—नव because the first few showers of the season bring forth blossoms in the कदम्ब। डम्बर is शोभा ; also array, preparation etc. as in आडम्बर।

(*xix*) **(ततः प्रविशति कुशः)।**

(Then enters Kuśa).

कुशः (साद्भ तहर्षधैर्य धनुरास्फालयन्)–

Kuśa (*Patting his bow with wonder joy and confidence*)—

दत्तेन्द्राभयदक्षिणैर्भगवतो वैवस्वतादा मनो–
दृप्तानां दहनाय दीपितनिजक्षत्रप्रतापाग्निभिः।
आदित्यैर्यदि विग्रहो नृपतिभिर्धन्यं ममैतत्ततो
दीप्रास्त्रस्फुरदुग्रदीधितिशिखानीराजितज्यं धनुः ।।18।।

Lucky is this bow of mine, with its string lighted up by the tops of the fierce flames shooting from the glowing weapons, if there is a fight with kings descended from the

Sun—kings who, beginning with Manu the worshipful, the Sun's son, have kindled the fire of their own Kṣattriya prowess to consume the arrogant and have bestowed the boon of safety of Indra.

(इति विकटं परिक्रामति)।

(*Walks with haughty strides*)

मित–।'अद्भुतम्' विस्मयः।'धैर्यम्' अप्रकम्पता निर्विकारता।'आस्फालयन्' ताड़यन्। प्रोत्साहनाय भृत्यादीनामपि पृष्ठे करेण ताड़नं दृश्यते हि लोके। दत्तेति।

अन्वयः–भगवती वैवस्वतात् मनोः आ दृप्तानां दहनाय दीपितनिजक्षत्रप्रतापाग्निभिः दत्तेन्द्राभयदक्षिणैः आदित्यैः नृपतिभिः यदि विग्रहः ततः मम एतत् दीप्रास्त्रफुर- दुग्रदीधितिशिखानीराजित्यं धनुः धन्यम्।

व्याख्या–'भगवतः वैवस्वतात्' सूर्यपुत्रात् 'मनोः' मनुनाम्नः सूर्यवंशीयानामादिपुरूषात् 'आ' ततः प्रभृति 'दृप्तानां' दर्पोद्धतानां 'दहनाय' दाहाय 'दीपितः' प्रज्वालितः 'निजः क्षत्रप्रतापाग्निः' क्षत्रतेजोहुताशनः यैः ततश्च दृप्तान् दग्ध्वा। 'दत्ता इन्द्राय अभयदक्षिणा' भयाभावरूपं दानं यैः तादृशैः 'आदित्यैः सूर्यवंशीयैः 'नृपतिभिः' सह 'यदि विग्रहः' युद्धं 'ततः मम एतत् दीप्रास्त्राणं भासुरायुधानां याः 'स्फुरन्त्यः' प्रकाशमाना 'उग्राः' करालाः 'दीधितिशिखाः' किरणाग्राणि ताभिः 'नीराजिता' वर्द्धितशोभा दीपिता इत्यर्थः 'ज्या' गुण यस्य तादृशं 'धनुः धन्यं' प्रशस्यम्। अत्र प्रथमार्द्धे असुरसमरः अध्वरत्वेन नीयते। तत्र आदित्या नृपतयो नृपतयो यज्वानः, क्षत्र तेज एव यज्ञियाग्निः, इन्द्रः पुरोहितः, अभयं दक्षिणा। इत्येतत् सर्वमद्भुतम्। ईदृशैरादित्यैः सह युद्धम् इति धन्यं धनुः। ततश्च हर्षः। तस्मिंश्च युद्धे दीप्राणि मम अस्त्राणि सहायाः तत् का चिन्ता इति धैर्यम् इत्यनु सन्धेयम्।

Notes. 1. साद्भुत etc.—अद्भुतञ्च हर्षश्च धैर्यञ्च अद्भुतहर्षधैर्याणि। तैः सह। अद्भुत because these kings are all wonderful fighters (see Ṭīkā). हर्ष because of the good luck in getting a chance to fight the best fighter of this wonderful group of kings. धैर्य is धीरता, *'i.e.'* absence of nevousness. This is because though of the fight is going to be a grim one, victory is assured through the resplendent weapons he possesses. This confidnece is already expressed in "अद्यास्तमेतु भुनेष्वधिराजशब्दः" etc., sl. 16. 2. दत्त etc.—The word दक्षिणा in place of दान is significant. An ordinary दान is not a दक्षिणा, but only the दान in an अध्वर। Hence, it implies that the fight was the अध्वर। See टीका। Also Indra was the instigator at the fight, hence he is the पुरोहित in the अध्वर and his

दक्षिणा is अभय (safety). 3. आदित्यैः–अदितेरपत्यं पुमान् इति अदिति +ण्य आदित्यः Sun. तस्म इमे इति आदित्य+ण्य आदित्याः descendants of the sun. 4. दीप्रास्त्र etc.—स्फुरत् shooting. दीधिति light. शिखा top सम्यक् राजिता शोभिता इति निर्+राज+क्त कर्मणि नीराजिता। The word is used on purpose. There is a ceremony called नीराजना at which horses, elephants weapons etc. of the warrior are honoured with light, obeisance, flowers etc. "ज्या was नीराजित" seems to hint at this नीराजनाविधि। 5. विकटम्–उद्धतं यथा तथा।

(*xx*) **रामः—कोऽप्यस्मिन् क्षत्तियपोतके पौरुषातिरेकः।**

Rāma—What an abundance of manliness in this strange Kṣattriya boy !

दृष्टिस्तृणीकृतजगत्रयसत्त्वसारा
धीरोद्धता नमयतीव गतिर्धरित्रीम्।
कौमारकेऽपि गिरिवद्गुरुतां दधानो
वीरो रसः किमयमैत्युत दर्प एव ।।18।।

Is this the sentiment of heroism of pride itself advances imparting, even in mere childhood, weights as in a mountain? The look rates as straw the quintessence of the might of the three worlds ; the steps, proud and steady, bend the earth down as it were (under them).

मित– 'क्षत्रियस्य पोतः' शिशुः 'क्षत्रियपोतः'। अज्ञातः क्षत्रियपोतः 'क्षत्रायपोतकः'। तस्मिन्। 'पौरुषस्य' पुरुषोचितस्य शौर्यस्य 'अतिरेकः' आतिशयम्।। दृष्टिरिति।

अन्वयः–दृष्टिः तृणीकृतजगत्रयसत्वसारा। धीरोद्धता गतिः धरित्रीं नमयति इव। किमयं वीरो रसः उत दर्प एव कौमारकेऽपिगिरिवत् गुरुतां दधानः ऐति।

व्याख्या–'दृष्टिः' अस्य नेत्रपातः 'तृणीकृतः' तृणमिव अनादृतः 'जगत्त्रयस्य' त्रिभुवनस्य 'सत्त्वसारः' वीर्योत्कर्षः यया तादृशी। 'धीरा' अविचलिता 'उद्धता' विकटा च 'गतिः' पादपातः 'धरित्रीं पृथ्वीं 'नमयति इव' अवनम्नां करोतीव। तत् 'किम् अयं वीरो रसः उत दर्प एव' मूर्त्तिमान् वीरो रसः दर्पी वा 'कौमारके अपि' बाल्ये अपि 'गिरिवत्' गिरौ इव 'गुरुतां दधानः' गौरवं भारम् आदधत् 'ऐति' आगच्छति।।

Notes. 1. क्षत्रिय etc.—क here is अज्ञाते। क्षत्रियपोत here means an unknown Kṣattriya lad. Next क is attached स्वार्थे to क्षत्रियपोत। 2. तृणीकृत etc.—तृणीकृत here does not mean actually transformed into straw, but only rated as straw. सत्त्वसार is usually explained differently thus—सत्त्व is प्राणी। सार is बल। सत्त्वानां सारः। In our explanation सत्त्व is बल ("सत्वं गुणे पिशाचादौ बले द्रव्यस्वभावयोः" इति विश्वमेदिन्यौ) and सार is स्थिरांश extract सत्तस्य सारः।3. कौमारकेपि–कुमारस्य भावः इति कुमार+अञ् कौमारः। The अपि here implies गर्हा। गर्हा is of कौमार। In the matter of imparting the weight of a mountain, कौमार is an unsuitable subject. Hence गर्हा attaches to कौमार। In other words कौमार is here कुत्सित् and क comes in स्वार्थे by the rule "कुत्सिते"।

(xxi) **लवः–(उपसृत्य)–जयति यजत्यार्यः।**

Lava (*Approching*)—Prosper, let noble brother prosper.

कुशः–नन्वायुष्मन् किमियं वार्त्ता युद्धमिति ?

Kuśa—Well, long-lived one, what is this talk of a fight ?

लवः–यत्किञ्चिदेतत्। दृप्तभावमुत्सृज्य आर्योऽस्मिन् विनयेन वर्त्तताम्।

Lava—It is trifle. In this matter, let my noble brother assume modesty casting off this haughty bearing.

कुशः–किमर्थम् ?

Kuśa—What for ?

लवः–एष देवो रघुपतिस्तिष्ठति, स च स्निह्यत्यसावयोः उत्कण्ठते च युष्मत्सन्निकर्षस्य।

Lava—Here is the king, the lord of the Raghus, waiting ; he again, is affectionate towards us and longing for your approach.

कुशः– (सतर्कम्)–स रामायणकथानायको ब्रह्मकोषस्य गोपायिता ?

Kuśa (*In doubt*)—The hero of the story of the Rāmāyaṇa, the guardian of the treasure of the Vedas ?

लवः–अथ किम्।

Lava—Who else ?

मित–।'उपसृत्य' कुशमिति शेषः।।'इयं वार्त्ता' एषा जनोक्तिः।।'यत् किञ्चित्'

तुच्छमित्यर्थः।'अस्मिन्' एतस्मिन् युद्धप्रस्तावे।।'आवयो' सम्बन्धे 'स्निह्यति' स्नेहवान् भवति।'तव सन्निकर्षः' सन्निधिः। तस्य सम्बन्धे 'उत्कण्ठते' अभिलष्यति, इच्छति च भवान् सन्निहितो भवतु इति।। 'तर्कः' शङ्का। तेन सह। 'ब्रह्म' वेदः। तद्रूपस्य 'कोषस्य धनस्य 'गोपायिता' रक्षिता।।

Notes. 1. उपसृत्य–It seems कुशमुपसृत्य is a better stage direction. 2. दृप्तभावम् etc.—दृप्तनाम् उद्धतानां भावः। तम्। It is a trifle, hence you need not trouble yourself about it ; lay aside this defiant attitude and resume your natural meekness. 3. एषः etc.—The king, with whose army the scuffle was, is himself present here ; and he is affectionate towards us and longs to see you. So, there is no room for defiance—विनयेन वर्त्तताम्। 4. युष्मत्सन्निकर्षस्य–The proper विभक्ति is the चतुर्थी। Thus युष्मत्सन्निकर्ष लब्धुम् उत्कण्ठते=युष्मत्सन्निकर्षाय उत्कण्ठते। सम्बन्धमाचविवक्षया षष्ठी। 5. गोपायिता–गुप+तृच् कर्त्तरि गोपायिता with आय added. The आय is optional, hence also गोपिता or गोप्ता without आय।

(xxii) **कुशः–आशंसनीयपुण्यदर्शनः स महात्मा, किन्तु कथमस्माभि-रुपगन्तव्य इति न सम्प्रधारयामि।**

Kuśa—The holy sight of that high souled king has to be desired, but I cannot make out in what style he is to be approached by name.

लवः–यथा गुरुस्तथोपचारेण।

Lava—With respect as one's father or uncle has to be approached.

कुशः–अयि कथं नामैतत् ?

Kuśa—Well. why thus ?

लवः–अत्युदात्तसुजनश्चन्द्रकेतुरौर्मिलेयः 'प्रियवयस्य' इति सख्येन मामुपतिष्ठते तेन तत्सम्बन्धेन धर्मतात एवायं राजर्षि रिति।

Lava—The exceedingly noble and good soul Candraketu, Urmila's son, treats me with friendship calling me "Dear friend" so, through his connection, this royal sage is indeed by custom our uncle.

कुशः–सम्प्रत्यवचनीयो राजन्येऽपि प्रश्रयः।

Kuśa—Now this humility is irreprochable even though towards a Kṣattiya.

मित– ।'आशंसनीयं' प्रार्थनीयं 'पुण्यं' पवित्रं 'दर्शनं' यस्य सः।'सम्प्रधारयामि' अवगच्छामि।।'उपाचारेण' पूजया सह उपगन्तव्यः।'यथा गुरुः' उपगन्तव्यः 'तथा'।। 'अयि' इत्यनभिमतौ। यथा गुरुरित्यनभिमतं मे।।'अत्युदात्तः' अतिशयेन महान् तथा 'सुजनः' सज्जनः 'और्मिलेयः' ऊर्मिलापुत्रः। 'उपतिष्ठते' सङ्गच्छते मैत्र्या। 'धर्मेण' लोकाचारेण 'तातः' पिता।। सम्प्रति' अधुना सति सम्बन्धे 'राजन्ये' क्षत्रिये 'अपि प्रश्रयः' विनयः 'अवचनीयः' अनिन्द्यो मे। क्षत्रियमपि धर्मतातं नमामि इति नास्ति निन्दा।

Notes. 1. अयि etc.—अयि here implies disapproval. Comp. अयि बहुतरं द्रष्टव्यामस्ति etc., Act I, para xxxi. 2. अत्युदात्त etc.—उदात्त is महत्। "उदात्तो दातृमहतोः" इत्यादि हैमः। Paratically it is the same as उदार here. वीरराघव has it uncompounded, which seems the better reading. 3. और्मिलेयः–ऊर्मिला is a human name, but it begins with ऊ which has बृद्धसंज्ञा। Hence the rule "अबृद्धाभ्यो नदीमानुषीभ्यस्तन्नामिकाभ्यः" does not apply and we get the usual ढक्। Thus ऊर्मिला+ढक्=और्मिलेय Urmilā's son. 4. उपतिष्ठते–सङ्गतिकरणे आत्मनेपदम् by "उपाद्देवपूजासङ्गतिकरण-मित्रकरणपथिषु"।5. धर्मतातः–धर्म is here आचार custom. "धर्मोऽस्त्री पुण्य आचारे" इत्यादि मेदिनी। 6. सम्प्रति etc.—A क्षत्रिय has to be उद्धत towards a क्षत्रिय who is an antagonist. But as the king is an affectionate धर्मतात्, antagonism is out of the question. So, there is no disgrace in being humble towards him.

(xxiii) **लवः–पश्यत्वेनम् आकारानुभावगाम्भीर्यसम्भाव्यमान-विविधलोकोत्तरचरितातिशयमार्यो महापुरुषम्।**

Lava—Let noble brother mark this great personage the grandeur of whose various super-human deeds may be inferred from his make, majesty and tranquillity.

कुशः (निर्वर्ण्य)–

Kuśa (*marking attentively*)—

अहो प्रासादिकं रूपमनुभावश्च पावनः।
स्थाने रामायणकविर्देवीं वाचं व्यवीवृतत् ।। 20।।

O the gracious form ! O the sanctifying majesty ! In the right place did the poet of the Rāmāyaṇa transform the Goddess of speech.

(उपसृत्य) तात प्राचेतसान्तेवासी कुशोऽभिवादयते।

(*Advancing*) Father, Prācetasa's disciple Kuśa bows unto you.

मित–।'आकारेण' आकृत्या 'अनुभावेन' प्रभावेण 'गाम्भीर्येण' अविचलतया च 'सम्भाव्यमानः' उत्प्रेक्ष्यमाणः 'विविधानां लोकोत्तराणाम्' अतिमानुषणां 'चरितानाम्' कर्मणाम् 'अतिशयः' उत्कर्षः यस्य तम्।। अहो इति।

अन्वयः–अहो प्रासादिकं रूपं पावनः अनुभावश्च। स्थाने रामायणकविः देवीं व्यवीवृतत।

व्याख्या–'अहो विस्मयकरमस्य 'प्रासादिकं' प्रसन्नतासमुद्भवं 'रूपम्' आकृतिः प्रसन्नतामयी अस्य आकृतिरिति भावः। विस्मयकरः अस्य 'पावनः' पवित्रः 'अनुभावश्च' प्रभावोऽपि। तत् 'स्थाने' यथास्थाने सुसदृशे नायके एव विषये 'रामायणस्य' तादख्यायाः कथायाः 'कविः' प्रणेता 'देवीं वाचं' वाग्देवीं 'व्यवीवृतत्' विवर्त्तयामास तादृशेन कथारूपेण परिणतामकरोत्। यादृशी रचना नायकोऽपि तादृश एव इति भावः।।

Notes. 1. आकार etc.—आकार refers to the build of the body. अनुभाव is तेजस् majesty. It is not *prowess*, for that cannot be inferred from a mere look at the person. लोकेभ्य उत्तरं श्रेष्ठम्। Now see टीका। 2. प्रासादिकम्–प्रसाद serenity. प्रसादे भवम् इति प्रसाद+ठञ् अध्यात्यादि प्रासादिकम्। 3. स्थाने–स्थाने is यथास्थान the right place. तस्मिन्। विषयाधिकरणे 7मी। See next. 4. व्यवीवृतत्–वि+वृत+णिच्+ल्युङ् तिप् transformed. The goddess was given a shape (व्यवीवृतत्) in the matter of राम। From what I see before me, it is evident that the grandeur of the style of the poem thus obtained and the grandeur of its subject-matter—the hero Rāma—suit each other.

(xxiv) **रामः–एह्येति आयुष्मन्।**

Rāma—Come, long-lived one, come.

अमृताध्मातजीमूतस्निग्धसंहननस्य ते !
परिष्वङ्गाय वात्सल्यादयमुत्कण्ठते जनः ।। 21।।

This person, through affection, longs for an embrace of your person that is like a water-laden cloud.

(परिष्वज्य स्वगतम्) तत् किमपत्यमयं दारकः,

(*Embracing—To himself*)—

अङ्गादङ्गात् स्नुत इव निजः स्नेहजो देहसारः
प्रादुर्भूय स्थित इव बहिश्चेतनाधातुरेव।
सान्द्रानन्दक्षुभितहृदयप्रस्रवेनेव सृष्टो
गात्रं श्लेषे यदमृतरसस्रोतसा सिञ्चतीव ।। 22 ।।

Well, whose son could this boy be that is as if the essence of my own body produced from affection and issued from every limb ; as if the element of the my conciousness itself, having become manifest, is standing outside ; as if made of the drippings of my heart when stirred by intense joy ; as if swashing my body, at embrace, with a stream of the juice of nectar.

मित– । अमृतेति।

अन्वयः–अयं जनः वात्सल्यात् ते अमृताध्मातजीमूत- स्निग्धसंहननस्य परिष्वङ्गात् उत्कण्ठते।

व्याख्या–'अयं जनः' एषः अहं 'वात्सल्यात्' स्नेहात् 'ते' तव 'अमृतेन' जलेन आध्मातः' पूर्णः यः 'जीमूतः' मेघः स इव 'स्निग्धं' नेत्रतर्पणं यत् 'संहननं' देहः तस्य 'परिष्वङ्गाय' आलिङ्गनाय 'उत्कण्ठते' औत्सुक्येन तिष्ठति।।'तत् किम्' इत्यादि परिवर्त्तिता श्लोकेन अन्वितम्। अङ्गादिति।

अन्वयः–तत् अङ्गात् अङ्गात् स्नुतः निजः स्नेहजः देहसार इव, चेतनधातुरेव प्रादुर्भूय वहिः स्थित इव, सान्द्रानन्दक्षुभितहृदयप्रस्नवेन सृष्ट इव अयं दारकः किमपत्यं यत् श्लेषे अमृतरसश्रोतसा गात्रं सिञ्चतीव।

व्याख्या–परिष्वज्य परमानन्दसन्दोहमनुभवम् प्राह 'तत्' तस्मात् यतोऽयमभूतपूर्व आनन्दः ततः पृच्छामि 'अङ्गात् अङ्गात्' सर्वेभ्यः अङ्गेभ्यः 'स्नुतः' क्षरितः निजः' स्वीयः मम इत्यर्थः स्नेहजः' जातः 'देहसारः' शरीरस्य स्थिरांशः स्नेहरूपं यत् एकमुपादानं देहे अस्ति तस्य निष्कर्षः 'इव' स्थितः। एतन्निष्ठ एव मदीयः स्नेह इति भावः। किञ्च 'चेतनरूपो' यो 'धातुः' उपादानं स 'एव प्रादूर्भूय' मूर्त्तिमान भूत्वा 'बहिः' शरीरात् वहिः 'स्थित इव'। एतदधीनं मे जीवनमित्याशयः। अपरञ्च 'सान्द्रेण' प्रगाढ़ेन 'आनन्देन क्षुभितं' विचलितं यत् 'हृदयं तस्य 'प्रस्नवेन' द्रवेण 'सृष्ट इव' निर्मित इव। एतद्गतो मे कृतस्न आनन्द इत्यर्थः। एवंविधः 'अयं दारकः' बालकः 'किमपत्यं' कस्य जनस्य अपत्यं स्यात् 'यत्' अपत्यं 'श्लेषे' आलिङ्गनकर्मणि 'अमृतरसस्य' सुधाद्रवस्य 'स्रोतसा' प्रवाहेण 'गात्रं सिञ्चतीव' प्लावयतीव। मृता

सीता विलुपञ्च तयैव सह मदीयमपत्यम्। एतत्तु पुनर्नजाने कस्यापत्यं निजमिव अपत्यमानन्दयति माम् इति कौतूहलम्।।

Notes. 1. अमृत etc.—अमृत is जल। "अमृतं यज्ञशेषे स्यात् पीयूषे सलिले घृते" इति विश्वमेदिन्यौ। जीभूत is मेघ। स्निग्ध literally opposed to परुष, hence *juicy*, here *pleasing*. संहनन गात्र। "गात्रं वपुः संहननम्" इत्यमरः। The derivation is uncertain. We offer संहन्यते अनेन इति सम्+हन+ल्युट करणे संहननम् that with which the soul is killed. Or say हन is here गतौ, then संहनन is that with which the world is reached. 2. किमपत्यम्–कस्य अपत्यम्, 6तत्–। 3. अङ्गादङ्गात्–वीप्सायां द्विवर्चनम्। It reminds us of the well-known words. "अङ्गादङ्गाद्विनिष्क्रान्तो (प्रभवति) हृदयादभिजायसे। आत्म वै पुत्र नामासि जीवस्व शरदां शतम्।।" Joy, affection, consciousness etc. are all seen in the body. The boy is my affection itself. Vidyasagara reads देहजः स्नेह–सारः। But अङ्गादङ्गात् स्रुतः seems to include देहज। Our reading appears in three of his manuscripts. 4. प्रादुर्भूय etc.—The boy is my consciousness itself, *'i.e.'* I shall lose consciousnes if he be away. 5. सान्द्र etc.—Compare "हृदयादभिजायसे" in the quotation above. The boy is my joy incarnate. 6. *Remark*—the sentiment raised is one of mere curiosity at this stage. Rāma knows this cannot be his boy ; well then whose is he that affects him so strangely ?

(*xxv*) **लवः–तात ललाटन्तपो घर्मदीधितिः, तदत्र शालच्छाये मुहूर्त्तमासनपरिग्रहं करोतु तातः।**

Lava—Father, the sun is heating you brow, so let father for a moment take a seat here in the shade of these *Śāla* trees.

रामः–यदभिरुचितं वत्साय। (इति सर्वे परिक्रम्योपविशन्ति)।

Rāma—As it pleases my child. (*All walk round and sit down*).

रामः (स्वगतम्)–

Rāma *(To himself)*—

अहो प्रश्रययागेऽपि गतिस्थित्यसनादयः।

साम्राज्यशंसिनो भावाः कुशस्य च लवस्य च ।। 13।।

Ha ! Even when modified (lit—accompanied) by humility

the bearing, such a gait, stance, seat etc. of both Kuśa and Lava declare their sovereignty.

मित–ललाटं तपतीति। 'ललाटन्तपः'। शलानां छाया 'शालच्छायम्'।। अहो इति।

अन्वयः–अहो कुशलस्य च लवस्य च गतिस्थित्यासनादयो भावाः प्रश्रययोगे अपि साम्राज्यशंसिनः।

व्याख्या–'अहो' आश्चर्यम् ! 'कुशलस्य लवस्य च गतिः' गमनं 'स्थितिः' अवस्थानम् 'आसनम्' उपवेशनम् 'इत्यादयो भावाः' चेष्टाः 'प्रश्रयेण' विनयेन यो 'योगः' संसर्गः तस्मिन् सति 'अपि' विनयेन तिरोहितस्वरूपेऽपि साम्राज्यं शंसन्ति सूचयन्तीति 'साम्राज्यशंसिनः'। समाट्सुतावेतौ इत्यनयोर्गत्यादिभिरेव निवेद्यते इत्यर्थः।।

Notes. 1. ललाटन्तपः–ललाट+तप+खश् कर्त्तरि। The sun was in his face. Lava notices this and suggests a seat elsewhere. 2. घर्म etc.—दीधिति। ray. धर्मः दीधितिरस्य। 3. शालच्छाये– ''बाहुल्ये'' इति नपुंसकत्वम्। 4. वत्साय–''रुच्यर्थानां प्रीयमाणः'' इति सम्प्रदाने चतुर्थी। 5. प्रश्रय etc.—प्रश्रय meeknes विनय। Modified by विनय, the movements are apt to appear as common-place. Even thus they declare sovereignty. 6. गति etc.—गति and स्थिति have already been seen. The आसन is seen just now when परिक्रम्य उपविशन्ति। 7. साम्राज्य etc.—साम्राज्यं साधु शंसन्ति इति साम्राज्य+शंस+णिनि कर्त्तरि साधुकारिणि। सम्राजो भावः साम्राज्यम्। They declare sovereignty. Hence they are of royal descent. 8. *Remark*—The vagueness of "whose son could he be" (किमपत्यम् etc.) is a bit removed. Rāma now knows that they are scions of *some* royal race.

(*xxvi*) **(रा–)**

वपुरविहितसिद्धा एव लक्ष्मीविलासाः
प्रतिजनकमनीयं कान्तिमत् केतयन्ति।
अमलिनमिव रत्नं रश्मयस्ते मनोज्ञा
विकसितमव पद्मं विन्दवो माकरन्दाः (24) (रा–)

The play of grace, not procured yet achieved, occupies their body which is beautiful and charming to every one, just as the attractive rays do the flawless gem, or the drops of honey do the full-blown lotus. (R—)

मित–। साम्राज्यसूचकतां दर्शयति वपुरिति।

अन्वयः–मनोज्ञाः ते रश्मयः अमलिनं रत्नमिव, माकरन्दाः विन्दवः विकसितं पद्ममिव, अविहितसिद्धा एव लक्ष्मीविलासाः कान्तिमत् प्रतिजनकमनीयं वपुः केतयन्ति।

व्याख्या–'मनोज्ञाः' मनोहराः 'ते रश्मयः' प्रसिद्धाः मासः 'अमलिनं' विशदं 'रत्नमिव', 'माकरन्दाः' मकरस्य मधुन इत्यर्थः 'विन्दवः विकसितं' प्रफुल्लं 'पद्ममिव' 'अविहिताः' अकृताश्च 'सिद्धाः' सम्पन्नाः 'एव' नैसर्गिका इति यावत् 'लक्ष्म्याः' शोभाया 'विलासाः' विभ्रमाः' 'कान्तिमत्' उज्ज्वलं 'प्रतिजनकमनीयं' सर्वमनोरमं 'वपुः' 'केतयन्ति' निवसन्ति'। अकर्मकत्वात् देशस्य कर्मता।।

Notes. 1. अविहित etc.—लक्ष्मीविलास is there and delights every one (प्रतिजनकमनीय) ; but this लक्ष्मीविलास is not secured by artificial means (अविहित) as in the case of an ordinary individual ; it comes natural to them (सिद्ध) as is expected in one of royal decent. अविहितसिद्धाः may also be explained thus :—विहितं विधानम् effort. विहितेन सिद्धाः विहितसिद्धाः secured with effort. न तया। 2. केतयन्ति–कित निवासे is चुरादि and अकर्मक। Hence the देश, *i.e.,* वपुः becomes कर्म by the maxim "देशश्चाकर्मणाम्"। 3. अमलिनम् etc.—The second half on the verse cites illustrative examples. The luster of the gem and the honey in the lotus come by nature and are not यत्नसिद्ध। 3. *Remark*—Verse 24. is in support of verse 23.

(xxvii) (रा–) भूयिष्ठाञ्च रघुकूलकुमारच्छायामेतयोः पश्यामि।

(R—) I also see in them great resemblance with boys of the race of Raghu.

कठोरपारावतकण्ठमेचकं वपुर्वृषस्कन्धमबन्धुरांसकम्।
प्रसन्नसिंहस्तिमितञ्च वीक्षितं ध्वनिश्च माङ्गल्यमृदङ्गमांसलः।। 25।।

(रा–)

The body is dark-blue like the throat of an adult piegon with the neck as of a bull and shoulders evently set. Also the look is steady as of a lion at ease ; the voice again is full like that of a festive drum. (R—)

मित–एवं सामान्यतो वालयो राजपुत्रतां निरूप्य विशेषं निरूपयति–'एतयोः कुशे लवे च 'भूयिष्ठां' समधिकां 'रघुकुलमाराणां छायां' प्रतिबिम्बं सादृश्यमित्यर्थः 'पश्यामि'।। तदेव दर्शयति कठोरेति।

अन्वयः–वपुः कठोरपारावतकण्ठमेचकं वृषस्कन्धम् अबन्धुरांसकम्, वीक्षितञ्च प्रसन्नसिंहस्तिमितम्, ध्वनिश्च माङ्गल्य- मृदङ्गमांसलः।

व्याख्या–'वपुः' शरीरं 'कटोरस्य' उपचितगात्रस्व प्राप्तयौवनस्य इत्यर्थः 'पारावतस्य' कपोतस्य 'कण्ठः' इव 'मेचकं' नीलम्, किञ्च 'वृषस्यस्कन्धः' इव 'स्कन्धः' यस्मिन् तादृशम्, अपि च 'अवन्धुरौ' अनुन्नतानतौ 'अंसौ' भुजसन्धी यस्मिन् तादृशम्। वीक्षितञ्च' अवलोकनमपि 'प्रसन्नस्य' प्रशान्तस्य 'सिंहस्य' इव स्तिमितम्' अव्याकुलम्। 'ध्वनिश्च' कण्ठध्वनिरपि 'मङ्गल्यस्य' 'मङ्गलकरस्य 'मृदङ्गस्य' इव, मांसलः' गम्भीरः। तत् किमेतौ ऐक्ष्वाकस्य कस्यचिद्राजर्षेः कुमारौ, तेन च गोत्रलक्ष्णैर्मदनुकारिणौ ? इति विस्मयवितर्कविलासः।।

Notes. 1. भूयिष्ठाम् etc.—Rāma's curiosity is now replaced by suprise. The boys look like princes of Raghu's race. This is detailed in the verse following. 2. कठोर etc.—कठोर adult, full-grown, Comp. "परिणतकठोर etc.", sl. 13. मेचक is blue as in "अये कोऽयमिन्द्रमणिमेचकच्छविः", sl. 17. 3. प्रसन्न etc.—प्रसन्न is undisturbed. प्रसन्नसिंह by लक्षणा here means प्रसन्नसिंहवीक्षित। प्रसन्नसिंह इव स्तिमितम्। वीक्षित has भावे क्त। 4. माङ्गल्य etc.—मङ्गलमेव इति मङ्गल+अण् स्वार्थे (प्रज्ञादि) माङ्गलम्। माङ्गले साधुः इति माङ्गल+य माङ्गल्यः। Hence again, by लक्षणा, माङ्गल्यमृदङ्ग stand for माङ्गल्यमृदङ्गध्वनि। माङ्गल्यमृदङ्ग इव मांसलः। 5. *Remark*—The surprise is mixed with deliberation. The boys seem to be princes of Raghu's race and through family likeness they resembles *me* in build etc. Well then who is that lucky Rāghava whose son they are ?

(xxviii) **(रा–) (सूक्ष्मं निरूप्य) अये न केवलमस्मत्संवादिन्याकृतिः,**

(R—) (Observing closely) Ha ! Their form resembles not mine alone.

अपि जनकसुतायास्तच्च तच्चानुरूपं
स्फटमिह शिशुयुगे नैपुणोन्नेयमस्ति।
ननु पुनरिव तन्मे गोचरीभूतमक्ष्णो-
रभिनवशतपत्रश्रीमदास्यं प्रियायाः ।।26।।

This and that again, similar to those of the daughter of Janaka also, are with a little skill, to be clarly guessed in these two boys. Nay, methinks the face of my darling, bearing the charm of a fesh-blown lotus, as if one again come within range of my eyes.

मित– । अस्माभि: मया संवादिनी सादृशी 'अस्मत्संवादिनी'।। अपीति।

अन्वय:–इह शिशुयुग्भे जनकासुताया अनुरूपमपि नैपुणौन्नेयं तच्च तच्च स्फुटम् अस्ति। ननु प्रियाया: तत् अभिनवशतपत्रश्रीमत् आस्यं पुन: मे अक्ष्णो: गोचरीभूतमिव।

व्याख्या–'इह' अस्मिन् 'शिशुयुग्भे' बालकयुगले 'जनकसुताया अनुरूपमपि' सदृशच्च 'नैपुणेन' निपुणतया 'उन्नेयं' निर्गाह्यं 'तत् च तत् च' एकाधिको भाव: 'स्फुटम् अस्ति' सुस्पष्टमास्ते। 'ननु' किं बहुना 'प्रियाया: तत् अभिनवस्य' सद्योविकसितस्य 'शतपत्रस्य' पद्मस्य 'श्री:' कान्ति: तद्युक्तम् 'आस्यं' मुखं 'पुन:' भूयो 'मे अक्ष्णो: गोचरीभूतम् इव' अक्षिविषयं गतिमित्युतप्रेक्षे। मनदनुकारिणी जनकजानुकारिणी च अनयोराकृतिक: अयि भो: किमेतत् इति भाव:।।

Notes. 1. अस्मत् etc.—संवाद is सादृश्य। अस्माभि: संवाद: अस्मत् संवाद: स: अस्ति अस्या: इति अस्मत्स वाद+इनि मत्वर्थे। Having resemblance with me. 2. तच्च तच्च–Refers to different things, such as ओष्ठमुद्रा, कर्णपाश, नेत्र etc. as detailed below. Hence तद् for each reference. It is not a case of वीप्सा। 3. नैपुणा etc.—निपुण clever. निपुणस्य भाव: इति निपुण+अण् नैपुणम् cleverness. The word is both युवादि (अण्) and ब्राह्मणदि (ष्यञ्) yielding two forms नैपुण and नैपुण्य। For the idea compare "विदग्धैर्निर्ग्राह्य:" (IV. 21). 4. ननु–This is an अव्यय modifying the previous statement (आक्षेप)। What do I say of resemblance here and three (तच्च तच्च)? It is the whole face as it were I see before me. 5. *Remark*—This raises a suspicion. Resemblance with myself can be explained by family likeness, but how is it that they are so much like my wife ? Who then are these ?

(xxix) **(रा–)**

मुक्ताच्छदन्तच्छविसुन्दरीयं सैवीष्ठमुद्रा स च कर्णपाश:।
नेत्रे पुनर्यद्यपि रक्तनीले तथापि सौभाग्यगुण: स एव ।।27।।(रा–)

(R—) This the very same closing of the lipe (Or—cover in the shape of lips) beautiful by the glimpse of the pearl-white teeth ; the same again are the beautiful ears. If, however, the eyes are blue and red (*i.e.,* not blue only like those of Sītā), the virtue of attractiveness is still the very same. (R—).

मित–। अनुरूपतां विशदयति मुक्तेति।

अन्वयः–इयं मुक्ताच्छदन्तछविसुन्दरी ओष्ठमुद्रा सा एव, कर्णपाशः स च। नेत्रे पुनः यद्यपि रक्तनीले तथापि सौभाग्यगुणः स एव।

व्याख्या–'इयम्' शिशुयुगले दृश्यमाना 'मुक्ताच्छानां' सुक्ताधवलानां 'दन्तानां छविभिः' कान्तिभिः 'सुन्दरी' शोभना 'ओष्ठमुद्रा' ओष्ठयोर्मुद्रणां मुद्रितौ ओष्ठौ इत्यर्थः 'सा एव' नूनं सीताया इव। कर्णपाशः' प्रशस्ती कर्णौ 'स च' स एव सीतायाः कर्णपाश इव नास्ति सन्देहः। 'नेत्रे पुनः' नयने तु यद्यपि' यदि च 'रक्तनीले' न हि सीताया इव केवलं नीले 'तथापि' सत्यपि एतावति भेदे 'सौभाग्यगुणः' सुभगतारूपो गुणः 'स एव' तद्देव वर्त्तते। तत् किमेतौ ममैव तनयौ इति वितर्कः।।

Notes. 1. मुक्ताच्छ etc.—The teeth are slightly visible (see next). 2. ओष्ठमुद्रा–Literally "closing of the lips". This means "the lips closed" by the maxim "भावानयने द्रव्यानयनम्"। When the lips close they do not press firmly against each other so as to give a determined expression to the face, but remain very slightly parted. Hence, the teeth are *slightly* visible. 3. कर्णपाशः–पाश in the उत्तरपद is प्रशस्तवचन। प्रशस्तः कर्णः कर्णपाशः। "प्रशंसावचनैश्च' इति समासः। A नित्यतत्पुरुष। 4. नेत्रे पुनः etc.—पुनः introduces a difference. The eyes of the boys are रक्तनील, *i.e.,* blue with a tinge of red ; but Sītā's eyes are blue only. The female eyes are often described as इन्द्रीवरद्यति। In the male a tinge of red is deemed auspicious. कौसल्या describes राम as "रक्ताक्षो दुन्दुभिस्वनः"। Perhaps it is for this reason that वीरराघव takes नेत्रे as referring to शिशुनेव and सीतानेत्र, hence dual. In consequence in रक्तनीले he supposes रक्त to refer to the boys, eyes—the boys are रक्ताक्ष–and नील to refer to the eyes of सीता alone. 5. सौभाग्यगुणः–सुभग is सुन्दर। तस्य भाव इति सुभग+ष्यञ् सौभाग्यम् सौन्दर्यम्। "हृद्भगसिन्ध्वते पूर्वपदस्य च" इत्युभयपदबृद्धिः। सौभाग्यमेव गुणः। This shows that there is अभेद in spite of the भेद noted above, 6. *Remark*—Note how राम is gradually drawing the boys towards him. He starts with the simple query "Whose children are they ?" (किमपत्यमयं दारकः)। He answers his query himself saying—They are certainly scions of some royal race साम्राज्यशंसिनो भावः कुशस्य च लवस्य च)। Soon he becomes more definite—They are princes of Raghu's race (भूयिष्ठाश्च रघुकुलच्छायमेतयोः पश्यामि)। Here however, he was reached the final stage—I see Sītā's face in them (अभिनवशतपत्रश्रीमदास्यं प्रियायाः); they are my boys. He realises the extreme unlikeliness of this conclusion hence he looks for corroborative evidence in the following para.

(xxx) (रा–) तदेतत् प्राचेतसाध्युषितमरण्यं यत्र किलदेवी परित्यक्ता, इयञ्चानयोराकृतिर्बत्सयोः। यदपि–स्वतः–प्राकाशान्यस्त्राणीति, तत्र विमृशामि अपि खलु तच्चित्रदर्शनप्रस्तावे अस्त्राभ्यनुज्ञानमुद्धूतं स्यात्, न ह्यसाम्प्रदायिकान्यस्त्राणि पूर्वेषामप्यनुशुश्रुमः। अयञ्च संप्लवमानमात्मानं सुखातिशयो हृदयस्य मे विस्त्रभ्यते। भूयिष्ठञ्च मया द्विधा प्रतिपन्नो देव्या गर्भभार आसीत्। (रा–)।

(R—) This indeed is that forest inhabited by Prācetasa where the queen was abandoned ; and such is the appearance of these dear boys. Again in the matter that the weapons are self-revealed, I surmise, might not the permission to the weapons, given on the occasion of inspecting the pictures, have taken effect ? For even of the ancients we have not heard of ultra-traditional (got without initiation) weapons. This excessive delight too of my heart steadies my drifting soul. And it was fully understood to me the queen's burden of foetus was divided into two.

मित–।'प्राचेतसेन' वाल्मीकिना 'अध्युषितं' कृतवसति। 'किलं' इत्यावधारणे। 'इयञ्च' सीतासदृशी च। इहैव सीता परित्यक्ता इहैव सीता परित्यक्ता इहैव बालौ सीतया मया च तुल्यरूपौ। तन्नैतदसम्भवं यत् ममैव सुतावेतौ क्रव्यद्भिर्भक्षितायामपि सीतायां दैवेन परिरक्षितौ। अस्य समर्थनमाह–'स्वतः प्रकाशानि अस्त्राणि' इति लवेनोक्तम्। 'तत्र विसृशामि' शङ्के 'अपि' सम्भाव्येत किं 'चित्रदर्शनप्रस्तावे तत् अस्त्राणाम् अभ्यनुज्ञानम्' अनुमतिः 'खलु' तदेव उद्धूतं' सम्प्राप्तं 'स्यात्'। ''सर्वथा त्वत्प्रसूतिमुपस्थास्यन्ति'' इति यत् चित्रदर्शन मया प्रोक्तं तदेव अनुज्ञारूपेण गृह्णती अस्त्रदेवता जन्मनि एतौ समाश्रिता तत एव उच्यते स्वतः प्रकाशानि अस्त्राणि इति। वस्तुतस्तु 'पूर्वषामपि' पूर्वाचार्यणामपि 'अस्त्राणि असाम्प्रदायिकानि' गुरूपदेशं विनैव स्वतः प्रकाशानि 'इति न हि अनुशुश्रुमः' नैव श्रूयते अस्माभिः। [अत्यन्तापह्नवे लिट्]। सर्वमेतदाशाजननं मे मन्दभाग्यस्य। तदुपरिं 'अयं मे हृदयस्य सुखातिशयश्च' कुशस्य परिष्वङ्गात् जातः 'संप्लवमानं' शङ्कासागरे सन्तरन्तम् अस्थिरम् 'आत्मानं विस्त्रम्भयते' विस्त्रम्भेण विश्वासेन योजयति तवैव तनयौ इति विश्वासमुत्पाद्य स्थिरीकरोति इत्यर्थः। द्वौ पुत्रौ तथा परित्यक्तायाः सीताया न सम्भवत इति न मन्तव्यम्। यतः–'देव्या गर्भभारः मया भूयिष्ठञ्च' बहुश एव 'द्विधा प्रतिपन्नः' द्विधाविभक्तत्वेन गृहीत 'आसीत्' ! तत् यमजावेतौ स्याताम्।

Notes. 1. तदेतत् etc.—Construe एतत् तत् अरण्यं यत्र etc. 2. इयञ्च–That is to say, like Sītā and like myself. Hence, the inference in natural that these are Sītā's sons. 3. चित्रदर्शनप्रस्तावे etc.—See Act I, para xxvi. अभ्यनुज्ञानम् command. It is not *permission* which usually is preceded by a prayer on the part of the party receiving permission. Here the weapons made no prayer to Rāma. A command again is addressed to the person commanded. The language used (त्वत्प्रसूतिम उपस्थास्यन्ति) is not of command. उपतिष्ठत commands, उपस्थास्यन्ति does not. The weapons cannot act on उपस्थास्यन्ति। Hence perhaps Rāma's doubt as expressed by विमृशामि अपि स्यात्। see next. 4. असाम्प्रदायिकानि–सम्+प्र+दा+घञ् भावे सम्प्रदायः formal gift, *i.e.*, gift by initiation. तत्र भवानि इति सम्प्रदाय+ठञ् साम्प्रदायिकानि। न तथा। There was no initiation in this case. Hence also the weapons could not pass over to the boys. Thus Rāma is not sure that the simple words त्वत्प्रसूतिम् उपस्थास्यन्ति have transferred the weapons. 5. अनुशुश्रुमः–We have not even heard, let alone actual seeing of it. This is total denial (अत्यन्तापह्नव)। Hence we have लिट् without परोक्षता। 6. संप्लवमानम्–प्लवमान is floating, floating in a sea of doubt. 7. विस्रम्भयते–विस्रम्भेन योजयति विस्रम्भ+णिच् (नाम धातु)+लट्ते। Comforts, steadies. कर्त्रभिप्रायविवक्षायामात्मनेपदम्। The rules "निगरणचनार्थे-भ्यश्च" "अणावकर्मकात्-" etc. have no application here, because these apply only when णिच् is added to certain roots (धातोः) ; here the णिच् comes after a प्रातिपदिक not a धातु। 8. भूयिष्ठञ्च etc.—This meets the objection that सीता could not have become the mother of *two* boys after her exile. She gave birth to twins. I am almost sure of this for I could percieve that her foetus was divided into two. The following verse is in support of this.

(*xxxi*) (रा–) (सास्त्रम्)–

(R—) (*With tears)*—

पुरारूढ़े स्नेहैपरिचयविकासादुपचिते
रहो विस्त्रब्धाया अपि सहजलज्जाजड़दृशः।
मयैवादौ ज्ञातः करतलपरामर्शकलया
द्विधा गर्भग्रन्थिस्तदनु दिवसैः कैरपि तया ।। 28 ।।

From shampooing with the palm of my hand is privacy (she having her eyes fixed through inborn bashfulness, though quite at ease, the affection that had previously grown having developed through growth of familiarity) the attachment of her foetus was first by me preceived to be in two places, and then by her in a few days.

(रुदित्वा) तत् किमेतौ पृच्छामि केनाप्युपायेन ?

(*Having wept*) Shall I then question them by some means or other ?

मित–। पुरेति।

अन्वयः–पुरा रुढ़े स्नेहे परिचयविकासात् उपचिते विस्रब्धाया अपि सहजल्लाजड़दृशः गर्भग्रन्थिः रहः करतलपरामर्शकलया आदौ मया एव द्विधा ज्ञातः तदनु कैरपि दिवसैः तया।

व्याख्या–'पुरा' पूर्वं विवाहात् परमेव इत्यर्थः 'रूढ़े' अङ्कुरिते 'स्नेहे' अनुरागे गच्छति काले 'परिचयस्य' परस्परहृदयविज्ञानस्य 'विकाससात्' स्फुरणात् 'उपचिते' प्रगाढ़े सति 'विस्रब्धायाः अपि' विश्वस्ताया अपि अनियन्त्रणाया अपि इत्यर्थः 'सहजया' प्रकृतिसुलभया 'लज्जया जड़दृशः' मदीयेन व्यापारेण स्तिमितनेत्रायाः सीतायाः 'गर्भग्रन्थिः' गर्भबन्धः 'रहः' एकान्ते 'करतलेन' यः परामर्शः संवाहनं तस्य 'कलया' कलनया अनुष्ठानेन इत्यर्थः 'आदौ' प्रथमं 'मया एव द्विधा' द्वयोः स्थानयोः 'ज्ञातः' अनुभूतः 'तदनु' ततः परं 'कैः अपि दिवसैः' कैश्चित् दिनैः 'तया' ज्ञातः।।

Notes. 1. पुरा etc.—पुरा may be compounded or left uncompounded with रूढ़े। 2. रहः–It seems better taken with करतलपरामर्शकलया then विस्रब्धायाः as is usual. The दूरान्वय is quite immaterial with भवभूति। 3. अपि–The force is this—First the affection was of long standing (पुरा); next, the affection had deepened (उपचित); as a consequence she left absolutely no restraint before me (विस्रब्धा); in spite of all this (अपि) etc. 4. सहज etc.—The जड़ता of the eyes was caused by her सहजलज्जा which overcame her विसम्भ। Of course the लज्जा was due to the shampooing. 5. द्विधा–द्विधा स्थित इति ज्ञातः। द्वयोः स्थानयोः इति द्वि+धाच् अधिकरणविचाले। अधिकरणविचाल is multiplication of location. गर्भग्रन्थि has one place usually for its location. Here we have two. One has become two. 6. तत् किमेतौ etc.—Rāma personally has no longer much doubt that the boys are his children. He now wants corroboration from the boys themselves.

(*xxxii*) **लवः–तात किमेतत्–**

Lava—Father, what is this ?

वाष्पवर्षेण नीतं वो जगन्मङ्गलमाननम्।

अवश्यायावसिक्तस्य पुण्डरीकस्य चारुताम् ।। 28 ।।

Thy face, the source of the world's welfare, is led to the beauty of a dew-besprinkled white lotus through the flow of tears ?

कुशः–अयि वत्स,

Kuśa.—O Dear brother.

विना सीतादेव्या, किमिव हि न दुःखं रघुपतेः
प्रियानाशे कृत्सनं किल जगदरण्यं हि भवति।
स च स्नेहस्तावानयमपि वियोगो निरवधिः
किमित्येवं पृच्छस्यनधिगतरामायण इव ।। 30 ।।

Without queen Sītā what is not a source of grief to the lord of the Raghus ? It is said that the whole world becomes indeed a wilderness on the loss of one's beloved wife. That love in that measure and this endless separation ! Why ask thus like one that has not learnt his Rāmāyaṇa ?

मित–। वाष्पेत्यादि।

अन्वयः–जगन्मङ्गलं वः आननं वाष्पर्षेण अवश्यायाव- सिक्तस्य पुण्डरीकस्य चारुतां नीतम्।

व्याख्या–'जगतां' मङ्गलं' मङ्गलावहं कल्याणकरं 'वः आननं वाष्पर्षेण' अश्रुतापेन 'अवश्य येन' तुषारेण 'अवसिक्तिस्य' प्रोक्षितस्य 'पुण्डरीकस्य' श्वेतपद्मस्य 'चारुतां नीतं' कान्तिं प्रापितम्। विरहपाण्डु वदनमण्डलं पुण्डरीकेण सवर्णं जातम्।। विनेति।

अन्वयः–सीतादेव्या विना रघुपतेः किमिव न हि दुःखम्। प्रियानाशे किल कृत्स्नं जगत् अरणयं हि भवति। स च तावान् स्नेहः अयमपि निरवधिः वियोगः। अनधिगतरामायण इव किमिति एवं पृच्छसि।

व्याख्या–'सीतादेव्या विना' सीतादेवीं विहाय स्थितस्य 'रघुपतेः' रामस्य 'किमिव' किं नाम वस्तु 'न हि दुःखं' नैव दुःखकरम्? सर्वमेव दुःखकरम् अतः सुलभमेव तस्य रोदनम्। कुत एवमित्याह 'प्रियनाशे किल' जनाः कथयन्ति दयिताया नाशे सति 'कृत्स्नं जगत्' निखिलं भुवनम् 'अरण्यं हि भवति' वनमिव नूनं प्रतिभाति। अतएव सर्वे दुःखकरम्। सत्यञ्चोक्तं "तदारम्याण्यरम्याणि प्रियाः शल्यं तदासवः।

तदैकाकी सबन्धुः सन्निष्टेन रहितो यदा।।"'स च' पूर्वानुभूतः लोकविदितश्च रामसीतयोः 'तावान्' अतिभूमिं गतः 'स्नेहः' प्रीतिः, पक्षान्तरे 'अयमपि' एषोऽधुना अनुभूयमानः 'निरवधिः' निरन्तरस्थायी 'वियोगः' सीताया सह विरहः-इति भूयान् अनयोः मीलनविरहयोः पठित्वापि अनधिगतम् भेदः, अतश्च कष्टदायक एव। 'अनधिगतरामायणः' रामायणं पठित्वापि अनधिगतम् अनधीतं रामायणं येन तादृशः जन 'इव', किमिति कस्मात् हेतोः 'एवं पृच्छसि' जिज्ञाससे। जिज्ञासा न त्वयि युक्ता इति भावः।

Notes. 1. अवश्याय etc.— अवश्यायते शीतो भवति इति अव+श्यै+ण कर्त्तरि अवश्यायः frost. 2. पुण्डरीकस्य–Rāma's face is expected to be श्याम। It had become पाण्डु, through grief. 3. प्रियनाशे etc.—किल shows that he is only repeating what people say ; he cannot have personal experience in the matter. 4. किमिति–A command अव्यय meaning 'why'. Also see next para.

(*xxxiii*) रामः (स्वगतम्)—अये तटस्थित आलापः, कृतं प्रश्नेन। दग्धहृदय, कोऽयमाकस्मिकस्ते पारिप्लवो विकारः ? एवं निर्भिन्नहृदयावेगः शिशुजनेनाप्यकम्पितोऽस्मि। भवतु तावदन्तरयामि (प्रकाशम्) वत्सौ, रामायणमिति श्रूयते भगवती वाल्मीकेः सरस्वतीनिस्यन्दः प्रशस्तिरादित्यवंशस्य, तत्र किञ्चित् कौतूहलेन श्रोतुमिच्छामि।

Rāma—(*To himself*) —Ha ! Their talk is indifferent ; away with questions. Blighted heart, what unaccountable unrestrained perturbation of thine is this ? With the hearts' commotion thus revealed I am being pitied by boyes even. Well, I will screen it over. (*Aloud*) Dear boys, a eulogy of the solar race the flow of the divine speech of the Worshipful Vālmīki is being spoken of. Through curiosity I wish to hear a little of it.

मित–।'तटे' कूले 'स्थितः जलं नावगाहते उदासीन इत्यर्थः। उदासीन 'आलापः' उदासीनस्येव आलापः। यदि सीतासुतः स्यात् कुशः तदा आप्तवत् ''बिना जनन्याः'' इति ब्रूयात् न तु ''बिना सीतदेव्या' इति ''तातस्य' इति च न तु ''रघुपतेः' इति। 'प्रश्नेन कृतं' ज्ञातं ज्ञातव्यं वृथा प्रश्नः। नेमौ सीतासुतौ इत्यर्थः। अकस्मादागत 'आकस्मिकः' अकारण इत्यर्थः।'पारिपूलवंः' चञ्चलः। निर्भिन्नः' प्रकटः 'हृदयावेगेः' मनोविकारो यस्य तादृशः। 'अन्तरयामि' प्रच्छादयामि अनिर्भिन्नो यथा स्यात् तथा करोमि इत्यर्थः 'सरस्वत्याः' वाग्याः 'निस्यन्दः' प्रवाहः। 'प्रशस्तिः' प्रशंसा। वाल्मीकिना विरचितः सूर्यवंशस्यप्रशंसामयः प्रबन्ध इत्यर्थः।।

Notes. 1. तटस्थितः–Primarily it means a person who stands at the margin of water and does not get down into it. Hence an indifferent *person*. Here again it is applied not to the person but to the आलाप of the person. Practically then तटस्थित आलापः is the same as तटस्थितस्य आलापः। 2. आकस्मिकः–अकस्मात् भव इति अकस्मात्+ठञ्। Unaccountable. 3. निर्भिन्न etc.—Comp. अनिर्भिन्नो गभीरत्वात्।"–III, sl. I. 4. अन्तरयामि–अन्तर is अन्तर्धि screen. "अन्तरमवकाशवधिपरिधानान्तर्द्धिभेदतादर्थ्ये" etc.—*Amara*. अन्तरेण योजयामि इति अन्तर+णिच् (नामधातु)+लट् मिन्। Having become निर्भिन्न the हृदयावेग stands uncovered, I will again cover it up. 5. कौतूहलेन etc.— He is trying to keep himself engaged and thus screen over his निर्भिन्नहृदयावेग।

(xxxiv) **कुशः–स कृत्स्न एव सन्दर्भः अस्माभिरावृतः, स्मृत्यपस्थितौ तावदिमौ बाचरितस्य अन्त्येऽध्याये श्लोकौ।**

Kuśa—The whole of that work has been read through by us. These two verses in the last chapter of the Bālacarita have now come up to memory.

रामः–उदीरयतु वत्सः।

Rāma—Let my darling repeat them.

कुशः– प्रकृत्यैव प्रिया सीता रामस्यासीन्महात्मनः।
प्रियभावः स तु तया स्वमुणैरेव वर्द्धितः ।। 31 ।।

Kuśa—To Rāma, the high-souled, by nature indeed, was Sītā dear ; but that dearnes she really enhanced by her own virtues.

तथैव रामः सीतायाः प्राणेभ्योऽपि प्रियोऽभवत्।
हृदयं त्वेव जानाति प्रीतियोगं परस्परम् ।। 32 ।।

In the very same manner Rāma became dearer than life to Sītā ; but their hearts alone knew the extent of each other's love.

मित–।'सन्दर्भः' प्रबन्धः।'आवृत्तः' अधीतः।'स्मृतौ उपस्थितौ' आगतौ। 'बालचरितस्यं बालकाण्ठस्य।।'उदीरयतु' उच्चारयतु।। प्रकृत्येपि।

अन्वयः–सीता प्रकृत्या एव महात्मनः रामस्य प्रिया आसीत्। स तु प्रियभावः तया स्वगुणैः वर्द्धित एव।

व्याख्या–सुगमा। स्वभावजा प्रियता स्वभावदत्तैर्गुणैः वर्द्धिता इति भावः।। तथेति।

अन्वयः–रामः तथा एव प्राणेभ्यः अपि सीतायाः प्रियः अभवत्। किन्तु परस्परं प्रीतियोगं हृदयमेव जानाति।

व्याख्या–'रामः' यथा सीता तस्य प्रिया 'तथा एव प्राणेभ्यः अपि सीतायाः प्रियः अभवत्'। 'तु' किन्तु 'परस्परम्' अन्योऽन्यं प्रति ईदृशं 'प्रीतियोगं' प्रेमबन्धनं तयोः 'हृदयम् एव जानाति' नान्यः कोऽपि।।

Notes. 1. तावत्–अवधारणे। Or say अवधौ, for the present स्मृत्युपस्थितौ। 2. बालचरितस्य etc.—The verses are re ıd differently in different editions of the Rāmāyaṇa. I am told that Gorresio's Rāmāyaṇa has Bhavabhūti' readings. 3. प्रियभावः—Here प्रियाया भाव would give प्रियाभावः। So first take प्रियम् in the neuter (सामान्ये नपुंसकम्), then say प्रियस्य भावः। 4. परम्परम्–Deriv. *ante.* द्वितीया in connection with प्रति understood.

(xxxv) **रामः–कष्टमतिदारुणोऽयं हृदयमर्मोपघातः। हा देवि, एवं किल तदासीत्। अहो निरन्वयविपर्यासविरसवृत्तयो विप्रलम्भपर्यवसायिनस्तापयन्ति संसारवृत्तान्ताः।**

Rāma—O woe ! This is a very heavy blow to the vitals of my heart, Alas ! my queen ! Such indeed was it then. O, they do afflict, these affairs of life that through unexepected (lit.—disconnected) reversals are better in their course and thus end in disappointment.

क्व तावानानन्दो निरतिशयविस्त्रम्भबहुलः
क्व तेऽन्योन्यं यन्ताः क्वचन गहनाः कौतुकरसाः।
सुखे वा दुखे वा क्व नु खलु तदैक्यं हृदययो-
स्तथाप्येष प्राणःस्फुरति न तु पापो विरमति।। (रा–)

Where now is that immense bless augmented by unsurpassed confidence ? Where are those mutual efforts ? Where are those indescribable tastes of fun (Or—festivities)? Where indeed is that union of hearts in joy as well as sorrow ? Yet *this* heart beats ; the thing does not indeed stop. (R—)

मित–। 'हृदयस्य मर्मणि' जीवस्थाने 'उपघातः' प्रहारः। 'एवं किल' ईदृश एव "प्रकृत्यैव" इत्यादिश्लोश्लोकोक्तप्रकार एव 'तदा आसीत्'। निर्गत।

अन्वयः अनुवृत्तिः यस्यस 'निरन्वयः' पूर्वर्त्तिसूचकशून्यः अतएव अननुमेयः यः 'विपर्यासः' अन्यथाभावः दशान्तरमित्यर्थः तेन 'विरसा' अप्रीतिकरा 'वृत्तिः' प्रसरो येषां तादृशं अतएव 'विप्रलम्भे' प्रतारणायां 'पर्यवस्यन्ति' ये तथाविधाः ईदृशत्वेन नीता अनीदृशा। जायमाना आपातसरसाः परिणमनीरसा इत्यर्थः। 'संसारवृत्तान्ताः' संसारभावाः।। क्वेति।

अन्वयः–निरतिशयविस्रम्भबहुलः तावान् आनन्दः क्व ? ते अन्योऽन्यं यत्नाः क्व? गहनाः कौतुकरसाः क्वचन ? तत् सुखे वा दुःखे वा हृदययोः ऐक्यं क्व नु खलु ? तथापि एष पापः प्राणः स्फुरति न तु विरमति।

व्याख्या–निर्भरः अतिशयः अस्य 'नितिशयः' भूया इत्यर्थः यः 'विस्रम्भः' अन्योऽन्यविश्वासः तेन 'बहुलः' विवृद्धः 'तावान्' तत्परिमितः महान् इत्यर्थः 'आनन्दः क्व ' कुच गतः ? गत एव आनन्दः। 'ते' पूर्वदृष्या 'अन्योऽन्यं' परस्परं प्रति 'यत्नाः' प्रीत्युत्पादनचेष्टाः 'क्व'? गता एव ते। 'गहनाः' सान्द्राः 'कौतुकस्य' प्रहासस्य उत्सवस्य वा 'रसाः' स्वादाः 'क्वचन' क्वापि? ते च गताः। 'तत्' पूर्वानुभूतं 'सुखे वा दुःखे वा हृदययोः ऐक्यं क्वनु खलु' क्ववा गतम् ? इत्थं सर्वमेव अपुनरावृत्तये गतं 'तथापि एष पापः' दुष्टः प्राणः' हन्मारुतः 'स्फुरति' चलति 'न विरमति' न प्रशाम्यति।।

Notes. 1. हृदयमर्म etc.—हृदयमर्मन् is the most sensitive spot in the heart. Bhavabhūti often refers to it, thus—"हृन्मर्मव्रण इव वेदनां करोति" (I, 30), "व्रणौ रूढग्रन्थिः स्फुटित इव हन्मर्मणि पुनः" (II, 26) etc. 2. निरन्वय etc.—अन्वीयते अनुगम्यते इति अनु+इ+अच् कर्मणि अन्वयः that which is followed ; hence *cause*, bacause it is always followed by the *effect*. In this sense, निरन्वय means अहेतुक। वि+परि+अस+घञ् भावे विपर्यास reversal. निरन्वयविपर्यास now means causeless, hence unexpected, reversal. The टीका gives a slightly different explanation. 3. विप्रलम्भ–etc.—For विप्रलम्भ in the sense प्रतारण comp. "मया एव विप्रलब्ध आर्यपुत्रः" (III). 4. कौतुक etc.—कौतुक is परिहास fun. रस is स्वाद taste. 5. प्राणः–This is singular masucline when meaning हृद्वायु the air that circulates in the heart. "प्राणो हन्मारुते" इत्यादि विश्वमेदिन्यौ। By हन्मारुत is probably meant the pulsation of the heart.

(xxxvi) **(रा–) भोः कष्टम्।**

(R—) O woe !

प्रियागुणसहस्राणामेकोन्मीलनपेशलः ।
य एव दुःस्मर कालस्तमेव स्मारिता वयम् ।। 34।।

I am reminded of that very period that is the most painful to think of because charming on account of the simultaneous (Or—wondrous) unveilling of the thousands of the virtues of my darling.

तदा किञ्चित् किञ्चित् कृनपदमहोभिः कतिपयै-
स्तदीषद्विस्तारि स्तनयुगलमासीन्मृगदृशः।
वयः स्नेहाकूतव्यतिकरघनो यत्र मदनः
प्रगल्भव्यापारः स्फुरति हृदि मुग्धश्च वपुषि ।।35।।

(The period) when Love, intensified by the union of age, affection and desire, germinates at heart with a vigorous move but is subdued in the body ; (for) then (तदा) the breasts of the fawn-eyed (girl) that had slowly made their mark became in but few days slightly expansive.

मित–।प्रियेति।

अन्वयः–प्रियागुणसहस्राणाम् एकोन्मीलनपेशलः यः एव कालः दुस्मरः तमेव वयं स्मारिताः।

व्याख्या–'प्रियायाः' सीतायाः 'गुणसहस्राणाम्' असंख्यानां गुणानां यत् 'एकोन्मीनं' युगपदुन्मेषः अद्भुतोन्मेषो वा तेन 'पेशलः' मधुरः 'यः एव कालः दुःस्मरः' स्मर्तुमशक्यः 'तमेव वयं स्मारिताः' स एव अस्माभिः स्मृतः। यस्य स्मरणं दुःसहं स एव कालः स्मृत इत्यर्थः।। कालं विश्निष्टि तदेति।

अन्वयः–यत्र वयः स्नेहाकूतव्यतिकरघनः मदनः हृदि प्रगल्भव्यापारः (सन्) स्फुरति वपुषि च मुग्धः। तदा किञ्चित् किञ्चित् कृतपदं मृगदृशः तत् स्तनयुगलं कतिपयैः अहोभिः ईषविस्तारि आसीत्।

व्याख्या–कं कालम् इत्यपेक्षायामाह 'यत्र' यस्मिन् काले 'वयसः' नवयौवनस्य 'स्नेहस्य' अन्योऽन्यानुरागस्य 'आकूतस्य' अभिलाषस्य च यः 'व्यतिकरः' एकत्र समावेशः तेन 'घनः' सान्द्रः 'मदनः हृदि' मनसि 'प्रगल्भः' प्रौढ़ः 'व्यापारः' प्रसरः यस्य तादृशः सन् 'स्फुरति' आविर्भवति 'वपुषि च' देहे पुनः 'मुग्धः' अप्रगल्भः। क्रिम्भूतं वय इत्याह–'तदा' तस्मिन् काले 'किञ्चित्' शनैः शनैः 'कृतपदम्' दीर्घणैव कालेन मुकुलितप्रायं 'मृगदृशः' हरिणलोचनाया सीतायाः 'तत् स्तनयुगलं कतिपयैः अहोभिः झटित्येव 'ईषविस्तारि' आभोगवत् 'आसीत्'। तत् हृदि प्रगल्भो मद्रनः नोचेत् कथं झटिति स्तनपरिणमणाहः।।

Notes. 1. प्रिता etc.—सहस्र here is merely a large number not actually a thousand. गुणानां सहस्राणि गुणसहस्राणि etc. 2. एक etc.—एक is, by transference of epithets. यौगपद्ययुक्त simultaneous. Or एक is श्रेष्ठ, hence अद्भुत wondrous. पेशल is रम्य charming. 'पेशलः कुशले रम्यै'' इति हेमः। Now see Tika. 3. दुःस्मर–दुखेन स्मर्यते इति दूर+स्मृ+खल् कर्मणि of painful memory. 4. तमेव etc.—स्मृ+णिच्+क्त कर्मणि caused to remember. Here before णिच् we had वयं तं स्मृतवन्तः। With णिच् the poet wants कुशः अस्मान् तं स्मारितवान्। Changing the voice कुशेन वयं तं स्मारिताः। According to Bhaṭṭoji, however, the अणिकर्त्ता does not become कर्म here and the form becomes कुशः अस्माभिः तं स्मारितवान् yielding the final form कुशेन अस्माभिः स स्मारितः। 5. तदा–etc. As already remarked this is against the Vīracarita where Sītā is seen to be an adult already at marriage.

(xxxvii) **कुशः–अयञ्च मन्दाकिनीचित्रकूटवनविहारे सीतादेवी-मुद्दिश्य रघुपतेः श्लोकः–**

Kuśa.—This again is Raghupati's verse intended for queen Sītā when sporting in the forest of Citrakūṭa by the river Mandākinī.

त्वदर्थमिव विन्यस्तः शिलापट्टोऽयमग्रतः।
यस्यायमभितः पुष्पैः प्रवृष्ट इव केशरः ॥ 36 ॥

For thee, as it were, has been laid this slab of stone, in front, on both sides of which this Vakula tree has showered heavily with flowers.

रामः (सलज्जास्मितस्नेहकरुणम्)–अति नाम मुग्धः शिशुजनः विशेषतस्त्वरण्यचरः ! हा देवि, स्मरसि तस्य प्रदेशस्य तत्समय-विस्रम्भातिप्रसङ्गमाक्षिणः ? कष्टं भोः कष्टम् !

Rāma *(With affection, pathos and a bashful smile)*—Boys are indeed very simple especially the dwellers in the woods. Ah ! Queen ; dost thou remember that place, witness of our excess of familiarity at the time ? Woe ! O woe !

श्रमाम्बशिशिरीभवत् प्रसृतमन्दमन्दाकिनी-
मरुत्तरलितालकाकुलललाटचन्द्रद्युति।
अकुङ्कमकलङ्कितोज्ज्वलकपोलमुत्प्रेक्ष्यते
निराभरणसुन्दरश्रवणपाशसौम्यं मुखम् ॥37॥ (रा–)

(By me) is being fancied before me thy face—beautiful though without decoration, glorious in its well-shaped ears, with cheeks bright and not defiled with saffron, at the time having the sweat of toil on it and becoming cool, with the lustre of your moon like brow ruffled by your tresses that were agitated by the mild breeze proceeded from the Mandākinī.

मित–। 'मन्दाकिनीगतं चित्रकूटवनम्' शाकपथिवादि। मन्दकिनीसमीपस्थं वनमित्यर्थः। तत्र विहारः।। त्वदर्थमिति।

अन्वयः–अयम् अगतः शिलापट्टः यस्य अभितः अयं केशरः पुष्पैः प्रवृष्ट इव, त्वदर्थम्, विन्यस्तः।

व्याख्या–'अयम् अग्रतः' पुरोवर्ती 'शिलापट्टः' प्रस्तरलम् 'यस्य अभितेः' उभयतः पार्श्वयोरित्यर्थः 'अयं केशरः' एष वकुलपादपः 'पुष्पैः प्रवृष्ट इव' वारिर्षणमिव पुष्पवर्षणं कृतवान्त्वदर्थम् इव' मन्ये तत्रैव प्रयोजने 'विन्यस्तः' स्थापितः तत् इह शेष्व।। लज्जाजनितं स्मितं 'लज्जास्मितम्'। प्राक्तनस्नेहस्मरणात् 'स्नेहः'। तत् सर्वं नास्ति 'करुणम्'। मुग्धः' सरलः। 'अरण्यचस्तु विशेषतो मुग्धः'। 'प्रदेशस्य' इति शेषविवक्षया षष्ठी। 'तत्समयः' इत्यादि व्याख्यातं प्राक्।। श्रमेति।

अन्वयः–श्रमाम्बुशिशिरीभवत् प्रसृतमन्दाकिनी मरुत्तरलिताल काकुलललाटचन्द्रद्युति अकुङ्कमकलङ्कितोज्जवलकपोलम् निराभरण-सुन्दरश्रवणपापसौम्यं (ते) मुखम् उत्त्प्रेक्ष्यते।

व्याख्या–'श्रमाम्बुभिः शिशिरीभवत्' शीततां गच्छत् 'प्रसृतः' प्रवृत्तः 'मन्दः मन्दाकिनीमरुत्' तेन 'तरलितैः' चञ्चलैः 'अलकैः' चूर्णकुन्तलैः ललाटपार्श्वस्थैः केशैः 'आकुला' विमिश्रा मन्दीकृता इत्यर्थः 'ललाटचन्द्रस्य' चन्द्रतुल्यस्य ललाटस्यद्युतिः' यस्मिन् तत् 'अकुङ्गमकलद्धितौ' कुङ्कुमेन अकलङ्कितौ 'उज्ज्वलौ कपोलौ' गण्डौ यस्मिन् तत् निराभरणौ च सुन्दरौ च यौ 'श्रवणपाशौ' प्रशस्ते श्रवणे ताभ्यां 'सौम्यं' ते 'मुखम् उत्पेक्ष्यते' अग्रतः परिदृश्यते इव मया।।

Notes. 1. यस्यायमभितः–अभितः requires द्वितीया by the Vārttika. "अभितः परितः–"। यम् अभितः is the form expected. निरङ्कुशाः कवयः। 2. पुष्पैः–The करण of वर्षणक्रिया। 3. प्रवृष्टः–प्र is intensive. The root is taken intransitively and the क्त is कर्त्तरि। Here the downpour is achieved with flowers not with water. 4. हा देवि etc.—Addresses Sītā in the air. He fancies he sees her there. प्रदेशस्य has षष्ठी by "अधीगर्थ दयेशां कर्मणि"। 5. अकुङ्कुम etc.—कुङ्कुमेन कलङ्कितौ shows that Sītā's complexion was brighter than the lustre of कुङ्कुम। This was due to the permanent अङ्गराग given her by अनसूया the wife of Atri. cf. "स्फुरत्प्रभामण्डलमानसूयं मा विभ्रती शाश्वतमङ्गरामगम्। रराजः शुद्धेति पुन स्वपुर्यैसन्दर्शिता वह्निगतेव भर्त्रा।।" *Raghu.* XIV. 6. निराभरण etc.—श्रवणपाश is a नित्यसमास of the तत्पुरुष class, पाश is प्रशंसावाची when it is final in the तत्पुरुष। The समास is by "प्रशंसावाची"। पाश is of the मतल्लिकादि class. "मतल्लिकोद्घमिश्राः स्युः प्रकाण्डस्थलभित्तयः। हस्तपाशतटाः पादपालीमचर्च्चिकादयः"–*Vardhamāna.* 7. *Remark*—For the moment it seemed to him that Sītā was actually present there and he was looking at her beautiful face. This gave him relief but he is soon dis-illusioned and exclaims in despair कष्टं भोः कष्टम् etc.

(xxxviii) **(रा–) (स्तम्भित इव स्थित्वा सकरुणम्)–अहो नु खलु भोः–**

(R—) *(With pathos after remaining as if paralysed)*—Ha O indeed !—

चिरं ध्यात्वा ध्यात्वा निहित इव निर्माय पुरतः
प्रवासेऽप्याश्वासं न खलु न करोति प्रियजनः।
जगज्जीर्णारण्यं भवति हि विकल्पव्युपरमे
कुकूलानां राशौ तदनु हृदयं पच्यत इव ।।38।।

Even in separation it is not that a dear one does not give consolation when created, as it were, by meditation—long meditation—and placed in front. At the cessation of the delusion, the world, verily becomes a bligted wilderness. Thereafter the heart is as though being baked in heap of husks a-glow.

मित–। सीतामुखदर्शनं विप्रलम्भमात्रम् इति ज्ञात्वा शोकक्षोभात् 'स्तम्भित इव स्थित्वा सकरुणम्' आह।। चिरमिति।

अन्वयः–प्रवासे अपि चिरं ध्यात्वा ध्यात्वा निर्माय पुरतः निहित इव प्रियजनः आश्वासं न करोति न खलु। विकल्पव्युपरमे जगत् जीर्णरण्यं हि भवति। तदनु हृदयं कुकूलानां राशौ पच्यते इव।

व्याख्या–'प्रवासे अपि' विरहे अपि 'चिरं ध्यात्वा ध्यात्वा' निरन्तरानुध्यानेन 'निर्माय' अलीकं कल्पयित्वा 'पुरतः निहित इव' निर्मातुरग्रे स्थापित इव 'प्रियजनः आश्वासम्' अवसितो विरह इति सान्त्वनां 'न करोति न खलु' करोत्येव। सीताया मुखमग्रतः कल्पयित्वा ममापि जातमेव क्षणं समाश्वासनम्। 'विकल्पस्य' अलीकस्य'

अलीकस्य, विपरीतायाश्च तस्याः कल्पनायाः 'व्य परमे' अवसाने अपयाते मोहे इत्यर्थः 'जगत् जीर्णारण्यं हि' अवदग्धं काननमिव हि 'भवति'। 'तदनु' ततः परं 'हृदयं कुकूलानां राशौ' महति तुषानले 'पच्यते इव' दह्यते, पाकं भजते इव। यथा अस्मिन् क्षणे मदीयं हृदयम्।।

Notes. 1. स्तम्भित इव etc.—He sees it is a delusion and the shock paralyses him for a moment. 1. a. पुरतः–It is an underived primitive word meaning 'in front'. अव्यय–अधि 7मी। "पुरत प्रथमे चाग्रे" इति विश्वः। Some derive it with अतसुच् after पूर्व, but in the case पुर् cannot be ordered in place of पूर्व! The rules being "पूर्वाधरावराणमपि पुरधवश्चैषाम्" and "अस्ताति च"। cp. "कथं...पुरत....कश्चितु विभाषाग्रहणं योगात् विभज्यते। तेन पूर्वशब्दादतसुच। 'अस्ताति च' इति सूत्रे चकारस्य अनुक्तसमुच्च्यार्थत्वात् पुरादेशः। तन्निमूलम्। पुरतः इति...अप्रामणिकमेव"—*Bhattoji*. 2. विकल्प etc.—कल्प्नते निर्मीयते इति कल्पः creation. विरुद्धः कल्पः विकल्पः false creation, delusion. 3. कुकूलानाम्–कुकूल is तुषानल। In this sense अमर takes it as masucline, but other authorities declare it to be always neuter. "कुकूलं शङ्कुभिः कीर्णे श्वभ्रे ना तु तुषानले" इत्यमरः। "कुकूलं तु तुषानले" इत्यादि हैमः etc. 4. पच्यते–Not burnt up but slowly being baked so as to feel it the more.

(*xxxix*) **नेपथ्ये–**

वशिष्ठो वाल्मीकिर्दशरथमहिष्योऽथ जनकः
महैवारुन्धत्या शिशुकलमाकर्ण्य सभयाः।
जराग्रस्तैर्गात्रैरथ खलु विदूराश्रमतया
चिरेणागच्छन्ति त्वरितमनसोऽपि श्रमजड़ाः ।।38।।

In the Tiring Room—Vaśiṣṭha even along with Arundhatī, Vālmīki, the queensof Daśaratha, and Janaka, alarmed on hearing of the boy's quarrel, are coming, slowly thogh their will is hurrying, landguid through fatigue because of their age-stricken limbs and especially because the hermitage is far away.

मित–। वशिष्ठ इति।

अन्वयः–अरुन्धत्या सह एव वशिष्ठः वाल्मीकिः दशरथमहिष्यः अथ जनकः शिशुकलहमाकर्ण्य सभयाः (सन्तः) त्वरितमनसोऽपि जराग्रस्तैः गात्रैः अथ विदूराश्रमतया श्रमजड़ाः चिरेण आगच्छन्ति खलु।

व्याख्या–सुगमा। 'दशरथमहिष्यः' कौसल्याकेकयीसुमित्राः। 'शिशुकलहं' लवचन्द्रकेत्वोः कलहम्। 'सभयाः' इति अरुन्धतीवशिष्ठवाल्मीकीनाम् उभयोरर्थे भयम् इतरेषां तु चन्द्रकेतोरर्थे। 'विदूरे आश्रमो' येषां तेषां भावेन। 'आगच्छन्ति' इहैव रणाङ्गने।।

Notes. 1. दशरथमहिष्यः–The queens had all gone to Ṛṣyaśṛṅga's sacrifice and from there had come over to Vālmīki's hermitage. See Act II. 2. अथ–Implies समुच्चय। 'अथायो संशये स्यातामधिकारे च मङ्गले। विकल्पानन्तप्रश्नकार्तस्न्यरम्भसमुच्चये।।" इति मेदिनी। 3. जराग्रस्तैः etc.—उपलक्षणे तृतीया। 4. विदूराश्रमतया–This is with respect to the old people. The hermitage was not actually very far away, but *to old people* the distance was rather long.

(*xl*) **रामः–कथं भगवन्तावरुन्धतीवशिष्ठौ अम्बा जनकश्च अत्रैव ! कष्टम् ! कथं खल्वेते द्रष्टव्याः। (सकरुणं विलोक्य) अहह तातजनकोऽप्यत्रैवायाति इति वज्रेण ताड़ितोऽस्मिमन्दभाग्यः।**

Rāma—How so ! Are the worshipful Arundhati and Vaśiṣṭha, my mothers and Janaka indeed here? O woe ! How can these be faced ? (*Observing—With pathos*) Oh ! ill-starred as I am, I am struck with a thunder-bolt as father Janaka too is coming this very way.

सम्बन्धस्पहणीयताप्रमुदितैर्जुष्टे वशिष्ठादिभि-
र्दृष्ट्वापत्यविवाहमङ्गलमहे तत्तातयोः सङ्गतम्।
पश्यन्नीदृशमीदृशे पितृसखं वृत्ते महावैशसे
दीर्ये किं न सहस्त्रधाहमथवा रामेण किं दुष्करम् ।।40।।

Having before witnessed the meeting of the two fathers at the auspicious marrige festivities of their children—festivities joined in by Vaśiṣṭha and others delighted at the desirability of the connection—Why, do I not burst into a thousand pieces now seeing my father's friend in this plight after the perpetration of such a terrible cruelty (to his daughter) ? Or, what cannot be suffered (lit.—done) by Rāma ?

मित–सम्बन्धेति।

अन्वयः–सम्बन्धस्पृहणीयताप्रमुदितै वशिष्ठादिभिः जुष्टे अपत्यविवाहमङ्गलमहे

तातयोः तत् सङ्गतं दृष्ट्वा ईदृशे महावैशसे वृत्ते ईदृशं पितृसखं पश्यन् किमहं सहस्राधा न दीर्ये ? अथवा रामेण किं दुष्करम् ?

व्याख्या–'सम्बन्धस्य' जनकानां रघूणाञ्च विवाहसम्बन्धस्य 'स्पृहणीयतया' प्रार्थनीयतया 'प्रमुदितैः' समधिकं हर्षमनुभवद्भिः वशिष्ठादिभिः' परमर्षिभिः 'जुष्टे' स्वोपस्थित्या सम्भाविते 'अपत्ययोः' मम न सीतायाश्च 'विवाहमङ्गलस्य महे' उत्सवे 'तातयोः' गुर्वोः जनकदशरथयोः 'तत्' आनन्दमयं 'सङ्गतं' समागमं 'दृष्ट्वा ईदृशे' एबंविधे 'महावैशसे' सीतानिधनरूपे घोरे घाते 'वृत्ते' जाते सति 'ईदृशम्' ईदृशीमवस्थां प्रपन्नं पितृसखं' पितुः सखायं तातजनकं 'पश्यन् किम अहं सहस्रधा ना दीर्ये' विदीर्णो न भवामि। 'अथवा' नैतदाश्चर्यम्। 'रामेण' वज्रयमेण 'किं दुष्करं' न किमपि। एतत् दृष्ट्वा अविदीर्णन देहेन अवस्थानं सुकरमेव तस्य।।

Notes. 1. सकरुणम्–etc.—कथं भगवन्ती etc. in uttered immediately on hearing what is said behind the scene. The party is not then within sight. Now they are all visible and the sight of Janaka deeply affects Rāma. 2. अत्रैव–Even here, *i.e.*, he is coming up to me. This is the first interview with these august personages after Sītā's exile. 3. सम्बन्ध etc.—Comp. 'जनकानां रघूणाञ्च सम्बन्धः कस्य न प्रियः'' (I, sl. 27). 4. दृष्ट्वा, पश्यन्–This is for contrast. I saw *that* and now seeing *this*. 5. वृत्ते महावैशसे–The वैशस was of my certain. I brought disunion in union. What was thought desirable by sages like Vaśiṣṭha was rendered most undesirable by my wicked self. 6. दीर्ये–दृ+लट्, कर्मकर्त्तरि। 7. रामेण etc.—रामोऽस्मि सर्वसहः। दुष्कर has खल कर्मणि। रामेण has अनुक्ते कर्त्तरि तृतीया because षष्ठी is barred by ''न लोकाव्ययनिष्ठास्वलर्थतृनान्''।

(xli) **नेपथ्ये–कष्टं कष्टम् !**

In the Tiring Room—Woe ! O Woe !

अनुभावमात्रसमुपस्थितश्रियं सहसैव वीक्ष्य रघुननाथमीदृशम्।
प्रथमप्रमूढ़जनकप्रबोधनाद्विधुराः प्रमोहमुपयान्ति मातरः ।। 41 ।।

After the reviving of Janaka, who fainted away first on suddenly beholding Raghunātha in this plight with beauty reduced to majesty only, the mothers distressed are falling into a swoon.

रामः–हा तात, हा मातरः, हा जनकः,

Rāma—Alas father ! Alas mother ! Alas Janaka.

जनकानां रघूणाञ्च यत् कृत्स्नं गोत्रमङ्गलम्।
तस्मिन्नकरुणे पापे वृथा वः करुणा मयि ।।42।।

Useless (misplaced) is your pity on me the sinner that was pitiless on what was the sum total of the blessings of the race of Janaka and Raghu.

यावत् सम्भावयामि। (इत्युत्तिष्ठति)।

Let me attend (upon). (Rises).

कुशलवौ–इत इतस्तातः।

Kuśa and Lava—This away, father, this way.

(इति सकरुणाकुलं परिक्रमय निष्क्रान्ताः सर्वे)।

(*Exeunt all walking with agitation and pathos*).

इति कुमारप्रत्यभिज्ञानो नाम षष्ठोऽङ्कः।

This is the Sixth Act named *Recognition of the princes.*

मित– । अनुभावेति।

अन्वयः–ईदृशम् अनुभावमात्रसमुपस्थितश्रियं रघुनाथं सहसैव वीक्ष्य प्रथमप्रमूढ़जनकप्रबोधनात् (परम) विधुराः मातरः प्रमोहम् उपयान्ति।

व्याख्या–'ईदृशम्' एतदवस्थम् 'अनुभावमात्रे' केवले महिम्नि 'समुपस्थितां पर्यवसिता 'श्री' कान्तिः यस्य तादृशं 'रघुनाथं सहसैव' अतिर्कितमेव 'वीक्ष्य' दृष्ट्वा 'प्रथम सर्वाग्रे 'प्रमूढ़स्य' मोहमुपगतस्य 'जनकस्य 'प्रबोधनात्' समाश्वासनात् परं 'विधुराः' शोकविह्वला 'मातरः प्रमोहम् उपयान्ति' विसंज्ञा भवन्ति।।'हा जनक' इति प्रक्षिप्तमिव प्रतिभाति।। जनकानामिति।

अन्वयः–सुगमः।

व्याख्या–सुगमा।'यत्' सीतारूपं वस्तु। पूर्वार्द्धं व्याख्यातं प्राक् प्रथमाङ्के।'पापे' पापिनि इत्यर्थः [पापशब्दात् मत्वर्थीयः अर्श आद्यच्] ।।'सम्भावयमि' समीपगमनेन सत्कारं करोमि इति भावः।।

Notes. 1. सहसैव–The एव may be taken either सहसा or वीक्ष्य। 2. प्रथम etc.—The sight distressed them all, but Janaka could not stand it at all. The mothers ran to his assistance. After he had revived, they were eased of apprehension on his account, but the sight of his emotion re-doubled their own distress and they too were falling into a swoon. 3. हा जनक–This seems to be an interpolation. Bare जनक is disrespectful coming from Rāma. Also हा तात is irrelevant now with reference to दशरथ। We believe the correct reading is हा तात, हा मातरः where तात refers to जनक and is mentioned first because it was he who fainted first and the voice behind the curtain mentions him first. 4. जनकानाम् etc.—See I, sl. 5. 5. सकरुणाकुलम्–आकुल perplexed. सकरुणञ्च आकुलञ्च यथा तथा। 6. कुमारप्रत्यभिज्ञानः–प्रत्यभिज्ञान is recognition. Though राम has still some doubts, the recognition of कुश and लव as his son is well-nigh complete.

सप्तमोऽङ्कः

(i) (ततः प्रविशति लक्ष्मणः)।

(*Then enters Lakṣmaṇa*).

लक्ष्मणः—भोः भोः। अध खलु भगवता वाल्मीकिना सब्रह्मक्षत्र-पौरजानपदाः प्रजाः सहास्माभिराहूय कृत्स्न एव सदेवासुरतिर्यगुरग-नायकनिकायो जङ्गमः स्थावरश्च भूतग्रामः स्वप्रभावेण सन्निधापितः। आदिष्टश्चाहमार्येण—वत्स लक्ष्मण, भगवता वाल्मीकिना स्वकृतिम-प्सरोभिः प्रयुज्यमानां द्रष्टुमुपनिमन्त्रिताः स्मः तत् गङ्गातीरम् आपोद्यस्थान-मुपगस्य क्रियतां समाजसन्निवेशः—इति। कृतश्च मर्त्यामर्त्तस्य भूतग्रामस्य समुचितस्थानेषु समुपवेशनं मया। अयञ्च—

Lak.—Ho ! Ho ! To-day by worshipful Vālmīki, after having summoned along with us the subject from the town and the country including Brāhmaṇas and Kshattriyas, even the entire world of creation, movable and immovable including the host of gods, demons and the leading Nagas, birds and beasts, has been caused to assemble through his spiritual power. And I am instructed by noble brothers—"Dear Lakṣmaṇa, we have been invited by worshipful Vālmīki to witness his own composition being staged by the celestial nymphs ; go then to the place of concert on the banks of the Ganges and get the audience seated". And the seating of all being mortal and immortal has been arranged for by me. And here,—

राज्याश्रमनिवासेऽपि प्राप्तकष्टमुनिव्रतः।

वाल्मीकिगौरवादार्य इत एवाभिवर्त्तते।। 1

Comes this very way, in deference to Vālmīki, my noble

brother who, though living in the hermitage of a kingdom, observes the rigorous vow of a hermit.

मित–। 'अद्य खलु भगवता वाल्मीकिना कृत्स्न एव भूतग्रामः' निखिला एव सृष्टिः स्वप्रभावेणा' आत्मनस्तपोबलेन 'सन्निधापितः' उपस्थापितः आश्रमं प्रापित इत्यर्थः। किम्भूतो भूतग्रामः ?–'जङ्गमः' चलः स्थावरश्च' अचलश्च अधिष्ठातृदेवतया। एवं कृत्स्नो भूतग्रामः। मन्ये जङ्गमेषु ये महान्तः तेषु तस्य प्रभावो न प्रसर्पति, ते नात्र समागताः–'देवासुरनिकायेन' देवदानवसमूहेन 'तिर्यगुरगनायकनिकायेन' नागेषु पशुपक्षिष च ये प्रधानं तेषामपि समूहेन 'सह' कृत्स्न एव भूतग्रामः। एत् एव किं यूयमपि इह प्राप्ताः ?–केनापि कारणेन, यत् स एव भगवान् जानाति, अस्माकम् अस्मत्प्रजानाञ्च पृथभाह्वानं कृतम्।'अस्माभिः सह सब्रह्मक्षत्रपौरजानपदाः प्रजाः आहूयं उपनिमन्त्र्य स्वप्रभावेण कृतस्न एव भूतग्रामः सन्निधापितः। स्वकृतिम्' आत्मना कृतं नाटकविशेषम्। 'प्रयुज्यमानाम्' अभिनीयमानाम्। 'आतोद्यस्थानं' वाद्यभूमिम। 'समाजसन्निवेशः' समागतानां प्रेक्षकाणमुपवेशनम्। 'मर्त्त्यस्य' मरणशीलस्य 'अमर्त्त्यस्य' चिरजीवनः।। राज्येति।

अन्वयः–राज्याश्रमनिवासे अपि प्राप्तकष्टमुनिव्रतः आर्यः वाल्मीकिगौरवात् इत एव अभिवर्तते।

व्याख्या–'राज्यपुरुषे आश्रमे' यो 'निवासः' स्थितिः तस्मिन् 'अपि प्राप्तम्' अनुभूतं 'कष्टं' क्लेशकरं 'मुनिव्रतं येन तथाविधः 'आर्यः' रामः 'वाल्मीकौ' यत् 'गौरवं' बहुमानः तस्मात् हेतोः न तु रङ्गदर्शनलालसया 'इत एव' इहैव आतोद्यस्थाने 'अभिवर्त्तते' आगच्छति।।

Notes. 1. खलु–This is here an expletive (वाक्यालङ्कारे)। "खलु स्याद्व्यक्यभूषाम्" इत्यादि विश्वमेदिन्यौ। 2. सब्रह्म etc.—ब्रह्मा ब्राह्मण जातिश्च क्षत्रं क्षत्रियजातिश्च ब्रह्मक्षत्रे। पौराश्च जानपदाश्च पौरजानपदाः। ब्रह्मक्षेत्राभ्यां सह सब्रह्मक्षत्राः। सब्रह्मक्षत्राः पौरजानपदाः। 3. आहूय–आह्वान here is निमन्त्रण। We have all been specially invited. Why this special treatment for us is more than I know. The staging was intended for Rāma and his subjects, the rest of the creation were to be witnesses only. Hence the difference in the treatment. 4. सदेवासुर etc.—निक्षीयते अस्निम् इति नि+चि+घञ् अधिकरणे निकायः a group. देवासुराश्च तिर्यगुरगनायकाश्च। तेषां निकायः समूहः देवासुरतिर्यगुरग–नायकनिकायः। तेन सह। Qual. भूतग्रामः। 5. भूतग्रामः–भूतानां समूह इति भूत+ग्रामच। This is by the Vārttika "गुणदिभ्यो ग्रामच् वक्तव्य' गुणादि being आकृतिगण। Certain lexicographers who come much later than Kātyāyana have ignored this Vārttika and taken राम as a प्रातिपदिक meaning समूह when final in a षष्ठी तत्पुरुष। Thus "शब्दादिपूर्वो वृन्देऽपि ग्रामः" इति हैमः। 6.

स्वप्रभावेण—No invitation was issued to these. 7. आतोद्यस्थानम्–आ सम्यक् तुद्यते ताड्यते इति आ+तुद+ण्यत् कर्मणि आतोद्यम् musical instruement. 8. राज्यश्रम etc.—The अपि in the verse is meaningless. If राज्य is an आश्रम then वष्टमुनिव्रत is expected. आश्रमनिवास is inseparable form मुनिव्रत। Thus अपि has no force. If we construe अपि with आर्यः, below, the criticism is avoided, thus राज्याश्रमनिवासे प्राप्तकष्टमुनिव्रतः आर्यः अपि etc. But the दूरान्वय becomes glaring in that case. Perhaps दूरान्वय is better than असङ्गति। राज्य is often identified with आश्रम। cp. "राज्याश्रममुनिं मुनिः"—*Raghu.*

(ii) (ततः प्रविशति रामः)।

(Then enters Rāma)

रामः–वत्स लक्ष्मण, अपि स्थिता रङ्गप्रेक्षकाः।

Rāma—Dear Lakṣmaṇa, are the spectators of the acting seated ?

लक्ष्मणः–अथ किम् ?

Lak.—What else ? (Yes)

रामः–इमौ पुनर्वत्सौ कुशलवौ चन्द्रकेतुसदृशीं स्थानप्रतिपत्तिं लम्भयितव्यौ।

Rāma—But these, two, dear Kuśa and Lava, have to be accorded the honour of seats like that of Candraketu.

लक्ष्मणः–प्रभुस्नेहप्रत्ययात् तथैव कृतम्। इदं तु आस्तीर्णं राजासनम्, उपविशत्वार्यः।

Lak.—That is just what has been doen by me from a knowledge of (lit.—through reliance : on) Master's affection (for them). Here again in the royal seat spread out, let my noble brother sit down.

रामः–(उपविशति)।

Rāma—(*Sit down*).

लक्ष्मणः–प्रस्तूयतां भोः।

Lak.—Let the play begin, ho !

मित– ।'रङ्गः' नृत्यम्। अत्र नृत्यमित्युपलक्षणं समग्रस्य अभिनयकर्मणः। तस्य 'प्रेक्षकाः'।"नृत्ये रणे खले रागे रङ्गः क्लीवे त्रपुण्यपि"इति त्रिकाण्डशेषः।'स्थिताः' आसीनाः।'स्थानस्य' आसनस्य 'प्रतिपत्तिः' गौरवम्। विशिष्टासनपरिग्रहात् यत् गौरवं तत्।'लम्भयितव्यौ' प्रापयितव्यौ।।'प्रभोः स्नेहः'। तस्मिन्।'प्रत्ययः' तस्मात्।।

Notes. 1. रङ्गः etc.—रज्यन्ते जना अस्मिन् इति रञ्ज+घञ् अधिकरणे रङ्गः dance; hence *music* in general. It also means the theatre and thence, by transference, the audience. Thus "आलिखित इव सर्वतो रङ्गः।"—*Śakuntala*. 2. लम्भयितव्यौ–लभ+णिच् तव्य कर्मणि। The roots is here गत्यर्थ। Hence, before णिच्—कुशलवौ (कर्त्ता) स्थानप्रतिपत्तिं लप्स्येते। Attaching णिच्—त्वं कुशलवौ (कर्म) स्थानप्रतिपत्तिं लम्भयिष्यसि। This is by the rule "गतिबुद्धि—। Changing the voice त्वया कुशलवौ (उक्तकर्म) स्थानप्रतिपत्तिं लम्भयिष्येते (=लम्भयितव्यौ)। See also our *Kirāt* I. sl. 15. and under "लम्भयेत्"—*Kirāt* XI. sl. 57.

(*iii*) (प्रविश्य) सूत्रधारः—भो भो भगवान् भूतार्थवादो प्राचेतसः सजङ्गमस्थावरं जगदाज्ञापयति–यदिदमस्माभिरार्षेण चक्षषा समुद्वीक्ष्य पावनञ्च करुणाद्भुतरसञ्च किञ्चिदुदनिबद्धं तत्र कार्यगौरवादवधातव्यम्—इति।

(Entering) Stage-Manager—Ho ! Ho ! The Worshipful Prācetasa, who speaks only of matters that are true, thus commands the world including the movable and the immovable—"Owing to gravity of the matter, attention has to be paid to that something which is sanctifying and at the same time marvellouos and pathetic in sentiment and which has been composed by my after having ascertained it with saintly vision."

रामः–एतदुक्तं भवति–साक्षात् कृतधर्माणो महर्षयः। तेषाममृतसाराणि परोरजांसि प्रज्ञानानि न क्वचिद्व्याहन्यते इत्यनभिशङ्कनीयानि–इति।

Rāma—This is what is being said—'The great seers have direct perception of the nature of things. Their knowledge transcends the range of passion, is immutalbe like nectar, is nowhere falsified, hence should never be doubted."

मित– ।'मूतार्थ' वदति' यः सः सत्यवचनः इत्यर्थः।'आर्षेण' ऋषिजनोचितेन

'चक्षुषा' न हि प्राकृतजनवत् चर्मक्षुषा। 'सम्यगुद्वीक्ष्य' वस्तूनामन्तस्लतमपि ज्ञानालोकेन दृष्ट्वा। 'करुणाः अद्भुतः' च द्वौ 'रसौ' यस्मिन् तत्। 'कार्यस्य' प्रस्तुतस्य कर्मणः 'गौरवात्' गुरुत्वात्। 'अवधातव्यम्' अवधानं कर्त्तव्यम्।। 'एतदुक्तं भवति' एष भगवद्वचनस्य निष्कर्षः। 'साक्षात्कृतः' ज्ञानमयेन चक्षुषा प्रत्यक्षीकृतः धर्मः' द्रव्यधर्मः वस्तुतत्वमित्यर्थः यैः ते। 'अमृतम्' इव 'साराणि' स्थिराणि अन्यन्यथाभावीनि इत्यर्थः। 'रजसः' कामादिकस्य 'पराणि' रजोगुणातीतानि शुद्धसत्वमयामि। 'प्रज्ञानानि' प्रकृष्ट-ज्ञानानि। 'व्याहन्यन्ते' अन्यथाभवति। 'अनभिशङ्कनीयानि' निःशङ्कं ग्राह्याणि। यदुच्यते महर्षिणा तत् सत्यं मन्यन्तां भवन्तः इति भावः।।

Notes. 1. भूतार्थ etc.—अर्थ is अभिषेच sense. भूत is सत्य true—"भूतं सत्योपमानयोः" इत्यादि हैमः। भूमतः अर्थः भूतार्थः true in its sense. भूतार्थ+वद+णिनि कर्त्तरि ताच्छील्ये। 2. समुद्वीक्ष्य—Having fully observed, throughly examined etc. 3. साक्षात् etc.—धर्म is स्वभाव nauture "धर्म पुण्ये यमे न्याये स्वभावाचारयोः क्रतौः" इत्यादि विश्वः। साक्षात् is प्रत्यक्ष directly preceived. An अव्यय। असाक्षात् साक्षात् सम्पद्यमानः कृतः इत्यर्थे साक्षात्+कृ+क्त कर्मणि साक्षात्कृतः, गतितत्—। Now see Tika. 4. अमृत etc.—सारयन्ति कालमतिवाहयन्ति इति मृ+णिच् कर्त्तरि साराणि that which defies time, imperishable; immutable etc. Now see Tika. 5. परोजांसि—Those that are beyond the sphere of action of रजोगुण, *i.e.*, untainted by passion and prejudices. Comp. also. परःसहस्राः (I, sl. 15). 6. प्रज्ञानानि—प्रकृष्टानि ज्ञानानि प्रज्ञाननि insight.

(iv) **नेपथ्ये—हा अज्जउत्त हा कुमार लक्खण एआदणिं मन्दभाइणिं असरणं अस्णेआसणप्पसववेअणं हदासं साबदा मं अहिलसन्ति। ता दाणीं मन्दभाइणी भाईरहीए अत्ताणअं निक्खिवेमि [हा आर्यपुत्र, हा कुमार लक्ष्मण, एकाकिनीं मन्दभागिनीम् अशरणाम् अरण्ये आसन्नप्रसव-वेदनां हताशां श्वापदा माम् अभिलषयन्ति। तदिदानीं मन्दभागिनी भागीरथ्यामात्मानं निक्षिपामि]।**

In the Tiring Room—Alas, husband ! Alas, prince Lakṣmaṇa ! Beasts of prey of longing after me, the ill-starred, alone as I am in this wilderness without a protection with the final throes near and with all hopes gone. I shall therefore, luckless I am, throw myself into the Bhāgīrathī.

लक्ष्मणः (आत्मगतम्)—कष्टं वत अन्यदेव किमपि।

Lak. (*To himself*)—O woe ! Alas ! This is indeed something quite different.

सूत्रधारः–

विश्वम्भरात्मजा देवी राज्ञा त्यक्ता महावने।
प्राप्तप्रसवमात्मनं गङ्गादेव्यां विमुञ्चति ।। 2।।
(इति निष्क्रान्तः)।

Manager—The queen, the daughter of Viśvambharā (Earth), abandoned by the king in deep forest, throws herself into the divine Ganges with the pangs of delivery on. *(Exit)*.

मित–। 'हता' गता 'आशा' जीविताशा यस्याः ताम्। 'वत' इत्यव्ययं खेदे। 'अन्यत्' यत् परिचिन्तितमत्माभिः ततो भिन्नम्। विश्वेति।।

अन्वयः–राज्ञा महावने त्यक्ता विश्वरम्भरात्माज देवी प्राप्तप्रसवम् आत्मानं गङ्गादेव्या विमुञ्चति।

व्याख्या–सुगमा। 'विश्वम्भरां' इति साभिप्रायम्। परिरेव पत्नीं भरति। इयन्तु पत्या त्यक्ता। समया पुनरस्य माता विश्वमेव भरति। तथापि इयं भरणकर्त्तारमलभमाना हताशा आत्मानं जले पातयति इत्यभिप्रायः।।

Notes. 1. हताशाम्म—She has lost all hope. Her husband had abandoned her, her mother, though close by, takes no notice of her. Who else would save her ? None. Hence in despair (हताशा) she says भागीरथ्यामात्मानं निक्षिपामि। 2. विश्वम्भरा etc.—विश्वं विभर्त्ति इति विश्व+भृ+खच् कर्त्तरि स्त्रियां विश्वम्भरा the all-sustainer, *i.e.*, the earth. Now see Ṭīkā. 3. गङ्गादेव्याम्—Taken along with भागीरथ्यामात्मानं निक्षिपामि above, the देवी seems misplaced. देवीत्व should be in the back-ground and नदीत्व made prominent, गङ्गाम्भसि seems to serve the purpose.

(*v*) **रामः–हा देवि, हा देवि, लक्ष्मण अवेक्षस्व।**

लक्ष्मणः–आर्य, नाटकमिदम्।

रामः–हा देवि दण्डकारण्यवासप्रियसखि, एष ते रामात् दैबदुर्विपाकः।

लक्ष्मणः–आर्य दृश्यतां तावत् प्रबन्धार्थः।

रामः–एष सज्जोऽस्मि वज्रमयः।

(ततः प्रविशति उत्सङ्गितैकैदारकाभ्यां पृथ्वीभागीरथीभ्याम् अवलम्बिता सीता)

रामः–वत्स लक्ष्मण, असंविज्ञातमनिबन्धमन्धतमसमिव प्रविशामि धारय माम्।

Rama—Ha, my Queen ! Ha, my Queen ! Lakshmana, go and see.

Lak.—Noble brother, this is a play.

Rāma—Alas Queen ! Dear companion of my sojourn in the forest of Daṇḍaka, such has been evil turn of fortune through Rāma.

Lak.—Noble brother, first see the matter of the composition.

Rāma—Here, my adamantine self is ready.

(Then enters Sītā supported by Pṛthvī and Bhāgīrathī with a boy in the lap of each).

Rāma—Dear Lakṣmaṇa, hold me I am as if entering a blinding gloom, unaccountable (अनिबन्धनम्) and never before experienced(असंविज्ञातम्)।

मित–।'अवेक्ष्स्व' पश्य।द्रतुं गच्छ कालोचितञ्च कुरु इत्यर्थः।'दैवस्य' भाग्यस्य 'दुर्विपाकः' विषमः परिणामः। 'तावत्' इत्यव्ययमवधौ। प्रथमं 'प्रवन्धस्य' अभिनीयमानस्य काव्यस्य 'अर्थः' वस्तु 'दृश्यतां' पश्चात् विचारस्य शुभं जातम् अशुभं वा।। 'उत्सङ्गितः' क्रीड़े कृतः 'एकैकः दारकः' बालः याभ्यां ताभ्याम्।। 'असंविज्ञातम्' अननुभूतपूर्वम्' 'अनिबन्धनम्' अज्ञातकारणम्।।

Notes. 1. दण्डकारण्य etc.—Comp. महारण्यवासप्रियसखि, Act I, para lxv. 2. तावत्—Here it means अवधि time-limit. 'यावत् तावच्च साकल्येऽवधौ मानेऽवधारणे'' इत्यमरः। The time-limit is still the acting is over. 3. उत्सङ्गित etc.—एकः एकः एकैकः। वीत्सायां द्विरुक्तिः। बहुव्रीहिवद्भावः। Now See Ṭīkā. 4. असंविज्ञातम्–सम्यक् विज्ञातमिति सम्+वि+ज्ञा+क्त कर्मणि। न तथा। I have never experienced this sort of thing before. 5. अनिबन्धनम्–निवध्यते अनेन इति नि+बन्ध+ल्युट् करणे निबन्धनम् cause. अविद्यमाणं निबन्धनमस्य etc. I do not know whence it comes. 6. अन्धतमसम्–अन्धं तमः इति अन्ध+तमस्+अच् समासान्त by the rule ''अवसमन्धेभ्यस्तमसः''। This emotion is owing to the sudden apparition of सीता।

(*vi*) **देव्यौ—** **समाश्वसिहि कल्याणि दिष्ट्या वैदेहि वर्द्धसे।**
अन्तर्जलं प्रसूतासि रघुवंशधरौ सुतौ ।।3।।

Goddesses—Blessed Vaidehi, be composed, luckily you prosper. Under water you are delivered of two boys, the upholders of the race of Raghu.

सीता (समाश्वस्य)—दिट्ठिआ दारए पसूद म्हि। हा अज्जउत्त [दिष्ट्या दारकौ प्रसूतास्मि। हा आर्यपुत्र]। (इति मूर्च्छति)।

Sītā (*Recovering*)—Luckily I am delivered of two boys ! Alas, husband ! (*faints away*).

लक्ष्मणः—(पादयोर्निपत्य)—आर्य दिष्ट्या वर्द्धामहे, कल्याणअरोहो रघुवंशः। (विलोक्य) हा हा कथं क्षुभितवाष्पोत्पीड़निर्भरः प्रमुग्ध एवार्यः। (इति वीजयति)।

Lak. (*Falling at the feet*)—Noble brother, luckily do we prosper. Raghu's race has now got blessed offshorts. (Observing) Alas ! Alas ! How so ! Powerless under an outbrust of tears that have been stirred, my noble brother has indeed fainted away. (*Fans him*)

मित—। समाश्वसिहीति।

अन्वयः—कल्याणि वैदेहि समाश्वसिहि, दिष्ट्या वर्द्धसे। अन्तर्जलं रघुवंशधरौ सुतौ प्रसूता असि।

व्याख्या—सुगमा।'अन्तर्जलं' जले। विभक्तार्थेऽव्ययीभावः।। आर्यपुत्रेण न दृष्टौ दारकौ इति दुःखेन प्राह 'हा आर्यपुत्र' इति।।'कल्याणः' मङ्गलमयः 'प्ररोहः' अङ्कुरः अस्य।'क्षुभितः' उद्वेलः यः 'वाष्पीत्पीड़ः' अश्रुप्रवाहः तेन 'निर्भरः' विह्वलः।'प्रमुग्धः' प्रमोहं गतः।।

Notes. 1. अन्तर्जलम्—A नित्यसमाससमास of the अव्यायोभाव class. The constituent are अन्तर्, an अन्तर्, an अव्यय meaning मध्ये, and जल। But the वाक्य must be अस्वपद, *i.e.,* it must not contain *both* अन्तर् and जल। Hence say जले इति अनतर्जलम् or अन्तर्जले। 2. हा आर्यपुत्र—Comp. "किं वा मया प्रसूतया...न परिचुम्बितमार्यपुत्रेण।"—Act III. 3. कल्याणप्ररोहकः etc.—This explains the joy of लक्ष्मण। It has been so long a permanent source of grief to Rāma's three brothers that with Rāma's loss of progeny the direct line of the kings of the solar race goes unrepresented. Comp. 'अप्रतिष्ठे रघुज्येष्ठे का प्रतिष्ठा कुलस्य नः।" etc., Act V, sl. 25.

(vii) पृथ्वी–वत्से समाश्वसिहि समाश्वसिहि।

Pṛthvī—Take heart, my child, take heart.

सीता (आश्वस्य)–भअवदि का तुमं इअं अ [भगवति का त्वम् इयञ्च]।

Sītā (*Coming round*)—Worshipful lady, who are you and this one ?

पृथ्वी–इयं ते श्वशुरकुलदेवता भागीरथी।

Pṛthvī—This is Bhāgīrathī the guardian deity of your father-in-a-law's house.

सीता–भअवदि णमो दे [भगवति, नमस्ते]।

Sītā—Salutation to thee, worshipful (deity).

भागीरथी–चारित्रोपचितां कल्याणप्तम्प्रदमधिगच्छ।

Bhāg—May you attain the profusion of belssings earned by your character.

लक्ष्मणः–अनुगृहीता स्मः।

Lak.—We are favoured.

भागीरथी–इयं ते जननी वसुन्धरा।

Bhāg.—This is your mother Vasundharā.

सीता–हा अम्ब एरिसी अहं तुए दिट्ठा [हा अम्ब, ईदृशी अहं त्वया दृष्टा]।

Sītā—Alas mother ! I am seen by thee in this plight !

पृथ्वी–एहि वत्से एहि पुत्रि। (इति सीतामालिङ्ग्य मूर्च्छति)।

Pṛthvī—Come darling ! Come daughter ! (Faints having embraced Sītā).

मित–।'चारित्रं' चरित्रं पातिब्रत्यादिभिः पूतं शीलम् ! तेन 'उपचितां' वर्द्धिताम् अर्जितामित्यर्थः।'कल्याणानां' मङ्गलानां 'सम्पत्' राशिः ताम्।

Notes. 1.अनुगृहीता :–अनु+ग्रह+क्त कर्मणि। Favoured. They were favoured, for Sītā's attainment of कल्याणसम्पद् through चारित्र will give them scope to take back Sītā. Thus Bhāgīrathī's uttering was hailed by Lakṣmaṇa—the spectator. See also next para.

(viii) **लक्ष्मणः (सहर्षम्)–दिष्ट्या पृथ्वीभागीरथीभ्यामभ्युपपन्ना आर्या ।**

Lak. (*With joy*)—O luck : Noble sister has been succoured by Pṛthvī and Bhāgīrathī.

रामः (अवलोक्य)–करुणतरं खल्वेतद्वर्त्तते ।

Rāma *(Observing)*—This is really supremely pathetic.

भागीरथी–विश्वम्भरापि नाम व्यथते इति जितमपत्यस्नेहेन ! यद्वा सर्वसाधरणो ह्येष मोहग्रन्थिरन्तरश्चेतनावतामनुपप्लवः संसारतन्तुः ।

Bhāg—Maternal affection has triumphed,for even Viśvambharā grieves. Or rather this unseverable bond of delusion—a chain to the world that operates on the heart of sentient beings—is common to all. Cheer up, child Vaidehi, goddess Bhūtadhātri, cheer up.

वत्से वैदेहि (?), देवि भूतधात्रि, समाश्वसिहि समाश्वसिहि ।

Pṛthvī (*Having recovered*)—Goddess, how can I cheer up after having given birth to Sītā ?

पृथ्वी (आश्वस्य)–देवि, सीतां प्रसूय कथमाश्वसिमि ?

एकश्चिरं राक्षसमध्यवासस्त्यगोद्वितीयश्च सुदुःसहोस्याः । (4–)

First her long stay in the midst of Rākṣasas ; second the abandonment ; both are extremly unbearable (to me).

भागीरथी–

को नाम पाकाभिमुखस्य जन्तोर्द्वाराणि दैवस्य पिधातुमीष्टे ।।4 ।।

Bhāg.—Who ever can close the gates of the fate of a creature when it is about to mature ?

मित– । 'अभ्युपपन्ना' अनुगृहीता साहायेन इति शेषः।। 'करुणतरम्' अतिकरुणम्।। 'एषः अनुपप्लवः' अभेद्यः 'मोहग्रन्थिः' मायाबन्धनं 'चेतनावतां' प्राणभृताम् 'अन्तश्चरः' हृदये व्यापारवान् 'संसारतन्तुः' संसारिणां बन्धनरज्जुः 'सर्वसाधरणो हि' अतएव विश्वम्भरापि व्यथते।। 'सीतां प्रसूय' तस्याः सुदुःसहेन दुःखेन पीड़िता 'कथमाश्वसिमि'। एक इति।

अन्वयः–अस्याः चिरं राक्षसमध्यवासः एकः, त्यागश्च द्वितीयः सुदुः सहः।

व्याख्या–'अस्याः' सीतायाः 'चिरं' दीर्घकालं 'राक्षसानां मध्ये वासः एकः' सुदुःसहः क्षोभो मम 'त्यागश्च भर्त्रा 'द्वितीयः' सुदुःसहः क्षोभः। कथमाश्वसिमि।।

अन्वयः–जन्तोः पाकभिमुखस्य दैवस्य द्वाराणि पिधातुं को नाम ईष्टे।

व्याख्या–'जन्तोः' प्राणिनः 'पाकभिमुखस्य' आसन्नपरिपाकस्य 'दैवस्य' नियतेः 'द्वाराणि' मार्गान 'पिधातुः' रोद्धुं 'को नाम ईष्टे' प्रभववति। न करोऽपि। सीताया भाग्याधीनं सवे जातम् अलमनुशोचनया।।

Notes. 1. दिष्ट्या etc.—लक्ष्मण is glad that Sītā is helped by Pṛthvī and Bhāgīrathī. Thus they had hopes of their कुलप्रतिष्ठा in Lava and Kuśa. 1. a. करुणतरम्–Pathetic because this happens while I am living and reigning. The stage-direction is defective. Rāma is in a swoon ("प्रमुग्ध एवार्यः"–para vi). Better say आश्वस्य अवलोक्य। 2. जितम्–जि here mens either उत्कर्षप्राप्ति or अभिभव। *Trans*—'has trimphed' or 'rules supreme'. 3. वत्से वैदेहि–This again in defective. Sītā has already recovered (see para vii, सीता आश्वस्य etc.).

(ix) **पृथ्वी–भागीरथि, सृदशमुक्तम्। युक्तमेतद्वा रामभद्रस्य ?**

Pṛthvī—Well said (lit. Suitably replied), Bhāgīrathī. For Rāmabhadra agains, has this been proper ?

न प्रामणीकृतः पाणिर्बाल्ये बालेन पीड़ितः।
नाहं न जनको नाग्निर्नानुवृर्त्तिने सन्ततिः ।। 5 ।।

No heed was paid to the hand taken in childhood by the child, nor to myself, nor to Janaka, nor or Fire, nor to devoted following, not to progeny.

सीता–हा अज्जउत्तं सुमराविदम्हि [हा आर्यपुत्रं स्मारितास्मि]।

Sītā—Alas ! I am reminded of husband.

पृथ्वी–आः कस्तवार्यपुत्रः ?

Pṛthvī—Who is thy husband, hey ?

सीता (सलज्जास्त्रम्)–जहा वा अम्बा भणादि [यथा वा अम्बा भणति]।

Sītā (*With shame and tears*)—Or (it is really) as mother says.

रामः–अम्ब पृथ्वि, ईदृशोऽस्मि।

Rāma—Mother Pṛthvī, so have I become.

भागीरथी–भगवति वसुन्धरे, शरीरमसि संसारस्य, तत् किमसंविदानेव जामात्रे कुप्यासि ?

Bhāg.—Worshipful Vasundharā, you are the body of this world, they why, as if in ignorance, are you angry with your son-in-law ?

घोरं लोके विततमयशो या च वह्नौ विशुद्धि-
र्लङ्काद्वीपे कथमिव जनस्तामिह श्रद्दधातु।
इक्ष्वाकूणां कुलधनमिदं यत् समाराधनीयः
कृत्स्नो लोकस्तदतिगहनं किं स वत्सः करोतुः ।।6।।

A dire infamy had spread among the people. How indeed could people here have faith in the purification in fire that happened in the island of Laṅkā ? The treasure of the race of Ikṣvāku is that people have allto be served. That is very hard task ; what could that child do ?

तथाप्येष तेऽञ्जलिः।

Still here is my fold of plams (Or—here are my palms folded) to you.

मित–।मेति।

अन्वयः–बाल्ये बालेन पीड़ितः पाणिः न प्रामणीकृतः, न अहम्, न जनकः, न अग्निः, न अनुवृत्तिः, न सन्ततिः।

व्याख्या–सीतापरित्यागे 'बाल्ये बालेन पीड़ित' परिणयविधौ गृहीतः 'पाणिः' सीतायाः करः 'न प्रमाणीकृतः' कर्त्तव्यनिर्णतृत्वेन न चिन्तितः। बाल्यादियं मे सहचारिणौ, ह्रदयमस्या जानामि नेयं परित्यागमर्हति इत्येव मन्तव्यं स्यादित्यर्थः। 'न अहं' पृथिवी प्रमाणीकृता। नरचितसाक्षिणी अहमपि न पृष्टा सीता त्याज्या न वा इति। 'न जनकः' श्वशुरः प्रमाणीकृतः। 'न अग्निः' नरचरितसाक्षी वह्निरपि न प्रमाणीकृतः। 'न अनुवृत्तिः' वनेऽपि सहगमनम्। न सन्ततिः' गर्भस्था प्रजा प्रमाणीकृता। अस्या विनाशे सन्ततिलोपः स्यात् तत् नेयं त्याज्या इत्येव मन्तव्यं स्यात्।। 'कस्तव आर्यपुत्रः' विधवा इव अनाथसि इत्यर्थः।। 'शर्रारम स सांरस्य' अतएव सर्वं जानासि तथापि 'असंविदाना' अनाजतौ 'इव किं कुप्यसि'।

अन्वयः–लोके घोरम् अयशवितितम्। या च लङ्काद्वीपे वह्नौ विशुद्धिः ताम् इह कथं जनः श्रद्दधातु। इदम इक्ष्वाकूणां कुलधनं यत् कृत्स्नो लोकः समाराधनीयः। तत् अतिगहमम्। स वत्सः किं करोतु।

व्याख्या–'लोके' जगति 'घोरम् अयशो विततम्' प्रमृतम्। ननु वह्नौ विशुद्धासा कथमयशः इत्याह–'या च' या पुनः दूरे 'लङ्काद्वीपे वल्हौ विशुद्धिः ताम्' तस्याम् 'इह' अयोध्यायां 'कथं जनः श्रद्दधातु' विश्वसितु। इत्थं सति अविश्वासे किं कर्त्तव्यमित्याह 'इदम् इक्ष्वाककूणां' रघूणां 'कुलस्य धनं' सर्वस्वभूतं 'यत् कृत्स्नः लोकः' 'निखिलाः प्रकृतयः 'समाराधनीयः' रञ्जनीयः। 'तत्' सर्वलोकरञ्जनम् 'अतिगहनं सुदुष्करम्। 'स वत्सः' रामः 'किं करोतु' सुकरं नान्यत् किञ्चिदासीत् येन सर्वलोकरञ्जनं स्यात्, दुष्करमपि सीतापरित्यागमेवाकरोत्।।

Notes. 1. नाहम्–This is because of two reasons. First she is Rāma's mother-in-law ; second because the Earth is one of the witnesses who see all that people do. Comp. "आदित्यचन्द्रावनिलोऽनलश्च द्यौर्भूमिरापो हृदयं यमश्च। अहश्च रात्रिश्च उभे च सन्ध्ये धर्मश्च जानाति नरस्य वृत्तम्"।। 2. आर्यपुत्रं स्मारिता—For grammer see under तमेव स्मारिता वयम्, VI, sl. 34. 3. कस्तवार्यपुत्रः–You have no longer a husband now. Forget that you bad one. 4. असंविदाना–सम+विद+शानच् कर्त्तरि संविदाना aware. It is used intransitively (no कर्मविवक्षा), hence the आत्मनेपद by "सभो गम्यच्छि-प्रच्छिस्वरत्यर्तिश्रुविदिभ्यः"।5. जामात्रे–"क्रियाग्रहणमपि कर्त्तव्यम्" इति सम्प्रदाने चतुर्थी as in पत्ये शेते। "क्रुधद्रुहेर्ष्यासूयार्थानां यं प्रति कोपः" does not apply. If it did, Pāṇini would have written यस्मै कोपः" 6. तामिह etc.—श्रत् is an अव्यय meaning भक्ति। It is treated like an उपसर्ग। Hence श्रत्+घ+लोट तु। श्रत् is the कर्म of धा, consequently ताम् here is irregular ; should be तस्याम्।7. तथापि etc.—Gaṅgā tries to appease her wrath.

(*x*) **लक्ष्मणः–अब्याहतान्तःप्रकाशा हि देवता भूतेषु विशेषेण गङ्गा।**

Lak.—In the matter of beings gods, especially Gaṅgā, are of unfailing inner illumination (*'i.e.'* they see everythig in its proper light).

रामः–अम्ब अनुवृत्तस्त्वया भागीरथगृहे प्रसादः।

Rāma—Mother, unceasing has been thy favour to the house of Bhāgīrathī.

पृथ्वी–देवि नित्यं प्रसन्नास्मि वः, किन्त्वापातदुःसहः शोकावेगः अपत्यस्य, न पुनर्न जानामि सीतास्नेहं रामभद्रस्य।

Pṛthvī—Goddess, I am always gracious towards (those that are) your own ; but the shock of an offspring's grief is hard to withstand at the time of the visitation. It is, however, not that I do not know of Rāmabhadra's love for Sītā.

दह्यमानेन मनसा दैबाद्वत्सां विहाय सः।
लोकोत्तरेण धैर्येण प्रजा पुण्यैश्च जीवति ।। 7 ।।

He, having abadoned my darling through fate, lives, with a burning heart, though his superhuman fortitude and the merits of his subjects.

रामः–सकरुणा हि गुरवो गर्भरूपेषु।

Rāma—Superiors are indeed kind to those that are like children unto them.

मित–।'अव्याहतः' अप्रतिहितः 'अन्तः' मध्ये मनसि इत्यर्थः 'प्रकाशः' स्फुरणं यस्याः सा। यद्वा–अव्याहतः' अनन्यथाभूतः 'अन्तस्थितिस्य' भूतमनीगतस्य 'प्रकाशे:' स्फुरणं यस्याः सा। या हि भूतानां मनोगतं तत्त्वतः पश्यति सा इत्यर्थः।। 'अनुवृत्तः' सातत्येन दर्शितः। उपसर्गवशात् वृतिः सकर्मकः।। 'नित्यं प्रसन्नास्मि वः' युष्मभ्यम् अञ्जलिबन्धनं बाहुल्यमेव ते। 'आपाते' आविर्भावकाले 'दुःसहः'। दह्यमानेनेति।

अन्वयः–दैवात् वत्सां विहाय दह्यमानेन मनसाः सः लोकोत्तरेण धैर्यण प्रजापुण्येश्च जीवति।

व्याख्या–'दैवात्' दैवकृतात् दुर्योगात् हेतोः 'वत्सां' सीतां 'विहाय' परित्यज्य 'दह्यमानेन' साक्षात् दाहसिव अनुभवता 'मनसा' सह, सत्यपि मरणकारणे इत्यर्थः 'स' रामभद्रः 'लोकोत्तरेण' अलौकिकेन 'धैर्येण' धीरतया हेतोः 'प्रजानां पुण्यैश्च' हेतुभिः। 'जीवति'।। 'गर्भः' अपत्यम्। 'गर्भः रूपम्' आकृतिः येषां तेषु विषये। पुत्रतुल्योऽहम् यस्या अतोऽनुकम्पते मां भगवती पृथ्वी इत्यर्थः।।

Notes. 1. अव्याहत etc.—For समास see टीका। They look within themselves (प्रणिधान) and have not to seek information outside like ordinary mortals. Their inner self is then illumined (अन्तः प्रकाश) and reveals to them whatever they want to know. Comp. "सोऽपश्यत् प्रणिधानेन सन्ततिस्तम्भकारणम्। भावितात्मा भुवो भर्त्तुरथैनं प्रत्यबोधयत्।।" *Raghu*. This is said because गङ्गा has spoken the truth. How could she know? She knew unerringly (अव्याहत) by प्रणिधान all that passed within Rāma when he abandoned सीता। 2. देवि नित्यम्–etc.—This is because भागीरथी has folded her palms to win prithvi's favour. Why supplication ? I am always pleased with you all. 3. आपात etc.—The शोकावेग of the अपत्य is दु:सह to the mother. Sītā weeps (शोकावेग) ; how can I bear it? 3. दश्चमानेन etc.—All this happended within a few hours of her exile. Hence "He is being consumed with grief ; merits of his people have kept him alive, etc." are, to say the least, premature at this stage.

(*xi*) सीता (रुदती कृताञ्जलिः)–णेदुमं अत्तणो अङ्गेसु विलअं अम्बा [नयतु मामात्मनः अङ्गेषु विलयम् अम्बा]

Sītā (Weeping—With palms joined)—Let mother lead me to mergence in her limbs.

रामः–किमन्यद्ब्रवीतु।

Rāma—What else could she say ?

भागीरथ–शान्तम् । अविलीना संवत्सरसहस्त्रं भूयाः।

Bhāg.—Peace ! Mayest thou be not extinct for a thousand years !

पृथ्वी–वत्से तावपेक्षणीयौ ते पुत्रौ।

Pṛthvī—Really, my child, my regard for your infants.

सीता–अणाध म्हि किं एदेहिं [अनाथास्मि किमेताभ्याम्]।

Sītā—I am helpless without a protector myself, what is the use of these ?

रामः–हृदय वज्रमयमसि।

Rāma—You are all adamant, oh heart.

भागीरथी–कथं त्वं सनाथाप्यनाथा।

Bhāg.—How having a husband, are you without a protector.

सीता–केरिसं मम अभवाए सणाधत्तणं [कीदृशं मम अभव्यायाः सनाथत्वम्]।

Sītā—What like is this possession of a husband for me the inauspicioius ?

देव्यौ– जगन्मङ्गलमात्मानं कथं त्वमवमन्यसे।
आवयोरपि यत् सङ्गात् पवित्रत्वं प्रकृष्यते ।। 8 ।।

Goddesses—Why do you despise your own self that is auspicious to the whole world through contact with which the purity even of us is enhanced ?

मित–। 'विलयः' अदृश्यता, विनाश इत्यर्थः।। 'अपेक्षणीयौ' चिन्तनीयौ। आत्मार्थे अन्यार्थे वा यदि नास्ति जीवितस्पृहा तथापि अपत्यार्थे अविलयो वाञ्छनीयस्ते इति भावः।।'अनाथा' अशरणा ? आत्मानमपि रक्षितुमशक्ताहम् अपत्यार्थे नास्ति मे अपेक्षा।। 'अभव्यायाः' अलक्षणायाः। सुलक्षणहि पतिसौभाग्यवती भवति अहं तु अलक्षणा। तन्नास्ति मे भर्त्रततीत्वम्।। जगदिति।

अन्वयः–जगन्मङ्गलमात्मानं–यत्सङ्गात् आवयोरपि पवित्रत्वं प्रकृष्यते–कथं त्वम् अवमन्धसे।

व्याख्या–'जगतां मङ्गलं' मङ्गलकरं भव्यजननम् 'आत्मानं यस्य' आत्मानः 'सङ्गात्' साहचर्यात् 'आवयो रपि पवित्रयोरपि 'परित्रत्वं प्रकृष्यते' प्रकर्ष लभते तादृशम् आत्मानं 'कथं त्वम् अवमन्यसे' अभव्या इति गर्हसे।।

Notes. 1. अङ्गेषु विलयम् etc.—Reminds of the विलय of सृष्टि in Brahman. विलय regression. 2. किमन्यत् etc.—Her regression into Earth, her orginal source, in the only proper things of rher now. 3. अपेक्षणीयी etc.,—For the sake of the infants at least you should avoid regression. Affection for the infants ought to hold you on the land of the living. The reading अवेक्षणीयौ implies the question—"Who is to guard your infants in your absence ?" This is reasily answered saying "you two will do it". But अपेक्षणीयौ raises a real difficulty with regard to पुत्र, and has to be preferred. 4. अभव्यायाः–भवतीति भूरुयत् कर्त्तरि भव्यम् blessing. तत् अस्ति अस्या इति भव्य+अच् भत्वर्थे भव्या blessed, auspicious. न भव्या अभव्या inauspicious. The current reading is मन्दभागिन्या। But मन्दभागिनी (unlucky) is not a निन्दा, while अभव्या certainly implies निन्दा। The verse following that अभव्या is the better reading. Desprecation of self should always, be avoided, especailly in your case, cp. "नात्मानमवसादयेत्"–*Gītā*. 5. जगन्मङ्गलम्–You bring belssings to the worlds, you cannot be अभव्या। 6. प्रकृष्यते–प्र+कृष+लट् ते कर्मकर्त्तरि or कर्मणि।

(xii) **लक्ष्मणः–आर्य श्रूयताम्।**

Lak.—Hear, my noble brother.

रामः–शृणोतु लोकः।

Rāma—Let the people hear.

(नेपथ्ये कलकलः)

(*A hubbub in the tiring room*)

रामः—अद्भुततरं किमपि।

Rāma—Somethings very stange (perhaps).

सीता—किं त्ति सअलं अन्तरिक्खं पज्जलदि [किमिति सकलमन्तरीक्षं प्रज्वलति]।

Sītā—Why is it that the whole vault of heaven is ablaze ?

देव्यौ—ज्ञातम् !

Goddesses—Found !

कृशाश्वः कौशिको राम इति येषां गुरुक्रमः।
आविर्भवन्ति तान्येव शस्त्राणि मह जृम्भकैः ।। 9 ।।

These very weapons including the Jrimbhakas, in the matter of which Kṛśāśva, Kauśaśva, Rāma are the gurus in or, do now make their appearance.

नेपथ्ये— देवि सीते नमस्तेऽस्तु गतिर्नः पुत्रकौ हि ते।
आलेख्यदर्शने देवो यथाह रघुनन्दनः ।।10 ।।

In the Tiring Room—Salutation be to thee, Queen Sītā. Your sons are, to be our destination as king Raghunandan had commanded while inspecting the picture.

मित—। 'अद्भुततरम्' अत्यद्भुतम्। यद्वा—अद्भुतं दृष्टं ततोऽद्भुतं दृष्टव्यम् इत्यतिशायने तरप्।। कृशाश्व इति।

अन्वयः—क्रशाश्वः कौशिकः रामः इति येषां गुरुक्रमः तान्येव शस्त्राणि सह प्रादुर्भवन्ति।

व्याख्या—'कृशाश्वः कौशिकः रामः इति येषां गुरुक्रमः' आचार्यपरम्परा 'तान्येव शस्त्राणि जृम्भकैः सह प्रादुर्भवन्ति प्रकटीभवन्ति। तेषामेव भासा अन्तरीक्षं ज्वलति।। देवीति। सुगमम्।।

Notes. 1. शृणोतु लोकः—I stand in no need to hear. I never doubted Sītā's purity. It is the people (लोकः), her calumniators, who should listen. 2. अन्तरीक्षम्—अन्तः मध्ये स्वर्गमर्त्ययोः मध्ये ईक्ष्यते इअि अन्तर्+ईक्ष+घञ् कर्मणिर अन्तरीक्षम् the sky. 3. प्रज्वलति—Sītā is startled. 4. गुरुक्रम—गुरुणाम् उपदेष्टणाम्

क्रमः परम्परा। 5. देवि सीते etc.—As already remarked under act VI, चित्रदर्शनप्रस्तावे अस्त्राभ्यनुज्ञानम् etc., the appearance of the weapons is not satisfactorily explained. गति is आश्रय resort, that which is reached. गम्यते इयम् इति गम्+क्तिन् कर्मणि।

(xiii) **सीता—दिट्ठिआ अत्थेदेअदाओ प्फुरन्दि [दिष्ट्या अस्त्रदेवताः स्फुरन्ति]।**

Sītā—Luckily it is the divine weapons a-glow.

लक्ष्मणः—उक्तमासीदार्येण ''सर्वथेदानीं त्वत्प्रसूतिमुपस्थास्यन्ति'' इति।

Lak.—It was declared by my noble brother—"They will now certainly serve your children."

देव्यौ— नमो वः परमास्त्रेभ्यो राघवस्य परिग्रहात्।
अनुध्यातैरुपेतव्यं वत्सयोर्भद्रमस्तु वः ।।11।।

Goddesses—Salutation to you the best of weapons from Rāghava's wife. You have to appear unto these dear boys when though of (Now) let blessings attend upon you.

रामः— क्षुभिताः कामपि दशां कुर्वन्ति मम साम्प्रतम्।
विस्म्नयानन्दसन्दर्भजर्जराः करुणोर्मयः ।।12।।

Rāma—The waves of grief, that have been raised, are now being broken into by joy, wonder and apprehension (Or—volumes of joy and wonder) throwing me into an idescribable condition.

मित—।'अस्त्राणं देवताः' अधिष्ठात्राः। नम इति।

अन्वयः—राघवस्य परिग्रहात् परमास्त्रेभ्यः वः नमः। अनुध्यातैः वत्सयोः उपेतव्यम्। भद्रमस्तु वः।

व्याख्या—व्याकुला निरुतरा सीता इति तदर्थे देव्यौ प्रतिवदतः 'राघवस्य' रामस्य 'परिग्रहात्' पत्न्याः सीतायाः सकाशात् 'परमास्त्रेभ्यः' शस्त्रोत्तमेभ्यः 'बः नमः'। वयं युष्मभ्यं सीताया प्रतिप्रणामं बूमः इत्यर्थः। 'अनुध्यातैः' स्मृतैः भवद्भिः 'वत्सयोः' दारकयोरेतयोः 'उपतेव्यं' समीपमागन्तव्यम्। सम्प्रति 'भद्रं' मङ्गलम् 'अस्तु वः' प्रतिनिवर्त्तध्वमिति भावः। क्षुभिता इति।

अन्वयः—क्षुभिताः करुणोर्मयः साम्प्रतं विस्यानन्दसन्दर्मजर्जराः (सत्यः) मम कामपि दर्शा कुर्वन्ति।

व्याख्या–'क्षुभिता:' प्राप्तविक्षोभा: उत्ताला इत्यर्थ: या: 'करुणोर्मय:' शोकतरङ्गा: ता: 'साम्प्रतम्' अधुना 'विस्मयेन' घटनाचक्रस्य अद्भुततया जातेन अद्भुतरसेन 'आनन्देन' सीताया विपन्निवारणात् सुतसम्प्राप्तेश्च जातेन हर्षेण तथा 'सन्दर्भेण' अत: परं किं वा स्यात् इति शङ्कया [यद्वा–'विस्मयस्य आनन्दस्य' च य: 'सन्दर्भ:' प्रवाह: तेन] 'जर्जरा:' विशीर्णा: सत्य: 'मम कामपि' अनिर्वचनीयां दशां कुर्वन्ति। विमिश्रा रसा: न जाने किमनुभवामि।।

Notes. 1. दिष्ट्या etc.—She was startled by the flash and is now assured that it is nothing but flash of weapons that have come to befriend. 2. नमो व: etc,—विद्यासागर assigns this verse too to राम reading धन्या: स्मो व: परिग्रहात् in the second quarter. But the greeting should come from सीता or her deputies. राम is only a spector and has no voice in the matter. If we say that राम in his emotion forgets that it is a play and replies to the weapons, then the address to सीता made by the weapon goes unanswered which creates an awkward situation ; because, apart from the discourtesy of the thing, the weapon cannot retire unless dismissed by either सीता or by पृथ्वी or गङ्गा as Sītā's deputies. We therefore prefer to give it to the goddesses. Sītā was too unwell and upset to reply herself परिग्रह is पत्नी wife. "पत्नीपरिजनादानमूलशापा: षरिग्रहा:" इत्यमर:। परिगृह्यते इति परि+ग्रह+अप् कर्मणि। अपादाने 5मी metal अपाय being assumed भद्रमस्तु व: like शिवास्ते पन्थान: is a formula of dismissal. 3. विस्मय etc.—सम्+दृभ+घञ् भावे सन्दर्भ apprehension, array. दृभ meaning भय gives apprehension' ; when meaning रचन we have 'array' For समास see टीका। 4. करुणा etc.—करुणा is grief. करुणस्य ऊर्मय: weaves of grief. This implies that राम compares his mind to a sea. He does not know the state of his mind (कामपि दशाम्) because there is करुणरस, अद्भुतरस (विस्मय), शान्त (आनन्द) and भयानक (सन्दर्भ) all mixed up in a confused mass.

(xiv) **देव्यौ–रमस्व वत्से, रामभद्रतुल्याविदानीं ते संवृतौ पुत्रौ।**

Goddesses—Rejoice, child your boys have now become the equals of Rāmabhadra.

सीता–भअवदीओ को एदाणं खत्तिओचिदं कर्म करिस्सदि [भगवत्यौ क एतयो: क्षत्रियोचितं कर्म करिष्यति]।

Sītā—Worshipful deities, who will render unto these the rites befitting a Kṣattriya ?

रामः– एषा वशिष्ठगगुप्तानां रघूणां वंशवर्द्धिनी।
कष्टं सीतापि सुतयोः संस्कर्त्तारं न विन्दति।।13।।

Rāma—Pity ! Even Sītā, here, does not find an expurgator for her boys after having added to the race fo the Raghus, the race cared for by Vaśiṣṭha himself.

भागीरथी–पुत्र किं तवानया चिन्तया ? एतौ हि वत्सौ स्तन्यत्यागात् परेण भगवतो वाल्मीकेरर्पयिष्यामि, स एतयो क्षत्रकृत्यं करिष्यति।

Bhāg.—Daughter, away with this thought [*Lit*—What have you to do with this thought]. I shall entrust these dear ones to worshipful Vālmīki after they are weaned of mother's milk ; he will render unto them the rites of Kṣattriyas.

यथा वशिष्ठाङ्गिउरसावृषी प्राचेतसस्तया।
जनकानां रघूणाञ्च वंशयोरुभयोर्गुरुः ।।14।।

Like the sages Vaśiṣṭha and Aṅgīrasa, Prācetasa also is and *guru* of the races of the descendants of both Janaka and Raghu (Or—As are the sages Vaśiṣṭha and Aṅgīrasa so is Prācetasa, and heis the *guru* of the races of the descendant of both Janaka and Raghu).

मित–।'रमस्व' मोदस्व।'क्षत्रियाणाम् उचितं' योग्यम्।। एषेति।

अन्वयः– कष्टम्। वशिष्ठगुप्तानां रघूणां वंशवर्द्धिनी एषा सीतापि सुतयोः संस्कर्त्तारं न विन्दति।

व्याख्या–अहो 'कष्टम्' दुःखम्। स्वयं 'वशिष्ठेन' ब्रह्मपुत्रेण 'गुप्तानां' रक्षितानां 'रघूणां' रघूवंशीयानां 'वंशवर्द्धिनी' अपत्येन कुलालाम्बनभूता 'एषा सीतापि सुतयोः संस्कर्त्तारं' क्षत्रियोचितं संस्कारं करिष्यन्तं जनं 'न विदन्ति' न लभते।। 'अनया' कः कर्म करिष्यति इत्येवंरुपया। 'क्षत्राणां कृत्यम्' कर्म। क्षात्र संस्कार मित्यर्थः।। यथैति।

अन्वयः–यथा ऋषी वशिष्ठाङ्गिरसौ तथा प्राचेतसः उभयोः जनकानां रघूणाञ्च वंशयोः गुरुः।

व्याख्या–सुगमा। 'आङ्गिरसः' शतानन्दः।।

Notes. 1. रामभद्र etc.—रामभद्रेण तुल्यौ। तादृशावेव वीरौ अस्त्रलाभात्। 2. वंश etc.—वंशवर्द्धयति इति वंश+वृध+णिच+णिनि कर्त्तरि। 3. सीतापि–She who is under the care of the illustrious Vaśiṣṭha himself cannot find one to purify her sons. O fate! 4. स्तन्यत्यागात् पेरण–See Act III,para 5. 5. वशिष्ठ etc.—

अङ्गिरस् was one of the mind borns sons of ब्रह्मन्। तस्य गोचापत्यं पुमान् इति अङ्गिरस्+अण आङ्गिरसः। Refers to शतानन्द।

(xv) **रामः–सुविचिन्तितं भगवत्या।**

Rāma—Well thought of by the worshipful (Bhāgīrathī).

लक्ष्मणः–आर्य, सत्यं विज्ञापयामि तैस्तैरुपायैर्वत्सी कुशलवावुत्प्रेक्षे।

Lak.—Noble brother, I tell thee the truth—From these clues I am thinking of dear Kuśa and Lava.

एतौ हि जन्मसिद्धास्त्रावुभौ प्राचेतसान्मनेः।
वीरौ सम्प्राप्तसंस्कारौ वयसा द्वादशाब्दिकौ ॥15॥

For, these two had the weapons revealed at birth, both the heroes received purification form the sage Prācetasa and both have completed their twelfth year of birth [Lit.—by birth have seen their twelfth monsoon].

रामः–वत्स इत्येवाहं परिप्लवमानहृदयः सम्प्रमुग्धोऽस्मि।

Rāma—Dear brother for this very reson, with an agitated heart, I am utterly unnerved (lit.—Stupefied).

पृथ्वी–एहि वत्से पवित्रोकुरु रसातलम्।

Pṛthvī—Come child, sanctify the nether regions.

रामः–हा प्रिये लोकान्तरं गतासि।

Rāma—Alas, darling, you are gone to another world !

मित–। 'सुविचिन्तितं' सुष्ठु निरुपितम्। 'उपायैः' हेतुभिः। 'उत्प्रेक्षे' ऊहे।। एताविति।

अन्वयः–उभौ हि एतौ वीरौ जन्मसिद्धास्त्रौ, मुनेः प्राचेतसात् सम्प्राप्तसंस्कारौ, वयसा द्वादशाब्दिकौ।

व्याख्या–उपायान् आह 'उभौ हि' उभावेव 'एतौ वीरौ जन्मनः सिद्धानि अस्त्राणि' ययोः तादृशौ, इत्येक उपायः। 'मुनेः प्राचेतसात् सम्प्राप्ताः संस्काराः याभ्यां तादृशौ, इत्यु पायो द्वितीयः। 'वयसा' हेतुना 'द्वादश अब्दाः' वर्षाः सन्ति ययोः तादृशौ, इति तृतीय उपायः।। 'परिप्लवमानं' चञ्चलं 'हृदयं' यस्य तादृशः। 'इत्येव' अस्मादेव

कुशलवोप्रेक्षणादेव। अहमपि कुशलबावुप्रेक्षे इत्यर्थः। 'लोकान्तरं' अन्यं लोकं लोकं रसातलमित्यर्थः। तत्र स्थिता भूलोकसम्पर्कविरहिता इति खेदः।।

Notes. 1. वत्सौ etc.—कर्म of उत्प्रेक्षे। 2. एतौ etc.—Three reasons are given to establish the pluarality of उपाय (उपायैः)। 3. द्वाशाब्दिकौ–द्वौ च दश च द्वादश। द्वादशानां पूरणः इति द्वादश+डट् द्वादश twelfth. अपः ददाति इति अप्+दा+क कर्त्तरि शब्दः monsoon ; by transference of epithets it means here वत्सर। द्वादशः अब्दः द्वादशब्दः। सः अस्ति अनयोः इति द्वादशब्द+ठन् द्वादशाब्दिकौ those that have completed their twelfth year. 4. हा etc.—Transferred to another world not dead.

(xvi) **सीता–णेदु मं अत्तणो अङ्गेसु विलअं अम्बा, ण सक्कम्हि एरिसं जीअलोअपरिवत्तं अणुभविदुं [नयतु मामात्मनः अङ्गेषु विलयमम्बा, न शक्त्रास्मि ईदृशं जीवलाकपरित्तंमनुभवितुम्]।**

Sītā—Let mother lead me to mergence in her own limbs. I am unable to bear such vicissitudes of the lad of the living.

रामः–किमुत्तरं स्यात्।

Rāma—What would the answer be ?

पृथ्वी–वत्से स्तन्यत्यागं यावत् मन्नियोगतः पुत्रयोरपेक्षस्व, परेण यथा रोचते तथा करिष्यसि।

Pṛthvī—Child, at my bidding, have regard for the boys until they are weaned of mother's milk. Thereafter yoiu will do as pleases you.

भागीरथी–एवं नाम। (ततो निष्क्रान्ताः गङ्गापृथ्वीसीताः)।

Bhāg.—Just so. (*Next exeunt Gaṅgā, Pṛthvī and Sītā*).

रामः–कथं विलय एव वैदेह्याः सम्पन्नः ! हा देवि दण्डकारण्य-वासप्रियसखि, हा चारित्रदेवते लोकान्तरं पर्यसितासि ! (इति मूर्च्छति)।

Rāma—How so ! Vaidehi's mergence itself has come about ! Alas, Queen, my dear companion in the sojourn in the forest of Daṇḍaka ! Alas, the presiding deity of character! You are gone to another world ! *(Faints away)*

मित–।'अङ्गेषु विलयं' विलीनतां 'नयतु' त्वदीयादङ्गात् मामसृजः तत्रैव सम्प्रति

मां प्रतिसंहर। सशरीरं वासं तु न रोचये। 'जीवलोकस्य' प्राणिजगतः 'परिवर्त्तं' दशाविपर्य्यासम् 'अनुभवितुं न शक्नोमि'। असह्योऽयं परिवर्त्तः तत् मां विल नयतु।। 'किम् उत्तरं' पृथ्व्याः प्रतिवचनं 'स्यात्' विलयम् अनुमोदेत न वा इत्यर्थः।। 'नियोगः' आदेशः। 'मम नियोगः' तस्मात। 'पुत्रयोः' सम्बन्धे 'अपेक्षस्व' पुत्रौ अपेक्षस्व इत्यर्थः। 'परेणा' परं स्तन्यत्यागात् परम्।। 'एवं नाम' इति पृथ्वीवाक्यस्य अनुमोदनम्।। 'कथम् इत्याश्चर्ये। 'विलय एव' इत्यनुमानम्। विलये वैदेह्या निश्चयः, देवीभ्याञ्च स्तन्यत्यागकालापेक्षा विहिता। स च गतः कालः। तत् "विलय एव सम्पन्नः" इति परिशुद्धमनुमानम्। 'चरित्रं' शीलम्'। तदेव 'चारित्रम्'। तस्य 'देवता'। 'पर्यवसिता' गता–अनेकार्थत्वात् धातूनाम्।।

Notes. 1. पुत्रयोः–The षष्ठो is peculiar ; we expect द्वितीया। But विवक्षावशात् कारकाणि। There is no कारकविवक्षा here, hence शेषे षष्ठी। 2. नाम–Implies अभ्युपगम assent. गङ्गा agrees with पृथ्वी। "नामकोऽभ्यप्रगमे" इत्यादि मेदिनी। 3. पर्य्यवसिता–परि+अव+सो+क्त कर्त्तरि। The root सो is अन्तकर्मणि, i.e., it implies the end (अन्त)। Thus पर्यवसान means end, finish etc. Comp. "अवसितं हसितम्", "दिनावसाने सन्ध्येव", etc. But the sense of roots enunciated by पाणिनि are illustrative not exhausetive. There are other senses besides those enunciated; these have to be inferred from usage. Here सो means 'to go'. A different explanation without change of meaning may be suggested, thus—परि stands uncompounded and is to be taken with लोकान्तरम्। अवसिता ended' vanished etc. in its usual sense. "लोकान्तरम् परि" पातालमभि लक्ष्य 'अवसिता' अन्तर्हिता। लोकान्तरम् has कर्मप्रवचनीययोगे द्वितीया। परि being a लक्ष्मण (indicator) is कर्मप्रवनीय by the rule "लक्षणेत्थम्भूताख्यानभागवीप्सासु प्रतिपर्यनवः"।

(xvii) **लक्ष्मणः–भगवन् वाल्मीके, परित्रायस्व परित्रायस्व। एष किं ते काव्यार्थः ?**

Lak.—Help ! Worshipful Vālmīki, help ! Is this the object of your poem ?

नेपथ्ये–अपनीयतामातोद्यकम्। भो भोः सजङ्गमस्थावराः प्राणभृतो मर्त्यामर्त्याः, पश्यत भगवता वाल्मीकिनानुज्ञातं पवित्रमाश्चर्यम्।

In the Tiring Room—Let the musical instruments be removed. Ho ! Ho ! living beings movable and immovlable mortal and immortal. behold the holy marvel approved by worshipful Vālmīki.

लक्ष्मणः (विलोक्य)–

मन्थादिव क्षुभ्यति गाङ्गमम्भो
व्याप्तञ्च देवर्षि भिरन्तरिक्षम्।
आश्चर्यमार्या सह देवताभ्यां
गङ्गामहीभ्यां सलिलादुदेति ।।16।।

Lak. *(observing)*—The current of Gaṅgā is being agitated as if from churning ; the sky again is crowded with gods and sages. O wonder ! Noble sister-in-law is emerging from water along with the goddesses Gaṅgā and Mahi.

मित–'काव्यस्य' अभिनीयमानस्य प्रबन्धस्य 'अर्थः' प्रयोजनम्। "विलय एव वैदेह्या सम्पन्नः" इत्येव किं ग्रन्थस्य प्रतिपाद्यम् ?' आतोधकं' वाद्ययन्त्रादि 'अपनीयताम्' अपसार्यताम् निवृतोऽभिनय इत्यर्थः। 'जङ्गमाः' चराः 'स्थावराः' अचराः 'मर्त्याः' मरणशीलाः 'अमर्त्या' चिरजीविनः इति प्रकारेण सर्वे 'प्राणभृतः'। 'वाल्मीकिना अनुज्ञातम्' अनुमोदितम्। स्वयं वाल्मीकिरेव इदमाश्चर्य दर्शयति व इति भावः।। आश्चर्य विवृणोति मन्थादिति।

अन्वयः–गाङ्गम् अम्भः मन्थादिव क्षुभ्यति अन्तरिक्ष च देवर्षिभः व्याप्तम्। आश्चर्यम् ! देवताभ्यां गङ्गामहीभ्यां सह आर्या सलिलात् उदेति।

व्याख्या–'गाङ्गम् अम्भः गङ्गाप्रवाहः 'मन्थनादिव' मन्थादिव 'क्षुभ्यति' आलोड़ितं भवति। न हि प्रकृत्या कृत एष क्षोभः यतः 'अन्तरिक्षं च 'आकाशं पुनः देवैः ऋषिभिः' च 'व्याप्तम्' इत्याश्चर्यम्। 'आश्चर्यम्' अद्भुततरं पुनरेतत् यत् देवताभ्यां गङ्गामहीभ्यां सह आर्या' वेदैही 'सलिलात्' गङ्गाम्भसः 'उदेति' उन्मज्जति।।

Notes. 1. एषः etc.—do you mean to inform us that सीता has merged in Earth ? 2. सजङ्गम etc.—प्राणभृतः is the विशेष्य and सजङ्गमस्थावराः and मर्त्यामर्त्याः are विशेषण। 3. वाल्मीकिना etc.—We should not be surprised if वाल्मीकि himself spoke these words. 4. देवर्षिभिः–देवाश्च ऋषयश्च देवर्षयः। तैः। The wonder lies in this—The gods and the sages are in eager expectation above ; the waters of the Ganges are being violently agitated ; and lo ; noble sister-in-law emerges from water ! Wonder indeed !

(xviii) **पुनर्नेपथ्ये–**

(Again in the Tiring Room)—

अरुन्धति जगद्वन्द्ये गङ्गापृथ्व्यौ भजस्व नौ।
अपितेयं तवाभ्यासे सीता पुण्यब्रता बधूः ।।17।।

Arundhati deserving the world's homage, do a favour unto us, Gaṅgā and Pṛthvī. Your daughter-in-law Sītā, here, of holy vow, is made over to your care.

लक्ष्मणः–आश्चर्यमाश्चर्यम्। आर्य पश्य पश्य। (विलोक्य) कष्टमद्यापि नीच्छ्‌वसित्थार्यः।

Lak.—Wonder,wonder ! Look, noble brother look ! (*observing*) O woe ! Even now noble brother does not come round.

(ततः प्रविशत्यरुन्धती सीता च)

(*Then enter Arundhati and Sītā*)

अरुन्धती–

त्वरस्व वत्से वैदेहि मुञ्च शालीनशीलताम्।
एहि जीवय मे वत्सं प्रियस्पर्शेन पाणिना ।।16।।

Arun.—Hasten, Child Vaidehi. Abandon bashfulness Come revive my child with your hand the touch of which is dear to him.

मित– । अरुन्धतीति।

अन्वयः–जगद्वन्द्ये अरुन्धति नौ गङ्गापृथ्व्यी भजस्व। इयं पुण्यव्रता वधूः सीता तव अभ्यासे अर्पिता।

व्याख्या–हे 'जगद्वन्द्ये' त्रिभुवनपूज्ये 'अरुन्धति नौ' आवां 'गङ्गापृथ्व्यी भजस्व' अनुगृहाणा। कथमनुग्रह इत्याह 'इयं पुण्यव्रता' पूतचरिता 'वधूः' स्नुषा त्वदीया 'तव अभ्यासे' समीपे 'अर्पिता' न्यस्ता। न्यासमङ्गीकृत्य आवामनुगृहाणा। त्वरस्वेति।

अन्वयः–सुगमः।

व्याख्या–सुगमा।। 'शाकलीनशीलताम्' लज्जाशीलाताम् इति भावः।।

Notes. 1. भजस्व–भज usually means 'to accept' , to worship' etc.

Here the sense is 'to favour'. 2. अभ्यासे–अभ्यास is अन्तिक neighbourhood. "अभ्यासोऽभ्यसनेऽन्तिके" इति विश्वमेदिन्यौ। 3. *Remark*—अरुन्धती was among the spectators. The stage direction is defective. After the verse should be added निष्क्रान्ता अरुन्धती। Without this ततः प्रविशति अरुन्धती etc. below becomes incongruous. 4. ततः प्रविशति etc.—Another defective stage-direction. Add पृथ्वी भागीरथी च। These two also must enter, for otherwise एषा, इयम् etc. below become inconsistent. 5. शालीन etc,— शालाप्रवेशमर्हति इति शालाप्रवेश+खञ् शालीनाः bashful. The उत्तरपद, *i.e.*, प्रवेश disappears by निपातन in the rule "शाकीनकौपीने अधृष्टाकार्य योः"। शीलनस्य शीलभिव यस्यसा, शालीनशीलम्। सामान्ये नपुंसकम्। तस्य भावः। ताम्। Avoid शील यस्या, because पुंवद्भाव will not then be available.

(*xix*) सीता (ससम्भ्रममुपसृत्य रामं स्पृशन्ती)–समस्स सदु अज्जउत्तो [सामश्वसितु आर्यपुत्रः]।

Sītā (*Advancing with agitation and touching Rāma*)—Let my husband take heart.

रामः (समाश्वस्य सानन्दम्)–भो किमेततत्। (दृष्ट्वा सहर्षाद्भुतम्) अये देवी, अरुन्धती सर्वे च प्रहृष्यदृष्यशृङ्गशान्तासमेता गुरवः।

Rāma (*With joy, having recovered*)—Ho ! What is this ? (*Observing—With joy and wonder*) Ha, the Queen ! Arundhatī and all elders overjoyed along with Ṛsyaśṛnga and Śānta !

अरुन्धती–वत्स एषा भगवती भागीरथगृहदेवता सुपसन्ना गङ्गा।

Arun.—My son, this is the worshipful deity of the house of Bhāgīratha the mightly gracious Gaṅgā.

भागीरथी–जगत्पते रामभद्र, स्मर्यतामालेख्यदर्शने मां प्रत्यात्मनो वचनम्, यथा–"सा त्वमम्ब स्नषायामरुन्धतीव सीतायां शिवानुध्यानपरा भव'–इति। तत्र अनृणास्मि।

Bhāg.—Rāmabhadra, the lord of the world remembers your words to me at the inspection of the painting, thus—With such traditions, mother, do thou be like Arundhatī watchful over the welfare of thy daughter-in-law Sītā". In the matter of that I am absloved.

मित–सविस्मयः प्राह 'किमेतत्' इति। 'हर्षेण अद्भुतेन' च 'सह'। 'प्रहष्यन्तश्च ऋष्यशृङ्गशान्तासमेताश्च गुरवः'।। इयतो वर्षान् सीतायाः समाश्रयः इति प्राह 'सुपसन्ना' इति।। अविद्यमानमृणमस्याः 'अनृणा'। इह ऋणमिति अवश्यकरणीयार्थे। प्रभोर्वचनम् अवश्यकरणीयमेव। अतएव "जगत्पते" इति सम्बोधनम्।।

Notes. 1. अये देवो etc.—The sight of सीता was अद्भुत to राम and caused him हर्ष। वाल्मीकि has invited the whole world, hence अरुन्धती etc. were all among the spectators unnoticed by राम so long. 2. सुपसन्ना–Through her spiritual power अरुन्धती was aware of the many invaluable services redered unto सीता by गङ्गा, hence the epithet is a happy one at this moment. 3. जगत् पते–This is a necessary epithet. Being king of the whole world he was king to गङ्गा also. Hence सा त्वमम्ब etc. is a king's command. Now see below. 4. तत्र–तस्मिन् वचने विषये, i.e., I have obeyed. 5. अनृणा–For समास see टीका। ऋण here is not a debt but by transference of epithets it means something unavoidable like the repayment of a debt. Such a thing is the king's command. गङ्गा has become अनृणा by executing the command.

(xx) **अरुन्धती–इयंते श्वश्रूर्भगवती वसुन्धरा।**

Arun.—This is your mother-in-law worshipful Vasundharā.

पृथ्वी–उक्तञ्च पूर्व मायुष्मता वत्पारित्यागे, यथा–"भगवति वसुन्धरे श्लाघ्यां दुहितरमवेक्षस्व जानकीम्"–इति। तदधुना कृतवचनास्मि प्रभोर्वत्सस्येति।

Pṛthvī—Verily at my child's renunciation afore it was said by the long-lived self, thus—"O mighty repository of riches (Earth), look after your worthy daughter Janakī". So I have now done the bidding of my son, my master.

रामः–कथम् ! कृतमहापराधो भगवतीभ्यामनुकम्पितः। (इति प्रणमति)।

Rāma—How ! I am commiserated by the worshipful goddesses though I gave great offence ! (*Bcws down*).

अरुन्धती–भो भोः पोरजानपदा इयमधुना भगवतीभ्यां जाह्नवी–

वसुन्धराभ्यामेवं प्रशस्य ममारुन्धत्या समर्पिता, पूर्वञ्च भगवता वैश्वानरैण निर्णीतपुण्यचारित्रा सब्रह्मकैश्च देवैः संस्तुता सवितृकुलबधूर्देवयजन-सम्भवा सीतादेवी परिगृहते इति कथं भवन्तो मन्यन्ते ?

Arun.—Ho ! Ho ! Citizens and Villagers, here is being taken back this daughter in law of the solar race, Queen Sītā, sprung from the sacrificial ground for the gods who again formerly with her holy character tasted by the divine fire was eulogised by the gods including Brahman, and who has just been committed to me, Arundhatī, by the worshipful Jāhnavī and Vasundharā after having belauded her. What do you think of it ?

मित–।'पूर्वम्' इत्यच प्रथमाङ्को द्रष्टव्यः।'प्रभोः' इति वचनस्य अवश्यकर्त्तव्यतां दर्शयति।'एवं प्रशस्य' इत्यत्र "अरुन्धति जगद्वन्द्ये" इत्यादिश्लोको द्रष्टव्यः।'पूर्वञ्च' इति रावणवधान्ते।'निर्णीतं' परिदृष्टं निश्चितं वा 'पुण्य चारित्रं' चरित्र यस्यासः। 'देवैः संस्तुता अग्निपरीक्षावसाने।'इति' एतत् सीतायाः ग्रहणं 'कथं भवन्ती मन्यन्ते' अयुक्तं वा मन्यन्ते।।

Notes. 1. श्वश्रूः–श्वशुरस्य स्त्री इति श्वशुर+ऊङ् श्वश्रूः by निपातन in the rule "श्वशुरः श्वश्रुवा"।2. प्रभोः–This is because he was the king. वत्सस्य because he was her son-in-law. 3. मम–शेषे विवक्षया षष्ठी। 4. वैश्वानरेण–विश्वे नरा अस्य विश्वानरः a certain sage (ऋषि)। विश्व becomes विश्वा by the rule "नरे संज्ञायाम्"। विश्वानरस्य अपत्यं पुमान् इति विश्वानर+अण् वैश्वानरः fire. 5. निर्णीतपुण्यचारित्रा–The पुण्यचारित्र was already there, the चारित्र was not made पुण्य by fire. Fire only declared the पुण्यचारित्र। 6. सब्रह्मकैः–ब्रह्मा एव इति ब्रह्मन्+क स्वार्थे ब्रह्मकः। ब्रह्मकेण सह सब्रह्मकाः। तैः। Arundhatī's words are sarcastic.

(xxi) **लक्ष्मणः–एवमार्या अरुन्धत्या निभत्सिताः प्रजाः। कृतस्नश्च भूतग्राम आर्यां नमस्करोति, लोकपालाश्च सप्तर्षयश्च पुष्पवृष्टिभिरुप-तिष्ठन्ते।**

Lak.—The subjects have been thus rebuked by noble Arundhatī. Also the entire creation are saluting my noble sister-in-law ; and the guardians of the Universe together with the Saptarṣis and honouring her with showers of flowers.

अरुन्धती–जगत्पते रामभद्र,

Arun.—Rāmabhadra, lord of the world.

नियोजय यथाधर्मं प्रिया त्वं धर्मचारिणीम्।

हिरण्मयाः प्रतिकृतेः पुन्यकृतिमध्वरे ।।18।।

Employ at the sacrifice, as is your duty, your dear co-worker in piety, the holy original of the golden image.

सीता (स्वागतम्)–जाणादि अज्जउत्तो सीतादुःक्खं पमज्जिदुं [जानाति आर्यपुत्रः सवीतादुखं प्रमार्ष्टम्]।

Sītā (*To herself*)—My husband knows how to wipe off Sītā's grief.

रामः–यथा भगवत्यादिशति।

Rāma—As your worshipful self commands.

लक्ष्मणः–कृतार्थोऽस्मि

Lak.—My purpose is served.

सीता–जीविद म्हि [जीवितास्मि]।

Sītā—I am enlivened (given back life).

मित–। सुरासुराणामनुमोदनसुल्लिख्य यदुच्यतेप्राकृतान् मर्त्यात् प्रति "किं भवन्तो मन्यन्ते" तत् निर्भर्तृ सनमेव प्रजानाम्। 'भूतग्रामः' भूतसमूहः।। नियोजयेति।

अन्वयः–त्वं हिरण्मयाः प्रतिकृतेः पुण्यप्रकृतिं प्रियां धर्मचारिणीं यथाधर्मम् अध्वरे नियोजय।

व्याख्या–'त्वं हिरण्मयाः प्रतिकृतेः सवुर्णप्रतिमायाः भवत्कृतायाः 'पुण्यप्रकृतिं' पवित्रम् आदर्श 'प्रियाम्' आत्मनः प्रीतिदायिनीं 'धर्मचारिणीं सहधर्मिणीं 'यथाधर्मं' शास्त्रमनुपालयन् 'अध्वरे' यागे प्रकान्तेऽस्मिन् अश्वमेधे 'नियोजय' व्यापारय। प्रतिगृहीणैनमित्यर्थः। एतेन प्रतिकृतिकरणेन यदद्भुतं प्रेम प्रख्यापितं तदर्थे कृतज्ञा पाह 'जानाति' इत्यादि। मदीया प्रकृतिरध्वरे नियोजिता इति सर्वथा प्रमृष्टं मे त्यागदुःखम् इत्यर्थः।।

Notes. 1. भूतग्रामः–भूतानां समूह इति+भूत+ग्रामच् समूहे भूतग्रामः the host of beings. 2. आर्याम् etc.—Here चतुर्थी in connection with नमस् is over-ruled by द्वितीया owing to कृ। "उपपदविभक्तेः कारकविभक्तिर्बलीयसी"। Comp.

"नारायणं नमस्कृत्य नरञ्चैव नरोत्तमम्। देवीं सरस्वतीञ्चैव ततो जमयुदीरयेत्।।" 3. उपतिष्ठन्ते–देवताबुद्ध्या पूजयन्ति। Hence आत्मनेपद by the Vārttika "उपाद्देवपूजा-सङ्गतिकरणमित्रकरणपथिषु"। By the force of her character she had become a veritable goddess (देवता)। Comp. "आवयोरपि यत्सङ्गात् पवित्रत्वं प्रकृष्यते"–sl. 9. *ante*. 4. यथाधर्ममम्–धर्मनतिक्रम्य नियोजय is the sense (अव्ययी भाव) which implies that if after all this your do not take her back धर्म पतितः स्याः–you will inculr demerit. 5. प्रियाम्–This is double-edged, meaning she please you (प्रीणतीति प्रिया) and also she is dear to you. Hence by taking her back you do nothing unpalatable (out of fear of धर्मलोप) like the sick man swallowing a bitter pill. 6. जानाति etc.—The golden image declares an unprecedented favour and सीता is grateful for it. Compare—"आर्यपुत्र इदानीमसि त्वम्। अहो उत्खातं मे इदानीं परित्यागलज्जाशल्यमार्यपुत्रेणा"–Act III.

(*xxii*) **लक्ष्मणः–आर्ये एष निर्लज्जो लक्ष्मणः प्रणमति।**

Lak.—Noble Sister-in-law, here shameless Lakṣmaṇa bows to you.

सीता–वच्छ एरिसो चिरं जोव [वत्स ईदृशश्चिरं जोव]।

Sītā—Dear one, may you live long just as you are.

अरुन्धती–भगवन् वाल्मीके उपनीयेतामिमौ सीतागर्भसम्भवौ रामभद्रस्य कुशलवौ। (इति निष्क्रान्ता)।

Arun.—Worshipful Vālmīki, let these two Kuśa and Lava born of Sītā's womb, be introduced (lit—brought up) to Rāmabhadra. (*Exit*)

रामलक्ष्मणौ–दिष्ट्या तथैव तत्।

Rāma and Lak.—O Luck ! It is just as we thought.

सीता (स वाष्पाकूतम्)–कहिं मे पुत्तआ [कुत्र मे पुत्रकौ]।

Sītā (*With tears and a look of enquiry*)—Where are my boys ?

(ततः प्रविशति वाल्मीकिः कुशलवौ च)

(*Then enter Vālmīki and Kuśa and Lava*)

वाल्मीकिः–वत्सौ कुशलवौ, एष रघुपतिः पिता युवयोः, लक्ष्मणः कनिष्ठतातः सीतादेवी जननी। एष राजनिर्षिर्जनको मातामहः।

Vālmīki—Dear Kuśa and Lava, here is your father the lord ofthe Raghus ; your uncle Lakṣmaṇa ; your mother queen Sītā. Here is your meternal-grandfather the royal sage Janaka.

मित–तथा वने परित्यज्य भूयोऽपि मुखं दर्शयति इति 'निर्लज्जः'।। 'ईदृशः' भ्रातुर्वचनकरः।। 'रामभद्रस्य उपनीयेताम्' इत्यन्वयः।। 'तत्' वस्तु यथा अस्माभिरुत्प्रेक्षितं 'तथा एव' कुशलवावे सीतासुतौ। 'आकुतम्' अभिप्रायः दर्शनाभिलाषा इत्यर्थः।।

Notes. 1. ईदृशः–Lakṣmaṇa was devotedly attached to सीता। To abandon her in the forest in that fashion merely because his brohter commanded was almost a death-blow to him. Yet he did without. demur. Such obdience was rare. May you remain such (ईदृशः) ever-obedient to your brother. 2. भगवान् वाल्मीके–वाल्मीकी was outside. She wants him to come in with कुश and लव। 3. सवाष्प etc.—She is to see them after a separation of nearly 12 years. Hence the tears. आकूत is अभिप्राय। वाष्पेण आकूतेन च सह। She asks the question *meaningly i.e.,* She wants to see them forthwith before they are brought up to her, 4. मातामहः–This is mother's father. मातुः पिता इत्यर्थ मातृ+डामहच्।

(*xxiii*) **सीता (सहर्षकरुणाद्भुतं विलोक्य)–कथं तादो (कथं तातः)!**

Sītā—(*Observing with joy and surprise*)—How so! my father !

कुशलवौ–हा तात, हा अम्ब, हा मातामह।

Kuśa and Lava—O father ! O mother ! O grand-father !

रामः (सहर्ष मालिङ्ग्य)–ननु वत्सौ, पुण्यैः प्राप्त्वौ स्थः।

Rāma (*Embracing with joy*)—Well, dear boys, through merit have you been restored.

सीता–एहि जाद कुश, एहि जाद लव, एहि जात लव, चिरस्स परिष्वजेथां पुनर्जन्मान्तरगतां जननीम्)।

Sītā—Come child Kuśa, come child Lava, embrace for long your mother who has come to a new life (lit.—new birth).

कुशलवौ (तथा कृत्वा)–धन्यौ स्वः।

Kuśa and Lava (*Doing as bid*)—We are blessed !

सीता–भअवं पणमामि (भगवान् प्रणमामि)।

Sītā—Worshipful Sir, I bow to you.

वाल्मीकिः–ईदृश्येव चिरं भूयाः।

Vālmīki—May you continue thus for long indeed.

मित–। पितुदर्शनात् 'हर्षः' अतीतस्मरणात् 'करुणात्, अचिन्तितोपस्थित्या 'अद्भुतम्'।। 'हा' इति खेदे। ईदृशी भवतां इति रामायाणपाटात् विदितसर्ववृत्तान्तौ अनुकम्पेते।। 'जन्मान्तरं गता' प्राप्ता। को नाम जन्तुः एकस्मिन्नेव जन्मनि ईदृशं दशाविपर्ययमनुभवति तत् विवासितां सीता मृतां मन्येथाम्, इयमपरा सीता जननी युवयोः इति भाव।। 'ईदृशी' भत्रां पुत्राभ्याञ्च अवियुक्ता।।

Notes. 1. कथं तातः–The is surprised that Janaka is there. She was not aware of the fact that a drama was to be staged and the whole world had been invited to witness the staging. Just then पृथ्वी and भागीरथी were commanded by वाल्मीकि to come over with her ; this is all she knew. 2. चिरस्य–An अव्यय meaning चिर। परिष्वजेथाम् is the sense. अत्यन्तसंयोगे द्वितीया which has disappeared because चिरस्य is an अव्यय।

(xxiv) **सीता–अमहे तादो कुलगुरु अज्जाअणो सभत्तआ अज्जा सन्तादेई सलक्खणा सुप्पतणा अज्जउत्तचलणा समं कुशलवा विदीसन्ति, ता ब्णिभरम्हि आणन्देण अहो ! तातः कुलगुरुः आर्याजनः, सभर्त्तका आर्या शान्तदेवी, सलक्ष्मण सुपसन्ना आर्यपुत्रचरणाः, समं कुशलवौ अपि दृश्यन्ते तत् निर्भरास्मि आनन्देन]।**

Sītā—Ha ! I am bewildered with delight, for here are seen simultaneously father, our family preceptor, my mothers-in-law, noble princess Śānta with her husband, the highly gracious feet of my husband together with Lakṣmaṇa and Kuśa and Lava as well.

(नेपथ्ये कलकलः)

(*A hubbub in the tiring room*)

वाल्मीकिः (उत्थायावलोक्य च)–उत्खातलवणो मधुरेश्वरः प्राप्त्वः।

Vālmīki—(*Rising and observing*)—The lord of Madhura has come having up-rooted Lavaṇa.

लक्ष्मणः–सानुषङ्गाणि कल्याणानि।

Lak.—Blessings have a following.

रामः—सर्वमिदमनुभवन्नपि न प्रत्येमि। यद्वा प्रकृतिरिय मभ्युदयानाम्।

Rāma—Throgh experiencing all this I do not believe it. Or this is the nature of blessings.

मित—। 'निर्भरा' विह्वला। 'मधुरा' मथुरा। तस्या 'ईश्वरः' स्वामी लवणस्य स्थाने नायकः शत्रघ्नुः।। 'अनषङ्गेणा' अनुवन्धेन सह वर्त्तमानामि सानुषङ्गाणि' कल्याणन्तरेण अनुगतानि इत्यर्थः।।

Notes. 1. निर्भरा—भरति इति भृ+अच् कर्त्तरि भरः that which supports, *i.e.*, strength etc. निर्गतः भरः अस्याः निर्भरा powerless, bewildered etc. 2. उत्खातलवणः etc.—This is incongruous (see *Intro.*) 3. सानुषङ्गाणि—अनुषज्यन्ते इति अनु+सञ्ज+घञ् कर्मणि अनुषङ्गः appendage. Vīrarāghava makes it neuter (अनुषङ्गम्)।

(xxv) वाल्मीकिः—रामभद्र, उच्यतां किं ते भूयः प्रियमुपकरोमि।

Vālmīki—Rāmabhadra, say that further joy can I bring unto thee.

रामः—अतः परमपि प्रियमस्ति ? तथापोदमस्तु—

Rāma—Is there and joy exceeding this ? However, be it thus.

पाप्मभ्यश्च पुनातु वर्द्धयतु च श्रेयांसि सेयं कथा
मङ्गल्या च मनोहरा च जगतो मातेव गङ्गेव च।
वाल्मीकेः परिभावयन्त्वभिनयैर्विन्यस्तरूपां वुधाः
शब्दब्रह्मविदः कवेः पिरणतप्रज्ञस्य वाणीमिमाम् ।। 20 ।।

May that story, auspicious and enchanting like Gaṅgā and the mother of the world, sanctify removing sins and augment blessings May the wise deem *this*—*this* to which has been imparted from by actings—as the speech of Vālmīki the poet of mature intellect who knows Brahman in the shape of word.

(इति निष्क्रान्ताः सर्वे)।

(Exeunt all).

इति समेलनं नाम सप्तोऽङ्कः।

This is the Seventh Act named Reunion.

मित–।'परम् अधिकम्।। अतः परं भरतवाक्यम् पाप्मभ्य इति।

अन्वयः–जगतो माता इव च गङ्गा इव च मङ्गल्या च मनोहरा च सा इयं कथा पाप्मभ्यः पुनातु च श्रेयांसि वर्द्धयतु च। अभिनवैः विन्यस्तरूपाम् इमाम् बुधाः शब्दब्रह्मविदः परिणत प्रज्ञस्य कवेः वाल्मीकैः वार्णीं परिभावयन्तु। यद्वा–इमां वार्णीं बुधाः परिभावयन्तु इति योजना।

व्याख्या–'जगतो माता' पृथ्वी 'इव च गङ्गा इव च मङ्गल्या च मङ्गलकरौ च 'मनोहरा च' हारिणौ च 'सा' वाल्मीकिप्रणीता प्रसिद्धा 'इयं' युष्मत्समीपे उपस्थापिता 'कथा पाप्मभ्यः' पापेभ्यः 'पुनातु च' शोधयतु च 'श्रेयांसि' मङ्गलानि 'वर्द्धयतु च' पुष्णातु च। 'अभिनवैः' प्रयोगैः 'विन्यस्तं' विहितं 'रूपं' स्वरूपं यस्याः ताम् 'इमां' सम्प्रति श्रुतां वाचं 'बुधाः' विद्वांस 'शब्दब्रह्मविदः' वागात्मनि ब्रह्मणि प्रबुद्धस्य अतएव 'परिणता' पूर्णतां प्राप्ता 'प्रज्ञा' धीर्यस्य तस्य 'कवेः वाल्मीकेः वार्णीं परिभावयन्तु' मन्यन्ताम्। अस्मिन् भवभूतिप्रोक्ते यच यत्र वाल्मीकिना विरोधो लक्ष्यते तत्तदपि वाल्मीकेरेव वाक्यं मन्यन्ताम् इत्यर्थः। यद्वा–'अभिनयैः विन्यरूपां शब्दब्रह्मविदः परिणतप्रज्ञस्य कवेः वाल्मीकेः इमां वार्णीं बुधाः परिभावयन्तु' चिन्तयन्तु सती वा असती वा इति विमृशन्तु।।

Notes. 1. सेयं कथा–सा refers to Vālmīki's story as in the Rāmāyaṇa. इयम् points at the same story now retold. The story in not a new one, but the memorable one as given to the world by Vālmīki. 2. वाल्मीकेः etc.—The second half of the verse is with special reference to Bhavabhūti's version. My version differs from Vālmīki's in certain matters. Do not therefore forthwith reject my version as unworthy of credence rather deem this too as spoken by Vālmīki himself. Here the construction is—सा इयं कथा। इमां वाल्मीकेः वार्णीं परिभावयन्तु। In this इमाम् being in an अन्वादेश ought to be एनाम्। A defence may be suggested. In the first half सा इयं कथा refers to the *substance* of the story—कथावस्तु। The second half speaks of the *form* of *body* of the story—कथारूप, *i.e.*, the रचना, भाषा etc. Thus, the reference being to different things, we have no अन्वादेश and इमाम् is in order. In the alternative construction given in the टीका and अन्वादेश seems to be unavoidable. The reading तामेताम् for वाल्मीकेः seems defective (see *Intro*). 3. *Remark*—This verse contains the same idea as the verse "प्रोचतसो मुनिवृषा प्रथमः कवीनाम्" etc. of the Vīracarita as discussed in the Introduction.

Index